FACES OF RULERSHIP IN THE MAYA REGION

Dumbarton Oaks Pre-Columbian Symposia and Colloquia

Series Editor
Frauke Sachse

FACES OF RULERSHIP IN THE MAYA REGION

PATRICIA A. MCANANY AND MARILYN A. MASSON
Editors

DUMBARTON OAKS | WASHINGTON, D.C.

© 2024 Dumbarton Oaks
Trustees for Harvard University, Washington, D.C.
All rights reserved.
Printed in the United States of America by Sheridan Books, Inc.

LIBRARY OF CONGRESS CATALOGING-IN-PUBLICATION DATA

NAMES: Pre-Columbian Studies Symposium "Faces of Rulership in the Maya Region" (2021 : Online) | McAnany, Patricia Ann, editor. | Masson, Marilyn A., editor. | Dumbarton Oaks, host institution.
TITLE: Faces of rulership in the Maya region / Patricia A. McAnany and Marilyn A. Masson, editors.
OTHER TITLES: Dumbarton Oaks Pre-Columbian symposia and colloquia.
DESCRIPTION: Washington, D.C. : Dumbarton Oaks, [2024] | Series: Dumbarton Oaks Pre-Columbian symposia and colloquia | "Volume based on papers presented virtually at the Pre-Columbian Studies symposium "Faces of Rulership in the Maya Region," organized by Dumbarton Oaks, Washington, D.C., and held on March 25–27, 2021."—Title page verso. | Includes bibliographical references and index. | Summary: "Authority—whether royal, divine, material, fleeting, or enduring—varied across space and time in the Maya region, from its Preclassic dynastic origins through the colonial encounters of the sixteenth century. The changing faces of Maya rulership and their foundational ties to symbolic material objects, architecture, ancestral beings, deities, and written monuments are fully explored in the fifteen chapters of *Faces of Rulership in the Maya Region*. The contributors track rulership—beyond the prevalent paradigm of divine kingship—by considering the power of queens and unraveling codes embedded in art and public buildings. Through the close study of the agency of rulers who often sought to distinguish themselves from other dynasts, the contributors come to an enhanced understanding of the relational dynamics between rulers and subject peoples. Chapters reveal that rulership was perpetually challenged in ways that impacted adjacent institutions of nobles and literati. Applying concepts of rulership outlined in the book *On Kings* by David Graeber and Marshall Sahlins, this volume brings Maya history and archaeology into the current, anthropological conversation about rulership in premodern times" —Provided by publisher.
IDENTIFIERS: LCCN 2024001478 | ISBN 9780884025207 (hardcover)
SUBJECTS: LCSH: Mayas—Politics and government—History—Congresses. | Mayas—Kings and rulers—History—Congresses. | Maya art—Congresses. | Mayas—Antiquities—Congresses. | Mexico—Antiquities—Congresses. | Central America—Antiquities—Congresses.
CLASSIFICATION: LCC F1435.3.P7 P74 2024 | DDC 972.81/016—dc23/eng/20240410
LC record available at https://lccn.loc.gov/2024001478

GENERAL EDITOR: Frauke Sachse
ART DIRECTOR: Kathleen Sparkes
DESIGN AND COMPOSITION: Melissa Tandysh
MANAGING EDITOR: Sara Taylor

Volume based on papers presented virtually at the Pre-Columbian Studies symposium "Faces of Rulership in the Maya Region," organized by Dumbarton Oaks, Washington, D.C., and held on March 25–27, 2021.

COVER PHOTOGRAPH: Queen in Maize Deity costume, Xupa, Chiapas © Fine Arts Museums of San Francisco. Photograph by Joseph McDonald.

www.doaks.org/publications

For David Graeber and Marshall Sahlins,
who collectively transformed anthropology in unparalleled ways.

CONTENTS

Preface | ix

1 Introducing the Faces of Rulership in the Maya Region | 1
   Patricia A. McAnany and Marilyn A. Masson

2 Rulers, Relatives, and Royal Courts:
   Excavating the Foundations of Classic Maya Alliance and Conflict | 27
   David Freidel

3 Whose Mountains?
   The Royal Body in the Built Environment | 47
   Alexandre Tokovinine, Francisco Estrada Belli, and Vilma Fialko

4 Masked Intentions:
   The Expression of Leadership in Northern Yucatán | 77
   William M. Ringle

5 Relatively Strange Rulers:
   Relational Politics in the Southern and Northern Maya Lowlands | 117
   Maxime Lamoureux-St-Hilaire and Patricia A. McAnany

6 Strange and Familiar Queens at Maya Royal Courts | 141
   Traci Ardren

7 Patron Deities and Rulership across the Maya Lowlands | 173
   Joanne Baron

8 Temporalities of Royal Costume in the Maya Lowlands | 191
   Christina T. Halperin

9 Maya Gastropolitics:
   Strategies, Tactics, Entrapments | 225
   Shanti Morell-Hart

10 *Le roi est mort, vive le roi*:
   Examining the Rise, Apogee, and Decline of Maya Kingship in Central Belize | 249
   Jaime J. Awe, Christophe Helmke, Claire E. Ebert, and Julie A. Hoggarth

11 Jaina Figurines:
    Contexts and Social Linkages on the Western Side of the Maya World | 285
        Antonio Benavides C.

12 Postclassic and Contact-Period Maya Rulership | 311
        Marilyn A. Masson

13 Denying the Rights of "Natural Lords":
    Maya Elite Struggles for Rewards and Recognition in Colonial Yucatán, 1550–1750 | 333
        John F. Chuchiak IV

14 Toward a New Framework for Comparing Ancient and Modern Forms of Social Domination
    (or, "Whatever Happened to the Archaic State?") | 369
        David Wengrow

15 Relationships of Command:
    From Sovereignty to Anarchy | 385
        Scott R. Hutson

Contributors | 397

Index | 403

PREFACE

The need to understand the forms of rulership and governance in the societies of the ancient Americas, as well as their relationship to political organization in other parts of the world, goes back to the days of first encounter, when different systems of world order clashed and Indigenous leaders across the continent had to succumb to European invaders. Bartolomé de Las Casas argued that these societies had legitimate governors and advocated for restoring the sovereignty of the Indigenous rulers who had been dispossessed by the Spanish Crown. In his *Apologética historia sumaria*, Las Casas provides detailed descriptions of different forms of rulership across the Americas, comparing them to contemporary and past systems of the "old world" to attain a new and integrated understanding of a general divine order.

These early attempts of "translating" the systems of governance have continued in modern scholarship, and the political organization of the Maya cultural area has received particular attention through time. What were the political units and how did they relate to each other? Who governed them and how were those rulers selected? Did forms of authority change over time or across space? Is there a connection between the cultural collapse of the Preclassic and the Classic and their forms of rulership? Mayanists have discussed these questions for several decades, balancing an ever-growing body of archaeological data with the insights gained from the epigraphic turn and, more recently, the increasing availability of scientific data from DNA or isotope analysis, among others.

The scholarship published by Dumbarton Oaks through the years has reflected the latest ideas and controversies about Maya political organization. But the annual symposium in 2021 was the first that dedicated itself exclusively to the subject of rulership and its regional developments and characteristics. Organizers Patricia McAnany and Marilyn Masson had been looking forward to discussing the topic with a group of renowned scholars in the Dumbarton Oaks Music Room, a place of political significance that had housed the Washington Conversations on International Peace and Security Organization in 1944, which constituted the first step in the formation of the United Nations. But the COVID-19 pandemic changed these plans and the symposium had to be moved into the virtual realm. Held on Zoom on March 25–27, 2021, the number of virtual attendees was three times higher than it would have been in the Music Room. Although the participants did not have the opportunity to meet in person, the organizers did the utmost to stimulate the exchange of ideas among the contributors during and after the symposium. The result is a marvelous volume that reflects the current scholarly debate on rulership in the field of Maya studies.

My thanks go to the volume editors and contributors for bringing together this tremendous collection of essays. The constructive suggestions of two anonymous reviewers who read the volume for Dumbarton Oaks were highly appreciated. Managing editor Sara Taylor and director of publications Kathy Sparkes deserve special thanks for the many hours they invested into producing this beautiful book.

I hope that this volume provides innovative perspectives on a current debate in a field that continues to generate new data and insights. Studying ancient Maya rulership and systems of governance opens up new pathways of learning about human organization and gives—in the spirit of Las Casas— the Indigenous peoples of the Americas a more prominent role as agents of world history.

Frauke Sachse
Director of Pre-Columbian Studies
Dumbarton Oaks

Introducing the Faces of Rulership in the Maya Region

PATRICIA A. McANANY AND MARILYN A. MASSON

Faces of Rulership in the Maya Region focuses on the faces of rulers rather than kings. The more abstract term "ruler" is gender-neutral and accommodates authority exerted outside of the exclusive domain of patrimonial rhetoric. Although the latter belongs squarely within any discussion of Maya rulers (Martin 2020:59–60), issues of succession, bloodline, pomp, adornment, and colorful corporeal presentation were neither the sole prerogatives of southern lowlands kings nor the sole modes of governance. Maya queens and other governing elites shared—or led—in the duties, execution, and symbolic foundations of ruling. They did so both in the southern Classic-period heartland of divine lordship as well as in northern contexts where political actors were veiled behind architectural grammar. This volume joins a recent body of work in anthropology and archaeology in striving toward a more nuanced understanding of rulership from a comparative spatial and temporal perspective within the Maya region.

As the following chapters illustrate, the roots of Maya principles of governance ran deep. Spatially, we detect variation in local historical choices of emphasis regarding the foundational legitimacies that bound lords and subject peoples (society) together. Temporally, evolutionary schemes of Maya political organization have typically dwelt on disjunctive reorganization associated with major breaks from the Late Preclassic to Classic period or the Terminal Classic to Postclassic period. More recent research recognizes not only diachronic cycling in the serial rise and fall of Maya states but also within regimes and within periods of lowlands subregions. Institutional reproduction and transformation are historically constituted (Sahlins 1981:7–8). Mesoamerican scholarship increasingly values a historical anthropology approach that recognizes that political change may invoke selected, valued structures of the past. Shifting forward-facing appearances and claims of Maya rulership may be driven by a plethora of social forces and natural pressures. Reproduced, reinvented, and derivative practices arise from the manipulation of history in processes of survival, resistance, revival, and ethnogenesis (e.g., Grube

2021; Kepecs and Alexander 2018; Smith 2011:425; Vail and Hernández 2011).

The definition of "ruler" varies from generic formulations such as "one who rules" to synonyms for sovereigns exercising supreme authority. The concept of rulership, as examined in this book, considers the fact that authority in some premodern states, including Maya examples, was shared, or at least periodically challenged by persons occupying royal, sub-royal, noble, and "ruler" statuses and titles (Arnauld et al. 2021:13). This volume's title uses the multifaceted term "face" with intentionality. According to *Merriam-Webster*, the word "face" refers to a demeanor (friendly face), a facade or other outward appearance (donning makeup, a disguise, a building's decorative program, putting on a good "face"), status (saving "face"), a surface (e.g., of a clock, coin, or planet), and persons themselves (as in seeing new "faces" or representing the "face" of an organization).

The faces of rulership in Maya history and archaeology include the well-studied portraits and dynastic records of southern Classic-period kings, authorities, and institutions; foreign and local claims to authenticity (including ancestral commemoration); architecture headlining sanctions of divine beings; and symbolic things that manifest rulership within or beyond generations. For the Classic Maya, hieroglyphic texts reveal the importance of the concept of personhood—*bah(h)*—the essence of which could be represented by a head, a face, or an object such as an effigy (Houston and Stuart 1998). Presentation, consumption, and enactment of ritual were practices that also defined the character and perception of rulership for the purpose of perpetuating or amplifying power. Spectacles were essential participatory practices, for rulers and attendees alike, that underwrote Maya polities' claims to power (Inomata and Coben 2006), including times when power was dissipating (Miller and Brittenham 2013:177). Performances and feasts symbolically united attendees in affirmations of polity and at the same time divided them by reiterating inequality (Dietler 2001:77; Smith 2011:421). Such occasions boosted efforts to reproduce and maintain sovereign rulership (Smith 2011:421). Cross-culturally, more dramatic spectacles involved public transcripts such as sacrifices (Miller and Brittenham 2013), or, as Dickson (2006) labels them, "theatres of cruelty" that underscored state power and inspired fear (see also Wengrow, this volume).

How faces of governing authorities worked and were materially manifested is treated in this volume, in a scope extending from the Preclassic to the colonial period in the southern and northern lowlands. Chapters vary in their foci on rulership. Some provide perspectives from single sites or classes of data, while others are topical and comparative. Syntheses of dynastic features of some of the largest Maya centers are accessible in recent treatments elsewhere (e.g., Martin 2020; Martin and Grube 2008); in particular, Martin (2020) offers a definitive synthesis of knowledge regarding southern lowlands Classic-period kingdoms, an effort this volume does not seek to replicate.

By dedicating this volume to David Graeber and Marshall Sahlins, we acknowledge the inspirational role that these two outsized intellectuals played in the conception of the 2021 Dumbarton Oaks symposium upon which this volume is based. For many of the contributors to this volume, *On Kings* offers a comparative framework by which Maya rulership and statecraft might be more fully comprehended (Graeber and Sahlins 2017). Characterizing kingship as one of the most historically prevalent forms of human governance, Graeber and Sahlins (2017:1) astutely commented on the ubiquity of kingship as well as its cosmic connections. This political form, manifested in pre-Hispanic Mesoamerica at various places and times, was not uniformly replicated. Distinctive modes of rulership emerged in the political cycles of Mesoamerica's states and empires. Archaeologists are still working to understand these shifting modes of governance. Foremost questions include how rulers presented themselves differently and how they related to each other, to parallel institutional authorities, and to their constituencies (Blanton and Fargher 2008; Blanton et al. 1996; Fash and López Luján 2009; Feinman and Carballo 2018; Martin 2020; Ringle and Bey 2009; Sugiyama et al. 2020). Chapters in *Maya Kingship: Rupture and Transformation from Classic to Postclassic Times*

table 1.1
Overlapping themes on the faces, places, and instruments of rulership treated in this volume.

GENERAL THEME	DETAILS	CHAPTERS
Monuments and symbols of the body politic	Edifices featuring sacred places and entities, ritual landscapes, palatial associations	Freidel (chapter 2), Tokovinine, Estrada Belli, and Fialko (chapter 3), Ringle (chapter 4), Awe, Helmke, Ebert, and Hoggarth (chapter 10)
	Importance of communal ritual	Freidel (chapter 2), Lamoureux-St-Hilaire and McAnany (chapter 5), Halperin (chapter 8), Awe, Helmke, Ebert, and Hoggarth (chapter 10), Benavides (chapter 11), Hutson (chapter 15)
	Animate objects or places as enduring (multigenerational) symbols of authority, and/or portraits of rulers, deities, and political groups	Freidel (chapter 2), Tokovinine, Estrada Belli, and Fialko (chapter 3), Ringle (chapter 4), Lamoureux-St-Hilaire and McAnany (chapter 5), Baron (chapter 7), Halperin (chapter 8), Awe, Helmke, Ebert, and Hoggarth (chapter 10), Benavides (chapter 11), Chuchiak (chapter 13), Hutson (chapter 15)
	Schismogenesis (polities and institutions self-defining in contrast to neighbors, promoting distinct community symbols)	Tokovinine, Estrada Belli, and Fialko (chapter 3), Lamoureux-St-Hilaire and McAnany (chapter 5), Baron (chapter 7)
Ties to productive places, landesque capital, land	Ancestors' links to fields, Postclassic concepts of territory from household to polity, lack of colonial proprietary land claims	Morell-Hart (chapter 9), Masson (chapter 12), Chuchiak (chapter 13)
Feasting, upward nobility, performance	Feasting as commensal politics, performance (at various occasions), affirmations of hierarchy, inclusive yet exclusive, asymmetrical reciprocal events	Lamoureux-St-Hilaire and McAnany (chapter 5), Baron (chapter 7), Halperin (chapter 8), Morell-Hart (chapter 9)
	Commensal feasting and monumental labor	Lamoureux-St-Hilaire and McAnany (chapter 5), Baron (chapter 7)
	Galactic mimesis (subordinate sites emulating titles and works of overlords, with a goal of upward nobility)	Lamoureux-St-Hilaire and McAnany (chapter 5)
	Social distancing of rulers	Lamoureux-St-Hilaire and McAnany (chapter 5), Halperin (chapter 8), Morell-Hart (chapter 9), Chuchiak (chapter 13), Hutson (chapter 15)
Dual sovereignty	Foreign ties, or additional variants of nonlocal "otherness," including stranger kings and queens as well as nonhumans	Tokovinine, Estrada Belli, and Fialko (chapter 3), Ardren (chapter 6), Morell-Hart (chapter 9), Masson (chapter 12), Chuchiak (chapter 13)
	Principles of dual sovereignty, tensions and reconciliations of local and nonlocal authentication	Freidel (chapter 2), Tokovinine, Estrada Belli, and Fialko (chapter 3), Ringle (chapter 4), Lamoureux-St-Hilaire and McAnany (chapter 5), Baron (chapter 7), Masson (chapter 12), Chuchiak (chapter 13), Hutson (chapter 15)
	Importance of queens and princess brides as rulers or otherwise as political actors	Freidel (chapter 2), Ardren (chapter 6)
	Local and nonlocal marriages and Indigenous/allochthonous duality	Lamoureux-St-Hilaire and McAnany (chapter 5), Ardren (chapter 6), Masson (chapter 12)

table 1.1 (continued)

GENERAL THEME	DETAILS	CHAPTERS
Authorities beyond rulers, including bureaucracies	Councils, secondary political officials, military orders, priesthoods, and other forms of negotiated authority	Freidel (chapter 2), Ringle (chapter 4), Lamoureux-St-Hilaire and McAnany (chapter 5), Morell-Hart (chapter 9), Masson (chapter 12), Wengrow (chapter 14), Hutson (chapter 15)
Ancestral ties, patron gods, local power	Importance of deep time and ancestral rulers (inscriptions or funerary features)	Tokovinine, Estrada Belli, and Fialko (chapter 3), Lamoureux-St-Hilaire and McAnany (chapter 5), Ardren (chapter 6), Awe, Helmke, Ebert, and Hoggarth (chapter 10), Hutson (chapter 15)
	Spatial association of rulers with palatial and royal funerary architecture	Tokovinine, Estrada Belli, and Fialko (chapter 3)
	Bundles pertaining to ancestors	Freidel (chapter 2), Tokovinine, Estrada Belli, and Fialko (chapter 3), Lamoureux-St-Hilaire and McAnany (chapter 5), Baron (chapter 7), Hutson (chapter 15)
	References to patron deities	Freidel (chapter 2), Tokovinine, Estrada Belli, and Fialko (chapter 3), Lamoureux-St-Hilaire and McAnany (chapter 5), Baron (chapter 7)
	Rulers as caretakers of supernaturals, feeding of ancestors	Baron (chapter 7), Morell-Hart (chapter 9), Awe, Helmke, Ebert, and Hoggarth (chapter 10), Hutson (chapter 15)
Transitions, transformations, violence, and "forms" of rulership	Transformation through time in legitimating programs, ancestors vs. supernaturals, foreign vs. local, via military intervention or other factors of shifting geopolitical landscapes	Freidel (chapter 2), Tokovinine, Estrada Belli, and Fialko (chapter 3), Ringle (chapter 4), Baron (chapter 7), Awe, Helmke, Ebert, and Hoggarth (chapter 10), Wengrow (chapter 14)
	Tenets of institutional capacities for violence, knowledge and charisma (political competition)	Wengrow (chapter 14)
	Rulers without "states"	Wengrow (chapter 14), Hutson (chapter 15)
Constraints and obligations	Adverse sacralization	Freidel (chapter 2), Hutson (chapter 15)
	Entrapment into performative roles, spaces, or economic obligations	Ardren (chapter 6), Morell-Hart (chapter 9), Hutson (chapter 15)
	Rulers and their relationship to subject peoples and to land	Lamoureux-St-Hilaire and McAnany (chapter 5), Benavides (chapter 11), Masson (chapter 12), Chuchiak (chapter 13), Hutson (chapter 15)

(Okoshi et al. 2021) also draw on the writings of Graeber and Sahlins (Andrieu 2021; Arnauld et al. 2021). The chapters published here complement one another by considering overlapping themes, as reviewed below, and summarized in Table 1.1. Before discussing the themes of this volume, we consider the historical dimension of scholarship on rulers and their courts.

A Historical Lens on Rulership in the Maya Lowlands

How did ideas about the faces of Maya rulership change over time? And how were Maya rulers thought to have related to their constituencies? Mayanists are justly criticized for an overemphasis on "all things royal" and a corresponding underemphasis on the many people (occupying varied statuses) who supported rulership through labor, crafting, and farming. Relations between royals and the remaining population are an underdeveloped area of scholarship; but arguably, such relationality cannot be understood without a deeper understanding of both sides of the coin. Through a historical lens, we examine the evolving face of rulership and ideas about the intermeshing of rulers with those who allied themselves (albeit conditionally) with a ruler.

During the sixteenth-century Spanish *entradas* into Yucatán, conquistadors quickly grasped the fact that they were attempting to subjugate a highly stratified society—one with many apical rulers. Although less centralized than their home kingdom of Castile, these Maya societies possessed many other similar characteristics, including monumental architecture, a writing system, and organized martial resistance to their conquest efforts. The early colonial capitals of Mérida and Valladolid (founded in 1542 and 1545, respectively) were built—not without resistance—on top of the large Postclassic royal courts of T'ho and Zací, which were occupied at the time of Spanish invasion. Spanish *encomenderos* used their knowledge of Postclassic tribute systems to justify their extraction of goods and services from peoples living within their *encomiendas*. In a 1579 mandatory report to the Spanish Crown, the *encomendero* Diego de Contreras wrote the following about the tributary relationship between the residents of the small town Tahcabo and the Postclassic royal court at Ek' Balam: "[he] was called Namon Cupul [and] was present at the head of Aquibalom [Ek' Balam], the town of a conqueror of this land . . . [T]hey had him as [their] lord, and to him they paid corn, chickens, fish, cotton and . . . small blankets" (Relaciones histórico-geográficas de las provincias de Yucatán 1900, translation by authors).

During the early colonial period, as Spaniards set about dismantling extant architecture to be reused in the construction of a conquest landscape that included European-style palaces and churches, they marveled at the engineering prowess of Yucatec Mayan peoples (see particularly López de Cogolludo 1688:176–177; Sánchez de Aguilar 1639).

There were few doubts about the existence of past rulers and, through the mid-nineteenth century, an acceptance—for the most part—of the historical connection between Yucatec descendants and the durable remains of their past (Catherwood 1844:3). One of the first references to Maya origins as something mysterious appeared in an 1822 travelogue by Don Antonio del Río focused on Palenque. He opined that the destruction of hieroglyphic texts and monuments by Spaniards during the conquest wars had "enveloped history in such a mazy labyrinth of doubt, that the most learned and experienced writers upon the subject have found it utterly impossible to solve the grand mystery of the origin of the Mexicans [Maya of Palenque]" (Río 1822:xiii).

Indeed, the "mystery" was enhanced by the complete opaqueness of Maya hieroglyphs. Over two hundred years earlier, Spaniards—clergy and bureaucrats alike—had forced Yucatec Maya scribes to adopt alphabetic writing, thus breaking the transmission of knowledge about hieroglyphic literacy. Equally relevant is the fact that until 1697, the central Maya Lowlands remained independent from Spanish rule and occupation (Jones 1998). Europeans had no knowledge of the many Classic-period royal courts at which hieroglyphic texts are particularly abundant. Directly relevant to evolving ideas about rulership is the fact that in areas of intensive colonization—such as northern Yucatán—Spaniards made it their business to emasculate Indigenous political authority and hierarchy, as historian Sergio Quezada (2014) has effectively documented and as further elaborated by John Chuchiak (this volume). In this way, colonialism wreaked havoc on Maya cultural heritage and obscured—quite purposefully—knowledge of past literacy and political hierarchies.

This attempted leveling of Maya peoples into an undifferentiated and landless peasant mass reverberated through time and arguably impacted the nineteenth-century nascent field of archaeology. Links with the past had been so severed that archaeologists focused on what could be learned through excavation. By the 1920s, Mexico adopted an official ideology of *indigenismo*—a celebration of the glories of an Indigenous past that operated simultaneously with programs of assimilation and cultural erasure

(Bonfil Batalla 1996). Powerful places of the past—such as Palenque—were groomed for a burgeoning heritage tourism industry. In 1952, archaeologist Alberto Ruz Lhuillier (1973) discovered a royal tomb within the Temple of the Inscriptions. In retrospect, it is hard to think of the tomb of K'inich Janaab Pakal I (d. 683 CE) as anything other than the interment of a royal ruler but archaeologists—particularly in the northern hemisphere—were slow to catch on.

In a revision of his popular book, *The Rise and Fall of Maya Civilization*, completed after the discovery of the Palenque tomb, J. Eric Thompson (1966:pl. 28) described the death mask of Pakal as a "[m]osaic jade mask which once covered the face of the *chief* [emphasis added] buried in the crypt of the Temple of the Inscriptions." Although a strong proponent of the glories of Maya civilization, Thompson was averse to thinking about the realpolitik of Maya central places before the sixteenth century, preferring the descriptor of "major ceremonial center" (Thompson 1966:89). Advocating for a model of theocratic leadership, he (1966:305) saw the Maya world as divided between ruling groups (with head chiefs) and Maya peasants. When the latter grew weary of the excesses of rulers, they abandoned them and the system collapsed.

By 1966, with a deluge of new hieroglyphic, calendric, and architectural evidence of rulers coming out of excavations at Tikal, even Thompson (1966:303) had to confess that "I once saw stelae as purely calendric and astronomical. It is now clear that there was no such abnegation of glory; *rulers* [emphasis added] did leave memorials of their accessions." The concession that carved monuments contained evidence relevant to piecing together biographies of rulers (and not just calendrical and astronomical ruminations) was underscored in publications by Tatiana Proskouriakoff (1960, 1963, 1964) based on the concordance between human life spans and Long Count dates at Piedras Negras and Yaxchilan. The colonial flattening of Maya political structure that had been superimposed on pre-colonial times was beginning to rebound.

There is little doubt that our understanding of pre-sixteenth-century rulership in the Maya Lowlands has been greatly impacted by the success (from the 1960s onward) of hieroglyphic decipherment based upon both phonetic and logographic readings of Classic-period texts (Coe 1992). When married to a more sophisticated art historical analysis of carved and painted imagery, much that had been incomprehensible to Thompson and others came into focus. *Blood of Kings: Dynasty and Ritual in Maya Art* (Schele and Miller 1986) arguably was the first book to codify a new interpretation of rulership, in which self-referential concepts—such as the term *k'uhul ajaw* (sacred ruler)—were invoked, and the notion of dynasty—i.e., the transmission of rulership across generations concentrated in a single family—was entertained. Enabled by the decipherment of the extremely large corpus of hieroglyphic texts and carved/painted imagery that had accumulated over decades of fieldwork, the old paradigm of theocratic chiefs crumbled under the weight of evidence. Although rulers featured in the *Blood of Kings* were not calendar priests, they nonetheless were deeply vested in ritual and sacrifice (Stuart 1988). In hindsight, this codification of what we might call southern-style rulership enriched Maya archaeology tremendously, but also opened a chasm between the south (where rulership was expressed in hieroglyphs and Long Count dates) and the north (where rulership was expressed primarily through monumental architecture, as William Ringle explores in further detail in this volume).

Long before the names and titles of rulers had been deciphered, a recurrent collocation of glyphic elements (dubbed "emblem glyphs") had been recognized by Heinrich Berlin (1958). Berlin's analysis was amplified by Joyce Marcus (1976), who linked emblem glyphs to places and the political process of state making. The exact meaning of emblem glyphs and their requisite *k'uhul ajaw* component has long been debated, but the research following Marcus refined our understanding of emblem glyphs and firmly established two ideas: a polity with an emblem glyph had a claim to some form of political autonomy; and those polities without emblem glyphs probably were not serious political players in the political ecosystem of the lowlands. Intense interactivity among polities was suggested by the fact that emblem glyphs often occurred at sites other than the ascribed home site and led to the idea that the lowlands contained "a forest of kings" (Schele and Freidel 1990). Epigraphers lined up on opposite sides to argue for and against the equality of rulers associated with emblem glyphs (Martin and Grube 1995; Mathews 1991).

As epigraphy and iconography revealed more about how rulers used ritual activities to promote the health and vitality of their polities, a parallel and contentious discussion ensued regarding whether rulers could be characterized as shamans (Freidel, Schele, and Parker 1993). Southern rulers also paid homage to royal ancestors, and it became increasingly clear that ancestor shrines (such as that of Pakal of Palenque) occupied key positions in the built environment of Classic-period capitals (Houston 1998; McAnany 1995, 1998). Along with ancestor veneration, authority might be concentrated within a family line through mechanisms of inheritance; as might be expected, the heir-designation ceremonies were increasingly identified hieroglyphically and iconographically (Miller 2001, among others).

A debate about whether Maya sites with ancestor shrines, palace precincts, and population estimates ranging from ten thousand to sixty thousand inhabitants could be called urban was finally laid to rest with the adoption of the term "royal court" to describe the core of large and largely influential places (Inomata and Houston 2000–2001). *Courtly Art of the Ancient Maya*, an exhibition and glossy catalogue with in-depth essays, soon followed (Miller and Martin 2004). The term "court" encompassed concentrations of monumental architecture, but could a court be called royal in the absence of an emblem glyph or ancestor shrines? Gargantuan political centers in the northern lowlands were more likely to lack both, and so the chasm widened. In great contrast to earlier ideas about sparse and perhaps seasonal populations residing at the center of Classic Maya aggregations, royal courts, such as Copan, were described as "peopled" by *Scribes, Warriors, and Kings* (Fash 2001).

The granularity of hieroglyphic texts allowed a synthesis, or *Chronicle of the Maya Kings and Queens* (Martin and Grube 2008), which featured eleven text-rich royal courts and a popular diagram of textually attested interaction among courts featuring conflicts, family ties, diplomatic contacts, and statements of hierarchy. The shorthand character of the *Chronicle of the Maya Kings and Queens* was amplified by Martin (2020) in *Ancient Maya Politics*, a comprehensive summary of evidence and a characterization of the Classic southern lowlands as a fraternity of kings. But there were gender issues afoot as Maya scholars grappled with the fact that most texts were written by males for other males (Houston 2009, 2018; Houston, Stuart, and Taube 2006). *Ancient Maya Women* (Ardren 2002) provided space for deepening our understanding of under-documented women in Maya society, and the field continues to grapple with the patrimonial rhetoric of Classic Maya texts (Martin 2020:59–64; Reese-Taylor et al. 2009; see also Ardren, this volume). In response to the outlandish prophecies proffered for the year 2012, David Stuart returned to the importance of time—especially the Long Count—to southern lowlands rulers. In some respects, *The Order of Days* (Stuart 2011) hearkens back to Thompson's assertions about the importance of time in Maya civilization, but it does so from a twenty-first-century understanding of hieroglyphic texts and calendrics.

The crisis faced by Late Classic rulers—especially in the southern lowlands—has been the subject of continuous debate ever since Thompson (1966:305) suggested that the crisis may have been caused by a revolt of the proletariat. Since that time, scores of paleoecological projects have searched—with varying success—for a smoking gun in the form of a killer drought (Iannone 2014). More likely, it was a concatenation of cultural and environmental factors that resulted in a pronounced population drawdown, first in the southern lowlands and later in the north. Recent scholarship has focused on the fragility of sacred rulership (McAnany 2019) and the political transformations that occurred at the end of the Classic period (Okoshi et al. 2021). Later in this volume, Marilyn Masson focuses on the regeneration of Maya society during the Postclassic period, considering how certain practices of rulership were continued while others were jettisoned (see also Arnauld et al. 2021:10; Masson, Hare, and Peraza Lope 2006; Masson and Peraza Lope 2014). The old moniker of "decadent" that the Carnegie Institution applied to the Postclassic period has been discarded. In its place, there is a new understanding of political cycles and the variable investment in the materiality and inheritance of rulership. In keeping with the goals of this volume, a new understanding of paramount rulers during the Postclassic period underscores that there is more than one face to rulership.

Strange and Familiar Rulers, People, and Places

As Graeber (2017b) observes, an important conceptual distinction separates divine kings from sacred ones. Divine kings assert considerable earthly power, sometimes acting with impunity and breaking rules or creating new ones (Graeber 2017b:378, 394). Sacred kings, on the other hand, may be constrained by their people, who employ institutional means to segregate and isolate them on the grounds of their sanctity. Graeber notes that "kings will . . . attempt to increase their divinity, and the people, to render them sacred" (2017b:402). Relevant to studies of Maya rulership is the idea that ancestral genealogies can challenge kings who draw upon a "stranger king" narrative, in which legitimization rests on foreign and exotic origins (Graeber 2017b:430, 436). In addition, as Graeber discusses, ancestral status deflates through time as descendants proliferate. For rulers, ancestors who are difficult to kill or to marginalize loom, a problem sometimes resolved by breaks in inheritance and the establishment of new dynasties (Freidel, this volume; Tokovinine, Estrada Belli, and Fialko, this volume). But in some cases, deep-time ancestry is the very lifeblood of the realm, and regimes may contrast sharply in the weight they accord to foreign versus local foundations of entitlement (Tokovinine, Estrada Belli, and Fialko, this volume).

Many of this volume's chapters consider the concept of the "stranger king," elaborated on by Sahlins (2008), as a key element in the formation of a "cosmic polity" (Graeber and Sahlins 2017:2–3). Within the Maya region, rulers were infused with qualities of strangeness, charisma, and sacredness based on spatial and social distance, place of birth, pilgrimage and investiture, marriage, and other rites of passage. Grappling with how strangeness coexisted with familiar, local legitimacies of rulership facilitates a better understanding of the contradictions of authority.

Pertinent to such inquiries are ongoing analyses of the historical impact over the longue durée of Early Classic–period Teotihuacan interventions, a topic that has long concerned Mayanists (e.g., Stone 1989; Stuart 2000). Political struggles to reconcile the dual heritage of local and nonlocal derivation are widely explored in interdisciplinary studies of Mesoamerica (e.g., Arnauld et al. 2021:14; Masson and Peraza Lope 2010; Pohl 2003a, 2003b; Restall 2001; Ringle 2004; Schele and Mathews 1998:197–256). The central paradox of rulership, in which rulers were both of the people and foreign to the people over whom they ruled, is a cross-cultural phenomenon of authentication (Kurnick 2016; Restall 2001:373–375). This paradox is inherent to the concept of dual sovereignty. The charisma of a stranger king is juxtaposed with the place-based authority of both a ruler and their Indigenous subjects (Sahlins 2017:230). As Sahlins states: "Summarising and at some risk generalising, in these stranger-kingships, two forms of authority and legitimacy coexist in a state of mutual dependence and reciprocal incorporation. The Native people and the foreign rulers claim precedence on different bases. For the underlying people it is the founder-principle: the right of first occupancy—in the maximal case, the claim of autochthony. Typically, then, there is some enduring tension between the foreign-derived royals and the Native people. Invidious disagreements about legitimacy and superiority may surface in their partisan renderings of the founding narratives, each claiming a certain superiority over the other" (Sahlins 2008:183–184).

Such forces are present even in the absence of archetypal "stranger king" scenarios, as explored by contributors to this book (Freidel, this volume; Tokovinine, Estrada Belli, and Fialko, this volume; Ardren, this volume; Hutson, this volume). Categories of otherness (stranger status), while typically drawn on claims of distant and/or mythical origins, also applied within regions, with respect to exchanges of royal brides (stranger queens) from powerful, legendary polities (Ardren, this volume). Of relevance to this argument are emic conceptualizations of local, hometown identity as distinctive, with "other" status accorded to residents living in different towns. Restall's work (1997, 2001) illustrates the importance of physical communities of origin, or *cahob* (towns and their affiliated land holdings), to Maya social identity in the contact and colonial periods. This prominent social marker likely has deep-time depth in the pre-Hispanic past, even in cases where house forms, material assemblages, and quotidian lifeways were shared (Marken, Guenter, and Freidel 2017). "Place," in other words, constituted a form of local ethnicity (Marken, Guenter, and Freidel 2017:192). Identities were further conceptualized in relation to features of local landscapes (Tokovinine 2013). Multiple local names are known for Palenque's lords and mythical localities within the settlement's landscapes (Marken, Guenter, and Freidel 2017) or places for ritual action (Tokovinine 2013:14–18). The importance of *cahob* is elaborated in subsequent chapters, which delve into ethnicity, place, authenticity, and the foundations of rulership rooted in places, architectural legacies, things, and the tensions accompanying exchanges and gatherings of people.

Communal and Collective Symbols of Authority

Some Mesoamerican scholars are now exploring the importance of collective action structures to state building and stability at the polity and community level. This body of work also considers the constraints placed on rulers—for example, among societies where material symbols or features embody the office and its power, rather than mortal personages (Blanton and Fargher 2016:147; Feinman and Carballo 2018). Community ritual, including the construction of impressive monumental landscapes, precedes offices of kingship in many areas (Blanton and Fargher 2016:324). However, it also accompanies ruler-centered regimes, representing the ongoing imperative of the "spatial reproduction of the polity" (Smith 2011:424). Early monumental centers such as Aguada Fénix (Tabasco) or Caral (Supe Valley, Peru), for example, lack evidence for centralized rulership or hierarchy (Inomata et al. 2020; Solis 2006). Similarly, large Preclassic Maya centers lack the conventional features associated with royal kings (Freidel, this volume; Freidel and Schele 1988). Like many other cases worldwide, they do not fit traditional expectations for early state societies (Wengrow, this volume).

Many years ago, Richard E. Blanton, Gary M. Feinman, Stephen A. Kowalewski, and Peter N. Peregrine (1996) defined regime structures as either corporate or exclusionary; the former was characterized as a relatively faceless government marked by shared power among different groups and institutions, with an emphasis on major public works and spaces for communal ritual. Public art in such cases adopts themes such as fertility, renewal, and cosmology with broad resonance in society (Blanton et al. 1996:6). Teotihuacan was presented as a foremost example of a corporate structure. Exclusionary regimes, on the other hand, featured visible rulers actively pursuing personalized control, patrimonial rhetoric, prestige, wealth, and patron-client relationships (Blanton et al. 1996:2–3). The Classic-period Maya were held up as a prime case of an exclusionary regime. These categories, as the authors acknowledge, coexist within many regimes; moreover, the fact that these modes can fluctuate through time within a given polity represents an important insight that moves beyond linear models of state development. In other influential recent works such as *The Dawn of Everything*, Graeber and Wengrow (2021:352–355) draw upon Mesoamerican case studies, such as that of Tlaxcala, to argue for kingless yet powerful premodern states (see Fargher et al. 2011). Teotihuacan's mode of governance likely changed over its long occupation, as it was initially led by influential sovereigns but subsequently moved to what may have been a more collective organization (as summarized by Carballo 2020:62, although the political structure at Teotihuacan represents an ongoing topic of debate [e.g., Headrick 2007; Sugiyama and Sugiyama 2020]).

Communal rituals at monumental places were important foundational elements in emergent complex societies (Earle 1997:171–173; Marken, Guenter, and Freidel 2017:200–202). Serving as community symbols writ large, monuments also embodied cosmological authentication of specific places, a status regenerated via ritual practice (e.g., Ashmore 2009; Doyle 2012; McAnany 2010:147; Rathje 2002). Ultimately, such monuments—emblematic of ties between gods and community members and tended by ritual leaders—evolved through time in the Maya area to become enduring symbols of inequality (McAnany 2010:150–153). They inspire awe and, at times, affection for authority (Smith 2011:425). On the other hand, communal rituals can be fraught with conflict and tensions that may be reflected in subversive aspects of the art programs that record them (Miller and Brittenham 2013:77–92). The naturalization of social inequality may have been rooted in the development of competitive (and ultimately hierarchical) grassroots community organizations (Freidel 2018:370; McAnany 1995). Things, including inalienable and durable monuments, depend on humans, as caretakers, to defend and maintain them. Given that humans also come to depend on things, this relationship becomes entangled and intensifies (Hodder 2011).

While ritual and religious monumental structures have been emphasized as indicators of collective authority and ideology for early complex societies, the chapters in this volume revisit these phenomena for Maya centers of the Preclassic through Classic periods. Faces of authority were not only symbolic—they were also represented in the person of a king or queen as well as by priests, council members, war leaders, and other officials. Bureaucratic institutions, even if headed by descendants of ruling elites, can potentially challenge political authority and pose fissures by which regimes can fracture (Eisenstadt 1980). Supernatural entities were also accorded power over kingdoms to which they granted authenticity and distinctive local status. Sacred things endured beyond generations in "monumental time" and embodied the office rather than the corporeal aspect of individuals (Freidel 2018:376–380, this volume; Halperin, this volume; see also Blanton and Fargher 2016:147). Chapters by Freidel; Tokovinine, Estrada Belli, and Fialko; Ringle; Lamoureux-St-Hilaire and McAnany; Baron; and Awe, Helmke, Ebert, and Hoggarth explore these recurrent themes within and between sites from the Preclassic or Classic periods, illustrating the meshed phenomenon of rulers, people, and patron gods. These analyses, collectively, track structures over the long run through ruptures and continuities in modes of rulership.

Bureaucracies and Pluralistic Ruling Authorities

Collective power attributed to bureaucratic institutions forms a key body of evidence in arguments for modes of leadership alternative to divine kingship. Officials participating in governance operated at various stations, from courts to local town administrations. The Tlaxcallan case involves developed bureaucracies or, more specifically, council rule. A pressing question for the Maya area is how institutions such as councils and the priesthood intersected with heads of state. In truth, they coexisted, even where rulers (mostly kings) reigned above them. Masson (this volume) reviews the relationships of Postclassic and contact-period Maya rulers with retinues of empowered officials who flanked (if not outranked) them, especially priests and secondary lords of town divisions or vassal kingdoms. Late Maya officials operated within hierarchies of scale, from towns to political capitals. Restall (2001) reviews an impressive array of early contact-period Maya offices by which constituents wielded degrees of authority in the affairs of state. A key question not yet fully answered is the time depth of these late Maya bureaucracies (Chichen Itza notwithstanding) (Ringle 2004). Although bureaucrats, war leaders, merchants, and priests were often sidelined in southern Classic-period Maya art and writing, greater numbers of secondarily ranked persons were portrayed in art programs toward the end of the period (e.g., Miller and Brittenham 2013:77–92). Epigraphers now find evidence for the existence of priests, priestesses, merchants, royal brides, and multiple categories of titles and roles in the Classic period, long before their well-known antecedents during and after Spanish contact (Martin 2020:85–101, 183–185, 324–325; Tokovinine and Beliaev 2013; Zender 2004). In examinations of the Puuc region, Ringle (this volume) identifies features attesting to authoritative organizations beyond the office of the ruler, such as the military, as reflected in the warrior sculptures that stand guard at Kabah and Labna. The Puuc sites that he analyzes have administrative facilities that would have housed paramounts, other authorities, and military officials.

Other places and times in deep Maya history that lacked strong evidence for ruler-centered leadership were presumably governed by similar institutions. Despite the renowned facelessness of Late Preclassic Maya rulership, the San Bartolo murals nonetheless attest to kingship, founded in recognizable mythic and cosmological principles of the later Classic period (Freidel 2018:369–370), formerly mostly hinted at from portable objects (Freidel and Schele 1988). Dichotomous models are inadequate. The observation by Blanton and colleagues (1996) that corporate and exclusionary principles coexist is especially prescient for our evolving understanding of Maya modes of governance. Rulers and institutions emphasizing collectivity, as well as strange and autochthonous emblems of authenticity, circulated and vied within dynamic cycles of polity reproduction. Variation is key, given the evidence for dynamic and distinctive political structures through time in the Maya area (and for complex societies in general) (Freidel 2018). Even at individual sites, such as Caracol, rulership modes were constantly changing (Chase and Chase 2021:244). Wherever dynastic rules of succession exist, cross-culturally, interventions occur, through "vetting by councils of sages, patriarchs, matriarchs, priests, nobles, and other factions" (Freidel 2018:370). Furthermore, Freidel argues that Preclassic Maya rulers were chosen in this way. The rites by which they were ordained into reign and transformed into divine status was weighted more heavily in certain cases than genealogical descent (Freidel 2018:370). We have long known that kinship and kingship presented dialectical conflicts in the emergence of Maya political complexity (McAnany 1995). Indeed, Ringle, Gallareta Negrón, and Bey (2021:250–251) detail the deposition of a stranger king at Ek' Balam by his subjects and the installation of a later ruler by a high-ranking auxiliary. The importance of council houses attached to administrative complexes has early origins in the Puuc region (Ringle, Gallareta Negrón, and Bey 2021:255). Ordinary people, bound to rulers as part of moral communities, also had options to exert power (Houston et al. 2003:233; Hutson, this volume; Joyce, Bustamante, and Levine 2001).

Feasting provided one important context for multivocal contributions to the affairs of state. The tensions and compatibilities of dual sovereignty are illustrated at the courts of La Corona and Kiuic, as discussed by Lamoureux-St-Hilaire and McAnany (this volume). They argue that the importance of royal feasting—whether diacritical feasting to shore up alliances between courts, or patron-sponsored feasting to reinforce sovereignty at home—is encoded within architecture, features, and artifacts of sites in both the northern and southern lowlands.

Female princesses of the Kaanul dynasty of Calakmul who married into the subordinate court of Late Classic–period La Corona illustrate the practice of royal hypogamy, in which royal women married "down" into lesser kingdoms, a pattern also observed at other sites (Canuto and Barrientos 2020; Lamoureux-St-Hilaire and McAnany, this volume). Upward nobility represents another key concept introduced by Graeber and Sahlins (2017:13). La Corona also provides an example of the process of upward nobility that was bolstered by alliance networks and marital arrangements. Rapid architectural expansion to accommodate royal brides and their entourages by the receiving royal court attests to this process (at great cost) of upward nobility at La Corona. In-marrying queens were personages who wielded dual branches of influence in polity governance, straddling the affairs of local kingdoms as mothers of heirs as well as bearing auras of non-local kingdoms (Ardren, this volume). They became entwined with what Adam T. Smith (2015) refers to as the political machinery of sovereignty, a concept closely related to dual sovereignty.

North and South

Despite their significant similarities in state religion, courtly elites, and political economies, lowland Maya courts differed in the degree to which faces of rulers were literally depicted in ceramic or sculptural art. Maya scholarship relies on the collaboration of those working with hieroglyphic decipherment and those working with evidence encoded in art, architecture, and archaeology. Ethnohistorical sources concerning Postclassic Maya states help to mitigate the scarcity of carved stone texts at late northern centers. Southern kingdoms are generally characterized as places where royal legitimacy leaned heavily upon the foundations of ancestral history, materialized in ancestor shrines (e.g., McAnany 1995). But this pattern was variable in emphasis and form, as Tokovinine, Estrada Belli, and Fialko (this volume) demonstrate for royal courts at Holmul and Naranjo. Architectural embellishment, whether the mosaic stone "masks" found at courtly buildings in the northern Puuc region (Ringle, this volume) or the large stucco masks so well-known for the Preclassic period (Freidel, this volume), materialized royal authority in a manner alternative to ancestral shrines and hieroglyphic histories.

The northern and southern lowlands were symbiotically bound by social and economic networks of exchange that carried information, ideas, people, and goods across the peninsula. Goods flowing in the north–south and inland–coastal directions (and the reverse) included salt, blue pigment, obsidian, cacao, cloth, fowl, fish, marine shell, dogs, deer, fruit, hides, feathers, thread, cloth, copal, stone tools, wood products, and other items documented in early colonial accounts and archaeological research (Masson and Peraza Lope 2010; Piña Chan 1978). Diverse environmental resources located within vegetation, topographic, and rainfall zones fostered long-term interdependencies and commercial exchange across subregions of the Maya area.

We know that the linguistic and sociopolitical gradient from north to south was permeable. Calakmul, one of the most powerful Classic-period states, was geographically located toward the northern edge of the southern lowlands, in a position advantageous for influencing—and exchanging with—northern polities. Given the erosion of many epigraphic records at Calakmul and other northern sites, we rely on archaeological evidence to document the northern interests and influences of southern hegemonic states (Freidel 2018, this volume).

Even as parallel and divergent materializations of rulership merit exploration across the north–south "divide," the long-term temporal comparisons are worth greater attention. Historical models drawn from the highly integrated, extensive regional political economies of the contact period hold much potential for archaeological testing and comparisons with the Classic period (Hanks 2010:32, 51–52; Jones 1989; Masson 2021; Masson and Peraza Lope 2014; Restall 1997:54, 173, 185). Sacred aspects of Maya rulership did not disappear at the end of the Classic period (Masson, this volume). Chloé Andrieu (2021:31) aptly observes that the concept of kings would have been historically powerful and lingering for Maya peoples, or "difficult to get rid of," building on the observation of Graeber and Sahlins (2017:12) that kings endure as a unifying principle.

Nonetheless, distinctions are important. The mosaic masks of the Puuc region and Chichen Itza have undergone multiple cycles of interpretation in Maya studies. Ringle (this volume) argues compellingly that many symbolize political and military institutions, rather than deities or other supernatural entities. Masks of different sites and time periods are associated with a diverse array of themes pertaining to governing and administrative bodies; some of them mark throne rooms or animate the sacred character of buildings where humans entreated deities. He further explores the significance of the mask programs to royal authority and rites of investiture and rulership. Later mosaic mask programs of the Terminal Classic period evince themes of emergence, particularly from the maw of the feathered serpent. While expressed differently at southern sites, the regimes of both regions shared concerns with investiture and the legitimacy of transmission of authority, always a perilous proposition. As Ringle observes, "mosaic masks represent an abstract embodiment of power—royal power, to be sure, but also the power possessed by other members of the nobility and military" (103).

Maya Women and Rulership

Gender dynamics of rulership are poorly understood, in part due to what Martin, following Richard Blanton and colleagues (1996), refers to as Classic Maya "patrimonial rhetoric" (Martin 2020:59–60). If agency—and thus the face—of female authority has been partially and intentionally obscured by the dominance of such rhetoric expressed in imagery and hieroglyphs, what paths of inquiry can illuminate female agency and authority? Graeber (2017a:85–87) explores key aspects of gender relations among royal Shilluk women of the African White Nile region, known ethnographically to have held "an extraordinary degree of power," even though the Shilluk were not organized as a matriarchy. He emphasizes that such power was negotiated rather than codified. Thus, understanding the complexities of gendered royal authority—official or in practice—may require reading between the lines of dynastic evidence.

Hieroglyphic texts at some of the royal courts provide counts of "kings" that omit intervals during which females ruled. For example, at Palenque and Tikal, Martin (2020:76) observes that known female rulers were skipped over in records detailing lineal accounts of succession. Notably, ruler titles were not gendered; cases are known where both male and female rulers held the titles of *ajaw* or *kaloomte'*. Compounding the challenges of seeing royal females is the tendency to ascribe male status to the often poorly preserved remains of burials, particularly if skeletal remains indicate robust muscle attachments. At Xunantunich, the remains of a female within a mortuary shrine constructed in the heart of the royal court were assumed to be that of a robust male until aDNA analysis revealed otherwise (Awe et al. 2020:501). Poor preservation of the pelvic bones, which are particularly diagnostic of sex, contributes to such biases (Geller 2017). With aDNA analysis now supporting reassessments of the sex of prominent individuals, female leaders and rulers have been resuscitated out of the murky past (Price et al. 2019).

While female royals stayed close to courtly spaces, they exerted considerable power and authority (Ardren, this volume). Shown in resplendent and richly brocaded *huipiles*, Lady Ix K'abal Xook represented a powerful local dynasty at Yaxchilan. Presiding from her personal living quarters, she was deeply involved in rituals preceding the martial campaigns of her husband and was a ritualist whose stone lintels commemorate her acts of bloodletting and conjuring an ancestral supernatural. In a different vein, Lady Ix Wak Jalam Chan of the Mutul dynasty traveled from Dos Pilas to rule Naranjo and represents a renowned example of a stranger queen. One of the few female royals shown standing atop a captive, she also presents a clear image of a warrior queen (Reese-Taylor et al. 2009). Hieroglyphic records indicate that she arrived at Naranjo with a large entourage of supporters and carried the rare high-status title of *kaloomte'*, generally associated with foreign overlords (Martin 2020:80, 83, 121). Reese-Taylor and colleagues (2009) provide additional examples of martial queens who filled roles generally associated with male rulers. But despite these exceptional cases, female sexuality, power, and authority would have loomed as unwanted challenges to hereditary male entitlements and as forces necessitating control (Joyce 2008). Such sentiments are encoded in Maya mythologies and codices (Chinchilla Mazariegos 2017; Vail and Stone 2002).

Whether they married locally, brought a foreign husband into their court, married into another court, or arrived as stranger queens, royal women played a critical role in the political economies of Classic-period centers. They oversaw and organized the production of elaborate cotton *mantas* that circulated as tribute payments from subject kingdoms to political capitals or bound elites together in webs of reciprocal obligation via lavish gifting (McAnany 2010:184–189, 2013a; Pohl 2003b).

Epigraphic records, along with spindle whorls and bone weaving tools found with high-status female burials, attest to the centrality of royal women's engagement with production at Classic Maya courts (Bell 2002; Hendon 2006; Miller and Martin 2004:94–95, 112–113). Ardren (this volume) emphasizes the ritual authority asserted by female royalty marrying into royal courts, who represented outsider stranger queens from other cities. Armed with a wealth of political knowledge, skilled in ritual fluency and potency, and accompanied by loyal entourages, females would have been deeply involved in political negotiations between royal courts, in effect serving as foreign consulates (Lamoureux-St-Hilaire and McAnany, this volume). *Entradas* of high-ranking brides into peer or subject kingdoms was not a neutral event, but rather one laden with threats to upset the status quo (Ardren, this volume). New brides inspired similar concerns at the scale of ordinary households in the contact period, resulting in complex social and ritual proscriptions for their control (Vail and Stone 2002).

Recognition of female actors in rulership is important, as are questions of use, control, and unequal entitlement along gender lines. Sovereign inclinations originate from and replicate elementary forms of domination within the domestic household (Wengrow, this volume), suggesting the embeddedness of mutually affirming institutions across class lines. Bride exchange, even when traditional and consensual from the perspective of women raised in societies where this was the norm, is a form of human exchange, often associated with an economic price (Ardren, this volume). Brides, like other captives, were sometimes acquired in war. While brides were integral to relational networks of debt and obligation between Maya families and polities (Harrison-Buck 2021), this practice was potentially fraught with tension and relations of dominance.

Nonhuman Faces of Sacred Authority

Graeber and Sahlins (2017:2) steadfastly reject a divide between cosmology and royal politics; instead, they characterize a royal realm as a "cosmic polity." Moreover, Graeber sides with A. M. Hocart, who opined that "what we have come to call 'government' originally derives from ritual" (Graeber 2017b:378). Thus, asymmetries in power and relations of domination are seen to flow from and through divine sanction. Within Maya archaeology, much ink has been spilled over whether a Maya ruler (*k'uhul ajaw*) was considered divine, sacred, or something else altogether (Freidel, Schele, and Parker 1993; Houston and Cummins 2004; Houston and Stuart 1996; Schele and Miller 1986). Martin (2020:71–73) notes that the term *k'uhul ajaw* is rarely found outside of emblem glyph collocations where the term, rather than designating a *k'uh* (a god or a divine thing), likely refers to a holy or sacred person (Jackson and Stuart 2001:224). In other words, something or someone can be regarded as sacred or holy without being divine or a god.

Nonetheless, a prominent facet of Maya rulership entailed channeling, conjuring, or effecting a "concurrence" (Houston 2006:148) with deities, spirits, and ancestors whose benevolence was key to prosperity, martial victories, and a general *buen vivir* within the realm. As Houston (2006:149) states: "'Transcendence' would be precisely the wrong word to describe this experience. The spectator and performer were not taken anywhere else; they did not lose themselves in their roles. Rather, divine essences came to visit, briefly, and were made animate by human flesh and motion. Practiced movement, especially of the feet, may have summoned these essences." In effect, Maya rulers were expected to possess a special ability to channel supernaturals and to solicit an efficacious intervention by deities or ancestors in human affairs. The faces and charisma of Maya rulership were thus intricately entangled with nonhuman faces of sacred authority.

The role of mediator between supernatural and human realms was both powerful and dangerous, the latter because of the real limits of rulers' power to effect positive outcomes over forces not entirely under their control (like rainfall). Smoke and mirrors were deployed, no doubt, and this vulnerability may have prompted regime changes when poor outcomes cascaded. The interlocutor role of rulers also indicates the affordance accorded to nonhuman deities and spirits (Bennett 2010; Latour 2007), entities that possessed agency and vibrancy potentially outstripping that of mortal ritualists (Arnold 2001; McAnany 2020). Summoning and negotiating with such forces was best handled by authoritative practitioners steeped in sacred status and practices (Houston 2014). The cosmic polity, as Graeber and Sahlins characterize a kingly realm, positioned a ruler in just this way, in juxtaposition with unpredictable and poorly controlled forces. Ritual practice also potentially buffered the vulnerability of royals to destabilizing threats—natural, social, or martial—by deflecting responsibility onto the shoulders of the gods.

Tokovinine, Estrada Belli, and Fialko (this volume) discuss how identity was vested in specific places. The commemoration of royal ancestors, while common, was manifested differently by local royal spatial associations with the venerated deceased. Classifications of ancestors, deities, and local patron gods sometimes overlapped, but Baron (this volume) clarifies some of the distinguishing features of the latter at Classic-period sites. Patron gods carried weighty importance for individual rulers and/or for community members (Baron 2016; Stuart 2011). Entities such as GI, GII, and GIII—the patron deities of the Palenque dynasty—pertained to royals, while others bolstered solidarity among all constituents within a realm. Baron maintains that during the Classic period, a conceptual separation existed between royal ancestors (*mam*) and patron gods (*k'uh*). This point is disputed by Tokovinine, Estrada Belli, and Fialko (this volume), who see slippage between the two at Naranjo and elsewhere. The centrality of patron deities—as reflected by shrine construction, particularly the massive pyramidal shrines of the Preclassic period that are generally devoid of ancestor interments (Ringle 1999)—suggests that there is validity and time depth to the distinction proposed by Baron. Like most patterns in the Maya region, the distinction was not absolute. Freidel's (this volume) argument for cenotaphs in the Preclassic is a case in point.

Baron emphasizes the intimacy of the connection between patron deities and the rulers who supported, fed, and nurtured them. She also notes that patron deities were tied to specific places, much more so than their ruler caretakers, helping to buttress the local dimension of dual sovereignty. Rulers politicized patron deity shrines to the extent that the rise and fall of the visibility of a patron deity at a site like La Corona correlated with regime change. Due to their influential roles at the heart of cosmic polities, patron deities were sensitive indicators of changing political organization. Baron distinguishes local patron gods from regionally shared founding deities such as K'uk'ulkan in the Terminal Classic and Postclassic periods.

Foundations and Flexibility of Rulership

Freidel (this volume) demonstrates that archaeological evidence can be brought to bear on the foundations of Classic Maya royal alliance and conflict. Drawing on artifactual, textual, and iconographic sources, he outlines rulership signatures in places and times with few hieroglyphic texts. Freidel tracks features attesting to rulers reaching back into the Preclassic period. In his view, distinctions of northern and southern styles of rulership widened during the Early Classic period. Considering the concept of "adverse sacralization" (Graeber and Sahlins 2017:8), Freidel fleshes out a model of sodality kings manifested at sites for which the impulse toward dynasty was muted.

Royal ancestor veneration, exemplified by the large pyramid shrines of the southern lowlands, is thought to be the sine qua non of southern courts and the practice by which royal succession was legitimated. Tokovinine, Estrada Belli, and Fialko (this volume) compare different royal practices and associations with ancestral monuments at the sites of Holmul and Naranjo. Holmul's built environment materialized authority through the construction of funerary shrines to royal ancestors. In contrast, the court of Naranjo concentrated on iconographic programs and shrines dedicated to patron deities, particularly one taking the form of a hummingbird. Mytho-historical narratives were expressed not only architecturally but also in art and writing programs at the sites.

In Martin's diagram (2020:fig. 75) of the political networks of Late Classic lowland courts based on hieroglyphic texts, many courts of northern or eastern coastal Yucatán are underrepresented, given that they have fewer or more poorly preserved records. However, a closer look reveals that these sites exhibit close ties to the Peten—and other centers of power—from the Preclassic through the Postclassic period, for example, on glyphs associated with stucco facades, stelae, altars, portable objects, and murals (Helmke 2020). Similarly, examples from the west coast of Campeche are reviewed by Benavides (this volume). Central Belize has long been identified as an area with direct political ties to major hegemonies of the Classic period (e.g., Chase and Chase 2021; LeCount and Yaeger 2010). Jaime Awe, Christophe Helmke, Claire Ebert, and Julie Hoggarth (this volume) interpret shifting signatures and cycles of rulership from the Preclassic through Classic periods at the Belize Valley sites of Cahal Pech, Blackman Eddy, and Xunantunich. Like the coastal center of Cerros (Freidel, this volume) and the central Peten, central Belize undergoes a florescence during the Middle and Late Preclassic periods, in terms of expanding populations and the cosmological foundations of rulership. This development is materialized explicitly in E-Group and triadic-shrine constructions (Awe, Helmke, Ebert, and Hoggarth, this volume). Subsequently, Awe and colleagues track strategies for the consolidation of local rulership, which are expressed in the idiom of the dynastic heartland with an emphasis on hieroglyphic records, royal ancestral veneration, and the construction and control of sacred landscapes. These sites negotiated advantageously in the contexts of fluctuating regional political alignments with larger, more powerful capitals.

Presentations and Practices of Kingship in Costuming, Adornment, and Feasting

Pervasive ruler portrait art is iconic of Late Classic southern courts, and this corpus permits an analysis of the varied costuming used to represent the social skins of rulers. Royals sometimes wear little more than a loincloth or gauzy *huipil*, while other times their attire was a weighty mix of fabrics and adornments of stone, papier mâché, cloth, feathers, and back racks. Christina Halperin (this volume) turns to the temporalities of kingly costume. She identifies items that commemorate the personage, lifetime, and feats of mortal kings, such as feathered capes, that are linked to martial achievements. Feathered capes are not durable and would not have been passed through generations, unlike adornments made of jade that were inherited and embodied titles, privileges, and capacities of rulers. More broadly, such inherited symbols of office carried the responsibilities of rulers to the body politic in monumental time, beyond the lifespan of individuals. On the other hand, feather capes were indicative of the performance of a particular kind of masculinity that could not be inherited and was not assured by birthright but rather was achieved by the corporeal essence of an adult male. Jade ornaments, in contrast, easily traversed gender distinctions and endured as multigenerational heirlooms. Other chapters also consider the power of embodied, sacred objects that symbolize rulership beyond individual reigns (Baron, this volume; Freidel, this volume; Lamoureux-St-Hilaire and McAnany, this volume; Tokovinine, Estrada Belli, and Fialko, this volume).

How mortal rulers were nourished in a very literal sense is treated by Shanti Morell-Hart (this volume). In her exploration of Classic Maya "gastropolitik," she reveals how modes of authority were created, managed, and subverted through culinary pursuits. Similarly, Lamoureux-St-Hilaire and McAnany (this volume) interpret feasting at La Corona as a strategy to manage the tensions of dual sovereignty within and across polity networks. Foodstuffs occupy a primary place in palace imagery, ranging from *kakaw* glyphs to food offerings, as Morell-Hart discusses. Food scarcity may have plagued some courtly feasts, standing in conflict with occasions meant to demonstrate abundance and largesse. She suggests that innovative culinary solutions, such as the savory plant-based sauces known in contemporary Yucatec feasting cuisine, resolved such dilemmas.

The social contexts of Jaina figurines have been poorly understood because the archaeological provenience is not known for some of the most exquisite examples. Antonio Benavides (this volume) amends this gap by reporting the details of archaeologically documented mortuary contexts with figurines at Jaina. These objects represent one of the richest and most ubiquitous artistic resources pertaining to the roles and adornments of Maya nobility, deities, and other personages. Benavides considers how the faces and corporeal representations of nobles—including seated rulers and courtly personages (such as dwarves)—came to serve as mortuary offerings for ordinary people, including children. He discusses how Jaina figurines embodied and expressed authority, gender roles, and other forms of cultural performance and, interestingly, how they exhibited potential ethnic differences. These patterns imply important social ideals and beliefs disseminated and embraced across class lines.

Elsewhere in the Maya area, figurine assemblages (like the war serpent headdresses that Benavides discusses) portray a similar array of entities and embellishments, and he observes close ties between Jaina and Palenque region sites. Halperin (2017:532–535) suggests that Peten figurines reflected traditions and roles that endured in a monumental, transgenerational timeframe, much like the jade objects she discusses in this volume. As portable objects, these figurines represented placemaking and mnemonic devices, connecting their owners to the events and places where they received them (Halperin 2014:112, 119, 2017:532). Jaina's ties to the Gulf Coast are reflected by INAA sourcing of figurines (Benavides, this volume), which identifies their production origins at influential political centers, such as Jonuta and Comalcalco, as well as at unknown localities in southern Veracruz. The figurines, while not made locally, were especially important to Jaina, a small island center, albeit one with dynastic records, along the coast of Campeche (Benavides, this volume).

Late Maya Rulers and Lords

Postclassic and contact-period Maya rulership is considered by Marilyn Masson (this volume), who argues that historical analogy holds much potential for exploring the divine and mundane faces of rulership over the longue durée. Primarily considered for their differences rather than their continuities with earlier political forms, the societies of the Postclassic and contact periods have for too long been considered emblematic of the collapse of Maya civilization. Masson reviews the archaeological and ethnohistorical evidence for the divine underpinnings and ritual obligations of late Maya rulers, as well as the critical placemaking foundations of political territory, monumental landscapes, and mythical and ancestral descent.

What happened to rulers and aristocracy after the Spanish incursions and ensuing wars of conquest? For the late sixteenth century, historians such as Quezada (2014) have documented the slow chipping away of the authority of "natural lords" and their right to draft labor and to be exempted from the burden of paying tribute to the Spanish Crown. John Chuchiak (this volume) considers the struggle of colonial-era Yucatec-Maya nobility to retain their rights under the Crown, as exemplified by the desire to sport coats of arms. Spanish authorities denied this recognition, based upon the claim that Maya lords lacked patrimonial landholdings. Yucatec lords were ultimately undeterred by failures to achieve this goal through official channels, and they created their own coats-of-arms, some of which adorned architectural facades and survived the ensuing centuries. Most students of Maya studies are familiar with the arborescent Xiu coats of arms that blends the traditional iconography of Spanish heraldic shields with Indigenous forms of ancestor imagery, demonstrating proclivity for assembling hybrid identities in the early colonial period.

Broader Picture Assessments

Further expanding the analytical lens of rulership, David Wengrow (this volume) deconstructs the study of the emergence of rulership and institutionalized inequality. He reconceptualizes this process according to three elementary forms of domination: *control of violence, control of knowledge,* and *charismatic politics*. His thought-provoking chapter takes these themes beyond the arena of Maya studies. Wengrow, building on his book with David Graeber (Graeber and Wengrow 2021), argues against traditional typological approaches to understanding civilization, advocating for a comparative approach that tracks differences and similarities among historical political forms. Variable societal investment in bureaucracy and sovereignty is gauged in terms of the latter's prerogative to violently enforce decisions. Political competition, in Wengrow's view, leads to dramatically different pathways to rulership. For the Classic Maya region, Wengrow (this volume) suggests the term "cosmic bureaucracy" as a good fit, given that the administration of royal courts was founded at least partially in the field of supernatural places, forces, and beings. Evidence for Maya area earthly bureaucracies, scarcely mentioned in hieroglyphic texts but perhaps hidden in plain sight, has not yet gained significant traction although chapters of this book speak to the issue (Masson, this volume; Ringle, this volume). Wengrow contrasts the covenantal overtones of cosmic bureaucracy with Mesopotamian statecraft, in which the heavens were perceived as places inhabited by gods who might intervene unexpectedly in human affairs and potentially instigate chaotic ruptures. Significantly, he proposes that the roots of these three elementary forms of domination can be found in households and small family groups, an idea that syncs with scholarship on the origins of inequality and the emergence of authority in the Maya area (e.g., McAnany 1995, 2010).

The last word on the faces of Maya rulership is provided by Scott Hutson (this volume), who dwells upon the notion of sovereignty and the many ways in which it could be compromised now and in the past. He rightly points out that faces of authority only existed in relation to the faces of the many constituents who chose to support their authority (or not). In other words, rulership is a deeply relational proposition in which a ruler is immersed in a dense network of relationships both within and among royal courts. By considering the potential fragility and limited agency of Classic Maya royal authority (McAnany 2019), he emphasizes the exertion of power by courtiers and households as the framework upon which political power depended.

Echoing the thoughts of Wengrow, Hutson notes that tropes of rulership in the Maya Lowlands often were based on concepts of hierarchy and authority as well as on the ritual and feasting activities that have domestic roots in nonroyal Preclassic households (see also Lucero 2003; McAnany 1995; Robin 2013). Thus, the "divine exceptionalism" (Hutson, this volume) that rulers claimed for themselves both held them aloft and simultaneously grounded them in deep time. But it was a fragile paradigm requiring balance, maintenance, and renewal, and it was subject to cycles of failure and reemergence by successor sponsors in shifting scenarios of place and time. Parallel frameworks for rulership from the Classic to the Postclassic period, despite more widely discussed differences, illustrate the ultimate durability of key elements of Maya rulership.

Final Thoughts

Taken altogether, the contributions to this volume expand our understanding of rulership and authority. Each places Maya rulership in dynamic conversation with comparative studies of politics and kingly authority, while not neglecting the distinctive cultural qualities and specific historical trajectories of rulership in the Maya region. Balancing general patterns with specific details represents a perpetual challenge of archaeology, a discipline that often tilts between overly generalized theoretical explanations that lack the richness of historical context and overly thick description of specific material cases with comparative implications left unexplored. We strive to achieve a balance between these two approaches in this volume.

REFERENCES CITED

Andrieu, Chloé
    2021   K'uhul Ajaw and Sacred Kings: Historicity and Change in Sacred Royalty / Divine Kingship Societies. In *Maya Kingship: Rupture and Transformation from Classic to Postclassic Times*, edited by Tsubaka Okoshi, Arlen F. Chase, Phillippe Nondédéo, and M. Charlotte Arnauld, pp. 21–34. University Press of Florida, Gainesville.

Ardren, Traci (editor)
    2002   *Ancient Maya Women*. AltaMira Press, Walnut Creek, Calif.

Arnauld, M. Charlotte, Tsubasa Okoshi, Arlen F. Chase, and Phillippe Nondédéo
    2021   Introduction to *Maya Kingship: Rupture and Transformation from Classic to Postclassic Times*, edited by Tsubaka Okoshi, Arlen F. Chase, Phillippe Nondédéo, and M. Charlotte Arnauld, pp. 1–20. University Press of Florida, Gainesville.

Arnold, Philip P.
    2001   *Eating Landscape: Aztec and European Occupation of Tlalocan*. University Press of Colorado, Niwot.

Ashmore, Wendy
    2009   Mesoamerican Landscape Archaeologies. *Ancient Mesoamerica* 20(2):183–187.

Awe, Jaime J., Christopher Helmke, Diane Slocum, and Douglas Tilden
    2020   Ally, Client, or Outpost? Evaluating the Relationship between Xunantunich and Naranjo in the Late Classic Period. *Ancient Mesoamerica* 31(3):494–506.

Baron, Joanne P.
    2016   *Patron Gods and Patron Lords: The Semiotics of Classic Maya Community Cults*. University Press of Colorado, Boulder.

Bell, Ellen E.
    2002   Engendering a Dynasty: A Royal Woman in the Margarita Tomb, Copan. In *Ancient Maya Women*, edited by Traci Ardren, pp. 89–104. AltaMira Press, Walnut Creek, Calif.

Bennett, Jane
    2010   *Vibrant Matter: A Political Ecology of Things*. Duke University Press, Durham, N.C.

Berlin, Heinrich
    1958   El glifo "emblema" en las inscripciones mayas. *Journal de la Société des Américanistes* 47(1):111–119.

Blanton, Richard E., and Lane Fargher
    2008   *Collective Action in the Formation of Pre-Modern States*. Springer, New York.
    2016   *How Humans Cooperate: Confronting the Challenges of Collective Action*. University Press of Colorado, Boulder.

Blanton, Richard E., Gary M. Feinman, Stephen A. Kowalewski, and Peter N. Peregrine
    1996   A Dual-Processual Theory for the Evolution of Mesoamerican Civilization. *Current Anthropology* 37(1):1–86.

Bonfil Batalla, Guillermo
    1996   *México profundo: Reclaiming a Civilization*. Translated by Philip A. Dennis. University of Texas Press, Austin.

Canuto, Marcello A., and Tomás Barrientos Q.
    2020   La Corona: Negotiating a Landscape of Power. In *Approaches to Monumental Landscapes of the Ancient Maya*, edited by Brett A. Houk, Barbara Arroyo, and Terry G. Powis, pp. 171–195. University Press of Florida, Gainesville.

Carballo, David M.
    2020   Power, Politics, and Governance at Teotihuacan. In *Teotihuacan: The World Beyond the City*, edited by Kenneth G. Hirth, David M. Carballo, and Barbara Arroyo, pp. 57–96. Dumbarton Oaks Research Library and Collection, Washington, D.C.

Catherwood, Frederick
    1844   *Views of Ancient Monuments in Central America, Chiapas, and Yucatan*. F. Catherwood, London.

Chase, Arlen F., and Diane Z. Chase
- 2021 The Transformation of Maya Rulership at Caracol, Belize. In *Maya Kingship: Rupture and Transformation from Classic to Postclassic Times*, edited by Tsubaka Okoshi, Arlen F. Chase, Phillippe Nondédéo, and M. Charlotte Arnauld, pp. 224–245. University Press of Florida, Gainesville.

Chinchilla Mazariegos, Oswaldo
- 2017 *Art and Myth of the Ancient Maya*. Yale University Press, New Haven.

Coe, Michael D.
- 1992 *Breaking the Maya Code*. Thames and Hudson, New York.

Dickson, D. Bruce
- 2006 Public Transcripts Expressed in Theatres of Cruelty: The Royal Graves at Ur in Mesopotamia. *Cambridge Archaeological Journal* 16(2):123–144.

Dietler, Michael
- 2001 Theorizing the Feast: Rituals of Consumption, Commensal Politics, and Power in African Contexts. In *Feasts: Archaeological and Ethnographic Perspectives on Food, Politics, and Power*, edited by Michael Dietler and Brian Hayden, pp. 65–114. Smithsonian Institution Press, Washington, D.C.

Doyle, James A.
- 2012 Regroup on "E-Groups": Monumentality and Early Centers in the Middle Preclassic Lowlands. *Latin American Antiquity* 23(4):355–379.

Earle, Timothy K.
- 1997 *How Chiefs Come to Power: The Political Economy in Prehistory*. Stanford University Press, Stanford.

Eisenstadt, Schmuel
- 1980 Cultural Orientations, Institutional Entrepreneurs, and Social Change: Comparative Analysis of Traditional Civilizations. *American Journal of Sociology* 85(4):840–869.

Fargher, Lane, Richard E. Blanton, Verenice Y. Heredia, John Millhauser, Nezahualcoyotl Xiuhtecutli, and Lisa Overholtzer
- 2011 Tlaxcallan: The Archaeology of an Ancient Republic in the New World. *Antiquity* 85(327):172–186.

Fash, William L.
- 2001 *Scribes, Warriors, and Kings: The City of Copán and the Ancient Maya*. 2nd ed. Thames and Hudson, London.

Fash, William L., and Leonardo López Luján (editors)
- 2009 *The Art of Urbanism: How Mesoamerican Kingdoms Represented Themselves in Architecture and Imagery*. Dumbarton Oaks Research Library and Collection, Washington, D.C.

Feinman, Gary M., and David M. Carballo
- 2018 Collaborative and Competitive Strategies in the Variability and Resiliency of Large-Scale Societies in Mesoamerica. *Economic Anthropology* 5(1):7–19.

Freidel, David
- 2018 Maya and the Idea of Empire. In *Pathways to Complexity: A View from the Maya Lowlands*, edited by M. Kathryn Brown and George J. Bey III, pp. 363–386. University Press of Florida, Gainesville.

Freidel, David, and Linda Schele
- 1988 Kingship in the Late Preclassic Maya Lowlands: The Instruments and Places of Ritual Power. *American Anthropologist* 90(3):547–567.

Freidel, David, Linda Schele, and Joy Parker
- 1993 *Maya Cosmos: Three Thousand Years on the Shaman's Path*. W. Morrow, New York.

Geller, Pamela L.
- 2017 *The Bioarchaeology of Socio-sexual Lives: Queering Common Sense about Sex, Gender, and Sexuality*. Springer, Cham.

Graeber, David
- 2017a The Divine Kingship of the Shilluk: On Violence, Utopia, and the Human Condition. In *On Kings*, by David Graeber and Marshall Sahlins, pp. 65–138. Hau Books, Chicago.
- 2017b Notes on the Politics of Divine Kingship: Or, Elements for an Archaeology of Sovereignty. In *On Kings*, by David Graeber and Marshall Sahlins, pp. 377–464. Hau Books, Chicago.

Graeber, David, and Marshall Sahlins
- 2017 *On Kings*. Hau Books, Chicago.

Graeber, David, and David Wengrow
    2021   *The Dawn of Everything: A New History of Humanity*. Farrar, Straus and Giroux, New York.

Grube, Nikolai
    2021   Nostalgic Kings: The Rhetoric of Terminal Classic Maya Inscriptions. In *Maya Kingship: Rupture and Transformation from Classic to Postclassic Times*, edited by Tsubaka Okoshi, Arlen F. Chase, Phillippe Nondédéo, and M. Charlotte Arnauld, pp. 35–50. University Press of Florida, Gainesville.

Halperin, Christina T.
    2014   Circulation as Placemaking: Late Classic Maya Polities and Portable Objects. *American Anthropologist* 116(1):110–129.
    2017   Temporalities of Late Classic to Postclassic (ca. AD 600–1521) Maya Figurines from Central Petén, Guatemala. *Latin American Antiquity* 28(4):515–540.

Hanks, William F.
    2010   *Converting Words: Maya in the Age of the Cross*. University of California Press, Berkeley.

Harrison-Buck, Eleanor
    2021   Relational Economies of Reciprocal Gifting: A Case Study of Exchanges in Ancient Maya Marriage and War. *Current Anthropology* 62(5):569–601.

Headrick, Annabeth
    2007   *The Teotihuacan Trinity: The Sociopolitical Structure of an Ancient Mesoamerican City*. University of Texas Press, Austin.

Helmke, Christophe
    2020   Under the Lordly Monarchs of the North: The Epigraphy of Northern Belize. *Ancient Mesoamerica* 31(2):261–286.

Hendon, Julia A.
    2006   Textile Production as Craft in Mesoamerica: Time, Labor, and Knowledge. *Journal of Social Archaeology* 6(3):354–378.

Hodder, Ian
    2011   Human-Thing Entanglement: Towards an Integrated Archaeological Perspective. *Journal of the Royal Anthropological Institute* 17(1):154–177.

Houston, Stephen D.
    2006   Impersonation, Dance, and the Problem of Spectacle among the Classic Maya. In *Archaeology of Performance: Theaters of Power, Community, and Politics*, edited by Takeshi Inomata and Lawrence S. Coben, pp. 135–155. AltaMira Press, Lanham, Md.
    2009   A Splendid Predicament: Young Men in Classic Maya Society. *Cambridge Archaeological Journal* 19:149–178.
    2014   *The Life Within: Classic Maya and the Matter of Permanence*. Yale University Press, New Haven.
    2018   *The Gifted Passage: Young Men in Classic Maya Art and Text*. Yale University Press, New Haven.

Houston, Stephen D. (editor)
    1998   *Function and Meaning in Classic Maya Architecture*. Dumbarton Oaks Research Library and Collection, Washington, D.C.

Houston, Stephen D., and Tom Cummins
    2004   Body, Presence, and Space in Andean and Mesoamerican Rulership. In *Palaces of the Ancient New World: Form, Function and Meaning*, edited by Susan Toby Evans and Joanne Pillsbury, pp. 359–398. Dumbarton Oaks Research Library and Collection, Washington, D.C.

Houston, Stephen D., Héctor Escobedo, Mark Child, Charles W. Golden, and René Muñoz
    2003   The Moral Community: Maya Settlement Transformation at Piedras Negras, Guatemala. In *The Social Construction of Ancient Cities*, edited by Monica L. Smith, pp. 212–253. Smithsonian Books, Washington, D.C.

Houston, Stephen D., and David Stuart
    1996   Of Gods, Glyphs, and Kings: Divinity and Rulership among the Classic Maya. *Antiquity* 70:289–312.
    1998   Pre-Columbian States of Being. Special issue, *RES: Anthropology and Aesthetics* 33:73–101.

Houston, Stephen D., David Stuart, and Karl Taube
    2006   *The Memory of Bones: Body, Being, and Experience among the Classic Maya*. University of Texas Press, Austin.

Iannone, Gyles (editor)
   2014   *The Great Maya Droughts in Cultural Context: Case Studies in Resilience and Vulnerability.* University Press of Colorado, Boulder.

Inomata, Takeshi, and Lawrence S. Coben (editors)
   2006   *Archaeology of Performance: Theaters of Power, Community, and Politics.* AltaMira Press, Lanham, Md.

Inomata, Takeshi, and Stephen D. Houston (editors)
   2000–2001   *Royal Courts of the Ancient Maya.* 2 vols. Westview Press, Boulder, Colo.

Inomata, Takeshi, Daniela Triadan, Véronica A. Vázquez López, Juan Carlos Fernandez-Diaz, Takayuki Omori, María Belén Méndez Bauer, Melina García Hernández, Timothy Beach, Clarissa Cagnato, Kazuo Aoyama, and Hiroo Nasu
   2020   Monumental Architecture at Aguada Fénix and the Rise of Maya Civilization. *Nature* 582:530–533.

Jackson, Sarah, and David Stuart
   2001   The Aj K'uhun Title: Deciphering a Classic Maya Term of Rank. *Ancient Mesoamerica* 12(2):217–228.

Jones, Grant D.
   1989   *Maya Resistance to Spanish Rule: Time and History on a Colonial Frontier.* University of New Mexico Press, Albuquerque.
   1998   *The Conquest of the Last Maya Kingdom.* Stanford University Press, Stanford.

Joyce, Arthur A., Laura Arnaud Bustamante, and Marc N. Levine
   2001   Commoner Power: A Case Study from the Classic Period Collapse on the Oaxaca Coast. *Journal of Archaeological Method and Theory* 8(4):343–385.

Joyce, Rosemary A.
   2008   *Ancient Bodies, Ancient Lives: Sex, Gender, and Archaeology.* Thames and Hudson, New York.

Kepecs, Susan, and Rani T. Alexander
   2018   Colonial and Postcolonial Change in Mesoamerica: An Introduction. In *Colonial and Postcolonial Change in Mesoamerica: Archaeology as Historical Anthropology*, edited by Rani T. Alexander and Susan Kepecs, pp. 1–10. University of New Mexico Press, Albuquerque.

Kurnick, Sarah
   2016   Paradoxical Politics: Negotiating the Contradictions of Political Authority. In *Political Strategies in Pre-Columbian Mesoamerica*, edited by Sarah Kurnick and Joanne P. Baron, pp. 3–36. University Press of Colorado, Boulder.

Latour, Bruno
   2007   *Reassembling the Social: An Introduction to Actor-Network Theory.* Oxford University Press, Oxford.

LeCount, Lisa J., and Jason Yaeger (editors)
   2010   *Classic Maya Provincial Politics: Xunantunich and Its Hinterlands.* University of Arizona Press, Tucson.

López de Cogolludo, Fray Diego
   1688   *Historia de la provincia de Yucathan.* Juan Garcia Infanzon, Madrid.

Lucero, Lisa J.
   2003   The Politics of Ritual: The Emergence of Classic Maya Kings. *Current Anthropology* 44(4):523–558.

Marcus, Joyce
   1976   *Emblem and State in the Classic Maya Lowlands: An Epigraphic Approach to Territorial Organization.* Dumbarton Oaks, Trustees for Harvard University, Washington, D.C.

Marken, Damien B., Stanley P. Guenter, and David Freidel
   2017   He's Maya, but He's Not My Brother: Exploring the Place and Ethnicity of Classic Maya Social Organization. In *"The Only True People": Linking Maya Identities Past and Present*, edited by Bethany J. Beyyette and Lisa J. LeCount, pp. 187–218. University Press of Colorado, Boulder.

Martin, Simon
   2020   *Ancient Maya Politics: A Political Anthropology of the Classic Period 150–900 CE.* Cambridge University Press, Cambridge.

Martin, Simon, and Nikolai Grube
   1995   Maya Superstates. *Archaeology* 48(6):41–46.
   2008   *Chronicle of the Maya Kings and Queens: Deciphering the Dynasties of the Ancient Maya.* 2nd ed. Thames and Hudson, New York.

Masson, Marilyn A.
- 2021 The "Othering" of Maya Political Economies. *Urban Commerce in the Ancient Americas*, special issue, *Archaeological Papers of the American Anthropological Association* 31(1):109–127.

Masson, Marilyn A., Timothy S. Hare, and Carlos Peraza Lope
- 2006 Postclassic Maya Society Regenerated at Mayapán. In *After Collapse: The Regeneration of Complex Societies*, edited by Glenn M. Schwartz and John J. Nichols, pp. 188–207. University of Arizona Press, Tucson.

Masson, Marilyn A., and Carlos Peraza Lope
- 2010 Evidence for Maya-Mexican Interaction in the Archaeological Record of Mayapan. In *Astronomers, Scribes, and Priests: Intellectual Interchange between the Northern Maya Lowlands and Highland Mexico in the Late Postclassic Period*, edited by Gabrielle Vail and Christine Hernández, pp. 77–114. Dumbarton Oaks Research Library and Collection, Washington, D.C.
- 2014 *Kukulkan's Realm: Urban Life at Ancient Mayapan*. University Press of Colorado, Boulder.

Mathews, Peter
- 1991 Classic Maya Emblem Glyphs. In *Classic Maya Political History: Hieroglyphic and Archaeological Evidence*, edited by T. Patrick Culbert, pp. 19–29. Cambridge University Press, Cambridge.

McAnany, Patricia A.
- 1995 *Living with the Ancestors: Kinship and Kingship in Ancient Maya Society*. University of Texas Press, Austin.
- 1998 Ancestors and the Classic Maya Built Environment. In *Function and Meaning in Classic Maya Architecture*, edited by Stephen D. Houston, pp. 271–298. Dumbarton Oaks Research Library and Collection, Washington, D.C.
- 2010 *Ancestral Maya Economies in Archaeological Perspective*. Cambridge University Press, New York.
- 2013 Artisans, *Ikatz*, and Statecraft: Provisioning Classic Maya Royal Courts. In *Merchants, Markets, and Exchange in the Pre-Columbian World*, edited by Kenneth G. Hirth and Joanne Pillsbury, pp. 229–253. Dumbarton Oaks Research Library and Collection, Washington, D.C.
- 2019 Fragile Authority in Monumental Time: Political Experimentation in the Classic Maya Lowlands. In *The Evolution of Fragility: Setting the Terms*, edited by Norman Yoffee, pp. 47–59. McDonald Institute Conversations, Cambridge.
- 2020 Soul Proprietors: Durable Ontologies of Maya Deep Time. In *Sacred Matters: Animacy and Authority in Pre-Columbian America*, edited by Steve Kosiba, John Wayne Janusek, and Thomas B. F. Cummins, pp. 71–104. Dumbarton Oaks Research Library and Collection, Washington, D.C.

Miller, Mary Ellen
- 2001 Life at Court: The View from Bonampak. In *Royal Courts of the Ancient Maya*, edited by Takeshi Inomata and Stephen D. Houston, vol. 2, pp. 201–222. Westview Press, Boulder, Colo.

Miller, Mary Ellen, and Claudia Brittenham
- 2013 *The Spectacle of the Late Maya Court: Reflections on the Murals of Bonampak*. University of Texas Press, Austin.

Miller, Mary Ellen, and Simon Martin
- 2004 *Courtly Art of the Ancient Maya*. Fine Arts Museums of San Francisco, San Francisco.

Okoshi, Tsubaka, Arlen F. Chase, Phillippe Nondédéo, and M. Charlotte Arnauld (editors)
- 2021 *Maya Kingship: Rupture and Transformation from Classic to Postclassic Times*. University Press of Florida, Gainesville.

Piña Chan, Román
- 1978 Commerce in the Yucatec Peninsula: The Conquest and Colonial Period. In *Mesoamerican Communication Routes and Cultural Contacts*, edited by Thomas A. Lee and Carlos Navarrete, pp. 37–48. New World Archaeological Foundation, Brigham Young University, Provo, Utah.

Pohl, John M. D.

    2003a   Creation Stories, Hero Cults, and Alliance Building: Confederacies of Central and Southern Mexico. In *The Postclassic Mesoamerican World*, edited by Michael E. Smith and Frances F. Berdan, pp. 61–66. University of Utah Press, Salt Lake City.

    2003b   Ritual Ideology and Commerce in the Southern Mexican Highlands. In *The Postclassic Mesoamerican World*, edited by Michael E. Smith and Frances F. Berdan, pp. 172–177. University of Utah Press, Salt Lake City.

Price, Neil, Charlotte Hedenstierna-Jonson, Torun Zachrisson, Anna Kjellström, Jan Stora, Maja Krzewińska, Torsten Günther, Verónica Sobrado, Mattias Jakobsson, and Anders Götherström

    2019   Viking Warrior Women? Reassessing Birka Chamber Grave Bj.581. *Antiquity* 93:181–198.

Proskouriakoff, Tatiana

    1960   Historical Implications of a Pattern of Dates at Piedras Negras, Guatemala. *American Antiquity* 25(4):454–475.

    1963   Historical Data in the Inscriptions of Yaxchilan, Part I. *Estudios de cultura maya* 3:149–167.

    1964   Historical Data in the Inscriptions of Yaxchilan, Part II. *Estudios de cultura maya* 4:177–201.

Quezada, Sergio

    2014   *Maya Lords and Lordship: The Formation of Colonial Society in Yucatán, 1350–1600*. Translated by Terry Rugeley. University of Oklahoma Press, Norman.

Rathje, Willam J.

    2002   The Nouveau Elite Potlatch: One Scenario for the Monumental Rise of Early Civilizations. In *Ancient Maya Political Economies*, edited by Marilyn A. Masson and David Freidel, pp. 31–40. Altamira Press, Walnut Creek, Calif.

Reese-Taylor, Kathryn, Peter Mathews, Julia Guernsey, and Marlene Fritzler

    2009   Warrior Queens among the Classic Maya. In *Blood and Beauty: Organized Violence in the Art and Archaeology of Mesoamerica and Central America*, edited by Heather Orr and Rex Koontz, pp. 39–72. Cotsen Institute of Archaeology Press, Los Angeles.

Relaciones histórico-geográficas de las provincias de Yucatán

    1900   *Colección de documentos ineditos relativos al descubrimiento, conquista y organización, de las antiguas poseiones espanolas de ultramar: Relaciones de Yucatán* 13, part 2. Real Academia de la Historia, Madrid.

Restall, Matthew

    1997   *The Maya World: Yucatec Culture and Society, 1550–1850*. Stanford University Press, Stanford.

    2001   The People of the Patio: Ethnohistoric Evidence of Yucatec Maya Royal Courts. In *Royal Courts of the Ancient Maya*, edited by Takeshi Inomata and Stephen D. Houston, vol. 2, pp. 335–390. Westview Press, Boulder, Colo.

Ringle, William M.

    1999   Pre-Classic Cityscapes: Ritual Politics among the Early Lowland Maya. In *Social Patterns in Pre-Classic Mesoamerica*, edited by David C. Grove and Rosemary A. Joyce, pp. 183–223. Dumbarton Oaks Research Library and Collection, Washington, D.C.

    2004   On the Political Organization of Chichen Itza. *Ancient Mesoamerica* 15(2):167–218.

Ringle, William M., and George J. Bey III

    2009   The Face of the Itzas. In *The Art of Urbanism: How Mesoamerican Kingdoms Represented Themselves in Architecture and Imagery*, edited by William L. Fash and Leonardo López Luján, pp. 329–383. Dumbarton Oaks Research Library and Collection, Washington, D.C.

Ringle, William M., Tomás Gallareta Negrón, and George J. Bey III

    2021   Stranger-Kings in Northern Yucatan. In *Maya Kingship: Rupture and Transformation from Classic to Postclassic Times*, edited by Tsubaka Okoshi, Arlen F. Chase, Phillippe Nondédéo, and M. Charlotte Arnauld, pp. 249–269. University Press of Florida, Gainesville.

Río, Antonio del

    1822   *Description of the Ruins of an Ancient City Discovered near Palenque, in the Kingdom of Guatemala, in Spanish America.*

Translated by Paul Felix Cabrera. Henry Berthoud, London.

Robin, Cynthia
   2013   *Everyday Life Matters: Maya Farmers at Chan.* University Press of Florida, Gainesville.

Ruz Lhuillier, Alberto
   1973   *El Templo de las Inscripciones, Palenque.* Instituto Nacional de Antropología e Historia, Mexico City.

Sahlins, Marshall
   1981   *Historical Metaphors and Mythical Realities: Structure in the Early History of the Sandwich Islands Kingdom.* University of Michigan Press, Ann Arbor.
   2008   The Stranger-King or, Elementary Forms of the Politics of Life. *Indonesia and the Malay World* 36:177–199.
   2017   The Stranger-Kingship of the Mexica. In *On Kings*, by David Graeber and Marshall Sahlins, pp. 223–248. University of Chicago Press, Chicago.

Sánchez de Aguilar, Pedro
   1639   *Informe contra idolorum cultores del obispado de Yucatán.* Por la viuda de Juan Gonzalez, Madrid.

Schele, Linda, and David Freidel
   1990   *A Forest of Kings: The Untold Story of the Ancient Maya.* W. Morrow, New York.

Schele, Linda, and Peter Mathews
   1998   *The Code of Kings: The Language of Seven Sacred Maya Temples and Tombs.* Scribner, New York.

Schele, Linda, and Mary Ellen Miller
   1986   *Blood of Kings: Dynasty and Ritual in Maya Art.* George Braziller, New York.

Smith, Adam T.
   2011   Archaeologies of Sovereignty. *Annual Review of Anthropology* 40(1):415–432.
   2015   *The Political Machine: Assembling Sovereignty in the Bronze Age Caucasus.* Princeton University Press, Princeton.

Solis, Ruth Shady
   2006   America's First City? The Case of Late Archaic Caral. In *Andean Archaeology III*, edited by William H. Isbell and Helaine Silverman, pp. 28–66. Springer, New York.

Stone, Andrea
   1989   Disconnection, Foreign Insignia, and Political Expansion: Teotihuacan and the Warrior Stelae of Piedras Negras. In *Mesoamerica after the Decline of Teotihuacan, AD 700–900*, edited by Richard A. Diehl and Janet Catherine Berlo, pp. 153–172. Dumbarton Oaks Research Library and Collection, Washington, D.C.

Stuart, David
   1988   Blood Symbolism in Maya Iconography. In *Maya Iconography*, edited by Elizabeth P. Benson and Gillett G. Griffin, pp. 175–221. Princeton University Press, Princeton.
   2000   "The arrival of strangers": Teotihuacan and Tollan in Classic Maya Study. In *Mesoamerica's Classic Heritage: From Teotihuacan to the Aztecs*, edited by David Carrasco, Lindsay Jones, and Scott Sessions, pp. 465–513. University Press of Colorado, Boulder.
   2011   *The Order of Days: The Maya World and the Truth about 2012.* Harmony Books, New York.

Sugiyama, Nawa, William L. Fash, Barbara W. Fash, and Saburo Sugiyama
   2020   The Maya at Teotihuacan? New Insights into Teotihuacan-Maya Interaction from the Plaza of the Columns Complex. In *Teotihuacan: The World Beyond the City*, edited by Kenneth G. Hirth, David M. Carballo, and Barbara Arroyo, pp. 139–171. Dumbarton Oaks Research Library and Collection, Washington, D.C.

Sugiyama, Saburo, and Nawa Sugiyama
   2020   Interactions between Ancient Teotihuacan and the Maya World. In *The Maya World*, edited by Scott R. Hutson and Traci Ardren, pp. 689–711. Routledge, New York.

Thompson, J. Eric S.
   1966   *The Rise and Fall of Maya Civilization.* 2nd ed. University of Oklahoma Press, Norman.

Tokovinine, Alexandre
   2013   *Place and Identity in Classic Maya Narratives.* Dumbarton Oaks Research Library and Collection, Washington, D.C.

Tokovinine, Alexandre, and Dmitri Beliaev

2013   People of the Road: Traders and Travelers in Ancient Maya Words and Images. In *Merchants, Markets, and Exchange in the Pre-Columbian World*, edited by Kenneth G. Hirth and Joanne Pillsbury, pp. 169–200. Dumbarton Oaks Research Library and Collection, Washington, D.C.

Vail, Gabrielle, and Christine Hernández

2011   The Construction of Memory: The Use of Classic Period Divinatory Texts in the Late Postclassic Maya Codices. *Ancient Mesoamerica* 22(2):449–462.

Vail, Gabrielle, and Andrea Stone

2002   Representations of Maya Women in Postclassic and Colonial Maya Literature and Art. In *Ancient Maya Women*, edited by Traci Ardren, pp. 203–228. Altamira Press, Walnut Creek, Calif.

Zender, Marc

2004   A Study of Classic Maya Priesthood. PhD dissertation, University of Calgary, Alberta.

Rulers, Relatives, and Royal Courts

Excavating the Foundations of Classic Maya Alliance and Conflict

DAVID FREIDEL

Invisible and Anonymous Rulers of the North

Something is different about kingship in northern Yucatan. This is probably due, in part, to the deep regional roots of social complexity, roots we now know extended well back into the Middle Formative period..." (Ringle, Gallareta Negrón, and Bey 2021:249)

The northern, central peninsular, and eastern Caribbean littoral lowland Maya did have divine or sacred rulers—cosmic strangers as David Graeber and Marshall Sahlins have lucidly described them (Graeber and Sahlins 2017)—even though they are rarely portrayed on stone stelae and even more rarely found interred. Acknowledging the nearly invisible rulers of the Maya north, central peninsular region, and Belize (Awe, Helmke, Ebert, and Hoggarth, this volume; Helmke, Guenter, and Wanyerka 2018) challenges and encourages a rethinking of current models of Maya history and evolution.

Of invisible rulers, Graeber and Sahlins say: "The chief weapon in the hands of those who oppose the expansion of royal power might be termed 'adverse sacralization'—to recognize the metahuman status of the monarch, to 'keep the king divine'... Kings become invisible, immaterial, sealed off from contact with their subjects or with the stuff and substance of the world—and hence, often, confined to their palaces, unable to exercise arbitrary power (or often any power) in any effective way" (Graeber and Sahlins 2017:8). Their arguments regarding invisibility and adverse sacralization become nuanced and complex, but the tensions and negotiations of power between rulers and followers remain a driving force of their explanations. Maya invisible emergent rulers, however, were demonstrably powerful from the Preclassic beginning, as manifest in royal jewels and central architecture, and remained so to the end. So the matter is not a simple one. However, I suspect that adverse sacralization was at work in keeping rulers beholden to their councils—that is, the men and women who divined their selection, their accession, and their initiation into the brotherhood of rulers. Ringle, Gallareta Negrón, and Bey (2021) demonstrate the enduring architectural design of northern lowland and central peninsular throne rooms and flanking court rooms in the Classic and Terminal Classic periods (Arnauld 2021). Rulership, relations, and royal courts were entangled for the ancient Maya (Martin 2020), as they were everywhere. It is no wonder that stranger rulership is a general strategy for establishing provisional political boundaries between them. Invisibility in rulership was a kind of koan for Maya divine rulers such as existed outside the southern Classic lowland civilization. People knew rulers when they saw them—knew them through their regalia, spectacles, acts, decisions, and architectural works (Ringle, this volume), even if they did not see them memorialized very much as human images. Even then, the rulers were generally seen as anonymous sacred beings, excepting remarkable breakout individuals who, late in the Classic period, revealed their faces on stelae and murals, declaring their dynasty as an institution. Hesitating well over half a millennium from the advent of dynasty in the southern lowlands in the Proto-Classic period (Martin 2020), the great majority of these rulers and their councils surely chose not to institute and publicize patrimonial succession. To suggest that these Preclassic and Classic rulers lacked the means to mobilize communities to build and sustain dynasties is simply not commensurate with the current archaeological record of precocious, pervasive, and enduring political power, particularly as expressed in architecture (Ringle, this volume; Ringle, Gallareta Negrón, and Bey 2021; Stanton et al. 2010; Tiesler et al. 2017).

Evidence in hand suggests that the invisible and anonymous Preclassic and Classic rulers of the north, as well as some of the eastern littoral of Belize (Awe, Helmke, Ebert, and Hoggarth, this volume; Helmke, Guenter, and Wanyerka 2018) did not feel compelled to embody themselves in stone stelae that detailed their lineages, even when they did commission stone monuments (Freidel 2012, 2018). Given their power to raise massive places of performance in centers and to commission a range of precious power objects, including some closely resembling or identical to those of the Classic dynasts in the south (Freidel and Suhler 1995), invisibility or anonymity hardly dampened their spirits. Their qualifications likely included demonstrated character and potential, the courage to undergo ritual death and resurrection (Garber and Awe 2008), and perhaps their stranger status (inherent to the resurrected in my view) distinguishing them from fellow *ajawtaak*. Rather than celebrate their kinship ties, I suggest that they appealed to their communities through patron deities and their councils. If I am right, surely qualified candidates came from distinguished families, and rulers had powerful kin supporters as well as sodality ones. Yet the importance of the office and its settings over the person is pervasively manifest in the Preclassic lowland material symbols of rulership (Freidel 1979, 1992; Freidel and Schele 1988) as well as in the symbolism of northern Classic rulers (Ringle, this volume; Ringle, Gallareta Negrón, and Bey 2021).

Bundles and Bundle Shrines: The Afterlife of Invisible Rulers

Some architectural, iconographic, and bioarchaeological evidence suggests that many rulers were materially present in death, through bundling and curation in bundle shrines (Acuña 2018; Reese-Taylor et al. 2006; Walker 2016). Maya mortuary practices from the Preclassic period onward (McAnany 2014:60–61) reveal the inclusion of extra body parts in graves; these are plausibly tokens from bundled ancestors. Undisturbed Maya tombs often reveal textiles indicating bundling of the deceased, including those in a prone position (Carrasco et al. 1999; Garcia-Moreno 2003, 2004; Guernsey 2006; Pendergast 1981, 1982). There are examples of seated rulers from as early as the Late Preclassic period whose remains were clearly bundled, such as Ruler Yax Ehb Xook of Tikal (Coe and McGinn 1963). Bundles in shrines are vulnerable to cremation by both enemies and friends (Headrick 1994), and hence may be preserved only in traces when interred. The advantage of ancestor bundles is

figure 2.1
Upper east panel, Structure 5C-2nd at Cerros. Reconstruction drawing by Kathryn Reese-Taylor.

figure 2.2
Lower east panel, Structure 5C-2nd at Cerros. Reconstruction drawing by Kathryn Reese-Taylor.

that they keep people present in the context of the living, and, as in the case of the Inka (Bauer and Covey 2002), the transformation of deceased rulers into bundles would have perpetuated a practice of making rulers divine during their living careers.

In general, the Maya constructed the divinity of their living rulers and queens in deity embodiments and power accoutrements (Freidel 1992); the divinity of their deceased royals was materialized in bundles, and buildings represented their sacred status in both life and in death (Freidel and Schele 1989). Graeber and Sahlins (2017:2) declare that people from deep antiquity in most places have lived in "cosmic polities" populated with hierarchically ordered "metahuman" powers. Divine rulers are imitations of the gods. This expansively animist manifesto is commensurate with views in *Maya Cosmos* (Freidel, Schele, and Parker 1993) about the pervasiveness of "soul force" in the ancient and modern Maya world and the potential sentience of things in it (Harrison-Buck and Freidel 2021). As the material symbols on buildings of Maya centers emerge, they are god masks, local variants of deities widely shared in the Maya Lowlands and beyond (Baron, this volume; McAnany 2019). Masks on buildings constructed after 500 BCE are not just representative of the gods but reveal the mindful and agentive character of the buildings themselves (Freidel and Schele 1989); they are the bundled bodies of gods (Guernsey 2006). Much evidence supports this hypothesis, including the depiction of animate *witz* mountain masks as portals of emergence for divine powers (Stuart 1987).

Ceremonial bundling of Classic Maya stelae (Stuart 1996) is exemplified by monuments at Late Preclassic Izapa and Chiapa de Corzo, which exhibit textile motifs that leave no doubt as to their symbolic wrapping (Guernsey 2006). The equivalence of bundles with stelae bridges the meanings of two classes of sacred things—royal ancestor bundles and royal embodiments in stone (Houston and Stuart 1998)—that will also be ancestors. Guernsey (2006) observes that the terrace panels on Structure 5C-2nd at Cerros (Freidel 1979) (Figures 2.1–2.2) feature the same textile motifs seen on the Izapa and Chiapa de Corzo stelae. She interprets these as extending the royal headbands of the upper monumental masks to bundle the whole building. Guernsey extends her argument to identify bound or bundled buildings in the Late Preclassic North Acropolis of Tikal (Coe 1965) and Group H at Uaxactun (Valdés 1987), affirmed in recent research by Acuña (2013, 2018). Acuña documented a Late Preclassic royal effigy turtle bundle shrine at El Achiotal in northwestern Peten. Structure 5C-2nd was possibly designed to curate royal bundles in its summit storage room in the southeast corner. Initiate rulers might have visited this space to retrieve the bundle of rulership while undergoing ritual death and resurrection, cycling counterclockwise out of the temple bearing the bundle onto the threshold of the temple following the path of the sun from east to west (Freidel and Schele 1988). In this perspective, the building's monumental masks assume the guise of bundle masks. The lower masks, conflating Sun God and Maize God symbolism, emerge or descend into turtle head chin masks. The elaborate ear flare assemblages framing them (Figures 2.1–2.2), elements of what would become the standard royal helmet crown of the Early Classic period, can be read as containing bundle knots, feathered mirrors, celts, and depending trefoil *Spondylus* shells, all signs of royal bundles. Together, the ear flare assemblages, with the central flare reading *be/bi* (Taube 2005:fig. 17), jewels, and pendants appear bundled in Cerros Cache 1 on the summit of Structure 6C, the royal accession building that replaced Structure 5C as discussed below (Garber and Awe 2008).

Preclassic Lowland Maya Rulers and Queens

The earliest lowland Maya rulers and queens of the Late Preclassic period (400 BCE–250 CE) were generally invisible in life; they were materialized as fragile mummy bundles or durable cenotaphic cached regalia bundles in death, manifesting mainly through their power instruments and architectural facilities (Freidel and Schele 1988). An exception to this pattern is the crowned ruler pictured on the west wall of the Pinturas shrine at San Bartolo (Saturno, Rossi, and Beltran 2018; Taube et al. 2010) (Figure 2.4). He is accompanied by an unreadable text that ends with *ajaw*. The west wall mural features a giant turtle portal discussed below. The north wall of this mural (Saturno, Stuart, and Taube 2005) suggests that it was a Late Preclassic royal bundle house, as argued for the aforementioned effigy turtle bundle shrine at El Achiotal (Acuña 2013, 2018). Preclassic buildings in Group H at Uaxactun, where the threshold shrine features effigy weaving, masks, and bundle knots, and Building B phase I at Holmul (Estrada Belli 2011) are also likely bundle houses.

The Pinturas mural's north wall (Figure 2.3) shows two young lords bearing rectangular objects with two bindings and triangular knots on top, moving toward a shrine that is also a Creation Mountain with a cave. The rectangular-bound objects, or bundles, have human face masks on the front with mirror shells across the mouths. Mouth mirrors, effigy shells, were already ancient symbols of divine rulership adorning wood, stone, and shell masks found with the sixth-century BCE Middle Preclassic royals discovered at Chiapa de Corzo (Bachand and Lowe 2012). The San Bartolo bundle masks wear, as crowns, the feathered mirror and celt of Olmec rulership identified by Kent Reilly (1990). The feathered mirror and celt are also featured in the elaborate ear flare assemblages framing deity masks on Structure 5C-2nd at Cerros, the first-century CE Late Preclassic bundle shrine and accession place (Harrison-Buck and Freidel 2021).

The west wall mural in the Pinturas shrine affirms that this is not only a bundle house but also an initiation and accession place for newly designated

figure 2.3
North wall mural, Pinturas shrine, San Bartolo. Drawing by Heather Hurst.

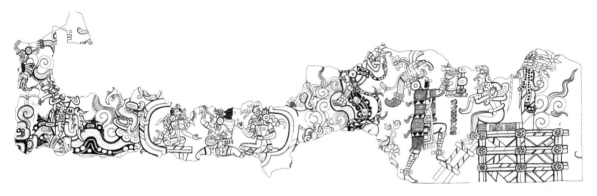

figure 2.4
West wall mural, northern sector, Pinturas shrine, San Bartolo. Drawing by Heather Hurst.

rulers. This pictorial narrative is a prelude to the accession and crowning of the human ruler through relating the story of the creation of the ordered world by youthful gods led by the Maize God, who is ultimately reborn and coronated on a scaffold throne. Saturno (2009) and Taube et al. (2010) identify the correlative story of his sacrifice of the Old Creator shaman's solar bird avatar (Figure 2.5), giving the Maize God power over time and the agrarian cycle of dry and rainy seasons. The human ruler is not only visible but also knowable in his transformation from human to divine: his initiation as a divine ruler is framed in the saga of the death and rebirth of the Maize God (Figure 2.4), dancing in the turtle on the way. Graeber and Sahlins are right when they say that divine rulers imitate gods. The mural is explicitly didactic. So if this was a bundle house, it likely was used only for ceremonial display and not for curation. A great east–west causeway led from the center of San Bartolo to this shrine when it was open and people attended to its story. And yet, while glyphs on the mural indicate that these painterly sages were literate, this ruler is still anonymous. Classic inscriptions accompanying rulers often reference parents or ancestors, but here we have seven inscrutable glyphs (syllabic *po*, *mo*, and *ja*) preceding logographic *ajaw*. Anonymity in the context of literacy, I would suggest, even more deliberately cuts him off from his human kin, ancestral, coeval, and future, and leaves him related only to the Maize God and the other deities central to the Pinturas mural story. Invisibility is partnered with anonymity in Preclassic Maya divine rulership.

Yet literacy is increasingly proving early in the southern lowlands with another San Bartolo inscription (Saturno, Stuart, and Beltran 2006) now documented to about 300 BCE, where again the readable glyph is *ajaw*. The name of rulership, if not the identified face, was established centuries before the Classic inscribed stela tradition. It was more likely a

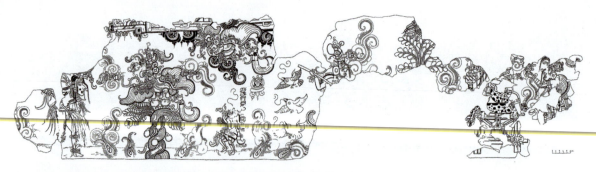

figure 2.5
West wall mural, central sector, Pinturas shrine, San Bartolo. Drawing by Heather Hurst.

predynastic than a preliterate era (Martin [2020:323] demurs in light of the retrospective insistence of some Classic rulers that their lineages extended well into the Late Preclassic period). And to be sure, Late Preclassic rulers did commission some stone monuments in the southern lowlands (Awe, Helmke, Ebert, and Hoggarth, this volume) and the craft of plain stela planting occurred even earlier in the highlands of Guatemala to the south (Arroyo 2007). Stela 1 at Nakbe provides another example of Late Preclassic anonymity for two rulers depicted decked out in royal jewels (Hansen 1993). This encounter-of-two-lords composition resembles La Venta Stela 3, an Olmec monument (Drucker 1981:44) of late Middle Preclassic date. It is probably not coincidental that the San Bartolo murals and the Nakbe stela are both found in the southern lowlands, where stela portraiture of dynasty takes hold in the third century CE (Martin 2020:390). Another anonymous Late Preclassic ruler on a stela at nearby Cival wears the solar bird as a belt mask (Estrada Belli 2011). The Early Classic tradition of named divine rulers on stelae grew out of this Preclassic tradition of anonymous stone rulers with its roots still further to the south (Lowe 1977). But these rare stone monuments occur in the midst of a much wider tradition of architectural symbolism in modeled and painted plaster (Freidel 1979) that evinces the presence of invisible rulers.

Cache 1 on the summit of Structure 6 at Cerros (Freidel 1979) contained a cenotaphic bundle with the deliberate arrangement of royal diadem jewels forming the crown surrounding a pectoral depicting a Maize God ruler (Freidel and Schele 1988; Garber 1986) (Figure 2.7). Along with the other materials in this offering (Figure 2.6), including *Spondylus* shell symbols of the cosmic womb and hematite crystal mouth-sized mirrors on mother-of-pearl backs, it is a bundle of rulership. Such royal insignia diadem jewels and other adornments illustrate the pan-Maya nature of Preclassic rulership and queenship (Freidel 1979, 1991, 1992, 1993; Freidel and Suhler 1995). But these insignia jewels of divine rulership surely belonged to human rulers like the one being crowned on the west wall of the San Bartolo mural in 100 BCE. At Cerros, insofar as the ruler had an enduring presence in death, it was mainly registered in such offerings as Cache 1. This offering likely marked the perishable summit structure as the new royal bundle house.

The earlier Structure 5C-2nd bundle house at Cerros was carefully buried as an animate being (Freidel and Schele 1988), a building designed to display the invisible human ruler when he performed on the central platform designed into the stairway. He was framed by the gods and by the reality of the cycle of the cosmos, the sun cycle of which he was the pivot. This architecture is profoundly political and religious in intention. As an apical member of the first sodality of rulers (Martin 2020:77), *ajawtaak*, the ruler of Cerros's legitimacy was declared by his central positioning in communal celebration. When they buried the building with exquisite care and offerings, they etched streams of tears below the eyes of the plaster image of the ruler masked as the creator, Itzamnaaj, entering the water of the west like the sun. To not see the invisible ruler here on the pivot platform in the middle of the stairway is to miss the entire point of the building's design.

figure 2.6
Cache 1, Cerros, shell mosaic mouth mirrors and *Spondylus* shells. Photograph by James F. Garber / Cerros Project.

figure 2.7
Cache 1, Cerros, arrangement of the diadem jewels and Maize God pectoral. Photograph by James F. Garber / Cerros Project.

The Selz Foundation Yaxuna Project (1989–1996) in north-central Yucatán was designed to investigate, among other things, the origins and development of northern lowland rulership (Stanton et al. 2010; Tiesler et al. 2017). Charles Suhler discovered two Late Preclassic bundle shrine–accession performance platforms designed for the simulation of death and resurrection, central rituals to the initiation of divine rulers (Freidel and Suhler 1999; Stanton and Freidel 2005). Present were cached royal signs, a jade mirror and celt, pierced for suspension and display, bundled with a large white stone ball under the floor of a subsurface sanctuary of one of the two effigy turtle platforms. Preclassic invisible rulership had a footprint at Yaxuna.

Current research in the northern peninsula continues to pursue the study of Middle Formative, Late Formative, and Preclassic bundle houses at multiple sites (Hutson and Welch 2014) and bundles in plazas that declare the presence of rulers less visible in monumental form (Parker 2021). Andrews (1986) reported a comparable Middle Preclassic cache of royal jades from Chaksinkin. Initially thought to be a reset offering because it was discovered by local people in a massive platform, we now know that such platforms were being constructed in the Middle Preclassic period (Ringle, Gallareta Negrón, and Bey 2021). A royal jade clam shell mirror featuring a bundle mask (also wearing a mouth mirror) is among the Chaksinkin jewels. This idea, likely derived from Olmec practice, evidently had been in the Maya Lowlands for many centuries prior to its depiction at San Bartolo on the north wall mural bundles. Preclassic sites north of the eighteenth latitude are massive and numerous. Most of them have been explored, many mapped, and some excavated. However, we know a lot more about the south in this era than the north. The data in hand indicate that the society of Preclassic kings and queens pervaded the lowlands. As Simon Martin declares, "this collective *ajawtaak* with its king in some sense the first among equals, points to, but does not yet fully illuminate, historical processes of great relevance to the formation of the Classic system" (Martin 2020:323).

In his brilliant and magisterial study of Classic Maya politics, Martin (2020:323) further suggests that the collapse of lowland Preclassic society and the fraught Proto-Classic era enabled a concentration of power by some southern lowlands rulers to establish patrimonial dynasties. His perspective resonates with the speculative model of "structural transformation" of the Maya mythic rationale for rulership from brotherhood to descent in the face of Late Preclassic emergent class strife and social inequality proposed in "history of the Maya Cosmogram" (Freidel and Schele 1988) and it is not far from the scenario elaborated by Freidel (2018). The challenge in revealing the changes is that they are, despite the presence of a small corpus of Preclassic texts, to be elucidated primarily by ahistorical archaeological data. The same challenge exists in those parts of the lowlands in which Classic societies evidently continued to be ruled by first among equals rather than patrimonial dynasts.

Early Classic Rulers in the North

There are Classic rulers in the north, but although their insignia and funerary arrangements, when scientifically observed, closely resemble southern practices, they remain rare and intriguing. The Yaxuna Project documented two Early Classic royal tombs in the city's north acropolis (Freidel and Suhler 1998; Freidel, Suhler, and Cobos Palma 1998; Tiesler et al. 2017). Both tombs were extraordinary, one improvised in a blocked-off section of subsurface corridor and one as much a sacrificial offering as a tomb. The first chamber was made of a section of subsurface corridor deep inside Structure 6F-3 (Suhler 1996). Ceramics date this tomb, Burial 23, to the late fourth century CE (Stanton et al. 2010), just before or during the Entrada of Sihyaj K'ahk' (Stuart 2000). The Preclassic turtle effigy platforms discussed above also had subsurface corridors surrounding their central bundle sanctuaries. Structure 6F-3 had later subsurface corridors framing a central underground chamber. Suhler and I (Freidel and Suhler 1999) identified this as a Classic accession ritual chamber because it has a raised doorway in the north wall that would have been accessed by a ladder, such as are depicted on the scaffold accession thrones of Piedras Negras stelae (Taube 1988). I now consider this chamber to be a possible curation place for royal bundles. Burial 23 (Figure 2.8) has a single individual bundled in the prone pose, buried with carved *Spondylus* sprocketed ear flares identifying him as GI, the Sun God in his aspect of One Tooth Person, Hun Yeh Winik Chaak, following Stuart's (2005) analyses of Palenque's creation texts. A stucco modeled, red-painted face fragment of GI was discovered in the terminal deposits of the royal palace in the south of Yaxuna (Freidel, Suhler, and Cobos Palma 1998). The context of Burial 24 expands these associations.

Burial 24, in Structure 6F-4, contained a complex tableau macabre (Tiesler et al. 2017:149–183). I now identify this as an offering dedicating the structure's complete rebuilding as a temple to embody the Moon Goddess of Teotihuacan. Along with the destruction and ritual termination of the royal palace in the southern neighborhood of the city (Freidel, Suhler, and Cobos Palma 1998), this temple rededication was part of the takeover of Yaxuna during the Entrada of Sihyaj K'ahk' and the ensuing New Order. The tableau offering included a sacrificed, and partially cremated, ruler identifiable by the white shell crown segments and name diadem jewel (quetzal, *k'uk'* in Mayan) of his cloth headband royal crown, accompanied by a queen identifiable by a similar crown (Figure 2.9) that was still on her skull, made of the same kind of white shell segments with a jade diadem jewel. This queen (Ardren 2001) was buried with a unique ceramic effigy of the Moon

figure 2.8
Yaxuna Burial 23 ruler with *Spondylus* GI ear flares, giant cowrie amulet, and divining shells. Photograph by Philip Hofstetter / Selz Foundation Yaxuna Project.

figure 2.9
Yaxuna Burial 24, shell crown of the queen. Photograph by Charles Suhler / Selz Foundation Yaxuna Project.

Rulers, Relatives, and Royal Courts   35

Goddess of Teotihuacan. She was transformed in death into a stranger queen and an embodiment of the Moon Goddess by conquerors from Teotihuacan and their Maya allies.

Study of the Yaxuna tombs, their contents, and their architectural contexts suggests that the earlier tomb, Burial 23, was that of a stranger ruler from the south, perhaps from Dzibanche in Quintana Roo, according to his bone chemistry (Baron, this volume; Tiesler et al. 2017). The later tomb represents a violent takeover of the city by another stranger ruler from (or affiliated with) Teotihuacan. The identity of the first ruler with the Kaanul regime rests, in part, on the fact that in the sixth century, Kaanul ruler Sky Witness (of Dzibanche) had a vassal queen at the city of Yo'okop, ninety kilometers south of Yaxuna (Nygard, Spencer, and Wren 2015). The Kaanul rulers may well have been operating as far north as Yaxuna, likely a strategic city in the control of salt production on the north coast of Yucatán and its distribution south (Stanton 2017). Secondly, the anonymous ruler in Burial 23 was accompanied by a concentration of shell-divining tokens next to a large Atlantic Deer Cowrie (*Macrocypraea cervus*) (Figure 2.9), so named in English for its tawny, fawn-like coloration, sometimes banded. There is a Classic-period supernatural (a *wahy* spirit) familiar of Kaanul regime rulers that has the head and limbs of a deer and a body often taken to be a bundle (Grube and Nahm 1994:fig. 15b). I identify this particular strange body, cartouched in a white rim, as the Deer Cowrie, and I argue that *wahy* spirits have several forms, some animals and insects, and that the spirit in question, whose formal name is Chijchan or Snake Deer, is embodied by the Deer Cowrie. This is a long way of saying that I think this ruler is a Kaanul regime agent from Dzibanche. Another clue that this may be the case is that the ruler was arranged with a scepter or drumstick above his head that was composed of deer antler. Another manifestation of the Chijchan is a supernatural snake with deer antlers, a *wahy* spirit depicted on codex-style vessels of the seventh and eighth centuries. Another (cut) Deer Cowrie amulet, associated with casting tokens, was present in a seventh-century tomb at El Peru Waka' that housed a known vassal ruler of the Kaanul regime (Freidel and Rich 2018). The fact that Teotihuacanos wanted to conquer Yaxuna in the era of the Entrada (378–520 CE) and that they were adversaries in that era to Kaanul rulers lends credence to this scenario. Although it remains challenging to graft the textual history of the southern lowlands visible rulers and queens onto the archaeology of the less visible and more anonymous ones in the north and east, there were clearly divine rulers and queens in the north in the Classic period.

Why are texts so rare or poorly preserved for Classic northern rulers and queens? Why don't these rulers just declare themselves on stelae like their southern lowlands contemporaries? Even when they evince ties to the south, as in the case of Classic rulers of Yaxuna, they do not reveal themselves in inscriptions that have survived. Divine rulers and queens at fourth-century Yaxuna performed in death much the same as their southern contemporaries, down to the use of carved white shell or coral curved tubular beads and a jade diadem sewn onto cloth crowns (Tiesler et al. 2017).

At Yaxuna, the New Order conqueror who sacrificed the ruler and queen arranged in Burial 24 was also a ruler. He placed a portrait jade diadem jewel with *Spondylus* beads symbolizing the cosmic womb in a red jar cache under the open summit of the pyramid of the tableau macabre tomb. That name diadem jewel looks like his depiction dancing as the Scarlet Macaw on the painted dish holding the head of his victim in Burial 24. The usurper collected the royal jewels, including Preclassic heirlooms, of his victim in a white jar from Oxkintok in western Yucatán, painted the jar black, the color of the west, and jammed a black axe carved as a god down onto the jades, to chop the rulership of his adversary (Tiesler et al. 2017:fig. 7.12). Early Classic northern rulers were evidently *ajawtaak* who could participate in hegemony without committing to dynasty.

Origins of the Kaanul Regime

The Preclassic settlement patterns of the north-central Peten reveal a clear hierarchy of sites surrounding the primate city of El Mirador (Hansen

1998). These satellite centers, such as El Tintal, are often connected to El Mirador by stone causeways of impressive intersite scale and length (Acuña and Chiriboga 2019:fig. 11). Following dramatic cessation of civic-religious construction at El Mirador and surrounding sites during the second century CE, this evident political collapse ushered in florescence of centers elsewhere, including Naachtun to the northeast and Tikal to the southeast, among others. Archaeological indices reveal Dzibanche's regional dominance over nearby sites such as Pol Box and Res Balam in the late Early Classic period (Velásquez García 2005), but no such pattern, so far determined, characterizes Late Preclassic Ichkabal, which also ceased major construction. While Ichkabal has enormous pyramids, and there are likely satellite sites in its vicinity, its status as a regional capital beyond southern Quintana Roo is unclear in terms of the material symbol systems and architectural decoration observed at contemporary sites (Freidel 1979). Ichkabal lacks preserved modeled stucco and polychrome painted decoration and other iconographic programs; it exhibits large buildings with traces of red painted plaster on the walls. The Preclassic center of Chakanbakan to the southwest of Dzibanche and near the Quintana Roo–Campeche border does have preserved monumental masks on a pyramid. Moreover, Debra Walker (2016) has identified a significant correspondence between the Late Preclassic ceramics of Ichkabal and Cerros. So perhaps this is just a matter of preservation. At El Mirador, the preserved decorated buildings evince god masks that conform to the regional style of masks at other Late Preclassic centers in widely dispersed corners of the lowlands, including at Cerros (Freidel 1979), Acanceh (Quintal Suaste 1999), El Achiotal (Acuña 2013), Calakmul (Garcia-Barrios 2009), Cival (Estrada Belli 2011), San Bartolo (Saturno, Stuart, and Taube 2005), and Chakanbakan (Salazar Lama 2015), among other sites. The mainstream-style monumental masks on Structure 5C-2nd at Cerros date to 100 CE (Vadala and Walker 2020), well after their inspirations at El Mirador. They are similar enough for me to posit that they are "colonial" emulations of El Mirador masks such as those found in the Danta Complex. Archaeological evidence suggests that if there existed a predominate city in the Preclassic Maya Lowlands, it was not Ichkabal but El Mirador. In contrast to other large sites (Reese-Taylor 2017; Šprajc 2008), El Mirador exhibits a complex range of building types representative of the variety found across the lowlands and is an urban site plan of great coherency. It is the primate Late Preclassic city in my view (Freidel 2018; Hansen and Guenter 2005).

Retrospective historical references from the Classic period allude to places and facilities of potential relevance to Late Preclassic Maya rulers and queens, providing windows into these less visible, earlier regimes. Grube (2004) discusses such legendary places as the "Chi Stone Throne Place," which was acknowledged by rulers throughout the region, implying the existence of an early regional capital. I have proposed (Freidel 2018) that the most plausible explanation for the sustained efforts of the Classic-period Kaanul regime to conquer the core area of the southern lowlands in the sixth through eighth centuries CE is that they were reasserting the hegemony that Kaanul had enjoyed in the Preclassic period. The geography of the lowlands suggests that such an earlier hegemony would have been centered in the middle of the country, at El Mirador (Marcus 2012), and not in the periphery at Ichkabal, just north of Dzibanche in Quintana Roo. There is a clear core area in the Preclassic Maya Lowlands, which, in terms of scale and concentration of large urban sites, is centered in the north-central Peten and adjacent upland areas in Maya Mexico.

The idea of regional hegemony supporting divine rulership makes sense as an innovation of major Preclassic polities, registered in their replicated architectural designs, coherent shared material symbol systems, and common ceramic styles. To be sure, there is variety in all these, as there is in any regional political system. But the sudden conversion (Vadala and Walker 2020) of Cerros from a small port town on a river route to the interior to a ceremonial center with a magnificent royal temple ornamented with the most sophisticated royal art of the kind perfected at El Mirador and adjacent Nakbe for centuries signals to me that it was part of such a hegemony. The same holds, in my view, for the extraordinarily sophisticated works of

Preclassic royal art in the northeastern Peten at sites like San Bartolo (Saturno 2009; Saturno, Stuart, and Taube 2005; Taube et al. 2010) and Cival (Estrada Belli 2011), situated in a strategic trade and transportation corridor linking the interior to the Caribbean littoral, and ornamented with polychrome painted monumental masks. But is this heartland core area of the Maya Lowlands Preclassic Kaanul? So far, there are no Preclassic texts that can support or deny this possibility. Kaanul as a name comes into focus in the Classic period, with the advent of glyphic texts, and Martin and Velásquez (2016) argue cogently that this names a place at Dzibanche, implying that it is a Classic-period emblem manifesting with the rise of a dynasty there. Still, Helmke and Kupprat (2016) suggest that Kaanul names a mythical place. It is in the nature and content of the known texts referencing Kaanul that I discern the prospect that the Classic rulers of the Kaanul regime were more like the posited sodality Preclassic rulers of El Mirador and other cities of that era, divine but not dynastic like their Classic contemporaries in the southern lowlands cities. That changed, of course, with Yuhknoom Ch'een II and the seventh-century Kaanul dynasty that he created.

Early Classic Kaanul Rulers: The Move to Visibility

Simon Martin (2020:409–411) details a brief for Early Classic Kaanul dynasts at Dzibanche. If the Calendar Round dates on the conquest treads there are correctly situated, then they date to the fourth century CE. At El Peru-Waka' in the northwestern Peten, the first glyphic evidence of Kaanul dates to the mid-sixth century CE. The Waka' discovery changed how epigraphers think about Early Classic Kaanul. Griselda Perez discovered Stela 44 cached inside the city temple (Structure M13-1) in 2014, while codirector Juan Carlos Perez tunneled along the centerline. Stanley Guenter, project epigrapher at the time, was able to read in the preserved text the name K'ahk' Ti' Chi'ch' as the overlord of an acceding ruler. Mary Kate Kelly took over as project epigrapher in 2016 and has drafted, formally deciphered, and published the monument (Kelly 2019), and Martin and Beliaev (2017; Beliaev and Martin 2021) situated this overlord as Kaanul ruler K'ahk' Ti' Chi'ch' in the Painted Ruler List, a list of Kaanul rulers painted in codex style on vases and drinking cups of the seventh and eighth centuries CE. The date of the Waka' accession, 556 CE, firmly places this overlord in the Early Classic period and—on the prospect that the ruler on the stela and on the cups were one and the same, along with other data—disconfirmed the hypothesis that the Painted Ruler List might be referring to Preclassic rulers (Martin 1997, 2017). This, in turn, opened the prospect that the list was of Early Classic rulers, as discussed below. An important thing to note about this ruler list, in all of its various expressions, is that there are no family ties between any of the emblem glyph–using rulers in the list. Instead, it is just a sequence of dated accessions. Martin (2020) references a new reading by Sergei Vepretski of Caracol Altar 21, who now identifies K'ahk' Ti' Chi'ch' as the Kaanul lord who defeated Tikal ruler Wak Chan K'awiil, last of the New Order rulers, and conquered Tikal in 562 CE, replacing Sky Witness (Martin 2005), who is now relegated to the status of junior ruler of Kaanul in the reign of K'ahk' Ti' Chi'ch'. The history of Kaanul continues to unfold. The relationship between these contemporary rulers remains to be elucidated with indications of multiple rulers in a given reign, but there are few genealogical clues in texts. I would suggest that is a true absence of evidence, because Kaanul rulers were sodality rulers, elected by council and not designated automatically by kin affiliation like dynastic rulers of the southern lowlands (Freidel 2018).

A perusal of Classic Maya ruler lists, like those of the Palenque dynasty (Schele and Freidel 1990:246–247) shows that the scribes sometimes did not include any explicit genealogical information. In the case of the Panel of the Cross at Palenque, it is just births and accessions. But generally, in the southern lowlands Classic dynasties, we do get some family ties, declarations of parentage and descent on carved stone stelae—one could say that such declarations were a principal point (Stuart 1996, 2005). The prospect that the Palenque dynasty is not, in fact, a genealogical dynasty is remote given the dramatic efforts of its rulers to heal disjunctions in it (Schele and Freidel 1990). Is the Painted Ruler List, now identified as Early Classic (Martin 2017) and compiled from several different seventh-century vessels, automatically a dynasty because it has a sequence of Kaanul rulers that starts with ruler Sky Lifter? I would suggest that the onus is on epigraphers to demonstrate that in the Early Classic period there are explicit declarations of parentage linking Kaanul rulers in the same way that there are explicit fourth- and fifth-century CE statements at Tikal linking divine rulers to their parents (Martin and Grube 2008:22–37). As Martin and Grube (2008:120–121) show, we have sixth-century genealogy at Yaxchilan, fifth-century genealogy at Copan (Martin and Grube 2008:192–194), and the list goes on. One can appeal to the inconstancies of the preserved record of Kaanul at Dzibanche, but, to my knowledge in the last analysis, there are no such genealogical Kaanul ruler ties there or anywhere else before the seventh-century rise of Yuhknoom Ch'een II (who may retrospectively declare his father to be Scroll Serpent, a sixth-century ruler, on Calakmul Stela 33).

The Painted Ruler List (and all known Early Classic inscriptions of Kaanul rulers) could be of sodality, elected kings initiated into divine status. If Martin (2017) is correct in his calculations of royal generational time, then the "sky lifter" of that sequence of Kaanul rulers acceded within a few generations of the dynastic founder Yax Ehb Xook of Tikal. In the time of the painting of the lists, the era of Yuhknoom Ch'een II's establishment of a "short count" Kaanul dynasty (Martin 2005), the contestation between Tikal and Kaanul was in full swing; the artists and their patrons may well have been simulating dynasty and recounting its stories as beginning in that earlier era. Indeed, as Martin (2020:72) observes, the qualification of rulers as sacred or divine is really a Late Classic practice, projected back in time on third- and fourth-century rulers of the painted list, enhancing their legitimacy much as contrived dynastic succession might have. Kaanul rulers could have had an actual aversion to declaring any family relations as their power and sanctity before Yuhknoom Ch'een II in the seventh century CE. The significant exception to this prospect would be the declaration of explicit kin ties when seventh-century Kaanul kings and queens engaged openly and historically in alliance building with existing royal families in the southern lowlands (Marcus 2012; Martin 2008).

Opponents of Tikal's suggested innovation of dynastic succession repeatedly desecrated the Late Preclassic and Terminal Preclassic North Acropolis after the founder Yax Ehb Xook's internment in Burial 85 (Freidel 2012; Freidel, MacLeod, and Suhler 2003). Coe and McGinn (1963), in their preliminary description of the excavation of the tomb of what we now believe was the founder and the platform over it, observe that the perishable structure I identify as the scaffold throne was burnt and the charred remains subsequently buried in a sealed pit in front of the platform. William Coe (1990) ultimately concluded that the burning of the buildings and patios of the early acropolis was desecratory. This destructive activity ceases at the end of the third century CE, around the time that ruler Foliated Ajaw Jaguar raised Tikal Stela 29 (Schele and Freidel 1990:fig. 4.11).

A Foliated Ajaw Jaguar occurs in the retrospective history of ruler Sihyaj Chan K'awiil II on Tikal Stela 31 (Martin 2020:120–121). Mathews (1985:44) surmised that this was the same ruler as on Stela 29. Schele demurred as royal names can certainly be reused (Schele and Freidel 1990:441), but I think Mathews was right about this for narrative contextual reasons that follow. The name on Stela 31 is in temporal position just prior to Unen Bahlam, the great Early Classic queen of Tikal (Freidel, MacLeod, and Suhler 2003), who is recorded as presiding over the period ending in 317 CE. One might suspect that Foliated Ajaw Jaguar was presiding at the prior period ending, for the preserved narrative going forward in time is strung together by *k'atun* Period Endings. In the text of Stela 31, Foliated Ajaw Jaguar is entitled *kaloomte'*, "supreme warrior," and this is a remarkable back projection of a title first used in the public Maya record at El Peru-Waka' on Stela 15 dedicated in 416 CE (Guenter 2005; Stuart 2000). The stranger Sihyaj K'ahk' used this title in January 378 CE when he "arrived" as a conqueror on 3 Kan in Waka' and then days later on 11 Eb in Tikal. His overlord, Ajaw Jatz'oom, Spearthrower Owl, was also a *kaloomte'*, as recounted on the Tikal Marcador (Laporte and Fialko 1995). The title *kaloomte'* was not used by a historical Maya ruler until the sixth century. So the back projection of the title to Foliated Ajaw Jaguar suggests that he was a conqueror like Sihyaj K'ahk'. Stela 29 depicts an ancestor floating above Foliated Ajaw Jaguar, and he wears as a headdress the name Chak Took Ich'aak. In the Stela 31 narrative, ruler Chak Took Ich'aak I of Tikal celebrates the period ending in 376 CE. The connection between these two namesake rulers seems to have been important to the narrative on Stela 31. If Muwaan Jol, ruler of Tikal and father of Chak Took Ich'aak I, usurped power from Queen Unen Bahlam and his son was likewise regarded as a usurper, this could have provided the justification for Sihyaj K'ahk' to break the line of succession and install a "new" stranger king.

The evidence of destruction in the early North Acropolis suggests (Freidel 2018) that sodality rulers of the north—inheritors of El Mirador, in my view, from soon after the declaration of dynasty at Tikal in the first century CE under Yax Ehb Xook—were determined to destroy or control this innovative institution of royal succession. Dynasty proved a resilient institution, as the many repairs and refurbishments of the North Acropolis of Tikal attest (during the second and third centuries), and so Kaanul rulers evidently chose to co-opt divine rulership at Tikal and other early dynastic capitals like Waka' that arose in the south. If this was the case, and later dynamics suggest that it was the long-term path to victory, then the Kaanul rulers and councilors were sophisticated, cosmopolitan, and ideologically flexible in their understanding of political power. They were prepared to support the insertion of stranger rulers and queens from the north into southern lowlands dynasties and, in so doing, they or their agents eventually became visibly part of the succession sequences that were fundamentally genealogical in purpose and spirit.

REFERENCES CITED

Acuña, Mary Jane
- 2013 Art, Ideology, and Politics at El Achiotal: A Late Preclassic Frontier Site in Northwestern Petén, Guatemala. PhD dissertation, Washington University, St. Louis.
- 2018 El Achiotal: An Interior Frontier Center in Northwestern Peten, Guatemala. In *Pathways to Complexity: A View from the Maya Lowlands*, edited by M. Kathryn Brown and George J. Bey, pp. 292–314. University Press of Florida, Gainesville.

Acuña, Mary Jane, and Carlos R. Chiriboga
- 2019 Water and the Preclassic Maya at El Tintal, Petén, Guatemala. *Open Rivers* 14, https://editions.lib.umn.edu/openrivers/article/water-and-the-preclassic-maya/.

Andrews, E. Wyllys
- 1986 Olmec Jades from Chaksinkin, Yucatan, and Maya Ceramics from La Venta, Tabasco. In *Research and Reflections in Archaeology and History: Essays in Honor of Doris Stone*, edited by E. Wyllys Andrews, pp. 11–49. Middle American Research Institute, Tulane University, New Orleans.

Ardren, Traci
- 2001 Death Becomes Her: Images of Female Power from Yaxuna Burials. In *Ancient Maya Women*, edited by Traci Ardren, pp. 68–88. AltaMira Press, Walnut Creek, Calif.

Arnauld, M. Charlotte
- 2021 Classic to Postclassic Maya Rulership: Changes in Military-Courtly Institutions. In *Maya Kingship: Rupture and Transformation from Classic to Postclassic Times*, edited by Tsubasa Okoshi, Arlen F. Chase, Philippe Nondédéo, and M. Charlotte Arnauld, pp. 133–151. University Press of Florida, Gainesville.

Arroyo, Barbara
- 2007 The Naranjo Rescue Project: New Data from the Preclassic Guatemala. Report submitted to the Foundation for the Advancement of Mesoamerican Studies, Inc., http://www.famsi.org/reports/06109/06109Arroyo01.pdf.

Bachand, Bruce R., and Lynneth S. Lowe
- 2012 Chiapa de Corzo's Mound 11 Tomb and the Middle Formative Olmec. In *Arqueología reciente de Chiapas: Contribuciones del encuentro celebrado en el 60° aniversario de la Fundación Arqueológica Nuevo Mundo*, edited by Lynneth S. Lowe and Mary E. Pye, pp. 45–68. New World Archaeological Foundation, Brigham Young University, Provo, Utah.

Bauer, Brian S., and R. Alan Covey
- 2002 Processes of State Formation in the Inca Heartland (Cuzco, Peru). *American Anthropologist* 104(3):846–864.

Beliaev, Dmitri, and Simon Martin
- 2021 Serpent Emperor: The Reign of K'ahk' Ti' Ch'ich' and the Origins of Dzibanché Hegemony. Paper presented at the 86th Annual Meeting of the Society for American Archaeology, San Francisco.

Coe, William R.
- 1965 Tikal, Guatemala, and Emergent Maya Civilization. *Science* 147:1401–1419, doi: 10.1126/science.147.3664.1401.
- 1990 *Excavations in the Great Plaza, North Terrace, and North Acropolis of Tikal: Tikal Report 14.* University of Pennsylvania Museum of Archaeology and Anthropology, Philadelphia.

Coe, William R., and John J. McGinn
- 1963 Tikal: The North Acropolis and an Early Tomb. *Expedition (Penn Museum)* 5(2):25–32, http://www.penn.museum/sites/expedition/?p=525.

Drucker, Philip
- 1981 On the Nature of the Olmec Polity. In *The Olmec and Their Neighbors*, edited by Elizabeth P. Benson, pp. 29–47. Dumbarton Oaks Research Library and Collection, Washington, D.C.

Estrada Belli, Francisco
- 2011 *The First Maya Civilization: Ritual and Power before the Classic Period.* Routledge, London.

Freidel, David
- 1979 Culture Areas and Interaction Spheres: Contrasting Approaches to the Emergence of Civilization in the Maya Lowlands. *American Antiquity* 44(1):36–54.
- 1991 The Jester God: The Beginning and End of a Maya Royal Symbol. In *Vision and Revision in Maya Studies*, edited by Flora S. Clancy and Peter D. Harrison, pp. 67–78. University of New Mexico Press, Albuquerque.
- 1992 The Trees of Life, Ahau as Idea and Artifact in Classic Maya Civilization. In *Ideology and Pre-Columbian Civilizations*, edited by Arthur A. Demarest and Geoffrey W. Conrad, pp. 115–133. School of American Research Press, Santa Fe.
- 1993 The Jade Ahau: Towards a Theory of Commodity Value in Maya Civilization. In *Precolumbian Jade: New Geological and Cultural Interpretations*, edited by Fredrick W. Lange, pp. 149–165. University of Utah Press, Salt Lake City.
- 2012 Maya and the Idea of Empire: A View from the Field. Gordon R. Willey Lecture, Peabody Museum of Archaeology and Ethnology, Harvard University, Cambridge, Mass.
- 2018 Maya and the Idea of Empire. In *Pathways to Complexity: A View from the Maya Lowlands*, edited by M. Kathryn Brown and George J. Bey, pp. 363–386. University Press of Florida, Gainesville.

Freidel, David, Barbara MacLeod, and Charles K. Suhler
- 2003 Early Classic Maya Conquest in Words and Deeds. In *Ancient Mesoamerican Warfare*, edited by M. Kathryn Brown and Travis Stanton, pp. 189–215. AltaMira Press, Walnut Creek, Calif.

Freidel, David, and Michelle Rich
- 2018 Maya Sacred Play: The View from El Peru-Waka'. In *Ritual, Play and Belief in Evolution and Early Human Societies*, edited by Colin Renfrew, Iain Morley, and Michael Boyd, pp. 101–115. Cambridge University Press, Cambridge.

Freidel, David, and Linda Schele
- 1988 Rulership in the Late Preclassic Lowlands: The Instruments and Places of Ritual Power. *American Anthropologist* 90(3):547–567.
- 1989 Dead Rulers and Living Temples: Dedication and Termination Rituals among the Ancient Maya. In *Word and Image in Maya Culture: Explorations in Language, Writing, and Representation*, edited by William F. Hanks and Don S. Rice, pp. 233–243. University of Utah Press, Salt Lake City.

Freidel, David, Linda Schele, and Joy Parker
- 1993 *Maya Cosmos: Three Thousand Years on the Shaman's Path*. W. Morrow, New York.

Freidel, David, and Charles K. Suhler
- 1995 Crown of Creation: The Development of the Maya Royal Diadems in the Late Preclassic and Early Classic Periods. In *The Emergence of Lowland Maya Civilization: The Transition from the Preclassic to the Early Classic*, edited by Nikolai Grube, pp. 137–150. A. Saurwein, Möckmühl.
- 1998 Visiones serpentinas y laberintos mayas. *Arqueología mexicana* 6(34):28–37.
- 1999 The Path of Life: Towards a Functional Analysis of Ancient Maya Architecture. In *Mesoamerican Architecture as a Cultural Symbol*, edited by Jeff Karl Kowalski, pp. 250–275. Oxford University Press, Oxford.

Freidel, David, Charles K. Suhler, and Rafael Cobos Palma
- 1998 Termination Deposits at Yaxuna: Detecting the Historical in Archaeological Contexts. In *The Sowing and the Dawning: Termination, Dedication, and Transformation in the Archaeological and Ethnographic Record of Mesoamerica*, edited by Shirley Boteler Mock, pp. 135–144. University of New Mexico Press, Albuquerque.

Garber, James F.
- 1986 The Artifacts. *Archaeology at Cerros, Belize, Central America: An Interim Report* 1:117–126.

Garber, James F., and Jaime J. Awe
- 2008 Middle Formative Architecture and Ritual at Cahal Pech. *Research Reports in Belizean Archaeology* 5:185–190.

Garcia-Barrios, Ana
- 2009 Chaahk, el dios de la lluvia, en el periodo clasico maya. PhD dissertation, Univeridad Complutense de Madrid, Madrid.

Graeber, David, and Marshall Sahlins
- 2017 *On Kings*. Hau Books, Chicago.

Grube, Nikolai
- 2004 El origen de la dinastía Kaan. In *Los cautivos de Dzibanché*, edited by Enrique Nalda, pp. 117–131. Instituto Nacional de Antropología e Historia, Mexico City.

Grube, Nikolai, and Werner Nahm
- 1994 A Census of Xibalba: A Complete Inventory of Way Characters on Maya Ceramics. In *The Maya Vase Book: A Corpus of Rollout Photographs of Maya Vases*, by Justin Kerr, vol. 4, pp. 686–714. Kerr Associates, New York.

Guenter, Stanley P.
- 2005 Informe preliminar de la epigrafía de El Peru. In *Proyecto arqueologia El Peru-Waka': Informe no. 2, temporada 2004*, edited by Hector L. Escobedo and David Freidel, pp. 363–399. Report presented to the Instituto de Antropología e Historia, Guatemala City.

Guernsey, Julia
- 2006 Late Formative Antecedents for Ritually Bound Monuments. In *Sacred Bindings of the Cosmos: Ritual Acts of Bundling and Wrapping in Mesoamerica*, special issue, *Ancient America* 3:22–39.

Hansen, Richard
- 1993 Investigations del Sito Arqueologico Nakbe, Peten, temporada 1989. In *III Simposio de Investigaciones Arqueológicas en Guatemala, 1989*, edited by Juan Pedro Laporte, Héctor L. Escobedo, and Sandra Villagrán de Brady, pp. 57–72. Ministero de Cultura y Deportes, Instituto Antropología e Historia, Asociación Tikal, Guatemala City.
- 1998 Continuity and Disjunction: The Pre-Classic Antecedents of Classic Maya Architecture. In *Function and Meaning*

Hansen, Richard D., and Stanley P. Guenter

 2005 Early Social Complexity and Rulership in the Mirador Basin. In *Lords of Creation: The Origins of Sacred Maya Rulership*, edited by Virginia M. Fields and Dorie Reents-Budet, pp. 60–61. Scala, London.

Harrison-Buck, Eleanor, and David Freidel

 2021 Reassessing Shamanism and Animism in the Art and Archaeology of Ancient Mesoamerica. *Religions* 12(6):394.

Headrick, Annabeth

 1994 The Street of The Dead . . . It Really Was: Mortuary Bundles at Teotihuacan. *Ancient Mesoamerica* 10(1):69–85.

Helmke, Christophe, Stanley P. Guenter, and Phillip Wanyerka

 2018 Kings of the East: Altun Ha and the Water Scroll Emblem Glyph. *Ancient Mesoamerica* 29(1):113–135.

Helmke, Christophe, and Felix A. Kupprat

 2016 Where Snakes Abound: Supernatural Places of Origin and Founding Myths and Titles of Classic Maya Kings. In *Places of Power and Memory in Mesoamerica's Past and Present: How Sites, Toponyms, and Landscapes Shape History and Remembrance*, edited by Daniel Grana-Behrens, pp. 33–83. Gebruder Mann Verlag, Berlin.

Houston, Stephen D., and David Stuart

 1998 The Ancient Maya Self: Personhood and Portraiture in the Classic Period. *RES: Anthropology and Aesthetics* 33:73–101.

Hutson, Scott R., and Jacob A. Welch

 2014 Sacred Landscapes and Building Practices at Uci, Kancab, and Ucanha, Yucatan, Mexico. *Ancient Mesoamerica* 25(2):421–439.

Kelly, Mary Kate

 2019 Documentación epigráfica: Ilustración de inscripciones jeroglíficas de El Perú-Waka'. In *Proyecto Arqueológico Waka': Informe no. 16, temporada 2018*, edited by Juan Carlos Pérez Calderón, Griselda Pérez Robles, and Damien Marken, pp. 349–361. Report submitted to the Dirección General del Patrimonio Cultural y Natural, Guatemala.

Laporte, Juan Pedro, and Wilma Fialko C.

 1995 Un reencuentro con Mundo Perdido, Tikal, Guatemala. *Ancient Mesoamerica* 6(1):41–94.

Lowe, Gareth

 1977 The Mixe-Zoque as Competing Neighbors of the Early Lowland Maya. In *Origins of Maya Civilization*, edited by Richard E. W. Adams, pp. 197–248. University of New Mexico Press, Albuquerque.

Marcus, Joyce

 2012 Maya Political Cycling and the Story of the Kaan Polity. In *The Ancient Maya of Mexico: Reinterpreting the Past of the Northern Maya Lowlands*, edited by Geoffrey E. Braswell, pp. 88–116. Equinox Press, London.

Martin, Simon

 1997 The Painted King List: A Commentary on Codex-Style Dynastic Vases. In *The Maya Vase Book: A Corpus of Rollout Photographs*, by Justin Kerr, vol. 5, pp. 846–867. Kerr Associates, New York.

 2005 Caracol Altar 21 Revisited: More Data on Double-Bird and Tikal's Wars of the Mid-Sixth Century. *The PARI Journal* 6(1):1–9.

 2008 Wives and Daughters on the Dallas Altar. Mesoweb, https://www.mesoweb.com/articles/martin/Wives&Daughters.html.

 2017 Secrets of the Painted King List: Recovering the Early History of the Snake Dynasty. Maya Decipherment, https://mayadecipherment.com/2017/05/05/secrets-of-the-painted-king-list-recovering-the-early-history-of-the-snake-dynasty/.

 2020 *Ancient Maya Politics: A Political Anthropology of the Classic Period 150–900 CE*. Cambridge University Press, Cambridge.

Martin, Simon, and Dmitri Beliaev

 2017 K'ahk' Ti' Ch'ich': A New Snake Ruler from the Early Classic Period. *The PARI Journal* 17(3):1–7.

Martin, Simon, and Nikolai Grube
- 2008 *Chronicle of the Maya Kings and Queens: Deciphering the Dynasties of the Ancient Maya.* 2nd ed. Thames and Hudson, New York.

Martin, Simon, and Erik Velásquez
- 2016 Polities and Places: Tracing the Toponyms of the Snake Dynasty. *The PARI Journal* 17(2):23–33.

Mathews, Peter
- 1985 Maya Early Classic Monuments and Inscriptions. In *A Consideration of the Early Classic Period in the Maya Lowlands,* edited by Gordon R. Willey and Peter Mathews, pp. 5–54. Institute for Mesoamerican Studies, State University of New York, Albany.

McAnany, Patricia A.
- 2014 *Living with the Ancestors: Kinship and Rulership in Ancient Maya Society.* 2nd ed. Cambridge University Press, Cambridge.
- 2019 Fragile Authority in Monumental Time: Political Experimentation in the Classic Maya Lowlands. In *The Evolution of Fragility: Setting the Terms,* edited by Norman Yoffee, pp. 47–59. McDonald Institute Conversations, Cambridge.

Nygard, Travis, Kaylee Spencer, and Linnea Wren
- 2015 Contemplating Carvings at the Feet of Queen Chaak Kab, Using Mixed Methodology to Understand Sculpture at Yo'okop. In *The Maya of the Cochuah Region: Archaeological and Ethnographic Perspectives on the Northern Lowlands,* edited by Justine M. Shaw, pp. 57–76. University of New Mexico Press, Albuquerque.

Parker, Evan
- 2021 Fields of Power and Fields of Play: Power, Inequality, and Sport at Middle Preclassic Paso del Macho, Yucatan. PhD dissertation, Tulane University, New Orleans.

Pendergast, David
- 1981 Lamanai, Belize: Summary of Excavation Results, 1974–1980. *Journal of Field Archaeology* 8(1):29–53.
- 1982 *Excavations at Altun Ha, Belize, 1964–1970.* 3 vols. Royal Ontario Museum, Toronto.

Quintal Suaste, Beatriz
- 1999 Mayas: Hallazgos recientes en el norte de Yucatan. *Aqueologia mexicana* 7(37).

Reese-Taylor, Kathryn
- 2017 Founding Landscapes in the Central Karstic Uplands. In *Maya E Groups: Calendars, Astronomy, and Urbanism in the Early Lowlands,* edited by David Freidel, Arlen F. Chase, Anne S. Dowd, and Jerry Murdock, pp. 480–513. University Press of Florida, Gainesville.

Reese-Taylor, Kathryn, Marc Zender, Pamela L. Geller, Julia Guernsey, and F. Kent Reilly
- 2006 Fit To Be Tied: Funerary Practices among the Prehispanic Maya. In *Sacred Bundles: Ritual Acts of Wrapping and Binding in Ancient Mesoamerica,* edited by Julia Guernsey and F. Kent Reilly, pp. 52–69. Boundary End Archaeology Research Center, Barnardsville, N.C.

Reilly, F. Kent
- 1990 Cosmos and Rulership: The Function of Olmec-Style Symbols in Formative-Period Mesoamerica. *Visible Language* 24(1):12.

Richards, Audrey I.
- 1968 Keeping the King Divine. *Proceedings of the Royal Anthropological Institute of Great Britain and Ireland* 1968:23–35.

Ringle, William M., Tomás Gallareta Negrón, and George J. Bey III
- 2021 Stranger-Kings in Northern Yucatan. In *Maya Kingship: Rupture and Transformation from Classic to Postclassic Times,* edited by Tsubaka Okoshi, Arlen F. Chase, Phillippe Nondédéo, and M. Charlotte Arnauld, pp. 249–269. University Press of Florida, Gainesville.

Salazar Lama, Daniel
- 2015 Formas de sacralizar a la figura real entre los maya. *Journal de la Société des Américanistes* 101(1–2):11–49.

Saturno, William A.
- 2009 Centering the Ruler: Maya Creation and Legitimization at San Bartolo. In *The Art of Urbanism: How Mesoamerican Kingdoms Represented Themselves in Architecture and Imagery,* edited by William L. Fash and Leonardo López

Luján, pp. 111–134. Dumbarton Oaks Research Library and Collection, Washington, D.C.

Saturno, Willliam A., Franco D. Rossi, and Boris Beltran

    2018   Changing Stages: Royal Legitimacy and the Architectural Development of the Pinturas Complex at San Bartolo, Guatemala. In *Pathways to Complexity: A View from the Maya Lowlands*, edited by M. Kathryn Brown and George J. Bey, pp. 315–335. University Press of Florida, Gainesville.

Saturno, William A., David Stuart, and Boris Beltran

    2006   Early Writing at San Bartolo, Guatemala. *Science* 311:1281–1283, doi: 10.1126/science.1121745.

Saturno, William A, David Stuart, and Karl A. Taube

    2005   La identificación de las figuras del Muro Oeste de Pinturas Sub-1, San Bartolo, Petén. In *XVIII Simposio de Investigaciones Arqueológicas en Guatemala*, 2004, edited by Juan P. Laporte, Barbara Arroyo, and Héctor E. Mejía, vol. 2, pp. 647–656. Ministerio de Cultura y Deportes, Instituto de Antropología e Historia, Asociación Tikal, Guatemala City.

Schele, Linda, and David Freidel

    1990   *A Forest of Kings: The Untold Story of the Ancient Maya*. W. Morrow, New York.

Šprajc, Ivan (editor)

    2008   *Reconociemento arqueológico en el sureste del estado de Campeche, Mexico, 1996-2005*. Archaeopress, Oxford.

Stanton, Travis W.

    2017   The Founding of Yaxuna, Place and Trade in Preclassic Yucatan. In *Maya E Groups: Calendars, Astronomy, and Urbanism in the Early Lowlands*, edited by David Freidel, Arlen F. Chase, Anne S. Dowd, and Jerry Murdock, pp. 450–479. University Press of Florida, Gainesville.

Stanton, Travis W., and David Freidel

    2005   Placing the Centre, Centering the Place, the Influence of Formative Sacbeob in Classic Site Design at Yaxuna, Yucatan. *Cambridge Archaeological Journal* 15:225–249.

Stanton, Travis W., David Freidel, Charles K. Suhler, Traci Ardren, James N. Ambrosino, Justine M. Shaw, and Sharon Bennett

    2010   *Excavations at Yaxuná, Yucatán, Mexico*. Archaeopress, Oxford.

Stuart, David

    1987   Ten Phonetic Syllables. *Research Reports on Ancient Maya Writing*, no. 2. Center for Maya Research, Washington, D.C.

    1996   Rulers of Stone: A Consideration of Stelae in Ancient Maya Ritual and Representation. *RES: Anthropology and Aesthetics* 29/30:148–171.

    2000   "The arrival of strangers": Teotihuacan and Tollan in Classic Maya Study. In *Mesoamerica's Classic Heritage: From Teotihuacan to the Aztecs*, edited by Davíd Carrasco, Lindsay Jones, and Scott Sessions, pp. 465–513. University Press of Colorado, Boulder.

    2005   *The Inscriptions from Temple XIX at Palenque*. Pre-Columbian Art Research Institute, San Francisco.

Suhler, Charles K.

    1996   Excavations at the North Acropolis Yaxuna, Yucatan, Mexico. PhD dissertation, Southern Methodist University, University Park, Tex.

Taube, Karl A.

    1988   A Study of Maya Scaffold Sacrifice. In *Maya Iconography*, edited by Elizabeth P. Benson and Gillett G. Griffin, pp. 330–351. Princeton University Press, Princeton.

    2005   The Symbolism of Jade in Classic Maya Religion. *Ancient Mesoamerica* 16(1):23–50.

Taube, Karl A., William A. Saturno, David Stuart, and Heather Hurst

    2010   *The Murals of San Bartolo, El Peten, Guatemala*, part 2, *The West Wall*. Boundary End Archaeology Research Center, Barnardsville, N.C.

Tiesler, Vera, Andrea Cucina, Travis W. Stanton, and David Freidel

    2017   *Before Kukulkan: Bioarchaeology of Maya Life, Death, and Identity at Classic Period Yaxuná*. University of Arizona Press, Tucson.

Vadala, Jeffrey R., and Debra S. Walker
　2020　The Rapid Rise and Fall of Cerros, Belize: A Generational Approach to Chronology. *Latin American Antiquity* 31(1):143–162.

Valdés, Juan Antonio
　1987　Uaxactún: Recientes investigaciones. *Mexicon* 8(6):125–128.

Velásquez García, Erik
　2005　The Captives of Dzibanche. *The PARI Journal* 6(2):1–4.

Walker, Debra S.
　2016　Life and Afterlife at Cerro Maya, Belize. In *Perspectives on the Ancient Maya of Chetumal Bay*, edited by Debra S. Walker, pp. 56–75. University Press of Florida, Gainesville.

3

Whose Mountains?

The Royal Body in the Built Environment

ALEXANDRE TOKOVININE, FRANCISCO ESTRADA BELLI, AND VILMA FIALKO

Introducing Authority and Legitimation

The relationship between political authority and landscape—either considered narrowly as the built environment of a regime or broadly as its material and discursive imprint onto actual and claimed territory—is one of the fundamental themes in the archaeological investigations of early complex polities. The "archaeology of the political" (Smith 2003, 2011) regards the spatial dimension of political life as shaped by the constant renegotiation of authority within a regime and between the regime and its subjects, but also as a structuring factor that enables and constrains sovereign power.

The present chapter examines the landscape-authority connection in the context of the Classic Maya early complex polities of the southern lowlands (Figure 3.1). It follows Smith's (2003) relational approach with one important modification. An emphasis is placed on identifying and assessing a set of practices and discursive strategies falling under the notion of legitimation (Gramsci 1971), defined as the co-optation of existing practices and beliefs by emergent political regimes to make authority appear natural and rooted in tradition. The notion of legitimation is useful in investigating sources and limits of political authority in situations when there is little evidence of outright coercion and violence.

Authority, Otherness, and Legitimating Strategies among the Classic Maya

Emergent political authority in early complex polities resolves the tension between a regime and its subjects by placing the ruler outside the society or even humanity, a topos commonly referred to as a "stranger king" (Graeber and Sahlins 2017; Houston and Stuart 1996). For the ancient Maya, the theme had at least two partially overlapping variants: ethnic/political others, and denizens of the wild/sacred landscape beyond the domesticated human space.

Maya elites could claim political or/and ethnic "otherness" along the dividing line of the "people-

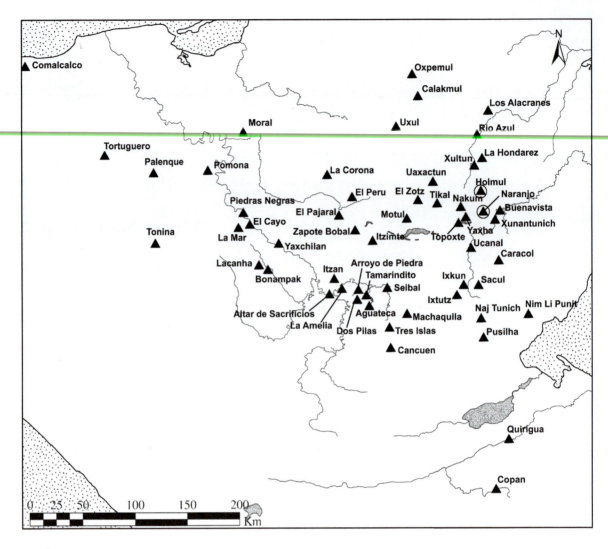

figure 3.1
Classic Maya political centers in the southern lowlands, including Naranjo and Holmul. Map by Alexandre Tokovinine.

aliens" (*winik-tz'ul*) dichotomy (see Lamoureux St-Hilaire and McAnany, this volume). For example, the authors of the Postclassic Dresden Codex (Figure 3.2a) depicted and mentioned "aliens in the west" (*tz'ul chikin*) when referring to Chontal and Nahua speakers of Zactam–Xicalango, a discourse that was part of the legitimating strategy of the Cocom dynasty (Beliaev 2013). The distinct double-line eye mark of the TZ'UL "alien" logogram is attested first in the AJAW "lord" sign at Late Preclassic San Bartolo (Figure 3.2b), implying a considerable depth to the concept and a link between "otherness" and kingship in Maya visual culture.

However, for the Classic period, there is only one unambiguous reference to a *tz'ul* ruler in the entire textual corpus (Krempel and Matteo 2016) (Figure 3.2c). Scholars infer the degree of one's political or ethnic "otherness" based on iconography and titles of origin, with no guarantee that the discourse at the time classified that visual symbolism and that part of the political landscape as *tz'ul*.

The second kind of "otherness" embedded in the "forest-field" (*k'ax-kol*) dichotomy is a fundamental trait of ethnographically documented and ancient Maya cosmologies (Hanks 1990; Taube 2003; Wilson 1993). The supernatural forces in the *k'ax* are

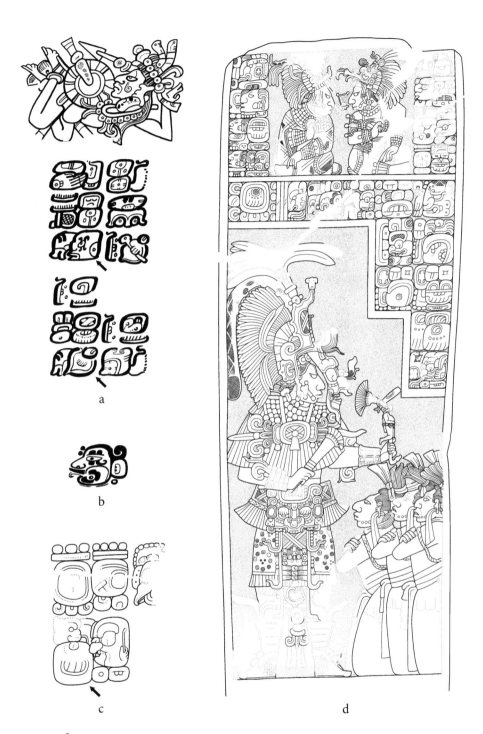

figure 3.2

Mayas and "others": a) visual and textual references to *tz'ul* of Zactam–Xicalango, Dresden Codex, page 50; b) AJAW grapheme with *tz'ul* markings, Structure Sub-1A, San Bartolo; c) *tz'ul kaloomte'*, unprovenanced monument fragment; and d) Yaxuun Bahlam as a "stranger king" on Yaxchilan Stela 11. Drawings by Alexandre Tokovinine.

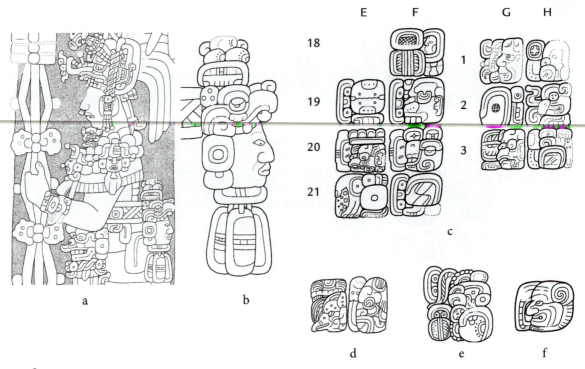

figure 3.3

Ancestors as *k'uh*: a) royal portrait on Naranjo Stela 48; b) close-up of the ancestral belt head on Naranjo Stela 48; c) possible reference to ancestral belt heads on Naranjo Stela 23; d) *mam k'uh* on Copan Stela 2; e) *mam k'uh sakun k'uh* on Copan Stela J; and f) MAM with a braiding pattern on Copan Papagayo step. Drawings by Alexandre Tokovinine.

the ultimate *tz'ul* of the landscape. Political authority is then created by negotiating with, possessing, and embodying these forces, even by transposing the wild "forest" sacred landscape onto the controlled human "field" space. The portrait of Yaxuun Bahlam on Yaxchilan Stela 11 (Figure 3.2d) exemplifies this topos. The king holds *k'awiil*, the token of his legitimacy (see below), and a tally of captives who kneel before him—an expression of his sovereign power. His body is visibly transformed into that of his patron god, whose very name, "Endless Drunkenness Fire O' (bird) Chahk" (Bolon Kalne'l Aj K'ahk' O' Chahk), implies control of natural phenomena (rain and fire) and altered mental states (drunkenness). But the most striking aspect of the king's portrait is that he is wrapped by a living mountain with a toponym. Yaxuun Bahlam's body is shown as simultaneously human and divine, in the capital and upon a distant mountain—a combination of concurrence with and transposition of the sacred "other," here explicitly linked to legitimacy and sovereignty.

The royal portrait on Yaxchilan Stela 11 features another crucial element of Classic Maya notions of sacred kingship: Yaxuun Bahlam's deceased parents witness the scene from above, transformed into the celestial bodies of the moon and the sun. There is evidence that ancient Maya gods and ancestors belonged to the same ontological category of *k'uh*. One of the common manifestations of the ancestral cult among the Classic Maya is belt heads (see Halperin, this volume). For instance, Naranjo Stela 48 shows its ruler, Ajnumsaaj Chan K'inich, with a life-size mask or head on the back of a rigid belt (Figure 3.3a). The head is labeled as his father, "Hearth" Chan Ahk (Figure 3.3b). If such belts were made of stone and used in the ballgame, they were called *ya' tuun*, "hip stones" (Houston and Stuart 2021). Therefore, the "hip" gloss is expected to index kinds of belts and belt items. According to the narrative on Naranjo Stela 23 (Figure 3.3c), when its holy ruler K'ahk' Tiliw Chan Chahk attacked Yaxha, the "head and bone" of the local ancestral king Yax

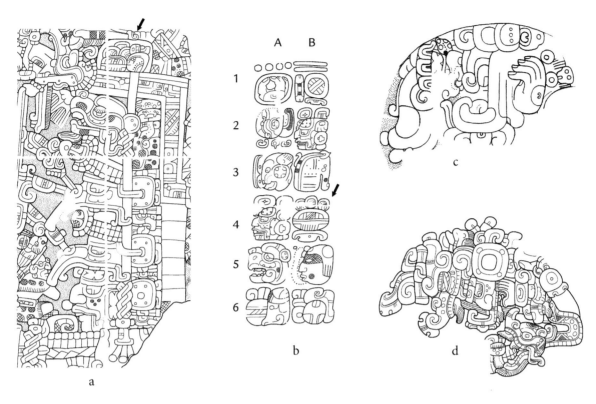

figure 3.4
Concurrence of ancestors and gods: a) "Hearth" Chan Ahk as K'inich Ajaw on Naranjo Stela 43; b) textual reference to "Hearth" Chan Ahk as K'inich Ajaw on Naranjo Stela 43; c) Tzik'in Bahlam concurrent with the patron deity on Naranjo Stela 45; and d) Yax Nuun Ahiin concurrent with the patron deity on Tikal Stela 31. Drawings by Alexandre Tokovinine.

Bolon Chahk "were opened and scattered on an island" (*pahsaj chok ti peten*). The victor "gathered the hip ancestor gods, his trophy" (*utz'akaw ya' mam k'uh yehte'*). Given that the narrative is about tomb opening, "hip ancestor gods" (*ya' mam k'uh*) must be the very same ancestral masks or heads such as the one depicted on Stela 48 at Naranjo. The *mam k'uh* expression occurs at Copan (Figure 3.3d), where it seems to be part of a *difrasismo*, most clearly spelled on Stela J as *mam k'uh sakun k'uh* (Figure 3.3e). The MAM sign on Stela J is partially occluded by K'UH. The visible part is not the typical lock of hair, but an earlier MAM on Copan Papagayo step has an identical element (Figure 3.3f). According to Davletshin (personal communication 2021), the *difrasismo* may be translated as "maternal ancestors, paternal ancestors," lending further support to the interpretation of the passage on Naranjo Stela 23 as a reference to ancestral belt masks. It should be noted, however,

that the English term "ancestor" and *mam k'uh* do not fully overlap. A jade belt head is a kind of other-than-human animate entity (see Baron, this volume), a *k'uh* created from an ancestor and, therefore, a *mam k'uh* or a *sakun k'uh*. But *k'uh* entities take different forms (for bundles, see Freidel, this volume) and may be created from other things/beings. There may be more than one *k'uh* from the same ancestor as implied by additional classifiers such as "hip *mam k'uh*."

The connection between ancestors and *k'uh* is complicated further by concurrence, *ubaahil aan* (Houston and Stuart 1996). For example, "Hearth" Chan Ahk of Naranjo mentioned above is depicted fully transformed into the Sun God (K'inich Ajaw) on Stela 43 from the site (Figure 3.4a). Only a name in the headdress indexes his human identity. The accompanying text clarifies that it was an act of *ubaahil aan* (Figure 3.4b). Moreover, deceased

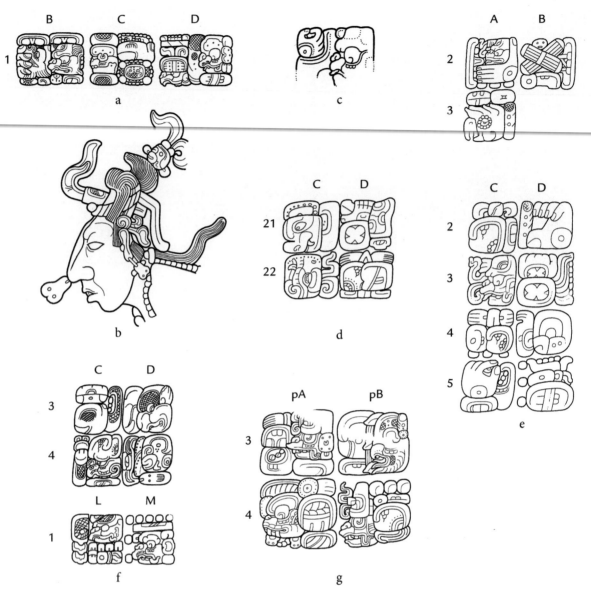

figure 3.5

Classic Maya concept of *k'awiilil*: a) *k'awiilil* summoned into an object (detail of Yaxchilan Lintel 25); b) a deceased ruler as K'awiil (detail of the sarcophagus, Temple of the Inscriptions, Palenque); c) dynastic founder as K'awiil on Tikal Stela 22; d) Sihyaj K'ahk's arrival as K'awiil (detail of Tikal Stela 31); e) Yax K'uk' Mo's arrival as K'awiil (detail of Copan Altar Q); f) K'awiil entering a temple (detail of an unprovenanced panel, Dumbarton Oaks, PC.B.528); and g) *k'awiilil* disappearing at Dzibanche and taking shape at Calakmul in the narrative on a panel at Xunantunich. Drawings by Alexandre Tokovinine.

royals may be continuously concurrent with deities. Naranjo ancestors are shown fully merged with the local divine founder (Figure 3.4c). Tikal ancestors appear merged with a similar deity, albeit with more solar attributes (Figure 3.4d). The hieroglyphic captions on Yaxchilan Stela 11 (Figure 3.2d)

unambiguously clarify that such ancestral transformations are *ubaahil aan* states.

The emic Classic Maya concept of legitimate authority is closely linked to K'awiil, such as the one held by Yaxuun Bahlam on Yaxchilan Stela 11 (Figure 3.2d). K'awiil—Schellhas's God K—is a deity of lightning (Taube 1992:69–79). It is also an immanent force or power—*k'awiilil* (Martin 2020:159)—related to and yet distinct from *k'uh*. The weapons of Yaxuun Bahlam's patron deity, Aj K'ahk' O' Chahk, have *k'awiilil* conjured into them by the king (Figure 3.5a). *K'awiilil* is specifically linked to the ancestors who are concurrent with God K, as in the posthumous portrait of K'inich Janaab Pakal of Palenque (Figure 3.5b). Dynastic founders may be referred to as K'awiil, sometimes with a place of origin, as in the "Chih Ka' K'awiil" title of the dynastic founder in the inscription on Tikal Stela 22 (Figure 3.5c). The narrative on Copan Altar Q (Figure 3.5e) describes the taking of K'awiil at Wiinte' Naah by the dynastic founder, followed by the journey and eventual arrival and "resting of K'awiil's feet" at Copan (*hili [y]ooke[l] k'awiil yita huli hux wintik*), perhaps intentionally failing to disambiguate between the founder and the K'awiil that he took. K'awiil may also represent a new source of authority with no implication of dynastic succession in the narrow sense. The text on Tikal Stela 31 (Figure 3.5d) describes the political change with the arrival of the foreign hegemon Sihyaj K'ahk' as "K'awiil of the West, kaloomte' Sihyaj K'ahk' came here walking" (*hulookaj ochk'in k'awiil siyaj k'ahk' kaloomte'*). K'awiil is what "activates" temples: according to a Palenque-area panel at Dumbarton Oaks (Figure 3.5f), "K'awiil entered the summit of Hux Bolon Chahk" (*ochi k'awiil ta titz hux bolon chahk*), "his foot was placed upon the mountain of his god" (*tehk'aj yook tuwitzil uk'uhuul*). The emphasis on foot movement in the three examples above indicates that *k'awiilil* is always an embodied force, that it is transferred through acts of performance and ritual motion. Finally, whole places may lose or acquire *k'awiilil* as a source of authority. According to the narrative on the Caracol hieroglyphic stairway section recovered from Xunantunich (Martin 2020:128–129; see Awe, Helmke, Ebert, and Hoggarth, this volume) that details the transfer of the main seat of the Kaanu'l royal dynasty from Dzibanche to Calakmul (Figure 3.5g), "*k'awiilil* is no more amid the city of Kaanu'l; *k'awiilil* is taking shape in Huxte' Tuun" (*machaj k'awiilil tahn ch'een kaanu'l pataal k'awiil[il] huxte' tuun*).

The notion of *k'awiilil* reflects a dual nature of Classic Maya legitimating practices: *k'awiilil* is embodied, derived from the ancestors and powerful foreigners, but also residing in certain places. A prior survey of the inscriptions (Tokovinine 2013) revealed that Classic Maya kings relied on two distinct strategies concerning the sources of their "otherness." Some royal dynasties insisted on *k'awiilil*'s nonlocal origins and placed greater emphasis on the *k'uh* from ancestors' bodies. Other royal houses claimed the indigeneity of their respective *k'awiilil* and relied more on the *k'uh* from local ancient places still populated by powerful animate entities. As a legitimating practice, each strategy presented a distinct set of challenges. Descendants of nonlocal dynastic founders faced the unpredictable nature of the actual biological succession and loss of control of the founder's essence gradually bleeding out in the form of cached possessions, bestowed gifts, and even body parts. The path of the indigeneity of rulers and sacred places implied that the landscape was filled with divine sources of authority that could be claimed by rival regimes or internal opponents.

The following section examines the cases of the two nearby archaeological sites in the Eastern Peten, Guatemala (Figure 3.1), Holmul and Naranjo, where the local political regimes diverged concerning the dominant legitimating strategies at the intersection of the dual concept of "otherness" ("people-aliens" and "field-forest") and the dual sources of politico-religious authority (*k'uh* and *k'awiilil* from ancestors and places). The regime at Holmul placed greater emphasis on the political/ethnic "otherness" and the ancestral sources of *k'uh* and *k'awiilil*. Its Naranjo counterpart was more closely tied to the local sacred landscape and the notion of its continuity. The dominant strategies corresponded to distinct practices that, in turn, resulted in differences in the material record at either site.

Holmul: A Landscape of Sovereign Bodies

The archaeological site of Holmul was occupied from the Middle Preclassic to the Terminal Classic periods. The first monumental structures with

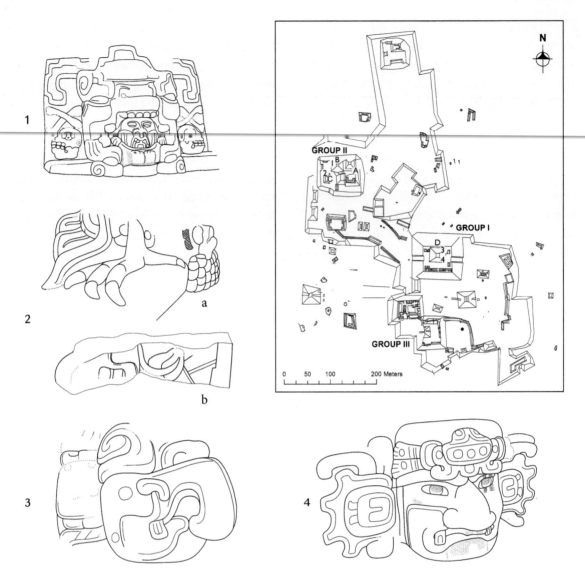

figure 3.6
Preclassic Holmul and its sacred landscape: 1) Building B, Group II; 2a) initial version of Building C, Group II; 2b) second version of Building C, Group II; 3) Building D, Group I; and 4) Building D, Group I. Drawings by Alexandre Tokovinine; map by Francisco Estrada Belli.

external decoration programs date to the beginning of the Late Preclassic period (Figure 3.6), when Holmul was a secondary center connected by a causeway to the larger site of Cival (Estrada Belli 2011). At the same time, several monumental platforms at Holmul were decorated with images of supernatural entities and locations pointing to an emergent local built landscape of powerful places and deities.

At least three locations with divine denizens may be identified in the Late Preclassic landscape of Holmul. The well-preserved phase of Building B in Group II featured representations of an animate jaguar mountain framed by jade jewels, skulls, and bones (Figure 3.6:1). An elderly Mam deity emerged from the mountain's mouth, clinging to the back of a serpent. The plan of the structure resembled an IK' "wind/air" logogram. The shrine could be a focal point of ancestral veneration and the notion of *ch'een* as a place of interaction between humans, deities, and ancestors (Tokovinine 2013:51–55). The

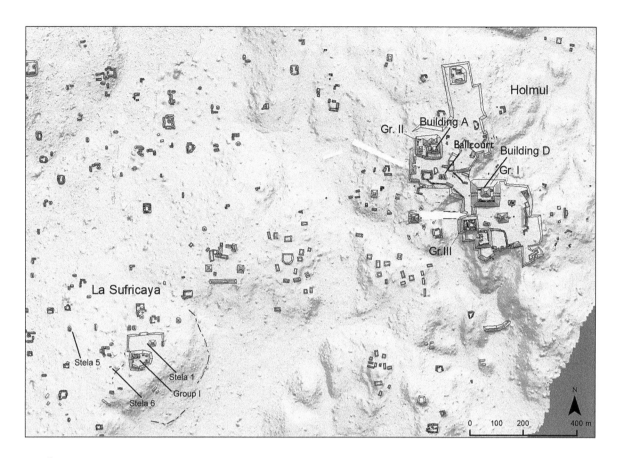

figure 3.7
Holmul and La Sufricaya. Map by Francisco Estrada Belli.

roughly contemporaneous Building C of Group II (Figure 3.6:2a) was decorated with a frieze showing a bird-human hybrid. A characteristic gorget of small feathers suggests that it could be a hummingbird. In Group I, the top level of the main platform featured the heads of a young deity with shell ear flares, a headband with the AK'AB element, and a TZ'UL/AJAW double line across one eye (Figure 3.6:4). The ear flares and the headband imply a connection to Itzam Kokaaj (God D), but facial marks do not fit that pattern and AK'AB seems to be framed by a 260-day cartouche and not a flower. The central pyramid of the same group (Figure 3.6:3) was decorated with images of a large eagle-like bird consistent with Late Preclassic versions of the Principal Bird Deity, an avian aspect of God D (Taube et al. 2010:29–57).

There were no clear statements of royal authority at Holmul during that period. At some point, however, the human-hummingbird platform in Group II was demolished and covered by a new structure decorated with large representations of the so-called avian variety of the Hux Yop Huun entity (Figure 3.6:2b), the divine symbol of kingship (Stuart 2012). The trend grew stronger at the beginning of the Early Classic period after the decline of Cival. A new version of Building B in Group II covered the IK'-shape temple with the emergent ancestral deities. Its external decoration continued with the air/wind/ancestor theme, but the interior spaces and the foundation became gradually filled with multiple elite burials (Merwin and Vaillant 1932:20–41). The inscription on an incised stingray spine from the funerary offerings in Room 2 identified the owner as Chak Tok Wayaab (Estrada Belli et al. 2009). It is the earliest occurrence of the local dynastic title. Building B, therefore, continued as a focal point in the sacred landscape, but the ritual shifted to accommodating the actual bodies of deceased rulers.

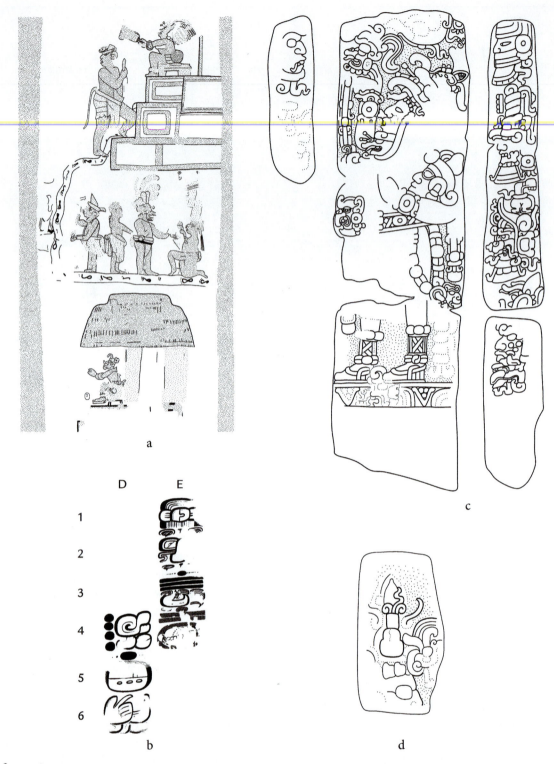

figure 3.8
New order at La Sufricaya: a) depiction of travel on Mural 6, Structure 1; b) arrival of K'awiil at Tikal in the narrative on Mural 7, Structure 1; c) ruler in the presence of deities on Stela 1; and d) deity head on Stela 6. Drawings by Alexandre Tokovinine.

The built environment of Holmul transformed dramatically around 379 CE, when its dynasty transplanted the residence and public spaces to a new complex of La Sufricaya located more than a kilometer away from the older core of Holmul (Figure 3.7). The shift was marked by adopting Teotihuacan traits in architecture and material culture (Estrada Belli et al. 2009). Figural and hieroglyphic murals in the palace at La Sufricaya depicted distant travel (Figure 3.8a) and celebrated the anniversary of "the arrival of K'awiil at Tikal" in 378 CE (Figure 3.8b). Therefore, Holmul rulers now saw themselves as part of a larger landscape with a global (Teotihuacan) and a local (Tikal) center. Their new *k'awiilil* was external and had a distinct place of origin in space and in time.

While changes at Holmul were part of a broader shift in Classic Maya political regimes and their legitimating strategies (Stuart 2000), no other archaeological site reveals such a clear separation at the level of the built landscapes. The shift also coincided with the emergence of carved stelae with the images of the ruler in the presence of patron deities. At least two gods may be identified: Chak Xib(?) Chahk rain deity on Stela 1 (Figure 3.8c) and Tajal Wayaab Sun God on Stela 6 (Figure 3.8d). The Preclassic cults evidenced in the architectural programs discussed above perhaps continued, but the divine list visibly expanded and the king's body was firmly placed in the center of the human-divine interaction. A funeral shrine was added to the main plaza north of the La Sufricaya palace complex shortly after (Tokovinine and Estrada Belli 2015), but its extensive deterioration complicated by looting means that little can be said of the ancestral cult at that time.

Around 550 CE, with the collapse of Teotihuacan and the incorporation of the Holmul region into the Kaanul (Dzibanche) hegemony, the Chak Tok Wayaab royal court moved back to the old core of Holmul. A new royal residence was constructed in Building A of Group II (Estrada Belli 2014), close to the Early Classic ancestral shrine of Building B (Figure 3.9, Phase A). Radiocarbon dates place the construction to around 545–645 CE (Estrada Belli 2015:10). It faced the Preclassic platform of Building C with the Hux Yop Huun frieze across the main courtyard of Group II (Figure 3.6). The royal status of the occupants is suggested by two hieroglyphic murals painted in the excavated southernmost room of the complex and by a cache on the central axis of the structure that contains a lidded vessel with a painted Hux Yop Huun symbol (Figure 3.9) (Díaz García 2012). The move meant that the built landscape of the ruling family once again overlapped with Late Preclassic monumental structures. Subsequent generations of Holmul rulers then "rewrote" that Preclassic landscape following the concept of political authority from the times of their stay at La Sufricaya.

The first visible step in the rewriting process was adding a tomb in front of the Preclassic platform with the Principal Bird Deity in Group I discussed above (Figure 3.10, Burial I). This burial (T84.14) with Early Classic vessels was followed by a cache (Figure 3.10, Cache 1) directly above the tomb (Shetler 2013). The burial/cache and the access steps of the platform were then covered by a temple structure (Figure 3.10, Phase D) dated to 420–588 CE (Estrada Belli 2020:8–10). Several Classic Maya inscriptions mention placing royal burials in structures called Wak Chanal Muyal Witz, the mountain-dwelling of God D or his avian alter ego (Tokovinine 2013:120–122). Given the possible connection of Holmul Group I to the Principal Bird Deity and a local variant of God D discussed above, it appears that this apparent funeral shrine conformed to a broader pattern of adding the royal dead to the pivotal point of the local sacred landscape. The funeral shrine did not fully cover the Preclassic platform, but rather fronted the structure, simultaneously restricting access to and deriving authority from it.

The funeral activity continued under the next generation of Holmul rulers, when burials dated to 546–609 CE (Figure 3.10, Burials II and III) were placed under the floor of the back room of the temple superstructure (Estrada Belli 2019:6–7; García Vázquez 2019:61–65). The building was then partially demolished to give way to a larger shrine (Figure 3.10, Phase E) directly over the burials accompanied by a new round of dedicatory caches (García Vázquez 2019:82–83). As a result of these

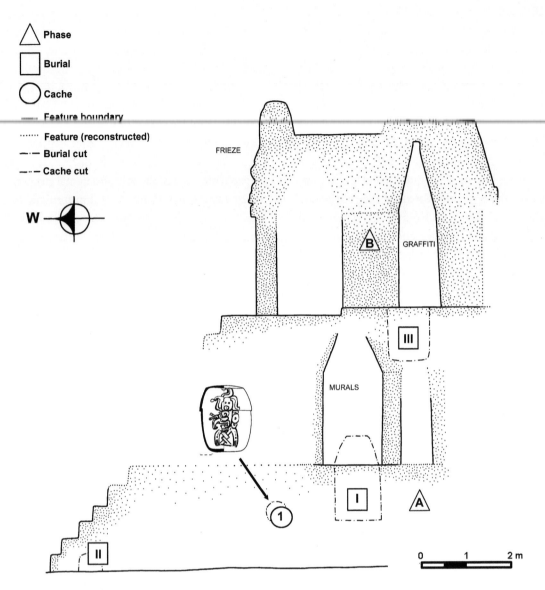

figure 3.9
Construction phases, burials, and caches in Building A, Group II, Holmul. Drawing by Alexandre Tokovinine.

modifications, the updated shrine became linked to at least three presumably royal ancestors. Its wider internal spaces, along with the presence of a large throne bench in the back room, imply that the range of its functions possibly expanded and included events with more participants in the presence of the dead and/or the living rulers.

Construction activities then shifted once again to the location of the palace of Building A in Group II. A vaulted tomb (Figure 3.9, Burial I) was added below what used to be its central room (Díaz García 2012; Estrada Belli 2015). The building was filled and incorporated into the foundation of a dynastic shrine (Figure 3.9, Phase B) with an elaborate frieze and a lengthy dedicatory inscription that may be dated to approximately 590 CE (Estrada Belli and Tokovinine 2016). At some point, a modest burial (Figure 3.9, Burial II) was added to the bottom section of the shrine's main access stairway (Díaz García 2012). Another burial (Figure 3.9, Burial III) was placed under the floor of the central room of the shrine.

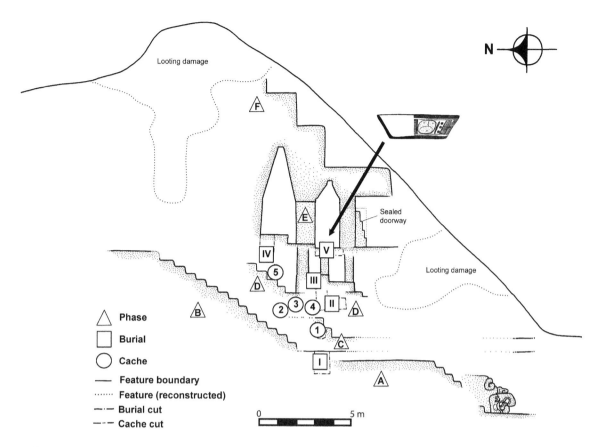

figure 3.10
Construction phases, burials, and caches in Building D, Group I, Holmul. Drawing by Alexandre Tokovinine.

In contrast to iterations of funeral structures in Group I, subsequent construction episodes fully preserved the facade of this new version of Building A. Its frieze (Figure 3.11) offers an insight into the role of the sovereign body in the ritual landscape of Holmul (Estrada Belli and Tokovinine 2016). The complex hieroglyphic emblems on the southern and northern sides of the temple (Figure 3.11b–c) label it as "Succession/Order House" (*tz'ak naah*). The dedicatory inscription along the western cornice of the building (Figure 3.11a) states that it was a "dwelling" (*otoot*) of the "five successors of the Wiinte' Naah lord" (a likely reference to the ruler with Teotihuacan connections who initiated the move from Holmul to La Sufricaya) and proceeds to list the five rulers, concluding with the likely occupant of the vaulted tomb below the temple, Tzahb Chan Yopaat Macha', and his son and successor K'inich Tajal Tuun/Chahk.

The narrative also reports that K'inich Tajal Tuun/Chahk was a vassal of Dzibanche kings, that his mother was a princess from Naranjo, and that the king of Naranjo Ajnumsaaj [Chan K'inich] was his maternal grandfather. The narrative thus firmly places the sources of political authority outside Holmul. First, it "clarifies" a line of rulers that connects Chak Tok Wayaab to Teotihuacan (the fact that there are only five generations between 378 and 590 CE implies some deliberate omissions here). Second, it mentions the political patronage of Dzibanche. Finally, it details a link to the royal bloodline of Naranjo and names the senior male relative from that dynasty.

The figural decoration on the western side of the temple roof (above the dedicatory text) is dominated by the representations of three animate mountains (Figure 3.11a–b). The mountains are not named (the cartouches appear eroded and painted

Whose Mountains? 59

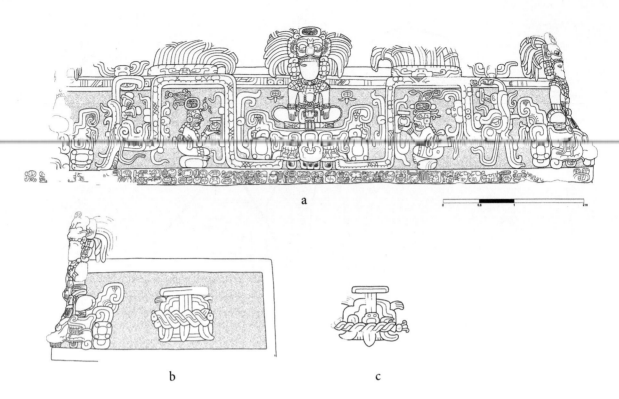

figure 3.11

The frieze of Building A, Group II, Holmul: a) western side; b) southern side; and c) northern side. Drawing by Alexandre Tokovinine.

over), but triads of mountains appear in Early Classic funeral contexts and seem to function as a way of orienting the body of a sovereign in a wider supernatural landscape (Acuña 2015). The central mountain is occupied by seated Tzahb Chan Yopaat Macha' concurrent with the sun in the eastern sky, much like one of the ancestors on Yaxchilan Stela 11 (Figure 3.2d). The scene on Holmul Building A takes this message one step further. It includes two feline star deities offering "first tamales" (*nah waaj*) to Tzahb Chan Yopaat Macha' as the Sun king. The deity to the left is labeled "commoner bone(s)/person(s)" (*paatkab baak/winik*). The deity to the right is labeled "... dynasty lord(s)" (... *tz'ak ajaw*) (Estrada Belli and Tokovinine 2016). The overall message is close to that in the scene on the lid of K'inich Janaab Pakal's sarcophagus (Chinchilla Mazariegos 2006), but rather than listing specific courtiers joining the Sun king as stars in the afterlife, the idea of the Holmul scene is that all of the kingdom, commoners and lords alike achieve a

form of celestial existence through what happens to the sovereign. The shrine's function expands beyond the funerary cult of Tzahb Chan Yopaat Macha' into veneration of the royal dynasty and divine kingship as a foundation of the social and cosmic order.

A palimpsest of graffiti inside the temple (Figure 3.12) is dominated by repetitive representations of helmeted ballplayers or/and ritual combatants. There is a ballcourt to the south of Building A (Figure 3.7), conforming to a pattern of ballcourts connected to funeral shrines (Houston 2014). The only glyphic commentary among the graffiti (see the close-up section in Figure 3.12) states that "she/he took the *k'uh*" (*uk'am[aw] k'uh*). The commentary seems to be associated with a large standing figure whose head is occluded by subsequent drawings. It is tempting to see a link between the shrine, the ballgame, and creating/obtaining ancestral *k'uh*.

The next generation of Holmul rulers resumed funeral activities in Group I with another set of

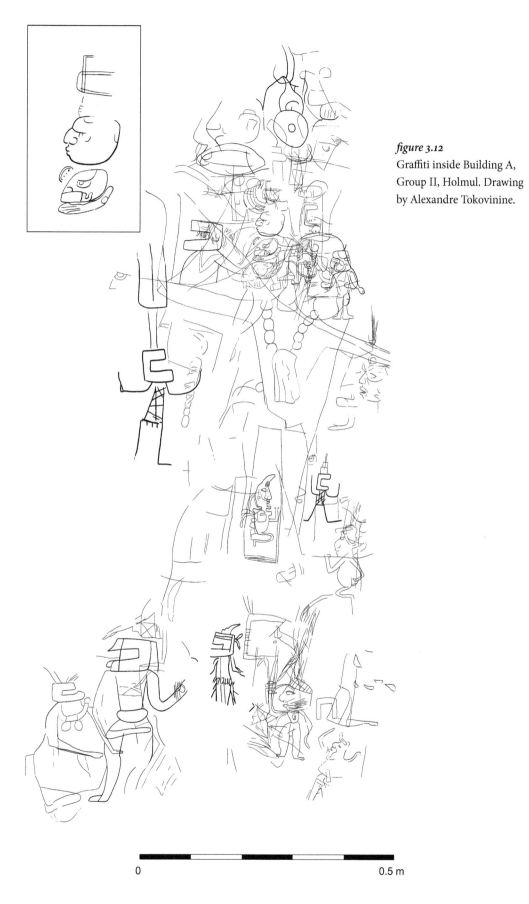

figure 3.12
Graffiti inside Building A,
Group II, Holmul. Drawing
by Alexandre Tokovinine.

Whose Mountains? 61

paired burials (Figure 3.10, Burials IV and V) around 615 CE (García Vázquez 2017:169–186, 2018:36–39). The funeral shrine was built over rather than demolished, and its internal rooms were repeatedly reentered with additional ritual deposits placed on top of the floors covering the burials (García Vázquez 2017:153–168). The succession of funeral shrines on the spot stops with the construction of that temple. The 8 Ajaw *tzolk'in* day name on one of the offering bowls (HOL.T.93.06.02.01/17.7.55.98, above Burial V in Figure 3.10) likely corresponds to the period ending ritual in 692 CE. The shape and type-variety classification of the vessel are consistent with the date. The implication is that the reentering episodes in Group I at Holmul occurred for nearly a century.

Therefore, by the early seventh century, the ritual landscape of Holmul had acquired two focal points: a dynastic shrine in Group II built on top of the first post-Sufricaya palace (at that point, the royal residence moved to Group III); and an accumulation of three funeral shrines gradually subsuming the Preclassic transposition of the celestial mountain in the center of Group I. The latter sequence may be described as a kind of occupation or substitution of an existing powerful place. The dynastic shrine of Building A, however, represented a somewhat different trajectory, as it began with a terminated royal residence that was replaced by a shrine venerating the posthumous concurrence of the former resident with a solar deity, the external sources of his authority, and the connection of his fate to that of his subjects. The overall message was that the ritual landscape was centered on the body of the sovereign in life and death. The dynastic shrine also attempted to resolve the question of legitimacy by presenting an uninterrupted line of succession from the "Wiinte' Naah lord" of La Sufricaya. It appears that the landscape somewhat stabilized because Building A of Group II and the funeral shrine over the last burials in the center of Group I functioned longer than the first two funeral shrines in Group I. Subsequent rulers were buried elsewhere, gradually "imprinting" the ancestral cult onto other monumental structures such as Ruin X, the main pyramid of the local E-Group.

Naranjo: A Landscape of Gods and Their Places

The archaeological site of Naranjo is located to the southwest of Holmul (Figure 3.1). The chronological framework of its occupation is comparable to Holmul. Yet during most of the Classic period, Naranjo was one of the larger cities in the region and its dynasty claimed ascendancy over most of the Eastern Peten, including Holmul (Fialko 2019; Martin and Grube 2008:69–83). Moreover, Naranjo was ruled by one of the oldest royal dynasties, with thirty-four rulers before Ajnumsaaj Chan K'inich's accession in 546 CE (Grube 2004).

In contrast to Holmul, the themes of the Late Preclassic architecture at Naranjo are largely unknown. But thanks to a large corpus of the inscribed monument and external references, the significance of the built landscape of Naranjo is much better understood. It is characterized by two distinct sacred geographies: several architectural compounds are indexed as deep-time places linked to the indigenous foundations of the local political regime, but the apparent royal residence contains an entire collection of distant places transposed as individual structures.

The urban core of Naranjo is dominated by a large triadic acropolis on its eastern side (Figure 3.13e). The main temple of the acropolis, Structure C-9, is the tallest building at the site. The impressive volume of the pyramid largely consists of the last two construction phases covering earlier features (at least two construction episodes) carved into the bedrock of the hill and dating to 554 CE and 682 CE (Fialko 2021; Tokovinine and Fialko 2007; Tokovinine et al. 2018). The inscriptions on Stelae 24 and 29, which detail the arrival of Ix Wak Jalam Chan Lem ("Lady Six Sky") at Naranjo (see Ardren, this volume) and subsequent dedication of the temple in 682 CE (Graham 1975:64, 1978:78), refer to the location as Wak Ihk' . . . Huun Nal Pek Sa'aal, which may be translated as "Six Black . . . Headbands Place, Flat hilltop, Sa'aal" (Tokovinine and Fialko 2007). The first part of this extended toponymical statement—Wak Ihk' . . . Huun Nal (Figure 3.13e)—also occurs on the fragments of Stela 45 buried in the

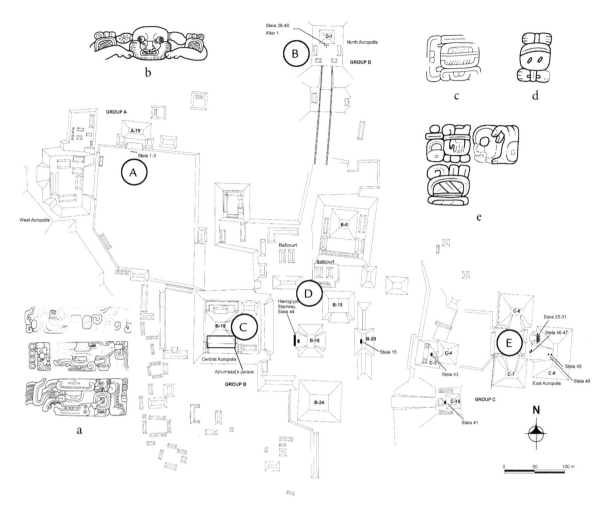

figure 3.13
Sacred landscape at Naranjo: a) toponyms associated with Structures A14–A16; b) Ti' (Sa'aal); c) Jo' Chan Naah; d) Maxam; and e) Sa'aal. Map and drawings by Alexandre Tokovinine.

554 CE version of the temple and on the basal registers of Stelae 22 and 46 placed in front of the 682 CE version of the shrine (Martin et al. 2017; Tokovinine and Fialko 2007). Therefore, the toponym Wak Ihk'... Huun Nal corresponds to the temple itself. The second half of the sequence contains a descriptive "flat hilltop" (*pek*) and probably refers to the whole triadic group. It concludes with the placename from the "emblem glyph" of Naranjo rulers, Sa'aal ("place where atole abounds"). The toponym of Sa'aal could denote the extent of the ancient city or even a wider realm. However, there are no references to events at Sa'aal outside the triadic acropolis. The earliest occurrence of the "Sa'aal lord" title is in a medallion of the royal crown of Naatz Chan Ahk depicted on mid-fifth-century Stela 45 (Tokovinine and Fialko 2007:9, fig. 4). Textual sources referring to Naatz Chan Ahk and his predecessor Tzik'in Bahlam cite the more common local royal title of Sak Chuween (Martin 1996:230–231). The "Sa'aal lord" appears in the texts on monuments commissioned in the 590s and later, during the second half of Ajnumsaaj Chan K'inich's reign (Stelae 38 and 43). The "divine (*k'uhul*)" prefix to "Sa'aal lord" was only added in the reign of K'ahk' Tiliw Chan Chahk and was never used in retrospective references (Martin et al. 2017). It has been argued previously that the title gradually evolved from something very specific

Whose Mountains? 63

and local to become the main marker of Naranjo's political community (Tokovinine 2011).

Additional insight into the significance of Sa'aal is provided by the inscription on Lintel 2 of Temple IV at Tikal (Figure 3.14a). The narrative details the defeat of the ruler of Naranjo Yax Mayuy Chan Chahk by his Tikal adversary (Martin 1996). Yax Mayuy Chan Chahk's "downfall" (Zender 2020) is alleged to have happened in the "city" (*kaaj*) and in a holy place (*ch'een*) of the "Ihk' Miin SNB ("Square-Nosed Beast"; the T1021 grapheme remains undeciphered) god." It also resulted in the capture of a deity of a "hummingbird palanquin" and "black headband" (recalling the "Six Black . . . Headbands Place" name of the C-9 shrine). The scene on the lintel shows the ruler of Tikal seated in a palanquin beneath a figure of a supernatural entity combining features of a hummingbird and Chuwaaj (the jaguar fire deity) and wearing the aforementioned headband. The basal register of the palanquin is marked with a repeated SA' logogram likely standing for the Sa'aal toponym. An earlier version of the same palanquin is represented on a vessel painted for Ajnumsaaj Chan K'inich (K7716) and possibly on a graffito at Tulix Mul in Belize (Helmke et al. 2019). Therefore, the toponym of Sa'aal denoted a place of holy relics that ultimately belonged to "Ihk' Miin SNB god." It is very likely that the temple on top of the C-9 pyramid was dedicated to Ihk' Miin SNB, although there yet is no direct textual reference naming him as the shrine's occupant. The more literal "cave" significance of the *ch'een* term (Vogt and Stuart 2005) may also relate to the carved bedrock features underneath the pyramid (Tokovinine and Fialko 2007).

Ihk' Miin/Mihiin SNB was a deep-time founder of the Naranjo royal dynasty, thirty-plus generations before the Late Classic lords (Figure 3.14b–c). The abovementioned text at Tikal calls him a *k'uh*. The inscription on Naranjo Stela 2 (Figure 3.14d) contains a list of the king's divine witnesses (*yichnal uk'uhuul*). Even though the section of the text is eroded, the name of Ihk' Miin SNB is discernible in Block B13, confirming his divine status.

It is significant that the two known Classic-period reconstructions of the C-9 pyramid, which coincided with a renewed emphasis on Ihk' Miin SNB and Sa'aal, correspond to periods of consolidation after times of crisis and uncertainty. Ajnumsaaj Chan K'inich began his reign in 546 CE as a child ruler installed after the fall of Naranjo under the sway of the Kaanuul hegemony (Martin and Grube 2008:72). His version of the temple was accomplished by the *k'atun* ending in 554 CE, and the corresponding Stela 48, embedded in the main stairway of the shrine, refers to the young king as *yax bolon tz'akb[uul] ajaw*—"new dynasty" or "new king eternal" (Tokovinine et al. 2018). The next renovation of the temple in 682 CE coincided with another dynastic reset marked by the arrival of Ix Wak Jalam Chan Lem and her regency over the reign of her child, K'ahk' Tiliw Chan Chahk. In either case, the inscriptions do contain more conventional claims of the royal status of the children's fathers, as reported on Stela 43 for Ajnumsaaj Chan K'inich and Stela 46 for K'ahk' Tiliw Chan Chahk (Martin et al. 2017; Tokovinine et al. 2018), but the cult of Ihk' Miin SNB tied to Wak Ihk' . . . Huun Nal Pek Sa'aal seemed to be the main source of royal legitimacy and claims to political authority.

The other key place in the sacred topography of Naranjo is Maxam (Figure 3.13d). The earliest references to Maxam are on Altar 1 (Graham 1978:103–104). The altar-stela pair of Altar 1 and Stela 38 (Graham 1978:97) are currently located in front of the pyramid D-9 of the North Acropolis, but the monuments were likely relocated there during the Terminal Classic period (Schuster 2012:32). The inscription on Altar 1 refers to the dedication of a temple in 577 CE as "stone-shaping of first/new . . . house [in] Maxam" (*pat-tuun yax* T593 *naah maxam*). The narrative further contextualizes Maxam as a deep-time place associated with Ihk' Miin SNB and a more recent ritual act by an otherwise unknown "Ich Puy lord" in 257 BCE. A connection to Ihk' Miin SNB is reinforced by the text and imagery on Stela 38 celebrating Ajnumsaaj Chan K'inich's act of *ubaahil aan* of Ihk' Miin SNB in 593 CE (Figure 3.14e). The only other toponymical information near D-1 is the basal register of later Stela 40 that simply states "edge" (*ti'*), although this allograph of TI' incorporates the main sign of the Sa'aal place-name (Figure 3.13b). As for Maxam, the

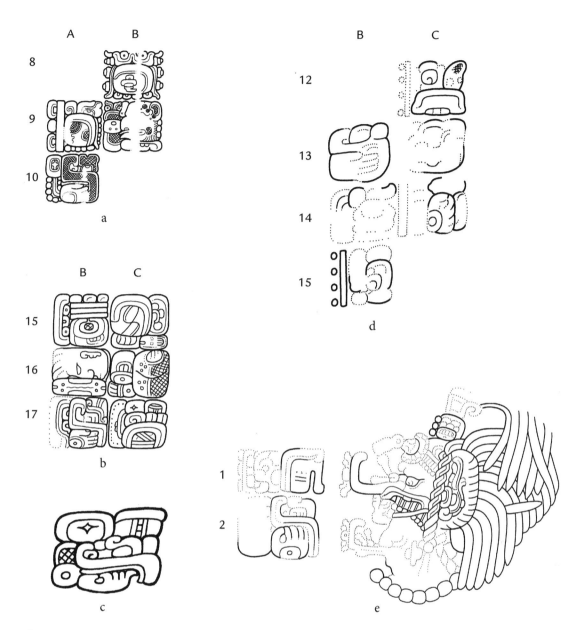

figure 3.14

Ihk' Miin SNB as a patron god of Naranjo: a) detail of Lintel 2, Temple IV, Tikal; b) detail of Stela 24, Naranjo; c) detail of Altar 1, Naranjo; d) detail of Stela 2, Naranjo; and e) detail of Stela 38, Naranjo. Drawings by Alexandre Tokovinine.

second direct reference to the place-name occurs on Stela 8 (Figure 3.13d), located in its original position in front of Structure B-4 north of the plaza formed by the Central Acropolis and the western pyramid of the E-Group. Although the statement on Stela 8 is poorly understood, it involves a public display of the captured Yaxha ruler that likely happened in this plaza given other monuments of similar themes nearby. Therefore, it is possible that Maxam denoted the area near the Central Acropolis and the E-Group, perhaps even as a kind of west (Maxam)–east (Sa'aal) pair.

The second kind of sacred geography at Naranjo—distant places transposed as local structures—is represented by the Central Acropolis (Figure 3.13). A massive five-level pyramid of B-15 takes a large portion of its basal platform. It sits on top of a Late Preclassic platform that also had five

Whose Mountains? 65

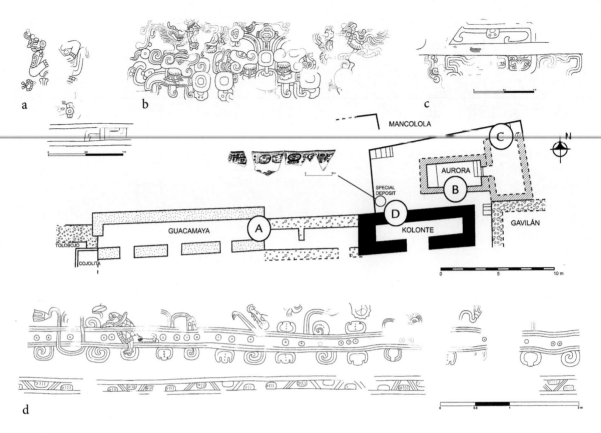

figure 3.15
Ajnumsaaj's palace as a transposition of sacred places: a) eastern frieze, Guacamaya structure; b) southern frieze, Aurora structure; c) northern frieze, Aurora structure; and d) northern frieze, Kolonte structure. Drawings by Alexandre Tokovinine.

distinct terraces (Fialko 2008, 2021). Fragments of an inscribed stucco frieze from the structure on the top level of the last construction phase of the pyramid contain the place-name of Nah Jo' Chan/Jo' Chan Naah (Figure 3.13c). Translated as "Five Sky House" or "First Five Skies," it corresponds to a celestial mountain dwelling of the Paddler deities (Stuart and Houston 1994:71). Given the emphasis on five levels in at least two iterations of the structure, it is plausible that it was meant to recreate this distant "mountain in the north" where one of the three stones was placed during the last creation (Looper 2003). A cluster of residential structures and at least one large throne room (Structure B-15A) occupied the space to the north of the B-15 pyramid during the last construction phases of the whole complex. This palatial compound may be attributed to the reign of Itzamnaaj K'awiil (Schuster 2012:30).

Investigations of the courtyard to the south of the B-15 pyramid revealed a set of earlier structures that were added to the still-visible Late Preclassic Mancolola central platform at the end of the Early Classic period (Fialko 2021) (Figure 3.15). Ajnumsaaj Chan K'inich was likely responsible for and resided in this cluster of adjacent buildings, as a special deposit associated with the filling of the area contained Tepeu 1 Saxche Orange polychrome pottery, including fragments of vessels that belonged to Ajnumsaaj Chan K'inich in the fourth *k'atun* of his life (Fialko 2005, 2008, 2021).

At least three of the buildings investigated so far are decorated by partially preserved roof and wall stucco friezes (Figure 3.15). The roof and wall friezes of the Aurora structure are the most well-preserved. The building consists of two segments that form an IK'-like shape in plan. A now-sealed doorway

figure 3.16
The Hummingbird God of Naranjo: a) detail of Ajnumsaaj's vessel from Burial T.93.76, Building D, Group I, Holmul; b) detail of an unprovenanced vessel (K1387); c) Saak/Xaak Witz as a mythical place, detail of an unprovenanced vessel (K1398); and d) Saak/Xaak Witz as an actual location, detail of the Komkom Vase, Baking Pot. Drawings by Alexandre Tokovinine.

connects the rooms. There is no other access to the eastern half and the main entrance to the building is in the southern wall of the western room. The southern and the northern sides of the roof of the western room of Aurora are decorated with elaborate molded and painted stucco landscape scenes. The two are very similar, although the southern version (Figure 3.15b) is of better quality and with additional details. Another frieze decorates the northern wall of the eastern room (Figure 3.15c). There is also a corresponding frieze on the same side of the roof of the room, but it was only partially exposed during excavation.

A frontal depiction of a living mountain occupies the central position in the scenes of the roof friezes of the western room of Aurora (Figure 3.15b). The mountain is marked by flowers with inscribed SAAK/XAAK ("seed"/"flower bud") logogram. The scene on the southern frieze contains two additional mountains shown in profile without additional elements. The central mountain on the southern frieze is also surrounded by images of flying or seated hummingbirds. The overall composition resembles the so-called Cosmic Vase from Rio Azul published by Adams (1999:85–86, fig. 36) and the unprovenanced Early Classic Deletaille

Whose Mountains? 67

tripod (Fields 2005:pl. 137), but it also recalls the organization of the frieze of Building A at Holmul and Rio Azul tomb paintings discussed above.

Two larger avian entities flank the central mountain in either scene. They seem to be identical down to the hieroglyphic name LEM-AAT or LEM-ne in the headdresses. They combine hummingbird beaks, chest pectorals, and AK'AB flower headbands of the *kokaaj* Principal Bird Deity and the youthful features of the young Maize/Wind God. The very same human-hummingbird hybrid (sometimes more avian and sometimes more humanoid) is depicted on multiple excavated and looted vessels produced by the Naranjo workshops during Ajnumsaaj Chan K'inich's reign (see also Chinchilla Mazariegos 2017:87–88) (Figure 3.16a). A late seventh-century painted vessel with an ownership statement naming the ruler of Zapote Bobal (Figure 3.16b) depicts a close approximation of the human-hummingbird entity of Aurora and provides it with a locative caption, "Sa'[aal]." There can be little doubt that the friezes represent a local patron deity and its mountainous dwelling, and that the same hummingbird deity appears on pottery and as part of a more complex composite entity on the royal palanquins at Naranjo.

Further clues about the function of the Aurora structure are provided by graffiti in the investigated western room (Tokovinine and Fialko 2018) (Figure 3.17a–d). Two hieroglyphic inscriptions mention a "priest" (*aj-k'uh*). One of the two is a tag on a doorjamb (Figure 3.17c), and the other is a caption *aj-bin ti aj-k'uh* ("*aj-bin* with/for the priest") next to an image of a speared deer (Figure 3.17a). There is at least one depiction of the Chuwaaj Fire God (Jaguar God of the Underworld), who was another divine patron of Naranjo royalty and was also part of the palanquin deity (Figure 3.17a). Wall counts indicate that the occupant of the room kept track of the 260-day calendar, lunar months, and some other cycles of unclear nature. At least one cruciform cosmogram is accompanied by a likely TZ'AK "order" symbol (Figure 3.17b). In summary, the graffiti are consistent with the building functioning as a temple occupied by a priest, presumably the one serving the cult of Lem Aat/Lem Neh.

If Aurora is a shrine, then the hummingbird flower mountain on the frieze likely evokes the deity's actual abode. Xaak/Saak Witz is a variant of a mythical Flower Mountain (Acuña 2015) that is transposed into specific shrines at other Classic Maya sites (e.g., the inscription on Tikal Stela 22 or Nim Li Punit Stela 1). The mythical narrative on the early eighth-century vessel K1398 likely made at Naranjo places the White Saak Mountain "in the north" (*Saak . . . Lem Witz Nal Xaman*; Figure 3.16c). However, the recently discovered account of the Naranjo-Yaxha wars on the early ninth-century Komkom Vase from Baking Pot, Belize (Helmke, Hoggarth, and Awe 2018), mentions the very same *Saak Witz* as a real place affected by the hostilities (Figure 3.16d). Other deep-time toponyms correspond to actual locales near Naranjo, including the yet-unidentified K'inchil Kab and Bahlam Jol-Witzna (Tokovinine 2020). Therefore, rather than projecting a potentially inaccessible deep-time landscape, the western room of Aurora likely transposed an actual mountain near Naranjo where the cult of the hummingbird deity had originated from. Moreover, the abovementioned hummingbird stucco frieze on a Late Preclassic building at Holmul (Figure 3.6:2a) attests to the antiquity of the cult and its presence at other sites in the region.

The frieze on the northern wall of Aurora's second (sealed) room depicts a large frontal view of a living mountain, but a hieroglyphic caption identifies it not as Saak/Xaak Witz, but as Lem Witz Nal (Figure 3.15c). Lem Witz Nal ("Shiny mountain place") is one of the more common place-names in painted cosmograms in Rio Azul tombs (Acuña 2015), but its placement on Aurora seems to be unrelated to funerary function. Instead, it continues by introducing landscape features to the palace compound. The Kolonte structure to the south of Aurora has its roof decorated with a massive "water band" symbolically adding a body of water to the palatial setting (Figure 3.15d). Finally, a preserved section of the roof frieze on a larger Guacamaya building shows a seated Chuween monkey above an eroded place glyph that seems to be otherwise unattested at Naranjo (Figure 3.15a). Given that the most common royal title at Naranjo is "White

figure 3.17
Graffiti as indicators of buildings' function in the Central Acropolis: a) interior wall, Aurora; b) detail of the interior wall, Aurora; c) doorjamb, Aurora; d) bench, Aurora; e) eastern doorjamb, Guacamaya; f) central doorjamb, Guacamaya; g) central doorjamb, Guacamaya; and h) detail of the interior wall, Guacamaya. Drawings by Alexandre Tokovinine.

Chuween" (*sak chuween*), the frieze decoration likely recreates the location of these supernatural artisans and/or refers to the royal ownership of the building. Preserved graffiti inside Guacamaya differ from those in Aurora and seem to be consistent with the political function of the space. The set features at least one eroded inscription left by a visiting king (Figure 3.17e), depictions of ballgames (Figure 3.17f), structures (Figure 3.17e, g), and possibly dedication of a stela in a setting that looks identical to that of Stela 48, the first monument erected by Ajnumsaaj Chan K'inich (Figure 3.17h).

If the proposed interpretation of Ajnumsaaj Chan K'inich's compound in the Central Acropolis is correct, it means that the ruler was constantly in place, not only in some beyond-the-see mythical locations but also in transposed focal points of the regional sacred landscape such as the mountain of the hummingbird deity. It is significant that this "landscape hoarding" had no clear funeral/ancestral connotations but rather strove to control the divine sources of royal authority. It likely happened in parallel with a process of collecting/extracting the *k'uh* from the landscape. Ajnumsaaj Chan K'inich

a

b

c

d

figure 3.18
The varying number of "lands" in Ajnumsaaj's titles at Naranjo: a) "five lands" (K8245); b) "six lands" (Stela 27); c) "seven lands" (K2704); and d) "ten lands" (K7716). Drawings by Alexandre Tokovinine.

claimed the title of "Seven Yopaat (rain gods)" (see the inscription in Figure 3.11a) in an apparent attempt to embody all of the rain deities of the "Seven Divisions" region/group of polities (Martin et al. 2016).

The strategy of deity/place hoarding was presumably aimed at maintaining a stable link between the body of the ruler and the divine sources of their power, as in the royal portrait on Yaxchilan Stela 11. While the palace compound transposed the outer sacred landscape, the sacred place at the inner heart of Naranjo—Sa'aal—along with the body of the ruler, could be extended into the outer landscape through the successive versions of the royal palanquin. While in a palanquin, the ruler, at least symbolically, never left Sa'aal while away. While in a palace, the ruler was constantly attending to key places and gods in a wider sacred landscape even while residing back at Naranjo. Moreover, the practice of giving away polychrome vessels with the images of the hummingbird deity may be interpreted as an effort to promote a specific vision of the regional sacred landscape as seen from Naranjo. It is unclear where the boundaries of the legitimating landscape were. It is revealing that there are at least four variants of the number + lands + *yok'in/yoon* royal title during the reign of Ajnumsaaj Chan K'inich—"five lands," "six lands," "seven lands," and even "ten lands"—as if the boundaries of the claimed area kept expanding or were perceived as such by the artists who worked for the king (Figure 3.18). The inscription with "ten lands" contains a reference to Ajnumsaaj's advanced age ("four *k'atun* lord") supporting the expansion interpretation, but the sample is too small to be certain of it.

Concluding Remarks: Gods, Places, Bodies

While the legitimating practices at Holmul and Naranjo share the theme of a sun-like ruler, the two communities diverge with respect to the source of the authority. Holmul's approach emphasizes relatively recent events and entails the periodic replacement of the currently most-venerated ancestor, perhaps to prevent loss of control of the ancestral cult and its takeover by competing descendants. Funeral shrines with repeated renovations occupy the central area of the site. Naranjo's discourse centers on an entrenched local and regional deep-time landscape with rulers constantly reaffirming their *ubaahil aan* with the patron deity and presence in the local landscape, which technically continues even when the ruler is not there (thanks to transportable places). At the same time, Naranjo kings seem to be concerned about other important spots in the local sacred geography and try to transpose such places and their deities to Naranjo. In other words, the sensibility of the Holmul political landscape is about access to the dead body or bodies, whereas the Naranjo model grapples with how to keep the living body of the sacred ruler in several places at once.

It is worth emphasizing that the built landscapes of Holmul and Naranjo were equally "strange" to the subjects of the political regimes, albeit in different ways. La Sufricaya palace at Holmul, in particular, exemplifies the notion of the ethnic/political "other." The Central Acropolis at Naranjo is a quintessential transposition of the entire "wild" sacred landscape, creating a "strange" core in the middle of the ordered landscape of the capital. It is also important that the two strategies were not mutually exclusive: Naranjo kings buried and venerated their ancestors; Holmul rulers placed their ancestors amid the sacred mountains. However, the relative dominance of either strategy potentially enabled distinct ways of opposing or questioning royal authority. The rulers of Holmul were vulnerable to challenges from other dynasties or even more distant members of their own family with the same Teotihuacan connections. They could also face rival ancestral cults or the gradual loss of ancestral relics through gifts or offerings. When viewed from this perspective, the likely "gaps" in the dynastic record between the "Wiinte' Naah lord" and the sixth-century rulers of Holmul indicated which former members of the dynasty no longer belonged to the pool of venerated ancestors because of links to failed or competing factions of the Chak Tok Wayaab royal house.

Their counterparts at Naranjo were dealing with an entrenched sacred landscape that could be highly resistant to any attempt to cut ties between specific political communities and their deities and associated holy places. Naranjo's strategy of "stretching" or "hoarding" was bound to encounter strong local resistance, which perhaps explains the amount of violence in the Late Classic narratives at the site. And yet even extreme violence was unsuccessful in breaking the links between local identities and sacred landscapes, as the case of the archaeological site of Witzna amply illustrates. The ancient toponym for the site, Bahlam Jol, appears on a sixth-century Naranjo vessel, suggesting that it was linked to the cult of Itzam Kokaaj/God D (Tokovinine 2020). Textual, paleoenvironmental, and archaeological data indicate that Naranjo attacked, burned, and depopulated Witzna in 697 CE (Wahl et al. 2019). However, when Naranjo itself was defeated by Tikal almost half a century later, the population and the royal family of Bahlam Jol returned and rebuilt Witzna. This level of resilience indicates greater social and ideological cohesion within ancient Maya political communities than implied by some models of the ancient Maya sociopolitical organization. And yet this entrenchment in sacred landscapes also explains why some Maya rulers with regional aspirations struggled to extend authority beyond their own polity (see Baron, this volume).

Although the cases of Holmul and Naranjo by no means cover the full range of legitimating strategies available to Classic Maya political regimes, the dual-strategy framework discussed here can help elucidate differences and/or changes in legitimating practices and their impact on the material record. The case of La Corona (Baron, this volume) exemplifies a shift in emphasis from ancestors to patron deities. On the other hand, the driving force behind political changes at La Corona—the Kaanu'l royal house at Dzibanche—moved in the opposite direction regarding its own legitimating practices. Textual sources indicate that it initially claimed indigenous origins in the area of Dzibanche (Martin 2020:136–142). Yet with the Kaanu'l regime transitioning to a hegemonic state, the emphasis in the rhetoric shifted to its ethnic and political otherness. An epithet of "those of Chih Ka' and Wiinte' Naah" was incorporated into the kings' titles (Tokovinine 2020). Sequential royal burials were placed in Building 2 decorated with Teotihuacan place glyphs (Nalda 2003). The trend culminated in a dislocation of the main seat of the Kaanu'l regime from Dzibanche and its transfer to Calakmul. Therefore, it appears that the political rise of Dzibanche necessitated an ideological shift from a Naranjo-type legitimating strategy to something resembling the case of Holmul. Freidel (this volume) characterizes the transformations at Dzibanche as a replacement of sodality kingship with a dynastic system. However, even at the peak of their hegemonic power, Kaanu'l rulers were organized as a corporate group where overall membership and placement in a hierarchy of rotating offices were more significant than kinship ties (Martin 2017). Therefore, what changed was not the organizational principles but the legitimating practices of the Kaanu'l royal house.

It is highly significant that, in pursuit of different sources of authority, Maya rulers still relied on a broadly shared system of beliefs that provided them with a range of available legitimating strategies but presumably constrained their ability to exercise sovereign power. Identifying the social and cultural institutions responsible for the maintenance of this common cosmovision remains one of the major goals of future Maya studies.

This discussion also contributes to the ever-present dilemma of how ancient Maya built landscapes should be classified by archaeologists. In the case of the Central Acropolis at Naranjo, there is a visible overlap of royal residences and divine dwellings (populated by human ritual specialists). At Holmul, the ancestral shrine of Building D in Group I could serve as a royal residence. These overlaps make sense considering the concurrence of human and other-than-human actors and landscape transpositions. Moreover, other-than-human entities likely existed as assemblages of artifacts of which some could be "borrowed" by human agents (e.g., an ancestral *k'oj* mask becoming a *ya' mam k'uh* belt head) or recombined into different supernatural patrons, such as the complex deity of the Naranjo royal palanquins, blurring the classificatory boundaries between architectural spaces hosting the entities, dividualizing discreet structures. Yet the present study also demonstrates that some of these epistemic challenges may be addressed by looking at graffiti. Data from Holmul and Naranjo show that certain graffito themes may serve as indicators of dominant (but not the only) ritual practices in any given interior space.

Acknowledgments

Research at Holmul was authorized by Guatemala's Ministry of Culture and Sports (convenio 2019–2025) and supported by grants from the Pacunam, Hitz, Alphawood, and National Science foundations as well as the National Geographic Society. Institutional support came from Tulane University, the Middle American Research Institute, and the University of Alabama. Excavations at Holmul were supervised by Berenice García Vásquez, Mauricio Díaz, and Anya Shetler, and excavations at Witzna were supervised by Bhanny Giron Miranda and Kaitlin Ahern. We are grateful to the organizers and participants of the Dumbarton Oaks symposium, Stephen D. Houston, and Dmitri Beliaev, as well as to the anonymous reviewers for the comments and suggestions that contributed to the improvement of the original manuscript.

REFERENCES CITED

Acuña, Mary Jane
    2015   Royal Death, Tombs, and Cosmic Landscapes: Early Classic Maya Tomb Murals from Río Azul, Guatemala. In *Maya Archaeology*, vol 3, edited by Charles Golden, Stephen D. Houston, and Joel Skidmore, pp. 168–185. Precolumbia Mesoweb Press, San Francisco.

Adams, Richard E. W.
    1999   *Río Azul: An Ancient Maya City*. University of Oklahoma Press, Norman.

Beliaev, Dmitri
    2013   Western Foreigners in the Dresden Codex. In *The Maya in a Mesoamerican Context: Comparative Approaches to Maya Studies*, edited by Jesper Nielsen

and Christopher Helmke, pp. 167–173. Acta Mesoamericana no. 26. Verlag Anton Saurwein, Markt Schwaben.

Chinchilla Mazariegos, Oswaldo

2006   The Stars of the Palenque Sarcophagus. *RES: Anthropology and Aesthetics* 49–50:40–58.

2017   *Art and Myth of the Ancient Maya*. Yale University Press, New Haven.

Díaz García, Mauricio R.

2012   HOL.L.20, Edificio A, Grupo II, Holmul. In *Investigaciones arqueológicas en la región de Holmul, Petén: Holmul y Dos Aguadas; Informe preliminar de la temporada 2012*, edited by Francisco Estrada Belli, pp. 179–201. Online document, https://www.bu.edu/holmul/reports/informe_2012_layout.pdf.

Estrada Belli, Francisco

2011   *The First Maya Civilization: Ritual and Power before the Classic Period*. Routledge, London.

2014   Resumen de las investigaciones de la temporada 2014. In *Investigaciones arqueológicas en la región de Holmul, Petén: Holmul y Cival; Informe preliminar de la temporada 2014*, edited by Francisco Estrada Belli, pp. 1–18. Online document, https://www.bu.edu/holmul/reports/informe_2014_layout.pdf.

2015   Resumen de las investigaciones de la temporada 2015. In *Investigaciones arqueológicas en la región de Holmul, Petén: Holmul y Cival; Informe anual de la temporada 2015*, edited by Francisco Estrada Belli, pp. 2–28. Online document, https://www.bu.edu/holmul/reports/informe_2015_layout.pdf.

2019   Investigaciones arqueológicas y conservación de arquitectura monumental en la región de Holmul. In *Investigaciones arqueológicas y conservación de la arquitectura monumental en la región de Holmul, temporada 2018*, edited by Francisco Estrada Belli, pp. 1–33. Departamento de Monumentos Prehispánicos y Coloniales, Dirección General del Patrimonio Cultural y Natural, and Ministerio de Cultura y Deportes de Guatemala, Guatemala City. Online document, https://www.bu.edu/holmul/reports/informe_2018.pdf.

2020   Resumen de la Temporada 2019 del Proyecto Arqueológico Holmul. In *Investigaciones arqueológicas en el noreste de Petén, temporada 2019*, edited by Francisco Estrada Belli, pp. 1–24. Departamento de Monumentos Prehispánicos y Coloniales, Dirección General del Patrimonio Cultural y Natural, and Ministerio de Cultura y Deportes de Guatemala, Guatemala City. Online document, https://www.bu.edu/holmul/reports/informe_2019.pdf.

Estrada Belli, Francisco, and Alexandre Tokovinine

2016   A King's Apotheosis: Iconography, Text, and Politics from a Classic Maya Temple at Holmul. *Latin American Antiquity* 27(2):149–169.

Estrada Belli, Francisco, Alexandre Tokovinine, Jennifer M. Foley, Heather Hurst, Gene A. Ware, David Stuart, and Nikolai Grube

2009   A Maya Palace at Holmul, Peten, Guatemala and the Teotihuacan "Entrada": Evidence from Murals 7 and 9. *Latin American Antiquity* 20(1):228–259.

Fialko, Vilma

2005   El Palacio Mayor de la Realeza de Naranjo, Petén, Guatemala. In *XIX Simposio de Investigaciones Arqueológicas en Guatemala, 2005*, edited by Juan Pedro Laporte, Bárbara Arroyo, and Héctor E. Mejía, pp. 325–332. Museo Nacional de Arqueología y Etnología, Guatemala City.

2008   Proyecto de investigación arqueológica y rescate en Naranjo: Documentación emergente en el Palacio de la Realeza de Naranjo, Petén, Guatemala. Online document, http://www.famsi.org/reports/05005es/05005esFialko01.pdf.

2019   The Maya State of Naranjo-Sa'aal and Its Peripheral Organization: A Vision of Expansion and Control. Mesoweb, www.mesoweb.com/CATNYN/Maya_State_of_Naranjo.pdf.

2021   Cultural Development of the Monumental Epicenter of the Maya City of Naranjo-Sa'aal, Northeast Peten, Guatemala. Mesoweb, http://www.mesoweb.com/Contributions/Cultural_Development.pdf.

Fields, Virginia M.
  2005 *Lords of Creation: The Origins of Sacred Maya Kingship.* Los Angeles County Museum of Art, Los Angeles.

García Vázquez, Berenice
  2017 Excavación de le Estructura 1, Grupo I de Holmul. In *Investigaciones arqueológicas y conservación de arquitectura monumental en la región de Holmul, temporada 2016*, edited by Francisco Estrada Belli, pp. 61–190. Departamento de Monumentos Prehispánicos y Coloniales, Dirección General del Patrimonio Cultural y Natural, and Ministerio de Cultura y Deportes de Guatemala, Guatemala City. Online document, https://www.bu.edu/holmul/reports/informe_2016_layout.pdf.
  2018 Excavaciones en el Edificio D del Grupo I de Holmul. In *Investigaciones arqueológicas y conservación de arquitectura monumental en la región de Holmul, temporada 2017*, edited by Francisco Estrada Belli, pp. 29–64. Departamento de Monumentos Prehispánicos y Coloniales, Dirección General del Patrimonio Cultural y Natural, and Ministerio de Cultura y Deportes de Guatemala, Guatemala City. Online document, https://www.bu.edu/holmul/reports/informe_2017.pdf.
  2019 Excavaciones del basamento I, Edificio B y Edificio D del Grupo I de Holmul. In *Investigaciones arqueológicas y conservación de la arquitectura monumental en la región de Holmul, temporada 2018*, edited by Francisco Estrada Belli, pp. 25–89. Departamento de Monumentos Prehispánicos y Coloniales, Dirección General del Patrimonio Cultural y Natural, and Ministerio de Cultura y Deportes de Guatemala, Guatemala City. Online document, https://www.bu.edu/holmul/reports/informe_2018.pdf.

Graeber, David, and Marshall Sahlins
  2017 *On Kings.* Hau Books, Chicago.

Graham, Ian
  1975 *Corpus of Maya Hieroglyphic Inscriptions*, vol. 2, pt. 1, *Naranjo*. Peabody Museum of Archaeology and Ethnology, Harvard University, Cambridge, Mass.
  1978 *Corpus of Maya Hieroglyphic Inscriptions*, vol. 2, pt. 2, *Naranjo, Chunhuitz, Xunantunich*. Peabody Museum of Archaeology and Ethnology, Harvard University, Cambridge, Mass.

Gramsci, Antonio
  1971 *Selections from the Prison Notebooks of Antonio Gramsci.* Edited and translated by Quintin Hoare and Geoffrey Nowell-Smith. Lawrence and Wishart, London.

Grube, Nikolai
  2004 La historia dinástica de Naranjo, Petén. *Beiträge zur Allgemeinen und Vergleichenden Archäologie* 24:197–213.

Hanks, William F.
  1990 *Referential Practice: Language and Lived Space among the Maya.* University of Chicago Press, Chicago.

Helmke, Christophe, Gail Hammond, Thomas Guderjan, Pieta Greaves, and Colleen Hanratty
  2019 Sighting a Royal Vehicle: Observations on the Graffiti of Tulix Mul, Belize. *The PARI Journal* 19(4):10–30.

Helmke, Christophe, Julie A. Hoggarth, and Jaime J. Awe
  2018 *A Reading of the Komkom Vase Discovered at Baking Pot, Belize.* Precolumbia Mesoweb Press, San Francisco.

Houston, Stephen D.
  2014 Deathly Sport. Maya Decipherment, https://mayadecipherment.com/2014/07/29/deathly-sport/.

Houston, Stephen D., and David Stuart
  1996 Of Gods, Glyphs, and Kings: Divinity and Rulership among the Classic Maya. *Antiquity* 70:289–312.
  2021 Captains of the Team. Maya Decipherment, https://mayadecipherment.com/2021/08/12/captains-of-the-team/.

Krempel, Guido, and Sebastián Matteo
  2016 U.S. Authorities Consign Seven Fragments of Looted Maya Monuments to Guatemala. *Mexicon* 38(4):77–112.

Looper, Matthew G.
  2003 *Lightning Warrior: Maya Art and Kingship at Quirigua.* University of Texas Press, Austin.

Martin, Simon

    1996   Tikal's "Star War" against Naranjo. In *Eighth Palenque Round Table, 1993*, edited by Martha J. Macri and Jan McHargue, pp. 223–236. Pre-Columbian Art Research Institute, San Francisco.

    2017   Secrets of the Painted King List: Recovering the Early History of the Snake Dynasty. Maya Decipherment, https://mayadecipherment.com/2017/05/05/secrets-of-the-painted-king-list-recovering-the-early-history-of-the-snake-dynasty/.

    2020   *Ancient Maya Politics: A Political Anthropology of the Classic Period 150–900 CE*. Cambridge University Press, Cambridge.

Martin, Simon, Vilma Fialko, Alexandre Tokovinine, and Fredy Ramirez

    2016   Contexto y texto de la estela 47 de Naranjo-Sa'aal, Peten, Guatemala. In *XXIX Simposio de Investigaciones Arqueológicas en Guatemala, 2015*, edited by Bárbara Arroyo, Luis Méndez Salinas, and Gloria Ajú Álvarez, pp. 615–628. Ministerio de Cultura y Deportes, Instituto de Antropología e Historia, and Asociación Tikal, Guatemala City.

Martin, Simon, and Nikolai Grube

    2008   *Chronicle of the Maya Kings and Queens: Deciphering the Dynasties of the Ancient Maya*. 2nd ed. Thames and Hudson, New York.

Martin, Simon, Alexandre Tokovinine, Elodie Treffel, and Vilma Fialko

    2017   Estela 46 de Naranjo Sa'al, Petén: Hallazgo y texto jeroglífico. In *XXX Simposio de Investigaciones Arqueológicas en Guatemala, 2016*, edited by Bárbara Arroyo, Luis Méndez Salinas, and Gloria Ajú Álvarez, pp. 669–684. Ministerio de Cultura y Deportes, Instituto de Antropología e Historia, and Asociación Tikal, Guatemala City.

Merwin, Raymond E., and George C. Vaillant

    1932   *The Ruins of Holmul, Guatemala*. Peabody Museum of American Archaeology and Ethnology, Harvard University, Cambridge, Mass.

Nalda, Enrique

    2003   Prácticas funerarias en Dzibanché, Quintana Roo: Los entierros en el Edificio de los Cormoranes. *Arqueología* 31:25–37.

Schuster, Angela M. H. (editor)

    2012   *Naranjo-Sa'aal, Peten, Guatemala: Preserving an Ancient Maya City; Plan for Documentation, Conservation, and Presentation / Naranjo-Sa'aal, Peten, Guatemala: La conservación de una antigua ciudad maya; Plan para documentación, conservación, y presentación*. World Monuments Fund, New York.

Shetler, Anya

    2013   Excavación HOL.T.84, Grupo I, Pirámide Norte (Edificio D), Holmul. In *Investigaciones arqueológicas en la región de Holmul, Petén: Holmul y Cival; Informe preliminar de la temporada 2013*, edited by Francisco Estrada Belli, pp. 76–88. Online document, https://www.bu.edu/holmul/reports/informe_2013_layout.pdf.

Smith, Adam T.

    2003   *The Political Landscape: Constellations of Authority in Early Complex Polities*. University of California Press, Berkeley.

    2011   Archaeologies of Sovereignty. *Annual Review of Anthropology* 40(1):415–432.

Stuart, David

    2000   "The arrival of strangers": Teotihuacan and Tollan in Classic Maya Study. In *Mesoamerica's Classic Heritage: From Teotihuacan to the Aztecs*, edited by David Carrasco, Lindsay Jones, and Scott Sessions, pp. 465–513. University Press of Colorado, Boulder.

    2012   The Name of Paper: The Mythology of Crowning and Royal Nomenclature on Palenque's Palace Tablet. In *Maya Archaeology*, vol. 2, edited by Charles Golden, Stephen D. Houston, and Joel Skidmore, pp. 116–142. Precolumbia Mesoweb Press, San Francisco.

Stuart, David, and Stephen D. Houston

    1994   *Classic Maya Place Names*. Dumbarton Oaks Research Library and Collection, Washington, D.C.

Taube, Karl A.

1992 *The Major Gods of Ancient Yucatan.* Dumbarton Oaks Research Library and Collection, Washington, D.C.

2003 Ancient and Contemporary Maya Conceptions about Field and Forest. In *The Lowland Maya Area: Three Millennia at the Human-Wildland Interface*, edited by Arturo Gómez-Pompa, pp. 461–492. Food Products Press, Binghamton, N.Y.

Taube, Karl A., William A. Saturno, David Stuart, Heather Hurst, and Joel Skidmore

2010 *The Murals of San Bartolo, El Petén, Guatemala*, pt. 2, *The West Wall*. Boundary End Archaeology Research Center, Barnardsville, N.C.

Tokovinine, Alexandre

2011 People from a Place: Re-interpreting Classic Maya Emblem Glyphs. In *Ecology, Power, and Religion in Maya Landscapes*, edited by Christian Isendahl and Bodil Liljefors Persson, pp. 81–96. A. Saurwein, Markt Schwaben.

2013 *Place and Identity in Classic Maya Narratives.* Dumbarton Oaks Research Library and Collection, Washington, D.C.

2020 Distance and Power in Classic Maya Texts. In *Reinventing the World: Debates on Mesoamerican Colonial Cosmologies*, edited by Ana Díaz, pp. 251–281. University of Colorado Press, Boulder.

Tokovinine, Alexandre, and Francisco Estrada Belli

2015 La Sufricaya: A Place in Classic Maya Politics. In *Classic Maya Polities of the Southern Lowlands: Integration, Interaction, Dissolution*, edited by Damien B. Marken and James L. Fitzsimmons, pp. 195–224. University of Colorado Press, Boulder.

Tokovinine, Alexandre, and Vilma Fialko

2007 Stela 45 of Naranjo and the Early Classic Lords of Sa'aal. *The PARI Journal* 7(4):1–14.

2018 En el cerro de los colibris: El patrón divino y el pasiaje sagrado de la ciudad de Naranjo. Paper presented at the XXXII Simposio de Investigaciones Arqueológicas en Guatemala, Guatemala City.

Tokovinine, Alexandre, Vilma Fialko, Fredy Ramirez, Simon Martin, and Sergey Vepretskii

2018 La estela 48 de Naranjo Sa'aal, Peten: Contexto, hallazgo y texto jeroglífico. In *XXXI Simposio de Investigaciones Arqueológicas en Guatemala, 2017*, edited by Bárbara Arroyo, Luis Méndez Salinas, and Gloria Ajú Álvarez, pp. 867–876. Ministerio de Cultura y Deportes, Instituto de Antropología e Historia, and Asociación Tikal, Guatemala City.

Vogt, Evon Z., and David Stuart

2005 Some Notes on Ritual Caves among the Ancient and Modern Maya. In *In the Maw of the Earth Monster: Mesoamerican Ritual Cave Use*, edited by James E. Brady and Keith M. Prufer, pp. 155–185. University of Texas Press, Austin.

Wahl, David, Lysanna Anderson, Francisco Estrada Belli, and Alexandre Tokovinine

2019 Palaeoenvironmental, Epigraphic, and Archaeological Evidence of Total Warfare among the Classic Maya. *Nature Human Behaviour* 3(10):1049–1054.

Wilson, Richard

1993 Anchored Communities: Identity and History of the Maya-Q'eqchi'. *Man* 28(1):121–138.

Zender, Marc

2020 Disaster, Deluge, and Destruction on the Star War Vase. *The Mayanist* 2(1):57–76.

4

Masked Intentions

The Expression of Leadership in Northern Yucatán

WILLIAM M. RINGLE

Although the restrained classicism of the Puuc Colonnette architectural style is widely admired, the facades of many of these structures, decorated with friezes of colonnettes or geometric designs (Figure 4.1a), may seem inscrutable when compared to the florid relief sculpture of the southern lowlands (see Freidel, this volume; Tokovinine, Estrada Belli, and Fialko, this volume). Likewise, the deep interest in dynastic descent and military achievements evident in southern inscriptions, not to mention religious and cosmological concerns of the most profound significance, is largely absent in the thin textual record of the north (Grube 1994, 2003). Consequently, while we have a relatively full understanding of political organization in the south (Freidel, this volume; Martin 2020), we have yet to achieve parity in the north.

This chapter argues that late Puuc political messaging was often expressed by means of zoomorphic mosaic masks, so called because they were assembled from several individually carved components (Figure 4.1b). Mosaic masks are usually placed in the upper wall zone of buildings, at corners and above doorways, sometimes in stacks of up to four masks, but are occasionally to be found in the lower wall zone or used as steps. Their meaning can be at least partially understood by means of a conjunctive approach integrating settlement patterns, architecture, iconography, and epigraphy.[1] As will be seen, the association of masks with specific building plans also aids in the interpretation of such structures. These can then be tested elsewhere, most notably at Chichen Itza, where a variety of structures were decorated with masks. Although a definitive solution to the meaning of these masks remains elusive, a more nuanced treatment of masking can at least establish a framework for future studies.

Puuc Masks

The practice of masking the facades of the most prominent Puuc buildings began in the Terminal Classic period, sometime around 830–850 CE,

a

b

figure 4.1
a) Huntichmul Structure N5065E5425, a Puuc Colonnette-style range structure (photograph by William M. Ringle); and b) Xlabpak Structure 1, a Puuc Mosaic-style structure with mask stacks (photograph by William M. Ringle).

following the earlier Colonnette Style.[2] Their meaning has been an enduring debate in Maya archaeology (see Kowalski 1987:182–202 for a summary of earlier research). Seler (1917:13[5])[3] may have been the first scholar to suggest that they were versions of certain long-nosed deities pictured in the Late Postclassic codices, specifically Chaak (God B) or another he identified as Ah Bolon Tz'acab, now referred to as God K or K'awiil. They were both, in his opinion, cases of sympathetic magic, designed to bring rain to a region lacking rivers and lakes (Seler 1917:15[6]). Variants of this idea continue to be popular, especially since depictions of Chaak and Chaak impersonators are frequent in the region.

In contrast, Linda Schele (1998:483–487; see also Schele and Mathews 1998:ch. 6) identified some masks as representations of Itsamna (God D) because their flowered headbands resemble those of that deity. At Uxmal, she argued that the placement of masks with flower headbands over doorways identified these spaces as *its am nahs*, or sorcery houses. In fact, she maintained that the entire Nunnery Quadrangle and most likely the Codz Pop of Kabah were *its am nahs* because both were covered with mosaic masks (Schele 1998:487). Why so many rooms were necessary for conjuring was left unexplained. She also argued that some masks were mountain zoomorphs, by analogy with the zoomorphic heads decorating Copan Temple 10L-22. This has become the received opinion of many scholars. David Stuart's (1987) decipherment of Glyph T529 as *wits* ("mountain") later led him to a brief study of mountain imagery (Stuart 1997). He noted examples of architectural masks marked with the attributes of T528 (*tun*, "stone") or T529, which, at first glance, were quite similar to mosaic masks (Figure 4.2a–e), but he stopped short of addressing northern architectural masks. That step was taken by Karl Taube (2004) and Erik Boot (2004). Taube believed that such masks represent "Flower Mountain," a paradisiacal peak forming part of the cosmography of several Mesoamerican societies, arguing that the volutes often seen emerging from the ear flares of such masks tied them to concepts of breath and spirit and, by analogy, to the wind and clouds emitted by mountain portals. Furthermore, he and others have cited the crossed band-and-disk (X-O) markings on the snouts of some masks as schematic versions of the "grape bunches" that characterize *tun* markings, citing somewhat similar examples from the Postclassic codices (Figure 4.2f).

In my view, this argument does not bear up under scrutiny. No Puuc mask, to my knowledge, exhibits the cleft forehead of *wits* zoomorphs or the "grape bunch" that usually marks stone objects and undoubted *wits* heads (compare Figure 4.2c–e). As for the argument that secondary attributes (i.e., flowers or earspool volutes) necessarily indicate that masks were zoomorphic mountains, Taube's (2001) own illuminating discussion of breath symbolism demonstrates that volutes commonly reference the breath spirit of royals, in keeping with the political interpretation advanced herein. Several objections can be raised regarding the identification of X-O designs as signs for *wits* or *tun*. First, they may mark other objects, such as the supraorbital X-Os of a feathered serpent sculpture from Chichen Itza (Figure 4.2g). Second, X-O markings are present only on a small minority of mosaic masks, primarily from Chichen Itza. Puuc masks are instead usually decorated with disks, which alone cannot denote "stone" (Figure 4.2h). Finally, the Xs of certain elaborately carved examples are clearly crossed sky signs, while the circles are internally divided into quarters and may be *k'in* signs (Figure 4.2i). Celestial associations are also evident in masks bearing Lamat ("star"/"Venus") markings, such as those from the House of the Governor (cf. Figure 4.12c).

A further reason for rejecting the *wits* interpretation is that some Puuc masks were clearly the heads of animate creatures, such as the mask from the Labna Palace (Figure 4.3a). Two further mask sets, although from different sites, are virtually identical serpents, both adorning the front corners of buildings with "Chenes" monster maw entrances. One set forms the lower facade of Structure 1A1 (Manos Rojas) of Kabah (see also Rubenstein 2015:108) (Figure 4.3b), the second forms stacks at the lower corners of the "Chenes" superstructure of the Adivino pyramid at Uxmal (Figure 4.3c). In both, the mask heads are attached to intertwined

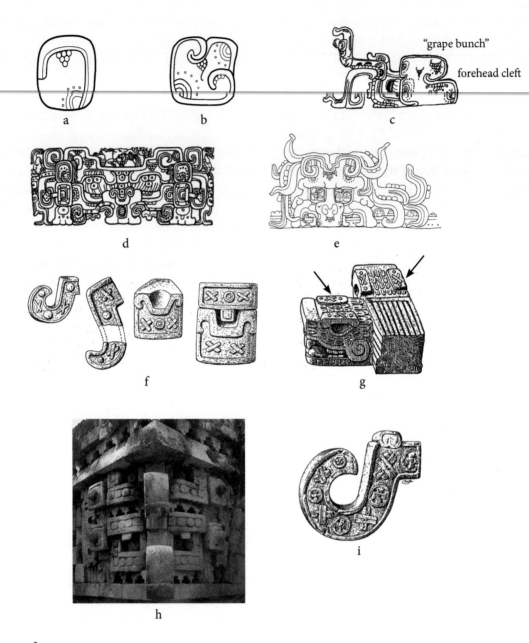

figure 4.2

Glyphs: a) T528 (TUN); and b) T529 (WITS) (drawings by William M. Ringle). Wits heads: c) polychrome pot detail (K521, drawing by Linda Schele © David Schele, courtesy Ancient Americas at LACMA); d) Bonampak St. 1 (drawing by Linda Schele © David Schele, courtesy Ancient Americas at LACMA); e) Palenque Tablet of the Foliated Cross (drawing by Linda Schele © David Schele, courtesy Ancient Americas at LACMA); f) X-O motif on mask fragments, Temple of the Little Tables, Chichen Itza (Seler 1998:figs. 259–260); g) feathered serpent with X-O motif on brows, Chichen Itza (Seler 1998:fig. 255); h) masks marked only by circles, Labna Palace (photograph by William M. Ringle); and i) mask nose from the Adivino, Uxmal (Seler 1917:Abb. 83).

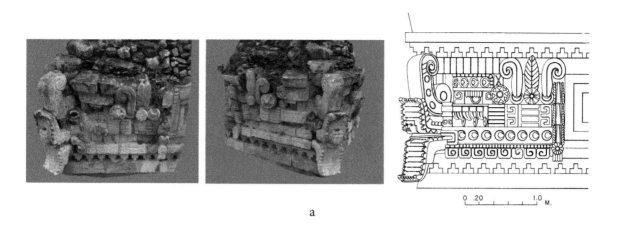

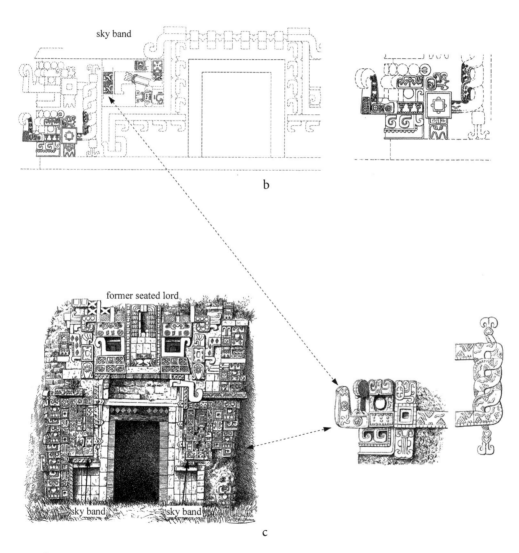

figure 4.3

Masks as animate creatures: a) Labna Palace, juncture of east and central patios (photogrammetric model by William M. Ringle; Pollock 1980:fig. 3); b) Structure 1A1 (Manos Rojas), Kabah (Pollock 1980:fig. 289); and c) "Chenes" Temple of the Adivino (Seler 1917:Abb. 94).

figure 4.4
Patterning of mask variants on the Codz Pop (2C6) of Kabah (see Rubenstein 2015). Note the binary division above the central entrance and the regular placement of variants. Reconstruction drawing by Gustavo Novelo Rincón and Lourdes Toscano Hernández, courtesy of the Proyecto Kabah, Instituto Nacional de Antropología e Historia.

serpent bodies and abut sky bands. Their noses are marked with "celestial" X-O motifs, while their lower eye surrounds or cheeks are decorated with motifs consisting of small circles and crescents unique to these masks, as are the unusual elements above their ear flares. That these were significant is indicated by the fact that they contrast with the facial decoration of the masks in the upper wall zone of the Adivino Chenes facade, with the mask stacks framing the stairway of the Adivino, and with the corner masks of Manos Rojas.

Any adequate and comprehensive explanation of Puuc masks must address the following general considerations:

1. Puuc masks are present only at some Puuc sites, chiefly east of Uxmal (Andrews 1995:fig. 68), and then only on a minority of structures within them. Furthermore, buildings may bear one or dozens of masks.
2. As defining traits of the Mosaic and Late Uxmal styles, Puuc masks were the product only of the last century of Puuc florescence (Andrews 1986, 1995). Therefore, they are likely to signify the changed circumstances of that period.
3. Masks were clearly associated with rooms and doorways, suggesting ties to the activities within those spaces. This is underscored

by several instances of masks marking rooms only accessible by internal doorways and thus not visible on the exterior, such as Room 27 of the Labna Palace (Figure 4.7a). Masks also sometimes functioned as steps, while a mask near the top of the west stairway of the Adivino at Uxmal probably served as a speaking podium.

4. Perhaps most importantly, masks vary significantly and systematically in their decoration. Puuc masks differ from site to site, from building to building within a given site, and even across the walls of a single structure. These variations were clearly intentional and pattern spatially, as can be seen in the Nunnery of Uxmal, where the sectors of Uxmal's leadership may be distinguished by their mask type (Ringle 2012). Another example, noted by Meghan Rubenstein (2015), is the facade of the Codz Pop of Kabah, the north half of which is composed of a single mask type, while the south half alternates two masks that differ slightly but undeniably (Figure 4.4).

One indication that masks functioned as political symbols is that mat signs were occasionally placed on the underside of their noses or snouts (Figure 4.5a–c; also note the left mask from Kabah illustrated in Figure 4.3b). Interestingly, mat signs accompany some masks from the Rio Bec region, whose architecture strongly resembles that of the Puuc, as indicated by an example from Chicanna (Figure 4.5a). Mosaic mask noses bearing mat signs have recently been unearthed at Kiuic, from what is probably a palace (George Bey, personal communication 2021). At Uxmal, a mask on Structure S of the Dovecote also had a mat sign on the underside of its snout, while below a head emerges from its maw (Figure 4.5b). A similar combination of mat signs and emergence can be found on the masks forming the extreme northwest corner of the Great Pyramid at Uxmal (Figure 4.5c; the extreme northeast masks are not present).[4] In these, mat signs are inscribed on the upper palate, contrasting with the chevrons in the same position on the inner northeast and northwest corner masks. The extreme northwest masks also differ in that only these masks have small heads placed within their maws (Figure 4.5d). Like the Dovecote head, these heads have brackets around their eye that unite to form a loop over their roman noses. A single pointed tooth resembling a sacrificial perforator extending from the upper lip identifies this as God G1 (Figure 4.5e).[5] As will be seen, this emergence theme is found not only in the Puuc, but even more consistently at Chichen Itza, where G1 also figures prominently. In another case, a miniature flying God K, universally associated with rulership throughout the lowlands, decorates an unusual mask nose from Xkipche (Figure 4.5f).

The roll perched on the nose of many Puuc masks (Figure 4.6a) may suggest the incorporation of features from another creature with highly charged political symbolism. The roll is pleated, flared at the ends, and bound in the center with one or two bands. To my knowledge, nose rolls are not otherwise part of lowland iconography, but an identical element is found on several Early Classic Teotihuacan–style *incensarios* from Central Mexico and the Tiquisate region of Guatemala (Berlo 1980; Hellmuth 1975; von Winning 1987) (Figure 4.6b, d, and e). These feature butterflies either on headdresses or in the uppermost register of these compositions, one of whose distinguishing features is the nose roll between its eyes that perhaps represents the hairy area covering the butterfly's ocellus (Figure 4.6c). Some *incensarios* are architectural (Chinchilla Mazariegos 2019), in that the butterfly surmounts a recessed room-like space containing a warrior or warrior effigy (Figure 4.6d–e), much as mosaic masks surmount the doors of Puuc buildings. These butterflies sometimes have Tlaloc-like upper jaws with fearsome teeth, as do many mosaic masks, while the long nose of Puuc masks may represent the butterfly's proboscis. As is well known, butterflies represent the souls of dead warriors in the highland Toltec tradition, from Teotihuacan to Tula to Tenochtitlan. This resonates with the general argument of this paper, that masks represent the powers animating the major political and military actors of the Puuc.

figure 4.5
Masks with mat signs: a) Chicanna (photograph by William M. Ringle); b) Dovecote, Uxmal (Seler 1917:Abb. 10); c) Great Pyramid, Uxmal (photograph by William M. Ringle); d) G1 head inside of maw (photograph by William M. Ringle); e) greenstone head of G1, environs of Rio Azul (redrawn after Wagner 2006:fig. 90); and f) mask nose with winged K'awiil figures from Xkipche (Prem 2003:fig. 130).

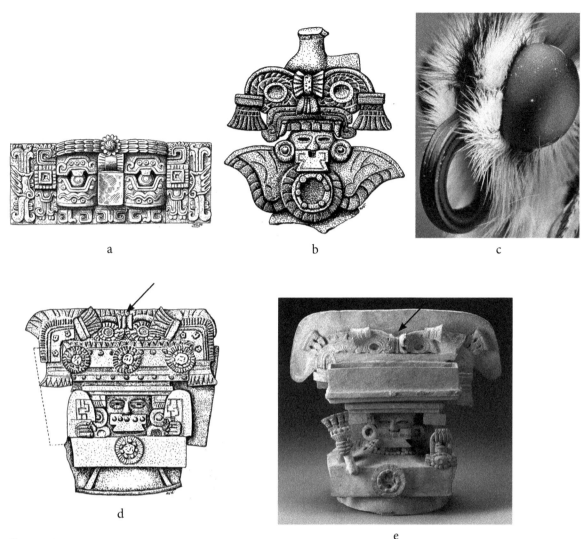

figure 4.6
Nose rolls and butterflies (arrows point to nose rolls): a) mask, House of the Governor, Uxmal (Seler 1917:Abb. 115); b) warrior with butterfly headdress on *incensario* lid (note the upper jaw [von Winning 1987:ch. 9, fig. 21a]); c) hairy area between the eyes of a butterfly; and d–e) *incensarios* with butterflies atop an architectural niche with a warrior within (von Winning 1987:ch. 9, fig. 18a).

The Architectural Placement of Puuc Masks

A further reason for arguing that Puuc masks functioned as political symbols is that they serve to distinguish domestic and administrative areas within Puuc palaces, as exemplified by the Labna Palace. Rooms 19–31 of the Labna Palace probably all had masks associated with them, as well as at the corners, while Rooms 1–18, in the eastern half of the palace, did not (Figure 4.7a), even though it was a later addition (Gallareta Negrón 2013). An even clearer example is the East Group of Kabah (Figure 4.8), probably the last seat of power at that site. The group consists of two adjacent quadrangles, Structures 2C1-4/1C3 (sometimes referred to as the "Palacio") and Structures 2C6/2B1-3,5 (the Codz Pop Group, after its most prominent structure, 2C6). Since in my view they both comprise a single palace, I will refer to them as the Northeast and Southwest Courts, respectively. The two appear to have been built and occupied at about the same time, since the quality of their masonry is quite similar and since both 2C2

Masked Intentions 85

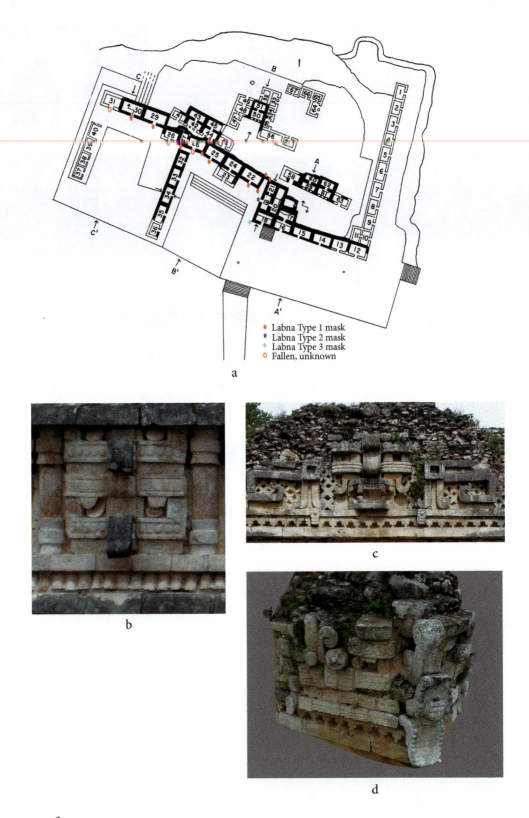

figure 4.7
a) Location of masks at the Labna Palace (Pollock 1980:fig. 3); along with b) Labna Type 1 mask; c) Labna Type 2 mask; and d) Labna Type 3 mask. Labna Types 2 and 3 masks are unique examples. Photographs by William M. Ringle.

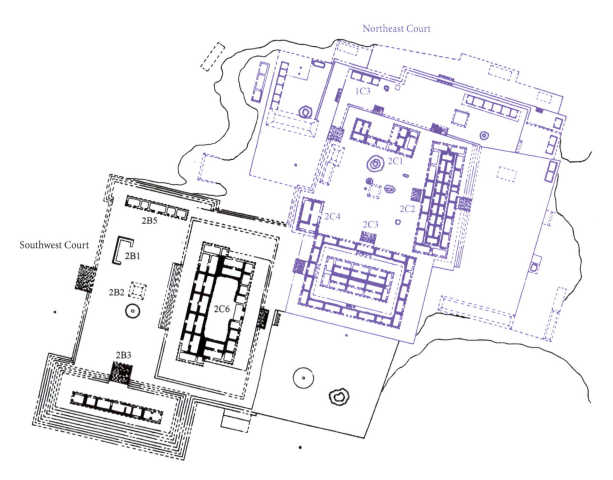

figure 4.8
The East Group of Kabah, showing the disposition of the Southwest and Northeast Courts (Codz Pop [2C6] in the former). Map reproduced from Pollock 1980:fig. 281.

and 2C6 had roof combs, a rarity on Puuc buildings of this period.

Several features indicate the administrative role of the Southwest (Codz Pop) Court. Most importantly for the purposes of this chapter, masks have only been identified on the facade of the Codz Pop, despite the fact that both Structures 2C2 and 2C3 of the Northeast Court have more rooms. In spectacular fashion, three of its sides are nearly completely enveloped by stacks of mosaic masks extending from the basal *zócalo* to the upper cornice (Figure 4.4). The Southwest Court also extends considerably more to the west, with a broad central stairway leading up to an expansive patio or plaza in front of the Codz Pop, not unlike Uxmal's House of the Governor. In contrast, the Northeast Court is set back from the Codz Pop, and its patio is less open to public view. The domestic orientation of the Northeast Court is further indicated by the several *chultuns* in and around it, plus an extensive kitchen area running along its northern side (Toscano Hernández and Novelo Rincón 2012). This segregation can also be observed in the Pajaros complex at Uxmal, probably the seat of rule prior to the occupant of the House of the Governor. There, masks were confined to the various stages of the Adivino, including the first stage when it was only a range structure, as discussed below. The association of masks with administrative buildings is further supported by their association with three specific floor plans from Labna, Uxmal, and Kabah: the tripartite throne room, the developed throne complex, and what I argue were military headquarters.

Tripartite Throne Room (Floor Plan 1)

Perhaps the simplest type of masked administrative structure is the first stage of the Labna Palace (Figure 4.9). Excavations by Tomás Gallareta Negrón's team established that Rooms 22–25 were the original throne complex, characterized by a central pair of tandem rooms flanked by rooms whose doorways were bordered by mat panels (Gallareta Negrón 2013). This stood at right angles to an Early Puuc range structure. Mosaic masks were placed above each doorway of the palace and at its corners (the northeast corner was not excavated, and the roof decoration of Room 23 is unknown). As Gallareta Negrón notes, the central tandem rooms (Rooms 23–24) seem to have been the office proper of the paramount, with Room 23, which extends outward from the plane of the palace, serving as a reception room fronting the inner Room 24, whose floor was significantly higher. The importance of these two rooms is also signaled by the step-frets framing the entrance to Room 24 and several images of God G1 in the lower molding of Room 23. Interestingly, the adjacent Rooms 22 and 25 are flanked by "mat" signs, rather than the central rooms.

This tripartite floor plan is repeated and elaborated upon throughout the Puuc and, indeed, at many sites across the northern plains, as noted by Gallareta Negrón. This same pattern is repeated in several Chenes structures and by Rooms 42, 49, 35, and 43 of Ek' Balam's acropolis, Structure GT-1. These comprise Ukit Kan Le'k's funerary chambers but perhaps originally were functioning offices (Ringle, Gallareta Negrón, and Bey 2021). There too, rooms bearing masks and "mat" signs flank a larger central room, but here a "monster maw" entrance substitutes for the central room mosaic masks, a point to which I will return.

Elaborations of this plan included raising the central room(s) to a second story by means of a central masonry platform between the flanking wings, often accessed by a "flying" staircase. Additional rooms—arranged in tandem and/or end to end—were sometimes added to the wings. Despite these innovations, the symmetry of the wings and the greater elaboration of the central rooms preserved the essentially tripartite organization of the Labna Palace throne room.

a

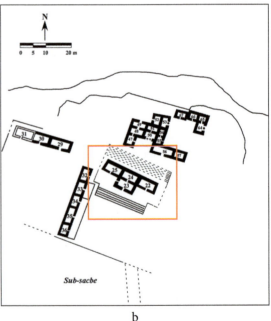

b

figure 4.9

The tripartite throne room: a) aerial view (photograph by William M. Ringle); and b) plan of throne complex (Gallareta Negrón 2013:fig. 16).

Developed Throne Complex (Floor Plan 2)

The second floor plan, which I refer to as the developed throne complex, is a range structure with rooms arranged in tandem fashion but distinguished by end rooms opening laterally (Figure 4.10). One example is the first construction stage of the Codz Pop, Rooms 1–14 (Novelo Rincón 2017:76) (Figure 4.10a; Construction Stage 1°A). Excavations by Lourdes Toscano Hernández and Gustavo Novelo Rincón established that the initial stage had just this pattern. The building may have been entirely covered with masks at this stage, but the rear facade was later dismantled when the structure was expanded. The tripartite theme is expressed by interior step masks between Rooms 7 and 8 and 9 and 10, and thus probably between 5 and 6. Rooms 5, 7, and 9 probably served as reception areas, since they are lower than the interior rooms, and the mosaic mask steps connecting them are especially elaborate.

Three important structures from Uxmal have similar floor plans. The first, and most like the Codz Pop, is the Adivino-sub, a range structure partially buried by the Adivino pyramid, but whose front was always left exposed (Huchim Herrera and Toscano Hernández 1999; Seler 1917) (Figure 4.10b). Like the Codz Pop, it had five front entrances leading to pairs of tandem rooms and lateral entrances at either end. The main differences between the two layouts are the internal divisions of the end rooms, but the end

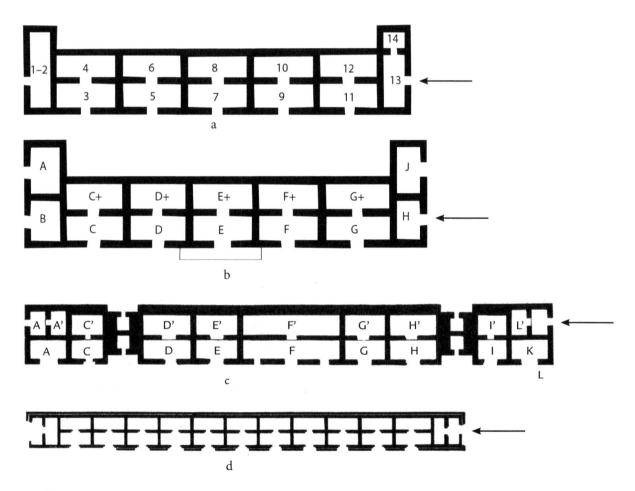

figure 4.10

The developed throne complex, with floor plans of the a) construction phase 1°A of the Codz Pop (after Pollock 1980:fig. 338, modified after Novelo Rincón 2017); b) Adivino-sub (Seler 1917:Abb. 81); c) House of the Governor, Uxmal (Seler 1917:Abb. 105a); and d) North Wing of the Nunnery (Seler 1917:Abb. 41).

rooms in both extended beyond the plane of the rear wall.

As noted, the Adivino-sub was the lone building in the Pajaros group with masks. Only the mask stacks over the central doorway and the door to the north of it survive (Doors E and F, Figures 4.11a, c–d, following Seler 1917:figs. 83a–b, 82, respectively), but possibly all doors may once have been crowned with masks. Slabs with images of Tlaloc, hewing closely to Central Mexican conventions, were almost certainly placed above the mask stacks, as they later were on the north building of the Nunnery. Ten of these were found and so could have marked all the doors of the substructure (Maldonado Cárdenas and Repetto Tío 1988; Sáenz Vargas 1969; Seler 1917:92, fig. 86) (Figure 4.11b). Three sculptures were also tenoned into the facade, above doorways and below mask stacks.[6] The central one, the so-called Queen of Uxmal, shows a young man with a headband of disks, possibly of jade, emerging from the mouth of a serpent with feathered eyebrows (Figure 4.11e), another example of the emergence theme. Feathered eyebrows are often markers of the feathered serpent in Postclassic Maya art (Taube 2010:172–177) and may well be here. The young man has a tattoo on his cheek that may also be a feathered serpent (Figure 4.11f), while the absence of any diagnostic iconographic traits suggests he is human. Two similar sculptures were later discovered by César Sáenz Vargas (1969) in the debris at either end of the building, except that in these God G1, previously mentioned with regard to the Great Pyramid and the Labna Palace, emerges from the maws of serpents with feathered bodies.

All in all, the floor plan of the Adivino-sub and its later memorialization by encasement within a massive pyramid suggest that it was not only the primary civic structure of the Pajaros quadrangle but also of Uxmal as a whole at this time. This is reinforced by links with two later examples of the developed throne complex, the House of the Governor (Kowalski 1987) and the North Building of the Nunnery (Figure 4.10c–d). These possess additional rooms (although the central section of the House of the Governor has five doors like the previous pair), and the end rooms do not extend beyond the plane of the rear wall, but in both cases they terminate in rooms opening laterally. Like the previous two examples, the central rooms are tandem pairs. They both have eleven front and two lateral doorways, although the House of the Governor achieved this by adding two end wings connected by portal vaults to the central block of rooms. This tripartite division of the House of the Governor is underscored by the small mat designs in the upper entablature of the wings, contrasting with the nested squares used in the entablature of the central block, an arrangement echoing the mat rooms flanking the throne room of the Labna Palace. These squares and the trapezoidally arranged mosaic masks serve to frame each of the front doorways of the House of the Governor, above which once sat seated lords arranged in ranked sizes, once again linking rulership with masks.

An important link between the Codz Pop, the central mask stack of the North Building of the Nunnery, and the House of the Governor is that their masks are virtually identical, except that the House of the Governor masks have a small "Lamat" sign below the eye, signaling "star" or perhaps "Venus" (Figure 4.12c).[7] They are also connected by skeletal motifs framing these masks (Ringle 2012). Termed "profile masks" by Novelo Rincón (2017) and Rubenstein (2015), these motifs run vertically alongside either side of the central mask stack on the North Wing and schematically frame the masks of the House of the Governor. Rotated ninety degrees, they also support the seated figures above the House of the Governor doorways (Ringle 2012) (Figure 4.12d). Novelo Rincón's analysis of the mosaic stones from the Codz Pop extends this pattern to Kabah:

> . . . on the west facade frieze, the continuous ornamentation of masks also changes at the height of the entrances, since above these there was a complex design formed by a stack of three masks flanked by profile masks with open maws, framed by a braided design (Novelo Rincón 2017:76, translation by author).

Their reconstruction drawing of part of the facade shows it to be virtually identical to the central stack of the North Wing of the Nunnery (Figure 4.12a–b).

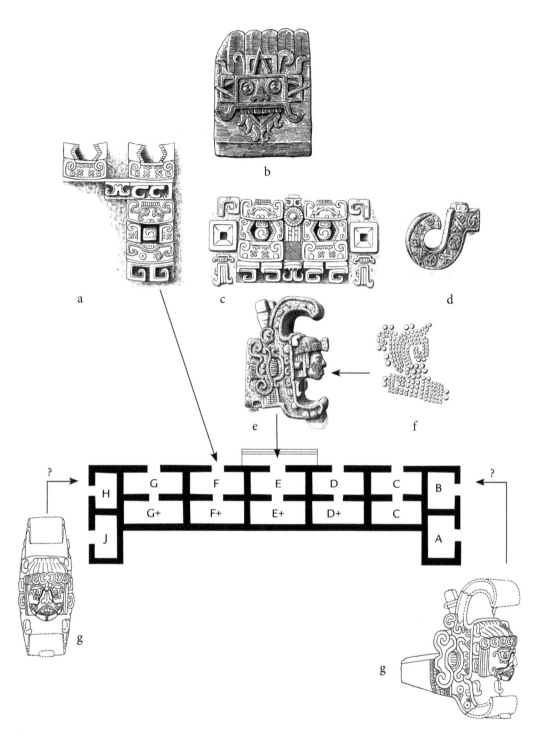

figure 4.11

Sculptures associated with the Adivino-sub: a) mask stack over Door F (Seler 1917:Abb. 82); b) Tlaloc mask, possibly over all doors (Seler 1917:Abb. 86); c) mask over Door E (Seler 1917:Abb. 83a); d) nose from mask over Door E (Seler 1917:Abb. 83b); e) sculpture tenoned into medial molding ("Queen of Uxmal") (Seler 1917:Abb 84a); f) facial markings on sculpture tenoned into medial molding (Seler 1917:Abb 84b); and g) sculptures tenoned into north and south ends, exact location unknown (Sáenz Vargas 1969; the drawings pertain to only one of these sculptures).

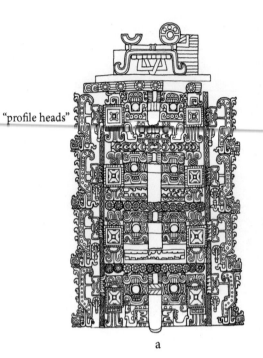
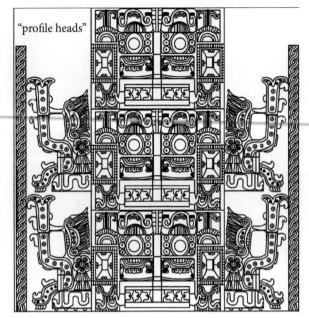

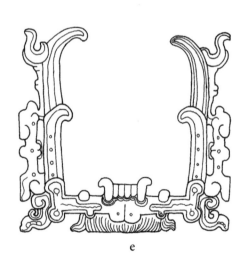

These "profile masks" are probably centipedes. In Classic Maya art, the centipede (*chapat*) is depicted with a bony head, gaping jaws, and curved fangs (Figure 4.12e). Centipedes are associated with death and served as a conduit to the underworld, but they also accompany images of the sun and may connote transformation and rebirth, Janab Pakal's sarcophagus being a prime example (Taube 2003; see also Stone and Zender 2011:179). Since on the House of the Governor facade the centipedes supported eleven statues arranged in three sizes, the latter are most probably ranked officials rather than dead rulers. The framing centipedes are thus another variant of the emergence theme, and the fact that they bracket both humans and mosaic masks suggests that the two may at some level be equated.

Military Offices (Floor Plan 3)

The diagnostic trait of the third floor plan is that the rooms forming the central axis of such structures communicate internally with adjacent rooms by means of doors piercing the end walls below the vault tympanum. This differs from most vaulted rooms, which are entered via doorways through the lateral walls below the vault spring (Figure 4.13a–b). The result is an internal suite of rooms that I believe served as military offices. One example is the East Building of the Nunnery, arguably the headquarters of the military "estate" of Uxmal because of the death imagery of its mask stacks and the owl-like sculptural medallions on its facade (Kowalski and Dunning 1999:285–286; Kowalski, Silverstein, and Follansbee 2002:n10; Ringle 2012; Taube 1992:60). As can be seen in Figure 4.13a, the central Rooms 7 and 8 are both flanked by smaller rooms entered through their end walls.

Two additional examples bear this association out: Rooms 20–22 of the Codz Pop (Novelo Rincón 2017) (Figure 4.13c) and Rooms 19–21 (and possibly Rooms 25–26) of the Labna Palace (Figure 4.13d). According to Novelo Rincón (2017:76–79), the rooms across the rear of the Codz Pop (Rooms 17–25) and the masonry core behind them were added during Construction Phase 1°D, Rooms 15–16 and 26–27 being the product of the earlier Phase 1°B. This also marked a radical shift in the decoration of the facade, in that mosaic masks were now confined to a few located below the basal molding on the north and south end walls, perhaps serving as steps up to a terrace surrounding the north end. The upper wall zone was instead covered by a simple lattice bordered by a dentate pattern consisting of triangles edging narrow vertical strips (Figure 4.14a), perhaps representing a series of weavings. (Note that this lattice also distinguishes the south and east buildings of Uxmal's Nunnery.)

Against this ground, seven nearly full-size, in-the-round sculptures of warriors were placed above the central three rooms (Rooms 20–22), the hypothesized suite of military offices (Carrasco Vargas and Pérez de Heredia Puente 1996:fig. 5; Novelo Rincón 2017:79; Rubenstein 2015:figs. 135–136) (Figure 4.14b–c). The central entrance (Room 21) to the suite was also framed by a pair of carved jambs (Pollock 1980:372–373; Rubenstein 2015:163–171, figs. 137–138) (Figure 4.14d) depicting warriors fighting and dancing and bearing the date 2 Chuen 3 Muan (859 CE).[8] Because the curved facial markings, either tattoos or scarifications, are common to both the facade sculptures and one of the principal figures in the jamb scenes, this figure has been identified as the "king of Kabah" (Carrasco Vargas and Pérez de Heredia Puente 1996; Novelo

---

figure 4.12

The mask common to Uxmal and Kabah and associated "profile" heads: a) central mask stack, Nunnery, Uxmal (drawing by Linda Schele © David Schele, courtesy Ancient Americas at LACMA); b) reconstructed mask stack above the west doors of the Codz Pop (courtesy of Lourdes Toscano Hernández, Proyecto Kabah, Instituto Nacional de Antropología e Historia); c) mask from the House of the Governor and flanking profile heads; d) seated lord above a profile head, House of the Governor (drawing by Frederick Catherwood in Stephens 1843:fig. 6); and e) centipede jaws from the Temple of the Inscriptions sarcophagus (drawing by Linda Schele © David Schele, courtesy Ancient Americas at LACMA).

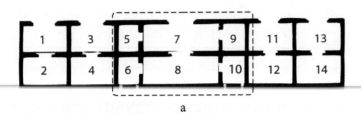

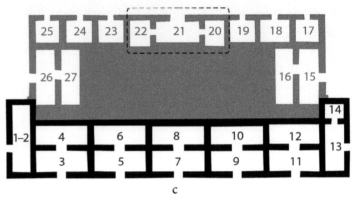

figure 4.13
Possible military offices: a) plan of the West Wing of the Nunnery, Uxmal (Seler 1917:Abb. 19); b) interior end wall (Stephens 1843:pl. X); c) final floor plan of the Codz Pop (after Novelo Rincón 2017); and d) Rooms 19–21 of the Labna Palace (Rooms 26–27 may be another set) (after Pollock 1980:fig. 3).

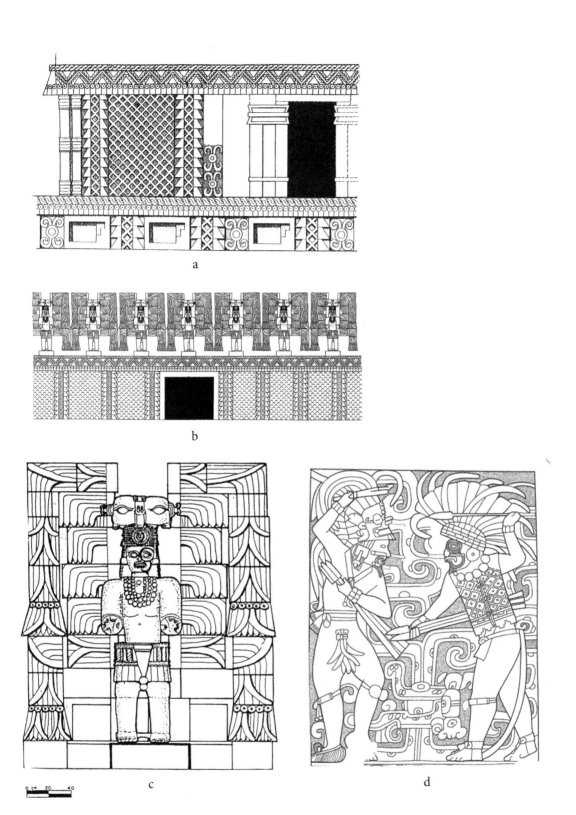

figure 4.14
a) Simple lattice background of the north end of the Codz Pop (Andrews 1990:fig. 44); b) arrangement of seven warriors placed between the central three doors (Andrews 1990:fig. 31); c) one of the standing warriors (Carrasco Vargas et al. 1992:fig. 5); and d) upper panel of a jamb from Room 21 of the Codz Pop (drawing by Meghan Rubenstein).

Masked Intentions 95

figure 4.15
Three views of the exterior of Rooms 19–21 of the Labna Palace: a) general view; b) detail of mask over doorway in Room 19; c) partial standing warrior to left of mask. Photographs by William M. Ringle.

a

b

c

Rincón 2017; Rubenstein 2015). But as Rubenstein (2015:161) notes, there are grounds for doubting this, since some of the warrior heads are marked on the opposite side of the face and differ in the belts they wear. Another reason for doubting that these sculptures were portraits of kings is the sheer number of them and their relatively obscure placement across the rear facade. It seems likely these were instead stylized images of warrior leaders. Another example of this floor plan from Kabah is Structure 2A3 of the West Group. Here, the three rear rooms are arranged according to the third floor plan, and the entrance to the central room was also framed by a pair of jambs depicting warriors. Adjacent was the probable administrative Structure 2A1.

Similar warriors (Figure 4.15) once stood guard over the entrance to Room 19 of the Labna Palace, flanking an unusual central mask above the doorway bearing the short count date "13th *tun* in *k'atun* 3 Ajaw" or 862 CE, perhaps its dedication date. Room 19 is the entrance to a truncated Floor Plan 3 internal suite, in this case with but a single flanking room (Room 21). Possibly the opposite pair was reconfigured when the East Wing was built. Alternatively, the similarly arranged Rooms 26 and 27 may have been designed to bracket the throne rooms, since they too share an internal passageway. The distinctive mask over Room 19 may, therefore, mark the military offices within. A final mask, over the southwest corner of the central court, shows a man emerging from the maw of the mask, invoking the emergence theme with respect to this sector of Labna's rulership (Figure 4.3a).

In sum, Puuc mosaic masks are strongly associated with each of the three floor plans. The first two appear to be versions of administrative structures, housing both paramounts, functionaries, and perhaps important nobles (e.g., Kabah Structure 2A1). The third is associated with the military, which architecturally appears to be subservient to administrative quarters. This is in keeping with my previous arguments (e.g., Ringle 2012) that the political organization of centers experiencing Central Mexican "Toltec" influence were conceptualized as being divided into four "estates": paramounts and their functionaries, religious functionaries, the military, and representatives of the nonroyal nobility and client rulers.

The Masks of Chichen Itza

The great center of Chichen Itza, with the largest collection of mosaic masks outside the Puuc heartland, provides a test of some of these assertions. Examples include the Casa Colorada, the House of the Three Lintels, the House of the One Lintel, Las Monjas, and La Iglesia, among others, all built in the Pure Florescent architectural style, very similar to Puuc Mosaic buildings (Figure 4.16). Since many of the mask-bearing structures also bear dedicatory inscriptions, it is also the best dated corpus of mosaic masks. Dates cluster within a very narrow range between 869 and 889 CE, or only about a decade after those from Labna and Kabah, but ten to thirty years before Uxmal's Nunnery.

Masks continued to adorn structures in the subsequent Modified Florescent, or "Toltec/International" style (Figure 4.17), after hieroglyphic writing generally ceased to be used. Pure and Modified Florescent masks differ in various details. The latter tend to be of poorer workmanship, flatter in relief, and have "X-O"–marked eye surrounds, while Pure Florescent eye surrounds contain a series of disks or scrolls and are carved in greater depth. Some Pure Florescent masks have trapezoidal pendants below their ear flares filled with small triangles, as if they were mosaics, while the ear flare pendants of several Modified Florescent masks consist of a series of pendant trapezoids. However, there is some overlap in traits. The Castillo, for instance, has ear flare pendants like the Pure Florescent examples just mentioned, and the Temple of the Three Lintels and the Caracol share distinctive scrolls emerging from their ear flares, despite the former being one of the purest expressions of Pure Florescent architecture while the Caracol is usually viewed as transitional Pure/Modified Florescent.

Another interesting trend concerns the emergence theme. During the Pure Florescent, many Chichen masks are distinguished from their Puuc counterparts by the replacement of nose rolls with

Type 1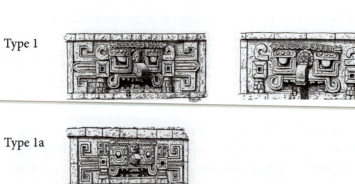

Type 1a

Type 1b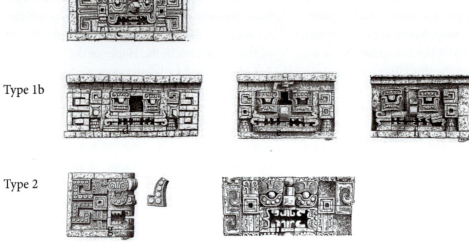

Type 2

Type 3

Type 4

Unclassified

figure 4.16
Pure Florescent masks from Chichen Itza, labeled according to Bolles's (1977) typology. Type 1: a) Las Monjas (Seler 1998:fig. 48); and b) Las Monjas (Seler 1998:fig. 35). Type 1a: c) Las Monjas (Seler 1998:fig. 16). Type 1b: d) La Iglesia (Seler 1998:fig. 53); e) La Iglesia (Seler 1998:fig. 55); and f) La Iglesia (Seler 1998:fig. 61). Type 2: g) Las Monjas (Seler 1998:fig. 33); and h) Uxmal, North Nunnery (Seler 1917:Abb. 60). Type 3: i) Las Monjas (Seler 1998:fig. 37). Type 4: j) Las Monjas (Seler 1998:fig. 38); k) Caracol turret (Ruppert 1935:fig. 338, detail); and l) Temple of the Three Lintels (Ruppert 1952:fig. 108). Unclassified: m) La Iglesia (Seler 1998:fig. 63); and n) Casa Colorada (Seler 1998:fig. 70).

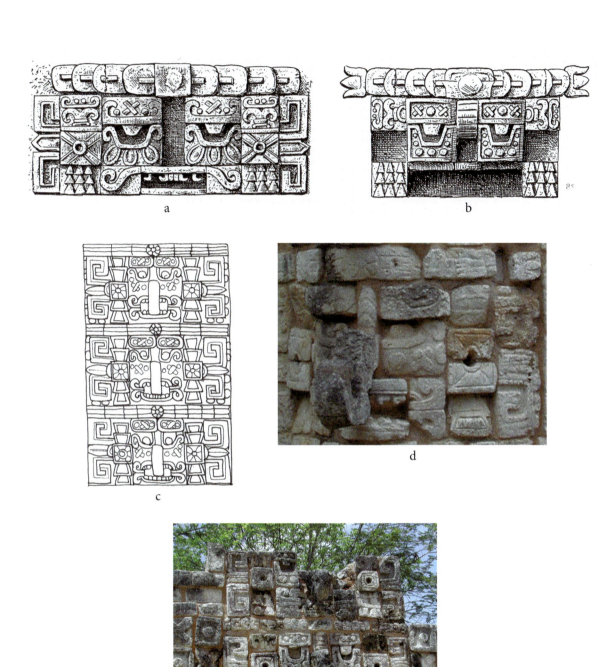

figure 4.17
Modified Florescent masks from Chichen Itza: a–b) masks from the west and south entrances to the Castillo (Seler 1998:figs. 84–85); c) Temple of the Warriors (drawing by Linda Schele © David Schele, courtesy Ancient Americas at LACMA); d) Osario (photograph by William M. Ringle); and e) Structure 3D7 (photograph by William M. Ringle).

Masked Intentions 99

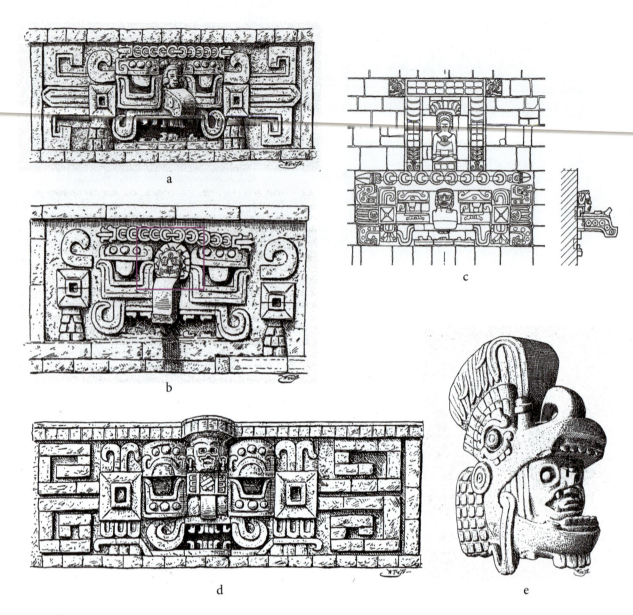

figure 4.18
The emergence theme on masks from Chichen Itza: a) head emerging from mosaic mask, Las Monjas, Caracol, Chichen Itza (Seler 1998:fig. 48); b) God G1 head emerging from mosaic mask, Las Monjas, Caracol, Chichen Itza (Seler 1998:fig. 72); c) God G1 head emerging from mosaic mask, Caracol, Chichen Itza (Ruppert 1935:fig. 338, 220–224); d) masked head emerging from mosaic mask, Casa Colorada (Seler 1998:fig. 72); and e) masked head emerging from Feathered Serpent, West Wing, Nunnery, Uxmal (Seler 1917:fig. 37b).

small heads (Figure 4.18a).[9] Most of these heads have few distinguishing features, but one, on a mosaic mask from the east facade of the East Wing of Las Monjas (Figure 4.18b), is probably another portrait of God G1. This deity also surmounts the noses of all the Caracol masks (Figure 4.18c), suggesting that the nose roll, God G1, and the small heads inter-substitute as components of the emergence theme. The heads on the roof comb masks of the Casa Colorada (Figure 4.18d) are unusual in that they seem to be wearing a facial mask of sorts, not unlike the heads emerging from the maw of the Feathered Serpent on the West Building of the Nunnery (Figure 4.18e). A rectangular panel or pectoral below the heads includes a mat motif, suggesting these were nobles or officeholders in the making, again underscoring the political dimension of mosaic mask facades.

During the Modified Florescent, the emergence theme disappears, as heads and nose rolls are absent on the masks of the Temple of the Warriors, the Osario, Structure 3D7, and Phase III of the Templo de la Serie Inicial. Unfortunately, the block where the head or nose roll might be is missing on two of the Castillo heads, but the other two noses appear to be tucked up against the face, rather than providing room for something above them. (Interestingly, a mat sign is inscribed on the underside of the nose of one mask.) The continued use of mosaic masks suggests some continuity of elite culture between the Pure and Modified Florescent periods, doubts about which have recently resurfaced, but the clear differences between the masks of the two periods suggests some change in practice, a point returned to in the conclusion.

The following discussion focuses chiefly on the Pure Florescent buildings of Old Chichen to determine whether commonalities of political structure were shared with the Puuc prior to the advent of strong non-Maya influence. As in the Puuc, Chichen masks of this period are highly variable, differing between buildings and across the facades of those with more complex iconographic programs. Like Puuc masks, they tend to be located over doorways and at the corners of structures, and tripartite arrangements are not uncommon (i.e., the House of the Three Lintels and the Casa Colorada).[10] Having said that, there is relatively little formal similarity between the masks of Chichen Itza and the Puuc. An exception is the lower two masks on the northeast and southeast corners of the East Wing of Las Monjas, whose eye surrounds are strikingly similar to the second-to-lowest mask above Room 4 of the Nunnery.

Las Monjas

Las Monjas, often identified as the probable seat of power during the Pure Florescent period, has Chichen Itza's largest and most varied collection of mosaic masks. Mosaic masks cover the front, east side, and part of the rear of the East Wing, and they completely encircle the upper entablature of the main platform (Figure 4.19a–b). Yet it is a decidedly odd building. The elaborate East Wing (Annex), a Pure Florescent range structure partially covered by the main platform, is without a balancing West Wing, resulting in an asymmetry unusual for public buildings in the north (Bolles 1977). Furthermore, the most elaborate relief sculpture is not centrally located, but is at the east end wall of the East Wing, where access was restricted by La Iglesia and later by the East Court.

In contrast, masks are absent from the second-story superstructure, built on the adjoining raised platform and probably the last building actually functioning in an administrative capacity. Built as a variant of Floor Plan 2, as was the East Wing, its end rooms (Rooms 16 and 20) extend across the width of the building and open laterally. Like the Codz Pop and Adivino-sub, it has five front entrances, though only three front rooms (Rooms 17–19). Seven hieroglyphic lintels record a dedicatory date of 880 CE (Bolles 1977). While no sculpture indicates a military role for the rear rooms, a mural depicting a war against a walled citadel decorated Room 22, although this was probably a later addition (Bolles 1977:197–218).

In Bolles's (1977) reconstruction of its building stages, Las Monjas originally consisted of a central raised basal platform (Platform 1) with flanking East and West Wings built at ground level, similar to several structures throughout the Puuc. However, only a small portion of the southwest and northwest corners of this platform (and Platform 2, built directly over it) was ever exposed. It was then encased by three later enlargements of the main basal platform, progressively engulfing the East Wing, so that the articulation of the latter with Platform 1 is unknown (Bolles 1977:281). No trace of a superstructure was ever found on Platforms 1 or 2. As for the putative West Wing, "except for the break at the west end of Platform 2 and the foundation steps in Platform 3, no other evidence of this construction was found" (Bolles 1977:88, cf. 284), this despite the relatively substantial exposure of the west side of Platform 3, where traces of the walls of a West Wing should have been visible, and despite

figure 4.19
a) Plan of Las Monjas (with third-story structure and infilling of rooms omitted) (adapted from Bolles 1977:39); and b) distribution of mask types on Las Monjas (adapted from Bolles 1977:248).

the absence of foundations in the open area west of the basal platform.

It therefore seems possible, if not probable, that the East Wing was originally a freestanding Floor Plan 2 building, prior to construction of Platform 1. If true, it may thus have been part of the original throne complex of Las Monjas, later supplanted by the second-story Floor Plan 2 superstructure atop Platforms 4 and 5 (Bolles 1977: 296–297). If true, the central room would originally have been Room 10. Unfortunately, excavations of the foundations of the East Wing buried by Platforms 3–5 revealed that the upper wall zone had been dismantled prior to infilling, so we have no evidence for the types of masks above those rooms.

Bolles (1977:121, 246–260) provides a five-category typology for the Las Monjas masks (Figure 4.16) and argues that formal differences may represent chronological renovations to facades. This seems unlikely, given that the disposition of masks by type shows that the same mask was employed at different stages of construction (Figure 4.19b). For instance, Type 3 masks were employed both on the East Wing and along much of the rear of Platform 5, which postdates it. Likewise, Type 1 masks, found on the east facade (Room 1) of the East Wing, are quite similar to the Type 1a masks decorating the upper edge of Platform 5. Formal differences seem more likely due to the overall semiotic program of the group.

In addition to its floor plans and numerous masks, the placement of a large relief of a seated lord above the entrance to Room 1 may provide another parallel with the Codz Pop (Figure 4.21b). The purpose of the lateral rooms of the Codz Pop, or at least the northern one, Room 1, has recently been illuminated by the discovery of a pair of carved jambs at its entrance. Rubenstein (2015:177) has convincingly argued that the jamb panels "depict a youth's rite of passage, most likely the installation of an heir to the throne." I would only add that the rites of investiture taking place in this room may also have included the military leadership and high nobility. The similarly positioned Room 1 of the Las Monjas East Wing may, therefore, have been the locus for such rites, as its iconography and sky band indicate,

either originally or following the construction of the second-story structure. (Bolles [1977] argues that this portion of the facade was a later renovation.)

There remains La Iglesia, a structure that has elicited remarkably little commentary aside from architectural descriptions. Unfortunately, Bolles (1977:31) was unable to tie La Iglesia to the construction sequence of the East Wing, but its construction techniques hew closer to the East Wing than the second-story building (compare the vault profiles in Bolles 1977:123, 136, 151), as does the emphasis on masked facades. I believe that La Iglesia originally stood at right angles to the East Wing, before construction of Platforms 1–5, and that together they formed the administrative core of Pure Florescent Chichen Itza, later to be supplanted by the enlarged Las Monjas. It is noteworthy that eight of the nine masks of La Iglesia were of a single type (Type 1b) not found on any of the other structures (Figure 4.16d–f), arguably marking a particular office.[11] The chief difference between Type 1 masks, framing Room 1 of the East Wing, and Type 1b is the absence of a disk headband in the latter, as well as differences in the decoration of the eye surround. The disk headband seemingly denotes a lesser rank at Chichen Itza and Uxmal, and its absence on La Iglesia masks suggests that it housed the office of the paramount. Further evidence is supplied below.

Conclusion: Masks, Power, and East–West Dynamics in Northern Yucatán

Mosaic masks represent an abstract embodiment of power—royal power, to be sure, but also the power possessed by other members of the nobility and military. A similar notion is championed by Rubenstein (2015:216), who argues that the Codz Pop was a living structure animated by its masks and that the multiple masks adorning Puuc buildings were, in effect, amplifications of this force, such that their number provides a rough index of the importance of a given structure. I would agree with this but would argue that these were in no way aspects of the natural world. Instead, the proliferation of masks in a relatively short space of time and their

Masked Intentions

confinement to certain buildings reflect a political landscape that was also rapidly changing and perhaps being consolidated under the suzerainty of a few large sites. However, this provides only a partial explanation for the differences between masks.

The significance and variety of masks can perhaps be refined by returning to Las Monjas. Plank's (2003, 2004) important study of the inscriptions of this building (especially the seven lintels from the second-story building) shows that all concerned dedicatory events, either of doorway lintels or glyphic texts. Following preliminary work by David Stuart (Stuart, Houston, and Robertson 1999), she demonstrates that many, if not most, of these formulaic expressions marked the possession of the object being dedicated—a lintel, a room, a text—by a god, who was, in turn, sometimes possessed by a human actor. Similar phrases occur on other Pure Florescent structures, such as the Temples of the One, Three, and Four Lintels, and the Casa Colorada. These were personal gods, not found outside of Chichen Itza, though some occurred across multiple structures (cf. Plank 2003:fig. 6.56).

She concludes that Las Monjas consisted of a series of room shrines to these gods (Plank 2003:433–444; see also Baron, this volume), becoming at its peak the principal religious structure of Old Chichen.[12] While not disputing her textual readings, I believe another interpretation is possible. Just as the link between modern patrons of civic and academic structures is often confined to their initial sponsorship and may have nothing to do with their use, the spirits mentioned in these dedications may be only tangentially related to room function. I would argue that masks were a formulaic way of "animating" an architectural component or space by a member of the nobility or military whose office it then became. In other words, the function of the second-story structure was primarily political and administrative rather than religious.

Nevertheless, if we accept Plank's central point that personal deities were involved in room dedications and perhaps then persisted as guiding spirits, it may be that mosaic masks performed a similar role. Thus, the differences we observe in mask design, as well as the regularities in their disposition, may reflect the particular function of architectural spaces, the office occupying them, or both, as I have attempted to show for the Nunnery (Ringle 2012). Plank is able to trace connections between buildings because of the repeated mentions of deities and humans, but unfortunately several of the structures with hieroglyphic dedications have completely collapsed, leaving the decoration of their facades unknown. And of course, the second-story building of Las Monjas, the product of the penultimate construction stage, lacks mosaic masks altogether, perhaps because the hieroglyphic lintels obviated their use.

There is, however, one supporting line of evidence. Plank (2003:427–433) documents a god she refers to as Chok Watab as being especially prominent on the central lintel (Room 18) of Las Monjas but also having mentions on Lintel 1a of that building, on the Temple of the Three Lintels (Lintel 3), the Temple of the One Lintel, the Initial Series Lintel, and on hieroglyphic band fragment 11 from the Caracol. We lack information regarding masks for the Temple of the One Lintel and the Initial Series structure, but interestingly the Caracol, the Temple of the Three Lintels, and the East Wing of Las Monjas all share a common mask. This mask, Bolles's Type 4, possesses distinctive volutes coming from its ear flares. Two of the three wear a feathered headband, the other wears a headband of linked disks. Thus, the placements of like masks on the facades of buildings later linked by mention of a common patron god strongly suggests the equivalence of mask and patron god and, by extension, mask and office.

Paralleling these developments was the increasing separation of a military estate or wing, sometimes housed in Floor Plan 3 structures. As we have seen, both the rear of the Codz Pop and Rooms 18–21 of the Labna Palace were later additions to existing structures. The date of the Labna nose is 862 CE and the date on the Codz Pop jamb is 859 CE, although it is not clear what events these reference. Another Floor Plan 3 building, the East Wing of Uxmal's Nunnery, is a freestanding structure that probably dates to around 900 CE. Thus, it seems likely that the development of separate military offices in the Puuc began around 850 CE and was an accepted division of governmental organization by 900 CE.[13]

George Bey and I have suggested that a similar process occurred in the transition from Pure to Modified Florescent Chichen Itza, as evidenced by the addition of warrior colonnades and gallery-patio structures to earlier elite compounds (Ringle and Bey 2009). As noted, only the mural in Room 22 of Las Monjas suggests military activities, as neither the second-story structure nor the East Wing have rooms arranged according to Floor Plan 3. However, and although they are later, two nearby structures are Modified Florescent versions of this plan—the south building of the Southeast Court and the east building of the East Court. Although both have a central room fronted by columns and the latter structure also has a colonnaded gallery, the central room is flanked by two rooms opening into it, like other Floor Plan 3 buildings (Figure 4.19a). Military associations are indicated by a bench frieze of warriors tied to possible captives in the former and a series of slabs decorated with shields in the latter (Bolles 1977:222–233). The jambs of the south building (Rubbings T20212 and T20213; Robertson 1995) also depict warriors, although one leg and one arm of the east warrior terminate in serpents. The west warrior bears a long lance while the eastern jamb is armed with darts.

Floor Plan 3 is rare at Chichen Itza, present in only two other structures (3D7 and 5B21) in Ruppert's (1952) architectural catalogue. Structure 3D7 forms part of the Thousand Columns Group, while Structure 5B21 belongs to the Grupo Principal del Suroeste. Each belongs to a typical complex of Modified Florescent buildings including serpent temples, ballcourts, gallery-patio structures, and colonnaded halls, though not all of these are present in each instance. Military associations of the two are fairly clear. Structure 5B21, known as the Temple of the Jaguar Atlantean Columns (Ruppert 1952:13), has a gallery portico of piers with sculpted warriors. Above, the superstructure has two sculptured Atlantean columns and two sculpted pilasters of individuals wearing jaguar masks and butterfly pectorals. Structure 3D7 was still largely buried in 1952, but Schmidt (2011:124–126) has since reported that it possesses carved warrior columns.

The Emergence Theme

The emergence theme is important to understanding these changes. Throughout much of Mesoamerica, the emergence of figures from the jaws of serpents, jaguars, coyotes, and other creatures suggests the mystical transformation of men into warriors, nobles, and kings through rites of initiation or investiture, to which can be added the figures emerging from mosaic masks. This can be demonstrated particularly clearly on the snout of the mask above the central doorway of La Iglesia (Figure 4.20). Although poorly preserved and mostly gone, a headdress decorated with disks is clearly visible above the weathered but distinguishable torso of a seated figure on the nose below. This theme is also present on mask panels of the Caracol (Figure 4.18c).

These provide a link to the so-called Chenes monster maw masks. Several of these occur at Puuc sites, such as the "Chenes" fourth stage of the Adivino temple (Figure 4.3c), one gracing a substructure of the House of the Governor, the upper doorway of Kabah 2A1 (Manos Rojas) (Figure 4.3b), and the Grupo Magaña of Huntichmul, although these are all damaged and only the Adivino temple has traces of a seated figure. The best-preserved example, however, is the seated figure perched on the nose of the monster around the door to Room 35 of Ek' Balam GT-1 (Ringle, Gallareta Negrón, and Bey 2021) (Figure 4.21a). A final example is adjacent to La Iglesia, on the east facade of the East Wing of Las Monjas (Figure 4.21b), where only the maw of the monster framing the doorway is represented. Above, where its nose would be, sits an elaborately feathered ruler. Below is an inscription with astronomical content (Bricker and Bricker 1995; Love 2015), the equivalent of a sky band. As noted, sky bands also accompany the Chenes facades of Manos Rojas and the Adivino temple and many thrones elsewhere in the lowlands (see Figure 4.3).

Why then the disappearance of the emergence theme on Modified Florescent masks? I suggest that changes in the political ideology of the period replaced the mosaic mask with the maw of the feathered serpent, as on the West Nunnery at Uxmal, or one of his avatars, such as the *hombre-pajaro-serpiente*

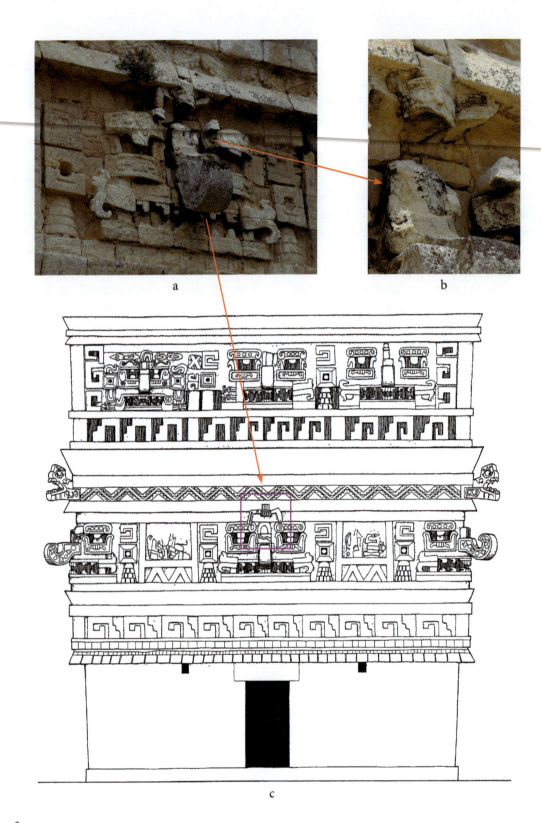

figure 4.20
The emergence motif, seating, and masks: La Iglesia, Chichen Itza. Elevation reproduced from Andrews 1991:78, and detail photographs by William M. Ringle.

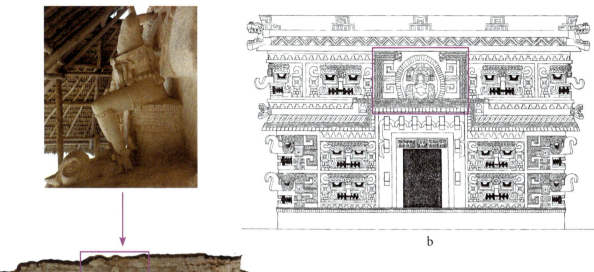

figure 4.21
Chenes masks and the emergence theme:
a) photogrammetric model of the facade of
Ek' Balam Room 35 and side view of seated figure
on nose (photographs by William M. Ringle);
and b) east face of the East Wing, Las Monjas
(Andrews 1991:57).

panels seen on the Temple of the Warriors and the Venus Temple, signaling the primacy of the feathered serpent. It thus appears that Chichen Itza shared a common presentation of rulership, if not the practice thereof, with the Puuc cities in the decades leading up to the transition to "Toltec" rule, after which mask use diverged somewhat.

Regarding the Puuc cities, what do masks indicate about the possible domination of the region by Uxmal or a coalition between Uxmal and Kabah? The variety of masks across the region suggests that individual sites still claimed their own expressions of power until mosaic masks ceased to be employed. With the exception of late Kabah and Uxmal, no mask is repeated at more than a single site. And although Chichen Itza seems to have embraced the symbolism of masks, its masks also differed from those of the Puuc, with the one exception mentioned earlier, suggesting it had no clients in the Puuc.

Nevertheless, the near identity of masks from the House of the Governor and the Codz Pop, and of Manos Rojas and the Adivino temple, is striking and can hardly be a coincidence, given the variety of masks at both sites and elsewhere. The hieroglyphic date from Manos Rojas is eight to twenty-two years earlier than those from the Codz Pop jambs (Table 4.1). One possibility is that Manos Rojas was inhabited by a cadet line of the occupants of the Pajaros quadrangle at Uxmal. It is, therefore, tempting to see the expanding fortunes of the parent dynasty, marked by the construction of the House of the Governor and Nunnery, reflected in the increased prominence of the cadet line, now housed in Kabah's West Group. However, if the hieroglyphic jambs reflect construction dates, then the Codz Pop must be earlier than either of the Uxmal complexes by several decades. At present, this difficulty cannot be resolved, but clearly the similarity in masking,

Masked Intentions 107

table 4.1

Hieroglyphic dates from Kabah.

2C6 Room 21	10.1.10.11.1	2 Chuen 4 Muan	October 18, 859
2C6 Room 1	10.2.3.11.5	8 Chicchan 8 Zotz	March 12, 873
Altar 3	10.1.0.0.0	5 Ajaw	November 28, 849
1A1 panel	10.1.1.3.19	2 Kawak 12 Wo	February 10, 851
(multiple possibilities)	10.1.1.5.19	3 Kawak 12 Zotz	March 22, 851
	10.1.1.7.19	4 Kawak 12 Xul	May 1, 851
	10.1.1.16.19	2 Kawak 12 Muwan	October 28, 851

Sources: Carrasco Vargas and Pérez de Heredia Puente 1996; Graña-Behrens 2002; Pérez de Heredia Puente 2001; Ringle and Bey 2009; Rubenstein 2015; Stuart and Rubenstein 2014; Thompson 1954

coupled with the construction of the Uxmal-Nohpat-Kabah *sacbe* (Carrasco Vargas 1993), indicates a very close relationship between these two centers, perhaps reflecting their emergence as the united center of power in the Puuc. Whether this represented outright domination of their neighbors or more indirect forms of hegemony remains to be seen: personally, I favor their roles as guarantors of legitimacy through sponsorship of investiture, accompanied by only modest influence over most affairs of state (Dunning and Kowalski 1994; Kowalski 2003, 2017).

The mask common to the House of the Governor, the central stack of the North Nunnery, and the Codz Pop has an interesting afterlife on the Late Postclassic colonnaded hall Q-151 of Mayapan (Masson and Peraza Lope 2014; Proskouriakoff 1962:113; Shook and Irving 1955) (Figure 4.22a).[14] Q-151 is located in the heart of Mayapan's civic core, just east of the Castillo (Q-162), and extends along one side of the basal platform supporting the Caracol (Q-152). It is otherwise typical of such structures, except that piers replace columns at two points along the facade, flanking the extension of the central stairway. Puuc masks were placed at the base of these piers, as well as at the base of the front corners, although these are poorly preserved. The interior bench was also decorated with carved stones from Terminal Classic Puuc structures, in this case, reliefs of either parrots or quetzals. Q-151 is the only colonnaded hall to be decorated in this manner. As recognized by the Carnegie archaeologists, the masks and slabs were almost certainly pulled from a Terminal Classic Puuc building, the masks, in particular, perhaps derived from the Codz Pop of Kabah (Proskouriakoff 1962:95). In support, Milbrath and Peraza Lope (2003:11) note that the dimensions of the mask do, in fact, correspond well with the size of the masks from that building. The Mayapan masks differ in several details from those of Uxmal and the Codz Pop (Figure 4.22b–c) and so were probably from other structures, but these authors are likely correct in identifying Kabah as the probable source.

Proskouriakoff had also argued that each of the colonnaded halls belonged to one of the principal factions or provinces comprising the Mayapan polity. Because of the masks on Q-151, we (Ringle and Bey 2001:286) hypothesized that these marked the building belonging to the Xiu faction residing at Mayapan, who claimed to have settled Uxmal and were for a period the rulers (or dominant faction) of Mayapan. As Masson cogently argues in this volume, Mayapan was not a replication of the Terminal Classic sites of Yucatán, but it did continue the tradition of northern Tollans. Organizationally Mayapan was apparently able to reconcile the competing Cocom and Xiu factions, descendants of the Terminal Classic Tollans of Chichen Itza and Uxmal, at least for a while. And although the landscape had shifted dramatically, the placement of

figure 4.22
Mask style common to: a) Mayapan Structure Q-151; b) House of the Governor; and c) Codz Pop. Photographs by William M. Ringle.

Masked Intentions 109

these masks surely indicates their value as memorials to a legacy of power that had begun three or four centuries earlier, even as it was experiencing its last gasp at Mayapan.

Acknowledgments

The arguments in this paper have evolved from conversations with my colleagues Tomás Gallareta Negrón and George Bey, although they may not agree with my interpretations, and with my former student Matt Morris. Much of my discussion of Kabah would not have been possible without Meghan Rubenstein's stimulating dissertation, emails, and generous provision of drawings. Lourdes Toscano Hernández also kindly lent unpublished reconstructions of the Codz Pop. Charles Rhyne's website (https://www.reed.edu/uxmal/) has been a valuable compendium of images of Uxmal and Kabah. Thanks also to the National Science Foundation, the National Geographic Society, and FAMSI for funding fieldwork in the Puuc, and to Mat Saunders for an invitation to present an earlier version of this paper at the 2015 "Maya at the Lago" meeting in Davidson.

NOTES

1 A pioneering example of such an approach is Kowalski's (1987) study of the House of the Governor. Much earlier, Seler (1917, 1998) recognized the importance of recording the diversity of architectural sculpture in the Puuc and at Chichen Itza.

2 Stone mosaic masks may descend from stucco antecessors, such as the stucco masks with attached twinned serpent bodies from the entablature of the House of the Seven Dolls-sub at Dzibilchaltun (Coggins 1983:figs. 7–10), dating to about 700 CE. Galván Bernal, Bey, and Ciau (2017) report on a dismantled modeled stucco facade from Kiuic. Although the fragments do not appear to belong to zoomorphic masks, they are of probable Late Classic date.

3 Bracketed page numbers refer to an unpublished, unaccredited English translation in the Peabody Museum Archives (SPEC.COLL.c.a.3 SE4 ruE Folio), probably sponsored by the Carnegie Institution and donated by H. E. D. Pollock.

4 In the north, rather than marking central rooms, mat signs consistently adorn those flanking them, perhaps marking them as the offices of the *holpop*.

5 God G1 is familiar as one of the three patron gods of Palenque, but he is found across the southern lowlands. Stuart (2005:161–174) notes instances from the Early Classic onward, though G1 does not seem to have survived the Classic period. Stuart distinguishes him from Chaak, noting that at Palenque he seems to have played a role in creation. He also seems to have been viewed as a mythical ancestor of the Palenque rulers; perhaps he played a similar role for the Puuc dynasts. G1 is also associated with bloodletting, as his protruding tooth indicates, and thus elite autosacrifice, but his function remains imperfectly understood.

6 Unpublished photos by Teobert Maler shows the central sculpture in situ: Uxmal Album 4-photos 5, 7, 9, and 11; https://digital.iai.spk-berlin.de/viewer/image/1049690117/1/LOG_0003/).

7 First noted by Seler (1917:136, Abb. 115a). Bricker and Bricker (1996) and Šprajc (2015) discuss the archaeoastronomical relationship between Venus and the House of the Governor.

8 The jamb date was originally read by Thompson (1954:97) as falling within the *tun* 10.1.10.0.0 (859 CE). Although Carrasco Vargas and Pérez de Heredia Puente (1996:302) argue for a later placement, Ringle and Bey (2009:343) note that the Calendar Round was correctly read as 2 Chuen 3 Muwan, almost certainly corresponding to 10.1.10.0.11. Stuart and Rubenstein (2014) later came to the same conclusion in a blog post.

9 The distinction is not complete. A mask on the right side of the roof comb of the Iglesia is an example of a Chichen mask with a nose roll. As noted, heads emerge from the maws of masks on the Dovecote and the Great Pyramid at Uxmal.

10 The Casa del Venado, adjacent to the Casa Colorada, also has three rooms and a roof comb, but no masks. Perhaps this again marks a separation of administrative and residential quarters.

11 The exception is the roof comb mask at the northwest corner. It is thoroughly aberrant, having a headband of four flower-like elements, pairs of which usually terminate a headband. It also has a nose roll, different eye-surround elements, and projects less than the other masks. The mask is present in early photographs of the structure, and so is not a later restoration error. It remains unexplained, unless it results from a repair to the building in pre-Hispanic times, after the meaning of the facade had been lost.

12 I would concur with her that the building is unlikely to have been a *popol nah*, or council house, since these usually are long, single-room halls, though some have smaller added rooms.

13 Xcalumkin's Initial Series Building may be a partial example of Floor Plan 3. If so, buildings dedicated to the military must already have been present by the mid-eighth century.

14 Masks continue to adorn Late Postclassic structures of the east coast, as at Tulum.

REFERENCES CITED

Andrews, George F.
- 1986 *Los estilos arquitectónicos del Puuc: Una nueva apreciación*. Instituto Nacional de Antropología e Historia, Mexico City.
- 1990 Architectural Survey at Kabah, Yucatan, Mexico. Report on file, University of Texas Library, Alexander Architectural Archive, http://hdl.handle.net/2152/13625.
- 1991 Architecture Survey at Chichén Itzá. Report on file, University of Texas Library, Alexander Architectural Archive, http://hdl.handle.net/2152/13489.
- 1995 *Pyramids and Palaces, Monsters and Masks: The Golden Age of Maya Architecture*, vol. 1, *Architecture of the Puuc Region and the Northern Plains*. Labyrinthos, Lancaster, Calif.

Berlo, Janet Catherine
- 1980 Teotihuacan Art Abroad: A Study of Metropolitan Style and Provincial Transformation in Incensario Workshops. PhD dissertation, Yale University, New Haven.

Bolles, John S.
- 1977 *Las Monjas: A Major Pre-Mexican Architectural Complex at Chichén Itzá*. University of Oklahoma Press, Norman.

Boot, Erik
- 2004 "Ceramic" Support for the Identity of Classic Maya Architectural Long-Lipped (Corner) Masks as the Animated Witz "Hill, Mountain." Mesoweb, www.mesoweb.com/features/boot/Masks.pdf.

Bricker, Harvey M., and Victoria R. Bricker
- 1996 Astronomical References in the Throne Inscription of the Palace of the Governor at Uxmal. *Cambridge Archaeological Journal* 6(2):191–229.

Bricker, Victoria R., and Harvey M. Bricker
- 1995 An Astronomical Text from Chichen Itza, Yucatan, Mexico. *Human Mosaic* 28:91–105.

Carrasco Vargas, Ramón
- 1993 Formación sociopolítica en el Puuc: El sacbé Uxmal-Nohpat-Kabah. In *Perspectivas antropológicas en el mundo maya*, edited by Ma. Josefa Iglesias Ponce de León and Francesca Ligorred Perramon, pp. 199–212. Sociedad Española de Estudios Mayas, Madrid.

Carrasco Vargas, Ramón, Josep Ligorred, Eduardo Pérez de Heredia, Antonio Centeno, and Fabienne de Pierrebourg
- 1992 Les fouilles du site de Kabah (Yucatán): Saison 1991. *Journal de la Société des Américanistes* 78(1):9–29.

Carrasco Vargas, Ramón, and Eduardo Pérez de Heredia Puente
- 1996　Los últimos gobernantes de Kabah. In *Eighth Palenque Round Table, 1993*, edited by Martha J. Macri and Jan McHargue, pp. 297–308. Pre-Columbian Art Research Institute, San Francisco.

Chinchilla Mazariegos, Oswaldo
- 2019　Temples to the Great Bird: Architecture, Mythology, and Ritual in Teotihuacan-Style Censers from Escuintla, Guatemala. *RES: Anthropology and Aesthetics* 71–72:78–96.

Coggins, Clemency
- 1983　*The Stucco Decorations and Architectural Assemblage of Structure 1-Sub, Dzibilchaltun, Yucatan, Mexico*. Middle American Research Institute, Tulane University, New Orleans.

Dunning, Nicholas P., and Jeff Karl Kowalski
- 1994　Lords of the Hills: Classic Maya Settlement Patterns and Political Iconography in the Puuc Region, Mexico. *Ancient Mesoamerica* 5:63–95.

Gallareta Negrón, Tomás
- 2013　The Social Organization of Labna, a Classic Maya Community in the Puuc Region of Yucatan, Mexico. PhD dissertation, Tulane University, New Orleans.

Galván Bernal, Melissa, George J. Bey III, and Rossana May Ciau
- 2017　From Temple to Trash: Analysis and Interpretation of a Dismantled Stucco Façade and Its Deposit from Kiuic, Yucatán. In *Recent Investigations in the Puuc Region of Yucatán*, edited by Meghan Rubenstein, pp. 39–58. Archaeopress, Oxford.

Graña-Behrens, Daniel
- 2002　Die Maya-Inschriften aus Nordwestyukatan, Mexiko. PhD dissertation, Rheinischen Friedrich-Wilhems-Universität zu Bonn, Bonn.

Grube, Nikolai
- 1994　Hieroglyphic Sources for the History of Northwest Yucatan. In *Hidden among the Hills: Maya Archaeology of the Northwest Yucatan Peninsula*, edited by Hanns J. Prem, pp. 316–358. Verlag Von Flemming, Möckmühl.
- 2003　Hieroglyphic Inscriptions from Northwest Yucatán: An Update of Recent Research. In *Escondido en la selva: Arqueología en el norte de Yucatán*, edited by Hanns J. Prem, pp. 339–370. Universidad de Bonn, Bonn; and Instituto Nacional de Antropología e Historia, Mexico City.

Hellmuth, Nicholas M.
- 1975　*The Escuintla Hoards: Teotihuacan Art in Guatemala*. Foundation for Latin American Anthropological Research, Guatemala City.

Huchim Herrera, José, and Lourdes Toscano Hernández
- 1999　El Cuadrángulo de los Pájaros de Uxmal. *Arqueología mexicana* 7(37):18–23.

Kowalski, Jeff Karl
- 1987　*The House of the Governor*. University of Oklahoma Press, Norman.
- 2003　Collaboration and Conflict: An Interpretation of the Relationship between Uxmal and Chichén Itzá during the Terminal Classic/Early Postclassic Periods. In *Escondido en la selva: Arqueología en el norte de Yucatán*, edited by Hanns J. Prem, pp. 235–272. Universidad de Bonn, Bonn; and Instituto Nacional de Antropología e Historia, Mexico City.
- 2017　The Nunnery Quadrangle at Uxmal: Creation, Captive Sacrifice, Ritual, and Political Authority in a Puuc Maya Palace Complex. In *Recent Investigations in the Puuc Region of Yucatán*, edited by Meghan Rubenstein, pp. 101–114. Archaeopress, Oxford.

Kowalski, Jeff Karl, and Nicholas P. Dunning
- 1999　The Architecture of Uxmal: The Symbolics of Statemaking at a Puuc Maya Regional Capital. In *Mesoamerican Architecture as a Cultural Symbol*, edited by Jeff Karl Kowalski, pp. 274–297. Oxford University Press, New York.

Kowalski, Jeff Karl, Rhonda Silverstein, and Mya Follansbee
- 2002　Seats of Power and Cycles of Creation: Continuities and Changes in Iconography and Political Organization at Dzibilchaltún, Uxmal, Chichén Itzá, and Mayapán. *Estudios de cultura maya* 22:87–111.

Love, Bruce
    2015   A Skyband with Constellations: Revisiting the Monjas East Wing at Chichen Itza. *The PARI Journal* 15(3):11–14.

Maldonado Cárdenas, Rubén, and Beatríz Repetto Tío
    1988   Los tlalocs de Uxmal, Yucatán. *Revista española de antropología americana* 18:9–19.

Martin, Simon
    2020   *Ancient Maya Politics: A Political Anthropology of the Classic Period 150–900 CE.* Cambridge University Press, New York.

Masson, Marilyn A., and Carlos Peraza Lope
    2014   *Kukulcan's Realm: Urban Life at Ancient Mayapán.* University Press of Colorado, Boulder.

Milbrath, Susan, and Carlos Peraza Lope
    2003   Revisiting Mayapan, Mexico's Last Maya Capital. *Ancient Mesoamerica* 14(1):1–46.

Novelo Rincón, Gustavo
    2017   Investigación y restauración arquitectónicas en el Codz Pop de Kabah, Yucatán. In *Recent Investigations in the Puuc Region of Yucatán*, edited by Meghan Rubenstein, pp. 71–80. Archaeopress, Oxford.

Pérez de Heredia Puente, Eduardo José
    2001   El Edificio de las Manos Rojas de Kabah, Yuc.: Datos para la cronología. Tesis de licenciatura, Universidad Autónoma de Yucatán, Mérida.

Plank, Shannon E.
    2003   Monumental Maya Dwellings in the Hieroglyphic and Archaeological Records: A Cognitive-Anthropological Approach to Classic Maya Architecture. PhD dissertation, Boston University, Boston.
    2004   *Maya Dwellings in Hieroglyphs and Archaeology: An Integrative Approach to Ancient Architecture and Spatial Cognition.* Hadrian Books, Oxford.

Pollock, H. E. D.
    1980   *The Puuc.* Peabody Museum of Archaeology and Ethnology, Harvard University, Cambridge, Mass.

Prem, Hanns J.
    2003   *Xkipché: Una ciudad maya en el corazón del Puuc*, vol. 1, *El asentamiento*. Universidad de Bonn, Bonn; and Instituto Nacional de Antropología e Historia, Mexico City.

Proskouriakoff, Tatiana A.
    1962   Civic and Religious Structures of Mayapan. In *Mayapan, Yucatan, Mexico*, edited by H. E. D. Pollock, Ralph L. Roys, Tatiana Proskouriakoff, and A. L. Smith, pp. 86–163. Carnegie Institution of Washington, Washington, D.C.

Ringle, William M.
    2012   The Nunnery Quadrangle of Uxmal. In *The Ancient Maya of Mexico: Reinterpreting the Past of the Northern Maya Lowlands*, edited by Geoffrey E. Braswell, pp. 191–228. Equinox Press, Sheffield.

Ringle, William M., and George J. Bey III
    2001   Post-Classic and Terminal Classic Courts of the Northern Maya Lowlands. In *Royal Courts of the Ancient Maya*, vol. 2, *Data and Case Studies*, edited by Takeshi Inomata and Stephen D. Houston, pp. 266–307. Westview Press, Boulder, Colo.
    2009   The Face of the Itzas. In *The Art of Urbanism: How Mesoamerican Kingdoms Represented Themselves in Architecture and Imagery*, edited by William L. Fash and Leonardo López Luján, pp. 329–383. Dumbarton Oaks, Washington, D.C.

Ringle, William M., Tomás Gallareta Negrón, and George J. Bey III
    2021   Stranger-Kings in Northern Yucatan. In *Maya Kingship: Rupture and Transformation from Classic to Postclassic Times*, edited by Tsubaka Okoshi, Arlen F. Chase, Phillippe Nondédéo, and M. Charlotte Arnauld, pp. 249–268. University Press of Florida, Gainesville.

Robertson, Merle Greene
    1995   *Merle Green Robertson's Rubbings of Maya Sculpture.* CD-ROM. Pre-Columbian Art Research Institute, San Francisco.

Rubenstein, Meghan L.
- 2015 Animate Architecture at Kabah: Terminal Classic Art and Politics in the Puuc Region of Yucatán, Mexico. PhD dissertation, University of Texas, Austin.

Ruppert, Karl
- 1935 *The Caracol at Chichen Itza, Yucatan, Mexico.* Carnegie Institution of Washington, Washington, D.C.
- 1952 *Chichen Itza: Architectural Notes and Plans.* Carnegie Institution of Washington, Washington, D.C.

Sáenz Vargas, César A.
- 1969 Exploraciones y restauraciones en Uxmal. *Boletín del Instituto Nacional de Antropología e Historia* 36:5–13.

Schele, Linda
- 1998 The Iconography of Maya Architectural Façades during the Late Classic Period. In *Function and Meaning in Classic Maya Architecture*, edited by Stephen D. Houston, pp. 479–518. Dumbarton Oaks, Washington, D.C.
- n.d. Schele Drawing Collection, Los Angeles Museum of Art, Los Angeles, http://ancientamericas.org/collection/browse/29.

Schele, Linda, and Peter Mathews
- 1998 *The Code of Kings: The Language of Seven Sacred Maya Temples and Tombs.* Scribner, New York.

Schmidt, Peter J.
- 2011 Birds, Ceramics, and Cacao: New Excavations at Chichén Itzá, Yucatan. In *Twin Tollans: Chichén Itzá, Tula, and the Epiclassic to Early Postclassic Mesoamerican World*, edited by Jeff Karl Kowalski and Cynthia Kristan-Graham, pp. 151–203. Dumbarton Oaks, Washington, D.C.

Seler, Eduard
- 1917 *Die Ruinen von Uxmal.* Verlag der Königlich Akadamie der Wissenschaften, Berlin.
- 1998 The Ruins of Chichen Itza in Yucatan. In *Collected Works in Mesoamerican Linguistics and Archaeology,* vol. 6, edited by J. Eric S. Thompson, Francis B. Richardson, and Frank E. Comparato, pp. 41–165. Labyrinthos, Lancaster, Calif.

Shook, Edwin M., and William N. Irving
- 1955 *Colonnaded Buildings at Mayapán.* Carnegie Institution of Washington, Washington, D.C.

Šprajc, Ivan
- 2015 Governor's Palace at Uxmal. In *Handbook of Archaeoastronomy and Ethnoastronomy,* edited by Clive L. N. Ruggles, pp. 773–781. Springer, New York.

Stephens, John Lloyd
- 1843 *Incidents of Travel in Yucatan.* 2 vols. Harper & Brothers, New York.

Stone, Andrea, and Marc Zender
- 2011 *Reading Maya Art: A Hieroglyphic Guide to Ancient Maya Painting and Sculpture.* Thames and Hudson, New York.

Stuart, David
- 1987 *Ten Phonetic Syllables.* Center for Maya Research, Washington, D.C.
- 1997 The Hills Are Alive: Sacred Mountains in the Maya Cosmos. *Symbols* 13:13–17.
- 2005 *The Inscriptions from Temple XIX at Palenque: A Commentary.* Pre-Columbian Art Research Institute, San Francisco.

Stuart, David, Stephen D. Houston, and John Robertson
- 1999 *Notebook for the XXIII Maya Hieroglyphic Forum at Texas, March 1999.* University of Texas at Austin, Austin.

Stuart, David, and Meghan Rubenstein
- 2014 The Reading of Two Dates from the Codz Pop at Kabah, Yucatan. Maya Decipherment, https://mayadecipherment.com/2014/10/30/the-reading-of-two-dates-from-the-codz-pop-at-kabah-yucatan/.

Taube, Karl A.
- 1992 The Temple of Quetzalcoatl and the Cult of Sacred War at Teotihuacan. *RES: Anthropology and Aesthetics* 21:53–87.
- 2001 The Breath of Life: The Symbolism of Wind in Mesoamerica. In *The Road to Aztlan: Art from a Mythic Homeland,* edited by Virginia M. Fields and Victor Zamudio-Taylor, pp. 102–123. Los Angeles County Museum of Art, Los Angeles.

2003   Maws of Heaven and Hell: The Symbolism of the Centipede and Serpent in Classic Maya Religion. In *Antropología de la eternidad: La muerte en la cultura maya,* edited by Andrés Ciudad Ruiz, Mario H. Ruz Sosa, and Ma. J. I. Ponce de León, pp. 405–442. Sociedad Española de Estudios Mayas, Barcelona; and Universidad Autónoma de México, Mexico City.

2004   Flower Mountain: Concepts of Life, Beauty, and Paradise among the Classic Maya. *RES: Anthropology and Aesthetics* 45:69–98.

2010   Gateways to Another World: The Symbolism of Supernatural Passageways in the Art and Ritual of Mesoamerica and the American Southwest. In *Painting the Cosmos: Metaphor and Worldview in Images from the Southwest Pueblos and Mexico,* edited by Kelley Hays-Gilpin and Polly Schaafsma, pp. 73–120. Museum of Northern Arizona, Flagstaff.

Thompson, J. Eric S.
1954   *The Rise and Fall of Maya Civilization.* University of Oklahoma Press, Norman.

Toscano Hernández, Lourdes, and Gustavo Novelo Rincón
2012   La cocina real de Kabah, Yucatán. Paper presented at the XXVI Simposio de Investigaciones Arqueológicas en Guatemala, Guatemala.

von Winning, Hasso
1987   *La iconografía de Teotihuacán: Los dioses y los signos.* 2 vols. Universidad Nacional Autónoma de México, Mexico City.

Wagner, Elizabeth
2006   Jade: The Green Gold of the Maya. In *Maya: Divine Kings of the Rainforest,* edited by Nikolai Grube, pp. 66–67. H. F. Ullmann, Rheinbreitbach.

Relatively Strange Rulers

Relational Politics in the Southern and Northern Maya Lowlands

MAXIME LAMOUREUX-ST-HILAIRE AND PATRICIA A. MCANANY

The relational dynamics that articulated Classic Maya rulership with the local and international political spheres blended the familiar with the strange and the sacred. As such, the model of divine stranger kingship, as proposed by Sahlins (2008) and Graeber (Graeber and Sahlins 2017), provides relevant concepts that can be deployed critically to understand how, for several centuries, Classic Maya royalty successfully managed large populations while maintaining an intricate network of alliances with external powers of varying degrees of cultural and linguistic difference. We also believe that the political dynamics of the southern and northern Maya Lowlands were comparable. After addressing underlying assumptions about the ancient Maya world, we discuss stranger queen/kingship (or more simply, rulership) and some key political dynamics—schismogenesis, galactic mimesis, and upward nobility—that accompany this kind of state-crafting. Importantly, we discuss how ubiquitous marital alliances between allochthonous and Indigenous nobles empowered royal courts by solidifying their sovereignty over both the local and international political spheres—something we refer to as dual sovereignty (for more on the coercive aspects of sovereignty, see Wengrow, this volume). After dwelling on rulership linked to a charter of strangeness, in which strange faces were highly valued, we turn to internal communicational mechanisms of statecraft exhibited in the feasting and gift giving (i.e., commensal politics) organized by royal courts for their allies and subjects.

Background

The deep history of the northern and southern Maya Lowlands (Figure 5.1) has long been conceived in binary terms. Morley (1917) first contrasted the Old and New Maya Empires as two loosely defined political entities subdividing Maya civilization chronologically and geographically between the supposedly older southern and newer northern lowlands. The post-1950s explosion of epigraphic

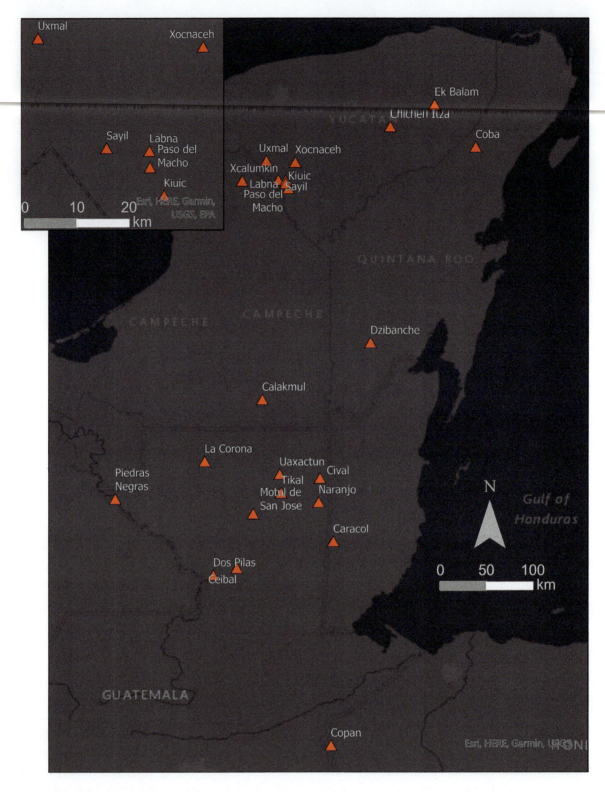

figure 5.1
Map of the Maya area, with sites mentioned in this chapter. Map by Maxime Lamoureux-St-Hilaire.

research further distanced the text-laden southern courts from their northern counterparts, where textual narratives are rarer. Meanwhile, the questionable idea of Maya exceptionalism flattened Maya civilization into a unique sociopolitical landscape that could not be compared to other premodern societies, especially not those of Europe (Chase and Chase 1992:307; Thompson 1954).

We now understand the ancient Maya world as a complex sociocultural and linguistic mosaic in constant geopolitical flux. This networked mosaic was unified by a linguistic family, coherent cultural and ideological traits, an expansive economic web, and an array of cogent political forces that articulated most ancient Maya regimes. Yet rarer data for the southern portions of the states of Campeche and Quintana Roo, which remain a relative terra incognita, complicate our holistic understanding of the lowlands and maintain a certain north–south dichotomy. But ancient Maya civilization did not undergo an exceptional development; the many tiles of its sociopolitical mosaic share traits with other parts of Mesoamerica and faraway, premodern civilizations. As anthropological archaeologists, we can utilize concepts drawn from structurally comparable, divine stranger kingdoms, which likely constituted "the dominant form of premodern state" (Sahlins 2017b:224).

A foundational tenet of this comparative approach is that no polity ever emerged in isolation (Graeber and Sahlins 2017:21; Sahlins 2017b:247; Wright 2006). The ancient Maya geopolitical landscape was relational, with political communities and institutions self-defining in contrast to neighboring polities—i.e., schismogenesis (following Graeber and Sahlins 2017, as adapted from Bateson 1935). Recurring exogamous marriages among complementary polities culminated in "international" aristocracies and, at localized courts, the presence of royal individuals of foreign origin, or "stranger rulers." Certain royal regimes superseded their neighbors, extending their dominion through exogamous marriage as well as hegemony, colonization, and conquest (Martin 2020; Martin and Grube 1994). These superordinate regimes directed or inspired subordinate courts to emulate their governmental practices—i.e., galactic mimesis (following Sahlins 2017a:365–376). Often, marginally powerful nobles adopted the titles, practices, and regalia of hegemonic courts—i.e., upward *nobility* (following Sahlins 2017b). Paradoxically, the same processes that "imported" foreign royals necessarily preserved some political power in the hands of local kin groups, creating dual sovereignties (Sahlins 2017b:231–232).

Ancient Maya rulers had privileged access to the gods and were engaged in international politics; as such, they did not fully belong to either the human world or to a specific political sphere. Stranger rulers, divine wielders of political and religious power, were contained in the royal precinct, or even within a regal palace (following Graeber 2017), thus leaving the handling of most earthly matters (like agriculture) to affines and traditional powerbrokers. Thus, ancient Maya divine royalty were simultaneously foreign and local, strange and familiar: "as their cosmic-cum-celestial powers derive from their external origins, the foreign identity of the kingship is perpetual, a condition of their sovereignty, in contrast to the earthly powers and identity of their indigenous subjects" (Sahlins 2017b:224).

Classic Maya rulership was articulated with international agents—overlords, allies, and subordinates—who largely defined the governmental superstructure, while articulations with local powerbrokers—noble members of the court, vassals, and leaders of communities of production—largely defined its infrastructure (Lamoureux-St-Hilaire 2018:468–470). This pairing of foreign and local political power, with obvious ramifications in the economic domain, makes it imperative for us to envision institutional royal courts (or governments) as the face of Classic Maya rulership, rather than focusing on individual rulers. As a ruling body, married foreign and local royals, along with their respective political networks, thus had dual sovereignty over both the local and international spheres.

While epigraphic and iconographic evidence document key aspects of these relational dynamics, especially external relations, the importance of non-textual or non-imagistic evidence cannot be underestimated (see Freidel, this volume). The archaeology of regal palaces is particularly relevant, since these complexes are the footprints of royal courts (Lamoureux-St-Hilaire 2018:43). In particular, the identification of rooms for hosting visitors and spaces for political gatherings is pivotal for studying the communicational practices that allowed royal courts to effectively manage their international and local relations. Studying the articulation of these key spaces can help us understand how ancient Maya politicians managed their networks and dual sovereignty. Below, we discuss the external and internal relational politics that were shared, via networked interaction, across most of the lowland Maya world. We provide examples from the northern and southern lowlands to further develop concepts and to close the gap between these regions.

Relational Regimes

> The kingdom is neither an endogamous formation nor does it develop in isolation: it is a function of the relationships of a hierarchically ordered, intersocietal historical field (Graeber and Sahlins 2017:5)

While written evidence is lacking for the Preclassic period, the degree to which Classic Maya texts sponsored by one royal court refer to others is remarkable. It is this very tendency that pushed Berlin (1958) toward his precocious discovery of "emblem glyphs." The realization that these emblems refer to royal houses, and not simply cities (Tokovinine 2013), emphasizes how they highlighted regimes—constellations of power—that were not always anchored in place. Upon closer inspection and embedded within the referential quality of emblem glyphs are the concepts of relationality and hierarchy. The royal Maya penchant for relationality is anything but exceptional; it is the founding principle of political networking strategies and of exogamy—a foundational topic in anthropological theory. There is solid evidence for continued emphasis on relationality and hierarchy during the Postclassic and colonial periods (Chuchiak, this volume; Cojti-Ren 2020; Masson, this volume; Masson and Peraza Lope 2014) and excellent reasons to believe that these forces were in full swing during Preclassic times. Indeed, the disparate sizes of Preclassic settlements and their massive architectural compounds suggest that hierarchy was etched into Preclassic political networks. The related concept of schismogenesis, or interactive emergence, is explored further while hierarchy is examined through the lens of galactic mimesis and upward nobility.

Stranger Rulership and Schismogenesis

PRECLASSIC PERIOD

Maya regimes did not emerge in isolation, but rather through interactions with neighbors, leading to both foundational alliances and antagonisms. While we lack textual evidence for the emergence of Preclassic Maya rulership, we know from both artifactual and architectural proxies that Preclassic levels of interactivity were high (see Awe, Helmke, Ebert, and Hoggarth, this volume). These vast material networks imply considerable social mobility and suggest that incipient polities were keenly aware of their peers and sought to forge foreign alliances.

As early as the Middle Preclassic period, settlements across the entire Maya Lowlands—from the sizable site of Ceibal (Inomata 2017a) to the diminutive center of Paso del Macho (Parker, Bey, and Gallareta Negrón 2020)—adopted symbols of power and centrality likely established by Olmec rulers. Artifacts were buried as community-anchoring foundational practices. Caches of polished greenstone objects, sometimes featuring Olmec symbols (Parker, Bey, and Gallareta Negrón 2020), were international instruments of authority with clear religious dimensions; they would become political regalia for subsequent generations. Additionally, the wide distribution of the Mamom and Chicanel ceramic spheres reflect civilizational levels of interaction. While containing locally specific forms and finishes (Bartlett and McAnany 2000), the reach and popularity of these redwares, which were present from the Pasión River to the Caribbean shore, were not again repeated until Postclassic times (Masson and Hare 2020).

Recent evidence suggests that the earliest monumental constructions in the Maya world were truly public, presenting no sign of pronounced inequality or incipient rulership (Inomata et al. 2020).

Yet the spread of E-Groups—the first clear institutional architectural compound (Inomata 2017b)—throughout southeastern Mesoamerica reflects the complementarity of cultural groups occupying the broader Yucatán Peninsula. As phrased by Inomata (2017b:215): "[t]his standardized spatial plan probably emerged through close interactions among diverse groups who lived on the southern Gulf Coast, in central Chiapas, and on the southern Pacific Coast of Mexico . . ." The subsequent spread of monumental Triadic Groups throughout most of the Maya Lowlands (Szymański 2014), however, reflected the high levels of mutually intelligible ideologies and the centralization of asymmetrical power relations. Clark and Hansen (2001) have argued persuasively for the presence of spatially expansive Preclassic kingdoms.

Our increasing comprehension of the pace and direction of the spread of institutional Preclassic architecture and artifacts underscores how incipient polities were enmeshed in socioeconomic networks akin to those better documented for later periods. Within this web, sets of minimally binary relationships led emerging polities to adopt shared or complementary political practices, some of which were more successful than others.

A handful of Classic texts referencing earlier times and dedicated by key rulers—that is, rulers of the Mutul and Kaanul dynasties—invoke two foreign places as sources of divine authority (Martin 2020:120–121). Known as "Moon Zero Bird" and "Maguey Metate/*chicha*," these places were seemingly visited by foundational political figures during Late Preclassic and Protoclassic times (between 158 and 317 CE), thus entangling foreign and local as sources of power (Martin 2020:120–121; Stuart 2014). By imposing, borrowing, and exchanging material/living embodiments of power, the Preclassic web of referential polities grafted onto existing processes of synergistic interaction a hierarchical structure that would come to permeate all textually documented interactions.

Classic Period

Texts from the Classic period regularly emphasize foreign places as sources of political power. Most famously, the "arrival of strangers" from Teotihuacan (Proskouriakoff 1993:4–10; Stuart 2000) led to the adoption of a new apical title (*kaloomte'*) first at Tikal, Uaxactun, and Piedras Negras (Martin 2020:80), then across the lowlands (Figure 5.2). This political inception, which brought new titles, regalia, and governing practices, shifted the area's hierarchical web of power while also transforming Tikal into a source of exotic, divine political credentials.

The "strangeness" of Maya royalty is thus relative. Stranger kings and queens need not have traversed cultural or linguistic boundaries to embody divine power. Affiliations with Tikal were suffused with Teotihuacan regalia and imagery. Blood ties with Tikal royalty would become transformative for localized sovereignty at centers such as Uaxactun, Caracol, Copan, and Motul de San José (Martin 2020).

Alliances solidified through inter-court marital exchanges produced stranger rulers at home courts, thus effectively anchoring myriads of dual sovereignties. While it is tempting to perceive the arrival of allochthonous rulers as disruptive for the organic solidarity promoted by the veneration of place-specific patron deities (Baron 2016, this volume; Tokovinine, Estrada Belli, and Fialko, this volume), the recurring, cyclical nature of these relational political practices suggest otherwise. Classic inscriptions make it clear that apical regimes exported members of their royal family, acting as centrifugal forces for stranger kingdom formation (following Graeber and Sahlins 2017:9), while peripheral and weaker regimes (or at least factions within them) welcomed or even sought these arrivals and benefited from newfound political status. For example, princesses from powerful courts were sent to marry royals of allied but less powerful courts, thereby solidifying marital alliances of support (Ardren, this volume; Sabloff 2018) as well as establishing the equivalent of a diplomatic consulate in a foreign court (Martin 2020:183). In the words of Sahlins (2017b:228):

> Yet most indicative of stranger kingship is the marriage to these powerful foreigners with native women—in the paradigmatic case, the union of the original stranger-king with the daughter or daughters of the autochthonous ruler—an alliance

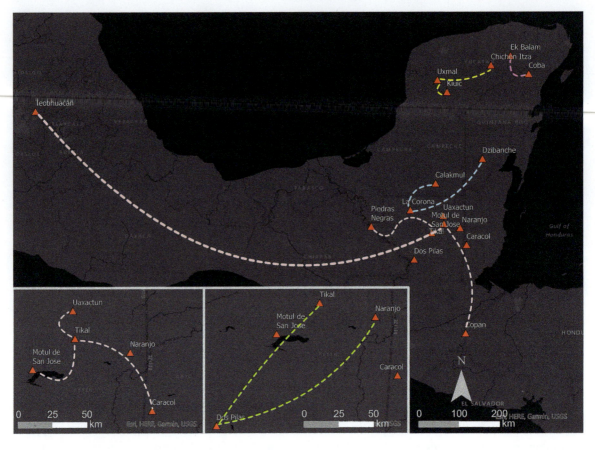

figure 5.2

Map of Mesoamerica, emphasizing the limited number of stranger-royalty connections mentioned in this chapter. Pink: the connection between Teotihuacan, Tikal, and its international allies. Green: the connection between Tikal, Dos Pilas, and Naranjo. Yellow: the connection between Uxmal and other sites sharing a Puuc architectural site. Purple: the connection between Ek' Balam and Coba. Blue: the connection between Dzibanche, Calakmul, and La Corona. Map by Maxime Lamoureux-St-Hilaire.

that is in effect the fundamental contract of the new society. Sovereignty here is embodied in and transmitted by women of rank. In the sequel, the union of the native woman with an immigrant prince engenders a succession of kings who combine in their own persons the essential components of the new regime: foreign and indigenous, celestial and terrestrial, masculine and feminine—each component incomplete in itself, but taken together they make a reproductive totality.

Always eluding absolute patterns, stranger and Native queens were equally common in the Classic Maya Lowlands. Textual (as well as skeletal isotopic) evidence from the Classic period abundantly documents these complementary exogamous political relations, although such relations often are phrased within the isotopic literature as patterns of mobility rather than marriage alliances (e.g., Freiwald 2020; Price et al. 2010; Somerville, Fauvelle, and Froehle 2013; Wright et al. 2010). This process, entangled with inter-polity hierarchies, is perhaps best exemplified by the ca. 643 CE departure of Bajlaj Chan K'awiil from Tikal, his arrival in the Pasión area, and his marriage into local royalty in the person of the so-called Lady of Itzan (Houston 1993:102–110; Martin 2020:250). The arrival of Bajlaj Chan K'awiil not only brought the foreign Mutul emblem glyph to the area but transformed the local hierarchy and defined a ceremonial core complete with a regal palace at Dos Pilas. Despite a history replete with conflict, this textbook example of stranger kingship was such a success that it was soon replicated by Bajlaj Chan K'awiil's daughter, Ix Wak Jalam Chan (aka "Lady Six Sky"), who moved northeast to Naranjo, where, as a stranger queen, she established a new regime in 682 CE (Closs 1985; Martin 2020:176–177). For both Dos Pilas and Naranjo, references to sovereignty were anchored in the allochthonous origins of Bajlaj Chan K'awiil and Ix Wak Jalam Chan, namely in the Mutul emblem glyph and iconographic references to Teotihuacan (Martin 2020:177), despite general allegiance to the rival hegemonic kingdom of Kaanul. These examples of schismogenesis and stranger rulership are clearly based on textual evidence. Yet archaeological evidence can also document this sort of complementary alliance, especially the architecture of regal palaces.

Galactic Mimesis and Upward Nobility

So far, we have discussed how idealized or apical political communities actively sent members of their royal families to cement alliances and establish hegemony over weaker, peripheral areas in a traditional top-down, core-periphery fashion. We also highlighted complementarity in the relationships articulating networked polities. Complementarity implies mutual benefit, even if framed in terms of asymmetrical reciprocity (Orenstein 1980). Based on broad comparative studies, Graeber (Graeber and Sahlins 2017) and Sahlins (2017a, 2017b) propose that the forces that sought the installation of stranger rulership often emanated from local, grassroot political factions rather than from external influences: "the elements of high political status, including kingship, are disseminated by a mimetic process through the region and on the initiative of the less powerful peoples" (Graeber and Sahlins 2017:14).

The arrival of a new stranger ruler and the creation of a dual sovereignty would likely have transformed palatial architecture and set into play heretofore unknown political practices. Simply housing a contingent of important foreigners would have required the expansion of court buildings and possibly the adoption of architectural styles that evoked a foreign court. The extent to which hypogamy—and polygyny—resulted in the renovation and expansion of the court, along with the spread of architectural styles, is underappreciated, since correlating architectural with fine-grained epigraphic accounts is often challenging. Nevertheless, there is mounting evidence that structures were built specifically to house the spouse(s) of nobility, whether foreign or local.

Galactic Mimesis in the North

At the Puuc site of Xcalumkin, carved doorjambs (8 and 9) identify the south structure of the Hieroglyphic Group as the house of "Lady Bone, fourth wife of (the) *itz'aat*" (Graham and von Euw 1992:170–171; Martin 2020:180). This text suggests that focused studies might reveal more temporal correlations between marital alliances and construction at royal courts. Where hieroglyphic records are sparse, there is reason to suspect that the spread of an architectural style throughout a region—such as the Puuc style in Yucatán—may have been intricately connected to hypogamy as Gallareta Cervera (2016) has suggested for the royal court at Kiuic. To recapitulate, the following linkages are possible: exogamous marriage → schismogenesis → expansion of royal courts → spread of regional architectural styles.

A closer look at the layout and architectural adornment of related royal courts is warranted. Uxmal is often described as the first among equals in the Puuc area, since it likely exerted hegemonic influence throughout the region (Dunning and Kowalski 1994) and beyond during Terminal Classic times. Similar to Tikal in exhibiting an architectural aesthetic that adroitly fused orthodoxy with innovation, Uxmal is situated at the entrance to the Puuc region in the fertile breadbasket of the Valle de Santa Elena. Although not well dated, Uxmal appears to have been founded earlier than other Puuc sites, and certainly earlier than Chichen Itza, since it displays the full Puuc architectural sequence (Ringle 2020:758). Ringle (2020:759; following Andrews 1995) suggests that Chichen Itza actively participated in what we would call galactic mimesis

figure 5.3
The west face of the Adivino pyramid of Uxmal, exhibiting the buried range structure at its base. Photograph by Maxime Lamoureux-St-Hilaire.

through the emulation of Uxmal's architectural innovations (Figure 5.2).

In terms of architectural practices, Uxmal may also have led the way by instituting the practice of burying range structures within pyramids. Described by Ringle (2020:762) as "fairly common" in the Puuc, this practice was enacted when the Adivino pyramid was built over a range structure (Figure 5.3), or "casa grande" (Arnauld 2001), that probably was a royal residence. Although likely commemorative in intent, the "unseen" (O'Neil 2009) within the Adivino was nevertheless a vaulted range structure rather than a royal tomb. A similar entombing of an earlier range structure within a pyramid would later occur at the smaller Puuc site of Kiuic (Bey 2004) (Figures 5.2 and 5.4)—perhaps another example of galactic mimesis in which a subordinate court emulates a superordinate kingdom.

The raising of pyramids over earlier buildings is well documented outside of the Puuc, but the importance and primacy of range structures as well as long stone buildings that lack internal wall divisions do separate the northern and southern lowlands (see Arnauld 2001; Ringle, Gallareta Negrón, and Bey 2021). This divergence apparently occurred during the Classic period. During earlier Preclassic times, massive pyramids were constructed in the north as well as in the south. Xocnaceh, located at the base of the Puuc (Gallareta Negrón 2005), provides a pointed example of massive shrine construction during the Middle Preclassic period. But in the Classic-period north, pyramidal shrines to patron deities are not accompanied by royal ancestor shrines except at a few very distinctive northern courts—such as Ek' Balam (Vargas de la Peña et al. 2020). There, galactic mimesis was expressed with an eye to the creation of an extraordinary ancestor

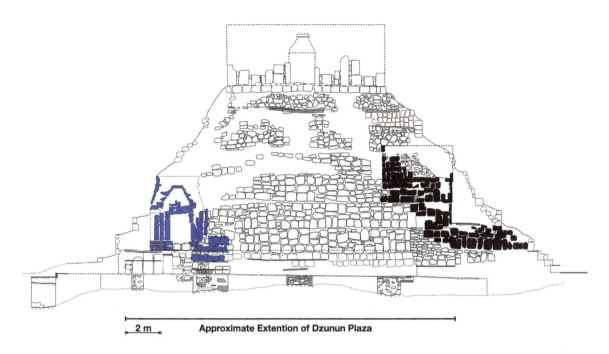

figure 5.4
Complete profile (looking north) of Structure N1065E1025, the pyramidal structure bordering Kiuic's Dzunun Plaza that buried the earlier range structure N1065-W, colored in blue and located to the left. Another buried structure, N1065-E, colored in dark grey, is located to the right (modified from Gallareta-Cervera 2016:180 [Figure 6.25] with permission).

shrine—a frequent dynastic practice in the southern lowlands. Ringle, Gallareta Negrón, and Bey (2021) have examined the entombment of Ukit Kan Le'k Tok' at Ek' Balam precisely in terms of the probability that he may have been a stranger king. Isotopic analysis of his skeletal remains suggests that he was not locally born, while epigraphic evidence from Room 22 of the Ek' Balam acropolis indicates that his mother was a stranger queen, possibly from Coba (Lacadena García-Gallo 2004; Vargas de la Peña et al. 2020:369, 371).

Because Puuc range structures are not always sequestered around private courtyards sitting atop an acropolis, these buildings tended to be more accessible than in the south. Testing this distinction through gamma maps of access patterns, Liendo Stuardo (2003:194) concluded that the looser access patterns at northern lowland sites might be indicative of greater reliance on bureaucratic structures of statecraft. Viewed differently, the greater accessibility of range structures at northern courts could be signaling that the authority accompanying rulership was less concentrated. Elsewhere in the Puuc region, at Xculoc and Xcalumkin, evidence for both an absence of inherited sacred rulership and the presence of multiple seats of power emphasizes the coexistence of multiple types of regimes in the Classic Maya Lowlands (Michelet 2002:82–84).

There are dramatic chronological and geographic distinctions between the northern and southern lowlands in the materialization of galactic mimesis. In the south, the culturally and linguistically foreign Entrada of the Early Classic period coincided with the death of at least one ruler, a dramatic and long-lasting restructuring of the visual cues of rulership, and the later destruction of what might be called the Mutul embassy located on the Street of the Dead at Teotihuacan (Sugiyama et al. 2020). The drama around these interactions may have been repeated shortly after 800 CE, when several local rulers were replaced by rulers with foreign names whose feats were commemorated in stone with foreign day signs (Martin 2020:279–294). In the southern lowlands, galactic mimesis over great distances equaled crisis even though an equilibrium between allochthonous and autochthonous sources of power might later be reestablished—as happened toward the end of the Early Classic period.

Such crises may have been exacerbated by the insularity of the southern lowlands and by heavy investments in hereditary rulership and the sacred quality of rulers (McAnany 2019). In the north—a peninsula surrounded on three sides by water—galactic mimesis was expressed with considerably less drama. During Late–Terminal Classic times, this process resulted in a creative fusion of allochthonous and autochthonous building styles, blending the sweeping corbelled vaults of Uxmal and Chichen Itza with plentiful representations of the feathered serpent. After a critical evaluation of the evidence for stranger kings in the northern lowlands, Ringle, Gallareta Negrón, and Bey (2021) demur on whether the extensive representation of material indicators of rulership in the discourse of the southern lowlands and of kingdoms to the west indicate *entradas* of foreign rulers or just savvy and integrative local statecraft.

Whether due to its geographic connectivity or a form of statecraft that may have had more in common with Classic-period western Mesoamerica than with the southern lowlands, the north was strengthened by what Martin (2020:283) and others refer to as the "early ninth century crisis" that destabilized the south. In the north, the ability to juggle a local Maya identity alongside strong external connections continued through the Postclassic and into the colonial period, when the aristocratic Xiu family famously claimed Mexican ancestry (Restall 1997).

Galactic Mimesis in the South

The small polity of La Corona (Figure 5.5), in the northwest Peten, provides an example of how these political processes operated in the southern lowlands. The rich textual record of La Corona—famous for the arrival of three powerful Kaanul princesses from the two historical seats of the Kaanul royal house, Dzibanche and Calakmul—is replete with manifestations of stranger rulership and galactic mimesis. By marrying La Corona kings (Canuto and Barrientos 2020:184–189; Stuart et al. 2014), the noble Kaanul women became prominent stranger queens. This enduring hypogamous practice integrated La Corona, its strategic location, and its resources within the Kaanul hegemony. Less mentioned but equally important is the accompanying economic boom, reflected in an influx of prestige goods, an increase in the dedication of hieroglyphic monuments, and a rise in serious architectural expansions—notably that of the site's royal acropolis (Canuto and Barrientos 2013, 2020; Lamoureux-St-Hilaire and Bustamante 2016).

The recurring arrivals at La Corona of Kaanul stranger queens—Ix Naah Ek' (520 CE), Ix Tz'ihb Winik (679 CE), and Ix Ti' Kaan (721 CE)—reflect the productivity of this practice for both political communities. Interestingly, the verb used to signify the arrival of these Kaanul noblewomen—*huli*—is used to describe politically transformative events, such as the arrival of dynastic founders at sites such as Tikal and Copan (Canuto and Barrientos 2020:184–185; Stuart 2000).

More evidence of stranger rulership comes from La Corona king Chak Ak' Paat Kuy, who came to power in 689 CE, corresponding to the apex of the Kaanul hegemony. The hieroglyphic monument Element 56 (Figure 5.6), found in the site's regal palace, describes key events framing this king's accession (Stuart et al. 2015). While we have no evidence that this ruler married a Kaanul noblewoman, we know he traveled to the royal court of Yuhknoom Yich'aak K'ahk of Calakmul (Stuart et al. 2015). Exactly what occurred during the nine-month sojourn of Chak Ak' Paat Kuy at his overlord's court is unknown, but his stay led him to receive a regnal name and title, along with distinct elements of regalia (Halperin, this volume; Lamoureux-St-Hilaire 2018:448). In fact, Chak Ak' Paat Kuy's elder brother, who ruled before him, lived through a similar, extended pre-accession travel to Calakmul. Canuto and Barrientos (2020:182) propose that "since the Kaanul lords hosted the successors of the La Corona throne, they were able to integrate and educate them into their hegemony, provide them a suitable Kaanul princess bride, and maintain leverage over their

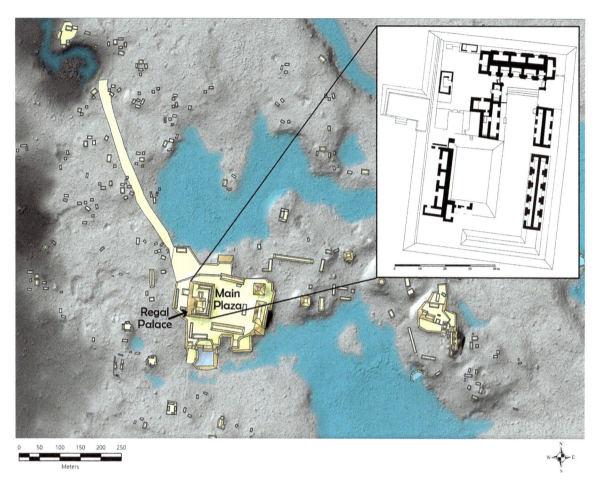

figure 5.5
Map of the site-core of La Corona, with a zoomed-in insert of its regal palace, Structure 13Q-4. Maps by Marcello A. Canuto, Maxime Lamoureux-St-Hilaire, and Eduardo Bustamante.

subordinate parents." Martin (2020:349) has called attention to the expansive palatial architecture of Calakmul, which contains a high frequency of range structures (over eighty in the West Acropolis alone), and suggests either an enormous cadre of noble inhabitants or frequent and long-staying noble "guests." Even in the much smaller palace of La Corona, at least one large vaulted room of the southeast group may have been the residence of a political administrator who responded directly to the Kaanul king—an *aj k'uhuun* named K'ahk' Way Na'—whose presence signified a Kaanul embassy (Lamoureux-St-Hilaire 2018:236–237, 450–451).

Interestingly, two other monuments found near Element 56 showcase the regalia that was bestowed upon La Corona kings-to-be. Elements 55 and 59 (Figure 5.7) respectively portray the almighty Kaanul king ? Ti' K'awiil and the humbler La Corona king Chakaw Nahb Chan (father of Chak Ak' Paat Kuy), both performing a period ending dance while wearing strikingly similar costumes. The notion that La Corona kings received regalia at their overlord's court and celebrated rituals in similar costumes resonates strongly with concepts of both galactic mimesis and upward nobility: "If you will forgive the English pun, galactic systems are marked by a politics of 'upward nobility,' whereby the chiefs of satellite areas assume the political statuses, courtly styles, titles, and even genealogies of their superiors in the regional hierarchy—who for their part imitate the galactic hegemon, while the latter, in invidious contrast to ambitious vassals and rival emperors,

Relatively Strange Rulers 127

figure 5.6
Field laboratory photograph of La Corona Element 56, found in the Northeast Courtyard of the site's regal palace. Photograph by Maxime Lamoureux-St-Hilaire.

figure 5.7
Composite photo of La Corona Elements 55 and 59, found in the Northeast Courtyard of the site's regal palace. Photograph by Maxime Lamoureux-St-Hilaire.

claims to rule the world. In the event, the structural effect is a certain 'galactic mimesis,' insofar as peripheral groups assume the polities and cosmologies of their regional superiors" (Sahlins 2017b:235).

Returning to the Element 56 narrative, Chak Ak' Paat Kuy founded two new communities upon his return (Stuart et al. 2015), likely displacing a portion of La Corona's community to populate them: "(On) 6 Ik 5 Yax, Ahktuun was established (and) he brought people there, (namely) those of Saknikte' [the ancient place-name of La Corona]" (Zender 2019:33–34). This enactment of divine power, upon Chak Ak' Paat Kuy's return as a Kaanul-sanctioned stranger king, adapts the practices of apical monarchs to local means, and may well have included sending off courtly members to outmarry and rule these new communities. This trickle-down stranger politics/colonization not only shaped the kind of regional politics worthy of recording on monuments but also the relationships that linked courts with local people. By invoking foreign sources of legitimacy and describing local political endeavors, this monument embodies the dual sovereignty of this small Classic Maya royal court. To delve deeper into this topic, we turn from epigraphic to archaeological evidence.

Relational Local Politics

The paradigmatic structure of stranger kingship is everywhere inherently ambiguous by virtue of the residual authority retained by the underlying native people as the original settlers and owners of the country . . . In critical respects the stranger kingdom is a system of dual sovereignties in which the immigrant rulers and the indigenous subjects reciprocally encompass one another (Sahlins 2017b:230).

In the southern lowlands, stranger rulers may have possessed divine powers connecting them with the gods and international networks, but they likely left land ownership in the hands of their local marital partner and their local networks (following Graeber and Sahlins 2017:7). Even if their sovereignty was not vested in foreign origins, Maya rulers required an effective system to negotiate with the communities of production who inhabited and worked the lands they ruled. Clearly, managing relationships with both international and local political networks represented logistical challenges for Classic Maya politicians (Figure 5.8). Their governments thus needed to engineer communicational practices to facilitate

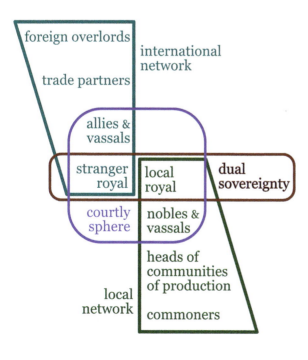

figure 5.8
The web of relations created by the dual sovereignty composed of local and stranger royals. Illustration by Maxime Lamoureux-St-Hilaire.

the operation of their dual sovereignty. These practices, anchored in the constructed landscape (i.e., temples, plazas, and palaces; see also Tokovinine, Estrada Belli, and Fialko, this volume), typically entangled the populace in state religion and foreign allies and local leaders in the exercise of courtly politics (Lamoureux-St-Hilaire 2018; McAnany 2001).

We contend that, while large-scale public ceremonies were key for strengthening political identity (e.g., Inomata 2006), the negotiation between royal courts and local, traditional powerbrokers (i.e., local nobles and heads of communities of production) occurred during more exclusive events inside regal palaces (Lamoureux-St-Hilaire 2020). While epigraphy and iconography, particularly polychrome scenes painted on vases, showcase small gatherings of nobles at royal courts inside audience chambers and their immediate surroundings (Foias 2013; Reents-Budet 2000), royal feasts likely involved larger groups that required more expansive exterior settings, such as the ubiquitous palace courtyards adjoining audiencias. By welcoming an exclusive political community within the divine household, such feasts empowered traditional powerbrokers by involving them in the exercise of courtly politics (Smith 2015:69) and in the experience of royal charisma. From a stranger royalty perspective, such feasts were key political-economic occasions to harness allochthonous sources of power (e.g., exotic foods [see Morell-Hart, this volume] and imported artifacts such as vessels, jewelry, and clothing) for securing the support of an autochthonous base and eliciting their earthly contributions to the regime (e.g., taxed foodstuffs and other commodities). As Graeber and Sahlins (2017:15) describe, "kingship is a political economy of social subjugation rather than material coercion." Thus, royal courts can be perceived as an institution engineered to simultaneously reproduce the regime and manage the political economy—two intricately connected spheres.

Commensal Politics and Communication

Commensal politics played a crucial role in facilitating political communication and economy. Classic Maya politicians were keenly aware of the importance of communication and vested in creating architectural settings to facilitate communication and host frequent commensal events. Semi-private courtyards and their associated "palace kitchens," which are increasingly recognized and investigated at Classic regal palaces, were a key apparatus of Maya rulership (see Morell-Hart, this volume). These complementary spaces—the reception-oriented courtyard and their ancillary complexes—allowed royal regimes to organize and host diacritical feasts that deliberately reproduced and reinforced political networks and their nested economies (Lamoureux-St-Hilaire 2020).

By their very definition, royal-sponsored diacritical feasts simultaneously excluded and included political agents, thus playing a critical role in "the enactment of sovereignty" (Smith 2015:69). The primary governmental functions of commensal politics were to: incentivize local leaders to gather regularly at the palace to pay homage and dues (taxes or tributes) and thus replenish the palace stores; reward subordinates with regalia and honor to reinforce their fealty; and facilitate communication among the many key political agents of the polity to ensure its coordinated success. Consequently, royal commensal politics transformed members of the community into agents central to the regime without whom it would have fallen apart. These asymmetrical reciprocal events—acting as context-renewing practices—both affirmed the sovereignty of rulers and vested traditional powerbrokers with authority. As such, royal-sponsored diacritical feasts were instruments of soft power held not only to extract resources from subjects (Helms 1993) but "to increase the number and loyalty of subjects, as by beneficial or awe-inspiring effects of royal largess, display, and consumption" (Sahlins 2017a:348).

Royal Commensal Politics at La Corona

The later Classic (700–850 CE) regal palace of La Corona (Figures 5.5 and 5.9), located on the west flank of the site's main plaza, provides a good example of an institution designed to facilitate royal commensal politics. The northern half of this palace was subdivided into two complementary groups connected by a single passageway. The large Northeast Courtyard was surrounded by masonry buildings

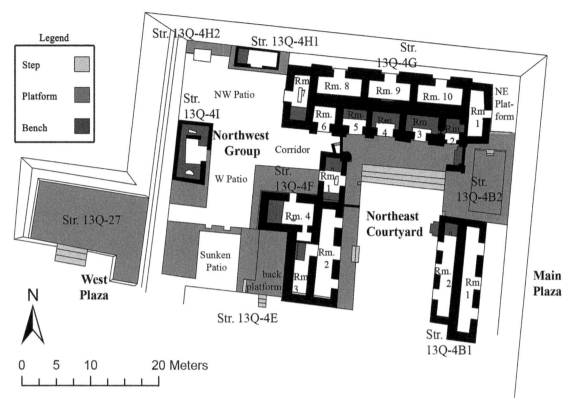

figure 5.9
Top plan of the northern half of the La Corona regal palace. Map by Maxime Lamoureux-St-Hilaire.

with royal residential, administrative, storage, and ceremonial functions; it was suitably adorned with an art program celebrating the kings of La Corona and their Kaanul overlords. Meanwhile, the adjacent Northwest Group housed a mix of sturdy masonry and semi-perishable buildings with ancillary, administrative, and nonroyal residential functions.

The ancillary Northwest Group, with its food-preparation, storage, and craft-oriented buildings, included open areas (Figure 5.10) adequately equipped to prepare both the court's daily meals and large feasts (Lamoureux-St-Hilaire et al. 2019). The personnel laboring in this group prepared massive amounts of food, as revealed by archaeological investigations in complementary activity areas and the multiple middens replete with vast quantities of preparation, storage, and serving vessels, cutting implements, and food waste (Lamoureux-St-Hilaire et al. 2020:113). A rich archaeological record attests to the regime's investment in the planning and preparation of feasts.

Anyone transiting from the Northwest Group to the Northeast Courtyard would have stepped through a tightly controlled passageway featuring two facing doorways and benches (Figure 5.11). The elaborate southern bench was administrative in function, while the northern bench was a low platform perfect for setting down objects, such as dishes, to be counted and inspected. Contextual and architectural evidence suggest that this room was managed by a high-ranking administrator, perhaps an *aj k'uhun*, who would have monitored the adequate purveying of meals during commensal events (Lamoureux-St-Hilaire 2018:287–291, 432–433).

The Northeast Courtyard featured a complementary set of buildings and rooms of mixed functions, all of which revolved around royal politics. The buildings displayed hieroglyphic monuments and stucco friezes and included elaborate residences, large audience rooms (including a throne room), and sizable storage and administrative rooms. The courtyard itself was subdivided into two tiers:

Relatively Strange Rulers   131

figure 5.10
Artistic reconstruction of the activities performed daily in the Northwest Group of the La Corona regal palace. Watercolor by Aaron Alfano.

figure 5.11
Room 1 of Structure 13Q-4F of the La Corona regal palace (looking west), which served as the passageway structure articulating the palace's two north groups. Photographs by Maxime Lamoureux-St-Hilaire.

a main lower courtyard (220 m²) and a stage (60 m²) that fronted the throne room and was accessed by a hieroglyphic staircase (Lamoureux-St-Hilaire 2018:100, 127). Beyond the audience rooms, which were ideal for hosting intimate gatherings, and the large courtyard, which could have hosted many guests (101–792 people, following Inomata 2006; Tsukamoto 2014), two reception areas were defined by elaborate exterior benches.

Its connection with the ancillary Northwest Group made this courtyard a perfect setting for hosting feasts. Different reception settings could have accommodated groups of distinct sizes, from intimate meals for emissaries to large feasts for local allies. The stage facing the throne room, framed by political art, would have facilitated verbal and material asymmetrical exchanges between the royals and their subjects. Interestingly, dishes served to guests in the courtyard would have been carried through the passageway, onto the stage, and down the hieroglyphic staircase, thus acquiring a ceremonial flavor emphasizing the regime's power to provide. Meanwhile, the courtyard's storage facilities and associated administrative rooms were perfect for safeguarding gifts for guests and tabulating the goods that subjects brought to their liege (Lamoureux-St-Hilaire 2022).

Summary

Despite its humble size, La Corona was intimately tied to the most potent kingdom of its time, Kaanul. La Corona rulers were instructed in the governing arts as predicated by a powerful regime, and they clearly harnessed this authority and behaved like divine kings. By hosting diacritical feasts in their regal palace, La Corona royals used their allochthonous power to establish an asymmetrical rapport with the local leaders who controlled the means of production. The energy invested in engineering this architectural institution, where the acquisition, storage, preparation, service, consumption, and discard of food occurred seamlessly, combined with its luxurious and overtly political settings reflect La Corona rulers' intent to please and impress their guests. The fine foods and drinks served in fancy imported vessels would have contributed to making these commensal political events efficient centralizing tools to gather vassals at court and to give them a taste of the allochthonous foundation of their authority.

By participating in these events, local followers established a certain status, which was no doubt bolstered by regalia, and absorbed elements of royal practices that they could use to their advantage in their local contexts: "a privileged relation to the metapersonal rulers of the human fate is the raison d'être of earthly social power... 'It's charisma'—in the original, god-infused sense" (Graeber and Sahlins 2017:3). These carefully crafted events and spaces anchored the dual sovereignty of Maya royal courts. Whereas petty kings emulated their overlords, local leaders emulated their liege and likely replicated elements of courtly grandeur—featuring regalia they received at court in exchange for their material contributions and fealty—during their own humbler feasts. As such, traditional powerbrokers living in the realm of La Corona participated in the sovereignty of their lord's overlord: "in these core–periphery configurations centered on dominant kingdoms, there are endemic impulses of 'upward nobility' at every level of the intersocietal hierarchy" (Graeber and Sahlins 2017:13).

Commensal Politics in the North

Local leaders were key agents for the cohesion of a political community. The variable presence and visibility of traditional powerbrokers within a court played a central role in perceived distinctions between northern and southern courts. On the one hand, the frequent presence and permanence of a council house or *popol nah* at northern sites suggest a large role for local powerbrokers, but, on the other hand, the sparseness, on the ground, of items construed as largesse distributed by noble courtiers to encourage fealty brings into question the authority of local powerbrokers or the extent to which vertical alliance building was materially expressed in durable items. Commensal politics and diacritical feasting may have taken on a different appearance in the northern lowlands.

In the northern Puuc region, for example, commensal politics is thought to have played a pivotal role due to the constant need to feed large labor parties assembled to construct and maintain the elaborate stone architecture. At the Late Terminal Classic Puuc site of Sayil, for instance, even middle-status domiciles were roofed with corbelled vaults (Carmean 1991). This elaborate architectural tradition began in the Late Preclassic, when "the widespread use of megalithic architecture indicate[s] a high quality of life for households" (Kidder et al. 2019:37). Beyond construction and maintenance tasks, more fundamental activities took place at quarries, lime kilns, and workshops where mosaic facades were fashioned (Carmean, McAnany, and Sabloff 2011; Parker, Bey, and Gallareta Negrón 2019). To be a member of a Puuc polity was to actively participate in building the kingdom, for many in a very muscular way. While labor parties no doubt were responsible for major constructions in the southern lowlands, the scale and elaboration of construction at Classic-period northern sites surpassed those of the south, partly because of readily available hard limestone. Moreover, construction appears to have been continuous. While one can find unfinished construction projects across lowland sites, the Puuc region contains some of the most dramatic examples: the unfinished Southern Palace complex of Sayil (Sabloff and Tourtellot 1991); the finished veneer stones arranged on the ground in front of Kiuic Structure N1000E0865 (Ringle, Gallareta Negrón, and Bey 2020:fig. 6.3), and the unfinished portions of the "Las Pulgas" group of Labna (Gallareta Negrón 2013), to name a few. These are strongly evocative of construction stopped dead in its tracks, illustrating moments when participation in labor parties ceased to hold attraction for the sustaining population.

The central role of feasting required to support these activities should be mirrored in the ceramic repertoire, perhaps with a preponderance and concentration of large cooking pots and serving bowls. In his analysis of pottery from the Yaxche sector of Kiuic, Gallareta Cervera (2016) found a negligible number of polychrome sherds, despite proximity of excavations to the political heart of Kiuic. Rather, the majority of sherds came from polished monochromatic slatewares or unslipped wares, mostly cooking pots. Gallareta Cervera (2016:140–149) found that large basins with a polished Puuc Slate finish and a diameter of 27–40 cm were most common, followed by unslipped jars, and thinner Puuc Fine Slate. The Dzunun Plaza of Kiuic featured a pottery assemblage resulting from large-scale food preparation and consumption. Smaller slipped jars—used to retrieve water from cisterns and to store and serve liquids—were spatially associated with a *chultun* in the Dzunun Plaza. Bey (personal communication 2022) reports the discovery of another large-scale food preparation area behind the unfinished Kuche palace at Kiuic, while Toscano Hernández and Novelo Rincón (2015) document a similar discovery from Kabah. These kinds of assemblages correlate with expectations for patron-role feasting (following Dietler 1996:97) and mirror the kitchen assemblage from La Corona.

The absence of polychrome ceramic production at northern sites has never been adequately explained, particularly considering the strong local tradition of polychrome mural painting and codex production. Conceivably, northern polities actively repudiated the flashy materiality of southern aristocracy that, in our minds, is linked to diacritical feasting. If polychrome ceramics were disdained in the north, then what sorts of diacritical feasting occurred at Classic-period northern sites? One of the most cited ethnohistoric texts relevant to this topic is the sixteenth-century *Relación de las cosas de Yucatán*, in which Bishop Diego de Landa describes in detail diacritical feasting and the items distributed as gifts at the end of the feast, including finely woven *manta*s and "a little stand and vessel, as beautiful as possible" (Tozzer 1941:92). Since Landa was stationed in the northern lowlands, his account reinforces the presence of diacritical feasting at least during the Postclassic period. In projecting back to the Classic period, we also need to consider the role played by organic and perishable luxury items, such as textiles.

Discussion and Concluding Thoughts

Rulership by strangers, as a complex and ubiquitous model of premodern politics, may yield some keys to help us unravel hitherto misunderstood aspects of ancient complex societies. This model is obviously easier to apply to premodern societies with a historical component like the Classic Maya. In fact, it appears that, within Classic Maya courts, stranger queenship and hypogamous practices were common (Ardren, this volume; Canuto and Barrientos 2020; Lamoureux-St-Hilaire 2018:452; Navarro-Farr et al. 2020; Reese-Taylor et al. 2009), even if the actual titles of queens seldom rivaled those of their male counterparts (Martin 2020:75). Significantly, this observation stands in contrast to Graeber and Sahlins's (2017:6) generalized dichotomy between stranger kings as allochthonous sources of powers versus queens as the indigenous roots of sovereignty.

Whether or not exogamy was equally popular among the rank and file of sub-royals, elites, and ordinary people has yet to be determined—though the question could possibly be answered through widespread stable isotope analyses performed on couple burials across different social segments of Classic Maya society. Within all sectors, exogamy likely existed in productive tension with endogamy—the former employed to strengthen alliances among communities, while the latter reinforced community solidarity. Although it is tempting to model ordinary people as principally endogamous and rooted in place—the veritable salt of the earth—oscillations in the size of the sustaining population around Classic-period courts as well as the great dispersion that took place during the Terminal Classic indicate that ordinary people could also call upon expansive social networks (McAnany et al. 2016).

Once stranger rulership has been recognized as a dominant regime-shaping force within a civilization, it is not far-fetched to extend its utility to reconstruct ahistorical components. In the ancient Maya case, we might extrapolate to forces at play during Preclassic times or among sociopolitical segments undocumented by the written record. We have established how some concepts underlying this model—schismogenesis, galactic mimesis, upward nobility, and dual sovereignty—can help us grasp the rise, development, and reproduction of ancient regimes. Conversely, these concepts also help us to understand how things fell apart.

In terms of the stated goals of this volume—to reveal the many faces of rulership across both the northern and southern lowlands—we suggest that the face(s) of rulership often were those of strangers. This desirable quality of strangeness, however, was achieved by different means that could include distant origins, a sojourn, and a return from a distant place—perceived as one of origins—or an in situ transformation of a local ruler into one suffused with radiant qualities and abilities to summon ancestors, patron deities, and critical forces of nature. Interestingly, this strangeness also went hand in hand with familiar roots: two faces of the royal coin that provided strong bases for royals to wield sovereignty both internationally and locally. These multiple faces of rulership were not chaotic but rather developed through understandable practices that have been studied and theorized for systems of kingship across a wide swath of time and space.

Acknowledgments

We thank Walter Witschey for his help in acquiring the site coordinates required to produce the two maps included in this chapter. We are also grateful to Tomás Gallareta Cervera for sharing data and an image from his doctoral research at Kiuic.

REFERENCES CITED

Andrews, George F.
    1995   *Pyramids and Palaces, Monsters and Masks: The Golden Age of Maya Architecture*, vol. 1, *Architecture of the Puuc Region and the Northern Plains*. Labyrinthos, Lancaster, Calif.

Arnauld, M. Charlotte
    2001   La "Casa Grande": Evolución de la arquitectura del poder del clásico al postclásico. In *Reconstruyendo la ciudad maya: El urbanismo en las sociedades antiguas*, edited by Andrés Ciudad Ruiz, María Josefa Iglesias Ponce de León, and María del Carmen Martínez Martínez, pp. 363–401. Sociedad Española de Estudios Mayas, Madrid.

Baron, Joanne
    2016   *Patron Gods and Patron Lords: The Semiotics of Classic Maya Community Cults*. University Press of Colorado, Boulder.

Bartlett, Mary Lee, and Patricia A. McAnany
    2000   "Crafting" Communities: The Materialization of Formative Maya Identities. In *The Archaeology of Communities: A New World Perspective*, edited by Marcello A. Canuto and Jason Yaeger, pp. 102–122. Routledge, New York.

Bateson, Gregory
    1935   Cultural Contact and Schismogenesis. *Man* 35:178–183.

Berlin, Heinrich
    1958   El glifo "emblema" en la inscripciones mayas. *Journal de la Société des Américanistes* 47:111–119.

Bey, George J.
    2004   Kiuic: Continuación del estudio del Grupo Yaxche'. In *Investigaciones arqueológicas en las ruinas de Kiuic y la zona Labna'-Kiuic, distrito de Bolonchén, Yucatán, México: Temporada de campo 2004*, edited by Tomás Gallareta Negrón, George J. Bey, and William M. Ringle, pp. 5-9-5-10. Informe Técnico al Consejo de Arqueología del Instituto Nacional de Antropología e Historia, Merida.

Canuto, Marcello A., and Tomás Barrientos Q.
    2013   The Importance of La Corona. *La Corona Notes* 1(1).
    2016   La Corona: Negotiating a Landscape of Power. In *Approaches to Monumental Landscapes of the Ancient Maya*, edited by Brett A. Houk, Barbara Arroyo, and Terry G. Powis, pp. 171–195. University Press of Florida, Gainesville.

Carmean, Kelli
    1991   Architectural Labor Investment and Social Stratification at Sayil, Yucatan, Mexico. *Ancient Mesoamerica* 2(2):151–165.

Carmean, Kelli, Patricia A. McAnany, and Jeremy A. Sabloff
    2011   People Who Lived in Stone Houses: Local Knowledge and Social Difference in the Classic Maya Puuc Region of Yucatan, Mexico. *Latin American Antiquity* 22(2):143–158.

Chase, Diane Z., and Arlen F. Chase
    1992   An Archaeological Assessment of Mesoamerican Elites. In *Mesoamerican Elites: An Archaeological Assessment*, edited by Diane Z. Chase and Arlen D. Chase, pp. 303–317. University Press of Oklahoma, Norman.

Clark, John E., and Richard D. Hansen
    2001   The Architecture of Early Kingship: Comparative Perspectives on the Origins of the Maya Royal Court. In *Royal Courts of the Ancient Maya*, vol. 2, *Data and Case Studies*, edited by Takeshi Inomata and Stephen D. Houston, pp. 1–45. Westview Press, Boulder, Colo.

Closs, Michel P.
    1985   The Dynastic History of Naranjo: The Middle Period. In *Fifth Palenque Round Table, 1983*, edited by Merle Greene Robertson and Virginia M. Fields, pp. 65–78. Pre-Columbian Art Research Institute, San Francisco.

Cojti Ren, Iyaxel
    2020   The Emergence of the Ancient Maya Kaqchikel Polity as Explained through the Dawn Tradition in the Guatemalan Highlands. *The Mayanist* 2(1):21–37.

Dietler, Michael
　1996　Feasts and Commensal Politics in the Political Economy: Food, Power, and Status in Prehistoric Europe. In *Food and the Status Quest: An Interdisciplinary Perspective*, edited by Polly Wiessner and Wulf Schiefenhövel, pp. 87–125. Berghahn Books, Providence.

Dunning, Nicholas P., and Jeff Karl Kowalski
　1994　Lords of the Hills: Classic Maya Settlement Patterns and Political Iconography in the Puuc Region, Mexico. *Ancient Mesoamerica* 5(1):63–95.

Foias, Antonia E.
　2013　*Ancient Maya Political Dynamics*. University Press of Florida, Gainesville.

Freiwald, Carolyn
　2020　Migration and Mobility in the Eastern Maya Lowlands. In *The Maya World*, edited by Scott R. Hutson and Traci Ardren, pp. 203–222. Routledge, New York.

Gallareta Cervera, Tomás
　2016　The Archaeology of Monumental Architecture and the Social Construction of Authority at the Northern Maya Puuc Site of Kiuic. PhD dissertation, University of North Carolina, Chapel Hill.

Gallareta Negrón, Tomás
　2005　*Proyecto Arqueologico Xocnaceh: Segunda temporada de campo; Informe técnico al consejo de arqueología del Instituto Nacional de Antropología e Historia*. Centro INAH Yucatán, Merida.
　2013　The Social Organization of Labna, a Classic Maya Community in the Puuc Region of Yucatan, Mexico. PhD dissertation, Tulane University, New Orleans.

Graeber, David
　2017　Notes on the Politics of Divine Kingship, or, Elements for an Archaeology of Sovereignty. In *On Kings*, by David Graeber and Marshall Sahlins, pp. 377–464. University of Chicago Press, Chicago.

Graeber, David, and Marshall Sahlins
　2017　*On Kings*. University of Chicago Press, Chicago.

Graham, Ian, and Eric von Euw
　1992　*Corpus of Maya Hieroglyphic Inscriptions*, vol. 4, pt. 3, *Uxmal, Xcalumkin*. Peabody Museum of Archaeology and Ethnology, Harvard University, Cambridge, Mass.

Helms, Mary W.
　1993　*Craft and the Kingly Ideal: Art, Trade, and Power*. University of Texas Press, Austin.

Houston, Stephen D.
　1993　*Hieroglyphs and History at Dos Pilas: Dynastic Politics of the Classic Maya*. University of Texas Press, Austin.

Inomata, Takeshi
　2006　Plazas, Performers, and Spectators: Political Theaters of the Classic Maya. *Current Anthropology* 47(5):805–842.
　2017a　The Emergence of Standardized Spatial Plans in Southern Mesoamerica: Chronology and Interregional Interactions Viewed from Ceibal, Guatemala. *Ancient Mesoamerica* 28(1):329–355.
　2017b　The Isthmian Origins of the E Group and Its Adoption in the Maya Lowlands. In *Maya E Groups: Calendars, Astronomy, and Urbanism in the Early Lowlands*, edited by David A. Freidel, Arlen F. Chase, Anne S. Dowd, and Jerry Murdock, pp. 215–252. University Press of Florida, Gainesville.

Inomata, Takeshi, Daniela Triadan, Verónica A. Vázquez López, Juan C. Fernandez-Diaz, Takayuki Omori, Maria Belén Méndez Bauer, Melina Garcia Hernández, Timothy Beach, Clarissa Cagnato, Kazuo Aoyama, and Hiroo Nasu
　2020　Monumental Architecture at Aguada Fénix and the Rise of Maya Civilization. *Nature* 582:530–533.

Kidder, Barry, Scott R. Hutson, Jacob Welch, and Shannon Plank
　2019　Building Quality of Life and Social Cohesion at Ucanha during the Terminal Preclassic. *The Mayanist* 1(1):37–58.

Lacadena García-Gallo, Alfonso
　2004　The Glyphic Corpus from Ek' Balam, Yucatán, México. Foundation for the Advancement of Mesoamerican Studies, http://www.famsi.org/reports/01057/index.html.

Lamoureux-St-Hilaire, Maxime

2018 Palatial Politics: The Classic Maya Royal Court of La Corona, Guatemala. PhD dissertation, Tulane University, New Orleans.

2020 Talking Feasts: Classic Maya Commensal Politics. In *Her Cup for Sweet Cacao: Food in Ancient Maya Society*, edited by Traci Ardren, pp. 243–273. University Press of Texas, Austin.

2022 The Tapir in the Room: Ancient Maya Storage Architecture. *Journal of Anthropological Archaeology* 68:101467.

Lamoureux-St-Hilaire, Maxime, and Eduardo Bustamante

2016 Investigaciones de desarrollo y funcionalidad en el palacio real de La Corona. *Simposio de Investigaciones Arqueológicas en Guatemala* 29:311–328.

Lamoureux-St-Hilaire, Maxime, Marcello A. Canuto, Tomás Barrientos, and Eduardo Bustamante

2020 Detachment from Power: Sequential Abandonment in the Classic Maya Palace of La Corona, Guatemala. In *Detachment from Place: Beyond an Archaeology of Settlement Abandonment*, edited by Maxime Lamoureux-St-Hilaire and Scott Macrae, pp. 103–119. University Press of Colorado, Louisville.

Lamoureux-St-Hilaire, Maxime, Marcello A. Canuto, E. Christian Wells, Clarissa Cagnato, and Tomás Barrientos Q.

2019 Ancillary Economic Activities in a Classic Maya Regal Palace: A Multi-Proxy Approach. *Geoarchaeology* 34(6):768–782.

Liendo Stuardo, Rodrigo

2003 Access Patterns in Maya Royal Precincts. In *Maya Palaces and Elite Residences: An Interdisciplinary Approach*, edited by Jessica Joyce Christie, pp. 184–203. University of Texas Press, Austin.

Martin, Simon

2020 *Ancient Maya Politics: A Political Anthropology of the Classic Period 150–900 CE*. Cambridge University Press, New York.

Martin, Simon, and Nikolai Grube

1994 Evidence for Macro-Political Organization amongst Classic Maya Lowland States. Mesoweb, https://www.mesoweb.com/articles/Martin-Grube/Macro Politics.html

Masson, Marilyn A., and Timothy S. Hare

2020 The Structures of Everyday Life in the Postclassic Urban Setting of Mayapan. In *The Maya World*, edited by Scott R. Hutson and Traci Ardren, pp. 794–812. Routledge, New York.

Masson, Marilyn A., and Carlos Peraza Lope

2014 *Kukulkan's Realm: Urban Life at Ancient Mayapán*. University Press of Colorado, Boulder.

McAnany, Patricia A.

2001 Cosmology and the Institutionalization of Hierarchy in the Maya Region. In *From Leaders to Rulers*, edited by Jonathan Haas, pp. 125–148. Kluwer Academic, New York.

2019 Fragile Authority in Monumental Time: Political Experimentation in the Classic Maya Lowlands. In *The Evolution of Fragility: Setting the Terms*, edited by Norman Yoffee, pp. 47–59. McDonald Institute Conversations, Cambridge.

McAnany, Patricia A., Jeremy Sabloff, Maxime Lamoureux-St-Hilaire, and Gyles Iannone

2016 Leaving Classic Maya Cities: Agent-Based Modeling and the Dynamics of Diaspora. In *Social Theory in Archaeology and Ancient History: The Present and Future of Counternarratives*, edited by Geoffrey Emberling, pp. 259–290. Cambridge University Press, New York.

Michelet, Dominique

2002 Del proyecto Xculoc al proyecto Xcalumkín: Interrogantes acerca de la organización política en la zona Puuc. *Estudios de cultura maya* 22:75–86.

Morley, Sylvanus G.

1917 The Rise and Fall of the Maya Civilization in the Light of the Monuments and the Native Chronicles. In *Proceedings of the Second Pan American Scientific Congress*, vol. 1, pp. 192–208. U.S. Government Printing Office, Washington, D.C.

Navarro-Farr, Olivia C., Keith Eppich, David A. Freidel, and Griselda Pérez Robles

2020 Ancient Maya Queenship: Generations of Crafting State Politics and Alliance Building from Kaanul to Waka'. In *Approaches to Monumental Landscapes of the Ancient Maya*, edited by Brett A. Houk, Barbara Arroyo, and

Terry G. Powis, pp. 196–217. University Press of Florida, Gainesville.

O'Neil, Megan E.
- 2009 Ancient Maya Sculptures of Tikal, Seen and Unseen. *RES: Anthropology and Aesthetics* 55/56:119–134.

Orenstein, Henry
- 1980 Asymmetrical Reciprocity: A Contribution to the Theory of Political. *Current Anthropology* 21(1):69–91.

Parker, Evan, George J. Bey, and Tomás Gallareta Negrón
- 2019 Organization of Masonry Technology in the Eastern Puuc: Evidence from Escalera al Cielo, Yucatán. *The Mayanist* 1(1):21–36.
- 2020 Centering the Early Maya Village: A Middle Preclassic Cosmogenic Jade Offering from Paso del Macho, Yucatán, México. Paper presented at the 2020 Mesoamerica meetings, University of Texas, Austin.

Price, T. Douglas, James H. Burton, Robert J. Sharer, Jane E. Buikstra, Lori E. Wright, Loa P. Traxler, and Katherine A. Miller
- 2010 Kings and Commoners at Copan: Isotopic Evidence for Origins and Movement in the Classic Maya Period. *Journal of Anthropological Archaeology* 29(1):15–32.

Proskouriakoff, Tatiana
- 1993 *Maya History*. University of Texas Press, Austin.

Reents-Budet, Dorie
- 2000 Feasting among the Classic Maya: Evidence from the Pictorial Ceramics. In *The Maya Vase Book*, vol. 6, edited by Justin Kerr, pp. 1022–1037. Kerr Associates, New York.

Reese-Taylor, Kathryn, Peter Mathews, Julia Guernsey, and Marlene Fritzler
- 2009 Warrior Queens among the Classic Maya. In *Blood and Beauty: Organized Violence in the Art and Archaeology of Mesoamerica and Central America*, edited by Heather Orr and Rex Koontz, pp. 39–72. Cotsen Institute of Archaeology Press, University of California, Los Angeles.

Restall, Matthew
- 1997 *The Maya World: Yucatec Culture and Society, 1550–1850*. Stanford University Press, Stanford.

Ringle, William M.
- 2020 The Northen Maya Tollans. In *The Maya World*, edited by Scott R. Hutson and Traci Ardren, pp. 752–772. Routledge, New York.

Ringle, William M., Tomás Gallareta Negrón, and George J. Bey
- 2020 Stone for My House: The Economic of Stoneworking and Elite Housing in the Puuc Hills of Yucatán. In *The Real Business of Ancient Maya Economies: From Farmers' Fields to Rulers' Realms*, edited by Marilyn A. Masson, David A. Freidel, and Arthur A. Demarest, pp. 98–116. University Press of Florida, Gainesville.
- 2021 Stranger Kings in Northern Yucatan. In *Maya Kingship: Rupture and Transformation from Classic to Postclassic Times*, edited by Tsubaka Okoshi, Arlen F. Chase, Phillippe Nondédéo, and M. Charlotte Arnauld, pp. 249–268. University Press of Florida, Gainesville.

Sabloff, Jeremy A., and Gair Tourtellot
- 1991 *The Ancient Maya City of Sayil: The Mapping of a Puuc Region Center*. Middle American Research Institute, Tulane University, New Orleans.

Sabloff, Paula L. W.
- 2018 How Pre-modern State Rulers Used Marriage to Reduce the Risk of Losing at War: A Comparison of Eight States. *Journal of Archaeological Method and Theory* 25(2):426–452.

Sahlins, Marshall
- 2008 The Stranger-King or, Elementary Forms of the Politics of Life. *Indonesia and the Malay World* 36:177–199.
- 2017a The Cultural Politics of Core–Periphery Relations. In *On Kings*, by David Graeber and Marshall Sahlins, pp. 345–376. University of Chicago Press, Chicago.
- 2017b The Stranger-Kingship of the Mexica. In *On Kings*, by David Graeber and Marshall Sahlins, pp. 223–248. University of Chicago Press, Chicago.

Smith, Adam T.
    2015   *The Political Machine: Assembling Sovereignty in the Bronze Age Caucasus.* Princeton University Press, Princeton.

Somerville, Andrew D., Mikael Fauvelle, and Andrew W. Froehle
    2013   Applying New Approaches to Modeling Diet and Status: Isotopic Evidence for Commoner Resiliency and Elite Variability in the Classic Maya Lowlands. *Journal of Archaeological Science* 40:1539–1553.

Stuart, David
    2000   The Arrival of Strangers: Teotihuacan and Tolan in Classic Maya History. In *Mesoamerica's Classic Heritage*, edited by David Carrasco, Lindsay Jones, and Scott Session, pp. 465–513. University Press of Colorado, Boulder.
    2014   A Possible Sign for Metate. Maya Decipherment, https://mayadecipherment.com/2014/02/04/a-possible-sign-for-metate/.

Stuart, David, Marcello A. Canuto, Tomás Barrientos Q., and Maxime Lamoureux-St-Hilaire
    2015   Preliminary Notes on Two Recently Discovered Inscriptions from La Corona, Guatemala. Maya Decipherment, https://mayadecipherment.com/2015/07/17/preliminary-notes-on-two-recently-discovered-inscriptions-from-la-corona-guatemala/.

Stuart, David, Peter Mathews, Marcello A. Canuto, Tomás Barrientos Q., Stanley Guenter, and Joanne Baron
    2014   Un esquema de la historia y epigrafía de La Corona. *Simposio de Investigaciones Arqueológicas en Guatemala* 27:435–448.

Sugiyama, Nawa, William L. Fash, Barbara W. Fash, and Saburo Sugiyama
    2020   The Maya at Teotihuacan? New Insights into Teotihuacan–Maya Interaction from the Plaza of the Columns Complex. In *Teotihuacan: The World Beyond the City*, edited by Kenneth G. Hirth, David M. Carballo, and Barbara Arroyo, pp. 139–171. Dumbarton Oaks Research Library and Collection, Washington, D.C.

Szymański, Jan
    2014   Between Death and Divinity: Rethinking the Significance of Triadic Groups in Ancient Maya Culture. *Estudios de cultura maya* 44:119–166.

Thompson, J. Eric S.
    1954   *The Rise and Fall of Maya Civilization.* University of Oklahoma Press, Norman.

Tokovinine, Alexandre
    2013   *Place and Identity in Classic Maya Narratives.* Dumbarton Oaks Research Library and Collection, Washington, D.C.

Toscano Hernández, Lourdes, and Gustavo Novelo Rincón
    2015   La Cocina Real de Kabah, Yucatán. Paper presented at the 80th Annual Meeting of the Society for American Archaeology, San Francisco.

Tozzer, Alfred M. (translator)
    1941   *Landa's* Relacion de las cosas de Yucatán. Peabody Museum of American Archaeology and Ethnology, Harvard University, Cambridge, Mass.

Tsukamoto, Kenichiro
    2014   Multiple Identities on the Plazas: The Classic Maya Center of El Palmar, Mexico. In *Mesoamerican Plazas: Arenas of Community and Power*, edited by Kenichiro Tsukamoto and Takeshi Inomata, pp. 50–69. University of Arizona Press, Tucson.

Vargas de la Peña, Leticia, Alejandra Alonso Olivera, Victor R. Castillo Borges, and Alfonso Lacadena García-Gallo
    2020   Ek' Balam: A Maya City in the Urban Landscape of Yucatan. In *The Maya World*, edited by Scott R. Hutson and Traci Ardren, pp. 364–383. Routledge, New York.

Wright, Henry T.
    2006   Early States as Political Experiment. *Journal of Anthropological Research* 62(3):302–319.

Wright, Lori E., Juan Antonio Valdéz, James A. Burton, T. Douglas Price, and Henry P. Schwarcz
    2010   The Children of Kaminaljuyu: Isotopic Insight into Diet and Long-Distance Interaction in Mesoamerica. *Journal of Anthropological Archaeology* 29(2):155–178.

Zender, Marc
    2019   The Classic Mayan Causative. *The PARI Journal* 20(2):28–40.

Strange and Familiar Queens at Maya Royal Courts

TRACI ARDREN

Scholars have often found it challenging to define the unique power of a queen (Stafford 1997, 1998). One solution is to understand a queen as an honorary man, especially when she holds what scholars commonly consider to be masculine titles. This solution suggests that power is masculine by definition, an assumption that rarely survives careful analysis in pre-Hispanic cultures of the New World. For the Maya of the ancient or Classic period (200–900 CE), the solution has often been to overlook the sizable evidence for the institution of queenship, instead focusing on the biographical details of select queens and their progeny. While individual royal women or noblewomen have long been identified through epigraphic decipherment or tomb excavations, their institutional role in the Maya monarchy is generally poorly understood.

This study presents an exploration of the nature of Indigenous Maya elite female power during the Classic period and considers how it is implicated in the office of formal queenship, exploring the ambiguities and paradoxes that emerge when the capacities of particular historical women are compared to what we know about Classic Maya power structures. Gender constructions were embedded in other social hierarchies during the Classic period (Joyce 2008), and precisely because gender conceptions were not stable or static over time, the rights and obligations of royal women were manipulated by women themselves, and by the centripetal forces of royal dynasties, to maintain and monopolize power. Maya queens of the Classic period were both secular authorities responsible for the protection of their polity and palace and divine authorities responsible for the recreation of the fertile world (see Tokovinine, Estrada Belli, and Fialko, this volume). Their experiences were varied at different urban centers, but the idealized representations they left behind allow us to grasp the profound role they played in elite culture and politics. Some queens held formal titles and were invested via political ritual, while other queens were known as such through their relationships to power-holding men. This diversity is to be expected in the study of queenship and is fundamentally shaped by the incomplete nature of the data available to us. This study asks how Indigenous Maya conceptualizations of gendered power contributed to the mechanisms of the state. Queens exercised power within structural power systems: How were the systems constituted? How did foreign or stranger queens maximize their unusual positionality within the formal roles available in the institution of Maya queenship? How did state-sponsored art and mythology control elite female sexuality to ensure succession? Why were queens essential to Maya rulership?

This chapter situates Maya queens within a framework informed by recent scholarship on queenship worldwide and the role of queens within the institution of monarchy. A fundamental precept of this scholarship is that royal women were part of the monarchy, not merely accessories. Female patronage was essential to sustaining a dynasty, as was the loyalty royal women generated through rituals and events at the heart of Classic Maya culture (Dunn and Carney 2018:2). Women's roles were shaped by the nature of specific monarchic institutions, which for the Classic Maya included competing dynastic lineages with supernatural origins that were governed by patriarchal descent. As fundamental features of how structures of authority were constituted, these characteristics of Maya monarchy both constrained the lives of royal women and allowed them room to function as essential actors in the perpetuation of dynastic or familial success. We have three major bodies of data from which to reconstruct the lives of ancient Maya queens and in which to see the patterns that emerge based on the institutional roles they played: hieroglyphic inscriptions, which emphasize kin relations and spiritual actions; tomb furniture and treatments, which emphasize the idealized productive activities of Maya queens; and elite art, which emphasizes ritual activities essential to the reproduction of the state.

Epigraphic data from the Classic period suggest that three basic categories of royal Maya women can be subsumed by the word "queen," which has a confounding number of meanings in modern English. Many royal women embodied more than one of these roles, and as such they had access to multiple avenues of power and influence. The most common and variable role included women who were mothers or wives of Maya rulers. A less common but more authoritative role included women who co-ruled with men, sometimes as regents for young sons but also as co-rulers with their husbands. Many of these women carried the royal *ajaw* (ruler) title during their lifetimes. The final role consisted of those queens who carried the *ajaw* title and ruled independently as queen. Seventeen Maya queens from the fourth through the eighth centuries across the southern lowlands are known to have held the supreme *kaloomte'* title during the Classic period, nearly 14 percent of all individuals known to carry this supreme title of independent authoritarian rule (Martin 2020:79) (Table 6.1). This is a strong demonstration that at the height of the Classic period certain royal women from across the lowlands were understood to embody the ultimate demonstration of diplomatic and political power. It is important to note that there is no Maya word for "queen" or "king." Power and authority were conveyed through titles, and the same titles were used by both male and female royals, although marked by a female prefix for women. But as Liz James writes in her exploration of Byzantian medieval queens, "titles are not the icing on the cake, but the essence of government" (James 1997:128). There was a unified system of title across the Maya Lowlands, and while titles indicate status rather than political office, they are a clear indication of the Indigenous system of hierarchical access to power and rank.

Any study of Maya queens and Indigenous female authority structures is situated within the ongoing evolution of Maya conceptualizations of gender as an axis of power. Maya queenship remains an evolving and salient cultural phenomenon at pageants held across Guatemala, where young women are elected as cultural ambassadors (Rasch 2020; Schackt 2005) (Figure 6.1). This study responds to a call by Indigenous feminists to address the long-term effects of colonialism by paying closer attention to the ways in which Indigenous women of the past shared power with men and the heterogeneous lives they lived (Cojti Ren 2006; Mihesuah 2003; Smith 1999; Speed 2019). As Devon Mihesuah

table 6.1

List of seventeen Maya queens known to carry the *kaloomte'* title. Table prepared by Simon Martin.

MONUMENT	PREFIXED BY	SPELLING	LONG COUNT	DATE CE	INDIVIDUAL
Calakmul Stela 51 (B#)		IX-KAL2-TE'2	9.15.0.0.0	731	1
Calakmul Stela 54 (B15)		*IX-KAL2-*TE'2	9.15.0.0.0	731	1?
Calakmul Stela 55 (D7)		IX-KAL2-TE'2	9.15.0.0.0	731	1?
Coba Spiral (19)		IX-KAL1[TE'1]-ma	?	?	2
Coba Stela 4 (I10)		KAL1[TE']-*ma	9.11.0.0.0	652	3
Coba Stela 1 (G20)		KAL1[TE']-ma	9.12.10.5.12	683	3
Dos Caobas Stela 1 (F1)	6-K'atun	IX[KAL2]-TE'2	9.15.0.0.0?		4
Dos Caobas Stela 1 (I2a)	6-K'atun	IX[KAL2]-TE'2	9.15.0.0.0?		4
Edzna Drum Altar	Ix- Name	KAL1[TE'1]-ma	c.9.11.0.0.0	652	5
El Perú Stela 34 (J?3)		IX[KAL2]-TE'2	9.13.0.0.0†	692	6
K4463 [Chochola]		IX KAL2-TE'2	?	?	7
K5976 [Xultun] (#)		IX KAL2-TE'2	?	?	8
La Corona (Panel 6)		IX[KAL2]-TE'2	9.15.0.0.0	731	9
La Corona Altar 4 (#)		IX[KAL2]-TE'	9.18.0.0.0	791+	10
Naranjo Stela 18 (D5)	West	KAL1[TE'1]-ma	9.14.10.0.0 LSS†	721	11
Naranjo Stela 24 (D10)	West	KAL1[TE'1]-ma	9.13.10.0.0*	702	12
Tikal Stela 12 (C5)		IX-KAL1[TE'1]-ma	9.4.13.0.0	527	13
Yaxchilan H.S.3 I (N1)	6-K'atun	IX-KAL2-TE'2	d. 9.13.13.12.5	705	14
Yaxchilan H.S.3 V (M2)		IX[KAL2]-TE'2	d. 9.13.13.12.5	705	14
Yaxchilan Lintel 23 (N8a)	Ix-West	KAL2-TE'2	9.14.14.13.17	726	15
Yaxchilan Lintel 24 (G4)		IX-KAL2-TE'2	9.13.17.15.12	709	15
Yaxchilan Lintel 25 (T1)		IX-KAL2-TE'2	9.14.11.15.1	723	15
Yaxchilan Lintel 27 (D1b)	6-K'atun	IX[KAL2]-TE'2	d. 9.13.13.12.5	705	14
Yaxchilan Lintel 32 (K3)		IX[KAL2]-TE'2	9.13.17.15.13	709	16
Yaxchilan Lintel 38 (C4-D4)	East-	KAL2-TE'2	9.16.12.5.14	763	17
Yaxchilan Lintel 53 (F2-G2)	East-	KAL2-TE'2	9.13.5.12.13	697	16
Yaxchilan Stela 10 (pC2)	East-	KAL2-TE'2	9.16.10.0.0	761	16

argues, the past impacts the present, and "knowing tribal traditions, including women's place in them, can help modern Natives cope with a complex—and impersonal—world by offering foundations to form their identities and to create strategies for dealing with adversity" (Mihesuah 2003:xv). Research on Native women that is nuanced and does not homogenize Indigenous cultures into a single stereotype is consistent with feminist approaches to social science in which "the social and political nature of the archaeological enterprise is acknowledged" and engagement with all forms of evidence has been

the institution of Maya queenship from our popular and scholarly interpretations of the Maya past, which damages not only Native history but also the scholarly understanding of Maya structural expressions of power. Native scholars such as Shannon Speed (2019:16) point out how the vulnerability of Native women today is tied directly to a structural condition imposed upon them in multiple and intersecting ways through structures of settler capitalist power, one of which is the production of historical narratives.

This study will seek out the evidence for women's agency and resistance, as well as attempt to highlight the power that Classic Maya queens exercised as "active manipulators rather than passive recipients" (Marcus 2020:59; Speed 2019) whenever possible. This is not to turn away from any available data or to highlight only positive anecdotes—just the opposite. By working carefully to see Indigenous principles at work, and by taking the reception of our research by Native peoples seriously, we can hope to remove our own embedded frameworks of masculinist and capitalist power structures from our reconstructions of the past and to reveal other ways of construing authority. As a White woman writing about Native culture, I take the advice of Mihesuah seriously—my writing not only must educate non-Natives about Native culture but also must be inspiring and educational to Natives (Mihesuah 2005:8).

figure 6.1

Qpoj Ajpetz'al 2018–2019 and Princesa Chnab'jul 2019–2021, Leidy Marily López Domingo from San Rafael Pétzal, Huehuetenango. Photograph by Julia Zabrodzka.

Patrilineality and Maya Queenship

In his study of the role of stranger kings within Taino history, William Keegan argued that archaeologists often overlook the role of kinship in our studies of the past, but that relations regulating social interactions, such as kinship systems, are key to understanding human culture (Keegan 2007:93). And while Sahlins (1985) argued that the transition to kingship implies a rejection of kinship, in the case of the Classic Maya, elites created and maintained their structural advantages by embodying a parallel system of divine kinship that simultaneously distanced them from the majority of the population and justified their rule through reference to kin relations

shown to yield a more accurate depiction of the past (Conkey 2005:22; see also Cojti Ren 2006; Mihesuah 1998; Smith 1999; Wylie 1997). Native women have been erased from the dominant historical narratives created by settler-colonial society, and their voices are still muted today, as an epidemic of violence against Native women rages through the New World (Speed 2019; Velasquez Nimatuj 2003). In our own way, until very recently Mayanists have erased

with distant (and often supernatural) ancestors (see Lamoureux-St-Hilaire and McAnany, this volume). As Keegan states, "even if the king's kinship is distinct from the kinship of others, it is still kinship" (Keegan 2007:94). Kin relations are often taught and reinforced through mythology, and as a form of social reproduction, mythology and beliefs coordinate disparate goals and structure social interactions. We will return to the role of Classic Maya mythology in constituting the institution of queenship, but first it is essential to understand how royal kinship systems both constrained women and provided them with ample opportunities to exercise power.

Although still a topic of some debate, most scholars accept that the Classic Maya practiced a system of patrilineal descent reckoning (Ensor 2013; Haviland 1970; Hopkins 1988; Josserand 2002; Martin 2020). In a recent synthesis and critique of previous research on Classic Maya kinship, Bradley Ensor notes that the use of the direct-historical approach to understand Classic kinship systems has resulted in a half decade of confusion and debate. Kinships systems are not static, and the expectation that, despite the cataclysmic impacts of colonialism, the kinship system of the Maya world would not have evolved or varied by region is unreasonable (Ensor 2013:3). And while Ensor does not reject completely the use of ethnohistoric or modern records, he does offer that archaeologists working in other parts of the world have had success modeling ancient kinship systems for larger explanatory purposes such as the role of kinship in socioeconomic and governance systems (Ensor 2013:3). If we view kinship as "forming concrete social relations that structure people's daily lives, which are indeed reflected in material remains," then kinship is very important to a study of rulership (Ensor 2013:6). To understand the structural avenues of power that Maya queens utilized, some of the specific characteristics of patrilineal succession are crucial.

Descent groups have important social qualities —they manage resources, support their members, share ceremonial responsibilities, etc. Highly relevant to archaeologists is the fundamental component of kinship, that without material functions, descent would cease to be relevant—in other words, your lineage provides many of the resources on which you rely (Ensor 2013:32). Likewise, kinship terminology structures most of the social interactions one has, including the interpersonal relationships, marriage opportunities, and gender and age cohort experiences. These interactions are the building blocks of social identities, how difference is understood, and group membership perpetuated. Patrilineal descent groups around the world and throughout history emphasize exogamy, or marriage outside the group/patrilineage. This is largely the result of competition between related male siblings for the resources available to their generation. It may also be why men were so heavily invested in negotiating marriage alliances for their royal daughters within the Classic Maya world—by leaving their homes, these women were no longer a draw on the material resources of the patriline, which were controlled by its male members and their unmarried sisters. Although such women would always remain a member of her father's patriline, when transferred from their home of origin to the home of their husband's patriline, they no longer could expect daily access to patriline material resources and, instead, had to negotiate for their needs within their new household of unrelated men and women (Figure 6.2). Eleanor Harrison-Buck (2021) explores the possibilities of bride wealth in Classic Maya marriage alliances, which may have mitigated the initial experience of moving from one royal household to another but would not have provided a permanent and secure resource base for royal brides. These structural patterns kept the power and influence of royal men localized and stable, while dispersing that of royal women. As David Wengrow states in his chapter on the origins of sovereign power, social domination operates at the household level in order to facilitate its operations at the societal level.

Resource management is also impacted by postmarital residence strategies, which dictate how adults are retained or passed to other households. While there is also debate about whether all Maya people were patrilocal in the Classic period, it is clear from the written record that many elites practiced patrilocality during the Classic period (Martin 2020:176). This system has implications for

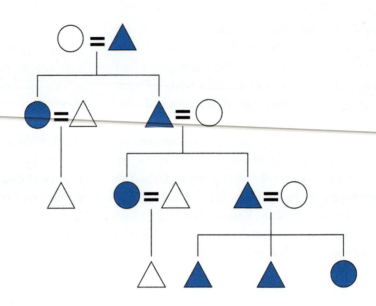

figure 6.2
Patrilineal descent group in which all blue shapes belong to the same patriline. Illustration by Traci Ardren.

the nature of household membership, access to resources, strategies for recruitment, residential identity, and postmarital mobility (Ensor 2013:31). For example, adult married women—as the only members of a patrilocal household who do not belong to the kin group where they reside—experience their household membership as contingent rather than innate, a tie that could be easily severed. This has a strongly gendered implication—men's relationships and interpersonal networks are structured and more stable throughout their lives, while women's relationships are destablized by postmarital patrilocal relocation. Kinship studies have long noted that there is an important distinction between residing in a household and belonging to a household. For example, a stranger queen who moved from one Classic Maya polity to another for marriage resided in the household of her husband but belonged to the lineage and spiritual resource group of her father—being physically separated did not necessarily mean forfeiting a social membership in her patrilineage, especially in matters of inheritance of spiritual knowledge and ancestral contacts. In fact, it is likely that marriage alliances were predicated on the ability of a royal woman to maintain her membership in her birth patriline and her relationships with her birth kin. In the hieroglyphic record, marriage alliances of high-status women to lower-status men are common; in these cases, the woman's birth patriline plays a crucial role in her reception at her new home. Likewise, when we see the marriage of a royal woman from a subjugated polity to her overlord, the woman functions as an object for the ongoing humiliation of her patriline. Ritual knowledge and ceremonial skills acquired from ancestors as a member of a patriline were clearly needed by women who left their homes, as we commonly see them commemorated in their new homes for their successful period ending rites or deity conjuration. And crucially, queens represented the promise that such ancestors, patron gods (see Baron, this volume), ritual knowledge, and skills would be passed to her husband's child.

Hereditary rule creates local factions, which are increasingly dangerous in polities with multiple royal sons. The texts are clear that primogeniture was not followed strictly, and Simon Martin argues that a capable or charismatic son may have been more likely to be seated as king than the firstborn (Martin 2020:104). A queen imported from another polity would not have ties to any local factions, thus making her a powerful tool to sidestep internal dynastic rivalry, rather than to enflame it. Because primogeniture was only a loose guideline, studies of queens in other cultures would suggest that a mother's advocacy for her son, especially in those polities with polygamous kings, may have been decisive. Even in polygamous kingdoms, such as Yaxchilan, the child of the senior wife was not always the one named to the throne. Martin (2020) has argued that polygyny provided greater vertical succession options—and it certainly did. It also could increase dynastic struggle by pitting wives against one another, or by allowing a dynasty to strengthen due to a broader network of interwoven kin relations among the various polities connected through marriage. We see these potentials in the history of Bird Jaguar IV at Yaxchilan, who took four wives, one a Snake Kingdom princess, two from Motul de San José, and one from Zapote Bobal (Martin 2020:192). Polygyny and alliance building was part of the court culture at Yaxchilan, and, in addition to celebrating his royal wives, Bird Jaguar IV used monumental art to celebrate his positive relationships with nobles and military captains. Bird Jaguar IV had grown up in a court with multiple queens, and his mother was likely a powerful woman from the Kaanul dynasty, who navigated the position of third wife of the king. The first wife, Queen K'ab'al Xook, was highly celebrated and undoubtedly a powerful influence in Bird Jaguar's life, even though (or perhaps especially because) she does not seem to have had any children of her own (cf. Josserand 2007).

Polygyny likely provided greater protection for those royal women who could not or did not wish to reproduce, enmeshed as they were within a royal court where their sister-wives would likely bear heirs. In cities with a history of polygynous marriage, such as Yaxchilan, we see the material record reflect aspects of female royal power other than motherhood and dynastic succession. These may have been some of the very few contexts where royal women were able to dedicate their lives to politics, ritual, or art without fear of banishment for their lack of offspring. It is important to consider the practice of polygyny as structurally advantageous to a patrilineal descent system that vested power in lineal continuity. It is also worth stating that this particular form of polygyny, in which marriage is highly politicized and strategic rather than based on modern notions of love or attraction, tells us nothing about the sexual lives of ancient Maya royals. It is simply one strategic political choice among many. It is quite likely some Maya kings had multiple sexual partners, given that they produced multiple offspring, but we are simply not able to conclude from the type of state-sponsored evidence in hand that royal women did not also take multiple sexual partners, or that Classic Maya cultural values prohibited less official sexual partnerships of all kinds. We will see that the control of female sexuality was a serious concern within Maya mythology of the Classic period, but this must be framed within the state-sponsored principles of a strict patrilineal succession model. Mythology of the Classic period, as depicted on painted vases and pots as well as in hieroglyphic texts, conveys state values and thus the importance of patrilineal succession as a basis for the orderly transfer of power. State rules of descent must be understood to be distinct from actual patterns of behavior, a fact well established in the global history of monarchy.

For this reason, it is important to refrain from using words that have a strong culturally specific character to describe patterns seen in other societies. The use of words such as "concubine" or "harem" to describe the multiple official wives or women of a Maya court fundamentally misconstrues the nature of those women's lives. Each of the royal women who appear on a monument, or an elite painted vase, had by dint of her appearance on such a rarified medium, an official role within Maya court culture. Each wife brought political connections and the power of her ancestral lineage to a marriage, and such arrangements had little to do with desire. In those cultures where actual harems and concubines originated, they were governed by strict rules because they were a tool of a patriline—a display of the power of the patriline, a display of male potency (not male pleasure), and a display of sex as a duty (not a choice) (Haboush 1988; Walthall 2008:14). Mayanists have drifted into projecting patriarchal fantasies onto the images of royal women depicted in Maya art, and into using borrowed language that distorts Indigenous evidence (Houston 2014; Miller 2018). Each wife of a polygynous Maya king represented an entire family or patriline that desperately sought a blood relationship with the king. Her retainers and other court women likewise held positions of privilege, even if they are depicted serving male elites.

These complex interdependencies deserve careful and respectful analysis.

Classic Maya Mythology and Queenship

Now that the structural relations of a patrilineal kinship system, coupled with patrilocal residence and polygynous marriage, have been explained, it is time to turn to the role of Classic Maya mythology, as a form of social reproduction that structured many of the options available to Maya queens and underscored their claims to authority. One basis for understanding the composition of Maya monarchy is the concept of gender complementarity, which not only structured the depictions of male and female interactions within ancient Maya culture but also influenced how dynastic power was constructed and shared. Complementarity or mutuality has been well established in other ancient cultures of Mesoamerica (Joyce 1993, 2000a; Kellogg 2005; Monaghan 2001; Nash 1997). A profound reliance upon the concept of complementary male and female productive roles is a consistent characteristic of ancient, historic, and modern Maya culture (Mathews 1985; Rosado Rosado 2001; Vogt 1969). As Joyce has noted for the Classic Maya, "the figures depicted in monuments offer a clear image of heterosexual adult gender performance that was simultaneously a precedent for the enactment of noble status and public formality" (Joyce 2008:99).

This principle, which enlarges the social body of a single ruler into an ideal of completion, is communicated via the paired images of king and queens on twin stelae at sites such as Calakmul, Yaxchilan, and Coba, as well as on many elite ceramic vases (Figure 6.3). The equivalency of wealth seen in the royal burials of both male and female elites is a further demonstration of this principle, as are royal parentage statements that conventionally mention both maternal and paternal lineages. Within the corpus of elite material culture available today, there is a relatively consistent communication of this principle. Complementarity—the concept that men and women mutually complete each other in order to achieve a greater whole that surpasses the value of each individually—is distinct from the ancient Mesoamerican concept of gender parallelism, where parallel lines of authority and institutional leadership are held by men and women (Kellogg 2005; Monaghan 2001:287; Silverblatt 1987). Complementarity is grounded in the productive activities of the natural world, and the obvious biological ramifications of male and female artistic pairings has fooled scholars into both overemphasizing the function of Maya queens as generators of heirs and underemphasizing the ideological role of queens in the fundamental reproduction of elite political and cosmological order.

As Kellogg and others have pointed out, the concept of complementarity can mask our understanding of inequality and subordination if not deployed carefully (Kellogg 2005:7; Klein 1994). For example, within elite Aztec society there was a clear ideology of gender parallelism—women and men had complementary tasks and religious obligations and were both very significant to bilateral lineage claims, yet elite women did not share social equality with men (Kellogg 2005; Klein 2001). Ideological complementarity does not preclude gender hierarchy. While mutuality has undergone tremendous challenges and modifications to its expression, both during the colonial period, when Spanish administration instituted female subjugation (Santana Rivas 2001), and within recent times, when out-migration changed the domestic gender dynamic toward female self-reliance (Weinstein Bever 2002), an ideology of gender complementarity exists in much of the modern Maya world alongside a hierarchical structure that privileges men. As with the Aztec, elite Maya women did not share social equality with men during the Classic period—the majority of sovereigns and administrators were male and Classic Maya art as a whole is dominated by a male-male gaze toward a youthful male body (Ardren 2020; Houston 2018; Joyce 2000b). Bioarchaeological studies reveal that while nutritional disparities along gender lines were more muted for elites than for commoners, elite women suffered a greater incidence of malnutrition in many regions of the Maya Lowlands (Ardren 2002; Storey 2008). Based on the impact of restricted literacy and our surviving corpus of royal art, elite

figure 6.3
Rollout photograph (K0554) of queens and kings in a paired ritual performance. Justin Kerr Maya archive, Dumbarton Oaks, Trustees for Harvard University, Washington, D.C.

male privilege was perhaps more pronounced and certainly is better documented in the Maya area than in the rest of pre-Hispanic Mesoamerica, and despite the presence of principles of gender complementarity in the expression of elite power, many aspects of daily life were characterized by male dominance. Complementarity also does not preclude the existence of nonbinary gender roles and expectations, which are hinted at in certain cave art and intoxication scenes, both of which depict male homosocial events with a fluidity of bodily contact (Ardren 2020:158). Clowns, jesters, dwarves, and other performers are often depicted in a manner that de-emphasizes gender as an identifying characteristic, in favor of other legitimizing scripts and cues.

In other words, complementarity, or what Susan Kellogg has called mutuality, is most visible in the cosmological or religious life of the ancient cultures of Mesoamerica (Kellogg 2005). Aztec, Mixtec, and Maya origin deities had features of both genders; in Native literature, the supreme creator deity was often portrayed as a married couple taking both male and female forms in order to cope with the enormity of the responsibility to create and maintain equilibrium in the world and humanity (Klein 2001; McCafferty and McCafferty 2009; Vail and Stone 2002). Classic Maya goddesses remain poorly defined, with recent scholarship leaning toward a pantheon of lunar and earth deities that take female form (Chinchilla Mazariegos 2017; Knowlton 2015; Taube 1994; Vail and Stone 2002).

An example of ideological complementarity in elite Maya cosmology is the persistent theme of two female deities who dress and care for the Maize Deity, or Juun Ixim ("One Maize"), during rebirth. This mythological scene is well attested in the artistic corpus from murals, ceramic vessels, and mortuary iconography. The prominence of this myth in the artwork of the San Bartolo murals has underscored the tremendous significance of the Dressing of the Maize Deity scene as the basis for elite supernatural power and its linkages to social order from the earliest emergence of royal culture (Saturno, Taube, and Stuart 2005) (Figure 6.4). There seems to be a very clear iconographic parallel between these female attendants dressing and feeding the reborn Maize Deity, attending to his birth, and providing sustenance, and the canon of images of Maya queens in service to their male relatives and the state. In palace scenes, queens are often depicted holding bowls of food or drink, presenting sacred bundles of cloth and ritual implements, and assisting at the bloodletting or

figure 6.4
Dressing of the Maize Deity scene, San Bartolo. Drawing by Heather Hurst.

figure 6.5
Rollout photograph (K956) of royal women assisting men with entheogenic rites. Justin Kerr Maya archive, Dumbarton Oaks, Trustees for Harvard University, Washington, D.C.

entheogenic enema rites of their male kin (Figure 6.5). These same themes of cultural reproduction through the domestic arts of raw to cooked are illustrated in the Dressing of the Maize Deity scene. Cosmological themes of parentage, creation, fecundity, and the power of birth are accentuated in the portraiture of Maya queens, whether they are shown as mothers of a king, as embodiments of the productive power of their dynastic houses, or as conjurers who summon spirits to control the portals through which such beings communicate with humans.

Oswaldo Chinchilla Mazariegos identifies the women who assist the Maize Deity as participants in an episode that relates the Maize Deity's fall into sexual temptation as the source of his death and ultimate rebirth (Chinchilla Mazariegos 2017:198). The Maize Deity is an active sexual being, who usually epitomizes the ideals of Classic Maya beauty and youth. In Chinchilla Mazariegos's reading, the Maize Deity embodies the magnetism of youthful sexuality, with all its fertile potential for bringing rain, ensuring crops, and perpetuating life. Yet sexuality is also a source of danger and potential pollution, a force that must be controlled in order to avoid overindulgence and ruin. Mesoamerican mythology is full of encounters with overly sexed women who lure men into danger and death (Vail 2019). While it is easy to see such myths as providing a script for the strict control of female sexual behavior (Klein 1994), such stories also reveal an acknowledgment of the profound and formidable power of female sexuality, as a force of both creation and destruction. The young women who dress and care for the Maize Deity (and ultimately lead him to death) are so beautiful as to be dangerous, and they simultaneously represent the danger of sexual attraction and its absolute necessity. As in other Mesoamerican traditions, this mythology serves to reinforce the state's control over not only women but also appropriate reproduction.

An additional source of spiritual authority for Maya queens came from claiming a metaphorical association with the Maize Deity and all the fertile potential this figure represents. Ideological complementarity made this association possible. In Maya art, the Maize Deity can take a gender ambiguous or intersexed form, with a costume that often

figure 6.6

Queen in Maize Deity costume, Xupa, Chiapas. © Fine Arts Museums of San Francisco. Photograph by Joseph McDonald.

figure 6.7
Rollout photograph (K4022) of God S with maiden. Justin Kerr Maya archive, Dumbarton Oaks, Trustees for Harvard University, Washington, D.C.

incorporates the same jade net skirt and *Spondylus* bivalve girdle worn by many Maya queens in official portraits (Figure 6.6). The *Spondylus* shell, in particular, has been noted as an overt symbol of feminine genitalia and reproductive potential (Miller and Martin 2004); Christina Halperin explains how royal costume was essential to the making of a queen later in this volume. To legitimate their power and privilege, royal women and men wore this costume while performing a ritualized version of the life cycle of the maize plant, a dual-sexed cultigen, who dies and is reborn each planting cycle (Taube 1985). Other scholars have elaborated upon the intersexed but often masculinized nature of the Maize Deity, but it is clear that while Maya kings very frequently personified the Maize Deity for purposes of royal legitimization, certain powerful and ambitious queens also embodied the Maize Deity role for the purposes of status enhancement and solidification of prestige (Bassie-Sweet 2002; Chinchilla Mazariegos 2017; Guenter and Freidel 2005; Joyce 2000a; Looper 2002; Taube 1985). The gender ambiguity of the Maize Deity, as a figure that surpassed the expectations of a single gender, lent itself to appropriation by ambitious queens seeking a means to expand upon their usual roles, or those who claimed to have access to supernatural levels of reproductive capability, such as giving birth to deities or protective spirits. A script for royal privilege based on the mythology of an intersexed or nonbinary deity is completely consistent with the principle of complementarity. Many Mesoamerican deities, especially those concerned with the powers of creation, blurred conventional gender boundaries in order to invert and thereby validate established gender norms (Klein 2001; Stone 2011).

The overt sexual power or potential of royal women is also present in mythological scenes of young and beautiful royal women interacting with various avatars of the Sun God, shown primarily on Classic-period ceramic vases (Figure 6.7). In this mythological cycle, a carefully guarded young woman is seduced by a roguish male hero in disguise, and their dalliance results in her impregnation. Perhaps best known in the story of Xquic, the mother of the Hero Twins in the Popul Vuh, Chinchilla Mazariegos suggests the same theme of fear/acknowledgment of female fertile potential is depicted on many Classic vases. Chinchilla Mazariegos also suggests that there are strong parallels between Xquic and Xochiquetzal, as noted first by eighteenth-century priest Francisco Ximenez, and explains that they are both sexually alluring young goddesses who trespassed prohibitions involving movement from home and magical trees—they both mothered important gods, and their "plight gave way to major cosmological events" (Chinchilla Mazariegos 2017:84). This story also touches on the themes of female sexuality and its powers of creation, by acknowledging a woman's ability to step outside the tightly prescribed rules of procreation and seize control of generational succession away from the state. In Classic iconography, Chinchilla Mazariegos identifies this young woman as the Moon Goddess, who is often depicted with an older male deity, perhaps her father or a creator deity

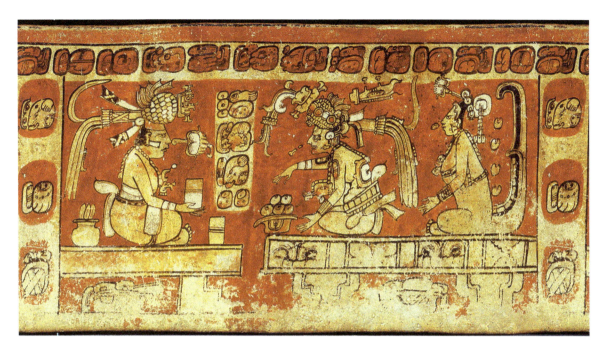

figure 6.8
Rollout photograph (K504) of God S with a long beak poking through a flower. Justin Kerr Maya archive, Dumbarton Oaks, Trustees for Harvard University, Washington, D.C.

like Itzamnaaj (Chinchilla Mazariegos 2017:87). On one Classic-period vase (K504), a young male figure on the left side of the scene is shown with a long beak poking through a flower—perhaps a mask meant to give him the appearance of a hummingbird, a common avatar of the Sun God (Figure 6.8). Hilda Delgado suggests that the common figurines that depict elite Maya women weaving with a bird perched on their loom are an iteration of this same theme, this time with the suitor disguised as a bird, and weaving is a well-known trope for sexual intercourse within Maya culture (Sullivan 1982; Vail 2019). A common scene that underscores the sexual nature of the relationship between bird and young woman often includes the bird in the act of biting or making some sort of contact with the breast of the young woman. Andrea Stone has observed that in the few instances in which a female breast of a young woman is depicted in Classic art, the exposed breast acted as an index of female power through "an associative chain that involved practices . . . or other domestic duties for women . . . as well as properties inherent to the body" (Stone 2011:180).

The suitor may also take the form of a supernatural insect, most commonly a mosquito. The infrequent appearance of an unclothed body in Classic Maya art emphasizes the importance of this iconography to our understanding of Classic values. The potency of the unclothed female body as a marker of female sexuality was used to indicate a danger to the order of the universe, a force so profound that it threatened to destabilize official and sanctioned reproduction, and thus patrilineal succession and dynastic claims to authority.

Domesticated female sexuality, harnessed in service to the patriline and thus to the controlled reproduction of the state, is also the topic of many Classic-period portraits of royal women, according to a new analysis by Chinchilla Mazariegos that builds on ideas proposed by David Freidel. The rituals performed by royal women on the Yaxchilan panels have long been understood to record these women conjuring what have been called vision serpents or ancestral spirits. Freidel was the first to suggest a similar act was depicted on La Corona Panel 6 (Figure 6.9), where three queens of the

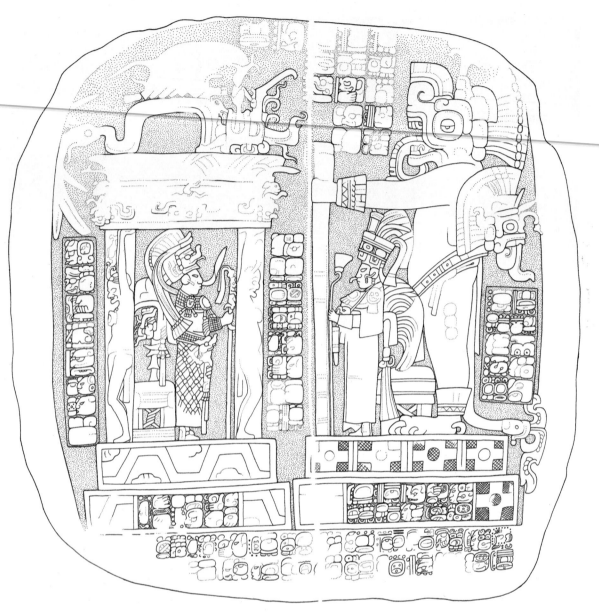

figure 6.9
La Corona Panel 6. Drawing by David Stuart.

Kaanul kingdom are engaged in ritually opening a portal to unleash their ancestral spirits (Freidel and Guenter 2003). Chinchilla Mazariegos makes a strong argument that what is often described as a vision serpent shares characteristics with a supernatural centipede—serpents and centipedes being creatures associated with the earth, fecundity, sexuality, and maternity in Mesoamerican myth (Chinchilla Mazariegos 2021:215). As powerful poisonous creatures, they embody the ambiguity with which Indigenous Mesoamerican peoples viewed sexuality—as a necessary and pleasurable force that was likewise dangerous and even ruinous if left uncontrolled. The sexual act not only brought fertility and rain but also unchecked license and unsanctioned reproduction.

The panels from Yaxchilan represent a claim by the royal family of this polity that queens conjure not only powerful ancestors from the past but also royal births for the patriline. As noted by Houston and Stuart, "conjuring K'awiil" seems to be a possible metaphor for the politicized and ritualized act of reproduction (Houston and Stuart 1989:8). The conjuration of K'awiil was a ritual recorded in many of the inscriptions accompanying queenly portraits, and this deity is known to have strong connections to dynastic legitimacy. Perhaps what Mayanists have long described as a stranger queen's ability to "improve the bloodline" of her new home, as in the history of Yaxchilan, La Corona, Naranjo, and Coba, among others, is an acknowledgment that this royal woman would conduct ceremonies to ensure the birth of a healthy and powerful royal heir. These rituals would thereby perform her loyalty to her family of marriage and maintain the status of her patriline by birth (see Baron, this volume; Tokovinine, Estrada Belli and Fialko, this volume). Of course, one can also imagine that a royal woman forced into marriage may have refused to perform such a ritual, or withheld her ceremonial skills from her husband's kin.

Given that Maya queenly power is situated at the intersection of cultural norms of gender and authority, queens did not utilize a single model or script for their legitimacy, especially over vast periods of time such as the Classic period. While certain Maya queens chose to infiltrate power bases normally monopolized by elite men and to embody the Maize Deity, other queens sought to stabilize their power by performing rituals associated with ensuring a successful birth and the perpetuation of their affinal patriline. The choices available to any historic queen are often limited to upholding the expectations of her gender, which in the case of Classic Maya queens might have included drawing spiritual authority from an association with attributes of K'awiil or the Female Attendant deities, or violating the expectations of her gender in order to fulfill the expectations of her office, which in the case of the Classic Maya might have led certain queens to embody attributes of the Maize Deity. The ideological script of gender complementarity was both utilized (as in stelae pairings) and deliberately violated (as in the portrait of an unaccompanied queen in warrior dress) during the Classic period. This paradox or ambiguity is to be expected in the materialization of the social discourse about gender conceptions that occurred within a society where elite women from powerful families were able to contest the largely masculine dominance of authority (Dunn and Carney 2018; Klein 2001; Walthall 2008). Each deviation from a gendered norm served to reinforce the norms overall. When a queen was able to deploy the resources of the state to commemorate her deviation, such as in the portraits the queen of Naranjo commissioned, we see that gender is neither static nor unyielding. With royal pedigree as a tool, certain Maya queens, such as Lady Yohl Ik'nal of Palenque and Lady Wak Jalam Chan Ajaw of Naranjo, contested the limitations of idealized masculine authority and co-opted a definition of gender complementarity that positioned them as dominant power holders within their polities.

Female Sexuality and Dynastic Success

Both a patrilineal system of kinship and much of the mythology of the Classic period support a pivotal role for royal women in ensuring dynastic success. Patrilineal descent created rivalries that exogamous marriage helped to neutralize. Mythological scenes of male–female mutuality, such as Dressing of the Maize Deity, provided a script for royal women and men to perform complementary court duties. A mythology that included acknowledgment of the potency of female sexuality and reproductive potential reified the interest of the state in controlled reproduction and the obligation of royal women to uphold that value.

The requirements of hereditary rule put women at the center of the Maya monarchy, as they had intimate access to the most powerful man in the kingdom (Walthall 2008:1). Each woman exploited this access in unique ways, and was controlled or restricted in different ways by the members of her court. But the comparative study of queenship makes very clear that nearly every queen was expected to produce an heir, preferably a male heir (Duggan 1997; Dunn and Carney 2018; Nelson 2003; Stafford 1998; Walthall 2008). The sexuality of a queen was conscripted into service to the state—it was politicized and laden with symbolic importance. She was, in fact, a conduit of state power, and her symbolic value as a font of legitimacy was unmatched (Heckel 2018). And while her reproductive potential, once harnessed to a king, was a source of legitimacy for the king's patriline, her own legitimacy was fragile, since it was vested so deeply in reproductive success. We have already seen that the practice of polygyny at some Maya cities may have offered some degree of protection from ostracization for those queens who chose not to, or were unable to, have a child. For Maya queens, their ability to perform other essential ritual roles, and their possession of esoteric ceremonial knowledge from their patriline of origin, seem to have also offered some counterweight to the need to reproduce. But motherhood was clearly the most fundamental avenue to power. Any queen in a rigidly patriarchal descent system was vulnerable to accusations of sexual impropriety or dishonor, which would be framed as dynastic disloyalty. Foreign queens were even more vulnerable to such accusations because they were outsiders, different, without kin, and exaggerated expectations of unification across dynasties or cultures were often projected upon them (Dunn and Carey 2018:6).

Parentage statements are the most common means by which we know the names and lives of ancient Maya queens (Martin 2020:179). Given the fact that most royal Maya marriages were arranged for political purposes, where husband and wife may not have shared any affection for one another, and that a patrilineal system generates friction and competition among male siblings, the easiest and most stable relationship within the court would have been between a queen mother and her son (or daughter, although they were often sent away in marriage). This maternal connection likely contributes to the prolific number of monuments depicting a royal mother commissioned by her son. The mother–son bond was a touchstone of Classic Maya culture that transcended generations. The invocation of the great ancestor Lady Yohl Ik'nal by Pakal two generations after she lived is a strong indication that legitimization could be achieved by commemorating (and thus laying claim to) female reproductive power in service to state-sanctioned generational succession.

Queen mothers were often chosen as regents over ministers who might have personal interest, because a queen's concern for the dynasty was presumed to be the same as that of their son (Walthall 2008:9). Even if they did not hold the role of regent, a queen mother likely oversaw palace administrative issues, provided intelligence to the king, and selected and trained members of her kin group or local faction for court positions (Walthall 2008:11). A stranger queen who arrived from elsewhere, produced an heir that was the beneficiary of both local and foreign dynasties, and lived a long life as queen mother was perhaps the most powerful person (after the king) in a Maya court. Here, we can think of the Red Queen, who arrived at Palenque from a small neighboring site, married the powerful king Pakal, birthed two sons, and lived a long and privileged life (Tiesler and Cucina 2006a). The benefits to a royal woman for the correct performance as generational wellspring and reproducer of dynastic success could be quite substantial.

I have stated that titles were the way in which power and authority were transferred within Maya elite society. Most mothers and wives carry a title in the hieroglyphic corpus known as the inverted vase, which has to date resisted decipherment (Martin 2020:191). Maria Eugénia Gutierrez has proposed that this glyphic complex is used as an adjective that describes only certain Maya queens (Gutierrez 2016) (Figure 6.10). Gutierrez suggests that the inverted vase is to be read as the adjective K'INAL / K'IHNAL / K'ÍILKAB / K'INTAHNAL (warm belly) + the noun IX-K'UH (goddess), the warm and wet woman—that is, the fertile woman who possesses (or has demonstrated) the ability to give birth and use her generative powers (Gutierrez 2016). Warmth as a characteristic of female reproductive power is also reflected in the modern Yucatec Maya concept of *kinam*, which is a variable force or heat possessed by some people more than others (Knowlton and Dzidz Yam 2019:726). The most common cause of an increase in someone's *kinam* today is exposure to pregnant women or sexual activity, and Knowlton and Dzidz Yam suggest that monitoring and controlling such a force is a community concern that helps explain

figure 6.10
Rollout photograph (K772) of inverted vase title. Justin Kerr Maya archive, Dumbarton Oaks, Trustees for Harvard University, Washington, D.C.

the three perinatal rituals recorded in the colonial-period books of Chilam Balam (Knowlton and Dzidz Yam 2019). Gutierrez's reading accords well with the emphasis placed on maternal roles as seen in the abundance of Classic-period parentage statements, and female reproductive power in service to the dynasty as seen in mythological art. It is quite likely that the successful production of an heir by a royal woman was status elevating, and perhaps even recorded in a title that, by its presence in an official script, reinforced yet again the desire and need for the state to harness the awesome power of female sexuality to its needs.

The Lives of Stranger Queens

Within this framework of patrilineal dynastic succession, female reproductive potency, spiritual midwifery of royal heirs, and the mother–son bond within Classic Maya society, we can now examine the phenomenon of stranger queens in greater detail. These royal women were sent from their palaces of birth to marry a king, sometimes hundreds of kilometers from their original homes. What could stranger queens do that other women could not? Why did Maya people choose a long-distance marriage alliance rather than wed the daughter of a local royal family? How did this choice function within Classic-period systems of governance and hierarchical power relations?

As the theory originally codified by Marshall Sahlins (1985) suggests, a stranger queen held the power of the Other, as she was a foreigner with magical faculties who could replace a worn out or ineffective ruler. As Maxime Lamoureux-St-Hilaire and Patricia McAnany explain in their chapter, the concept of the stranger queen or king captures the nature of Maya sovereignty that displayed a strong preference for royal identities that blended the familiar with the strange. Given that Maya queenship had an ideological basis in the performance of esoteric ceremonial actions that summoned the power of ancestors and royal heirs, we might expect that stranger queens within Maya history had a clear expectation of magical aptitude, or supernatural capabilities that would add to what the local family already possessed. In this sense, they provided a particular kind of calculation for dynastic success, one based in ritualized access to supernatural power in addition to female reproductive power. Stranger queens likely introduced new deities and rituals to their affinal kin; as others have noted, this is certainly the case with the Kaanul princesses who married into the many cities allied with Calakmul (Canuto and Barrientos 2020; Freidel and Guenter 2003; Navarro-Farr and

Rich 2014; Navarro-Farr, Kelly et al. 2020; Navarro-Farr, Pérez Robles et al. 2020). Stranger queens enlarged the network of contacts held by the kin of their marriage partner, thus broadening cosmological claims to authority as well as augmenting trade relations, exchange brokers, and other economic or artistic agents available to the court. Finally, given the importance of controlling elite female sexuality (and the fear of its corruption), the stranger queen, due to her arrival from a distance, brought the plausible illusion (or reality) of sexual purity. Her actual history at home could conveniently be erased or ignored, were her affines so inclined. With sexual conformity came the power to deploy one's sexuality in service of the state, which we have seen was one of the most immediate means to power that Maya queens exercised and a key component of why queens were essential to Maya rulership. The following discussion of three cities with powerful stranger queens draws extensively on the brilliant synthesis of Maya epigraphic history by Simon Martin (2020); it will illustrate all of these observations and hopefully provoke further questions.

Queens of La Corona

The small but very important vassal of Calakmul known today as La Corona was the beneficiary of at least three foreign queens from the Kaanul dynasty during the Classic period (Canuto and Barrientos 2020). We know about these women from an extraordinary monument commissioned by a local king who married the third stranger queen. La Corona Panel 6, a carved stone monument originally designed to adorn the walls of an elite palace and now housed in the Dallas Museum of Art, makes clear that the ritual skills and ancestral connections that these women possessed as members of the Kaan patriline were highly valued within their adopted home and perhaps viewed as essential to its dynastic success (Figure 6.9). While La Corona and Calakmul are only one hundred kilometers apart, this distance is likely farther than most royal women ever traveled from their palace compounds, and it is quite clear from the emphasis placed on the actions and titles of these women that they were seen as sacred Others who arrived to bring changes to La Corona.

The detailed panel depicts a remarkable series of creation rituals to birth or unleash war gods upon enemy dynasties, conducted by two queens from Calakmul who arrive in the vassal site of La Corona in the midst of Calakmul's wars of expansion (Freidel and Guenter 2003). The queens each stand in front of a throne decorated with symbols of creation and rebirth. The woman on the right is dressed in a Teotihuacan-style headdress and costume framed by an enormous anthropomorphic serpent with jaguar claws that Freidel and Guenter identify as the Teotihuacan deity Waxaklajuun Ubaah Kaan, a war god that she has summoned to assist her dynasty to victory (Freidel and Guenter 2003). The text suggests that she is the first stranger queen to arrive at La Corona; she may have originated in the court of Dzibanche, the center of the Kaanul dynasty when she arrived at La Corona in 520 CE. She is clearly named as the daughter of a powerful king of the Kaanul dynasty, Tuun K'ab Hix, though her mother's name is illegible. Because this monument was commissioned over a hundred years after her arrival at La Corona, we can read in this text that later descendants wished to make very clear that the first stranger queen to arrive at La Corona was from a distinguished patriline and that she transferred the power of her ancestral and reproductive potential to her descendants at La Corona. Their implication is that the first Kaanul queen performed in exactly the way a Classic Maya stranger queen was meant to uphold her role, by bridging two polities, reinforcing the elevated status of one by arriving at the other, and joining them forever in the form of royal heirs with shared ancestry and history.

The text continues with the arrival of the next foreign queen in 679, over one hundred and fifty years later; this woman is identified as the "Second Snake Lady" (Martin 2020:188). The name of her local husband is given, as well as a long list of her relatives from Calakmul, including the king, a consort queen, and other kin, including her son who was later to rule at La Corona and order the creation of this monument. The Third Snake Lady, Lady Ti', arrived forty-two years later and is the figure represented on the left side of Panel 6. She is described as an *ix kaloomte'*, or a royal woman of supreme influence, and her Kaanul kin are named in detail. An important distinction in the biographical detail of the Third Snake Lady is her participation with her husband in a period ending ritual on 9.15.0.0.0. The third stranger queen is depicted in the full regalia of a Classic Maya queen, including the use of the Maize Deity costume of jade netted skirt and *Spondylus* girdle. She stands in a temple decorated with the iconography of birth and fertility, such as the supernatural serpent-centipede and aged earth lords. This woman arrives at La Corona at the close of the seventh century, a time in which her Kaanul patriline is aggressively rebuilding and consolidating its influence in the region, following the epic wars with its greatest rival, Tikal. The king ruling at Calakmul when the Third Snake queen arrives commissioned many monuments to the grandeur and power of the Kaanul dynasty, and the deployment of this stranger queen likely was part of a multipronged approach to shore up the alliances of the Kaanul state and to maintain control of La Corona and the overland trade route to the south (Martin 2020:189). The fact that her husband, the king, ordered her depiction in full regalia performing a ceremony to ensure reproductive success, suggests that he too was concerned with reinforcing the message that the Kaanul dynasty was not damaged or weakened. Given the repeated attacks on his overlords by the leaders of Tikal, it may have been a strategic choice to depict the spiritual power of these queens, a source of authority that did not rely upon success in war or battles over territory. In many historical contexts, queens have occupied a unique position from which to claim spiritual authority, as a benefit of their gendered expectations that generally do not include military or other arenas of masculine competition. Yet female relatives of the La Corona queens went into battle (see below) so it is not clear that Maya conceptualizations of elite gendered performance followed a strict dichotomy between spiritual ministrations and martial activities (see Bassie-Sweet 2021 for more detail on elite women and war).

In understanding how stranger queens contributed to the maintenance of hierarchical power structures during the Classic period, La Corona Panel 6 gives us a unique perspective into one particular aspect of royal queenly power, the queen's role as spiritual authority. It is notable that the only parentage statements included in the panel are for the queens themselves, to document their illustrious heritage and connections to a supremely powerful patriline. Their children are not mentioned in the lengthy text, and clearly these women did not achieve the status sufficient to inspire such a complex and unique monument through motherhood alone. They are commemorated here for their roles as representatives of the patronage of the Kaanul dynasty over hundreds of years, for their essential roles as the connection points between a small and vulnerable polity and its huge and powerful protector, and as the individuals who transferred the spiritual potency of the Kaanul ancestral deities to their adopted home. We have less information about what other connections they may have provided—whether that was food, goods, or military services—but what was of utmost importance to the local king at the end of the seventh century, at least in terms of what he chose to commemorate in state propaganda, were the religious ceremonies performed by these women over the history of his dynasty.

There is a wide variety of epigraphic and artistic evidence available on the many opportunities Maya royal women had to act as religious specialists (Bassie-Sweet 2021; Guenter and Freidel 2005; Josserand 2002; Navarro-Farr, Kelly et al. 2020; Navarro-Farr, Pérez Robles et al. 2020; Stone 1988; Taube 1994; Vail and Stone 2002). Maya queens cared for sacred bundles, commemorated important calendrical moments, carried priestly titles, summoned ancestral spirits, and participated in the preeminent royal Maya ritual act of blood sacrifice. While many monuments show women with bloodletting implements, depictions of royal women actually performing the act of blood sacrifice are relatively rare. Images of royal men performing blood sacrifice are more common, and this practice was understood as a fundamental component of the ritual life of kings (Ardren and Hixson 2006).

The obligations of royal women of Calakmul to aid their dynasty in its wars of expansion were not limited to ritual actions. Kathryn Reese-Taylor and colleagues discuss depictions of Calakmul warrior queens from the late seventh century to the early eighth century (Reese-Taylor et al. 2009). After examining eleven depictions of queens dressed in warrior costume from Calakmul and three other Classic Maya sites, Reese-Taylor and colleagues suggest that the images and texts from these sites indicate strong political and cultural ties and show these royal women participated in battle, took captives, and were taken captive. Although most striking at this cluster of sites, other scholars have noted iconographic and ethnohistorical evidence for elite Maya women warriors and the more common image of queens reviewing prisoners of war (Ayala 2002; Valckx, Stanton, and Ardren 2011). There is good documentation that Central Mexican women went into battle prior to Spanish contact, but while Aztec literature was full of metaphorical references to childbirth as warfare and spindle whorls as shields, going into battle was not an expected component of the lives of high-status Aztec women, and as Cecelia Klein explains, "the ideological parallel between the domestic, reproductive woman and the militarily successful man was intrinsically asymmetrical and fictive" (Klein 1994:141; see also Kellogg 2005). Thus, while the images of royal Maya women in battle dress discussed above are rare, these representations clearly show that some particularly fierce Maya queens, such as Lady Ti' from Calakmul, resisted a purely liturgical role in military campaigns and instead positioned themselves within the main arena of a very high-status elite activity. Such ambitious queens contributed to the aggressively expansive nature of the Calakmul dynasty and created opportunities that did not generally exist for elite women. We can see a continuum of images relating elite Maya women to a range of war-related activities as an acknowledgment by elites that high-status women could be effective agents in situations of conflict—whether as ritual specialists or as actual combatants.

Naranjo Queens

At Naranjo, we find another polity with a long history of stranger queens, although here the practice has a much more sinister cast. Nonetheless, one Naranjo queen becomes arguably one of the most famous in Maya history, due to her ambition, opportunity, and success. After a long period of stable growth, in 626 CE, Naranjo was defeated by its local rival Caracol; then in 631 CE, it suffered an even worse "star wars" event, this time at the hands of Calakmul, which had once been an ally (Martin and Grube 2000:72). Two weak kings about which we know very little presided at Naranjo during this time, and the second was able to mount an attack on Caracol in 680 CE, in retaliation for the "star wars" event fifty years earlier (recorded, ironically, by Caracol) (Martin and Grube 2000:73). Nearly immediately after the retaliation, in 682 CE, a stranger queen from Dos Pilas arrived into this highly unstable and conflict-ridden milieu. Lady Six Sky, or Ix Wak Jalam Chan Ajaw, was the daughter of the founding king of Dos Pilas, a man who broke with his patriline of Tikal to found a new polity, although throughout his lifetime he continued to claim to have access to the gods and ancestors of Tikal. This king saw the weakness of Naranjo and, in a campaign to enlarge his political power throughout the region, likely reached out to the floundering Naranjo kings to offer his daughter in marriage.

It is unlikely that the royal family of Naranjo, or what was left of it at least, knew anything about the character of Queen Wak Jalam Chan Ajaw, other than that she was a foreign princess with ties to an ambitious king. From the historical record we have of her actions, this queen likewise perceived the weakness of her affines and, perhaps following in the footsteps of her father, set about creating a kingdom of her own. She married the local Naranjo lord, who is mentioned only once in all the inscriptions of Naranjo, while she is mentioned frequently. Her prominence in the hieroglyphic record has long been understood to be the result of the loyalty of her son, who commissioned the monuments—but structurally we can see that her arrival from afar to reinforce a weakened but once great dynasty allowed Naranjo to rebuild in a manner that would never have been possible with a local queen (Figure 6.11). This stranger queen was her father's daughter in

figure 6.11
Naranjo Stela 24, a portrait of Queen Wak Jalam Chan Ajaw, commissioned by her son. Illustration by Ian Graham © President and Fellows of Harvard College, Peabody Museum of Archaeology and Ethnology, 2004.15.6.2.45.

every sense, and she clearly understood her mandate to be extraordinary and to achieve extraordinary things. A patrilineal descent system allows for a woman to take the throne when there is no suitable male heir, and it appears that Wak Jalam Chan Ajaw grew up understanding this principle. To this end, she arrived at Naranjo with an entourage of retainers, likely members of her kin group that may have included artists, cooks, medics, or other skilled members of her court (Martin 2020:127). Three days after arriving at Naranjo, she performed an elaborate ritual that was remembered for many generations as part of her enduring legacy and proved her legitimacy as queen.

Through good fortune and a willingness to stick strictly to the script of queenly expectations, Queen Wak Jalam Chan Ajaw bore a son and heir six years later. We know little of what transpired during those six years, but by reference to queens in other cultures, we can imagine that she was only able to achieve what transpired after her son's birth by spending those first years cultivating the local court, nobles, and population of Naranjo. Perhaps she fostered patronage through good works, or further spiritual acts, or perhaps her presence as a representative of the Dos Pilas and Kaanul lineages created a stability that is not reflected in epigraphic inscriptions. But it is clear that she cemented a reputation for leadership and ambition with the local community, for when her husband died and their son was only five years old, Wak Jalam Chan Ajaw assumed the regency by putting her tiny son on the throne. As we have seen, patrilineal dynasties are inherently at risk of competition for the throne, and while it is possible there were secondary royal families at Naranjo that might have attempted to seat their own king, it is quite clear that the ambition and strategic intelligence of Wak Jalam Chan Ajaw, as well as her nonlocal connections, won over the local court and left no room for any other candidate. Once queen regent, she assumed all of the roles usually associated with a king, including leading campaigns of warfare, taking captives, and commemorating calendrical rituals on behalf of her city. On a series of stelae, she compared herself to the last great king of Naranjo who died almost a hundred years earlier, and performed rituals that may have called upon him as a powerful ancestral spirit of her kingdom. Not content to rule only her adopted city, she led campaigns of terror against two neighboring cities, B'ital and Tuub'al, burning them and taking captives (Martin and Grube 2000:76). Soon she was drawn into the wars between Calakmul and Tikal, and sent Naranjo warriors to attack Tikal, capturing a lord. Wak Jalam Chan Ajaw may have performed the role of dutiful queen when she first arrived at Naranjo, but she stepped far beyond what most Maya queens are recorded as having accomplished by continuing to direct, alongside her son as he came of age, military action throughout the region.

Wak Jalam Chan Ajaw's son, K'ahk' Tiliw Chan Chahk, eventually married a stranger queen from Tuub'al, one of the cities his mother had destroyed. Lady Unen Bahlam's marriage was likely a trophy won from the subjugation of Tuub'al by Naranjo and the desire of the older stranger queen to cement her control over the smaller site. By arranging for her son to marry a royal daughter of a subjugated center, she strengthened her position as patron of Tuub'al, styling herself, as her father had done, as a great ruler with many dependencies. Like other Maya captive brides, the unfortunate Lady Unen Bahlam likely did not experience the positive reception offered to her mother-in-law; instead, she served not as a symbol of the power of the Other but as a symbol of the power of the elder queen to control the lives and reproductive potential of her patriline. Unen Bahlam bore a son, fulfilling her obligations to concretize the legacy of the more powerful stranger queen, in the form of a direct lineal descendant. This son, once he took the throne, also married a stranger queen, this time from Yaxha, a polity seized and burnt by his father (and grandmother). This young woman was also a pawn in the perpetuation of Naranjo's history of using royal women as war booty, deploying marriage not to bring two dynasties together but to keep alive long-standing feuds and resentments. The stranger queen from Yaxha gave birth to a son, who would take the throne of Naranjo and invade the city of his mother's birth—a clear indication that Naranjo, perhaps because of a culture of calculated aggression initiated by Queen

Wak Jalam Chan Ajaw, constantly asserted itself through violence toward its neighbors and potential allies.

The power that royal women had to leverage their reproductive potential through rituals to contact supernatural patrons and deities likely made them especially vulnerable to the humiliations of war. To capture the generative potential of a dynasty and make it your own, in the form of a forced marriage between victor and vanquished, may have been a strategic form of spiritual warfare irresistible to certain cruel and ambitious Maya elites. In this rather tragic history of the generations of stranger queens brought to Naranjo, we note that except for the *ix kaloomte'* Queen Wak Jalam Chan Ajaw, the stranger queens are mentioned in the inscriptions not for their spiritual power but as mothers of men who would perpetuate the violence of taking wives, possibly as captives of war. These marriages relied upon the ability of stranger queens to enlarge the network of the overlord's dynasty. By absorbing the royal families of Tuub'al and Yaxha into the domain of Wak Jalam Chan Ajaw, the queen who rebuilt the Naranjo dynasty through her own offspring and external connections fulfilled the mandate of her father and his overlord. It was a campaign that capitalized on the strong relationship between queen and son, but one that reproduced the institutionalized violence of Maya patterns of bride capture in service to patriarchal power structures.

Palenque Queen

The tomb of the Red Queen at Palenque, which likely houses the remains of Lady Tz'akab Ajaw, the wife of the most famous king of Palenque, K'inich Janaab Pakal, rivals the richness of the better-known tomb of her husband (Tiesler and Cucina 2006a). A woman who died between forty and forty-five years of age, the Red Queen (so called due to the enormous amount of cinnabar covering her remains) was buried inside a limestone sarcophagus housed by a mortuary pyramid that contained large amounts of ceramics, jade, shell, and pearl objects, including ceremonial weaving implements. A funerary mask made of 1,140 plaques, a diadem, ear flares, multiple necklaces, a belt and wristlets, all made of jade, covered her body (Gonzalez Cruz 2000) (Figure 6.12). As with many royal Maya burials, two sacrificial victims were placed alongside the sarcophagus of the queen: a young woman and a ten-year-old child were found face down with their arms bound behind their backs (Tiesler and Cucina 2006b:501).

Inscriptions confirmed by dental isotope testing indicate that Lady Tz'akab Ajaw was a stranger queen who grew up in a much smaller secondary center known as "Three Gods," in the rural area surrounding Palenque (Martin 2020:412; Tiesler, Cucina, and Romano Pacheco 2008). Even though she was not from the royal court of Palenque, Tz'akab Ajaw may have enjoyed a positive reception when she arrived to marry the king. Her funerary monuments demonstrate a tremendous commitment of resources; she is the only wife of Pakal mentioned in the hieroglyphic corpus and, most importantly, Pakal was very sensitive to the power of female relatives to contribute to his dynastic success. A number of artworks commissioned during his reign, such as the famous Oval Palace Tablet, conspicuously feature his mother, Queen Sak K'uk'. Likewise, his mother is given prominence in the genealogical statements that he commissioned, where he went so far as to state that he was not the son of a king, a dramatic act that could only be taken by someone certain of their maternal royal legitimacy (Martin 2020:104; Schele and Freidel 1990:221).

Only twenty years before Pakal was born, a queen ruled alone at Palenque. Lady Yohl Ik'nal was the daughter of the previous king and inherited the throne in the absence of a male heir. She reigned during a time of increasing misfortune, when Palenque suffered repeated military attacks from the Kaanul dynasty. This historical situation may account for the total absence of texts from her reign. Despite these challenges, Yohl Ik'nal maintained her power and influence within courtly politics because her son acceded to the throne after her death twenty years later, in 604 CE. She was remembered by her grandson, King K'inich Janaab Pakal, who accorded her an exalted place in the dynastic history that he ordered inscribed on his famous sarcophagus. Pakal's inclusion of two great queens in this text, his

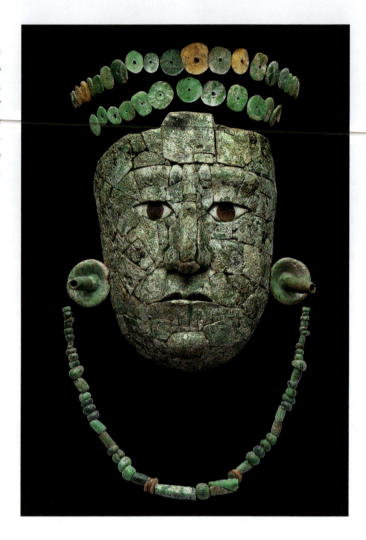

figure 6.12
Funerary mask of Queen Tz'akab Ajaw of Palenque. Photograph by Jorge Pérez de Lara, courtesy of Coordinación Nacional de Conservación del Patrimonio Cultural del Instituto Nacional de Antropología e Historia de México.

great grandmother Lady Yohl Ik'nal and his mother Muwaan Mat (which was likely a ruling name for Lady Sak K'uk'), despite the attacks on Palenque during their reigns, demonstrates the importance of queenly rule to one of the most well-known, successful, and paradigmatic male rulers in Classic Maya culture. For Pakal, his legitimacy as king was enhanced by the glorification of these queens and their accepted roles within the dynastic history of his polity.

Once Pakal was born, the pressure must have been intense to install him on the throne as soon as possible, given the expectation throughout the Maya world of male rulership, even at places such as Palenque, with a history of powerful queenship. Pakal's mother maintained her solo rule until he reached the age of twelve, when Pakal was installed as king. This delay speaks to her diplomatic skills within the court, where she must have had to convince other elites that Pakal did not need to be seated on the throne any earlier, even though this was the practice in other polities. With a son, her position of dynastic regenerator was secure, and while she was not named as ruler, she must have enjoyed the support of her court in order to delay the seating of her son, even though the polity was under siege from the Kaanul dynasty. Her reign, like that of her mother, transitioned normally to the next heir in line, at a pace in keeping with established practice throughout the Classic world. This indicates that local elites did not see her rule as terribly aberrant, and that the court did not understand dynastic succession to be in crisis. There are plenty of examples from nearby Maya cities where dynastic succession was interrupted, and a sitting ruler killed or removed in order to install a new king. The normal transition of power from Lady Sak K'uk' to Pakal indicates that local stakeholders accepted her period as effective regent, as did Pakal.

These influential women were the context into which the stranger queen Lady Tz'akab Ajaw arrived to marry Pakal when he was twenty-three years old. Given that Pakal later commissioned monuments that commemorated the influence of his mother, we can be certain that Lady Sak K'uk' played a large role in choosing his bride, as she was still very much alive and likely involved in court affairs. From a later event in his life, we gain some insight into why a foreign queen was chosen over one of the royal women from the local court. Palenque was not a polity that chose to commemorate its military campaigns against neighbors like Naranjo, nor was it allied with a single superpower, so it is unlikely that an alliance with the small (to date unidentified) site of "Three Gods" was the only motivation for a marriage alliance. From the Tablet of the Slaves and other inscriptions that postdate Pakal's reign, it is clear that he was very concerned to name his successor and to avoid competition for the throne among his two, or likely three, sons. On the same day that Pakal and Tz'akab Ajaw's eldest son acceded to the throne, their second son was named heir apparent (Martin 2020:132). There is evidence that the third son died at a young age, but his son eventually took his father's place on the Palenque throne (Martin 2020:133; Ringle 1996:55). Thus, we see Pakal as a king who wished to ensure a clear transfer of power, who acceded without overt conflict between factions, and who married an outsider who would be unlikely to foster any factionalism within the court, given her lack of kinship connections to anyone but him. Their sons took over in an orderly manner, and thus the stranger queen served the purposes of a king who sought to minimize conflict at succession but who also understood (and we might say respected) the role of queens within the Maya system of governance. That the dynasty did not last much longer after Pakal's death may suggest that the status enhancement of a stranger queen could not, in this instance at least, mitigate the undercurrents of dissent and disorder within the polity.

Conclusion

This chapter began with a series of questions meant to enlarge how we think about and understand Indigenous Maya conceptualizations of gendered power as a mechanism of the state, specifically as it applies to the institution of queenship and stranger queens. I have embraced the ambiguities and paradoxes that emerge in the increasingly well-documented historical biographies of many of these extraordinary women, and view these ambiguities as evidence of the agency such women were able to exercise within Classic Maya power structures. Gendered expectations intersected with the privileges of divine lineage, and some Maya queens leveraged their elite familial connections to stretch or contest those gendered expectations. Even when royal women ruled alone, or as queen regent, or carried the supreme *kaloomte'* title of independent authoritarian rule, their structural access to power was situated within a framework of gender complementarity and patriarchal descent. Both of these social constructions emphasized royal women as guarantors of dynastic succession, whether they facilitated succession through biological or ceremonial means. In this way, royal women occupied a fundamental role in Maya systems of social domination and sovereignty. They were literally the perpetuators of political control, through the conjuration of spiritual forces and offspring who would reproduce the power structures of the state.

In this analysis, stranger queens held a uniquely potent position as those who blended the familiar with the strange in order to become magical. In hypogamous arrangements where high-status women wed lower-status men, daughters of ambitious and successful kingdoms were sent to marry into subjugated or incipient dynasties. Newly formed kinship relations facilitated the flow of economic and other resources, but most importantly for a study of sovereignty, they enlarged the social influence of both polities in an asymmetrical arrangement. These exogamous marriages helped diffuse competition for resources within a patriline, transmit specialized ceremonial and artistic knowledge within elite society, and keep male power localized and

figure 6.13
Rollout photograph (K5847), showing royal women carried into a new polity, perhaps as part of marriage negotiations. Justin Kerr Maya archive, Dumbarton Oaks, Trustees for Harvard University, Washington, D.C.

stable. Hypogamy could also be wielded as a tool of oppression—when elite women were captured in war or forced to marry into the dynasty of an overlord, they became living monuments to the social costs of competition and domination inherent in the Classic dynastic state (Figure 6.13).

By seeking evidence for women's agency and resistance, I have also shown that while royal women reproduced many of the patriarchal power structures of Classic Maya society—especially what Wengrow has described as the patriarchal organization of the household as a model for the social domination of the kingdom—these same women often acted in their own self-interest. I have suggested that they were capable of withholding specialized ceremonial skills needed by their male kin, such as summoning dynastic supernatural patrons that could assist in war, and that they maximized affective ties to their sons as a robust source of social capital. Moreover, I have argued that polygamous kingdoms may have provided a milieu in which women who chose not to have children could thrive, perhaps by commissioning important artwork such as the panels of Structure 23 commissioned by Queen K'ab'al

Xook of Yaxchilan. Power holders within the state apparatus saw the potency not only of female reproductive power but also of female sexuality as a force in need of control, and the Classic Maya elite artistic record demonstrates the use of imagery and mythology deployed in order to direct what was understood as appropriate female behavior. Yet these same images reveal an acknowledgment of the fragility of divinely sanctioned patrilineal succession. The literature on global traditions of queenship makes clear that without the investment of royal women in dynastic success, kingdoms fail.

The stranger queens of La Corona, Naranjo, and Palenque present three very different cases of polities where royal women played key roles in the perpetuation and success of rulership in the form of social domination. In all three polities, multiple women leveraged their specialized ability to wield violence, control the circulation of knowledge, and exercise political charisma—the cornerstones of social domination and state-level power, as identified by Wengrow (this volume). Their royal birthright, as well as their gender and age, contributed to the choices they could make within their unique historical settings.

At La Corona, generations of women from Calakmul were commemorated for their specialized ritual skill and dynastic connections to supernatural patrons. At Naranjo, the extraordinary Queen Wak Jalam Chan Ajaw from Dos Pilas and the Kaanul dynasty is remembered for founding a legacy of military success built upon the exploitation of her stranger queen status and the subjugation of royal women from within her territory. Finally, at Palenque, we see an example of a strong and powerful king, Pakal, who was raised within a dynasty that acknowledged influential stranger queens who improved the fortune of a smaller, cosmologically preoccupied polity.

In each case, these queens brought something unique to the exercise of sovereign power. They brought expanded familial connections, both literal and supernatural. They brought a magical persona and a specialized knowledge of ceremonies essential to the perpetuation of the dynasty. And they brought the charismatic performance of the idealized values of their gender—as displayed in art, myth, and ritual. These mainstays of statecraft were the building blocks that allowed for the perpetuation, constitution, and durability of Classic Maya kingdoms. Stranger queens were strategic, both in their individual lives to survive the challenges of leaving all they had known to live with strangers, and as a tool of sovereign diplomacy. These princesses were politicized gifts, weapons even, in ongoing wars of dynastic competition. With ties to their birth patrilineage and to their family of marriage, they straddled two worlds of kin relations, supernatural obligations, and court politics. Their exchange maintained a form of structural violence inherent in monarchies that depend upon women for dynastic succession and thus also seek to control the reproductive process. Maya stranger queens may have been subject to the inequities of this system, but they were active agents in the exercise of formal authority, central to the monarchy rather than accessories, and they utilized the institution of queenship in a rich assortment of ways to glorify their kin groups, their polities, and themselves.

Acknowledgments

A great number of colleagues have shared their ideas and data with me over the course of writing this chapter and thinking about Maya queens for many years. I thank all of them, and hope to repay their generosity in the future. For hours of conversation and debate about Maya queens, I thank Karen Bassie-Sweet, Marcello Canuto, Nicholas Carter, Michael D. Coe, David Freidel, Pamela Geller, Stanley Guenter, Annabeth Headrick, Nicholas Hopkins, Stephen Houston, Rosemary Joyce, Maxime Lamoureux-St-Hilaire, Simon Martin, Mallory Matsumoto, Alexandre Tokovinine, and Gabrielle Vail. I especially wish to thank Oswaldo Chinchilla Mazariegos, Eugénia Gutierrez, and David Stuart as well as two anonymous reviewers for comments on an earlier draft of this chapter. Heather Hurst, David Stuart, and Julia Zabrodzka were particularly generous with illustrations and photographs.

REFERENCES CITED

Ardren, Traci
    2002   Death Became Her: Images of Female Power from Yaxuna Burials. In *Ancient Maya Women*, edited by Traci Ardren, pp. 68–88. AltaMira Press, Walnut Creek, Calif.

    2020   Gender and Sexuality. In *The Maya World*, edited by Scott R. Hutson and Traci Ardren, pp. 147–163. Routledge, New York.

Ardren, Traci, and David Hixson
    2006   The Unusual Sculptures of Telantunich, Yucatán: Phalli and the Concept of Masculinity among the Ancient Maya. *Cambridge Archaeological Journal* 16(1):7–25.

Ayala F., Maricela
    2002   Lady K'awil, Goddess O, and Maya Warfare. In *Ancient Maya Women*, edited by Traci Ardren, pp. 105–113. AltaMira Press, Walnut Creek, Calif.

Bassie-Sweet, Karen
    2002   Corn Deities and the Male/Female Principle. In *Ancient Maya Gender Identity and Relations*, edited by Lowell S. Gustafson and Amelia M. Trevelyan, pp. 169–190. Bergin and Garvey, Westport, Conn.
    2021   *Maya Gods of War*. University Press of Colorado, Boulder.

Canuto, Marcello A., and Tomás Barrientos Q.
    2020   La Corona: Negotiating a Landscape of Power. In *Approaches to Monumental Landscapes of the Ancient Maya*, edited by Brett A. Houk, Barbara Arroyo, and Terry G. Powis, pp. 171–195. University Press of Florida, Gainesville.

Chinchilla Mazariegos, Oswaldo
    2017   *Art and Myth of the Ancient Maya*. Yale University Press, New Haven.
    2021   Where Children Are Born: Centipedes and Female Sexuality in Ancient Mesoamerica. In *Sorcery in Mesoamerica*, edited by Jeremy D. Colton and John M. D. Pohl, pp. 206–235. University Press of Colorado, Boulder.

Cojti Ren, Avexnim
    2006   Maya Archaeology and the Political and Cultural Identity of Contemporary Maya in Guatemala. *Archaeologies* 2(1):8–19.

Conkey, Margaret
    2005   Dwelling at the Margins, Action at the Intersection? Feminist and Indigenous Archaeologies 2005. *Archaeologies* 1(1):9–59.

Duggan, Anne G. (editor)
    1997   *Queens and Queenship in Medieval Europe*. Boydell Press, Rochester, N.Y.

Dunn, Caroline, and Elizabeth Carney (editors)
    2018   *Royal Women and Dynastic Loyalty*. Palgrave Macmillan, Cham.

Ensor, Bradley E.
    2013   *Crafting Prehispanic Maya Kinship*. University of Alabama Press, Tuscaloosa.

Freidel, David A., and Stanley P. Guenter
    2003   Bearers of War and Creation. *Archaeology*, www.archaeology.org/online/features/siteq2/index.html.

Gonzalez Cruz, Arnoldo
    2000   The Red Queen. Mesoweb, www.mesoweb.com/palenque/features/red_queen/01.html.

Guenter, Stanley P., and David A. Freidel
    2005   Warriors and Rulers: Royal Women of the Classic Maya. In *Gender in Cross-Cultural Perspective*, edited by Caroline B. Brettell and Carolyn F. Sargent, pp. 74–80. Prentice Hall, Englewood Cliffs, N.J.

Gutierrez, Maria Eugénia
    2016   Reinas y guerreras mayas en inscripciones del periodo clásico. Paper presented at the X Congreso Internacional de Mayistas, Izamal.

Haboush, JaHyun Kim
    1988   *A Heritage of Kings: One Man's Monarchy in the Confucian World*. Columbia University Press, New York.

Harrison-Buck, Eleanor
    2021   Relational Economies of Reciprocal Gifting: A Case Study of Exchanges in Ancient Maya Marriage and War. *Current Anthropology* 62(5):569–601.

Haviland, William A.
    1970   A Note on the Social Organization of the Chontal Maya. *Ethnology* 9(1):96–98.

Heckel, Waldemar
    2018   King's Daughters, Sisters, and Wives: Fonts and Conduits of Power and Legitimacy. In *Royal Women and Dynastic Loyalty*, edited by Caroline Dunn and Elizabeth Carney, pp. 19–30. Palgrave Macmillan, Cham.

Hopkins, Nicholas A.
    1988   Classic Maya Kinship Systems: Epigraphic and Ethnographic Evidence for Patrilineality. *Estudios de cultura maya* 17:87–121.

Houston, Stephen D.
- 2014 Courtesans and Carnal Commerce. Maya Decipherment, https://decipherment.wordpress.com/2014/06/08/courtesans-and-carnal-commerce/.
- 2018 *The Gifted Passage: Young Men in Classic Maya Art and Text*. Yale University Press, New Haven.

Houston, Stephen D., and David Stuart
- 1989 *The Way Glyph: Evidence for "Co-essences" among the Classic Maya*. Center for Maya Research, Washington, D.C.

James, Liz
- 1997 Goddess, Whore, Wife, or Slave? Will the Real Byzantine Empress Please Stand Up? In *Queens and Queenship in Medieval Europe*, edited by Anne G. Duggan, pp. 170–189. Boydell Press, Rochester, N.Y.

Josserand, J. Kathryn
- 2002 Women in Classic Maya Hieroglyphic Texts. In *Ancient Maya Women*, edited by Traci Ardren, pp. 114–151. AltaMira Press, Walnut Creek, Calif.
- 2007 The Missing Heir at Yaxchilan: Literary Analysis of a Maya Historical Puzzle. *Latin American Antiquity* 18(3):295–312.

Joyce, Rosemary A.
- 1993 Women's Work: Images of Production and Reproduction in Pre-Hispanic Southern Central America. *Current Anthropology* 34(3):255–274.
- 2000a *Gender and Power in Prehispanic Mesoamerica*. University of Texas Press, Austin.
- 2000b A Pre-Columbian Gaze: Male Sexuality among the Ancient Maya. In *Archaeologies of Sexuality*, edited by Robert A. Schmidt and Barbara L. Voss, pp. 263–283. Routledge, New York.
- 2008 *Ancient Bodies, Ancient Lives: Sex, Gender, and Archaeology*. Thames and Hudson, New York.

Keegan, William F.
- 2007 *Taíno Indian Myth and Practice: The Arrival of the Stranger King*. University Press of Florida, Gainesville.

Kellogg, Susan
- 2005 *Weaving the Past: A History of Latin America's Indigenous Women from the Prehispanic Period to the Present*. Oxford University Press, Oxford.

Klein, Cecelia
- 1994 Fighting with Femininity: Gender and War in Aztec Mexico. In *Gender Rhetorics: Postures of Dominance and Submission in History*, edited by Richard C. Trexler, pp. 107–146. Medieval and Renaissance Texts and Studies, Binghamton, N.Y.

Klein, Cecelia (editor)
- 2001 *Gender in Pre-Hispanic America*. Dumbarton Oaks Research Library and Collection, Washington, D.C.

Knowlton, Timothy
- 2015 The Maya Goddess of Painting, Writing, and Decorated Textiles. *The PARI Journal* 16(2):31–41.

Knowlton, Timothy, and Edber Dzidz Yam
- 2019 Perinatal Rites in the Ritual of the Bacabs, a Colonial Maya Manuscript. *Ethnohistory* 66(4):721–744.

Looper, Matthew G.
- 2002 Women-Men (and Men-Women): Classic Maya Rulers and the Third Gender. In *Ancient Maya Women*, edited by Traci Ardren, pp. 171–202. AltaMira Press, Walnut Creek, Calif.

Marcus, Joyce
- 2020 Maya Usurpers. In *A Forest of History: The Maya after the Emergence of Divine Kingship*, edited by Travis W. Stanton and M. Kathryn Brown, pp. 49–66. University Press of Colorado, Boulder.

Martin, Simon
- 2020 *Ancient Maya Politics: A Political Anthropology of the Classic Period 150–900 CE*. Cambridge University Press, New York.

Martin, Simon, and Nikolai Grube
- 2000 *Chronicle of the Maya Kings and Queens: Deciphering the Dynasties of the Ancient Maya*. Thames and Hudson, London.

Mathews, Holly F.
- 1985 "We Are Mayordomo": A Reinterpretation of Women's Roles in Mexican Cargo System. *American Ethnologist* 12(2):285–301.

McCafferty, Sharisse, and Geoffrey McCafferty
    2009   Alternative and Ambiguous Gender Identities in Postclassic Central Mexico. In *Que(e)rying Archaeology*, edited by S. Teredy et al., pp. 196–206. University of Calgary Press, Calgary.

Mihesuah, Devon
    1998   *Natives and Academics: Researching and Writing about American Indians*. University of Nebraska Press, Lincoln.
    2003   *Indigenous American Women: Decolonization, Empowerment, Activism*. University of Nebraska Press, Lincoln.
    2005   *So You Want to Write about American Indians? A Guide for Writers, Students, and Scholars*. University of Nebraska Press, Lincoln.

Miller, Mary E.
    2018   Were They Enslaved? A New Look at Maya Figurines. Jane Powell Dwyer Memorial Lecture, Haffenreffer Museum of Anthropology, Brown University, Providence.

Miller, Mary E. and Simon Martin
    2004   *Courtly Art of the Ancient Maya*. Thames and Hudson, London.

Monaghan, John
    2001   Physiology, Production, and Gendered Difference: The Evidence from Mixtec and Other Mesoamerican Sources. In *Gender in Pre-Hispanic America*, edited by Cecelia Klein, pp. 285–304. Dumbarton Oaks Research Library and Collection, Washington, D.C.

Nash, June
    1997   Gendered Deities and the Survival of Culture. *History of Religions* 36(4):324–333.

Navarro-Farr, Olivia C., and Michelle Rich (editors)
    2014   *Archaeology at El Perú-Waka': Ancient Maya Performances of Ritual, Memory, and Power*. University of Arizona Press, Tucson.

Navarro-Farr, Olivia C., Mary Kate Kelly, Michelle Rich, and Griselda Pérez Robles
    2020   Expanding the Canon: Lady K'abel the Ix Kaloomte' and the Political Narratives of Classic Maya Queens. *Feminist Anthropology* 1(1):38–55.

Navarro-Farr, Olivia, Griselda Pérez Robles, Damaris Menéndez, and Juan Carlos Pérez Calderón
    2020   Forest of Queens: The Legacy of Royal Calakmul Women at El Perú-Waka's Central Civic-Ceremonial Temple. In *A Forest of History: The Maya after the Emergence of Divine Kingship*, edited by Travis W. Stanton and M. Kathryn Brown, pp. 73–90. University Press of Colorado, Boulder.

Nelson, Sarah M.
    2003   *Ancient Queens: Archaeological Explorations*. AltaMira Press, Walnut Creek, Calif.

Rasch, Elisabet Dueholm
    2020   Becoming a Maya Woman: Beauty Pageants at the Intersection of Indigeneity, Gender and Class in Quetzaltenango, Guatemala. *Journal of Latin American Studies* 52:133–156.

Reese-Taylor, Kathryn, Peter Mathews, Julia Guernsey, and Marlene Fritzler
    2009   Warrior Queens among the Classic Maya. In *Blood and Beauty: Organized Violence in the Art and Archaeology of Mesoamerica and Central America*, edited by Heather Orr and Rex Koontz, pp. 39–72. Cotsen Institute of Archaeology Press, University of California, Los Angeles.

Ringle, William M.
    1996   Birds of a Feather: The Fallen Stucco Inscription of Temple XVIII, Palenque, Chiapas. In *Eighth Palenque Round Table, 1993*, edited by Martha Macri and Jan McHargue, pp. 45–61. Pre-Columbian Art Research Institute, San Francisco.

Rosado Rosado, Georgina (editor)
    2001   *Mujer maya: Siglos tejiendo una identidad*. Universidad Autónoma de Yucatán, Merida.

Sahlins, Marshall
    1985   *Islands of History*. University of Chicago Press, Chicago.

Santana Rivas, Landy
    2001   La mujer en la sociedad maya, la ayuda idónea. In *Mujer maya: Siglos tejiendo una identidad*, edited by Georgina Rosado Rosado, pp. 33–70. Universidad Autónoma de Yucatán, Merida.

Saturno, William, Karl Taube, and David Stuart
- 2005 *The Murals of San Bartolo, El Peten, Guatemala*, pt. 1, *The North Wall*. Center for Ancient American Studies, Barnardsville, N.C.

Schackt, Jon
- 2005 Mayahood through Beauty: Indian Beauty Pageants in Guatemala. *Bulletin of Latin American Research* 24(3):269–287.

Schele, Linda, and David Freidel
- 1990 *A Forest of Kings: The Untold Story of the Ancient Maya*. William Morrow, New York.

Silverblatt, Irene
- 1987 *Moon, Sun, Witches: Gender Ideologies and Class in Inca and Colonial Peru*. Princeton University Press, Princeton.

Smith, Linda Tuhiwai
- 1999 *Decolonizing Methodologies: Research and Indigenous Peoples*. St. Martin's Press, New York.

Speed, Shannon
- 2019 *Incarcerated Stories: Indigenous Women Migrants and Violence in the Settler-Capitalist State*. University of North Carolina Press, Chapel Hill.

Stafford, Pauline
- 1997 Emma: The Powers of the Queen in the Eleventh Century. In *Queens and Queenship in Medieval Europe*, edited by Anne G. Duggan, pp. 3–26. Boydell Press, Rochester, N.Y.
- 1998 *Queens, Concubines, and Dowagers: The King's Wife in the Early Middle Ages*. Leicester University Press, London.

Stone, Andrea
- 1988 Sacrifice and Sexuality: Some Structural Relationships in Classic Maya Art. In *The Role of Gender in Pre-Columbian Art and Architecture*, edited by Virginia E. Miller, pp. 75–103. University Press of America, Lanham, Md.
- 2011 Keeping Abreast of the Maya: A Study of the Female Body in Maya Art. *Ancient Mesoamerica* 22(1):167–183.

Storey, Rebecca
- 2008 Los hombres y las mujeres mayas en el mundo prehispanico. In *Tendencias actuales de la bioarqueología en México*, edited by Patricia O. Hernández, Lourdes Márquez, and Ernesto González Licón, pp. 235–261. Escuela Nacional de Arqueología e Historia, Instituto Nacional de Antropología e Historia, Mexico City.

Sullivan, Thelma D.
- 1982 Tlazolteotl-Ixcuina: The Great Spinner and Weaver. In *The Art and Iconography of Late Post-Classic Central Mexico*, edited by Elizabeth Hill Boone, pp. 7–35. Dumbarton Oaks Research Library and Collection, Washington, D.C.

Taube, Karl
- 1985 The Classic Maya Maize God: A Reappraisal. In *Fifth Palenque Round Table, 1983*, edited by Merle Greene Robertson, pp. 171–183. Pre-Columbian Art Research Institute, San Francisco.
- 1994 The Birth Vase: Natal Imagery in Ancient Maya Myth and Ritual. In *The Maya Vase Book*, vol. 4, edited by Justin Kerr, pp. 650–685. Kerr Associates, New York.

Tiesler, Vera, and Andrea Cucina
- 2006a *Jaanab Pakal of Palenque: Reconstructing the Life and Death of a Maya Ruler*. University of Arizona Press, Tucson.
- 2006b Procedures in Human Heart Extraction and Ritual Meaning: A Taphonomic Assessment of Anthropogenic Marks in Classic Maya Skeletons. *Latin American Antiquity* 17(4):493–510.

Tiesler, Vera, Andrea Cucina, and Arturo Romano Pacheco
- 2008 El enigma de la Reina Rojo de Palenque. In *Palenque as Never Seen Before*, edited by Mayo Möller and Edwin Barnhart, pp. 190–195. Virtual Archaeologic, Mexico City.

Vail, Gabrielle
- 2019 The Serpent Within: Birth Rituals and Midwifery Practices in Pre-Hispanic and Colonial Mesoamerican Cultures. *Ethnohistory* 66(4):689–719.

Vail, Gabrielle, and Andrea Stone
- 2002 Representation of Women in Postclassic and Colonial Maya Literature and Art. In *Ancient Maya Women*, edited by Traci Ardren, pp. 202–228. AltaMira Press, Walnut Creek, Calif.

Valckx G., Aimée, Travis Stanton, and Traci Ardren
- 2011 Mujeres en la guerra: Una vista desde la arqueología. *Anales de antropología* 45:123–152.

Velasquez Nimatuj, Irma Alicia
- 2003 Ways of Exclusion: Maya Dress and Racism in Contemporary Guatemala. In *With Their Hands and Their Eyes: Maya Textiles, Mirrors of a Worldview*, edited by Mirelle Holsbeke and Julia Montoya, pp. 157–165. Etnografisch Museum Antwerpen, Antwerp.

Vogt, Evon
- 1969 *Zinacantan*. Harvard University Press, Cambridge, Mass.

Walthall, Anne
- 2008 *Servants of the Dynasty: Palace Women in World History*. University of California Press, Berkeley.

Weinstein Bever, Sandra
- 2002 Migration and the Transformation of Gender Roles and Hierarchies in Yucatan. *Urban Anthropology* 31(2):199–230.

Wylie, Alison
- 1997 Good Science, Bad Science, or Science as Usual? Feminist Critiques of Science. In *Women in Human Evolution*, edited by Lori D. Hager, pp. 29–55. Routledge, New York.

Patron Deities and Rulership across the Maya Lowlands

JOANNE BARON

Graeber and Sahlins (2017:3) hold that divine rulers "control nature itself... There are no secular authorities: human power is spiritual power." The editors of this volume, and the organizers of the Dumbarton Oaks symposium that brought us all together in 2021, have asked us to consider not only the operation of divine rulership among the Pre-Columbian lowland Maya but also whether we can recognize regional and temporal distinctions among diverse Maya peoples. In this chapter, I explore how Maya rulers drew spiritual power from patron deities—local gods of independent polities. I also consider the implications of Maya patron deity veneration to Sahlins's (2008) stranger-king model. By promoting themselves as caretakers for these community gods, rulers walked the fine line between maintaining social distance from their followers and being seen as community members themselves, a tension that Sahlins (2017:230) refers to as "dual sovereignty" (see Lamoureux-St-Hilaire and McAnany, this volume) and that Kurnick (2016) calls the "contradiction" of political authority.

Patron deity veneration occurred in cultures across Mesoamerica. Among the Classic period lowland Maya, rulers claimed exclusive purview over the cults of these gods and periodically introduced new deities to their polities' pantheons. These traditional practices corresponded to the political organization of this period: small-scale, semi-autonomous polities each ruled by its own local dynasty and caught in wider webs of patronage and economic exchange. During the ninth century, subtle changes can be observed, which may reflect new political configurations and relationships between Maya ethnic groups. The greatest shifts in deity veneration, however, appear to come in the Postclassic period, with the Mayapan confederacy and its new political institutions.

This chapter will focus on three closely related Maya groups that occupied the lowlands of Guatemala, Honduras, Belize, the Yucatán Peninsula, and the Gulf Coast of Tabasco during the Classic and Postclassic periods. These groups can be identified linguistically based on pre- and post-contact

Native-authored texts as well as Spanish-authored accounts. While these texts probably obscure a significant amount of intragroup linguistic diversity, this three-part classification is a useful starting place to describe the complex interactions that took place across the Maya Lowlands. The first group produced the Classic Ch'olti'an inscriptions of the southern lowlands (Houston, Robertson, and Stuart 2000). Whether this language constituted a true vernacular across this region or only a written prestige language, or somewhere in between, remains uncertain. Yet the widespread use and standardization of hieroglyphic inscriptions points to a significant portion of the elite population either speaking or reading and writing this language throughout the Classic period. The second group is speakers of Yukatekan languages, originally occupying the northern lowlands and then, in the Postclassic, moving south into the Peten and Belize. Finally, the third group is speakers of Chontal, a language closely related to Classic Ch'olti'an. This language originated in the Gulf Coast of Tabasco, where vestiges continue to this day. It also spread along the coast around the Yucatán Peninsula, moving inland from the Caribbean coast into Belize and the Peten in the ninth century. While linguistic and cultural differences existed among these three groups, they are so closely related that tracing cultural innovation and borrowing between them is challenging, as we will see.

This chapter also addresses chronologies spanning the Classic, Postclassic, and colonial periods. But the divisions between these periods are defined differently by scholars working in the southern lowlands and the northern lowlands. Specifically, in the south, the period between 800 and 900 CE is considered the Terminal Classic period, a time of political upheaval and demographic collapse. Meanwhile, in the north, the definition of the Terminal Classic is extended to around 1100 CE, to encompass the Puuc florescence as well as the apogee and decline of Chichen Itza. Because of these differing definitions of the Terminal Classic, I will endeavor to specify dates where possible.

Defining Patron Deities

The nature of Mesoamerican divinity has been investigated by many. In Maya studies, some of the most important early work was done by Schellhas (1904), who assigned letters to frequently recurring deities whose names we now know better—for example, "God K" for K'awiil and "God G" for the sun god K'inich Ajaw. Taube (1992) built on Schellhas's work, making connections between Classic and Postclassic iconography. More recently, Martin's work (2007) has demonstrated that these individual god entities can fuse with one another to create compound concepts—for example, the deity labeled "God N" (the "old man") can fuse with the Principal Bird Deity to form the entity labeled "God D." We can now firmly read the Classic Maya glyph for "god" as *k'uh* (Ringle 1988). Once labeled as "God C" by Schellhas, this glyph depicts a face resembling that of a monkey, which is meant to depict a generic god head. In front of this face appear droplets, indicating the substance with which gods were fed: incense, blood, or other ritual liquids (Baron 2016:46–51). The glyph also makes up the root of the *aj k'uhun* title for important court officials (Jackson and Stuart 2001; Zender 2004) and appears as the adjective *k'uhul*, meaning "god-like" in royal titles, in keeping with Graeber and Sahlins's (2017:3) observation that "kings are imitations of gods rather than gods of kings."

Classic-period gods had a dual nature. On the one hand, they were representations of natural phenomena like wind or sun. In this state, they appeared in mythic narratives explaining the cosmos. Rulers could embody their powers and re-enact these mythic narratives through the ritual act of deity impersonation (Houston and Stuart 1996). But these gods were distant from human life, not involving themselves in human affairs like their Greco-Roman counterparts. On the other hand, these same impersonal gods could become patron gods, developing personal relationships with particular Maya communities. This covenant allowed the deity to shed its aloof nature and take physical form as an effigy. My own work on the topic has focused on how and why these relationships were formed, as well as on the ritual practices used to venerate these patron gods and their role in human political relationships (Baron 2016).

Classic Ch'olti'an Patron Deity Veneration

A traditional set of patron deity veneration practices appears in the inscriptions of Maya Lowland sites starting as early as the third century on the Hauberg Stela, now housed in the Princeton Museum of Art, where a young ruler performs a bloodletting ritual before his god(s) (see Stuart 2008). Numerous Classic Ch'olti'an inscriptions reveal that patron deities were fed (often with ritual liquids such as chocolate, pulque, or human blood), clothed in garments and jewelry, bathed, and housed in temples. Their effigies were also periodically renewed or replaced, with elaborate ceremonies described at Palenque (Stuart 2006a). Inscriptions suggest that the majority of these duties were performed by the ruler and his associates—in fact, rulers claimed ownership of these gods in terms of intimate possession (*uk'uhil*) (Houston, Robertson, and Stuart 2001) and expressed their relationship as one similar to parents and children, with rulers providing loving care (Baron 2016:87; Houston and Stuart 1996:294).

Yet although patron gods are discussed in many inscriptions, distinguishing their veneration in the archaeological record from other kinds of ritual behavior is extremely difficult. Thus, when I began this research for my dissertation (Baron 2013), my initial goal was to establish some sort of pattern or "signature" that could be used to identify patron deity veneration in the absence of hieroglyphic inscriptions. One might expect that an archaeological signature of patron deity veneration would include patron deity effigies themselves. Descriptions at Palenque suggest the firing of clay effigies (Stuart 2006a). And depictions at Tikal show the capture of massive deity effigies from Calakmul, El Peru, and Naranjo (Martin 1996, 2000). So where are the effigies? In fact, they are extremely rare. The only example I could identify in this manner— pointed out to me by Bob Sharer—is El Porton Structure J7-4B-2, where excavators found a terminated deity effigy in an earlier phase of construction (Sharer and Sedat 1987). At Palenque, researchers found an abundance of large effigy incense burners buried inside the platforms of the Cross Group temples—known epigraphically to be the temples of the site's patron gods (Cuevas García and Bernal Romero 1999). Yet contrary to their interpretation, a close look at those effigies reveals that they do not share obvious iconographic features with Palenque's patron gods and are thus unlikely to represent the patrons themselves. This lack of deity effigies might have several explanations. First, it is possible that most of them were made from more perishable materials. This would certainly be the case for the giant effigies depicted at Tikal, which were apparently carried into battle; one can imagine the difficulty in hauling a towering clay statue into combat (Martin 1996, 2000). Another possibility is that leaving effigies behind was unthinkable, and that they were either destroyed or carried away when sites were abandoned. Whatever the case, this lack of Classic-period effigies can be contrasted to the overwhelming number of effigy censer fragments recovered at Postclassic sites, a point to which we will return.

In the absence of effigies, patron deity temples can be identified using accompanying inscriptions. Here, temples are usually called *wayib* meaning "place for sleeping" (Houston and Stuart 1989). Unfortunately, only a handful of structures can be securely identified as patron deity shrines by means of associated hieroglyphic labels. In the southern lowlands, these most famously include the Cross Group temples at Palenque, but also Tikal Temple VI (Temple of the Inscriptions), the small and poorly preserved Yaxchilan Temple 3, and four structures at La Corona, where I did my dissertation work. In addition, Tokovinine, Estrada Belli, and Fialko (this volume) also identify Naranjo structure C-9 and the Aurora structure within a palace compound as shrines for two Naranjo patron deities. If we examine all these architectural spaces, however, there is no obvious pattern that sets deity shrines apart from other ritual structures.

Digging deeper, I sought at La Corona to determine whether temple assemblages might be useful for identifying patron deity veneration. To do this, I excavated four temples at La Corona that could be identified as patron deity shrines by associated inscriptions (Baron 2013, 2016). I found that each of them had undergone a change in function, starting their construction sequences as funerary shrines over bedrock tombs and eventually changing to patron deity temples. This change in function was indicated by both a change in architectural features, as well as a change in midden assemblages located behind the temples and on their front terraces: patron deity veneration involved far more consumption of liquids, as indicated by an increase in bowls and an introduction of vases. The temple midden assemblages also suggested that, while the site's inscriptions focus entirely on the ruler's role in caring for patron gods, in fact, common people at La Corona may also have made offerings to their gods on these public temples, though the process was likely closely supervised by the royal court.

What did Classic Maya rulers and communities gain by all of this effort and attention to patron gods? Inscriptions detail how deities provided benefits to the whole community, specifically the safe passage of time and success in war. Deities oversaw period ending rituals and they were carried into battle (Baron 2016:78–84; Houston and Stuart 1996:302; Martin 1996, 2000). A god's presence could also sanction a friendly relationship between polities, as seen on a carved stairway block from Calakmul that appears to record a friendly get-together between patrons of Calakmul and its client, El Peru (Baron 2016:76–77) and on a stairway from El Palmar, in which a messenger of the El Palmar court recounted meeting the Copan patron gods during a diplomatic mission (Tsukamoto 2014:282–287). Gods also offered divine sanction to specific rulers, overseeing their accession ceremonies. The implication of these hieroglyphic narratives was that a) since patron gods protected and benefited the whole community, particularly in its relationships with other communities and b) since rulers took responsibility for the care of these gods, then c) rulers were owed obedience and material wealth in exchange for their ritual service. (The possibility that commoners were also participating in the care for patron gods, as suggested by the assemblages at La Corona, would likely have undermined this logic and is conveniently omitted from these narratives.)

Spatial Distribution

Since each polity had its own gods and traditions, and rivalries between polities were frequently represented as rivalries between patron gods, this basic social contract outlined in hieroglyphic narratives was specifically a *local* contract. Thus, while other aspects of Classic Maya rulership emphasize the ruler's foreign associations (Ardren, this volume; Graeber and Sahlins 2017; Kurnick 2016; Lamoureux-St-Hilaire and McAnany, this volume), patron deity veneration specifically framed the ruler as part of the local community. Therefore, as certain ambitious polities attempted to expand their authority through networks of alliance and patronage, they faced a challenge in trying to redefine this locally based authority. The Kaanul rulers of Dzibanche and Calakmul appear to have experimented with expanding the spatial confines of traditional patron deity cults. One, for example, gifted a new effigy of Caracol's patron god to the Caracol ruler, apparently to try to "sponsor" that local cult. Much later, a text from Cancuén relates how that site's ruler acceded to power under the auspices of Calakmul's gods, rather than his own. Earlier in this volume, Tokovinine, Estrada Belli, and Fialko reveal similar attempts by the rulers of Naranjo to stretch the boundaries of their realm through the distribution of vessels depicting a local patron god. Yet such experiments do not seem to have worked in the long term: Naranjo encountered violent resistance, and Calakmul's hegemony in the southern lowlands fluctuated over time, never really integrating into a recognizable empire.

But how local was local? Was the veneration of patron deities coterminous with the polity as a whole? Or were there also hyperlocal patron gods of households, neighborhoods, or districts? In answering this question, we are confronted again with the limits of evidence: the lack of inscriptions authored by non-elite people; the difficulty in distinguishing

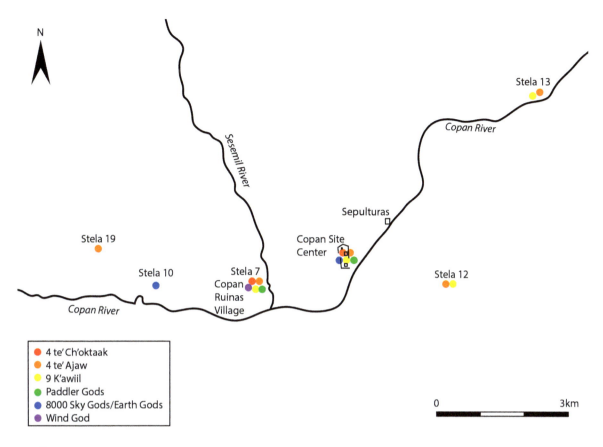

figure 7.1
Map of Copan and outlying stelae. Illustration by Joanne Baron, after Morley 1920:pl. 3.

patron deity veneration from other rituals at the household level; and the challenges of identifying political administration within a polity itself. Yet the available evidence suggests that Classic Ch'olti'an patron gods belonged to *whole* polities, rather than to political subdivisions.

Probably the best case study proving the unity of patron gods across the whole polity can be found at Copan. Copan's monuments discuss patron deity veneration at length, naming at least twenty-nine different gods. Several of Copan's monuments were erected at locations throughout the valley, outside of the polity's governing and ceremonial core. Thus, if the Copan polity had emic district divisions with corresponding gods, they would most likely be revealed in these outlying stelae. Five of these stelae discuss patron gods (Figure 7.1). The gods Chan te' Ch'oktaak ("four princes"), for example, are mentioned on Stela 7, but also on numerous monuments

in the site's ceremonial core. Chan te' Ajaw ("four lords") are similarly named on Stelae 7, 12, 13, and 19 as well as on numerous monuments in the site core. This same distribution occurs with the god Baluun K'awiil. In fact, these latter two gods are named on a hieroglyphic stairway hundreds of miles away at El Palmar, where a local official commemorated his diplomatic trip to Copan, during which he met these very god effigies (Tsukamoto 2014). They are also among those gods named as "guardians of Ux Wintik," the whole Copan polity, on the Bench of Temple 21a (Lacadena and Wichmann 2004). Deity sets also occur on these outlying stelae: the Paddler Gods appear on Stelae 7 and 13, while "8000 Sky Gods and 8000 Earth Gods" are named on Stela 10 and on Stela B in the site core. The only god who appears to be unique to any of these outlying stelae is the Wind God, named along with other deities on Stela 7. While it is possible that the Wind

Patron Deities and Rulership across the Maya Lowlands

God is somehow unique to the Copan Ruinas district of the Copan polity, where Stela 7 was found, his appearance on this stela within a longer list of gods instead points to his associations with the polity more broadly. Thus, although Copan inscriptions had ample opportunity to name gods of particular districts, they instead focused on deities that were also discussed in the site core, who played a role in the ruler's diplomatic relations with other polities, and who were considered "guardians" of the polity as a whole. This is strong evidence indicating that Copan did not recognize district gods, only polity-wide patron gods during the Classic period.

Another illustrative example can be found at the Yaxchilan polity. Yaxchilan's most prominent patron god was Aj K'ahk' O Chaak, who is mentioned in inscriptions dating from 537 all the way to 808, shortly before the polity's demise. The site of Dos Caobas, about thirteen kilometers southeast of Yaxchilan, was clearly part of the polity, as it depicted Yaxchilan rulers on its monuments. The only god mentioned at Dos Caobas was Aj K'ahk' O Chaak on Stela 1, suggesting once again that the polity venerated one set of gods, and Aj K'ahk' O Chaak in particular, rather than district gods.

It is possible, of course, that more localized district or neighborhood gods existed at Copan, Yaxchilan, and other sites, but that they were unimportant or even suppressed in official royal narratives. Either scenario, as we will see, contrasts to the directional, regional, or district gods revealed in official narratives of Chontal and Itza polities. Overall, Ch'olti'an inscriptions leave the impression of unified, polity-wide patron deity cults.

Temporal Distribution

These spatial patterns reveal that Classic Ch'olti'an patron deities corresponded to entire political entities rather than to neighborhoods or divisions. But what of chronology? The most noticeable pattern is that patron gods gradually accumulated into larger and larger pantheons at each site. This occurred as new patron gods were introduced periodically throughout a polity's history but did not replace the old. The inscriptions of Copan are also illustrative of this process, indicating that an astonishing number of deities had accumulated by the time of the site's abandonment (Baron 2016; Prager 2013). The same process can be observed at La Corona on a smaller scale. By correlating the construction histories of its temples with the historical record from the site's monuments, I argue (Baron 2013, 2016) that the introduction of new gods—and the change of function from ancestor shrines to deity shrines—was the result of political conflicts at the site between at least two rival elite families. Tokovinine, Estrada Belli, and Fialko (this volume) also propose a renewed emphasis on deity veneration in the C-9 structure of Naranjo after political upheavals of the polity. Thus, patron deity introduction and veneration may have been used by Maya rulers to remind their subjects of their local bona fides during periods of political weakness or stress.

But while pantheons expanded over time as new patron deities were added, there is no evidence that Classic Ch'olti'an populations *rotated* their gods or changed them in concert with calendrical cycles. In many cases, the same core patron gods appear in cycle after cycle while secondary gods are occasionally mentioned, seemingly at random. This is very clear at Palenque, for example, in its Temple of the Inscriptions text. The text gives a long historical account going back to the 9.4.0.0.0 period ending and proceeding through to 9.12.0.0.0. At each *k'atun* ending (except 9.6.0.0.0) as well as on a few year-ending dates, the same three principal patron deities are given gifts of bundles, clothing, and jewelry (Guenter 2007; Macri 1988:116–117; Stuart 2006b:166–168). The only other gods that appear in the text seem to be visiting with dignitaries from conquered polities (Baron 2013:481; Guenter 2007:48–49).

Patron Deities among the Chontal Maya

Chontalli is a Nahuatl term meaning "foreigner" that originally applied to diverse peoples inhabiting the Gulf of Mexico (Scholes and Roys 1968:15). Today, we use "Chontal" to refer specifically to speakers of Chontal Maya, a language closely related to Classic Ch'olti'an and more distantly related to Yukatek.

It is difficult to know the extent to which Classic Chontal populations saw themselves as distinct from their Maya neighbors to the east. During the Classic period, Ch'olti'an populations traded with the Tabasco region, importing fine paste ceramics and figurines. Tabasco's ethnic and political disposition in the Classic period is somewhat unclear. What is clear is that over the course of the seventh century, Piedras Negras, Palenque, and Calakmul undertook a series of military actions vying for control over eastern Tabasco (see Martin and Grube 2008), possibly, as I have argued elsewhere (Baron 2018), to control its supply of cacao.

While we cannot know for certain, it is possible that Comalcalco, the westernmost recognizable Classic Maya polity, was of Chontal extraction, given its Gulf Coast location. Originally an independent polity, Comalcalco came under the influence of Tortuguero in 649 after a military conquest (Zender 2001, in Martin 2020:97). The Tortuguero polity, in turn, may share origins with Palenque, as both use the *baak* emblem glyph. Later rulers of Comalcalco used this emblem as well, identifying themselves as stranger-king descendants of the conquerors from Tortuguero (and by extension, as affiliates of Palenque).

Archaeologists working at Comalcalco have recovered more than two dozen burials of individuals inside of urns, a mortuary pattern distinct from Classic Ch'olti'an sites (Armijo Torres 2018). One of these burials contained numerous inscriptions on small bone pendants and stingray spines, which have been analyzed by Marc Zender (2004). As a whole, this set of texts records a series of bloodletting rituals performed by the priest Aj Pakal Tahn starting in 765 and lasting until 777. Each year, on or near the spring equinox, Aj Pakal Tahn performed a bloodletting ritual before a different god. Not only are these repeated equinoctial rituals unique among Maya inscriptions, but the presence of a new god each year for thirteen years in a row is also unusual and can be contrasted to the Palenque pattern described above. Furthermore, as one reviewer has noted, the important role of the priest (as opposed to the ruler) in these rituals is also unusual. However, these funerary inscriptions also indicate that Aj Pakal Tahn performed rituals for the more conventional 9.17.0.0.0 period ending. The god who presided over this period ending, Unen K'awiil, is one of the same three principal gods of Palenque, and it is likely that he was brought to Comalcalco with the Tortuguero conquerors (Martin 2020:162–163). While it is difficult to make any firm conclusions using only one set of inscriptions, it is possible that the Comalcalco texts represent a Chontal practice—equinox rituals performed annually by a priest for new calendrical gods—upon which was grafted a Ch'olti'an practice—*k'atun* ending rituals for ancestral gods—introduced after the Tortuguero conquest. If so, these texts might reflect a hidden tension between the local populace and the patron deities of the foreign dynasty.

Ninth-Century Powerbrokers

The next possible glimpse of Chontal Maya that we see in the inscriptions comes in the ninth century. Simon Martin (Martin 2020:284–299), drawing on his own and previous observations by Guenter (1999) and Carter (2014), has recently argued that the eastern Peten and Belize came under the sway of foreigners during the ninth century. Their foreignness is evident in their unusual names, which were often spelled phonetically, as if adapting a foreign tongue, and which sometimes include Mexican-style square day names. Some specific features of these names point to a Chontal origin. Martin (2020:295–296) compares them to names listed in the colonial-era Paxbolon-Maldonado Papers, a document to which we will return shortly. Martin observes that the name Papmalil, recorded at Ucanal and Ixlu, contains the prefix *pap-* common in colonial surnames, while Petol, recorded at Tikal and on an unprovenienced vase K6437, contains the Chontal suffix *-ol*. Further, the colonial text documents the influence of Nahuatl on Chontal speakers, including as calendrical names.

In addition to Chontal-style names, these individuals were depicted with foreign clothing and grooming styles. Martin (2020) observes that in the inscriptions, they hold lofty *kaloomte'* titles, appearing alongside rulers of once powerful dynasties such as Caracol, Naranjo, and Tikal, who they now supervise or outrank. It appears that these new foreign powerbrokers used Ucanal as a base of operations, eventually sending offshoots to establish courts at Nakum and Ceibal. Archaeological changes that accompany these epigraphic clues include the appearance of circular structures and Paballon ceramics.

Did these Chontal powerbrokers bring changes to patron deity veneration at the sites they dominated? There are some hints that they did. At Ceibal, Wat'ul K'atel's stela program on and around a new radial pyramid A-3 places his expansionist political aspirations within a cosmological quadripartite scheme. A-3 and its associated stelae celebrate the 10.1.0.0.0 *k'atun* ending in 849. Four stelae mark the cardinal points and celebrate visits by subordinate Maya dignitaries (Carter 2014:196; Just 2007:22; Stuart 2016). Stela 11, facing east, depicts Wat'ul K'atel impersonating the Waterlily Serpent deity. It tells of Wat'ul K'atel's arrival in Ceibal exactly one solar year prior to the *k'atun* ending from Ucanal, located to the east (Stuart 2016). Stela 10, facing north, tells of lords from Tikal, Calakmul, and Motul de San José, all north of Ceibal, "witnessing" the ceremonies. This stela shows Wat'ul K'atel in the guise of "GI-K'awiil," the traditional patron god of the Ceibal polity and surrounding Petexbatun landscape. Stela 9, facing west, mentions a lord from Lakamtuun, which Stuart (2016) identifies with the Río Lacantún to the west. It shows Wat'ul K'atel as Chaak. Stela 8, facing south, records a visit from an unknown site called Puh (Carter 2014:196), which one suspects lies to the south. Wat'ul K'atel is dressed as the Jaguar God of the Underworld. Stela 21, placed in the shrine on the top of the structure, does not refer to visitors, but rather to the mythological creation date of 13.0.0.0.0 and links the Ceibal toponym to its mythological precursor (Stuart 2016). Wat'ul K'atel's headdress on Stela 21 is difficult to identify with any particular god.

None of the individual elements of this A-3 program at Ceibal appear out of place in the Classic Ch'olti'an world. Indeed, it is likely that the platform was meant to echo ancient mythological themes. And yet, GI-K'awiil, the principal patron god of Ceibal, has been demoted to just one of four directional gods. These directional gods are associated with Ceibal's new political hegemony, which is similarly conceptualized as a four-part scheme. While Classic Ch'olti'an polities, notably Copan, similarly described a four-part division of the Maya world, the Ceibal program seems unique in claiming hegemony over all of it. Whether those claims were more real or aspirational is still unclear.

There are other hints of Chontal-introduced changes as well. Ceibal Stela 19, dated to 10.3.0.0.0 in 889, records a unique ritual, in which four thirteen-day intervals are counted, for a total of fifty-two days after the period ending (Carter 2015). After each interval (or perhaps only after the full fifty-two days), some event occurred involving a god carried on a palanquin. The stela depicts the ruler in an unusual costume of the duck-billed Mexican wind deity. Other Mexican-style deities appear on Ceibal Stela 3 (the wind god and two Tlalocs) as well as on stelae at Ixlu and Ucanal (Carter 2014:218).

Acalan Chontal

We are not offered another glimpse into Chontal patron deity veneration practices until the colonial era. The Paxbolon-Maldonado Papers, written in the early seventeenth century, record the merits of Don Pablo Paxbolon, governor of Tixchel (Scholes and Roys 1968). Not only does the document give a history of the ruling dynasty of the Chontal of Acalan-Tixchel, it is one of few colonial-era documents to record the Chontal language, thus giving us valuable information about place-names and surnames (see above). Don Pablo descended from the rulers of the Acalan polity, whose capital at the time of the conquest was Itzamkanac. This town played a minor role in the conquest, being visited by Cortés on his way across the Maya region to Honduras. After much scholarly debate, the location of Itzamkanac can be placed on the Candelaria River (Scholes and Roys 1968) and likely corresponds to the site of El Tigre (Vargas Pacheco and Teramoto Ornelas 1996).

The Paxbolon-Maldonado Papers describe how the first ruler of the lineage, Auxaual, came to the Chontal area from Yukatek-speaking Cozumel Island, together with his principal men, probably in the fourteenth century (Scholes and Roys 1968:73).

Auxaual is not a Yukatek name, but instead can be found on an early colonial map as a village name in Tabasco. This suggests that Auxaual's Cozumel origins may have been contrived or exaggerated to give this ruler legitimacy (Scholes and Roys 1968:79, 838n5). But, it appears, the stranger-king narrative was counterbalanced by local patron deity veneration practices.

After the arrival of Cortés, a few generations later, the document describes "four divisions of the land" (*chan tzucul cab*): Tadzunum, Tachabte, Atapan, and Taçacto, each led by a principal man who the ruler consulted before making major decisions (Scholes and Roys 1968:390). A few decades later, the document recounts a visit by Fray Diego de Béjar to convert the Acalan Chontal to Christianity: "He wanted everyone to come and display his idols. Having heard what the father told them, they began to bring out their idols, first the idol of the ruler which bears the name of Cukulchan, and also the devil of Tadzunum, and those of Tachabte, Atapan, and Taçacto, and the other idols" (Scholes and Roys 1968:395). Note that the same four divisions of the land are mentioned, each with its own idol, distinct from the ruler's idol, Cukulchan (K'uk'ulkan, the Feathered Serpent). Further down in the same paragraph, the text lists other gods: "the idols hidden in their secret places by the Indians, such as Ykchua, for so this idol was called, another called Tabay, another called Ixchel, another called Cabtanilcabtan, and many other places of idols were sought out in all the pueblos." It is possible that the four named gods correspond to the four named "divisions of the land" listed above.

But what are these "divisions of the land"? Scholes and Roys (1968:54–55) note that the four named divisions do not appear on the document's list of Acalan towns, thus suggesting that they may be neighborhoods or divisions of the capital, Itzamkanac. Vargas Pacheco (2013), on the other hand, argues that these are four divisions of the entire Acalan polity, which then dominated the Candelaria River watershed to the Gulf Coast and south to Tenosique. He suggests that the four divisions of the land correspond to two Candelaria tributaries, the middle Candelaria itself, and the coast, each of these regions having a principal site. It is notable that Tixchel, the coastal site to where the Acalan Chontal eventually moved their capital, is named for Ixchel, one of the four deities listed during Diego de Béjar's conversion efforts. Itzamkanac, meanwhile, is an ancient theonym seen at Piedras Negras, Copan, and Xcalumkin (Martin 2015). Might these god names also refer to these communities' patron deities?

What to make of this evidence for Chontal patron deity veneration? Most of our information comes from locations and periods of substantial cultural mixing: Comalcalco after its conquest by Tortuguero, the eastern Peten after Chontal incursions, and the colonial period after Christian missionizing efforts. Yet we can identify three subtle changes. First, in terms of geopolitics, the Chontal powerbrokers of eighth-century eastern Peten, as well as the Postclassic- and colonial-era Acalan Chontal, had (or at least aspired to have) more geographically expansive hegemonies than their Classic Ch'olti'an counterparts. Second, there are hints that these hegemonies were divided by cardinal directions, each associated with different patron gods. And finally, there are hints of more complex calendrical rituals associated with patron deity veneration than those of Classic Ch'olti'an populations.

Patron Deities among the Yukatek Maya

While the northern Yucatán Peninsula was somewhat removed geopolitically, many Classic-period sites have material culture and inscriptions that show strong linkages to the elite prestige culture of the Classic Ch'olti'an polities to the south. Nevertheless, most of these sites do not address patron deity veneration explicitly in their hieroglyphic record, making it difficult to compare northern and southern traditions. The one exception to this pattern is Chichen Itza, which has a number of ninth-century inscriptions related to patron deities. And while these inscriptions clearly display Yukatekan cultural traits—linguistic, calendrical, and graphical differences from Ch'olti'an texts—the veneration practices they record are remarkably similar to their counterparts to the south.

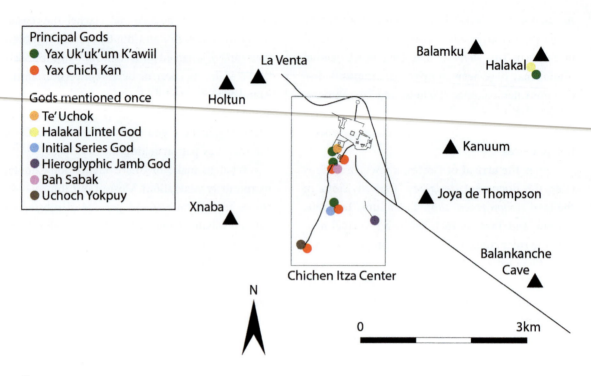

figure 7.2
Map of Chichen Itza and outlying groups. Illustration by Joanne Baron, after Stuart 1989:2–3.

Based on the work of previous authors, I identified ten patron deities named at Chichen Itza (see Boot 2005; Grube, Lacadena, and Martin 2003). (This is a conservative estimate, as other named characters may also have been gods [see Plank 2003].) First, many of the specific patron gods use similar names and epithets. For example, one of the two most prominent patron gods in the inscriptions of Chichen Itza was named Yax Chich Kan, who Boot (2005:321) argues was the Yukatekan version of the vision/waterlily serpent usually called Yax Chit Jun Witz' Naah Kaan in Classic Ch'olti'an. This god (or an aspect of him) was venerated as a patron deity at Calakmul, Copan, and Tikal (Baron 2016). Several patron deities at Chichen Itza are called *chanal k'uh* ("sky gods")—a slight variation from the *chanal k'uh kabal k'uh* ("sky gods and earth gods") seen in the inscriptions of Copan, Tikal, and Palenque (Baron 2013, 2016). Another is referred to as *ohlis k'uh* ("heart god") (see Stuart, Houston, and Robertson 1999:II–44), an epithet also found at Chinikiha, Comalcalco, and Palenque.

We can also see that, like the Classic Ch'olti'an polities, ninth-century Chichen Itza royal narratives did not seem to recognize distinct patron gods for different neighborhoods or quarters of the city (Figure 7.2). This is somewhat harder to prove at Chichen Itza than it is at Copan, because there is a smaller sample size, leading many deities to only be mentioned once in the inscriptions. Furthermore, there are fewer inscriptions in Chichen Itza's hinterlands. But there is one outlying area that records patron deity veneration: a lintel from a structure in Halakal, approximately five kilometers south of the site center. The Halakal inscription names one god who is not mentioned elsewhere, as well as Yax Uk'uk'um K'awiil ("Green-feathered K'awiil") (Grube, Lacadena, and Martin 2003), one of the more prominent gods of Chichen Itza. If we zoom into the center of Chichen Itza itself, a number of inscriptions mention gods who only appear once, but they are almost always together in a group with one or both of Chichen Itza's two most prominent deities, Yax Uk'uk'um K'awiil and Yax Chich Kan. Mapping the distributions of these two principal gods reveals no geographical pattern. Thus, while it is possible that Chichen Itza associated some minor gods with specific temples or areas only, the evidence suggests that overall, these two principal gods were considered patrons of the entire polity, including at least as far as Halakal. Similarly, ninth-century inscriptions of Chichen Itza reveal no calendrical patterning of patron deity veneration rituals, though this again may be the result of a small sample size. Most dates refer to temple dedications, which do not seem to follow obvious calendar cycles.

Like their counterparts to the south, the patron gods of Chichen Itza appear to be an important aspect of royal legitimation. Inscriptions clearly link these gods to the ruler and his close associates. One of the site's two principal gods, Yax Uk'uk'um K'awiil, as well as a deity named on the Initial Series Lintel, are explicitly described as belonging to the ruler (Boot 2005:321). This is quite similar to the rhetoric from southern Maya sites, where rulers frequently described their gods in terms of intimate possession (*uk'uhil*) (Houston, Robertson, and Stuart 2001). While the inscriptions of Las Monjas and the Temple of the Four Lintels at Chichen Itza also name different human owners of a set of patron gods, these owners are still closely and explicitly associated with the ruler K'ak'upakal. One of these is the ruler's mother, while others are his associates, explicitly said to "accompany" him.

When the Chichen Itza inscriptions cease to record patron deity veneration rituals after the ninth century, we lose a key source of evidence about these traditions. Ringle (this volume) proposes that the Puuc-style masks at Chichen Itza and other sites might refer to patron deities, which would open up a new avenue of future iconographic investigation. We can continue to rely on archaeology, and we gain colonial-era histories, such as the Chilam Balams and Landa's accounts. Yet these histories present a very different picture from what has been described in the epigraphic record: instead of traditional patron deity veneration, the colonial-era accounts emphasize the importance of K'uk'ulkan, the Feathered Serpent deity known in Nahuatl as Quetzalcoatl. According to these chronicles, K'uk'ulkan had a multifaceted identity as a ruler, priest, and deity, who arrived intrusively into the Yucatán Peninsula and ruled, seemingly repeatedly at multiple cities (see Landa 1978:10). Ringle, Gallareta Negrón, and Bey (1998:185) characterize this Feathered Serpent tradition as "a network of major shrines that transcended ethnic and political divisions," with Chichen Itza serving as the easternmost node in that network. At Chichen Itza itself, Landa (1978:10) associates K'uk'ulkan's veneration with the Castillo. Other structures of the "International style" at Chichen Itza bear strong resemblance to those of Tula, Hidalgo, another important site in Quetzalcoatl myths.

But whether these architectural and religious innovations were truly intrusive or indigenous, as well as the exact timing of these innovations, has been subject to heated debate. Volta and Braswell (2014), citing newly reanalyzed ceramic data, architectural data, and carved hieroglyphic dates, and applying Bayesian analysis to radiocarbon dates, present a convincing argument that the "International style" structures at Chichen Itza, which can be best associated with K'uk'ulkan and Toltec-style traits, were built around 950–1000 CE, postdating the Indigenous "Maya-style" ("Puuc-style"), which was built during the ninth century.

While debate continues about the exact dating of these styles, what is important here is that the inscriptions discussed above, which outline highly traditional patron deity veneration practices, correspond to this earlier "Puuc-style" architecture, and none of them make any mention of K'uk'ulkan or the Feathered Serpent cult. To me, this supports the notion that the K'uk'ulkan cult was introduced later, in conjunction with the "International-style" architecture, rather than the earlier Puuc style. While K'uk'ulkan has sometimes been called a patron deity of Chichen Itza and later of Mayapan, his cult is quite distinct from the traditional form of patron deity veneration that I have been describing. Rather than a local deity through which polities could define themselves in contrast to others, he was a pan-Mesoamerican phenomenon that invited pilgrimage to important shrine centers (Ringle, Gallareta Negrón, and Bey 1998). Thus, the promotion of the K'uk'ulkan cult among Maya polities represented a shift from the traditional narrative of locally based authority to one of true stranger-kings: rulers with foreign connections and a corresponding foreign god. The best evidence for these profound changes can be seen in the archaeology of Mayapan and its clients.

Mayapan

Mayapan innovated a dramatic break with the past. First and foremost, this break was political: Mayapan accomplished a remarkable feat in its confederacy. While previous hegemonies, especially Tikal and Calakmul, likely held sway over larger populations, it is important to remember that they were unstable networks, flickering in and out of regional dominance. Mayapan, in contrast, united a large territorial extent under a stable, multigenerational ruling structure (Masson and Peraza Lope 2014a). This was accomplished through its political system, in which leaders of subject towns came together to live in Mayapan, supported by their home populations. Though this council was likely presided over by a traditional paramount (Peraza Lope and Masson 2014a; Ringle and Bey 2001), the sheer territorial size and success of the Mayapan confederacy, as compared to Classic polities, suggests some sort of political innovation.

In what might this innovation consist? One Mayapan strategy appears to have been violence: Masson and Peraza Lope (2014b) detail evidence for war and human sacrifice on a larger scale than is typical in the Classic period. But I believe religious innovation also played an important role. I have argued that one of the many reasons this kind of stable territorial entity was not possible among Classic Ch'olti'an polities is that patron deity veneration couched royal authority in local terms: the ruler was responsible for caring for the community's local gods. How could the community trust a distant overlord to do the same? How could they trust that a distant overlord's local gods would have their interests at heart? While Classic Ch'olti'an rulers did promote narratives emphasizing their foreign origins (Ardren, this volume; Lamoureux-St-Hilaire and McAnany, this volume), it appears that they needed to be *physically* present in their polities in order to carry out their duties to local patron deities. Hare, Masson, and Peraza Lope (2014) reflect on the inherent tension among Mayapan's inhabitants between hometown loyalties and the greater confederacy. It is this very tension that may have eventually led to the city's demise after the Xiu uprising against Cocom rule. But for a few hundred years, Mayapan was able to navigate this tension, and one of the ways they did so was by simply discarding the traditional patron deity model altogether. Neither Landa nor the Chilam Balam books give any reference to specific patron gods of Mayapan or other Postclassic communities. This presents a striking contrast to the Native-authored documents from the highlands: patron gods play a major role in texts such as the Popol Vuh, Titulo de Totonicapan, and Memorial of Solola. And they play a major role in the Native-authored histories of the Nahuas.

In the place of traditional patron gods, we see new religious practices at Mayapan: Temple Q-162 was apparently built to emulate Chichen Itza's Castillo and to continue the cult of the Feathered Serpent, while Mayapan's Q-152 is similar to Chichen Itza's Caracol structure. But Mayapan also innovated an extreme proliferation of deity effigies representing numerous supernatural characters from both the Maya and Mexican pantheons. These came in the form of clay effigy censers and were introduced at some point after Mayapan's founding. Unlike in the Classic period, where effigies are almost impossible to find archaeologically, they are recovered in great quantities at Mayapan. Peraza Lope and Masson's (2014b) careful analysis of the distribution of these effigies demonstrates that while elites maintained control of their production and use, they were not confined to the main temple complex of Q-162. Iconographic analysis revealed that although there was some variation in which gods were represented in which ritual structures, each group contained a wide variety of effigies, including Q-162. In fact, while ostensibly the principal religious structure, this complex contained fewer effigies than other temple groups and no effigies of K'uk'ulkan himself (though it did contain three effigies of Ehecatl, the Mexican wind god sometimes associated with Quetzalcoatl).

We also see an extreme proliferation of calendar associations documented in the chronicles, with different deities presiding over *k'atuns* and years, often in a way that corresponded to rotational power-sharing arrangements (Edmonson 1982, 1986). While these calendar associations have not been explicitly documented archaeologically at Mayapan itself, researchers at Zacpeten were able to do so. Zacpeten is a Kowoj site in the Peten whose inhabitants claimed to have come from Mayapan (Rice 2009). There, excavators used precise point-proveniencing to show that old, well-used censers were often paired with newer censers. They interpreted this pattern to reflect Landa's account, in which a certain god would preside over a *k'atun*, with the upcoming god joining it at the ten-year mark (Pugh, Rice, and Cecil 2009). The fact that Mayapan religious practices documented in the chronicles can be observed at places as far away as the Peten, Eastern Yucatán, and Belize demonstrates Mayapan's political influence even in areas beyond its direct control.

Peten Itza

It is interesting to observe that the Itza of the Peten, the last independent Maya polity, may have been more traditional in their religious practices than Mayapan. Various Spanish eyewitnesses described the temples and idols of the capital, Noj Peten. Notably, none of them mention the cult of K'uk'ulkan, although Jones (1998:74) suggests that the description of the largest temple sounds similar to the K'uk'ulkan temples at Mayapan and Chichen Itza. Instead, eyewitnesses described two idols, Pakok and Hexchunchan—they burned incense, danced, and carried these idols into battle against their enemies (Villagutierre Soto-Mayor 1983:302–303). Eyewitnesses disagreed on the total number of temples at Noj Peten. The Franciscan missionary Avendaño reported nine (Means 1917:18), while General Ursua and his men reported twenty-one, including the principal temple, when they invaded the island the following year (Villagutierre Soto-Mayor 1983:313). Jones (1998:73) reconciles these accounts by arguing that there were nine principal temples—corresponding to eight districts of the Itza polity, with the extra (main) temple corresponding to the capital itself—and that the remaining twelve were of lesser importance. If he is correct, this might suggest an arrangement similar to the Acalan Chontal with district gods.

The Itza of the Peten traced their origins to Chichen Itza, claiming to have migrated south during K'atun 8 Ajaw after a conflict at a royal wedding. This account seems to refer to an episode from the Chilam Balams involving Hunac Ceel, who different scholars place at different times in Yucatán's chronology (Jones 1998:11–13). It is possible that the contrast between the traditionalist Itza and their Mayapan-aligned neighbors, the Kowoj, might be explained by the timing of their migrations to the Peten: the Itza before Mayapan's religious innovations, and the Kowoj after.

The Bigger Picture

In this chapter, I have examined patron deity veneration among the Classic Ch'olti'an, Chontal, and Yukatek populations of the Maya Lowlands from the Early Classic period until the conquest of the last independent Maya polity in 1697. This survey has revealed many continuities but also many distinctions among these groups. Ethnic differences appear to play only a minor role in these religious differences. While Chontal groups appear to have incorporated more elaborate calendrical rituals into patron deity veneration and may have arranged patron gods according to quadripartite schemes, they nevertheless continued to venerate particular gods of specific towns or districts. Of the three groups, the Chontal are the most difficult to reconstruct, a situation that can hopefully be remedied through future investigations of their archaeological sites. Chichen Itza, meanwhile, shows clear distinctions in its epigraphy and material culture from Ch'olti'an sites, but nevertheless records remarkably similar patron deity veneration practices in the ninth century. And the Peten Itza, though very late chronologically, continued to maintain similar traditions.

The biggest distinctions that we can see in this long history comes with the rise of the Mayapan Confederacy. The importance of the pan-Mesoamerican cult of the Feathered Serpent, the proliferation of gods and their effigy censers, and the complexity of calendrical rituals all left a lasting impact on the Yucatán Peninsula even after the city's demise. As I have argued throughout the chapter, the religious distinctions that we see across these groups and time periods were likely driven primarily by differences in political organization and strategies of legitimation. Most of the polities of the Classic Ch'olti'an were small in scale, with corresponding local gods and fine-grained distinctions between communities. While larger hegemonies did emerge, particularly those led by Calakmul and Tikal, neither of these polities introduced major religious innovations, and their hegemonies remained unstable and short-term. The territorial ambitions of the ninth-century Chontal newcomers are reflected in Ceibal's A-3 program and its designation of gods for each of the four corners of the political hegemony. And the Mayapan confederacy, uniting diverse communities under a single, stable political system, avoided the community distinctions represented by patron deities altogether. In their place, it emphasized an all-encompassing K'uk'ulkan cult and a complex calendrical power-sharing system presided over by innumerable gods, whose effigies were manufactured under elite supervision at the capital.

When considering these various practices in light of the stranger-king model, I would argue that "traditional" patron deity practices emphasized the ruler as a local. In caring for the community's supernatural patrons, the ruler created social distinction, but also set himself, along with his followers, in contrast to rival polities. Therefore, patron deity veneration was likely used as a counterbalance to the ruler's other political strategies, which emphasized his foreign connections and stranger status (Ardren, this volume; Lamoureux-St-Hilaire and McAnany, this volume). Thus, in times of strife or competition with other contenders to the throne, rulers could lean into the patron deity narrative, introducing new gods in the process. In contrast, the political strategies evident at Mayapan represented a jettisoning of these old strategies, focusing first on the international cult of the Feathered Serpent deity (a stranger-king par excellence) and then on the proliferation of calendrically linked gods uniting widespread territories into a single set of cult practices. Maya rulers across time and space had to balance the contradictions in their positions, and this meant cleaving to tradition, introducing new gods, and experimenting with new ideas, as the situation demanded.

A final note of caution: it is possible that at least some of the patterns described in this chapter are a result of the limitations of available data. After all, much of what we know of Chontal and late Yukatek practices come from colonial-era texts not available for earlier periods. And we would know virtually nothing about Classic-period patron deities if it were not for carved monuments, which disappeared by around 1000 CE. While archaeology is a valuable source of data in all periods, it is often difficult to interpret without emic descriptions of corresponding beliefs. So it is possible that the break with tradition that I am proposing for Mayapan is illusory. On the other hand, one could argue that the cessation of the monumental record is itself a piece of evidence. The act of commemoration, including inscribing in stone, of the ruler's great acts of reverence must have been part of the point of patron god cults. With new political arrangements came new religious practices that reduced the importance of these commemorative acts.

REFERENCES CITED

Armijo Torres, Ricardo

    2018   La investigación integral del INAH en Comalcalco de 1993 a 2018. *Nuevo mundo, mundos nuevos*, https://doi.org/10.4000/nuevomundo.74569.

Baron, Joanne P.

    2013   Patrons of La Corona: Deities and Power in a Classic Maya Community. PhD dissertation, University of Pennsylvania, Philadelphia.

    2016   *Patron Gods and Patron Lords: The Semiotics of Classic Maya Community Cults.* University Press of Colorado, Boulder.

    2018   Making Money in Mesoamerica: Currency Production and Procurement in the Classic Maya Financial System. *Economic Anthropology* 5(2):210–223.

Boot, Erik

    2005   *Continuity and Change in Text and Image at Chichén Itzá, Yucatán, Mexico: A Study of the Inscriptions, Iconography, and Architecture at a Late Classic to Early Postclassic Maya Site.* CNWS Publications, Leiden.

Carter, Nicholas

    2014   Kingship and Collapse: Inequality and Identity in the Terminal Classic Southern Maya Lowlands. PhD dissertation, Brown University, Providence.

    2015   An Innovative Ritual Cycle at Terminal Classic Ceibal. Maya Decipherment, https://mayadecipherment.com/2015/09/17/an-innovative-ritual-cycle-at-terminal-classic-ceibal.

Cuevas García, Martha, and Guillermo Bernal Romero

    1999   P'uluut K'uh, "dioses incensario": Aspectos arqueológicos y epigráficos de los incensarios palencanos. In *La organización social entre los mayas prehispánicos, coloniales y modernos: Memoria de la Tercera Mesa Redonda de Palenque*, edited by Vera Tiesler Blos, Rafael Cobos, and Merle Green Robertson, vol. 1, pp. 376–400. Instituto Nacional de Antropología e Historia, Universidad Autónoma de Yucatán, Mexico City.

Edmonson, Munro S. (editor and translator)

    1982   *The Ancient Future of the Itza: The Book of Chilam Balam of Tizimin.* University of Texas Press, Austin.

    1986   *Heaven Born Merida and Its Destiny: The Book of Chilam Balam of Chumayel.* University of Texas Press, Austin.

Graeber, David, and Marshall Sahlins

    2017   *On Kings.* Hau Books, Chicago.

Grube, Nikolai, Alfonso Lacadena, and Simon Martin

    2003   *Chichen Itza and Ek' Balam: Terminal Classic Inscriptions from Yucatan.* Proceedings of the Maya Hieroglyphic Workshop. University of Texas, Austin.

Guenter, Stanley

    1999   The Classic Maya Collapse. Unpublished manuscript.

    2007   The Tomb of K'inich Janaab Pakal: The Temple of the Inscriptions at Palenque. Mesoweb, www.mesoweb.com/articles/guenter/TI.pdf.

Hare, Timothy S., Marilyn A. Masson, and Carlos Peraza Lope

    2014   The Urban Landscape. In *Kukulcan's Realm: Urban Life at Ancient Mayapán*, edited by Marilyn A. Masson and Carlos Peraza Lope, pp. 262–321. University Press of Colorado, Boulder.

Houston, Stephen D., John Robertson, and David Stuart

    2000   The Language of Classic Maya Inscriptions. *Current Anthropology* 41(3):321–356.

    2001   *Quality and Quantity in Glyphic Nouns and Adjectives.* Research Reports on Ancient Maya Writing 47. Center for Maya Research, Washington, D.C.

Houston, Stephen D., and David Stuart

    1989   *The Way Glyph: Evidence for "Co-essences" among the Classic Maya.* Research Reports on Ancient Maya Writing 30. Center for Maya Research, Washington, D.C.

    1996   Of Gods, Glyphs, and Kings: Divinity and Rulership among the Classic Maya. *Antiquity* 70(268):289–312.

Jackson, Sarah, and David Stuart
- 2001 The Aj K'uhun Title: Deciphering a Classic Maya Term of Rank. *Ancient Mesoamerica* 12(2):217–228.

Jones, Grant D.
- 1998 *The Conquest of the Last Maya Kingdom.* Stanford University Press, Stanford.

Just, Bryan R.
- 2007 Ninth-Century Stelae of Machaquila and Seibal. Foundation for the Advancement of Mesoamerican Studies, http://www.famsi.org/reports/01050/01050Just01.pdf.

Kurnick, Sarah
- 2016 Paradoxical Politics: Negotiating the Contradictions of Political Authority. In *Political Strategies in Pre-Columbian Mesoamerica*, edited by Sarah Kurnick and Joanne P. Baron. University Press of Colorado, Boulder.

Lacadena, Alfonso, and Søren Wichmann
- 2004 On the Representation of the Glottal Stop in Maya Writing. In *The Linguistics of Maya Writing*, edited by Søren Wichmann, pp. 100–164. University of Utah Press, Salt Lake City.

Landa, Diego de
- 1978 *Yucatan Before and After the Conquest.* Translated by William Gates. Dover, New York.

Macri, Martha J.
- 1988 A Descriptive Grammar of Palenque Mayan. PhD dissertation, University of California, Berkeley.

Martin, Simon
- 1996 Tikal's "Star War" Against Naranjo. In *Eighth Palenque Round Table, 1993*, edited by Martha J. Macri and Jan McHargue, pp. 223–236. The Pre-Columbian Art Research Institute, San Francisco.
- 2000 Nuevos datos epigráficos sobre la guerra maya del dlásico. In *La guerra entre los antiguos mayas: Memoria de la Primera Mesa Redonda de Palenque*, edited by Silvia Trejo, pp. 107–124. Instituto Nacional de Antropología e Historia, Consejo Nacional Para la Cultura y las Artes, Mexico City.
- 2007 Theosynthesis in Ancient Maya Religion. Paper presented at the 12th European Maya Conference, Geneva.
- 2015 The Old Man of the Maya Universe: A Unitary Dimension to Ancient Maya Religion. In *Maya Archaeology 3*, edited by Charles Golden, Stephen D. Houston, and Joel Skidmore, pp. 186–228. Precolumbia Mesoweb Press, San Francisco.
- 2020 *Ancient Maya Politics: A Political Anthropology of the Classic Period, 150–900 CE.* Cambridge University Press, New York.

Martin, Simon, and Nikolai Grube
- 2008 *Chronicle of the Maya Kings and Queens.* 2nd ed. Thames and Hudson, New York.

Masson, Marilyn A., and Carlos Peraza Lope
- 2014a Archaeological Investigation of an Ancient Urban Place. In *Kukulcan's Realm: Urban Life at Ancient Mayapan*, edited by Marilyn A. Masson and Carlos Peraza Lope, pp. 30–85. University Press of Colorado, Boulder.
- 2014b Militarism, Misery, and Collapse. In *Kukulcan's Realm: Urban Life at Ancient Mayapan*, edited by Marilyn A. Masson and Carlos Peraza Lope, pp. 695–825. University Press of Colorado, Boulder.

Means, Philip Ainsworth
- 1917 *History of the Spanish Conquest of Yucatan and of the Itzas.* Peabody Museum of Archaeology and Ethnology, Harvard University, Cambridge, Mass.

Morley, Sylvanus G.
- 1920 *The Inscriptions of Copan.* Carnegie Institution of Washington Publication 219. Carnegie Institution of Washington, Washington, D.C.

Peraza Lope, Carlos, and Marilyn A. Masson
- 2014a Politics and Monumental Legacies. In *Kukulcan's Realm: Urban Life at Ancient Mayapan*, edited by Marilyn A. Masson and Carlos Peraza Lope, pp. 86–189. University Press of Colorado, Boulder.
- 2014b Religious Practice. In *Kukulcan's Realm: Urban Life at Ancient Mayapan*, edited by Marilyn A. Masson and Carlos Peraza Lope, pp. 695–825. University Press of Colorado, Boulder.

Plank, Shannon E.
- 2003 Monumental Maya Dwellings in the Hieroglyphic and Archaeological Records: A Cognitive-Anthropological Approach to Classic Maya Architecture. PhD dissertation, Boston University, Boston.

Prager, Christian
- 2013 Übernatürliche Akteure in der Klassischen Maya-Religion: Eine Untersuchung zu intrakultureller Variation und Stabilität am Beispiel des k'uh "Götter"-Konzepts in den religiösen Vorstellungen und Überzeugungen Klassischer Maya-Eliten (250–900 n.Chr.). PhD dissertation, Rheinischen Friedrich-Wilhelms-Universität zu Bonn, Bonn.

Pugh, Timothy, Prudence Rice, and Leslie Cecil
- 2009 Zacpeten Group 719, the Last Noble Residence. In *The Kowoj: Identity, Migration, and Geopolitics in Late Postclassic Peten, Guatemala*, edited by Prudence M. Rice and Don S. Rice, pp. 192–216. University Press of Colorado, Boulder.

Rice, Prudence
- 2009 The Kowoj in Geopolitical Perspective. In *The Kowoj: Identity, Migration, and Geopolitics in Late Postclassic Peten, Guatemala*, edited by Prudence M. Rice and Don S. Rice, pp. 21–54. University Press of Colorado, Boulder.

Ringle, William M.
- 1988 *Of Mice and Monkeys: The Value and Meaning of T1016, the God C Hieroglyph*. Research Reports on Ancient Maya Writing 18. Center for Maya Research, Washington, D.C.

Ringle, William M., and George J. Bey
- 2001 Post-Classic and Terminal Classic Courts of the Northern Maya Lowlands. In *Royal Courts of the Ancient Maya, Volume 2: Data and Case Studies*, edited by Takeshi Inomata and Stephen D. Houston, pp. 266–307. Westview Press, Boulder, Colo.

Ringle, William M., Tomás Gallareta Negrón, and George J. Bey
- 1998 The Return of Quetzalcoatl: Evidence for the Spread of a World Religion during the Epiclassic Period. *Ancient Mesoamerica* 9(2):183–232.

Sahlins, Marshall
- 2008 The Stranger-King or, Elementary Forms of the Politics of Life. *Indonesia and the Malay World* 36(105):177–199.
- 2017 The Stranger-Kingship of the Mexica. In *On Kings*, edited by David Graeber and Marshall Sahlins, pp. 223–248. University of Chicago Press, Chicago.

Schellhas, Paul
- 1904 *Representations of Deities of the Maya Manuscripts*. Peabody Museum of Archaeology and Ethnology, Harvard University, Cambridge, Mass.

Scholes, France V., and Ralph Roys
- 1968 *The Maya Chontal Indians of Acalan-Tixchel: A Contribution to the History and Ethnography of the Yucatan Peninsula*. University of Oklahoma Press, Norman.

Sharer, Robert J., and David W. Sedat
- 1987 *Archaeological Investigations in the Northern Maya Highlands, Guatemala: Interaction and Development of Maya Civilization*. University Museum, University of Pennsylvania, Philadelphia.

Stuart, David
- 2006a *Sourcebook for the 30th Maya Meetings, March 14–19, 2006*. The Mesoamerican Center, Department of Art and Art History, University of Texas, Austin.
- 2006b *The Inscriptions from Temple XIX at Palenque*. The Pre-Columbian Art Research Institute, San Francisco.
- 2008 A Childhood Ritual on the Hauberg Stela. Maya Decipherment, http://decipherment.wordpress.com/2007/04/13/reading-the-water-serpent/.
- 2016 Ceibal in Historical Context: Geo-Politics, Cosmology, and the Design of Structure A-3. Paper presented at the Maya Meetings, University of Texas, Austin.

Stuart, David, Stephen D. Houston, and John Robertson
- 1999 Recovering the Past: Classic Maya Language and Classic Maya Gods. In *Notebook for the XXIIIrd Maya Hieroglyphic Forum at Texas*. Department of Art and Art History, College of Fine Arts, and the Institute of Latin American Studies, Austin.

Stuart, George E.
- 1989 Introduction: The Hieroglyphic Record of Chichen Itza and Its Neighbors. Mesoweb, https://www.mesoweb.com/bearc/cmr/RRAMW23-25intro.pdf.

Taube, Karl
- 1992 *The Major Gods of Ancient Yucatan.* Dumbarton Oaks Research Library and Collection, Washington, D.C.

Tsukamoto, Kenichiro
- 2014 Politics in Plazas: Classic Maya Ritual Performance at El Palmar, Campeche, Mexico. PhD dissertation, University of Arizona, Tucson.

Vargas Pacheco, Ernesto
- 2013 Patrón de asentamiento y organización sociopolítica de la provincia de Acalan (Campeche–Mexico). *Revista de arqueologia americana* 31:81–112.

Vargas Pacheco, Ernesto, and Kimiyo Teramoto Ornelas
- 1996 Las ruinas arqueológicas de El Tigre: Campeche; ¿Itzamkanac? *Mayab* 10:33–45.

Villagutierre Soto-Mayor, Juan de
- 1983 *History of the Conquest of the Province of the Itza: Subjugation and Events of the Lacondon and Other Nations of Uncivilized Indians in the Lands from the Kingdom of Guatemala to the Provinces of Yucatan in North America.* Edited by Frank E. Comparato, and translated by Robert D. Wood. Labyrinthos, Culver City, Calif.

Volta, Beniamino, and Geoffrey E. Braswell
- 2014 Alternative Narratives and Missing Data: Refining the Chronology of Chichen Itza. In *The Maya and Their Central American Neighbors: Settlement Patterns, Architecture, Hieroglyphic Texts, and Ceramics*, edited by Geoffrey E. Braswell, pp. 356–402. Routledge, New York.

Zender, Marc
- 2001 The Conquest of Comalcalco: Warfare and Political Expansion in the Northwestern Periphery of the Maya Area. Paper presented at the 19th Maya Weekend, University of Pennsylvania Museum, Philadelphia.
- 2004 A Study of Classic Maya Priesthood. PhD dissertation, University of Calgary, Alberta.

Temporalities of Royal Costume in the Maya Lowlands

CHRISTINA T. HALPERIN

Part of the enduring power of Maya rulership was its ability to embody the memory, experience, and movement of time. While much is known about the dynastic histories of Maya kings and queens and their memorialization in carved stone monuments during key moments in the Maya calendar, this chapter explores the temporality of Maya *k'uhul ajawob* through their costume. Drawing inspiration from Ernst Kantorowicz's (1957) notion of the king's two bodies, I examine Maya costuming as a part of a central contradiction of kingship—that is, the ruler's body as both a natural body, limited in time by aging and the human life course, and a body politic, an enduring dynastic tradition grounded in divine kingship.

Although many different types of royal costume elements capture the temporalities of both personal narrative and enduring dynastic tradition, I turn to two elements in particular: feathered capes and carved jade ornaments. Carved jade ornaments were intertwined in the biography of individual rulers, both male and female, but also materialized dynastic connections that linked royal individuals to ancestors and deities of the deep past and ensured continuity of spirit and political legitimacy into the future. In contrast, I argue that feathered capes were more closely linked to the living, perishable body, where they marked key historic events in the individual life history of a king, most notably those involving war, conflict, and captive-taking. In this latter case, such costuming was also a critical part of the performance of a particular form of masculinity expressed by a mature adult whose status was not awarded at birth but was lived in the historical moment.

Bodily Dress and the Making of History

Costume, dress, body modifications, and ornament are often examined as a way to understand social identities, what Terence Turner (2012) has called the "social skin," the interface of an individual and society. And as Pierre Bourdieu's (1977, 1990) concept of *habitus* has emphasized, it is through bodily

figure 8.1
Egyptian *nemes* and *uraeus* as pharonic symbols of power over the longue durée: a) Den, 1st Dynasty (British Museum); b) Senwosret III, Middle Kingdom, 12th Dynasty (British Museum); and c) Hatshepsut, New Kingdom, 18th Dynasty (Metropolitan Museum of Art).

practices that social phenomena are internalized and take more concrete forms. Thus, in the context of this volume, the task would naturally focus on royal identities as they intersect with other identity formations in Maya society. Although this chapter does indeed explore kingly social identities, it more specifically examines the intersection of costume and time—that is, the ways in which costume elements were part of the making and memory of history and of the temporality of both personal lives and royal legacies. Throughout history, the body has always been a central symbol of both the living sovereign and sovereignty as a concept, institution, and ideal. As Kantorowicz (1957) underscores for medieval political theology, kingship attempts to balance the basic contradiction of body and soul, human and immortal, natural and mystical, and the natural body and the body politic—all summed up in the statement, "The king is dead. Long live the king."

Costume plays intimately into this very contradiction. It helps to produce an enduring kingly body politic—an institution, a governing body, and a legacy that does not die but continues over the longue durée—and a sensate body that becomes and changes through lived experience. For example, one of the best examples of costume in ancient Egypt as a participatory part of the enduring body politic was the pharaoh's *nemes* and *uraeus* (Figure 8.1), which served as the principal symbols worn by Egyptian pharaohs over thousands of years beginning with the 1st Dynasty (Den) and continuing through the Old, Middle, and New Kingdom periods.

Changes in royal costume can also be examined as gradual, multigenerational changes over the centuries, similar to cultural-historical perspectives of artifact styles that are often seen as the unconscious product and replication of tradition throughout history (Conkey and Hastorf 1993; Hegmon 1992; cf. Pauketat and Alt 2005; Robb and Pauketat 2013). In this case, long-term sartorial trends, on the temporal order of Fernand Braudel's (1960, 1992) *conjuntures*, mark particular eras of rulership rather than embodying an individual king or queen or rulership in general. Royal dress during the Golden Age of the Spanish Empire, for instance, was characterized by the wearing of black garments over the course of two centuries (Figure 8.2). While the color black was previously associated with monastic orders and a rejection of elaborate, luxurious, polychrome, and highly decorated textiles, the Habsburg royal family elevated black to become the new symbol of luxury and royalty. This new color of royal

figure 8.2
Black clothing of Habsburg royalty as defining an era of rulership in the Spanish Golden Age: a) Charles V, Holy Roman Emperor, King of Spain (painting by Titian, 1548, Alte Pinakothek); b) Joanna, Princess of Portugal, Regent of Spain (painting by Alonso Sánchez Coello, ca. 1557, Bilbao Fine Arts Museum); and c) Charles II, King of Spain (painting by Juan Carreño de Miranda, ca. 1685, Kunsthistorisches Museum Wien, Bilddatenbank).

garb was due, in part, to Spanish access to logwood dyes, which came from the Maya area, and produced a rich, dark, and very deep black that was superior to European dyes (Colomer 2014; Schneider 1978). In turn, the spread and popularity of particular types of costume and ornamentation may be seen as an emulation of prominent royal families, as noblemen and women throughout Europe also began to wear black clothing to symbolically capture the power of royal dominance and privilege through dress.

Although emulation and symbolic appropriation are certainly multidirectional and polyvalent, whereby trends emerge from all types of peoples, social classes, and contexts, there is no denying that elite practices often set the standard—something is alluring, pleasing, and commanding because it is elite. As Bourdieu (1986:5) noted: "Taste classifies, and it classifies the classifier. Social subjects, classified by their classifications, distinguish themselves by the distinctions they make, between the beautiful and the ugly, the distinguished and the vulgar, in which their position in the objective classifications is expressed or betrayed."

At the same time, costume has the potential to play a critical part of the making of temporalities—the experiences of being and becoming in a given moment or period of time (Csordas 1990, 1994; Joyce 2000a). In particular, when focused on personal narratives, costume and ornament are instrumental in producing particular life stages and in linking past events with the making of the present. In their depictions on stone and in painting, these costumes arguably make history as much as the written texts accompanying them. Of course, the histories that are often produced are those that embody monumental time—the official events of the state (Rankean history) rather than what Michael Herzfeld (1991:10–11) calls social time, the "grist of everyday experience." In our contemporary era of the modern nation-state, the role of costume in writing these types of histories is highly feminized. For example, while John F. Kennedy's suits are largely forgettable, Jacqueline Kennedy's dresses mark the historical moments of some of the most important political exchanges during his term. Likewise, it is Jacqueline Kennedy's pink Chanel

figure 8.3
Pink Chanel suit worn by Jacqueline Kennedy on November 22, 1963, the day of John F. Kennedy's assassination. JFKWHP-1963-11-22-B, Cecil Stoughton, White House Photographs, John F. Kennedy Presidential Library and Museum, Boston.

dress—not the garb of the deceased president—that captures in the public imagination JFK's assassination on November 22, 1963 (Figure 8.3). She understood the power of images to convey meaning as she refused to take the blood-stained dress off after leaving the hospital, indexically underscoring the tragedy of the moment in her donning of the dress at the swearing in of the 36th president, Lyndon B. Johnson. This event-based, lived aspect of costume is more difficult to examine archaeologically since many costume elements are perishable. Nonetheless, I rely here on the rich iconographic record of monuments, paintings, and ceramic media as well as durable stone ornaments to highlight two elements of Maya royal costume.

Feathered Capes: Militarism and the Making of Masculinities

One of the costumes that embodied the temporality of a Maya king's achievements and the unique historic moments of his lifetime was the feathered cape.[1] Although Nahautl peoples lauded the Toltec as the original feather workers in Mesoamerica and much has been written about Aztec feather producers (Berdan 2009, 2016; Caplan 2020; Filloy Nadal and Moreno Guzmán 2017; García Granados 1939; Haag et al. 2012; Sahagún 1959:61), the Maya were also masters of the feathered arts. Not only did Maya peoples have easier access to a large array of brilliant feathers from tropical birds than their Central Mexican counterparts, but extant imagery reveals that they prolifically incorporated feathered plumes in their headdresses, ceremonial back racks, weapons, and clothing. In fact, feathered capes may be closely associated with Classic Maya peoples, as they appear to be more commonly depicted in Maya iconography than elsewhere in Mesoamerica (Anawalt 1981:30, 1996; cf. Jiménez García 2010:12, 26, 29; Taube 2004:107, fig. 48c, 50c–d). Despite the relatively frequent appearance of feathered capes in Late and Terminal Classic sculpture, painting, and ceramics across the Maya Lowlands, however, they have never been the subject of a systematic study, and as such I take the opportunity to elaborate on them here.

I argue that feathered capes were tied to critical events of militaristic conflict and its aftermath of captive display, sacrifice, and goods transfer (Figures 8.4–8.9). Arguably, they were not only memorials of these historic events but also part of the making of mature masculinities in the life cycle of the king. Depictions of feathered capes are systematically associated with weapons, shields, and other militaristic accoutrements, such as pendants with upside-down sacrificial heads (Figure 8.5; see also Appendix 8.1). Many of the scenes also depict the presentation of, or kingly dominance over, war captives (Figures 8.4–8.5, 8.7d). One detailed example is Piedras Negras Stela 12, which depicts what scholars believe to be Ruler 7, who is being presented with captives by two subsidiary nobles (Figure 8.7d). Texts from the stela underscore that this event celebrates two wars against the city of Pomona, events that may have been in reprisal for an attack by Pomona centuries earlier (Houston, Stuart, and Taube 2006:202–203). This type of scene is repeated many times in Late Classic polychrome ceramic scenes, in which kings with feathered capes are presented with captives and war booty from military leaders or subordinate lords, some of whom also wear feathered capes (Figure 8.5; Appendix 8.1). In some cases, such as at Bonampak Lintel 3, Late Classic Maya kings are depicted in active poses of combat (Mathews 1980:fig.7) (Figure 8.8). Similar scenes of direct combat are also found at the site of Chichen Itza in the northern lowlands, where military leaders are depicted donning feathered capes, such as in the painted battle scene murals from the Upper Temple of the Jaguar (Ringle 2009) (Figure 8.9).

In the battle scene murals as well as in sculptural programs throughout Chichen Itza, it is clear that feathered capes were worn by many dominant military figures, such as the leading feathered serpent figure in the southwest mural (Ringle 2009:31–33) (Figure 8.9b), but almost never by everyone in the scene (see, for example, the dais from the North Colonnade, the carved panels on the south and west walls of the Lower Temple of the Jaguar, and the sculpted warrior costumes from columns in the Temple of the Warriors) (Baudez and Latsanopoulos 2010:fig. 6; Coggins 1992:43, 50, 60; Florescano 2009:VI.21, VI.22; Morris, Charlot, and Morris 1931:295, 310, fig. 257; Schele and Mathews 1998:219, fig. 6.14, A6, 241–243). This restricted use of the cape may denote differences in the ethnic identity, lineage, or regional affiliation of the different individuals, as well as differences in the social context of its use. In contrast, however, almost all of the fifteen sculpted Atlantean figures hold up the stone bench, although each cape is unique despite some overlapping design patterns (Schele and Mathews 1998:241–243) (Figure 8.10).

Although the militaristic use of the feathered cape continued uninterrupted from lowland cities to Chichen Itza in the northern lowlands, some variants in the basic form of the feathered cape can be detected and, in some cases, tied to political affiliations and regional trends. Feathered capes from Chichen Itza are systematically long, hanging below the waist, while southern lowlands examples vary in length with long, medium (waist-length), and short varieties (above the elbow; earliest possible example of a short cape dates to around 527 CE from Tikal Stela 10 and later examples span the eighth century). Another variant, a feathered tunic-cape, appears on Maya kings from Piedras Negras (Stela 7 [721/731 CE]) (Figure 8.7b), Tikal (Stela 34), Naranjo (Stelae 11 [777 CE?] and 21 [706 CE]), and Sacul (Stela 6 [780 CE]), in which the cape was counterbalanced with a frontal feathered strip over the chest. In both Naranjo Stelae 11 and 21, clear references to conflicts are detailed in the texts, with Stela 21 referencing K'ahk' Tiliw Chan Chahk's invasion of Yootz (*ubaah ti ochch'e'n yootz*) and Stela 11 mentioning a "land-burning" (*pulkab*) event afflicted on a rival. Nicholas Carter (2019:7–8) has argued that the Sacul king, K'iyel Janab, drew inspiration from Naranjo military symbolism, which included not only a similar feathered tunic-cape but also a similar feathered helmet and circular shield of the Jaguar God of the Underworld (possibly depicted only three years after the more recent Naranjo stelae). Such emulations parallel the growing popularity of black clothing among nobility during the reign of the Hapsburgs already mentioned and highlight what Graeber and Sahlins (2017:236, 247, 370) (see also Lamoureux-St-Hilaire and McAnany, this volume) call "galactic mimesis."

As has been evident in all the known examples, Classic feathered capes were clearly restricted to men.

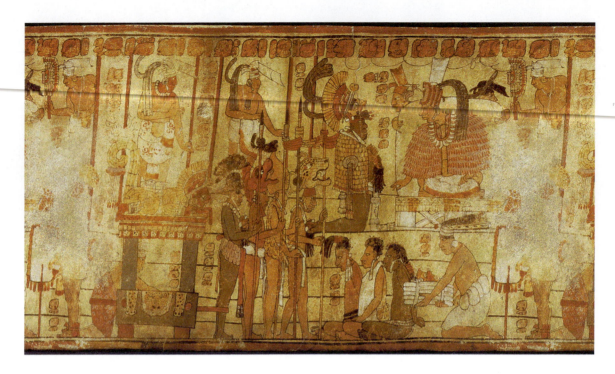

figure 8.4
Late Classic ceramic vase (K3412) depicting a Maya king with pinkish-red feathered cape receiving tribute and captives during the aftermath of war. Note that the military captain wears a yellow and red feathered cape and a trophy head pendant. Justin Kerr Maya archive, Dumbarton Oaks, Trustees for Harvard University, Washington, D.C.

figure 8.5
Feathered capes and trophy head pendants: a) Late Classic unprovenienced ceramic vase (L6416, Justin Kerr Maya archive, Dumbarton Oaks, Trustees for Harvard University, Washington, D.C.); and b) Terminal Classic figurine-ocarina, Tikal, PP7TT, cat. no. 154 (photograph by Christina T. Halperin).

figure 8.6
Young nobleman with long feathered cape standing across from Shield Jaguar III of Yaxchilan, Lintel 1, Site R. Drawing by Peter Mathews.

In general, the cloak—whether of cotton, maguey, or string—in Mesoamerica was a highly masculine garment (Anawalt 1981; Olko 2014:84; Thompson 1951:397). In addition, on the monumental examples in which militarism is emphasized with weapons or captives, the king is almost always an adult and never a child (although see Figure 8.6 for a young lord wearing a feathered cape). In this sense, the donning of feathered capes likely produced a sense of virile masculinity. The comparison of feathered capes with other types of capes, such as the long white cotton cloaks worn by subordinate noblemen labeled as y*ebeet* (messengers) (Houston, Stuart, and Taube 2006:243–248) and the black and white step-fret brocaded and fringed cape of the elderly, wrinkled God L (see also discussion of dotted thick-leaf cape below) (Taube 1992), underscores that masculinities were multiple and dynamic rather than singular and fixed (see also Ardren 2015; Houston 2009, 2018).

Arguably, these feathered capes were unique costumes made specifically for individual kings and military leaders during momentous occasions in their lives rather than as heirlooms passed down through the generations. The longevity of feathered capes is limited, due, in part, to their organic, perishable nature within the context of hot, humid environments whose exposure to bacteria, dust, light, and insects cannot be controlled, as is the

Temporalities of Royal Costume in the Maya Lowlands 197

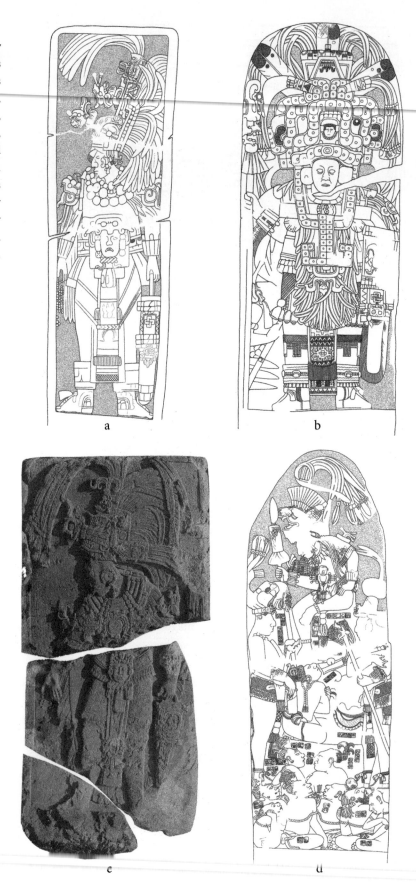

figure 8.7
Changes in feather cape styles by ruler over time on Piedras Negras monuments: a) Stela 2, Ruler 3 (697 CE); b) Stela 7, Ruler 3 (AD 721? CE); c) Stela 13, Ha' K'in Xook (771 CE); and d) Stela 12, Ruler 7 (795 CE). Drawings and photographs courtesy of the Peabody Museum of Archaeology and Ethnology, Harvard University, Cambridge, Mass.

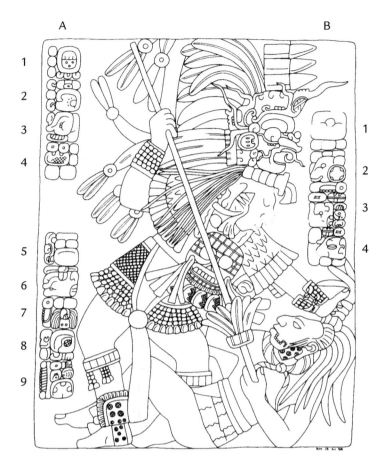

figure 8.8
Bonampak lord with short feathered cape in combat scene, Bonampak Lintel 3. Drawing by Peter Mathews.

case within museum settings in which feathers can be preserved, in some cases, for hundreds of years (Hudon 2005). Comprised principally of beta keratins, feathers typically decompose in less than a year when exposed to the ground surface, but can usually last fifteen to twenty years in more sanitary conditions. Likewise, changes in the depictions of feathered capes over time also suggest that these costume elements were not passed down from one generation to the next. For example, at the site of Piedras Negras, where the monumental record documented short time intervals (sometimes on the scale of the five-year *hotuns*), the style of feathered capes changes with each ruler (Figure 8.7). Perhaps the only possible example of generational sharing is the case of the Bonampak king Chaan Muan, who appears on Stela 1 with a very similar feathered cape as his father, Aj Sak Teles, seen on Bonampak Lintel 3 (Mathews 1980:fig.7; Miller and Brittenham 2013:240) (Figure 8.8).

Elsewhere in Mesoamerica, cotton and maguey capes (*mantas*) were active in molding key life stages and historic events within a person's biography (Olko 2014:84–106). The Aztec emperor awarded warriors capes for their achievements. For example, those who took their first captive were given an orange cape with a striped border and scorpion design, and those who took three captives were given a cape decorated with the "jewel of *ehecatl*" (Anawalt 1981:29). In turn, Aztec warriors of the highest rank had the privilege of wearing long red capes (*tilmatli*) with the *tenixyo* border ("having eyes on the edge"), which was tied on the right shoulder (and accompanied by the *quetzallalpiloni*, a hair ornament with quetzal plumes) (Anawalt 1981:30–31). Mexica emperors wore the *xiuhtlalpilli*, the indigo blue *tilmatli* decorated with the *tenixyo* border and often tied in the back. The cape was accompanied by his nose jewel and kingly head diadem or *xiuhuitzolli*, but unlike the Maya examples,

figure 8.9
Battle mural scenes from the Upper Temple of the Jaguar showing warriors with feathered capes (highlighted with black ovals): a) close-up of northwest mural showing warriors in active combat (Adela Breton watercolors, Ea8487, courtesy of the Bristol Museums, Galleries and Archives © Bristol Culture); and b) close-up of southwest mural showing leaders with feathered capes receiving tribute and gestures of submission after battle (Adela Breton watercolors; Ea8451c, courtesy of the Bristol Museums, Galleries and Archives © Bristol Culture).

a

b

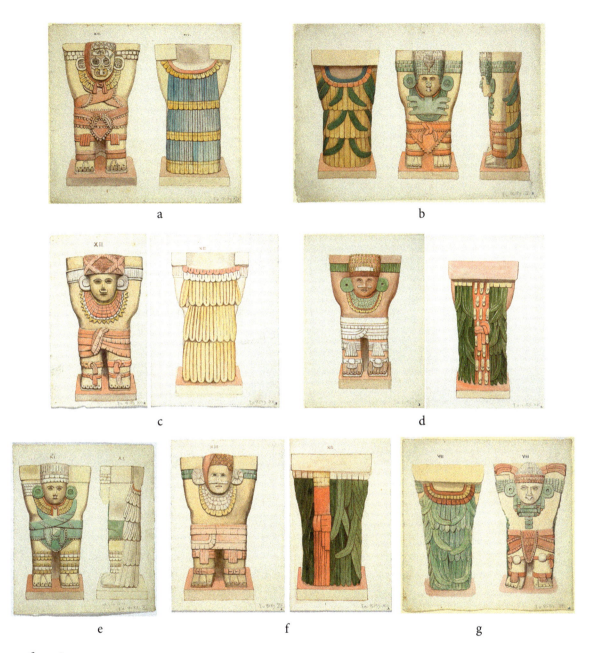

figure 8.10
Atlantean sculptures from Temple A, ballcourt, Chichen Itza: a) Ea8189 (XIV); b) Ea8189 (IV); c) Ea8189 (XII); d) Ea8189 (XV); e) Ea8189 (XI); f) Ea8189 (XIII); and g) Ea8189 (VIII). Adela Breton watercolors, courtesy of the Bristol Museums, Galleries and Archives © Bristol Culture.

figure 8.11
Calakmul Stela 51, showing Yuknoom Took' K'awiil, depicted at least twenty-nine years of age. Gift of the Carnegie Institution of Washington, 1958 © President and Fellows of Harvard College, Peabody Museum of Archaeology and Ethnology, 58-34-20/61919.1.

it was not overtly associated with militaristic events (Anawalt 1996).

Not all Maya iconographic scenes that feature feathered capes, however, involve references to conflict, captive-taking, and warfare. Although less common, there are some examples of elite and royal figures wearing decorated capes during acts of auto-sacrificial bloodletting or holding what appear to be sacrificial knives. One set of scenes involves what appear to be feathered capes decorated with *Spondylus* shells or similarly-shaped *adornos*.[2] Another set of examples is of young royal male individuals, labeled as *ch'ok* ("sprout" to signify status as an adolescent, young, or unmarried), who wear capes decorated with thick, dotted, green, leaf-like embellishments, as seen on the capes of K'inich Ahkal Mo' Nahb and Upakal K'inich on the throne panel from Palenque Temple XXI (see Appendix 8.1) (Figure 8.12). Although these leaf-like embellishments have often been interpreted as feathers (González Cruz and Bernal Romero 2012:98–103; Pillsbury et al. 2012:411–415), it is more likely that they were green leaves, perhaps green tobacco leaves (see comparative depictions of tobacco leaves with three dark dots and smaller dots on Tikal Altar 2 in Houston, Stuart, and Taube 2006:fig. 3.9, 114). Such leafy capes, as well as leafy bibs and baskets, are specifically associated with scenes of sacrifice and burning (Bassie-Sweet 2021:14–16; Scherer and Houston 2018:117–128). In this sense, a very specific type of cape—different from more typical feathered capes—appears to have played a vital role in initiation ceremonies that involved blood sacrifice, often from the penis, and that were a part of the making of boys into men and, more specifically, princes into kings.

Although feathered capes were a part of the personal biographies of kings, they were not specifically an emblem of the kingly body politic—that is, a bodily symbol of the *k'uhul ajaw* institutional system. As mentioned earlier, not just kings, but military leaders and noblemen, appear to have had the privilege of wearing and likely owning these exquisite coverings (Figures 8.4 and 8.6). What is clear is that they were unique items of tremendous wealth and prestige. As many have underscored, portable Maya wealth was often worn (as feathers, jade, marine shell, and cloth), whereby its value was highly performative (Houston, Stuart, and Taube 2006:244–249; McAnany 1993, 2010).

Feathered capes would have required an enormous number of feathers as well as skilled artisans with experience in the feathered arts. Aztec feather workers described by Bernardino de Sahagún (1961:92, 166) often glued feathers to textiles or leather, an artistic tradition later adopted by European artisans in the early modern period

figure 8.12
Sacrificial leaf cape and bibs with dots: a) Upakal K'inich as a young prince wearing the leaf cloak in a scene of blood sacrifice, throne panel, Palenque Temple XXI (after González Cruz and Bernal Romero 2012:fig. 14); b) young prince wearing a leaf cape and in the midst of an act of sacrificial penis bloodletting, Dos Pilas Panel 19 (drawing by Christina T. Halperin, after Houston 1993:fig. 4-9); and c) detail of a seated sacrificial victim wearing a leaf bib, from an unprovenanced Late Classic Maya vase (K1645; drawing by Christina T. Halperin).

(Filloy Nadal and Moreno Guzmán 2017; Russo, Wolf, and Fane 2015), but feathers could also be spun and woven into textiles (Johnson 1957; McCafferty and McCafferty 2000:47; Morris and Karasik 2003). Because of the flowing nature of the cape against the body, however, Maya artisans likely produced them by sewing bunches of feathers to either a cloth base, as hinted at in Maya imagery (see Figures 8.6 and 8.7c), or to an open netted base similar to Polynesian feathered capes (Buck 1943, 1944). Netted feathered cape bases may have been more conducive to "flying" or catching wind when worn while running or dancing. Hawaiian feathered capes were royal regalia that symbolized chiefly divinity and power. According to Bishop Museum records, Kalaniʻōpuʻu's feathered cloak (*ʻahu ʻula*), which was given to Captain James Cook, bore feathers from approximately twenty thousand birds.[3] Not only was the labor to collect such large quantities of feathers enormous, but the matching of the correct size and types of feathers represented detailed and skilled work (Cummins 1984:6).

The polychrome depictions of Maya capes indicate that the types of bird feathers incorporated into capes may have varied considerably.[4] In two unprovenanced Late Classic ceramic vases (K0767 and K3412) that depict the same tribute and captive display scene, the king wears a pinkish-red feathered cape that may have depicted feathers from the Roseate spoonbill (Figure 8.4). It contrasts with the yellow and red trimmed cape of the military leader presenting the captives. Other feathers, such as those from the cape of Calakmul Stela 51 (Figure 8.11), were long and thin, likely representing quetzal feathers. Part of the value of feathers was their ability to capture the spirit or essence of a particular bird or bird-deity and to fuse this essence with the person wearing the cape, in which human-animal-spirit divides were blurred (Bassie-Sweet 2008; Harris and Robb 2012; Houston and Stuart 1998). Among the Aztec, certain types of feathers—though by no means all—possessed *tonalli*, a solar-driven animating force (Caplan 2020). In turn, the feathered capes depicted in the polychrome battle murals as well as on the sculpted Atlantean figures from Chichen Itza reveal that each cape is unique with bird feathers of different types of birds (with blue, yellow, white, green, and other color feathers), decorative fringes, and design placements (Figures 8.9 and 8.10). Such a diversity of styles underscores the highly personalized nature of feathered capes in Maya society.

Jade Ornaments

In contrast to feathered capes, an extensive body of literature exists on jade ornaments (Azarova 2016; Digby 1972; Freidel, Reese-Taylor, and Mora-Marin 2002; Halperin, Hruby, and Mongelluzzo 2018; Joyce 2003; Kovacevich 2013; Kovacevich and Callaghan 2019; Proskouriakoff 1974; Stuart 2006; Taube and Ishihara-Brito 2012). These studies underscore the longer temporalities of these ornaments as they anchored royal individuals—both male and female—into extensive dynastic histories and helped produce an institutional body politic over the long term. Jade itself was the material embodiment of life-giving maize, wind, and the vital energy associated with the breath soul (Taube 2005).

The longevity of jade ornamentation as symbols of elite status dates back to at least the Middle Preclassic period from places such as La Venta and Chiapa de Corzo, where they are found in elaborate tombs (ca. 800–700 BCE). As Clark and Colman (2014:185) argue, by 700 BCE, jade ear spools, bead belts, and pendants became international symbols of kingship throughout Mesoamerica. By the Late Preclassic period, jade and white bark paper diadems, known as *sak hu'n* or *sakhuun* (white headband), became standard symbols of rulership in the Maya area, as seen from carved jade diadems from Tikal Burial 85, Cerros Cache 6B, imagery from the San Bartolo murals, and the Dumbarton Oaks jade pectoral (Freidel and Schele 1988; Saturno, Taube, and Stuart 2005), and arguably continued into the Postclassic period (Taube et al. 2010:fig. 41c) (Figure 8.13). As part of its performative value, they were presented to the *ajaw* during accession ceremonies and memorialized in more permanent sculpture and other artistic works recalling these dynastic ceremonies (Bonampak Panel 1; Taube et al. 2010:figs. 61, 63). The potency of this headdress for signifying rulership is also emphasized in hieroglyphic texts in which the headband forms a logograph (the headband alone or affixed to a head) used to write the word *ajaw* (Stuart 2015).

Although people of different social statuses had access to jade beads and other ornamentation, elite and royal families, in particular, enjoyed privileged access to a suite of finely sculpted jade ornaments. In addition to the *sak hu'n* diadem, these jade ornaments also included large sculpted belt pendants, funerary mosaic masks worn by the king or queen after death, and netted jade capes, huipils, and skirts, worn during accession and period ending ceremonies and donned by the Moon Goddess and Maize God during the Early and Late Classic periods (Joyce 1996, 2000b; Quenon and Le Fort 1997; Vázquez López 2017) (Figure 8.14).

In addition to the longevity of the use of jade ornaments as symbols of rulership, scholars have also pointed to the materiality of jade as critical in the recalling of generational dynastic connections in the past and the forging of dynastic succession for the future. Jade heirlooms were inalienable possessions that were often passed down from generation to generation, often regardless of gender. One of the

figure 8.13
An heirloom or ancient Middle Preclassic jade piece (top) reused as a pectoral, with new inscriptions during the Late Preclassic period on the back side (bottom). Royal *sak hu'n* headdress is highlighted in black. PC.B.538.22, Pre-Columbian Collection, Dumbarton Oaks, Washington, D.C.

most famous examples of an heirloom jade ornament is the Piedras Negras belt pendant that may have first belonged to Ruler 3, K'inich Yo'nal Ahk II (Figure 8.15). The texts celebrate his completion of thirteen calendrical cycles as lord of Piedras Negras and names a date seven years into the future (Joyce 2003:119; Proskouriakoff 1974). The carved image is likely a portrait of an *ajaw*, if not Ruler 3, then perhaps one of his ancestors. As depicted on Piedras Negras Stela 2 (697 CE, Ruler 3), Stela 4 (702 CE, Ruler 3), Stela 10 (736 CE, Ruler 4), Stela 40 (746 CE, Ruler 4), and Stela 13 (771 CE; Ha' K'in Xook), at least three different rulers, and likely more, wore his jade belt ornament (Figures 8.7 and 8.15). Eventually, its biography met a different fate as it was deposited in the Sacred Cenote at Chichen Itza (Clancy 2009), alongside many other offerings of jade jewelry from throughout the Maya realm (Proskouriakoff 1974). Thus, while the rulers' feathered capes from Piedras Negras change from stela to stela, the jade head pendant endured through the generations.

These heirloom jade pieces were not central to the performances of gendered identities. They were worn by royal males and females (Figure 8.14), they appear in both male and female tombs, and their hieroglyphic inscriptions, when present, often trace the owner to both male and female ancestors (Joyce 2000b, 2003; Navarro-Farr et al. 2020). Rosemary Joyce, for example, has argued that the carved jade head belt ornament recovered from Comayagua, Honduras, which is inscribed with a text naming a lord of Palenque, was likely an heirloom object brought to the Copan region by a royal woman from Palenque who may have married into the Copan dynasty: "Whenever it was reused, or even simply circulated on to other points on its journey, it carried along the record of its initial preparation and use, as a 'history object'" (Joyce 2003:116).

Temporalities of Royal Costume in the Maya Lowlands   205

figure 8.14
Lady Sak K'uk' wearing a jade headdress with *sak hu'n* jade diadems and a jade skirt and cape. She presents a jade headdress with a *sak hu'n* diadem to her son, K'inich Janaab Pakal. Oval Palace Tablet, Palenque (drawing by Linda Schele © David Schele, courtesy Ancient Americas at LACMA).

In some cases, jade jewelry may have invoked not just named dynastic connections over the generations, but a deep history, one that referenced mythical time. In many sacred Mesoamerican narratives, royal history is foregrounded with, and thus connected to, a mythic history of the deep past in which creator deities put in order the cosmic realms and embarked on a series of adventures (Bassie-Sweet 2008; Schele and Mathews 1998; Tedlock 1996, 2003). This possible tapping into mythic time is indicated, in part, by the reuse of Olmec-style jade objects by later Late Preclassic and Classic period Maya peoples (Fields and Reents-Budet 2005:182,

191–194; Schele and Miller 1986:119–120) (Figure 8.13). For example, a royal tomb from Nakum dating to the Late Classic period (ca. 650–870 CE) contained a jade pectoral with inscriptions and imagery stylistically dated to the Early Classic period (Żrałka et al. 2011:895–899) (Figure 8.16). The text names the owner of the pectoral as possibly a lord from Yaxha, while the imagery on the other side depicts a floating ancestor, perhaps a deceased ancestor of the named lord. Archaeologists, however, suggest that the pendant may have been produced before 600 BCE, based on its spoon or clamshell shape and the style of its drilled suspension holes. The known

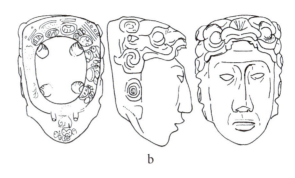

figure 8.15
Heirloom jade pendant: a) detail of Piedras Negras Stela 40, showing Ruler 4 wearing the heirloom jade head pendant on his belt, 9.15.15.0.0.9 (746 CE) (drawing by Christina T. Halperin); and b) jade head pendant from Piedras Negras recovered from the Sacred Cenote at Chichen Itza (drawing by Christina T. Halperin, after Proskouriakoff 1974:140–141).

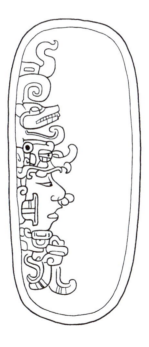
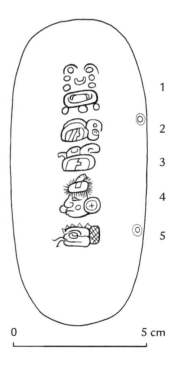

figure 8.16
Heirloom jade pectoral possibly dating back to the Middle Preclassic period, with inscriptions and imagery dating to the Late Preclassic or Early Classic period, found in a royal tomb, Burial 1, at Nakum dating to the Late Classic period. Photograph and drawing courtesy of Jarosław Źrałka, drawing by Simon Martin.

age or history of this particular piece or others like it, however, may have been irrelevant, as even more recently carved jade jewelry may have had the power to embody the Maize God or Wind God (Taube 2005), thus forging connections between mythic time and contemporary moments.

During the Postclassic period, the potency of jade ornamentation as a symbol of kingship continued but seemed to have greatly diminished in its overall significance. Although rulers continued to don jade ornaments after the Classic period, these ornaments were often much simpler and often in the form of circular or roughly shaped beads (Orellana 1984:77; Proskouriakoff 1974; Schele and Mathews 1998:306–307). As such, jade jewelry largely lost the embellishments of skilled carving and iconic symbolism referencing ancestors or deities. In this sense, they mark a shift in the *k'uhul ajaw* system of rulership of the Late Preclassic and Classic periods. In some cases, metal pendants and bells may have helped to create new kingly temporalities at the end of the Postclassic period—ones that were linked to the calling of rain deities and ancestors or beings further afield in Mesoamerica (Coggins 1992; Paris 2008; Simmons and Shugar 2013). By the end of the sixteenth century, Spanish colonial restrictions to the economic livelihood of Maya lords (Chuchiak, this volume) resulted in the fading of many Indigenous luxury items, which included the disappearance of feather workers (Orellana 1984:179).

Discussion

Costume simultaneously anchored the king's body in a longstanding legacy of divine dynastic history and served as instrumental components in the personal biography of a king or queen in the making of royal personhood through lived experience. As such, sartorial devices and bodily ornamentation helped bridge the contradiction of the king's two bodies: the tangible living body of short duration and the symbolic body politic, which was connected to the mythic and deeper histories of ancestors and deities. In this way, they also play into different kingly politics of varying efficacies, namely the ongoing establishment and legitimization of institutional sovereignty (jade) and the more punctuated and highly personal charisma of leaders (feathered capes) mentioned by David Wengrow (this volume). Although feathered capes and jade ornaments highlight two extremes of these kingly temporalities, many other different costume elements may be called upon to reveal the ways in which kingly costume and adornments were both "signs in history" *and* "signs of history" (Parmentier 1987:11–12).

Largely ignored in these examples are queens who showcased some of the most exquisite textile arts of Mesoamerica—those that involved skilled abilities in the dyeing, stamping, and painting of cloth; in the spinning of fibers; and in the weaving, brocading, and embroidering of cloth (Halperin 2017; Holsbeke and Montoya 2003; Morris 1984; Pincemin Deliberos 1998; Taylor 1992). Depictions of royal women often highlight their richly decorated huipils and skirts, which would have not only been emblematic of their elite status but also intimately tied to historical events in their kingdoms, their personal life stages, and their own political achievements (see Ardren, this volume). The perishable nature of textiles as well as the relatively fewer narratives and iconographic depictions of royal women render many of these textiles as part of forgotten histories. And of course, even more fleeting and forgettable were undergarments for royal women and quotidian loincloths for kings—the well-worn items that cycle in and out more quickly, embodying the "social time" of the everyday. Nonetheless, royal women shared with their male counterparts in the embodiment of long-term divine royal traditions and dynastic connections in their donning of durable jade ornamentation, as well as many other accoutrements not discussed here, such as shell, pyrite, and bone jewelry and headdresses of myriad materials. In this sense, royal jewels were gender-neutral. All of these adornments from textiles to feathered capes to stone ornaments collectively touch on a third body politic not discussed in detail here—that the royal body and, in turn, the state was both literally and metaphorically constituted of the contributions of its diverse people and their networks far and wide (although see Halperin 2014:ch. 1; Hutson, this volume).

In returning to the earlier comparison of John F. Kennedy and Jacqueline Kennedy, however, it is clear that contemporary kings and heads of state have lost their capacity to be peacocks (or, in emic Maya terms, quetzals). They have lost their capacity not only to be highly expressive in bodily costume but also to produce event-based history in and through dress. Although semiotics are never absent, the dark suit of male leaders and, more recently, the monochrome pantsuit of female leaders today reflect a relatively passive adherence to a modern, international sensibility (Hollander 2016). The conformity to this standardized, internationally recognized aesthetic seeks to displace sartorial commentary with what is seen as more important: actions and words. Yet ancient Maya kings and queens—and ancient and early modern kings and queens across the world—would likely disagree on this point, as costume for them was not just important, but essential in making oneself king or queen and in positioning oneself in history. The fact that male Maya artisans frequently depicted elite Maya men and male deities being ceremonially dressed with great care in their plumes, jewels, body paints, ritual accoutrements, and elaborate garments underscores that "being a peacock" during this time was highly masculine. In turn, the fact that elaborate and highly expressive costuming in contemporary-era politics has become feminized stimulates thoughtful reflection not just on changing gendered dynamics over the long term but also on the current state of the study of ancient costume, what has been a relatively marginalized domain of ancient history.

Appendix 8.1
Possible feathered capes.

ARTIFACT	MEDIUM	GENDER	TYPE	SCENE
Bonampak Lintel 3, Structure 1	Lintel	M	Short	Warfare; attacking enemy with spear in right hand
Bonampak Stela 1	Stela monument	M	Short	Warfare; holding spear and shield
Calakmul Stela 51	Stela monument	M	Long	Warfare; holding lance
Upper Temple of the Jaguars, Atlantean platform	Painted limestone sculptures	M	Long	Atlantean figures holding up bench
Temple of the Warriors, Column 17	Carved column	M	Long	Warfare; holding darts, atlatl, and stick of some sort
Temple of the Warriors, Column 25	Carved column	M	Long	Warfare; captive warriors with wrists bound
Temple of the Warriors, Column 37	Carved column	M	Long	Warfare; captive warriors with wrists bound
Temple of the Warriors, Column	Carved column	M	Long	Warfare; holding darts and atlatl
Lower Temple of the Jaguars, south and west walls	Carved limestone panel	M	Long	Warfare
Temple of the Wall Panels, slab covering cache	Carved slab	M	Long	Warfare; holding curved stick, darts, and atlatl
Lower Temple of the Jaguars, west wall	Carved limestone panel	M	Long	Warfare; holding atlatl and darts
Dais from North Colonnade, west side	Carved bench	M	Long	Warfare; procession of warriors
Northwest mural, Upper Temple of the Jaguars	Mural	M	Long	Warfare; battle scene; feathered cape figures stand over victims
Southwest mural, Upper Temple of the Jaguars	Mural	M	Long	Warfare; battle scene; receiving subordinate figures
Jade bead, Peabody Museum of Archaeology and Ethnology, 10-71-20/C6351	Jade bead	M	Medium	Sacrifice (?); holds sacrificial knife and textile/rope/sling
Disk F	Gold disk	M	Medium	Warfare; holding atlatl and two darts in a combat scene

SITE/REGION	DATE	PERIOD	INDIVIDUAL'S IDENTITY	REFERENCE
Bonampak	740 CE	Late Classic	Aj Sak Teles, possible father of Chaan Muan	Mathews 1980:69–71, fig. 7; Miller and Brittenham 2013:240
Bonampak	780 CE	Late Classic	Chaan Muan; celebration of first *hotun* ending	Mathews 1980:fig. 3; Schele and Miller 1986:fig. 28
Calakmul	731 CE	Late Classic	Yuknoom Took' K'awiil, lord of Calakmul (at least twenty-nine years or older)	Martin and Grube 2008:113
Chichen Itza		Terminal Classic	Fourteen of the fifteen Atlantean figures wear feathered capes	http://museums.bristol.gov.uk/list.php?keyword=chichen+itza
Chichen Itza		Terminal Classic	Possibly two individuals with feathered capes; one holds a dart, atlatl, and stick, while the other does not appear to have a weapon	Schele Drawing no. 5029
Chichen Itza		Terminal Classic	Four individuals with possible feathered capes; all of them have their wrists tied	Florescano 2009:VI.22
Chichen Itza		Terminal Classic	Three possible individuals with feathered capes; all of them have their wrists tied; all of them have name glyphs	Schele Drawing no. 5027
Chichen Itza		Terminal Classic	Wears butterfly pendant necklace; descending bird headdress; holds darts	Florescano 2009:VI.21
Chichen Itza		Terminal Classic	Three warriors on the left side of the panel wear long feathered capes; two of these figures hold long darts	Schele and Mathews 1998:219, fig. 6.14, A6
Chichen Itza		Terminal Classic	Jaguar figure who faces a serpent figure	Baudez and Latsanopoulous 2010:fig. 6
Chichen Itza		Terminal Classic	Figure in Row C with goggle eye mask, back mirror, and butterfly pendant	Tozzer 1957:fig. 526
Chichen Itza		Terminal Classic	Central figure on the west side	Morris, Charlot, and Morris 1931:295, 310, fig. 257
Chichen Itza		Terminal Classic	Possibly three warriors with feathered capes standing over victims	Ringle 2009:fig. 10, 11d
Chichen Itza		Terminal Classic	At least four warriors with feathered capes; some are receiving subordinate figures	Ringle 2009:fig. 4
Chichen Itza		Terminal Classic	Descending figure	Coggins and Shane 1984:60
Chichen Itza, Sacred Cenote		Terminal Classic	Military figure; subsidiary figure in the scene	Coggins and Shane 1984:43

Appendix 8.1 (continued)

ARTIFACT	MEDIUM	GENDER	TYPE	SCENE
Disk H	Gold disk	M	Medium	Warfare; scene of sacrifice after capture
K3412	Polychrome vase	M	Medium	Warfare and presentation of captives and tribute
P1040824	Ceramic figurine	M	Short	Fragment of male figurine
Naranjo Stela 8	Stela monument	M	Short	Warfare; holding shield and lance
Nim Li Punit Stela 2	Stela monument	M	Medium	Standing ruler in profile
Piedras Negras Stela 13	Stela monument	M	Long	Standing, scattering ritual
Piedras Negras Stela 5	Stela monument	M	Medium or long	Seated on throne; holds a bag and God K scepter
Piedras Negras Stela 2	Stela monument	M	Medium (?)	Standing, scattering ritual
Piedras Negras Stela 12	Stela monument	M	Short	Warfare; holding spear and presiding over bound captives
PP7TT154	Ceramic figurine	M	Long	Standing; wears decapitated head necklace similar to Piedras Negras Stela 12
Tikal Stela 10	Stela monument	M	Short	Captive-taking; holding flexible shield (?)
K7998	Polychrome vase	M	Medium	Royal court scene
SAMA.74.103	Ceramic figurine	M	Medium	Seated figure, possibly holds a knife
K1151	Polychrome vase	M	Medium	Warfare; holding spear and flexible shield; presentation of tribute (textiles and feathers)
K1151	Polychrome vase	M	Medium	Warfare; holding spear and flexible shield; presentation of tribute (textiles and feathers)
K8526	Polychrome vase	M	Medium	Presentation of tribute

SITE/REGION	DATE	PERIOD	INDIVIDUAL'S IDENTITY	REFERENCE
Chichen Itza, Sacred Cenote		Terminal Classic	Military figures; one emerges from a cloud serpent and holds darts and the other holds a captive	Coggins and Shane 1984:50
Dos Pilas/Petexbatun style		Late Classic	King wearing feathered cape is presented with captives and tribute by warriors; military leader appears to also wear a feathered cape and possesses a trophy head necklace	Justin Kerr Maya archive, Dumbarton Oaks, Trustees for Harvard University, Washington, D.C.
Lubaantun		Late Classic	Fragment of male figurine with short feathered cape	Norman Hammond, personal communication 2021
Naranjo	800 CE	Late Classic	Itzamnaaj K'awiil (twenty-nine years old)	Graham and Von Euw 1975
Nim Li Punit		Late Classic	Profile of standing lord, fragmentary part of stela	Norman Hammond, personal communication 2021
Piedras Negras	771 CE	Late Classic	Stela 13 celebrates the accession of Ruler 6	Clancy 2009:141; Martin and Grube 2008:151
Piedras Negras	716 CE	Late Classic	Ruler 3 at fifty-two years old; Ruler 3 celebrating either a preaccession ceremony or a memorial event for Ruler 2	Clancy 2009:93
Piedras Negras	697 CE	Late Classic	Ruler 3 (thirty-three years old); Ruler 3's cape is similar to his cape in Stela 5 almost a *katun* later	Clancy 2009:fig. 8.5
Piedras Negras	795 CE	Late Classic	Ruler 7	Martin and Grube 2008:153
Tikal		Terminal Classic	At least three figurines of this type	Reported here, Figure 8.5b, as well as Laporte 2009:fig. 15
Tikal	527 (?) CE	Late Early Classic	Kaloomte' Bahlam, nineteenth Tikal king; see also Tikal Stela 12	Jones and Satterthwaite 1982:25–26
Tikal, Burial 116		Late Classic	Seated lord with feathered cape receives subordinate, kneeling figure	Culbert 1993:fig. 72
Unprovenienced		Late Classic	Seated, portly figure with deer headdress and possible knife	San Antonio Museum of Art online collections
Unprovenienced		Late Classic	Military figure with pink and white feathered cape, subsidiary to main kneeling figure and standing ruler	Justin Kerr Maya archive, Dumbarton Oaks, Trustees for Harvard University, Washington, D.C.
Unprovenienced		Late Classic	Military figure with gray (green?) feathered cape, subsidiary to main kneeling figure and standing ruler	Justin Kerr Maya archive, Dumbarton Oaks, Trustees for Harvard University, Washington, D.C.
Unprovenienced		Late Classic	Male figure with white feathered cape (?); sits on throne facing ruler	Justin Kerr Maya archive, Dumbarton Oaks, Trustees for Harvard University, Washington, D.C.

Appendix 8.1 (continued)

ARTIFACT	MEDIUM	GENDER	TYPE	SCENE
K8526	Polychrome vase	M	Medium	Presentation of tribute
K6416	Polychrome vase	M	Long	Warfare; presentation of captive
K6187	Polychrome plate	M	Medium	Warfare; presentation of tribute
K5513	Polychrome vase	M	Medium	Presentation of tribute; feasting
K4825	Polychrome vase	M	Medium	Royal court scene
K4825	Polychrome vase	M	Medium	Royal court scene
K3478	Polychrome vase	M	Medium	Warfare; presentation of captives
K767	Polychrome vase	M	Medium	Warfare; presentation of captives
PC.B.200 Dumbarton Oaks figurine	Ceramic figurine	M	Medium	Sacrifice; holding a sacrificial knife in right hand
PUAM 2000-318; K3325	Ceramic figurine	M	Medium	Unknown, but right hand could have held a spear
K3412	Polychrome vase	M	Medium	Warfare; presentation of captives and tribute

SITE/REGION	DATE	PERIOD	INDIVIDUAL'S IDENTITY	REFERENCE
Unprovenienced		Late Classic	Male figure with white feathered cape (?); sits holding tribute bundle and facing ruler	Justin Kerr Maya archive, Dumbarton Oaks, Trustees for Harvard University, Washington, D.C.
Unprovenienced		Late Classic	Military leader at the center of the scene wears red feathered cape with decapitated head pendant, shield, and spear; stands in front of two other military figures and bounded and bleeding captive	Justin Kerr Maya archive, Dumbarton Oaks, Trustees for Harvard University, Washington, D.C.
Unprovenienced		Late Classic	Military leader with pinkish-red feathered cape is kneeling in front of ruler who holds a spear; ruler's throne contains tribute bundle	Justin Kerr Maya archive, Dumbarton Oaks, Trustees for Harvard University, Washington, D.C.
Unprovenienced		Late Classic	Ruler wears feathered cape (?) with tassels; sits on throne carved with glyphs; has pulque in front of him and tribute bundle behind him; two subsidiary figures present ruler with large bowl and vase full of unknown objects	Justin Kerr Maya archive, Dumbarton Oaks, Trustees for Harvard University, Washington, D.C.
Unprovenienced		Late Classic	Elite figure with black feathered cape and red lining seated in front of ruler seated on throne	Justin Kerr Maya archive, Dumbarton Oaks, Trustees for Harvard University, Washington, D.C.
Unprovenienced		Late Classic	Elite figure with cream-colored feathered cape and red lining dancing in front of ruler seated on throne	Justin Kerr Maya archive, Dumbarton Oaks, Trustees for Harvard University, Washington, D.C.
Unprovenienced		Late Classic	Military ruler wearing red feathered cape and holding spear; presents two captives who are seated in front of ruler who is also holding a spear and brandishing a shield	Justin Kerr Maya archive, Dumbarton Oaks, Trustees for Harvard University, Washington, D.C.
Unprovenienced		Late Classic	Similar scene to K3412; king wearing feathered cape is presented with captives and tribute by warriors; military leader appears to also wear a feathered cape and possess a trophy head necklace	Justin Kerr Maya archive, Dumbarton Oaks, Trustees for Harvard University, Washington, D.C.
Unprovenienced; Campeche style		Late Classic	Seated figure with sacrificial knife, two dot sacrification on nose, short beard, stiff cloth headdress with feathers	O'Neil 2012:pl. 77
Unprovenienced; Campeche style		Late Classic	PUAM	Justin Kerr Maya archive, Dumbarton Oaks, Trustees for Harvard University, Washington, D.C.
Unprovenienced; Dos Pilas/Petexbatun style		Late Classic	King seated on throne wears a cape possibly made from a red spoonbill water fowl	Justin Kerr Maya archive, Dumbarton Oaks, Trustees for Harvard University, Washington, D.C.

Appendix 8.1 (continued)

ARTIFACT	MEDIUM	GENDER	TYPE	SCENE
MNA-5-1045	Ceramic figurine	M	Medium	Unknown
Dumbarton Oaks panel	Limestone panel	M	Medium	Warfare; holding flexible shield and spear
Limestone panel from private collection	Limestone panel	M	Long	Warfare; holding elaborate axe and facing Shield Jaguar III, who holds a spear and flexible shield
K8017	Incised vase	M	Long	Royal court scene
Site R Lintel 3	Lintel	M	Short	Warfare; holding flexible shield and circular banner
Variant: Feathered Tunic/Cape				
Naranjo Stela 21	Stela monument	M	Tunic	Warfare; holding spear and shield and standing on bound captive
Sacul Stela 6	Stela monument	M	Tunic	Warfare; holding spear and shield
Naranjo Stela 11	Stela monument	M	Tunic	Warfare; holding spear and shield and standing on bound captive
Piedras Negras Stela 7	Stela monument	M	Tunic	Warfare; holding spear and shield
Tikal Stela 34	Stela monument	?	Tunic (?)	Unknown

M=Male; F=Female; Short=To elbows; Medium=To waist; Long=Below waist

SITE/REGION	DATE	PERIOD	INDIVIDUAL'S IDENTITY	REFERENCE
Unprovenienced; Jaina/Campeche style		Late Classic	Seated figure with beaded necklace, loincloth, slight belly	O'Neil 2012:fig. 227
Unprovenienced; Piedras Negras, El Cayo area		Late Classic	Chak Tun Ahk Kimi, *sajal* (noble status) wears a possible feathered cape	Jackson 2013:44–47
Unprovenienced; Yaxchilan region	after 723 CE	Late Classic	Young noble wears a long feathered cape and faces Yaxchilan's Shield Jaguar who holds a spear and flexible shield	Houston 2018:fig. 86
Unprovenienced; Xcalumkin		Late Classic	Ruler seated on perishable throne or bench and facing seated figure in position of submission or peace	Justin Kerr Maya archive, Dumbarton Oaks, Trustees for Harvard University, Washington, D.C.
Unprovenienced; Site R		Late Classic	Ruler with short feathered cape faces kneeling subordinate	Mayer 1995:pl. 258
Naranjo	706 CE	Late Classic	Texts describe military conquests and commemoration of K'ahk' Tiliiw Chan Chahk's entering the cave of Yootz	Carter 2019:6–8, fig. 7
Sacul	780 CE	Late Classic	Sacul ruler, K'iyel Janab	Carter 2019:6–8, fig. 7
Naranjo	777 CE?	Late Classic	Land-burning on a rival; K'ahk' Ukalaw Chan Chaak?, if so he would be older than twenty-two years old	Carter 2019:6–8, fig. 7
Piedras Negras	721/731 CE	Late Classic	Ruler 3, K'inich Yo'nal Ahk II (fifty-seven years old)	
Tikal		Late Classic	Too fragmentary for identification	Jones and Satterthwaite 1982:75, fig. 55c

NOTES

1. Feathered capes are different from the string capes and brocaded capes discussed elsewhere (Brittenham 2015; Winzenz 2014). They also differ from feathered back racks, which are easily confused with feathered capes.

2. Winzenz (2014:388–390) identifies both the penis-bloodletting kings on the Dumbarton Oaks vase (PC.B.568) and Yaxchilan Stela 9 as wearing "string" rather than feathered capes. I am not convinced that this identification is correct, as the embellishments are not thin and are not of uniform thickness as is the case with other string capes. Nevertheless, the identification of garment raw materials is notoriously difficult and multiple interpretations are possible.

3. https://www.bishopmuseum.org/feather-cloak-and-helmet-gifted-to-captain-cook-to-return-permanently-to-hawaii/

4. Colonial documents suggest that bird feathers were obtained in sustainable ways. Martin Tovilla reports that in the early seventeenth century, Indigenous inhabitants of the Verapaz region would lure birds to water pools and use some sort of adhesive to capture the feathers without killing the birds: "They value the birds so much that they never catch them, but each year harvest new feathers, and [so] they have great interest in them. Not everyone can collect the feathers but only those who have sites inherited from their fathers, and the dead, have these watering places" (Feldman 2000:96–97).

REFERENCES CITED

Anawalt, Patricia R.
- 1981 *Indian Clothing before Cortés: Mesoamerican Costumes from the Codices.* University of Oklahoma Press, Norman.
- 1996 Aztec Knotted and Netted Capes: Colonial Interpretations vs. Indigenous Primary Data. *Ancient Mesoamerica* 7(2):187–206.

Ardren, Traci
- 2015 *Social Identities in the Classic Maya Northern Lowlands: Gender, Age, Memory, and Place.* University of Texas Press, Austin.

Azarova, Mayya
- 2016 Maya Jade T-Shape Pendants within Mesoamerican Wind-Jewel Tradition. Master's thesis, University of California, San Diego.

Bassie-Sweet, Karen
- 2008 *Maya Sacred Geography and the Creator Deities.* University of Oklahoma Press, Norman.
- 2021 *Maya Gods of War.* University Press of Colorado, Louisville.

Baudez, Claude-François, and Nicolas Latsanopoulos
- 2010 Political Structure, Military Training, and Ideology at Chichen Itza. *Ancient Mesoamerica* 21(1):1–20.

Berdan, Frances F.
- 2009 Production and Use of Orchid Adhesives in Aztec Mexico: The Domestic Context. In *Housework: Craft Production and Domestic Economy in Ancient Mesoamerica*, edited by Kenneth G. Hirth, pp. 148–156. American Anthropological Association, Arlington, Va.
- 2016 Featherworking in the Provinces: A Dispersed Luxury Craft under Aztec Hegemony. *Ancient Mesoamerica* 27(1):209–219.

Bourdieu, Pierre
- 1977 *Outline of a Theory of Practice.* Cambridge University Press, Cambridge.
- 1986 *Distinction: A Social Critique of the Judgement of Taste.* Translated by Richard Nice. Routledge and Kegan Paul, London.
- 1990 *The Logic of Practice.* Stanford University Press, Stanford.

Braudel, Fernand
    1960   History and the Social Sciences: The Long Duration. *Political Research, Organization, and Design* 3(6):3–13.
    1992   *The Mediterranean and the Mediterranean World in the Age of Philip II*. Rev. ed. University of California Press, Berkeley.

Brittenham, Claudia
    2015   *The Murals of Cacaxtla: The Power of Painting in Ancient Central Mexico*. University of Texas Press, Austin.

Buck, Peter H.
    1943   The Feather Cloak of Tahiti. *Journal of the Polynesian Society* 52(1):12–15.
    1944   The Local Evolution of Hawaiian Feather Capes and Cloaks. *Journal of the Polynesian Society* 53(1):1–16.

Caplan, Allison
    2020   The Living Feather: Tonalli in Nahua Featherwork Production. *Ethnohistory* 67(3):383–406.

Carter, Nicholas P.
    2019   The Lord of the Yellow Tree: A New Reference to a Minor Polity on Sacul Stela 9. *PARI Journal* 19(4):1–9.

Clancy, Flora S.
    2009   *The Monuments of Piedras Negras, an Ancient Maya City*. University of New Mexico Press, Albuquerque.

Clark, John E., and Arlene Colman
    2014   Dressed Ears as Comeliness and Godliness. In *Wearing Culture: Dress and Regalia in Early Mesoamerica and Central America*, edited by Heather Orr and Matthew G. Looper, pp. 145–205. University of Colorado Press, Boulder.

Coggins, Clemency C.
    1992   *Artifacts from the Cenote of Sacrifice, Chichen Itza, Yucatan: Textiles, Basketry, Stone, Bone, Shell, Ceramics, Wood, Copal, Rubber, Other Organic Materials, and Mammalian Remains*. Peabody Museum of Archaeology and Ethnology, Harvard University, Cambridge, Mass.

Coggins, Clemency Chase, and Orrin C. Shane III (editors)
    1984   *Cenote of Sacrifice: Maya Treasures from the Sacred Well at Chichén Itzá*. University of Texas Press, Austin.

Colomer, José Luis
    2014   Black and the Royal Image. In *Spanish Fashion at the Courts of Early Modern Europe*, edited by José Luis Colomer, pp. 77–112. Centro de Estudios Europa Hispánica, Madrid.

Conkey, Margaret W., and Christine A. Hastorf
    1993   *The Uses of Style in Archaeology*. Cambridge University Press, Cambridge.

Csordas, Thomas J.
    1990   Embodiment as a Paradigm for Anthropology. *Ethos* 18(1):5–47.
    1994   Introduction: The Body as Representation and Being-in-the-World. In *Embodiment and Experience: The Existential Ground of Culture and Self*, edited by Thomas J. Csordas, pp. 1–25. Cambridge University Press, Cambridge.

Culbert, T. Patrick
    1993   *The Ceramics of Tikal Part A: Vessels from the Burials, Caches and Problematical Deposits*. Tikal Report No. 25. University Museum, University of Pennsylvania, Philadelphia.

Cummins, Tom
    1984   Kinshape: The Design of the Hawaiian Feather Cloak. *Art History* 7(1):1–20.

Digby, Adrian
    1972   *Maya Jades*. Trustees of the British Museum, London.

Feldman, Lawrence H.
    2000   *Lost Shores, Forgotten Peoples: Spanish Explorations of the South East Maya Lowlands*. Duke University Press, Durham, N.C.

Fields, Virginia M., and Dorie Reents-Budet
    2005   *Lords of Creation: The Origins of Sacred Maya Kinship*. Scala, London.

Filloy Nadal, Laura, and María Olvido Moreno Guzmán
    2017   Precious Feathers and Fancy Fifteenth-Century Feathered Shields. In *Rethinking the Aztec Economy*, edited by Deborah L. Nichols, Frances F. Berdan, and Michael E. Smith, pp. 156–194. University of Arizona Press, Tucson.

Florescano, Enrique
    2009   *Los orígenes del poder en Mesoamérica*. Fundo de Cultura Económica, Mexico City.

Freidel, David A., Kathryn Reese-Taylor, and David Mora-Marin
- 2002 The Origins of Maya Civilization: The Old Shell Game, Commodity, Treasure, and Kingship. In *Ancient Maya Political Economies*, edited by Marilyn A. Masson and David A. Freidel, pp. 41–86. Altamira Press, Walnut Creek, Calif.

Freidel, David A., and Linda Schele
- 1988 Kinship in the Late Preclassic Maya Lowlands: The Instruments and Places of Ritual Power. *American Anthropologist* 90(3):547–567.

García Granados, Rafael
- 1939 Mexican Feather Mosaics. *Mexican Art and Life* 5:1–4.

González Cruz, Arnoldo, and Guillermo Bernal Romero
- 2012 The Discovery of the Temple XXI Monument at Palenque: Kingdom of Baakal during the Reign of K'inich Ahkal Mo' Nahb. In *Maya Archaeology 2*, edited by Charles W. Golden, Stephen D. Houston, and Joel Skidmore, pp. 82–103. Precolumbia Mesoweb Press, San Francisco.

Graeber, David, and Marshall Sahlins
- 2017 *On Kings*. Hau Books, Chicago.

Graham, Ian, and Eric von Euw
- 1975 *Corpus of Maya Hieroglyphic Inscriptions*, vol. 2, pt. 1, *Naranjo*. Peabody Museum of Archaeology and Ethnology, Harvard University, Cambridge, Mass.

Haag, Sabine, Alfonso Maria y Campos, Lilia Rivero Weber, and Christian Feest (editors)
- 2012 *El penacho del Mexico antiquo*. ZKF Publishers, Altenstadt.

Halperin, Christina T.
- 2014 *Maya Figurines: Intersections between State and Household*. University of Texas Press, Austin.
- 2017 Textile Techné: Classic Maya Translucent Cloth and the Making of Value. In *Making Value, Making Meaning: Techné in the Pre-Columbian World*, edited by Cathy L. Costin, pp. 433–467. Dumbarton Oaks Research Library and Collection, Washington, D.C.

Halperin, Christina T., Zachary X. Hruby, and Ryan William Mongelluzzo
- 2018 The Weight of Ritual: Classic Maya Jade Head Pendants in the Round. *Antiquity* 92(363):758–771.

Harris, Oliver J. T., and John Robb
- 2012 Multiple Ontologies and the Problem of the Body in History. *American Anthropologist* 114(4):668–679.

Hegmon, Michelle
- 1992 Archaeological Research on Style. *Annual Review of Anthropology* 21(1):517–536.

Herzfeld, Michael
- 1991 *A Place in History: Social and Monumental Time in a Cretan Town*. Princeton University Press, Princeton.

Hollander, Anne
- 2016 *Sex and Suits: The Evolution of Modern Dress*. Bloomsbury Academic, London.

Holsbeke, Mirelle, and Julia Montoya (editors)
- 2003 *With Their Hands and Their Eyes*. Etnografisch Museum Antwerpen, Antwerp.

Houston, Stephen D.
- 1993 *Hieroglyphs and History at Dos Pilas: Dynastic Politics of the Classic Maya*. University of Texas Press, Austin.
- 2009 A Splendid Predicament: Young Men in Classic Maya Society. *Cambridge Archaeological Journal* 19(2):149–178.
- 2018 *The Gifted Passage: Young Men in Classic Maya Art and Text*. Yale University Press, New Haven.

Houston, Stephen D., and David Stuart
- 1998 The Ancient Maya Self: Personhood and Portraiture in the Classic Period. *RES: Anthropology and Aesthetics* 33:73–101.

Houston, Stephen D., David Stuart, and Karl A. Taube
- 2006 *The Memory of Bones: Body, Being, and Experience among the Classic Maya*. University of Texas Press, Austin.

Hudon, Jocelyn
- 2005 Considerations in the Conservation of Feathers and Hair, Particularly Their Pigments. In *Fur Trade Legacy: The Preservation of Organic Materials*, edited by Margot Brunn, pp. 127–147. Canadian Association for Conservation of Cultural Property, Ottawa.

Jackson, Sarah E.
- 2013 *Politics of the Maya Court: Hierarchy and Change in the Late Classic Period.* University of Oklahoma Press, Norman.

Jiménez García, Esperanza Elizabeth
- 2010 Sculptural-Iconographic Catalogue of Tula, Hidalgo: The Stone Figures. Foundation for the Advancement of Mesoamerican Studies, http://www.famsi.org/reports/07027/.

Johnson, Irmgard Weitlaner
- 1957 Survival of Feather Ornamented Huipiles in Chiapas, Mexico. *Journal de la Société des Américanistes* 46:189–196.

Jones, Christopher, and Linton Satterthwaite
- 1982 *The Monuments and Inscriptions of Tikal: The Carved Monuments.* Tikal Report no. 33A, University Museum Publications, University of Pennsylvania, Philadelphia.

Joyce, Rosemary A.
- 1996 The Construction of Gender in Classic Maya Monuments. In *Gender and Archaeology*, edited by Rita P. Wright, pp. 167–195. University of Pennsylvania Press, Philadelphia.
- 2000a Girling the Girl and Boying the Boy: The Production of Adulthood in Ancient Mesoamerica. *World Archaeology* 31(3):473–483.
- 2000b *Gender and Power in Prehispanic Mesoamerica.* University of Texas Press, Austin.
- 2003 Concrete Memories: Fragments of the Past in the Classic Maya Present (500–100 AD). In *Archaeologies of Memory*, edited by Ruth M van Dyke and Susan E. Alcock, pp. 104–127. Blackwell, Malden, Mass.

Kantorowicz, Ernst H.
- 1957 *The King's Two Bodies: A Study in Mediaeval Political Theology.* Princeton University Press, Princeton.

Kovacevich, Brigitte
- 2013 The Inalienability of Jades in Mesoamerica. In *The Inalienable in the Archaeology of Mesoamerica*, edited by Brigitte Kovacevich and Michael G. Callaghan, pp. 95–111. Archaeological Papers of the American Anthropological Association 23. Wiley Periodicals, Malden, Mass.

Kovacevich, Brigitte, and Michael G. Callaghan
- 2019 Fifty Shades of Green: Interpreting Maya Jade Production, Circulation, Consumption, and Value. *Ancient Mesoamerica* 30(3):457–472.

Laporte, Juan Pedro
- 2009 El embrujo del tecolote y otras historietas: Algunas consideraciones sobre los silbatos del Clásico en Tikal. In *XXII Simposio de Investigaciones Arqueológicas en Guatemala, 2008*, edited by Juan Pedro Laporte, Bárbara Arroyo, and Hector Méjia, pp. 1021–1050. Museo Nacional de Arqueología y Etnología, Guatemala.

Martin, Simon, and Nikolai Grube
- 2008 *Chronicle of the Maya Kings and Queens: Deciphering the Dynasties of the Ancient Maya.* Thames and Hudson, London.

Mathews, Peter
- 1980 Notes on the Dynastic Sequence of Bonampak, Part 1. In *Third Palenque Round Table, 1978*, edited by Merle Greene Robertson, pp. 60–73. University of Texas Press, Austin.

Mayer, Karl H.
- 1995 Stela 1 from Balamtun, Peten, Guatemala. *Mexicon* 17(4):62.

McAnany, Patricia A.
- 1993 The Economics of Social Power and Wealth among Eighth-Century Maya Households. In *Lowland Maya Civilization in the Eighth Century A.D.*, edited by Jeremy A. Sabloff and John S. Henderson, pp. 65–89. Dumbarton Oaks Research Library and Collection, Washington, D.C.
- 2010 *Ancestral Maya Economies in Archaeological Perspective.* Cambridge University Press, Cambridge.

McCafferty, Sharisse D., and Geoffrey G. McCafferty
- 2000 Textile Production in Ancient Cholula, Mexico. *Ancient Mesoamerica* 11(1):39–54.

Miller, Mary Ellen, and Claudia Brittenham
- 2013 *The Spectacle of the Late Maya Court: Reflections on the Murals of Bonampak.* University of Texas Press, Austin.

Morris, Earl H., Jean Charlot, and Ann Axtell Morris
- 1931 *The Temple of the Warriors at Chichen Itza, Yucatan.* Carnegie Institution of Washington, Washington, D.C.

Morris, Walter F.
- 1984 *A Millennium of Weaving in Chiapas.* Gobierno del Estado de Chiapas, Chiapas.

Morris, Walter F., and Carol Karasik
- 2003 Chiapas Textiles: The Art of Ancient Dreams. In *With Their Hands and Their Eyes,* edited by Mirelle Holsbeke and Julia Montoya, pp. 72–91. Etnografisch Museum Antwerpen, Antwerp.

Navarro-Farr, Olivia C., Mary Kate Kelly, Michelle Rich, and Griselda Pérez Robles
- 2020 Expanding the Canon: Lady K'abel the Ix Kaloomte' and the Political Narratives of Classic Maya Queens. *Feminist Anthropology* 1(1):38–55.

Olko, Justyna
- 2014 *Insignia of Rank in the Nahua World: From the Fifteenth to the Seventeenth Century.* University Press of Colorado, Boulder.

O'Neil, Megan E.
- 2012 Jaina-Style Figurines. In *Ancient Maya Art at Dumbarton Oaks,* edited by Joanne Pillsbury, Miriam Doutriaux, Reiko Ishihara-Brito, and Alexandre Tokovinine, pp. 400–430. Dumbarton Oaks Research Library and Collection, Washington, D.C.

Orellana, Sandra L.
- 1984 *The Tzutujil Mayas: Continuity and Change, 1250–1630.* University of Oklahoma Press, Norman.

Paris, Elizabeth H.
- 2008 Metallurgy, Mayapan, and the Postclassic Mesoamerican World System. *Ancient Mesoamerica* 19(1):43–66.

Parmentier, Richard J.
- 1987 *The Sacred Remains: Myth, History, and Polity in Belau.* University of Chicago Press, Chicago.

Pauketat, Timothy R., and Susan M. Alt
- 2005 Agency in a Postmold? Physicality and the Archaeology of Culture-Making. *Journal of Archaeological Method and Theory* 12(3):213–236.

Pillsbury, Joanne, Miriam Doutriaux, Reiko Ishihara-Brito, and Alexandre Tokovinine (editors)
- 2012 *Ancient Maya Art at Dumbarton Oaks.* Dumbarton Oaks Research Library and Collection, Washington, D.C.

Pincemin Deliberos, Sophia
- 1998 Tejidos del poder: Ejemplos de textiles en los murales de Bonampak, Chiapas. *Anuario* 1998:452–470.

Proskouriakoff, Tatianna
- 1974 *Jades from the Cenote of Sacrifice, Chichen Itza, Yucatan.* Peabody Museum of Archaeology and Ethnology, Harvard University, Cambridge, Mass.

Quenon, Michel, and Genevieve Le Fort
- 1997 Rebirth and Resurrection in Maize God Iconography. In *The Maya Vase Book: A Corpus of Rollout Photographs of Maya Vases,* by Justin Kerr, vol. 3, pp. 884–902. Kerr Associates, New York.

Ringle, William M.
- 2009 The Art of War: Imagery of the Upper Temple of the Jaguars, Chichen Itza. *Ancient Mesoamerica* 20(1):15–44.

Robb, John E., and Timothy R. Pauketat (editors)
- 2013 *Big Histories, Human Lives: Tackling Problems of Scale in Archaeology.* School for Advanced Research Press, Santa Fe.

Russo, Alessandra, Gerhard Wolf, and Diana Fane
- 2015 *Images Take Flight: Feather Art in Mexico and Europe 1400–1700.* Hirmer, Munich.

Sahagún, Bernardino de
- 1959 *Florentine Codex: General History of the Things of New Spain,* bk. 9, *The Merchants.* School of American Research, Santa Fe.
- 1961 *Florentine Codex: General History of the Things of New Spain,* bk. 10, *The People.* School of American Research, Santa Fe.

Saturno, William A., Karl A. Taube, and David Stuart
- 2005 *The Murals of San Bartolo, El Petén, Guatemala,* pt. 1, *The North Wall.* Center for Ancient American Studies, Barnardsville, N.C.

Schele, Linda, and Peter Mathews
- 1998 *The Code of Kings: The Language of Seven Sacred Maya Temples and Tombs.* Scribner, New York.

Schele, Linda, and Mary Ellen Miller
- 1986 *The Blood of Kings: Dynasty and Ritual in Maya Art.* Kimbell Art Museum, Fort Worth.

Scherer, Andrew K., and Stephen D. Houston
- 2018 Blood, Fire, Death: Convenants and Crises among the Classic Maya. In *Smoke, Flames, and the Human Body in Mesoamerican Ritual Practice*, edited by Vera Tiesler and Andrew K. Scherer, pp. 109–150. Dumbarton Oaks Research Library and Collection, Washington, D.C.

Schneider, Jane
- 1978 Peacocks and Penguins: The Political Economy of European Cloth and Colors. *American Ethnologist* 5(3):413–447.

Simmons, Scott E., and Aaron N. Shugar
- 2013 Maya Metallurgical Technology in Late Postclassic–Spanish Colonial Times: The View from Lamanai, Belize. *ArcheoSciences* (37):105–123.

Stuart, David
- 2006 Jade and Chocolate: Bundles of Wealth in Classic Maya Economics and Ritual. In *Sacred Bundles: Ritual Acts of Wrapping and Binding in Mesoamerica*, edited by Julia Guernsey and F. Kent Reilly, pp. 127–144. Boundary End Archaeology Research Center, Barnardsville, N.C.
- 2015 The Royal Headband: A Pan-Mesoamerican Hieroglyph. Maya Decipherment, https://mayadecipherment.com/2015/01/26/the-royal-headband-a-pan-mesoamerican-hieroglyph-for-ruler/.

Taube, Karl A.
- 1992 *The Major Gods of Ancient Yucatan*. Dumbarton Oaks Research Library and Collection, Washington, D.C.
- 2004 *Olmec Art at Dumbarton Oaks*. Dumbarton Oaks Research Library and Collection, Washington, D.C.
- 2005 The Symbolism of Jade in Classic Maya Religion. *Ancient Mesoamerica* 16(1):23–50.

Taube, Karl A., and Reiko Ishihara-Brito
- 2012 From Stone to Jewel: Jade in Ancient Maya Religion and Rulership. In *Ancient Maya Art at Dumbarton Oaks*, edited by Joanne Pillsbury, Miriam Doutriaux, Reiko Ishihara-Brito, and Alexandre Tokovinine, pp. 136–153. Dumbarton Oaks Research Library and Collection, Washington, D.C.

Taube, Karl A., William A. Saturno, David Stuart, and Heather Hurst
- 2010 *The Murals of San Bartolo, El Petén, Guatemala*. Boundary End Archaeology Research Center, Barnardsville, N.C.

Taylor, Dicey
- 1992 Painted Ladies: Costumes for Women on Tepeu Ceramics. In *The Maya Vase Book: A Corpus of Rollout Photographs of Maya Vases*, by Justin Kerr, vol. 3, pp. 513–525. Kerr Associates, New York.

Tedlock, Dennis
- 1996 *Popul Vuh: The Maya Book of the Dawn of Life*. Touchstone, New York.
- 2003 *Rabinal Achi: A Mayan Drama of War and Sacrifice*. Oxford University Press, Oxford.

Thompson, J. Eric S.
- 1951 The Itza of Tayasal, Peten. In *Homenaje al Doctor Alfonso Caso*, edited by Juan Comas, Manuel Maidonado-Koerdell, and Eusebio Dávilos Hurtado, pp. 389–400. Nuevo Mundo, Mexico City.

Tozzer, Alfred
- 1957 *Chichén Itzá and Its Cenote of Sacrifice: A Comparative Study of Contemporaneous Maya and Toltec*. Peabody Museum of Archaeology and Ethnology, Harvard University, Cambridge, Mass.

Turner, Terence S.
- 2012 The Social Skin. *HAU: Journal of Ethnographic Theory* 2(2):486–504.

Vázquez López, Verónica Amellali
- 2017 Pact and Marriage: Sociopolitical Strategies of the Kanu'l and Its Allies during the Late Classic Period. *Contributions in New World Archaeology* 11:9–48.

Winzenz, Karon
- 2014 The Symbolic Vocabulary of Cloth and Garments in the San Bartolo Murals. In *Wearing Culture: Dress and Regalia in Early Mesoamerica and Central America*, edited by Heather Orr and Matthew G. Looper, pp. 373–411. University Press of Colorado, Boulder.

Źrałka, Jarosław, Wiesław Koszkul, Simon Martin, and Bernard Hermes
- 2011 In the Path of the Maize God: A Royal Tomb at Nakum, Petén, Guatemala. *Antiquity* 85:890–908.

9

Maya Gastropolitics

Strategies, Tactics, Entrapments

SHANTI MORELL-HART

Across ancient Maya courts and council halls, rulers were "eating to make friends, and eating to make enemies" (to paraphrase Sutton 2001:5). Although modes of rulership in the ancient Maya world took a number of forms, all rulers engaged with foodways. Beyond famines and feasting, food politics were manifested in tributary offerings, trade goods, mobilized labor, appeals to deities, and basic everyday subsistence. Here, I frame the emergence, transformation, and persistence of the authority to rule by making arguments for "how to do things with foods" (with apologies to Austin 1975) and by tracking how modes of authority were created, managed, maintained, and subverted through culinary pursuits. Certain foods, much like regalia and thrones, offered synecdoches of rulership, tokens indexing a larger thing of which they were a part.

Some ruler obligations in the Maya area were in a managerial vein: maintaining resources through territory and trade, eliminating disruptions to supply chains through political negotiations, reducing threats to crops through landesque capital, and increasing crop yields through labor assignments. But sumptuous food procurement and elite culinary performance were also requirements for successful rulership. As described by Stephen Houston and colleagues, ruler-gifted foods could "confirm alliances, affirm agreements, and bind centers and peripheries of Classic polities," while imbibing drinks from gifted vessels could "seal bargains or celebrate important meetings" (Houston, Stuart, and Taube 1992:153).

Our basic ideas of rulership in the ancient Maya world have tended to center on a few formulations. Classic-period models tend to focus more on sovereigns, realms, and courts. Types of rulership included heterarchies (Hendon 2020; Scarborough, Valdez, and Dunning 2003), polyarchies (Dahlin and Ardren 2002:271–272), and hierarchies—all represented in the archaeological record, whether the period of rulership lasted an entire dynasty or a single yearly cycle. But rulers in the Postclassic period, primarily in the northern Yucatán, present alternate models to dynastic rulership, operating confederacies such as at Mayapan, with noble councils headed by paramount leaders and complex religious hierarchies (Masson 2021; Masson and Hare 2020:795; see also Baron, this volume). Whatever the form of rulership, activities of Maya rulers are represented in the archaeological record through quotidian and specialized culinary practice: administration, adjudication, ritualized activities, redistribution of resources, and diplomatic efforts.

For key ideas in this paper, I owe primary debt to Arjun Appadurai (1981). In his writings on gastropolitics, Appadurai illuminated the many ways conflict can arise between groups or individuals and examined how this conflict can be negotiated through food. Appadurai drew critical attention to foodways as active agents in economic movement, broader political ecologies, and spiritual practice. Using a broader working definition, I here characterize gastropolitics as: intentional, but sometimes having unintended consequences; lateral (peer-to-peer) as well as vertical (ruler-to-divinity and ruler-to-ruled); related to peace diplomacy and trade, but also to threats of war; related to sacred matters as much as economic matters (themselves intertwined); encompassing unique or recurring practices as well as semifixed cultural logics; and grounded in pragmatics, though "common sense" itself is culturally and historically constituted. I should emphasize that this understanding of gastropolitics folds in the spiritual realm, especially as Maya rulers engaged the divine and the deceased (e.g., Baron, this volume; Coe 1994:160; Freidel, this volume; McAnany 1995; Morehart and Butler 2010; Schele and Freidel 1990) as much as the human and the living (e.g., Golden et al. 2020; McAnany 2019; Rich and Eppich 2020; Yaeger [2010] 2018).

Like other forms of political maneuvering, we find evidence that gastropolitics infused ancient Maya statecraft from the earliest nascent cities through the arrival of the Spaniards. Scholars have already inferred many of the basic elements involved in the practice of gastropolitics. Analyses of food storage and serving places help us to understand aspects such as relative access to rulers, manifested in public versus secluded meal settings that represent relative degrees of performance and privacy. Ingredients and sources of food materials index trade and negotiation, bulk feast quantity, and degrees of connoisseurship. Prepared foods are represented in imagery alongside raw ingredient tribute, perhaps demonstrating both the munificence of rulers when hosting guests as well as the power of rulers to obtain their cut of foodstuffs. Culinary equipment was diverse, as we see in vessel imagery of courts, residues of offerings in tombs, and arrays of ceramics in middens. Food preparations and labor are harder to parse, with only faint suggestions from imagery and architectural layouts.

Our general understandings of Maya rulership come primarily from pottery and stone—the focus of many of the papers in this volume. But here I focus on foodstuffs and gastronomic practice, using a number of proxies. By combining paleoethnobotanical evidence, faunal evidence, iconographic representations, and ethnohistoric documents, I track the workings of gastropolitics as an often unstable foundation for ancient Maya rulership. I begin with the basic ingredients, then present several manifestations of gastropolitics: in haute cuisine, elite performance, and times of strife. I then point to a few ways that food practice operated as realpolitik, sometimes through the use of culinary deception. I finish by considering the ways that rulers were entrapped by their own gastropolitical maneuvers, sometimes with severe consequences.

Ingredients for Rulership: Players, Foods, Places, Things

In the very broadest brushstrokes, Classic-period polities in the northern Maya Lowlands are known for large and elaborate stone complexes, with more small-scale food ceremonialism, as well as centrally placed and accessible locations to perform large-scale ceremonial feasts and ritualized food offerings. Meanwhile, Classic-period polities in the southern Maya Lowlands are known for carved and painted texts, some with sacred food associations and culinary imagery, as well as elaborate royal funerary ceremonies, including sumptuous tombs with culinary offerings. Over time, Preclassic-period feasting and nascent culinary regionalism transitioned to Classic-period elaboration and formalization of foodways, which transitioned into Postclassic-period renegotiations and large-scale trade of commodities. Such broad brushstrokes necessarily obscure the pronounced heterogeneity that we actually see on the ground in different places and over time.

The roster of key food ingredients varied across the Maya Lowlands, in diversity and relative abundance, both for rulers and the ruled. Plant food ingredients numbered in the hundreds (Fedick 2020; Lentz 1999), yielding a diverse larder from which cooks could construct elaborate dishes. Most people are familiar with the "triumvirate plus," the maize, beans, squashes, and chiles that formed the cornerstones of Maya daily fare and continue to serve as key staples in the contemporary Maya area. A number of recent studies have also highlighted geophytes in elite Maya cuisine, including sweet potatoes, yams, achira, jicama, makal, arrowroot, and manioc (Cagnato 2016; Fernández Souza, Zimmermann, and Jiménez Álvarez 2020; Morell-Hart et al. 2021; Novelo-Pérez et al. 2019; Venegas Durán, Herrera-Parra, and Novelo Pérez 2020, echoing Coe 1994). Faunal resources also likely numbered over a hundred species, including terrestrial and aquatic meats (Emery 2002) as well as insects. Ducks, dogs, and turkeys were all domesticated (Boileau, Delsol, and Emery 2020), and some people may have kept deer and peccaries in pens (Hamblin 1980) and trapped fish in weirs (Chmilar 2013:210). Cooks incorporated a number of common aquatic species in meals (Boileau, Delsol, and Emery 2020), including fresh- and saltwater shellfish, fresh- and saltwater fish (Emery 2002), turtles, and various mollusks, as well as the occasional crocodile (Masson et al. 2020) or shark. Salt, though a critical food resource, is only epigraphically referenced once in the Maya area, on the murals at Calakmul (Martin 2012:68), whereas salt-making apparatuses have been recovered inland (Woodfill et al. 2015) and on the coasts (Andrews 2020; McKillop and Sills 2017). Salt supplies would have been critical as lowlands populations soared in the Classic period.

Whether for quotidian consumption or specialized culinary affairs, ancient Maya people left little evidence of large-scale food preparation in Classic-period centers. As Inomata and Houston ([2001] 2018) note, royal courts may have sponsored feasts, but not necessarily provided the banquet. In spite of frequent evidence of feasting consumption and discard, we have only limited evidence of large-scale food preparations directly associated with southern royal courts—such as those at Tikal (Harrison 1970:248, in Miller and Martin 2004:22), Xunantunich (LeCount 2001), and La Corona (Lamoureux-St-Hilaire 2020:246)—or with northern administrative and elite complexes—such as those at Sihó (Fernández Souza, Zimmermann, and Jiménez Álvarez 2020:200), Kiuic (Gallareta Cervera 2016:296), and Mayapan (Masson and Hare 2020:798).

Small-scale kitchens in palaces and elite complexes seemed more common than large-scale preparation facilities (e.g., Chase and Chase 2017; Inomata 2001). One such layout was documented at the site of Lacanjá Tzeltal (Morell-Hart and Ojeda González 2018). When looking for food preparation and disposal areas during the 2019 field season, researchers targeted the interior of the palace complex patio, two exterior locations adjacent to the palace complex, and a nearby house mound (of several in the area). Materials in the uppermost fills of the palace patio and house mound fall within a normal pattern across sites in southeastern Mesoamerica: the likely reuse of nearby and friable trash deposits as architectural fills. But one rich deposit on the "back" (south) side of the palace yielded large fragments of finer ceramics in what appeared to be a primary deposit of royal household trash.

Where did Maya sovereigns, councilors, and their entourages actually consume food? We have archaeological and iconographic evidence that the Maya elite consumed food in public places like plazas, semipublic places like shrines and colonnaded patios, and private locations like sacred caves (Morehart 2011; Spenard et al. 2020). They sometimes feasted near temples, sometimes inside palaces, sometimes during funerary rites, and sometimes atop platforms that were later filled in and constructed over, as documented at Classic-period Budsilhá in Chiapas (Morell-Hart et al. 2018).

figure 9.1
Rollout photograph (K6418) of a ceramic vessel, showing a ruler speaking to a kneeling attendant, while a large three-legged dish of sauce-covered tamales is situated prominently in the foreground. Justin Kerr Maya archive, Dumbarton Oaks, Trustees for Harvard University, Washington, D.C.

Rulers would have required people with specialized expertise to cook large quantities for their sponsored feasts and higher-quality elaborations for their daily meals, along with spiritually specific foodstuffs for the dead and the divine that were sometimes prepared by rulers themselves. Thus far, it is unclear who was "downstairs," preparing and serving these foods: attached specialists, lesser nobility, immediate members of a governing household, and/or enslaved laborers might all have played a role. Given what we know about other sorts of specialists, from scribes to ceramic artists to masons, we might also expect culinary specialists who accommodated gourmand tastes and brought artistry to food crafting. Rulers must have valued culinary elaboration very highly, given the frequency of foodstuffs in imagery, the epigraphic specifications of concoctions on vessels, and the marking of specific food purveyors in the murals at Calakmul (Carrasco Vargas, Vázquez López, and Martin 2009).

Although foods in imagery are almost never seen in banquet quantities, some portions seem generous, perhaps indicating a sort of snack tray offered to guests (Figure 9.1). Or perhaps these vessels held refreshments exclusively intended for rulers and royal households, while visiting dignitaries and tributaries looked on hungrily. Power plays between rulers and secondary lords (Houston and Stuart [2001] 2018) unfolded in such courtly settings, whether some stomachs were growling.

Supernatural Nourishment and Noblesse Oblige

As Simon Martin has noted (drawing from Marshall Sahlins), Maya rulers were not "free-floating agents, but grounded participants possessed of responsibilities as well as privileges" (Martin 2020b:69). Many—if not most—of these responsibilities were related to food. Some obligations were discharged through spiritual means: petitioning the divine for future abundant harvests, expressing gratitude for past harvests, interpreting auguries of weather conditions, and feeding divinities with vapors and blood. Linda Schele and David Freidel framed such relationships

figure 9.2

Bloodletting: ritualized practice and equipment. Images of Bonampak Stela 2, depicting ruler Yajaw Chan Muwaahn II about to engage in bloodletting. He is assisted by his mother, Ix Ahku'ul Patah (right), and his wife, Ix Yax Chiit Jun Witz' Naah Kan (left). Ix Ahku'ul Patah holds a vessel of paper strips and a stingray spine. Inset is an example of a stingray spine, recovered from Str. 766A-l, Cache 2, Zacpeten. Photograph of Bonampak Stela 2 by Shanti Morell-Hart; line drawings of Bonampak Stela 2 by Peter Mathews; photograph of stingray spine from Zacpeten by Timothy Pugh.

between ancient Maya people and the divine in this way: "The people reaped the benefits of the [ruler's] intercession with the supernatural world and shared in the material wealth a successful performance brought to the community" (Schele and Freidel 1990:98; see also Ardren, this volume; Baron, this volume; Freidel, this volume; Houston 2018:85). Even the ability to host feasts may have been directly linked to the divine, if ritual wealth was seen as objectivized spiritual power, physically manifesting the blessings and protections of spirits (Sahlins 2017:61).

For many rulers, regular intermediation with gods and other supernaturals transpired by offering specialized sacred materials, including sanctified foods and beverages, incense, body parts, blood, and even entire infants (see Baron, this volume; Chuchiak 2003; Houston 2018; Houston, Stuart, and Taube 2006; Tiesler and Scherer 2018)—though all may have been considered "food" of a sort (Monaghan 1999). The deities that fed from various smokes and vapors, odors and essences, were thus made sympathetic to human petitions, or simply kept nourished. In this sense, what Andrew Scherer and Stephen Houston (2018:142) have framed as offerings "to honor covenants with supernaturals, to appeal to their senses, and to satiate their appetites" is effectively strategic cooking. In this way, rulers preparing "foods" and feeding the gods are not only intermediaries with ancestors and other divine beings (Figure 9.2). They are the cooks (*ch'aajom* title, overseer of bloodletting), while bloodletting and sacrificial instruments—obsidian blades and flakes, stingray spines, cord—could be considered types of sacred culinary equipment. Feeding deities thus runs metaphorically parallel to feeding human beings, and both are critical for survival.

Deceased ancestors were often at least semi-deified, if not fully deified, and acted simultaneously

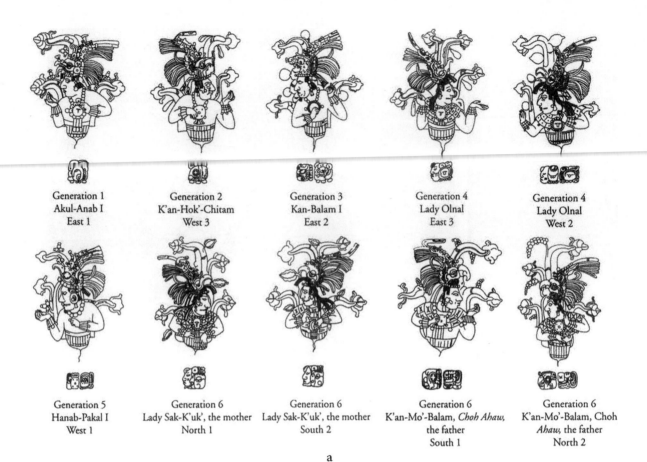

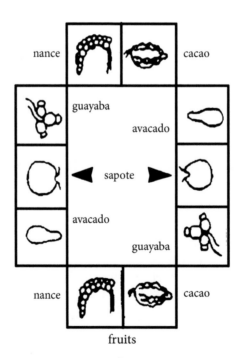

figure 9.3
Ancestors reborn as various fruit-bearing trees in an orchard, on K'inich Janaab Pakal sarcophagus. Illustrations by Peter Mathews, reproduced from Schele and Mathews (1999:121).

230　MORELL-HART

as owners, anchors, and managers of productive places, from garden to orchard to field. Their favor and intercession initially required special funerary ceremonies, then constant renewal and maintenance of obligations through ongoing offerings and gifts (see Awe, Helmke, Ebert, and Hoggarth, this volume; Benavides, this volume; Howie, White, and Longstaffe 2010; Morehart and Butler 2010). McAnany has argued that the interment of deceased individuals was linked directly to the establishment and maintenance of claims to agricultural land, "on loan" from ancestors who needed "payments" for use rights (McAnany 1995:100; see also Baron, this volume; Chuchiak, this volume). Ancestors are directly linked to orchards, most famously on the sarcophagus of K'inich Janaab Pakal at Palenque (Schele and Mathews 1999:119–125), where side panels show his ancestors reborn as various fruit-bearing trees in an orchard (Figure 9.3). Agricultural metaphors in Maya funerary practice abound: interment and descent to the netherworld were equated with the sowing of maize kernels; the soul's separation from the body in the tomb was equated with the germinated maize seed sprouting; ritualized decapitation was equated with the harvest of maize cobs; and the bones of ancestors were equated with fertilizer for the earth (see Ardren, this volume; Awe, Helmke, Ebert, and Hoggarth, this volume; Martin 2020b:149; O'Neil 2009:119; Taube 1989).

Initial funerary practices may have served to nourish interred individuals en route to or during the afterlife (Tozzer 1941:129–131), to awaken and rebirth the spirit, and/or to propitiate other divinities on behalf of the deceased (McNeil 2010). In the Postclassic period, when divine rulers were no longer the norm, we still find funerary offerings similar to those in the Classic period, although with much more overlap between daily foods and specialized funerary offerings in the latter period, whether ceramic containers (Howie, White, and Longstaffe 2010) or faunal foods (Masson and Hare 2020).

Gastropolitics between rulers, gods, and the deceased thus involved a number of ritualized food offerings, from everyday fare to human flesh and blood. Smoke could be the offering medium, though supernaturals were sometimes fed directly through their images and carved figures. Rulers negotiated the divine as farmers negotiated the soils, and all had different strategies for coaxing crops to grow.

Gastropolitics in Haute Cuisine

Beyond the diverse staples that provided the bulk of nutritional needs, sumptuary foodstuffs also made their way into elite ceremony and cuisine. In terms of raw ingredients, cacao ruled the roost, meriting epigraphic note across pre-Hispanic time periods (Stuart 2006) and remaining well-documented into the colonial period (see Chuchiak, this volume). Cacao orchards may have even factored into marriage dowries (Harrison-Buck 2017), helping to establish and maintain social relations between groups and mirroring the marriage alliance itself. Tributes of cacao, often depicted as bags with numerical markings (Figure 9.4), appear on painted vases, as well as in Room 1 of the Bonampak paintings (Houston 1997; Miller and Martin 2004:62). Other costly plant ingredients likely included vanilla beans and annatto, as documented alongside salt in trade wars during the Postclassic period in the Peten region (Caso Barrera and Aliphat Fernández 2006). But Maya rulers appeared to tie the values of most plant foodstuffs more closely to modes of preparation and serving, given the specific recipes noted epigraphically and the vessel forms associated with specific plant residues (e.g., Powis et al. 2002; Spenard et al. 2020). Ground spice mixtures (*recados*) commonly seen in markets today (Fedick 2017) may also have been viewed as sumptuous, especially if transporting exotic flavor combinations to distant places.

The relative value of animals seemed entirely dependent on access and degree of domesticity, with hunted meats holding a special place in iconographic representations. Dogs, turkeys, iguanas, and rabbits are more common overall in faunal assemblages across social strata, though relative quantities vary (Emery 2002). Deer meat was imported into island settings, although deer and peccary consumption varied, with more restricted use in certain places and time periods (Sorayya Carr 1996). Marine materials made their way into inland settings (Masson and

figure 9.4
Rollout photograph (K2914) of a ceramic vessel, showing a marriage negotiation. Tribute featured in the lower half includes three bags of beans (*ux ka bu'l*, "three are our bean [bundles]"), cloth, and possibly a cone of salt. Denver Art Museum, 2003.1. Justin Kerr Maya archive, Dumbarton Oaks, Trustees for Harvard University, Washington, D.C.

Peraza Lope 2013), frequently recovered as stingray spines and shell, but also likely transported as dried shrimp and fish. Anthony Andrews describes how traders navigated rivers, lakes, and the coast, from the Preclassic through the colonial periods, to move fishes, shellfishes, and marine mammals, alongside condiments and salt (Andrews 2020; see also Sorayya Carr 1996). Generally, the highest stratum of society was more closely linked to higher meat consumption, as evidenced in isotopic studies (Chase and Chase 2017; Wright 2003 in Fernández Souza, Zimmermann, and Jiménez Álvarez 2020:193), spot-test chemical studies of proteins (Fernández Souza, Zimmermann, and Jiménez Álvarez 2020), and faunal remains (Emery 2002; Götz 2011 in Fernández Souza, Zimmermann, and Jiménez Álvarez 2020:192; Masson et al. 2020). However, some sites, such as Piedras Negras, evidence no such obvious distinctions (Scherer, Wright, and Yoder 2007).

Other sumptuous ingredients likely included honeys and salts. Particular regional honeys (Bianco, Alexander, and Rayson 2017) may have been valued, especially if floral flavors were distinct from region to region, linking honeys to terroir and perhaps perceived medicinal qualities. Salts from inland and coastal production areas, with different mineral profiles, may have also invoked specific terroirs and medicinal applications. These ingredients were rarely under absolute ruler control of production and distribution (Batún Alpuche 2009; Caso Barrera and Aliphat Fernández 2006; McKillop and Sills 2017), with few exceptions (Martin 2020b; Woodfill et al. 2015). Rather, rulers may have had more commonly held rights over human labor to produce such ingredients, as in colonial examples of salt production (see Chuchiak, this volume).

Prestige foods were not simply sumptuous ingredients, traded from distant places or grown in restricted orchards. They were also elaborately prepared, presented, and consumed. Consumption of specially prepared balché alcohol, at least in the colonial period, was used to mark insiders and outsiders of a community—Maya and non-Maya alike (Chuchiak 2003:153–154). A variety of named cacao drinks reveals differences in cacao preparation that may have indexed social distinctions and cultural refinement (Henderson and Joyce 2006; Houston 2018:83). In the part of the corpus dating to the Early Classic period, at least seven cacao drink preparations are represented, though by the Late Classic period, only three are documented on ceramic vessels (Carter and Matsumoto 2020). Atole also appears in a wide number of mixtures and flavors (Beliaev, Davletshin, and Tokovinine 2010; Houston, Stuart, and Taube 2006:108) and is even named on a monument (see Tokovinine, Estrada Belli, and Fialko, this volume), indicating that elite foods were not limited to those made from precious ingredients (see also Loughmiller-Newman 2013). Particular types of atole preparations are sometimes indicated—e.g., "not of the common kind" (Tokovinine 2016:17)—in some cases where fresh maize appeared to be preferred.

We can thus consider the relative value of foodstuffs that had difficult modes of preparation: tamales were more labor-intensive than atoles, while tamales with ground sauces were more elaborate still. Deer may have been more exotic, restricted, or even sacred (Looper 2019; Sorayya Carr 1996), and thus deer tamales with elaborate sauces were perhaps the costliest and most elaborate of all.

Gastropolitics in Elite Performance

Elite membership, as with membership in other communities, could be expressed through dress, work, speech, walk, and tool use—as well as through ways of eating. Embodying rulership required costuming and adornment (see Halperin, this volume), but also specific consumption practices, including the performance of table manners, the control of sumptuous supplies and stores, and the show of munificence to guests at banquets and feasts. Whether dynastic rulers in the south, engaging in the performance of royal duties, or non-dynastic rulers in the north, expressing both symmetrical and asymmetrical relationships, ruler legitimacy was based on intelligibility, not only in brute expressions of power but also in how they ate, feasted, and fed the gods. Through food practices, rulers presented themselves as rulers in ways that were understood by other rulers—similarly to inscribing mutually intelligible texts (see Martin 2020b)—as well as by the ruled and the divine. Foodscapes, like landscapes and architecture, were subject to periodic remodeling (see Ringle, this volume; Tokovinine, Estrada Belli, and Fialko, this volume), but were never reformulated in such a way that made no sense.

What evidence do we have of culinary diglossia (sensu Houston and Inomata 2009:45; Houston et al. 2000) between nobility and non-elites? That is, to what extent were some elite foodways akin to a separate language, inscrutable to the average person? Establishing distinction (Bourdieu [1979] 1984) was a necessary part of rulership, similarly to processes of *aggrandizement*, described by Awe, Helmke, Ebert, and Hoggarth (this volume); *legacy*, described by Halperin (this volume); and *legitimation*, described by Tokovinine, Estrada Belli, and Fialko (this volume). Conspicuous consumption of specialized foods could bolster or create authority, whether for a divine ruler, high council leader, or primary lineage head. As previously noted, differential access to sumptuary foods was a key marker, as were certain kinds of serving ware, specific sorts of serving places (Inomata 2001), and certain elaborate preparations, including the brewing of cacao beverages (Henderson and Joyce 2006) and the performance of frothing (Coe 1994:141–144). But gestural distinctions in the performance of table manners may have been more subtle and less perceptible to everyone. To the non-elite, some table manners may have seemed overly fussy, if noticed at all. Such gestural messages would also have landed differently on foreigners in Maya courts.

"Stranger" rulers (see Ardren, this volume; Lamoureux-St-Hilaire and McAnany, this volume; Masson, this volume; Ringle, this volume) would have followed some local conventions to ensure relevancy, but also established legitimacy through a number of esoteric and exotic foodways. Maya aristocratic traditions included serving ware used during politically transitional periods, and different types of vessels were sometimes marked with glyphs related to contents, ownership, or patronage (Stuart 1989). But vessel forms shifted over time, related

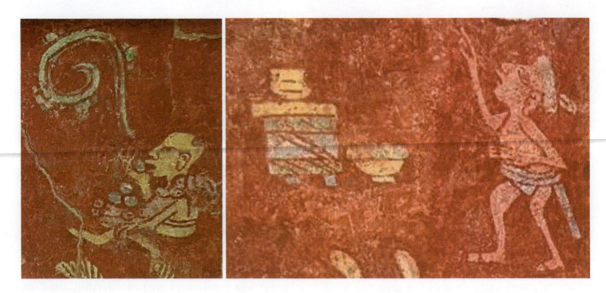

figure 9.5
Details of foodstuffs from the Tepantitla compound murals at Teotihuacan. Photographs by Shanti Morell-Hart.

to shifts in ruler performance as well as to changes in broader preferences and availability. Houston (2012:92) describes more skeuomorphs of gourds in the Early Classic period, likely requiring a two-handed cupping approach to consuming atoles or liquid chocolate. The Late Classic flat-bottomed cylinders represented a shift toward clarifying activities in displays and possibly stabilizing vessels while at rest on flat surfaces. Terminal Classic vessels included new barrel-like forms with restricted openings and other forms potentially used for frothing. Perhaps the grater bowls and comales described by Traci Ardren (2020) for the Late Classic to Postclassic transition were rooted in similar processes, though were also related to the arrival of foreign influences.

The Central Mexican influences evident in serving ware and dynastic records were probably also manifested in the foodstuffs themselves. The actual foreign-born, such as the Teotihuacan founders of new patrilines at Tikal, Uaxactun, and Copan after 378 CE (Martin 2020b:390), likely missed some foods from home (Figure 9.5). For visiting foreign dignitaries—did Maya state banquets include a touch of the familiar (similarly to Fitzpatrick 2016) or simply dazzle with local delights? We do know that in later periods, the Maya people of Xuenkal "learned how to be the Itzá, by eating correctly with food made on highly charged objects provided by the new state" as well as by consuming new types of foods such as tortillas (Ardren 2020:291).

At state dinners, whether served to local or foreign dignitaries, a number of considerations would have been managed by chefs, attaches, and servers: where to seat people relative to the ruler; which dishes to offer to best express the relative status of the host and guests; and which culinary equipment to use to most astound foreign dignitaries and future in-laws. In such performances, physical and social proxemics were likely closely related (similarly to Appadurai 1981), whether foods were shared from a single dish or individually served. That is, the politically closer to the ruler, the bodily closer to the ruler, in state dinners as much as public feasts. But there would also have been a sort of spatial deixis in play: at a large-scale feast, nobles jockeying for position in the immediate environs of a ruler all probably seemed relatively close together to farmers watching from a more distant vantage point.

Much has been written about feasting in the Maya area, and even more specifically the role of feasting in political relationships (e.g., Brown and Freiwald 2020; Brown and Gerstle 2002; Halperin and Foias 2016; LeCount 2001; Reents-Budet 2000). Through feasts, rulers circulated wealth, celebrated

figure 9.6
Rollout photograph (K1092) of feasting imagery painted on a ceramic vessel, showing (over)abundant fermented beverages and general drunkenness. Justin Kerr Maya archive, Dumbarton Oaks, Trustees for Harvard University, Washington, D.C.

ancestors, and cemented alliances—sometimes raucously (Figure 9.6). Feasting debts were very real (Houston 2018:84), sometimes gravely so. Rulers in the Postclassic period used the pretense of feasting to massacre banquet guests (Pohl and Pohl 2003:141), and rulers in the colonial period dodged reciprocal feasting obligations by ratting out former hosts to authorities (Chuchiak 2003:150). During the performance of any ruler-hosted meal, social distinctions could be enunciated or subverted, while loops of obligation were formed and upheld or broken.

The spectacle of a feast might pertain to what has been termed a "theatre state" by Clifford Geertz (1980), where "organized power was realized only periodically, in grand but fleeting spectacles, and anything we might consider 'statecraft'—from diplomacy to the stockpiling of resources—existed in order to facilitate the rituals and ceremonies, rather than the other way around" (see Wengrow, this volume). But in Maya gastropolitics, pomp also served power (to paraphrase Geertz 1980:13). The feasts themselves helped to extend and stabilize rulership, through the ingestion of gifted food, bodily affirmation of commensality, creation of obligation, and inculcation of a "natural" social order, as in colonial period balché rituals described by Chuchiak (2003:147–150). The feast could help to temporarily reconcile the "paradox of cultural megalomania with organizational pluralism" (Geertz 1980:19), through the spectacle itself, alongside structurating processes of mobilization.

Over the long term, recurring feasts (among other activities) would have required more investment than a stone stela. Although political discourse in stone offered relative durability (see Ringle, this volume), labor for a feast had to be amassed at a much larger scale to deliver the same message. This is not to spiral into an argument about relative material values or the notion of value itself, but rather to point toward how much work, how many resources, and how many people were mobilized for a banquet.

Let Them Eat Cacao

Up to this point, I have devoted the bulk of my narrative to the workings of gastropolitics in "good times." Now, however, I turn to the hard times. We have incontrovertible evidence that multiple regions of the Maya area—at different points in time—faced severe strife, whether sociopolitically motivated (e.g., warfare), naturally onset (e.g., droughts), or some combination of the two. Social unrest may have been initiated or exacerbated by environmental factors at various points in time (Aimers and Hodell 2011; Yaeger 2020). Such environmental factors included droughts (Iannone, Yaeger, and Hodell

2014), soil erosion and exhaustion, and drinking water scarcity and contamination. Nicholas Dunning, Timothy Beach, and Sheryl Luzzadder-Beach (2020) address the ways that rulers may—or may not—have interceded with farmers at such times, to amplify agricultural output and to reduce risk, by developing alliance and trade networks.

In preparing for war, it appears that rulers prioritized agricultural necessities over other factors such as astronomical phenomena (Martin 2020b). Martin found that key peaks in recorded warfare events were connected to dry periods, when "there was not only available manpower" but readily available food in the granaries of the enemy "to extort, loot, or destroy" (Martin 2020b:227). Dry periods were also "the easiest for travel, the least demanding of labour in the fields, as well as when food stocks were most vulnerable" (Martin 2020b:227).

Whether issues with water or scarcity of maize and other agricultural staples were primary factors, a breakdown in supply chains is clear. Perhaps the gods were not fed enough, and crops shriveled or drowned. Or the ruled were not fed enough, and the discontents of the people translated into withering supply streams. Or perhaps the "long-term nature of antagonisms . . . and a tenacious memory for aggrievement that borders on vendetta" (Houston and Inomata 2009:48) led the rich to eat the rich. The tempo of food supply disruptions varied, as did the severity, and the ways that different social sectors were affected.

But not all was so grim. We do find some evidence of resilience during these periods of strife, if not for everyone. Some places fared better than others, where we find ongoing resource availability such as salt production (Woodfill et al. 2015) or robustly sustained trade connections (Howie, White, and Longstaffe 2010:372). In such stable, long-term occupations, with Preclassic through Postclassic components, there was overall good population health, evident in the paleo diet and dental pathology (Howie, White, and Longstaffe 2010). Maya farmers may have had greater food resilience (Ebert et al. 2019; Somerville, Fauvelle, and Froehle 2013) after one or several seasons of poor productivity, given a more diverse suite of crops and food-production strategies than is usually calculated in bare-bones algorithms of carrying capacities and seasonal timing. Such resilience might even be suggested in findings by Hoggarth et al. (2017), in their calculations of demographic recovery during the colonial period.

Yet maize supplies—and specifically, their disruption through drought or trade route shifts—usually lie at the heart of most collapse models in the Maya area, whether implicitly or explicitly framed. Agricultural yields in such models are invariably constructed around the biological properties of maize, and the productive capacity of socionatural systems to maintain its supply (Fedick, Morell-Hart, and Dussol 2023; Morell-Hart et al. 2022). Our definitions of staple foods continue to overweigh maize—alongside swidden and extensive agricultural practices—across environments, time periods, and demographic sectors. But as discussed in previous passages, increasing evidence of geophytes (Morell-Hart et al. 2022), tree crops, wild game and fish, and managed fauna, in addition to widespread landesque investments (Fedick, Morell-Hart, and Dussol 2023), reveals a broad range of managing and buffering strategies. The question remains as to what extent these affordances were available to rulers and elites. Elite segments of the population, in times of crisis, arguably had less direct physical access to farmlands, less direct knowledge of food production and gathering strategies, and were more invested in retaining the old lifeways that privileged their position.

Rulership—whether monarch or confederate—was dependent on supply maintenance, with failures leading to warfare and the dissolution of elite systems. Regardless of the reasons for abandonment and radical demographic shifts, the Terminal Classic period saw dramatic changes to rulership and how it was constituted. Postclassic shifts in governance may have gone hand in hand with reimagining the movement and distribution of food supplies for the populace—though the gods were still fed with apportionments of blood well into the colonial period (Tozzer 1941). Opulent and centralized palace receiving halls of the Classic period were reimagined in multiplicate at Postclassic Mayapan (Masson 2021), perhaps also reconfiguring feasting ceremonialism in the many council halls.

Gastropolitik, Rulership, and Culinary Lies

I now turn to what I term "gastropolitik," a portmanteau here operating as shorthand. I borrow heavily from notions of realpolitik (loosely following Waltz 2014)—a term that may encompass foodways but does not focus on them—and gastropolitics (following Appadurai 1981)—a term that may encompass realpolitik but does not focus on its practice. Realpolitik involves pragmatism; public-facing activities and private transactions where rhetoric and action are sometimes at odds. The impetus for realpolitik may be the amplification or consolidation of political power, but may also be a more benign pursuit of security or basic survival (Waltz 2014; similar to Kennan 1991). Such "politik" can involve the strategies of the state or institution, as well as the tactics of various actors. The dynamics of realpolitik—between tactical maneuvers and strategic policies—can also result in entrapment, for some or all parties.

Apart from general negotiations surrounding food, a key feature of gastropolitik is the occasional mismatch of public-facing narratives and private actions when pursuing pragmatic remedies for various issues and crises. From the negotiation with divinities to the management of recalcitrant nobles, Maya rulers pursued solutions to complex problems that may not have matched their public or recorded rhetoric. Making use of a sort of gastronomic code-switching, rulers sometimes used cuisine to appear wealthier, more refined, more foreign, more divine, or more closely allied to others than they actually were (similar to notions of galactic mimesis and upward nobility described by Sahlins 2017; see Halperin, this volume; Lamoureux-St-Hilaire and McAnany, this volume).

First, did rulers display particular table manners differently—or consume different foods—in public-facing ceremonies, versus privately in their own chambers (similarly framed in Graeber 2017:407)? It may be that for some Maya leaders, "symbolic extravagance masked political fragility" (Martin 2020b:30), and performances of opulence may not have represented the actual size of supply stores. Rulers may have concealed a lack of plenty, thus also hiding their fall from divine favor. Furthermore, minor nobles may have attempted to put on airs by eating specialized foods, making lavish funerary offerings, or engaging in ruler-like gestures at banquets (similarly to Houston 2012:90; Jackson 2009:75; Lamoureux-St-Hilaire and McAnany, this volume).

Ana García Barrios (2017:186) argues that imagery of lavish foodstuffs in courtly scenes was more effective in a context of scarcity, and that such representations of plenty carried a message of general well-being and abundance. Even without a context of scarcity, however, many elaborate foodstuffs—presented in fine serving wares—look costly in ingredients and/or preparation: frothed cacao beverages, tamales with fine sauces, fermented pulques. Times of hunger would amplify the message of such foods, in both edible and painted versions. But such messages could also have gone beyond simply expressing social distinction to actively inculcating social divisiveness.

Conversely, rulers may have tried to connect with the "little people" by eating "low-brow" foods at feasts or by democratizing modes of serving. Tokovinine, drawing on work by Baron, has described transformations in types of wares over time, including fewer plates, from sixth- to seventh-century feasting deposits at La Corona. These transformations are tied to shifts in temple use from ancestor veneration to local deities, and a concomitant "shift from [an] exclusive, diacritical mode of feasting to a more inclusive, patron-client mode, in which the ruling lineage of La Corona offered food and drinks to the commoners" (Tokovinine 2016:18). Even so, Tokovinine finds evidence of continued diacritical feasting during the same time period, in fine serving vessels found in an elite residence midden—vessels that included dedicatory inscriptions marking their relative exclusivity.

Second, ostensibly cemented alliances were sometimes shifting behind the scenes. As suggested in work by Christina Halperin and Antonia Foias (2010:407), vessels gifted from one polity (see Tokovinine, Estrada Belli, and Fialko, this volume) could be "be hidden away from view or brought out into view" in banquet settings, as a sly strategy to form sometimes conflicting alliances with multiple rulers. In this sense, allies could be gained "almost in secret rather than publicly and permanently proclaiming [them] on stone monuments" (Halperin and Foias 2010:407).

Third, in marketplace settings, rulers may have quietly rigged exchange behind public-facing assertions of "fair prices." This returns us to questions of direct ruler control over food-surplus production and redistribution, versus the relative autonomy offered by marketplaces. Formal marketplaces could also have reflected "efforts at political control, with the major hegemons making themselves the centers of [the] regional exchange system" (Martin 2020a:468). Marketplaces were certainly witness to duplicitous food exchanges, as evidenced by the fake cacao beans sometimes put into circulation by Aztec counterfeiters (Coe and Coe 2013).

Finally, rulers may have put on airs before local nobility, by serving "foreign" foods in "foreign" ways, paralleling generations of Teotihuacan-inspired imagery at Tikal and many other Classic-period centers. We see replacements in modes of frothing chocolate (Brittenham 2019; Houston 2017) and modes of preparing maize dough (Taube 1989), in ceramic forms and imagery of foods alike. Were Teotihuacan-inspired foodways initially "kept distinct from Maya forms, thereby putting acute emphasis on foreignness" (Stone 1989 in Martin 2020b:245)? Did Maya rulers make efforts to actually eat as Teotihuacanos ate, and did "stranger" rulers attempt to similarly localize themselves through food? We see some evidence for duplicity, or at least multisited identities. In portraits of Ceibal ruler Wat'ul K'atel, a likely foreigner, we see him portrayed both as Central Mexican and quintessential Maya king (Martin 2020b:297). A cacao vessel from Burial 10 at Tikal, made with Teotihuacan mold technology, was simultaneously Maya in form, "the inclusion of the figural lid a way of naturalizing a [Teotihuacan] vessel shape through the [Maya] metaphor of a local body, now a marked category in a way that it was not a generation earlier" (Brittenham 2019:114). Food recipes and performance were likely equally polyvalent, much as Traci Ardren postulates (2020) for later Itza foodways at Postclassic Chichen Itza.

Food Inside the Gilded Cage

Engaging in gastropolitics was hardly a recipe for success in rulership. The deliberate strategies pursued by rulers could be confounded, to borrow from Michel de Certeau, with the tactics of the ruled. I have focused here on ruler strategies that "bet on place" more than on tactics of the ruled that "bet on time" (Certeau 1984:37–39). Strategies of rulers were also confronted by the entropy of reality, where trappings of rulership could become heavy burdens under new circumstances (Graeber 2017).

As we have seen, acts of diplomacy deployed by rulers in the negotiation of real situations made clear use of food. But gift giving and reciprocal feasting, as documented long ago by Marcel Mauss (1954), easily became bonds of obligation for royalty, rulers, and others. Rulers were entrapped into giving blood, providing sacrifices, and feeding divinities and ancestors. Apart from moving goods and giving blood, rulers were also entrapped into the public performance of their role. Such public performances, in turn, furthered expectations of maintaining food supply, effecting diplomacy, and so on. The pressure for rulers to conform to expectations inhered a rigidity that could prove uncomfortable or even fatal. As Takeshi Inomata and Stephen Houston have framed it ([2001] 2018:3, drawing from David Webster [2001] 2018): "All courts change through time, if in a manner conditioned by the inertia of courtly protocol, habitual practice, and monumental setting—what David Webster . . . has called the 'hermit-crab' effect, but from which these royal crabs could not so easily extract themselves!" (see also Awe, Helmke, Ebert, and Hoggarth, this volume).

The perpetual insecurity of rulership led to commissioned artisans etching statements of alliance, fealty, and domination into monuments and murals. But other artisans expressed these relationships through food, which could serve simultaneously as medium and message of rulership (Morell-Hart 2020). Such expressions included dramatic gestures in feasts and regular tribute, but also in the small-scale and quotidian—who had access to particular foods, who distributed them, and how. The hegemonic balance of power that Martin describes, in which smaller individual units have more dynamic fortunes while the broader society evidenced relative stability for centuries, is rooted in the exercise of "conventions, protocols, norms" (Martin 2020a:471), including foodways.

The permanence of ceramic, obsidian, and stone, when compared to the impermanence of food, has implications for symbolic durability, paralleling contrasts between jade objects and featherwork (Halperin, this volume). That is, simple iterations of legitimacy, authority, and alliance were not enough—ongoing reiteration was necessary (similarly to iterative practice as described by Butler 1990 and Certeau 1984). Food impermanence meant that Maya rulers could not simply rely on one feast, one cacao tithe, one bloodletting. Gastropolitics eased the process of perpetual upkeep and the constant maintenance of relations. The higher frequency of upkeeping acts for consumable products meant that there were more openings for transformation through reiteration. In feasts, gift giving, and bloodletting, each iteration of "feeding" offered opportunities for heterodoxy, in how foods were distributed, in how gifts were apportioned, and in how supernaturals responded (or did not).

Final Thoughts

Making food, like making war, is a matter of life and death, and Maya rulers were mediators engaged in a number of critical culinary practices. Here, I have presented arguments for the political heft of foodways in ancient Maya society—not simply as the caloric base for survival. Gastropolitics in the Maya area took many forms, with different types of food serving to craft, maintain, and transform critical social relations, through forward-facing performances and hidden activities and agendas. We find the specific potency of foodways in all sorts of political negotiations—symmetrical and asymmetrical alike—through standard gastropolitical channels as well as the back channels emergent in gastropolitik. We see food competition and conflict, but also food cooperation and reciprocation, and sometimes pragmatic approaches to social and environmental issues occurring in the shadow of public protestation. Rulers were meant to seize crops in war and receive them in tithe; negotiate favorable trade agreements for exotic sumptuous goods; entertain dignitaries with feasts; negotiate with ancestors and divinities for agricultural yields, sometimes by feeding them blood; manage food surpluses; and preside over community feasts. Rulers were responsible both for managing the flow of staple foods to drought-stricken areas as well as for demonstrating proper table manners when entertaining foreign dignitaries. Quotidian foodways, foodstuffs in mortuary contexts, foodstuffs as tax and tithe, and social distinctions were all established through actions of rulers, as much as rulers were entrapped into taking these actions and then repeating them.

Ancient Maya rulership was thus manifested in performance (sometimes of distinct foodways), in munificence (such as in banquets and feasts), in spiritual authority (partially gained by feeding the right blood and offerings), in management of supplies (through agriculture and trade), and in diplomacy (including marriage alliances and state banquets). Images of warfare were meant to commemorate, inspire, or subject; feast foods were meant to satiate, socialize, or distinguish. Commensal acts reinforced the authority to rule, as messages themselves were ingested. The endurance, durability, and persistence of monuments—as markers and actants—can be contrasted with the embodiment, repetition, and incorporation of food. The impermanence of foodstuffs stands in contrast to the rigidity of food expectations, a rigidity that entrapped rulers in bonds of obligation. But rulers continually laid these traps for themselves, accustomed as they were to creature comforts, regular food supplies, and sumptuous dishes.

We see divergences and commonalities in gastropolitics between northern and southern polities, and over time. But as I alluded earlier, "certain features of cuisine are sometimes retained even when the original language of the culture has been forgotten" (Fischler 1988:280). Memories and social expectations are encoded in food (Sutton 2001), whether consciously or unconsciously, bidden or unbidden, consumed or offered to the divine. Food is perpetually reiterative and inalienable once ingested. For these reasons, cuisines, like languages, are often more durable than rulership.

Acknowledgments

My thanks to Patricia McAnany and Marilyn Masson, for framing the original Dumbarton Oaks symposium, for their invitation to participate, and for their thoughtful comments about the manuscript. John Chuchiak, David Wengrow, Traci Ardren, and Mary Miller provided helpful comments during the original symposium, while David Freidel and John Henderson provided further comments just after. My thanks to Andrew Scherer and Stephen Houston for directing me toward helpful literature and imagery, as well as to the two anonymous reviewers. The paper is more robust following these suggestions; any errors or omissions are my own. My gratitude as well to the many farmers, cooks, and other stewards of Maya culinary heritage who have shared their knowledge—and food! Developing the ideas presented here was made easier with direct understanding of how culinary delight can affect basic sociality.

REFERENCES CITED

Aimers, James J., and David Hodell
    2011   Societal Collapse: Drought and the Maya. *Nature* 479:44–45.

Andrews, Anthony P.
    2020   Ancient Maya Ports, Port Facilities, and Navigation. In *The Maya World*, edited by Scott R. Hutson and Traci Ardren. Routledge, New York.

Appadurai, Arjun
    1981   Gastro-Politics in Hindu South Asia. *American Ethnologist* 8(3):494–511.

Ardren, Traci
    2020   Thinking (and Eating) Chichén Itzá: New Food Technology and Creating the Itzá State at Xuenkal. In *Her Cup for Sweet Cacao: Food in Ancient Maya Society*, edited by Traci Ardren, pp. 274–296. University of Texas Press, Austin.

Austin, John L.
    1975   *How to Do Things with Words*. Edited by J. O. Urmson and Marina Sbisà. 2nd ed. Clarendon Press, Oxford.

Batún Alpuche, Adolfo Iván
    2009   Agrarian Production and Intensification at a Postclassic Maya Community, Buena Vista, Cozumel, Mexico. PhD dissertation, University of Florida, Gainesville.

Beliaev, Dmitri, Albert Davletshin, and Alexandre Tokovinine
    2010   Sweet Cacao and Sour Atole: Mixed Drinks on Classic Maya Ceramic Vases. In *Pre-Columbian Foodways: Interdisciplinary Approaches to Food, Culture, and Markets in Ancient Mesoamerica*, edited by John E. Staller and Michael D. Carrasco, pp. 257–272. Springer, New York.

Bianco, Briana, Rani T. Alexander, and Gary Rayson
    2017   Beekeeping Practices in Modern and Ancient Yucatán. In *The Value of Things: Prehistoric to Contemporary Commodities in the Maya Region*, edited by Jennifer P. Mathews and Thomas H. Guderjan, pp. 87–103. University of Arizona Press, Tucson.

Boileau, Arianne, Nicolas Delsol, and Kitty F. Emery
    2020   Human-Animal Relations in the Maya World. In *The Maya World*, edited by Scott R. Hutson and Traci Ardren, pp. 164–182. Routledge, New York.

Bourdieu, Pierre
    (1979) 1984   *Distinction: A Social Critique of the Judgement of Taste*. Harvard University Press, Cambridge, Mass.

Brittenham, Claudia
    2019   When Pots Had Legs: Body Metaphors on Maya Vessels. In *Vessels: The Object as Container*, edited by Claudia Brittenham, pp. 81–120. Oxford University Press, Oxford.

Brown, Linda A., and Andrea I. Gerstle
    2002   Structure 10: Feasting and Village Festivals. In *Before the Volcano Erupted: The Ancient Cerén Village*, edited by Payson Sheets, pp. 97–103. University of Texas Press, Austin.

Brown, M. Kathryn, and Carolyn Freiwald
    2020   Potluck: Building Community and Feasting among the Middle Preclassic Maya. In *Her Cup for Sweet Cacao: Food in Ancient Maya Society*, edited by Traci Ardren, pp. 25–46. University of Texas Press, Austin.

Butler, Judith
    1990   *Gender Trouble: Feminism and the Subversion of Identity*. Routledge, New York.

Cagnato, Clarissa
    2016   A Paleoethnobotanical Study of Two Classic Maya Sites, El Perú-Waka' and La Corona. PhD dissertation, Washington University, St. Louis.

Carrasco Vargas, Ramón, Veronica Vázquez López, and Simon Martin
    2009   Daily Life of the Ancient Maya Recorded on Murals at Calakmul, Mexico. *Proceedings of the National Academy of Sciences* 106(46):19245–19249.

Carter, Nicholas, and Mallory E. Matsumoto
    2020   The Epigraphy of Ancient Maya Food and Drink. In *Her Cup for Sweet Cacao: Food in Ancient Maya Society*, edited by Traci Ardren, pp. 87–123. University of Texas Press, Austin.

Caso Barrera, Laura, and Mario Aliphat Fernández
    2006   Cacao, Vanilla and Annatto: Three Production and Exchange Systems in the Southern Maya Lowlands, XVI–XVII Centuries. *Journal of Latin American Geography* 5(2):29–52.

Certeau, Michel de
    1984   *The Practice of Everyday Life*. Translated by Steven Rendall. University of California Press, Berkeley.

Chase, Diane Z., and Arlen F. Chase
    2017   Caracol, Belize, and Changing Perceptions of Ancient Maya Society. *Journal of Archaeological Research* 25:185–249.

Chmilar, Jennifer A.
    2013   Ancient Maya Cultivation in a Dynamic Wetland Environment: Insights into the Functions of Anthropogenic Rock Alignments at El Edén Ecological Reserve, Quintana Roo, Mexico. PhD dissertation, University of California, Riverside.

Chuchiak, John F.
    2003   "It is their drinking that hinders them": Balché and the Use of Ritual Intoxicants among the Colonial Yucatec Maya, 1550–1780. *Estudios de cultura maya* 24:137–171.

Coe, Sophie D.
    1994   *America's First Cuisines*. University of Texas Press, Austin.

Coe, Sophie D., and Michael D. Coe
    2013   *The True History of Chocolate*. Thames and Hudson, New York.

Dahlin, Bruce H., and Traci Ardren
    2002   Modes of Exchange and Regional Patterns: Chunchucmil, Yucatán. In *Ancient Maya Political Economies*, edited by Marilyn A. Masson and David A. Freidel, pp. 249–284. Altamira Press, Walnut Creek, Calif.

Dunning, Nicholas P., Timothy Beach, and Sheryl Luzzadder-Beach
    2020   Ancient Maya Agriculture. In *The Maya World*, edited by Scott R. Hutson and Traci Ardren, pp. 501–518. Routledge, New York.

Ebert, Claire E., Julie A. Hoggarth, Jaime J. Awe, Brendan J. Culleton, and Douglas J. Kennett
    2019   The Role of Diet in Resilience and Vulnerability to Climate Change among Early Agricultural Communities in the Maya Lowlands. *Current Anthropology* 60(4):589–601.

Emery, Kitty F.
    2002   The Noble Beast: Status and Differential Access to Animals in the Maya World. *World Archaeology* 34:498–515.

Fedick, Scott L.
- 2017 Plant-Food Commodities of the Maya Lowlands. In *The Value of Things: Prehistoric to Contemporary Commodities in the Maya Region*, edited by Jennifer P. Mathews and Thomas H. Guderjan, pp. 163–173. University of Arizona Press, Tucson.
- 2020 Maya Cornucopia: Indigenous Food Plants of the Maya Lowlands. In *The Real Business of Ancient Maya Economies: From Farmers' Fields to Rulers' Realms*, edited by Marilyn A. Masson, David A. Freidel, and Arthur A. Demarest, pp. 224–237. Oxford University Press, Oxford.

Fedick, Scott L., Shanti Morell-Hart, and Lydie Dussol
- 2023 Agriculture in the Ancient Maya Lowlands (Part 2): Landesque Capital and Long-Term Resource Management Strategies. *Journal of Archaeological Research* 32:103–154.

Fernández Souza, Lilia, Mario Zimmermann, and Socorro Pilar Jiménez Álvarez
- 2020 Celebrating Sihó: The Role of Food and Foodways in the Construction of Social Identities. In *Her Cup for Sweet Cacao: Food in Ancient Maya Society*, edited by Traci Ardren, pp. 188–218. University of Texas Press, Austin.

Fischler, Claude
- 1988 Food, Self and Identity. *Social Science Information* 27(2):275–292.

Fitzpatrick, Meagan
- 2016 Trudeau's State Dinner Menu Blends American and Canadian Flavours. CBC News, Toronto, https://www.cbc.ca/news/world/trudeau-obama-state-dinner-1.3481896.

Gallareta Cervera, Tomás
- 2016 The Archaeology of Monumental Architecture and the Social Construction of Authority at the Northern Maya Puuc Site of Kiuic. PhD dissertation, University of North Carolina, Chapel Hill.

García Barrios, Ana
- 2017 The Social Context of Food at Calakmul, Campeche, Mexico. In *Constructing Power and Place in Mesoamerica: Pre-Hispanic Paintings from Three Regions*, edited by Merideth Paxton and Leticia Staines Cicero, pp. 171–190. University of New Mexico Press, Albuquerque.

Geertz, Clifford
- 1980 Political Definition: The Sources of Order. In *Negara: The Theatre State in Nineteenth Century Bali*, pp. 11–25. Princeton University Press, Princeton.

Golden, Charles W., Andrew K. Scherer, Stephen D. Houston, Whittaker Schroder, Shanti Morell-Hart, Socorro Pilar Jiménez Álvarez, George Van Kollias, Moises Yerath Ramiro Talavera, Jeffrey Dobereiner, and Omar Alcover Firpi
- 2020 Centering the Classic Maya Kingdom of Sak Tz'i'. *Journal of Field Archaeology* 45(2):67–85.

Götz, Christopher M.
- 2011 Diferencias socioeconómicas en el uso de animales vertebrados en las tierras bajas mayas del norte. In *Vida cotidiana de los antiguos mayas del norte de la Península de Yucatán*, edited by Rafael Cobos and Lilia Fernández Souza, pp. 45–65. Ediciones de la Universidad Autónoma de Yucatán, Mérida.

Graeber, David
- 2017 Notes on the Politics of Divine Kingship. In *On Kings*, by David Graeber and Marshall D. Sahlins, pp. 377–464. Hau Books, Chicago.

Halperin, Christina T., and Antonia E. Foias
- 2010 Pottery Politics: Late Classic Maya Palace Production at Motul de San José, Petén, Guatemala. *Journal of Anthropological Archaeology* 29(3):392–411.

Hamblin, Nancy Lee
- 1980 Animal Utilization by the Cozumel Maya: Interpretation through Faunal Analysis. PhD dissertation, University of Arizona, Tucson.

Harrison, Peter D.
- 1970 The Central Acropolis, Tikal, Guatemala: A Preliminary Study of the Functions of Its Structural Components during the Late Classic Period. PhD dissertation, University of Pennsylvania, Philadelphia.

Harrison-Buck, Eleanor
- 2017 The Coin of Her Realm: Cacao as Gendered Goods among the Prehispanic

and Colonial Maya. In *The Value of Things: Prehistoric to Contemporary Commodities in the Maya Region*, edited by Jennifer P. Mathews and Thomas H. Guderjan, pp. 104–123. University of Arizona Press, Tucson.

Henderson, John S., and Rosemary A. Joyce

2006 Brewing Distinction: The Development of Cacao Beverages in Formative Mesoamerica. In *Chocolate in Mesoamerica: A Cultural History of Cacao*, edited by Cameron L. McNeil, pp. 140–153. University Press of Florida, Gainesville.

Hendon, Julia A.

2020 Cuisine and Feasting in the Copán and Lower Ulúa Valleys in Honduras. In *Her Cup for Sweet Cacao: Food in Ancient Maya Society*, edited by Traci Ardren, pp. 219–241. University of Texas Press, Austin.

Hoggarth, Julie A., Matthew Restall, James W. Wood, and Douglas J. Kennett

2017 Drought and Its Demographic Effects in the Maya Lowlands. *Current Anthropology* 58(1):82–113.

Houston, Stephen D.

1997 A King Worth a Hill of Beans. *Archaeology* 40.

2012 The Best of All Things: Beauty, Materials, and Society among the Classic Maya. In *Ancient Maya Art at Dumbarton Oaks*, edited by Joanne Pillsbury, Miriam Doutriaux, Reiko Ishihara-Brito, and Alexandre Tokovinine, pp. 85–99. Dumbarton Oaks Research Library and Collection, Washington, D.C.

2017 Forgetting Chocolate: Spouted Vessels, Coclé, and the Maya. *Maya Decipherment: Ideas on Ancient Maya Writing and Iconography*, https://maya-decipherment.com/2017/09/24/forgetting-chocolate-spouted-vessels-cocle-and-the-maya/, accessed 2021.

2018 *The Gifted Passage: Young Men in Classic Maya Art and Text*. Yale University Press, New Haven.

Houston, Stephen D., and Takeshi Inomata

2009 *The Classic Maya*. Cambridge World Archaeology. Cambridge University Press, Cambridge.

Houston, Stephen D., John Robertson, David Stuart, Jill Brody, John G. Fought, Charles Andrew Hofling, Patricia A. McAnany, John M. D. Pohl, Andrea Stone, and Judith Storniolo

2000 The Language of Classic Maya Inscriptions. *Current Anthropology* 41(3):321–356.

Houston, Stephen D., and David Stuart

(2001) 2018 Peopling the Classic Maya Court. In *Royal Courts of the Ancient Maya*, vol. 1, *Theory, Comparison, and Synthesis*, edited by Takeshi Inomata and Stephen D. Houston, pp. 54–83. Routledge, New York.

Houston, Stephen D., David Stuart, and Karl A. Taube

1992 Image and Text on the "Jauncy Vase." In *The Maya Vase Book: A Corpus of Rollout Photographs of Maya Vases,* vol. 3, edited by Justin Kerr, pp. 504–523. Kerr Associates, New York.

2006 *The Memory of Bones: Body, Being, and Experience among the Classic Maya*. University of Texas Press, Austin.

Howie, Linda, Christine D. White, and Fred J. Longstaffe

2010 Potographies and Biographies: The Role of Food in Ritual and Identity as Seen through Life Histories of Selected Maya Pots and People. In *Pre-Columbian Foodways in Mesoamerica*, edited by John E. Staller and Michael D. Carrasco, pp. 369–398. Springer, New York.

Iannone, Gyles, Jason Yaeger, and David Hodell

2014 Assessing the Great Maya Droughts: Some Critical Issues. In *The Great Maya Droughts in Cultural Context*, edited by Giles Iannone, pp. 51–70. University of Colorado Press, Boulder.

Inomata, Takeshi

2001 The Classic Maya Palace as a Political Theater. In *Reconstruyendo la ciudad maya: El urbanismo en las sociedades antiguas*, pp. 341–362. Sociedad Española de Estudios Mayas, Madrid.

Inomata, Takeshi, and Stephen D. Houston

(2001) 2018 Opening the Royal Maya Court. In *Royal Courts of the Ancient Maya*, vol. 1, *Theory, Comparison, and Synthesis*, edited by Takeshi Inomata and Stephen D. Houston, pp. 3–23. Routledge, New York.

Jackson, Sarah E.
   2009   Imagining Courtly Communities: An Exploration of Classic Maya Experiences of Status and Identity through Painted Ceramic Vessels. *Ancient Mesoamerica* 20(1):71–85.

Kennan, George F.
   1991   Morality and Foreign Policy. In *Morality and Foreign Policy: Realpolitik Revisited*, vol. 6, edited by Kenneth Martin Jensen and Elizabeth P. Faulkner, pp. 59–76. United States Institute of Peace Press, Washington, D.C.

Lamoureux-St-Hilaire, Maxime
   2020   Talking Feasts: Classic Maya Commensal Politics at La Corona. In *Her Cup for Sweet Cacao: Food in Ancient Maya Society*, edited by Traci Ardren, pp. 243–273. University of Texas Press, Austin.

LeCount, Lisa J.
   2001   Like Water for Chocolate: Feasting and Political Ritual among the Late Classic Maya at Xunantunich, Belize. *American Anthropologist* 103(4):935–953.

Lentz, David L.
   1999   Plant Resources of the Ancient Maya: The Paleoethnobotanical Evidence. In *Reconstructing Ancient Maya Diet*, edited by Christine D. White, pp. 3–18. University of Utah Press, Salt Lake City.

Looper, Matthew G.
   2019   *The Beast Between: Deer Imagery in Ancient Maya Art.* University of Texas Press, Austin.

Loughmiller-Newman, Jennifer
   2013   The Analytic Reconciliation of Classic Mayan Elite Pottery: Squaring Pottery Function with Form, Adornment, and Residual Contents. PhD dissertation, State University of New York, Albany.

Martin, Simon
   2012   Hieroglyphs from the Painted Pyramid: The Epigraphy of Chiik Nahb Structure Sub 1-4, Calakmul, Mexico. In *Maya Archaeology* 2, edited by Charles W. Golden, Stephen D. Houston, and Joel Skidmore, pp. 60–81. Precolumbia Mesoweb Press, San Francisco.
   2020a   Classic Maya Geopolitics. In *The Maya World*, edited by Scott R. Hutson and Traci Ardren, pp. 459–476. Routledge, New York.
   2020b   *Ancient Maya Politics: A Political Anthropology of the Classic Period 150–900 CE.* Cambridge University Press, Cambridge.

Masson, Marilyn A.
   2021   Resiliency and Cultural Reconstitution of the Postclassic Mayapan Confederacy and Its Aftermath. In *Mesoamerican Archaeology: Theory and Practice*, edited by Julia A. Hendon, Lisa Overholtzer, and Rosemary A. Joyce, pp. 278–314. 2nd ed. John Wiley and Sons, Hoboken, N.J.

Masson, Marilyn A., and Timothy S. Hare
   2020   The Structures of Everyday Life in the Postclassic Urban Setting of Mayapan. In *The Maya World*, edited by Scott R. Hutson and Traci Ardren, pp. 794–812. Routledge, New York.

Masson, Marilyn A., Timothy S. Hare, Bradley W. Russell, Carlos Peraza Lope, and Jessica L. Campbell
   2020   Faunal Foods as Indices of Commoner Wealth (or Poverty) in Rural versus Urban Houselots of the Terminal Classic and Postclassic in Northwest Yucatán. In *Her Cup for Sweet Cacao: Food in Ancient Maya Society*, edited by Traci Ardren, pp. 297–333. University of Texas Press, Austin.

Masson, Marilyn A., and Carlos Peraza Lope
   2013   Animal Consumption at the Monumental Center of Mayapán. In *The Archaeology of Mesoamerican Animals*, edited by Christopher M. Götz and Kitty F. Emery, pp. 233–279. Lockwood Press, Atlanta.

Mauss, Marcel
   1954   *The Gift: Forms and Functions of Exchange in Archaic Societies.* Free Press, Glencoe, Ill.

McAnany, Patricia A.
   1995   *Living with the Ancestors: Kinship and Kingship in Ancient Maya Society.* University of Texas Press, Austin.
   2019   Fragile Authority in Monumental Time: Political Experimentation in the Classic Maya Lowlands. In *The Evolution of Fragility: Setting the Terms*, edited by Norman Yoffee, pp. 47–60. McDonald Institute for Archaeological Research, University of Cambridge, Cambridge.

McKillop, Heather I., and E. Cory Sills

    2017   The Paynes Creek Salt Works, Belize: A Model for Ancient Maya Salt Production. In *The Value of Things: Prehistoric to Contemporary Commodities in the Maya Region*, edited by Jennifer P. Mathews and Thomas H. Guderjan, pp. 67–86. University of Arizona Press, Tucson.

McNeil, Cameron L.

    2010   Death and Chocolate: The Significance of Cacao Offerings in Ancient Maya Tombs and Caches at Copan, Honduras. In *Pre-Columbian Foodways: Interdisciplinary Approaches to Food, Culture, and Markets in Ancient Mesoamerica*, edited by John E. Staller and Michael D. Carrasco, pp. 293–314. Springer, New York.

Miller, Mary Ellen, and Simon Martin

    2004   *Courtly Art of the Ancient Maya*. Fine Arts Museums of San Francisco, San Francisco.

Monaghan, John

    1999   *The Covenants with Earth and Rain: Exchange, Sacrifice, and Revelation in Mixtec Society*. University of Oklahoma Press, Norman.

Morehart, Christopher T.

    2011   *Food, Fire and Fragrance: A Paleoethnobotanical Perspective on Classic Maya Cave Rituals*. Archaeopress, Oxford.

Morehart, Christopher T., and Noah Butler

    2010   Ritual Exchange and the Fourth Obligation: Ancient Maya Food Offering and the Flexible Materiality of Ritual. *Journal of the Royal Anthropological Institute* 16(3):588–608.

Morell-Hart, Shanti

    2020   Plant Foodstuffs of the Ancient Maya: Agents and Matter, Medium and Message. In *Her Cup for Sweet Cacao: Food in Ancient Maya Society*, edited by Traci Ardren, pp. 124–160. University of Texas Press, Austin.

Morell-Hart, Shanti, Lydie Dussol, and Scott L. Fedick

    2022   Agriculture in the Ancient Maya Lowlands (Part 1): Paleoethnobotanical Residues and New Perspectives on Plant Management. *Journal of Archaeological Research* 31(2023):561–615.

Morell-Hart, Shanti, Sarah Newman, Joshua Schnell, Meghan MacLeod, Sarah Watson, Harper Dine, and Mallory E. Matsumoto

    2018   Capítulo 2: Budsilha: Operación 1: Investigaciones en el Grupo Principal. In *Proyecto Arqueológico Busiljá-Chocoljá: Informe de la temporada de investigación*, edited by Andrew K. Scherer and Charles W. Golden, pp. 6–46. Instituto Nacional de Antropología e Historia, Mexico City.

Morell-Hart, Shanti, and Sonny Moisés Ojeda González

    2018   Capítulo 7: Lacanjá Tzeltal; Operación 8: Investigaciones del Palacio. In *Informe de la décima temporada de investigación presentado ante el Consejo de Arqueología del Instituto Nacional de Antropología e Historia*, edited by Andrew K. Scherer and Charles W. Golden, pp. 218–252. Instituto Nacional de Antropología e Historia, Mexico City.

Morell-Hart, Shanti, Melanie Pugliese, Cameron L. McNeil, and Edy Barrios

    2021   Cuisine at the Crossroads. *Latin American Antiquity* 32(4):689–704.

Novelo-Pérez, María J, E. Moisés Herrera-Parra, Lilia Fernández-Souza, Iliana Ancona-Aragón, and Socorro Jiménez-Álvarez

    2019   Pre-Columbian Culinary Landscapes: Reconstructing Elite Gastronomy at Sihó, Yucatán. *STAR: Science & Technology of Archaeological Research*:1–13.

O'Neil, Megan E.

    2009   Ancient Maya Sculptures of Tikal, Seen and Unseen. *RES: Anthropology and Aesthetics* 55(1):119–134.

Pohl, John M. D., and Mary E. D. Pohl

    2003   Cycles of Conflict: Political Factionalism in the Maya Lowlands. In *Factional Competition and Political Development in the New World*, edited by Elizabeth M. Brumfiel and John W. Fox, pp. 138–157. Cambridge University Press, Cambridge.

Powis, Terry G., Fred Valdez Jr., Thomas R. Hester, W. Jeffrey Hurst, and Stanley M. Tarka Jr.

    2002   Spouted Vessels and Cacao Use among the Preclassic Maya. *Latin American Antiquity* 13(1):85–106.

Reents-Budet, Dorie
    2000   Feasting among the Classic Maya: Evidence from the Pictorial Ceramics. In *The Maya Vase Book: A Corpus of Rollout Photographs of Maya Vases*, vol. 6, edited by Justin Kerr, pp. 1022–1037. Kerr Associates, New York.

Rich, Michelle, and Keith Eppich
    2020   Statecraft in the City of the Centipede: Burials 39, 38, and Internal Alliance Building at El Peru-Waka', Guatemala. In *A Forest of History: The Maya after the Emergence of Divine Kingship*, edited by Travis W. Stanton and M. Kathryn Brown, pp. 88–106. University Press of Colorado, Louisville.

Sahlins, Marshall D.
    2017   The Original Political Society. In *On Kings*, edited by David Graeber and Marshall D. Sahlins, pp. 23–64. Hau Books, Chicago.

Scarborough, Vernon L., Fred Valdez, and Nicholas P. Dunning
    2003   *Heterarchy, Political Economy, and the Ancient Maya: The Three Rivers Region of the East-Central Yucatán Peninsula.* University of Arizona Press, Tucson.

Schele, Linda, and David A. Freidel
    1990   *A Forest of Kings: The Untold Story of the Ancient Maya.* Morrow, New York.

Schele, Linda, and Peter Mathews
    1999   *The Code of Kings: The Language of Seven Sacred Maya Temples and Tombs.* Simon and Schuster, New York.

Scherer, Andrew K., and Stephen D. Houston
    2018   Blood, Fire, Death: Covenants and Crises among the Classic Maya. In *Smoke, Flames, and the Human Body in Mesoamerican Ritual Practice*, edited by Vera Tiesler and Andrew K. Scherer, pp. 109–150. Dumbarton Oaks Research Library and Collection, Washington, D.C.

Scherer, Andrew K., Lori E. Wright, and Cassady J. Yoder
    2007   Bioarchaeological Evidence for Social and Temporal Differences in Diet at Piedras Negras, Guatemala. *Latin American Antiquity* 18(1):85–104.

Somerville, Andrew D., Mikael Fauvelle, and Andrew W. Froehle
    2013   Applying New Approaches to Modeling Diet and Status: Isotopic Evidence for Commoner Resiliency and Elite Variability in the Classic Maya Lowlands. *Journal of Archaeological Science* 40(3):1539–1553.

Sorayya Carr, Helen
    1996   Precolumbian Maya Exploitation and Management of Deer Populations. In *The Managed Mosaic: Ancient Maya Agriculture and Resource Use*, edited by Scott L. Fedick, pp. 251–261. University of Utah Press, Salt Lake City.

Spenard, Jon, Adam King, Terry G. Powis, and Nilesh W. Gaikwad
    2020   A Toast to the Earth: The Social Role of Beverages in Pre-Hispanic Maya Cave Ritual at Pacbitun, Belize. In *Her Cup for Sweet Cacao: Food in Ancient Maya Society*, edited by Traci Ardren, pp. 47–86. University of Texas Press, Austin.

Stone, Andrea
    1989   Disconnection, Foreign Insignia, and Political Expansion: Teotihuacan and the Warrior Stelae of Piedras Negras. In *Mesoamerica after the Decline of Teotihuacan AD 700–900*, edited by Richard A. Diehl and Janet Catherine Berlo, pp. 153–172. Dumbarton Oaks, Washington, D.C.

Stuart, David
    1989   Hieroglyphs on Maya Vessels. In *The Maya Vase Book: A Corpus of Rollout Photographs of Maya Vases*, vol. 1, edited by Justin Kerr, pp. 149–160. Kerr Associates, New York.
    2006   The Language of Chocolate: References to Cacao on Classic Maya Drinking Vessels. In *Chocolate in Mesoamerica: A Cultural History of Cacao*, edited by Cameron L. McNeil, pp. 184–201. University Press of Florida, Gainesville.

Sutton, David E.
    2001   *Remembrance of Repasts: An Anthropology of Food and Memory.* Berg, Oxford.

Taube, Karl A.

    1989   The Maize Tamale in Classic Maya Diet, Epigraphy, and Art. *American Antiquity* 54(1):31–51.

Tiesler, Vera, and Andrew K. Scherer

    2018   *Smoke, Flames, and the Human Body in Mesoamerican Ritual Practice*. Dumbarton Oaks Research Library and Collection, Washington, D.C.

Tokovinine, Alexandre

    2016   "It is his image with pulque": Drinks, Gifts, and Political Networking in Classic Maya Texts and Images. *Ancient Mesoamerica* 27(1):13–29.

Tozzer, Alfred M.

    1941   *Landa's Relación de las cosas de Yucatan: A Translation*. Peabody Museum of American Archaeology and Ethnology, Cambridge, Mass.

Venegas Durán, Benito Jesus, E. Moisés Herrera-Parra, and María Novelo Pérez

    2020   Análisis e identificación de almidones arqueológicos en instrumentos líticos y ceramica del Conjunto Residencial Limón de Palenque, Chiapas, Mexico. *Revista de arqueología*:1–20.

Waltz, Kenneth

    2014   Anarchic Orders and Balances of Power. In *The Realism Reader*, edited by Colin Elman and Michael A. Jensen, pp. 113–124. Routledge, New York.

Webster, David

    (2001) 2018   Spatial Dimensions of Maya Courtly Life: Problems and Issues. In *Royal Courts of the Ancient Maya*, vol. 1, *Theory, Comparison, and Synthesis*, edited by Takeshi Inomata and Stephen D. Houston, pp. 130–167. Routledge, New York.

Woodfill, Brent K. S., Brian Dervin Dillon, Marc Wolf, Carlos Avendaño, and Ronald Canter

    2015   Salinas de los Nueve Cerros, Guatemala: A Major Economic Center in the Southern Maya Lowlands. *Latin American Antiquity* 26(2):162–179.

Wright, Lori E.

    2003   La muerte y el estatus económico: Investigando el simbolismo mortuorio y el acceso a los recursos alimenticios entre los mayas. *Publicaciones de la SEEM*:175–193.

Yaeger, Jason

    (2010) 2018   Commodities, Brands, and Village Economies in the Classic Maya Lowlands. In *Cultures of Commodity Branding*, edited by Andrew Bevan and David Wengrow, pp. 167–195. Routledge, New York.

    2020   Collapse, Transformation, Reorganization: The Terminal Classic Transition in the Maya World. In *The Maya World*, edited by Scott R. Hutson and Traci Ardren, pp. 777–793. Routledge, New York.

10

Le roi est mort, vive le roi

Examining the Rise, Apogee, and Decline of Maya Kingship in Central Belize

JAIME J. AWE, CHRISTOPHE HELMKE, CLAIRE E. EBERT, AND JULIE A. HOGGARTH

Le roi est mort, vive le roi
(The king is dead, long live the king)

The French phrase that titles this paper can be traced back to the funeral of Charles VIII in 1498 (Giesey 1987:123). By this simple proclamation and ritual act, the transition of hereditary rulership in European monarchies was confirmed and iterated in the face of death; the proclamation equally served to publicly convey that there would be stability and continuity in the kingdom despite the loss of the country's previous monarch and liege. Hereditary rulership and related rites of intensification like that alluded to above have a long history in human societies, and they continue to be a major topic of interest for archaeologists studying the institution of kingship in the Maya world (Okoshi et al. 2021). Indeed, the study of lowland Maya kingship can be traced back to the early "Thompsonian" view of ruler priests who periodically conducted sacred rituals atop gaudily painted pyramids while members of their community observed from below (Thompson 1927; see also Becker 1979). Some five decades later, with the publication of *The Blood of Kings: Dynasty and Ritual in Maya Art*, Schele and Miller (1986) introduced the idea of divine kingship, and the "importance of lineage [or genealogical descent] in the legitimation of Maya kingship" (Stuart 2005:262). Less than a decade later, Schele and Freidel (1990) proposed a model of Maya "shaman-kings," in which Maya rulers were thought to derive "power" through their "ability to access a spirit world" (Stuart 2005:263). More recently, and partly as a result of major advances in epigraphic research and the decipherment of Maya texts, it has become widely accepted that, at its peak, kingship in Maya culture was hereditary, dynastic, complex, dynamic, and often manifested quite differently from one region to another (Chase et al. 2021; Freidel and Schele 1988; Houston and Inomata 2009; Houston and Stuart 1996; Martin 2003, 2020; Martin and Grube 2008; McAnany 1995; Rice 2008; Ringle, Gallareta Negrón, and Bey 2021; Stuart 1996, 2005; Stuart and Houston 1994).

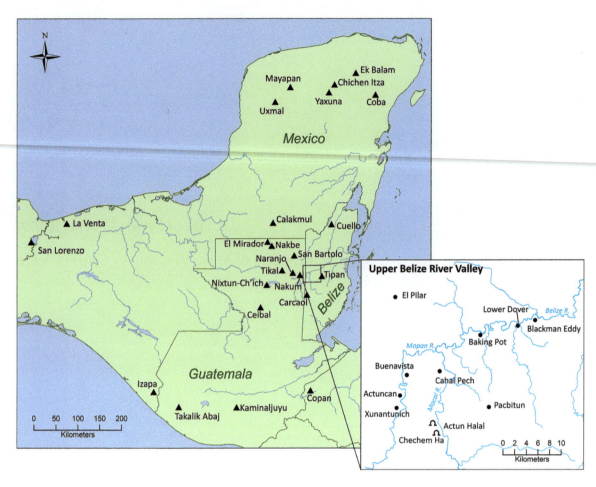

figure 10.1
Map of the Belize Valley, with sites mentioned in text. Map by Claire E. Ebert, courtesy of the BVAR Project.

Even a cursory review of the various hypotheses about the nature of Maya rulership reveals that most research on this topic has predominantly focused on the Classic period (Chase et al. 2021; Martin and Grube 2008; Okoshi et al. 2021; Sharer and Traxler 2006). The reasons for this bias are quite understandable, as there is simply more archaeological evidence in the form of hieroglyphic texts, carved monuments, tombs, material culture, and iconography to facilitate the identification of Classic-period rulers, the activities they engaged in, and the political authority they held over their subjects. In contrast to the study of Classic-period kingship, only a few researchers have addressed questions regarding the emergence of Maya rulership during the Formative period, and even fewer have examined changes in the institution of kingship during the transition from the Terminal Classic to the Postclassic period (see Awe n.d.; Brown and Bey 2018; A. Chase and D. Chase 2021; D. Chase and A. Chase 2021; Estrada Belli 2006, 2011; Fields and Reents-Budet 2005; Hansen 2012; Inomata 2016; Okoshi et al. 2021; Ringle, Gallareta Negrón, and Bey 2021; Yaeger and Brown 2019). Whereas the sum of the latter research represents commendable efforts to understand the institution of kingship during specific times and places, even fewer scholars have attempted to examine diachronic changes in the manifestation of rulership, and how this sociopolitical institution developed and changed from Formative times to the Terminal Classic period. It is this latter topic that we address in this paper. The Belize Valley (Figure 10.1)—particularly the centers of Cahal Pech, Blackman Eddy, and Xunantunich, with their two-thousand year history of occupation—is an ideal

table 10.1

Diachronic changes in the faces of rulership in the Belize River Valley.

DATE/PHASE	POLITICAL STRUCTURE	METHODS USED FOR ATTAINING/ MAINTAINING STATUS	ARCHAEOLOGICAL EVIDENCE
Late Early Formative to Early Middle Formative 1200–750 BCE	Aggrandizers	Created social obligations by sponsoring public rituals steeped with cosmological significance and through conspicuous disposal of wealth.	Feasting deposits; fine-paste ceramics decorated with cosmological symbols; exotics unevenly distributed in community; specialized non-residential architecture.
Late Middle Formative 750–300 BCE	Emerging *Ajawtaak*	Continued above; appropriated religious symbols; co-opted community rituals; promoted deification of deceased ancestors; associated themselves with the Maize God; reoriented site cores as axis mundi through the construction of monumental architecture along cardinal directions; and presided over public events and rituals.	Figurine production/use in household rituals disappear; E-Groups constructed in site cores; exhumation of ancestral remains and reburial in shrines; placement of center-line caches in public spaces; evidence for public cyclical celebrations (e.g., rain ceremonies and the passage of solstices and equinox); clear evidence of settlement hierarchy.
Late Formative 300 BCE–300 CE	*Ajawtaak*	Rulers continued to preside over public events; made decisions on behalf of community; dedicated monuments that identified their exalted statuses and associated them with ancestors, deities, and cosmos; and established dynastic rulership.	E-Groups converted to Eastern Triadic Assemblages (ETA); tomb and crypt burials in ETA; stucco masks on buildings; carved stelae depicting a ruler emerging from the maws of supernatural beings/sacred landscapes or performing public rituals; use of *ajaw* glyph on art, monuments, and portable objects.
Early to Late Classic 300–800 CE	*K'uhul Ajawtaak*	Performed public cyclical rituals on behalf of the populace; incorporated theonyms in their titles that reflected their exalted status and linked them with deities and deified ancestors; sponsored construction of public ceremonial architecture (e.g., temples and ballcourts); engaged in military expeditions; and established alliances with other royal houses.	Carved and inscribed monuments that focused on the ruler; plain stelae erected predominantly in site cores; sequential interment of dynastic lineage in ETA; sumptuous grave goods in tombs of the ruler featuring Maize God imagery; use of theonyms and royal epithets in the titles of rulers; inscriptions describing activities of royals; construction of royal palaces in site acropolises with very restricted access.
Terminal Classic 800–1000 CE	Perpetuators	Rulers clung to past traditions by continuing to commission carved stone monuments with inscriptions describing their elevated statuses; buried their dead in tombs and in site core shrines; and tried to maintain alliances with other royal houses.	Carved and inscribed stelae that identified Terminal Classic rulers; inscriptions that continued to use royal epithets for rulers and for establishing their descent from royal ancestors; tomb construction and tombs containing remains of individuals with royal accoutrements away from ETA; declining number of elite burials.

region to examine the latter question and to explore the rise, apogee, and decline of kingship in the Maya Lowlands. Additionally, our more than three decades of research in central Belize, and the large database produced by this work, allow us to compare the diachronic changes in the faces of rulership (Table 10.1) in the Belize River Valley with that of other neighboring regions in the Maya Lowlands.

The Aggrandizers: The Late Early Formative to Early Middle Formative (Cunil to Jenney Creek Phases 1200–750 BCE)

Evidence for late Early Formative to early Middle Formative occupation in the lowlands continues to be sparse, making it almost impossible to determine the true nature of political organization during this precocious period of Maya development. Despite this overall paucity of data, a few sites in the Belize River Valley, such as Cahal Pech, Blackman Eddy, and Xunantunich, have produced information that facilitates a cursory examination of the nature (presence or absence) of rulership at this time. We know that some of the earliest settlements in the valley were established during the Cunil/Kanocha (1200–900 BCE) and Early Jenney Creek (900–750 BCE) phases, and that they were located on the summits of hills overlooking the Belize River and its Macal and Mopan tributaries. These elevated locations were likely chosen for early settlements for practical reasons, and possibly because they conformed to important features of sacred landscapes. Excavations at the three sites indicate that the earliest settlements were relatively small, consisting of modest domestic buildings. At Cahal Pech, however, one of these early buildings, Structure B4, served as a special function structure, or possibly as the residence of an important kin group within the community. These functions are indicated by the presence of several significant Cunil-phase caches that we discovered along the central, north–south, axis of Structure B4. The first cache, which was located below the floor of the earliest building platform, contained the mandible of a crocodile (*Crocodylus moreletii*). The second cache contained several fragments of decorated fine-paste ceramic bowls and dishes (Figure 10.2). The third cache, located in a subsequent phase of construction, contained a large and diverse number of cultural remains that included nine perforated disks produced from imported marine shells, twenty-seven obsidian flakes, three jadeite objects, seventy-seven chert flakes, numerous faunal remains, and cave pearls (Awe 1992:341). In yet another Cunil-phase cache, there were several fragments of marine shells, plus a shell pendant that was carved in the form of a quatrefoil motif, likely representing a portal to the underworld (Garber and Awe 2009:153–155) (Figure 10.2). Interestingly, we have found no formal burials dating to either the Cunil/Kanocha or early facet Jenney Creek phases in the Belize Valley (Ebert et al. 2019). Human remains from these early phases continue to be solely represented by burnt fragments of long bones recovered below the floors of early building platforms, possibly suggesting that cremation, or exhumation and reburial, were part of the reverential disposal of human remains at that early date in central Belize.

The marine shells, obsidian, and jadeite in the Cahal Pech caches indicate that at least some members of the Cunil-phase community had the means both to acquire and to dispose of high-status, exotic objects. The same is true of the fine-paste ceramic vessels at Cahal Pech and Blackman Eddy, some of which were carved with symbols representing the *k'an* cross, the lightning motif, and the Principal Bird Deity (Awe et al. 2021; Brown, Awe, and Garber 2018; Garber and Awe 2009) (Figure 10.2a–b, e). Two of the jadeite objects in the third cache were also in the form of a "flame eyebrow" and a fang (Figure 10.2c–d), and were likely part of a mosaic mask (Awe 1992:308). Garber and Awe (2009) previously suggested that the presence of these various iconographic motifs, including the crocodile mandible, the flame eyebrow, and the cave pearls, together with the quatrefoil opening, provides solid evidence that the Cunil-phase Maya in the Belize Valley were participating in a pan-Mesoamerican symbol system and that they were cognizant of the Maya creation narrative and of the complex structure of their cosmos. But how does all this relate to the emergence of rulership in the Belize Valley?

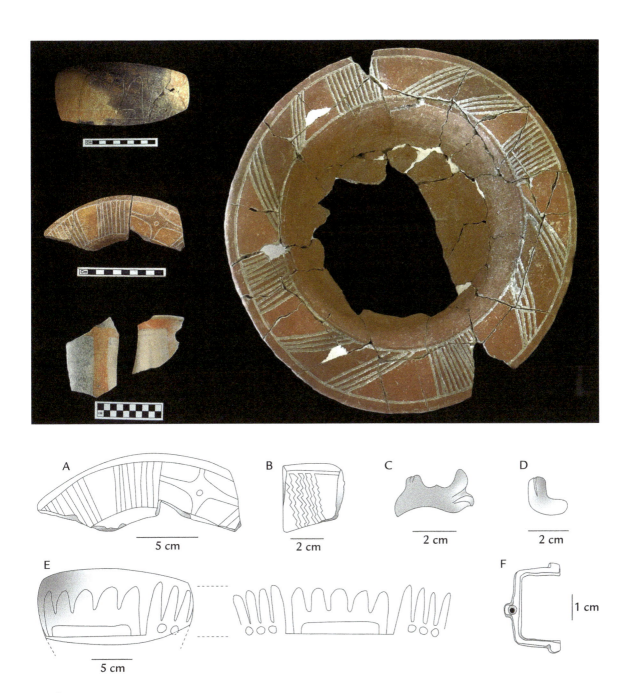

figure 10.2
Examples of Cunil-phase fineware ceramics: top, a selection of illustrative examples (photographs by Jaime J. Awe, courtesy of the BVAR Project); and bottom, Cunil-phase (1200/1100–900 BCE) symbols incised on fine-paste ceramics, including a *k'an* cross (a), lightning motif (b), flaming eyebrow (greenstone adorno) (c), fang (greenstone adorno) (d), crest of the Principal Bird Deity (e), and shell half quatrefoil pendant (f) (drawings by Sean Goldsmith and digitized by Claire Ebert, courtesy of the BVAR Project).

Le roi est mort, vive le roi

Sharer and Traxler (2006:581) suggest that, given the absence of significant status markers in the Early and Middle Formative period, a decentralized council system of governance (which they equate with the *multepal* system known for Late Postclassic Yucatán) may have been in operation in early Maya communities. The problem with this proposal is that, archaeologically, such a diffuse system of governance is particularly difficult to determine. This is true even for the Terminal Classic period, when evidence for sociopolitical change is far more archaeologically visible than in Formative-period contexts. Based on the evidence from Cahal Pech and Blackman Eddy, as well as data from other regions in Mesoamerica (see Blake and Clark 1999), we suggest that during these early stages of cultural development, aggrandizers had already begun accruing elevated status for themselves and their kin. Clark and Blake (1994) have argued that Early Formative aggrandizers likely invested in the acquisition and disposal of exotics; were involved in the production of specialized crafts, such as the production of marine shell beads and fine-paste ceramics; and commissioned the construction of special function structures. Cunil-phase aggrandizers in the Belize Valley can also be characterized in this way, and our data suggest that they appropriated iconographic motifs to demonstrate special knowledge of their creation narrative and cosmos. Status in Cunil communities was probably created and maintained through the conspicuous disposal of wealth items and the sponsoring of rituals steeped with cosmological significance, during which fine-paste ceramic vessels incised with iconographic motifs were publicly used and discarded. The motifs on the various portable Cunil-phase objects clearly reflect knowledge of early pan-Mesoamerican symbols that were interwoven with concepts of a sacred cosmos. Brown, Awe, and Garber (2018) further suggest that the decorated Cunil fine-paste ceramics were used in feasts sponsored by the emerging Belize Valley elite in their effort to create "obligations of reciprocity" or for the purpose of self-aggrandizement.

Our investigations in nearby subterranean sites also suggest that Cunil-phase aggrandizers may have sponsored rituals in caves along the Macal River Valley (Awe et al. 2021). At both Chechem Ha Cave and Actun Halal Rockshelter, for example, we have evidence of possible ritual activity as far back as the late Early Formative to early Middle Formative period (Awe, Helmke, and Morton 2019; Lohse et al. 2006; Moyes 2006). Cultural remains in these subterranean sites include dated charcoal, ceramics, lithics, and macrobotanicals, perhaps associated with agricultural fertility rituals (Awe et al. 2021; Moyes 2006:583–584; Moyes et al. 2017). The marine shell effigy in the form of the quatrefoil motif, the cave pearls in Cunil/Kanocha-phase caches at Cahal Pech and Blackman Eddy (Awe 1992; Brown 2003), and the coeval use of nearby caves provide compelling evidence that, from quite early, caves in the Belize Valley were perceived as nodal points in the sacred landscape and that they were being used for ritual purposes at this early date. Evidence for Early to Middle Formative–period cave rituals are not unique to the Belize Valley. These activities also have been recorded in Juxtlahuaca and Oxtotitlan Caves in Guerrero (Coe, Urcid, and Koontz 2015), in Cuyamel and Gordon's Caves in Honduras (Brady 1995; Healy 1974), and in Oaxaca (Flannery and Marcus 1983). Once established, the tradition of cave rituals officiated by leaders of the community continued throughout the Classic period and remains an important practice in modern times (Halperin 2002, 2005).

Coeval with these developments, most Belize Valley community members continued to conduct their own household rituals. A key component of these private rituals was the use of hand-modeled figurines, the majority of which are represented by female effigies (Awe et al. 2021; Brown 2003). According to Marcus (1998, 1999), Early Formative figurines were associated predominantly with female fertility rites. Marcus (1993:2–6) further notes that women used figurines to petition ancestors "for guidance" and that figurines "provided a medium which the spirits of specific ancestors could return to and inhabit during this petitioning." At Cahal Pech and Blackman Eddy, most early figurines date to the Cunil/Kanocha phase of occupation and are generally found in deposits below the floors of building platforms (Awe 1992; Brown, Awe, and Garber 2018; DeLance 2016; Peniche May 2016; Peniche May, DeLance, and Awe 2018). Most of these domestic buildings, however, lack the relatively rich exotic and symbolically laden cache deposits, like those found in Structure B4, signaling that social inequalities were already emerging. We suggest that these social differences were possibly fueled by aggrandizers seeking to elevate their status within their communities.

Contemporaneous and somewhat similar changes have been detected at Ceibal in Guatemala. At the latter site, Inomata and his colleagues (2013) recorded an E-Group assemblage that was first constructed ca. 950 BCE. An offering, Cache 108, dating to 800 BCE was subsequently deposited below plaza level along the east–west axis of the E-Group (Inomata 2016). Inomata (2016:48) notes that a carved shell pendant found in the cache represents "a decapitated head," suggesting "that human sacrifice was already part of public ritual held in the plaza." This interpretation is based on the subsequent discovery of a "series of decapitated or dismembered bodies [that] were deposited in the plaza" about four centuries later (440 BCE). While Inomata's interpretation of the shell pendant is certainly plausible, we believe that the prevalence of maize symbolism and the incorporation of creation narratives in Formative-period iconography and ritual makes it more likely that the shell pendant symbolically represented the decapitated head of the Maize God (see below).

The Emerging *Ajawtaak*: The Late Middle Preclassic Period (750–300 BCE)

The late Middle Preclassic witnessed considerable social, political, architectural, and ritual changes in the Belize Valley. Within the site cores of Cahal Pech, Blackman Eddy, and Xunantunich, these changes are reflected by the construction of the first monumental architecture, including E-Groups and Eastern Triadic complexes (see Awe, Hoggarth, and Aimers 2017; Ebert and Awe 2020), as well as other large, non-domestic buildings. At Cahal Pech,

AMS ^{14}C dating of the western radial pyramid of that site's E-Group (Figure 10.3) as well as cultural remains in the central structure of the associated Eastern Triadic building, place construction sometime between ~735 and 405 cal BCE (Ebert, McGee, and Awe 2021:5). Several other buildings, including large platforms, were constructed to the north and south flanks of Plaza B, where the E-Group is located. Recent research at the easternmost architectural complex of "Early Xunantunich," the site's Preclassic center, has documented a contemporaneous E-Group complex at that site (Brown 2017). Blackman Eddy also possesses a sequence of platforms, including a triadic arrangement, dating to the Middle Preclassic period (Brown and Garber 2008). Other non-domestic structures, including two-tiered platforms with stucco masks flanking their central stairways (Awe 1992; Brown 2017; Brown, Awe, and Garber 2018:108; Garber et al. 2004) and large circular platforms that were likely used as forums for public ritual performances (Aimers, Powis, and Awe 2000; Peniche May 2016), were built at these sites. At the same time, differential growth among the rising centers of the Belize Valley provides strong evidence for increasing site hierarchy in the region, with Cahal Pech, Blackman Eddy, and Xunantunich representing the primary centers at the time (Ebert 2017).

Changes in ritual associated with emergent elites are particularly significant during the late Middle Formative period and are reflected by site alignments, architecture, and caching activity. Site cores of Middle Formative centers in central Belize, for example, were predominantly constructed with east–west orientations, in alignment with the pathway of the sun. Caches, often emulating cosmological concepts and creation narrative symbolism, were also placed in public courtyards, especially along the centerline between E-Groups and their western radial pyramids (Brown, Awe, and Garber 2018; Porter 2020) as well as on the corners of some buildings (Garber and Awe 2009). Examples of these centerline caches come from Cahal Pech, where Cache 2017-1 and Cache 2017-2 were placed along the centerline of the E-Group during the late Middle Formative period. Cache 2017-1 contained thirteen

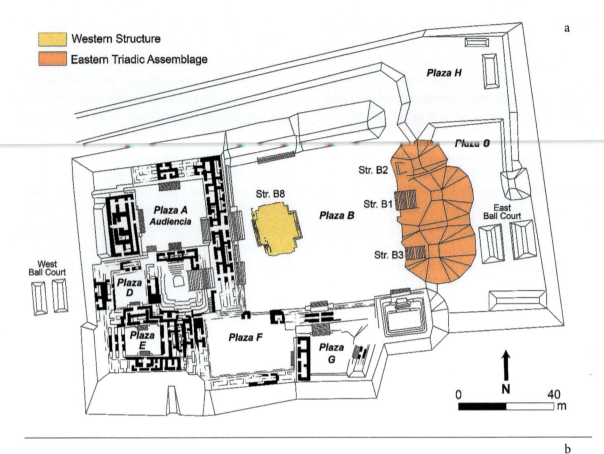

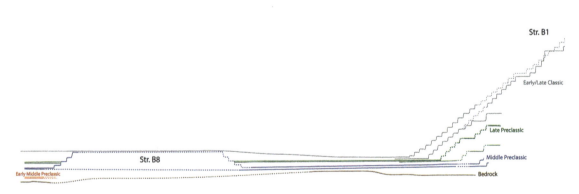

figure 10.3
a) Cahal Pech site core, showing location of Middle Preclassic E-Group (after Ebert, McGee, and Awe 2021:fig. 2); and
b) E-Group section, Plaza B, Cahal Pech (after Ebert, McGee, and Awe 2021:fig. 5).

reconstructable/partial ceramic vessels, and Cache 2017-2 contained twenty-six reconstructable/partial ceramic vessels as well as thirty fragments of jadeite beads that had been smashed and placed within and around the ceramic vessels. Below and around the ceramics and fragmented jadeite beads were 245 marine and freshwater shells, thirty-five chert flakes, and two figurine heads. Charcoal associated with this cache produced a Middle Formative date between 765 and 515 cal BCE (PSUAMS-5857) (Porter 2020). Though ^{14}C data from Cache 2017-1 suggested a Late Formative date, both caches contained Middle Formative pottery, and both were associated with a small cobble platform, suggesting contemporaneous placement. In his interpretation of the caches, Porter (2020) noted that the number of ceramic vessels was important. While one contained the sacred thirteen, the other had twenty-six, which has a numerological association with the Maya celestial realm (e.g., Sharer and Traxler 2006:730). Porter also suggests that jadeite beads likely represented kernels of maize (see Taube 2000, 2005), and that the shells and chert flakes symbolically represented water and the underworld.

Garber and Awe (2009) reported on several other cache deposits that were placed at the corners of a Middle Preclassic building below Plaza B at Cahal Pech. The deposit at the northeastern corner of the building included thirteen jadeite triangulates, a headless figurine, and three slate bars. The northwestern deposit had three polished river stones, a figurine head, and thirteen obsidian blade fragments. The southwestern deposit contained a single figurine head. The southeastern corner appears to have contained another figurine head, but this deposit was disturbed by the subsequent placement of a Late Formative burial that intruded into the Middle Formative context. Garber and Awe (2009:187–190) previously noted that the deposits at the corners of the Middle Formative building were part of a ritual program that clearly reflects knowledge of a structured cosmos, including the division of the celestial realm (represented by the thirteen greenstones and thirteen obsidian fragments). Likewise, they identify key episodes of the Maize God's myth, including his decapitation (represented by the figurine heads) and his subsequent resurrection at the Three Stone Place of creation (represented by the three slate bars and river stones). Similar ritual events, associated with the construction of public buildings, are evident at Blackman Eddy. The construction of Structure B1-5th, for example, was celebrated by the caching of numerous ceramic vessels at the base of the building (Brown, Awe, and Garber 2018:103).

The late Middle Preclassic Belize Valley also witnessed the onset of burials that were placed in special contexts and deposited in patterns that reflect ancestor worship and cosmological associations. At Xunantunich, a burial in the E-Group Plaza contained the headless remains of an adult male (Brown, Awe, and Garber 2018:109). The burial showed signs of reentry and the removal of the skull. Robin et al. (2012:128) recorded evidence for a similar and coeval practice at the nearby site of Chan, where a burial that had been placed in the middle of the E-Group Plaza was reopened and several skeletal elements, including the skull, were removed. Brown, Awe, and Garber (2018:109) propose that the "placement of honored deceased persons within the heart of the community's ceremonial space" is a clear indication that specific deceased ancestors were beginning to be elevated, and venerated, above others in the community.

At Xunantunich, Brown (2017; Brown, Awe, and Garber 2018) also found multiple post holes in front of the E-Group that were likely used for erecting periodic altars in front of the building. Brown and her colleagues propose that the altars were likely used during rituals related to "annual solar events such as the equinoxes and solstices" (Brown, Awe, and Garber 2018:107). We further propose that these ceremonies, along with many of the caches deposited in open plazas, were sponsored and officiated by emerging elite during the Middle Formative period. By sponsoring these public events, emerging rulers were able to transmit and solidify their growing political stature in the community. Significantly, and likely associated with these changes, the production of figurines, which were previously used in private household rituals, began to decline (Awe n.d.). The practice of decorating ceramics with iconographic motifs and cosmological symbols, which was evident during Cunil times and greatly reduced during the Jenney Creek phase, was also discontinued at the onset of the late Middle Preclassic period, suggesting a shift in the function of ceramics and their consumption by different social sectors.

To the west of the Belize Valley, communities in the central Peten and eastern Pasión regions of Guatemala experienced similar changes, albeit with a few regional nuances and differences. By 700 BCE, the inhabitants of Ceibal had created a formal plaza, along a north–south alignment, by constructing large residential platforms on the north and south flanks of their E-Group courtyard (Inomata 2016). Inomata (2016:51) claims that this allowed the site's emerging elite to perform communal ceremonies in the plaza, but that there was "no clear indication that these emergent elites had strong power to impose their will on others by coercion." He proposes that the continued semimobile lifeway of the site's inhabitants allowed them "to escape from the imposition of elite power." Whether late Middle Formative inhabitants of all lowland Maya sites were still practicing mobile lifestyles is debatable, as is the role of coercion in the construction of monumental architecture. Instead, it is likely that emergent elite were still in the process of establishing control over the mostly autonomous populace, and that their sponsorship of monumental architecture and public rituals in site cores was part of an ongoing strategy to accomplish this goal. In this context, the construction of monumental architecture likely served to transform the human-made site cores into emulations of ideational landscapes, to convert them into the axis mundi of rapidly growing communities, and as a setting/theater in which the emerging elite could perform public rituals on behalf of the community at large.

Closer to the Belize Valley, the emerging elite at Cival also constructed a Middle Preclassic E-Group, which Estrada Belli (2006:62, 2011) suggests was created as an "architectural device... to celebrate the four divisions of the calendar year." Somewhat related to this idea, Rice (2008) as well as Aimers and Rice (2006) suggest that emerging rulers began to identify themselves with the sun and that this is "best exemplified by the plethora of constructions of so-called 'E-Group' assemblages, paired structures commemorating sight lines to solstitial and equinoctial sunrises beginning in the Middle Preclassic period" (Rice 2008:290). Wright (2011:41) adds that E-Groups were used by emerging elite to perform public rituals that celebrated "celestial and agricultural cycles and to reenact creation events." He further proposes that radial pyramids could be "microcosmic representations of the quadripartite earth, and as such, a ruler performing rituals on the platform would become the axis mundi at the center of the cosmos" (Wright 2011:41).

The First *Ajawtaak*: The Late Preclassic Period (300 BCE–300 CE)

The cultural changes that occurred in the Belize Valley during the Late Formative period, particularly regarding the institution of kingship, were quite profound. These changes are highly visible archaeologically and are manifested by several innovations and by a few cultural continuities, albeit writ large. Monumental architecture, for example, continued to be constructed, but the pace of construction and the scale of new buildings dwarfed the efforts evident in the late Middle Formative period (Awe 1992:356). Architectural changes are also evident by the discontinuance of certain types of structures and the introduction of new forms. The construction of large circular platforms, for example, was gradually discontinued and these were replaced by more imposing, multitiered, and rectilinear structures with central stairways leading to their summits (Aimers, Powis, and Awe 2000; Awe 1992, 2008; Brown 2003; LeCount, Mixter, and Simova 2017; Mixter 2016; Robin 2012). Stucco masks, many depicting the Principal Bird Deity, the Sun God, and other deities, decorated the flanks of stairways on these pyramids. One example of these large pyramidal buildings at Cahal Pech, Structure A1, was raised fifteen meters above the plaza surface (Awe 1992:356). Elite residences bordering the courtyards at Cahal Pech also increased in size and were elevated above the surfaces of their corresponding courtyards.

Among the most important architectural changes revealed by investigations at the sites of Cahal Pech, Blackman Eddy, Actuncan, and Chan is the transformation of E-Group complexes into Eastern Triadic Shrines (Awe, Hoggarth, and Aimers 2017; Ebert, McGee, and Awe 2021). At Cahal Pech, this is evident by the demolition of the upper tiers of the E-Group's western radial pyramid, and by its "burial" beneath Plaza B (Ebert, McGee, and Awe 2021). At the eastern end of Plaza B, the earlier E-Group platform was modified, enlarged, and replaced by three in-line pyramidal structures. The central structure was also raised several meters higher than its northern and southern counterparts. These Belize Valley innovations stand in contrast to changes in the Peten and

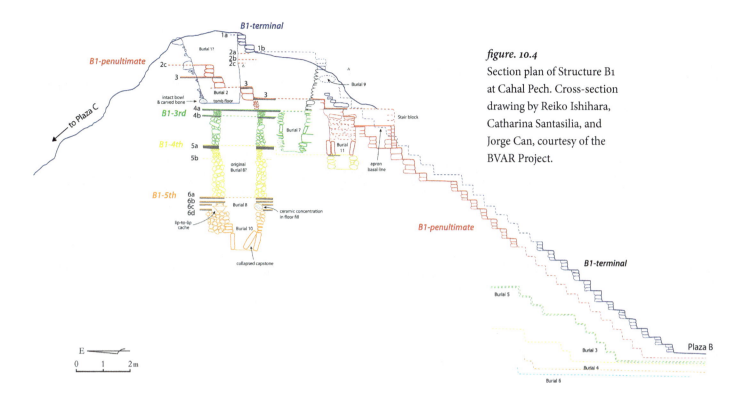

figure. 10.4
Section plan of Structure B1 at Cahal Pech. Cross-section drawing by Reiko Ishihara, Catharina Santasilia, and Jorge Can, courtesy of the BVAR Project.

northern Belize (e.g., at Lamanai), where E-Groups were replaced by Triadic Groups rather than by in-line triadic assemblages (Awe, Hoggarth, and Aimers 2017; Saturno, Rossi, and Beltran 2018).

A significant innovation that accompanied these architectural changes was the placement of the first tombs and crypts within the structures (Figure 10.4) of Eastern Triadic Assemblages (Awe 2013; Mitchell 2006; Novotny 2012). Burials B1-8 and B1-10 at Cahal Pech provide two examples of these elite graves (Awe 2013). Elsewhere in the valley, similar graves are represented by Burials 8, 9, and 10 at Chan (Keller 2012:263; Novotny 2012:236–238), and by a tomb in the E-Group at Early Xunantunich. The Xunantunich tomb appears to have been reentered in antiquity, possibly for the removal of skeletal remains (Brown, Awe, and Garber 2018:111–112). A slate slab at the top of the filled-in chamber was decorated with an incised image in low relief depicting an individual that "appears to be wearing a headdress" and holding either a staff or ceremonial bar in front of his body. At both Cahal Pech and Chan, the Late Formative tombs/crypts predominantly contained the remains of male individuals accompanied by jadeite and marine shell jewelry, stingray spines, obsidian blades, fine-paste ceramics, and heads of Middle Formative figurines (Figures 10.5–10.6). At Chan, Keller (2012:263) notes that the "specific ornaments interred with each man, a possible headdress piece and matched ear flares, suggest that they were attired in the garb of rulers." We also suggest greenstone pendants in Late Formative burials likely represented images of the Maize God and it is possible that the figurine heads may have served as symbolic representations of earlier ancestors.

The association of Late Formative *ajawtaak* with revered ancestors and the Maize God is best represented by Burial B4-3 at Cahal Pech. This burial (Figure 10.7a), which was axially located beneath the summit platform of Late Formative pyramid Structure B4, contained two large lip-to-lip, Sierra Red ceramic basins. The vessels were framed or bordered by several long bones placed along the four cardinal directions. A Middle Formative figurine head and the spout of a chocolate pot were located on each of the four cardinal points. Enclosed within the ceramic vessels were large fragments of an adult human skull and two jadeite triangulates. Below the bottom vessel, and at the center of the bone rectangle, was a carved conch shell figure in the form

Le roi est mort, vive le roi

figure 10.5
Grave goods in Cahal Pech Burial B1-8. Photographs by Catharina Santasilia, courtesy of the BVAR Project.

figure 10.6
Grave goods in Cahal Pech Burial B1-10. Photographs by Catharina Santasilia, courtesy of the BVAR Project.

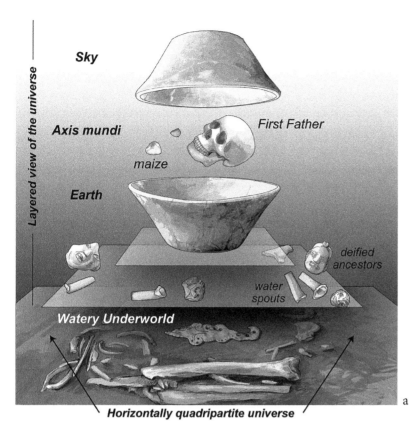

figure 10.7
Artistic reconstruction of Burial B4-3 from Cahal Pech (a), showing the quadripartite arrangement of human remains in Burial B4-3 with crocodilian shell effigy at center (b). Drawings by Sarah Sage, courtesy of the BVAR Project.

of a crocodile (Figure 10.7b). Our analysis of the human remains noted that the skeleton was incomplete, missing all the teeth and most of the small bony remains. The absence of small bones is consistent with secondary burials that contain human remains exhumed from their original place of interment (Awe 2013). More importantly, the structured arrangement of the human remains and grave goods in Burial B4-3 clearly reflects a Maya cosmogram as well as the Formative-period origin of the concept of "the myth of the hero twins and the resurrection of the maize god" (Awe 2021). It is quite obvious, for example, that the long bones bordering the deposit along the four cardinal directions served to represent the quadripartite nature of earth. Completing the quincunx are the lip-to-lip vessels at the center of the bone quadrangle. The figurines on the four sides of the quadrangle represent the aged Atlantean deities with quadripartite associations, tied to the four cardinal directions, typically subsumed under the heading of God N in the Classic Maya pantheon (see Boot 2017; Martin 2015). The vertical division of the universe is represented by the crocodilian shell effigy and the lip-to-lip vessels above it. The skull within the lip-to-lip vessels is akin to the decapitated head of the Maize God within a

Le roi est mort, vive le roi   261

cave in a sacred mountain. This sacred mountain, in turn, rests on the back of the crocodile (earth), which floats in the primordial sea (see Houston and Taube 2011:29). Among the most significant artifacts in the entire assemblage are the chocolate pot spouts and the two jade triangulates that were placed with the skull in the lip-to-lip vessels. Awe (2013:40) suggests that the spouts "reflect the concept of *pars pro toto*," in that they are meant to represent complete "chocolate" pots. In Yucatán, as well as in the Maya Highlands (where they are called *pichingas*), these spouted ceramic vessels are not only used for serving chocolate drinks but also serve as water containers (Powis et al. 2002:96). On the "Resurrection" plate, the Hero Twins are depicted pouring water onto a fissure on the back of the earth turtle. The water is directed to the remains of their father, the Maize God, who, through this action, is resurrected like maize that sprouts at the coming of the rains (e.g., Miller and Martin 2004:56–57). The chocolate pot spouts in Burial B4-3 were, therefore, purposely placed with the deposit to convey this subtle message. Awe (2013:39, 2021) suggested that the two jadeite triangulates next to the skull were symbolic representations of maize. The association of jade with maize was originally proposed by Adrian Digby (1964:25–26, pl. xivb) and more recently by Karl Taube (2005). When we combine all of this information, it is clear that the message that this deposit was meant to convey is that the exhumed remains of the deceased ancestor were being accorded qualities of the Maize God, and that, like that deity, he would resurrect and rise to the heavens. Equally significant is that the burial served to establish that the ancestors of certain families had become considerably more important than others, and that access to these deified ancestors allowed their descendants to communicate with powerful beings in the universe. If our interpretation of this change is accurate, it could explain why Middle Formative figurines, which were previously used to petition ancestors in household rituals, completely disappear during Late Formative times. From here onward, it was the responsibility of the *ajaw* to communicate with deities and his deified ancestors to ensure stability and prosperity for subjects and community (see Freidel and Schele 1988).

The disappearance of figurines at the start of the Late Preclassic period across the central Maya Lowlands (Awe 1992:270–285; DeLance and Awe 2021; Rands and Rands 1965:536) is most certainly associated with these sociopolitical changes. In her study of figurines from San José Mogote, for example, Marcus (1999, 2009) notes that prior to the emergence of rank in the Early Formative period, figurines were used by women "for invoking the spirits of their ancestors." When males in the community began to appropriate religion to legitimize their growing social statuses in the Middle Preclassic period, female figurines were replaced by male effigies, a change that coincided with the construction of monumental architecture and elite burials (Marcus 1999:94). By the start of the Late Preclassic Monte Albán period (300–100 BCE), "the small, handmade pottery figurines of the Formative period gradually disappeared," coinciding with the consolidation of "Formative chiefdoms" in the Valley of Oaxaca (Marcus 2009:31).

The introduction and dedication of the first carved and plain stelae represent one of the most salient types of evidence for the Late Formative establishment of the first *ajawtaak* in the Belize River Valley. This change at Cahal Pech is best represented by Stela 9, one of the earliest lowland Maya examples of these new monuments as well as of their use to portray the elevated status of particular individuals, *ajaw*, in the community (Awe, Grube, and Cheetham 2009; Helmke 2019:33). Stela 9 (Figure 10.8a) is a "wrap-around" type of monument whose style is more typical of monuments found along the Pacific Coast and Guatemalan Highlands (Awe, Grube, and Cheetham 2009:182; Guernsey 2010). The stela depicts a human emerging from "the wide-open maw" of a "supernatural feline, replete with a serpentine bifid tongue," an iconographic theme that is also recorded on Formative-period monuments at Izapa (e.g., Miscellaneous Monument 2), Takalik Abaj (Monument 67), and across Mesoamerica (Awe, Grube, and Cheetham 2009:182; Helmke 2019:33). Awe, Grube, and Cheetham (2009:182) previously argued that the "style, iconography, size, and execution" of Stela 9, along with "the absence of hieroglyphs," all indicate

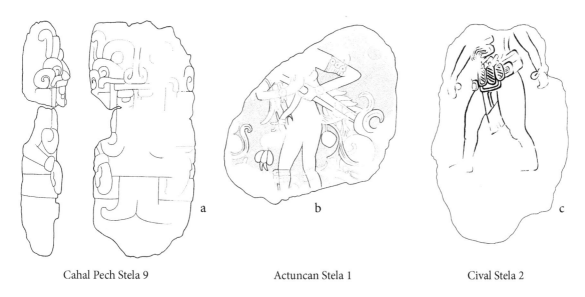

figure 10.8
Formative-period monuments from the Belize River Valley and Cival, Guatemala: a) Cahal Pech Stela 9 (drawing by Nikolai Grube, courtesy of the BVAR Project); b) Actuncan Stela 1 (drawing by Nikolai Grube, courtesy of the BVAR Project); and c) Cival Stela 2 (drawing by Christophe Helmke, courtesy of the BVAR Project).

that this monument was carved and erected "before the development of Maya writing" or before inscriptions began to be transferred to carved monuments. Based on these characteristics, and the fact that no other Formative-period stela in the Maya Lowlands shares these traits, it is likely that Cahal Pech Stela 9 dates to at least the early facet of the Late Formative period, if not earlier. Helmke adds: "The iconography of this stela is fascinating for the hybridity of its style, showing a transitional form between the large stucco masks of deities and the supernatural that adorn temple structures in the Late Preclassic, and the Classic period focus on the ruler as the sole subject of representation . . . Preserving the depictions of the deities of old, the king [depicted on Cahal Pech Stela 9] is now seen as emerging from these, supporting and validating his rule, and anticipating the figural motifs of the ensuing Classic period" (Helmke 2019:34).

Actuncan Stela 1 (Figure 10.8b) represents another Late Formative monument from the Belize Valley. Postdating Cahal Pech Stela 9, the Terminal Formative Actuncan monument depicts "a ruler brandishing a rigid ceremonial bar, although the dynamic stance, with legs apart, is analogous to" other Late Formative monuments, like Cival Stela 2 (Figure 10.8c) and Nakum Stela 4 (Helmke 2019:33; Żrałka et al. 2018:9). Żrałka and his colleagues (2018:9) add: "The striding pose with legs apart and the manner of representing the feet, as well as the pointed adornments worn on the ankles, are highly comparable to such early Maya monuments as Kaminaljuyu Stela 11, [and] Takalik Abaj Stela 5." Other early monuments discovered at Peten sites include stelae from Nakbe, El Mirador, and Cival. Nakbe Stela 1 has no hieroglyphic texts but depicts two male figures facing each other. According to Helmke (2019), some of the traits associated with the figure on the left suggest that he may represent the Sun God, while the Jester God in the headdress of the figure on the right suggests that this individual was a human ruler. What is remarkable here is that both are rendered in anthropomorphic form and at equal scale, as if homologous rulers of each of their respective realms. Despite this apparent equality, the human ruler has his arm folded across his chest as a sign of deference. These entities appear to be in the midst of a deliberation, the Sun God calling to attention an important point with raised index finger. This deliberation may well entail the negotiation

Le roi est mort, vive le roi

of incipient godliness, with human rulers increasingly ascribing themselves divine attributes in their service as mediums with the divine.

In addition to Stela 9, Cahal Pech also has several plain (uncarved) stelae. A cache below one of the plain stelae contained the headless and armless torso of a Middle Formative figurine that was placed in an upright seated position beneath the butt of the stela. Two eyes and a mouth were incised on the chest of the figurine in an apparent attempt to modify it sometime after its primary function had ceased (Awe n.d.). At Early Xunantunich, Brown, Awe, and Garber (2018:97) suggest that some plain monuments at that site could likely date to the Late Formative period. A similar observation has been made by Guernsey and Love (2005:41; see also Pereira 2009) for plain monuments at sites along the Pacific coastal region. Whether or not the plain monuments at Cahal Pech are Late Formative in date is almost impossible to determine. What is significant, however, is that when we consider the other unequivocal Late Formative Belize Valley stelae in tandem, they provide solid evidence "for increasing social stratification, as encoded in complex symbolism and representational conventions, and testify to the incipience and expansion of centralized rulership across the region" (Helmke 2019:34).

Murals from San Bartolo and Tikal, as well as the introduction of hieroglyphic texts, provide even more compelling evidence for the establishment of *ajawtaak* during the Late Formative period (Hansen 1991; Justeson and Mathews 1990; Martin 2003; see also Martin 2020:113). The murals on the west wall of the Pinturas Group at San Bartolo, for example, depict the coronation scenes of a human ruler in a complex backdrop recounting the role of the Maize God in the advent of cultigens and the epic battles of a culture hero, in the defeat of the great celestial bird (Saturno 2005; Saturno, Rossi, and Beltran 2018; Saturno, Taube, and Stuart 2005; Urquizú and Hurst 2011). A single vertical band of hieroglyphs at San Bartolo also may contain one of the earliest uses of the glyph for *ajaw* (Helmke 2012:106–107; Saturno, Stuart, and Beltran 2006:1282). Another possible early representation of the *ajaw* glyph appears on a carved parietal that was discovered at Cuello (Hammond 1999:54, fig. 2). These various lines of evidence, both in the Belize Valley and the Peten, indicate that by the start of the Christian era, Maya *ajawtaak* were fully established in communities across the central lowland region.

The *K'uhul Ajawtaak*: The Early and Late Classic Periods (300–800 CE)

Hereditary rulership in the Belize Valley, like everywhere else in the Maya Lowlands, reached its apogee during the Early and Late Classic periods. This rise is quite evident in the archaeological record of Classic-period sites and is reflected by some important changes in the way that rulers began to manifest their elevated status. What is also evident in the Belize Valley is that not long after the start of the Early Classic period, local rulers were forced to adjust to external pressures brought on by "foreign" overlords, particularly those who ruled over Tikal, Caracol, and Naranjo (Awe, Helmke, Aimers et al. 2020; Helmke 2019; Helmke and Awe 2012).

Compelling evidence for the establishment of hereditary rulership, and for the continuity of power held by particular lineages and households, is clearly indicated by the continued and sequential interment of rulers in tombs within the Eastern Triadic Shrines at Cahal Pech, Baking Pot, Blackman Eddy, Buena Vista, and Pacbitun (Audet 2006; Awe 2013; Garber et al. 2004; Healy 1990; Novotny et al. 2018; Yaeger and Brown 2019; Yaeger et al. 2015). Concurrent with these activities, Belize Valley elite began constructing their palatial residences in elevated acropolises within the site cores, with accesses that became increasingly restricted. Separating the private living spaces of the *k'uhul ajawtaak* from public courtyards were imposing multiroom buildings that likely served as audiencias (Awe 2008). In central Belize, particularly at Cahal Pech, Xunantunich, and Caracol (e.g., the Caana temple complex), these audiencias consist of thirteen doorway palace-type buildings that overlooked the largest open access plazas, and in locations that clearly separate the public plazas from the royal residences at the sites (Awe 2008). Awe (2008) previously noted that the thirteen doorways of these imposing structures were purposeful features of these buildings, for they served as not too subtle heuristic and symbolic devices for manifesting the elevated and deified statuses of the rulers who lived in the lofty palaces above them.

The burial of deceased rulers in pyramidal eastern shrines also provided opportunity for the heirs of dead rulers to publicly affirm and declare their right to rule by virtue of their descent. Here again, the location and morphology of Eastern Triadic Shrines, and their exclusive use by the elite to bury their lineage heads, likely served to convey important political, social, and religious messages. The burial of rulers in eastern shrines, with their in-line triadic pyramids, which likely symbolized the three-stone place of creation, may have also conveyed the idea that, like the sun that is reborn in the east, so too would the deceased ancestors who were interred in these sacred locations.

Like their contemporaries in neighboring regions, Early Classic *k'uhul ajaw* in the Belize Valley also began to use carved stelae and other media to declare their authority. Stelae with calendar dates, rulership-related iconography, and hieroglyphic inscriptions are evident on Blackman Eddy Stela 1, Pacbitun Stela 6, and Pacbitun Altar 3, all dating to the fourth and fifth centuries CE (Garber 1992; Helmke 2019; Helmke and Awe 2008; Skaggs et al. 2017). Two Early Classic ceramic vessels from an elite burial at Baking Pot (Colas et al. 2002) also are decorated with "some of the earliest examples of dedicatory inscriptions (i.e., Primary Standard Sequences) anywhere in the Maya Lowlands" (Helmke 2019:34). The text on one of the vessels indicates that it was owned by a royal personage named Lem? Tz'unun Tok Suutz'. A dynastic title on yet another Baking Pot vessel suggests that it once named a monarch of Caracol, and given its date, may have once belonged to either Yajawte' K'inich II (r. 553–593+ CE) or his son K'an II (r. 618–658 CE) (Helmke 2019:35). These texts, and other shared cultural traditions, like finger caches at Cahal Pech and Baking Pot, clearly reflect overtures by Caracol to exert influence over the smaller Belize Valley polities toward the end of

figure 10.9
Grave goods from Burial B1-7 at Cahal Pech. Photographs by Catharina Santasilia, courtesy of the BVAR Project.

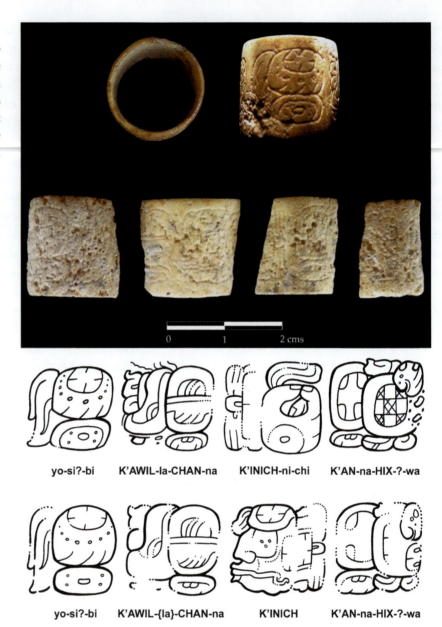

figure 10.10
Inscriptions on bone rings from Cahal Pech Burial B1-7. Photographs and drawing by Marc Zender, courtesy of the BVAR Project.

the Early Classic period. More importantly, these overtures were harbingers of important political changes that ensued during the Late Classic period.

Caracol's influence in the Belize Valley, for example, begins to wane toward the end of the seventh century CE, when it was replaced by Naranjo as the primary regional overlord. One of the last vestiges of Caracol's influence at Cahal Pech is made evident by a multiple, sequential burial in a tomb (Burial B1-7) discovered in the central structure (Structure B1) of the site's Eastern Triadic Shrine. Multiple sequential interments are a hallmark of burial traditions at Caracol (D. Chase and A. Chase 1996) and examples of this tradition are present at sites throughout Caracol's area of influence (Healy, Awe, and Helmuth 1998). In addition to reflecting the last traces of Caracol's influence at Cahal Pech, Burial B1-7 also reflects the continued affluence and stature of the site's rulers. This is reflected in the lavish and sumptuous grave goods (Figure 10.9) in the burial, and in the two bone rings and turtle plastrons that were inscribed with the regnal name and the royal title of the local dynasts (Awe and Zender 2016; Helmke 2019; Novotny et al. 2018) (Figure 10.10).

The royal title of the kings of Cahal Pech is only partly deciphered, but can be read as K'an Hix . . . w, wherein the final segment involves an as yet undeciphered sign (Awe and Zender 2016:163). This dynastic title is preceded by the regnal name of a particular monarch, K'awiil Chan K'inich (possibly "the radiant one is powerful in the sky"), which is significant as it provides solid evidence that Belize Valley *ajawtaak* were using royal epithets that included theonyms like those used by their exalted counterparts in other regions of the Maya Lowlands. Houston and Inomata (2009:3; see also Martin and Grube 2008:15) note that at the time of coronation, Classic-period rulers would take on theonyms, such as K'awiil and K'inich, that "likened them to gods," thereby reflecting their "divine" status. This onomastic principle, in fact, marked the enthroned monarch as a particular incarnation of one specific aspect of a greater deity, with all the initial elements of these regnal names specifying the attributes of this aspect (Colas 2014).

A subsequent royal tomb in Structure B1 at Cahal Pech, Burial B1-2, also contained fragments of an incised turtle carapace. The partially preserved turtle shell fragments with inscriptions suggest the regnal name of the Late Classic king K'awiil Chan K'inich was repeated on these remains (Awe and Zender 2016:160). Together with the lavish display of wealth (Figure 10.11) in Burial B1-2, they serve as testimony of the hereditary nature and success of the royal lineage at the site. The presence of Cahal Pech's dynastic title on a jadeite plaque that was discovered along with the remains of a female individual in a royal tomb at Nim li Punit further suggests that royal houses in the Belize Valley were also involved in fomenting alliances with sites in other lowland Maya regions (Prager and Braswell 2016). On the jadeite plaque from Nim li Punit, the dynastic title occurs as part of a parentage statement, naming the mother of the original owner as one from the dynastic house of Cahal Pech (Helmke 2019:36).

With the waning of Caracol at the start of the Late Classic period, the political focus of Belize Valley rulers turned west toward their new overlords residing at Naranjo. Present evidence suggests that, for the most part, the royal houses of the Belize Valley quietly, if not begrudgingly, acquiesced to their changing political circumstances. That their royal houses continued to flourish under this new regime, however, is made evident by various gifts, particularly in the form of polychrome vessels, that Naranjo rulers bestowed upon them (see Helmke et al. 2019:27–30). The gifting of the Buenavista vase, and other ceramic vessels in tombs at Baking Pot, Xunantunich, and Cahal Pech, is testimony to this new arrangement with Naranjo. So too are Panels 3 and 4 (see Helmke 2019:fig. 7) at Xunantunich, which represent sections of the Caracol hieroglyphic stairway that was removed from the latter site following its defeat by Naranjo in 680 CE. Awe, Helmke, Slocum, and Tilden (2019, 2020), as well as Helmke and Awe (2016a, 2016b) suggest that the panels were likely obtained by Xunantunich's ruler for their participation as Naranjo's ally in this star war event. A tomb within Structure A9 at Xunantunich, the pyramid on which Panels 3 and 4 were displayed, also contained the remains of an elite woman with several ceramic vessels, including some that were likely gifts from the royal house of Naranjo (Awe, Helmke, Slocum et al. 2019, 2020). Political connections between Naranjo and valley-wide rulers are also evident in a throne room on Structure A1 at Cahal Pech, and on monuments from Tipan Chen Uitz. On the rear wall of the Cahal Pech throne room, a poorly preserved text records a royal accession at the site, and also mentions "an ethnonym and the dynastic title of Naranjo" (Helmke 2019:37; Helmke and Awe 2008:80–82). At Tipan Chen Uitz, located on the Roaring Creek tributary of the Belize River, inscriptions on ballplayer panels appear to refer to a Late Classic figure from Naranjo (Helmke et al. 2015).

In spite of these obvious connections to Naranjo's more dominant royal house, it appears that Belize Valley rulers were still able to maintain a patron-client relationship with their more powerful neighbor and to remain relatively autonomous during the turbulent years of the Late Classic period (Awe, Helmke, Slocum et al. 2019). This is perhaps best illustrated by our discovery of Panel 2, secondarily placed beside one of the doorways of the audiencia (Structure 32) on the Castillo (see Helmke 2019:fig. 8). This very well-preserved and inscribed

figure 10.11
Grave goods from Cahal Pech Burial B1-2. Photographs by Jaime Awe and Catharina Santasilia, courtesy of the BVAR Project.

monument contains part of a clause that ends with *ta-uutz witz ajaw*, clearly in reference to the "title ascribed to the kings of Xunantunich" (Helmke 2019:39). These hieroglyphic texts, like those in the throne room at Cahal Pech and on the ballplayer panels at Tipan Chen Uitz, are clear testimony that Belize Valley sites were full participants in a system of kingship in which rulers were considered "holy" or "divine" lords, and in which these regional *ajawtaak* enjoyed similar prerogatives to those of the lordly rulers of the larger and more dominant polities of the central Maya Lowlands.

The Perpetuators: The Terminal Classic Period (800–900 CE)

The Terminal Classic period brought tumultuous changes to most of the cities in the central lowlands. For reasons that are still being debated, many royal houses, and the cities they governed for many centuries, began to decline (see Martin 2020 for a recent overview). Many cities were gradually and eventually abandoned, and all vestiges of their previous glory, and the rulers who presided over them, faded away. This so-called period of collapse, however, was never even across the lowland Maya landscape, and the pace of decline and abandonment differed within individual regions, as well as from polity to polity (e.g., Ebert et al. 2014). In the Belize Valley region, for example, the decline of some sites preceded that of others. The decline of Classic-period seats of hegemonic power, such as Naranjo, also served to liberate their Belize Valley vassals from their previous political control. Some royal houses celebrated the decentralization of power brought about by these events. Others were as stricken as their overlords and were apparently unable to take advantage of the opportunity to prosper outside the shadow of their previous benefactors. Below we describe how Belize Valley monarchs and their kingdoms reacted to the diverse ecological and sociopolitical changes that ensued during this period of transformation and decline.

Cahal Pech appears to be one of the first sites in the valley to buckle under the various economic and sociopolitical stressors that define the Terminal Classic period. Following an initial spurt in building activity, major construction efforts in the site core gradually ceased, and buildings began to fall into disrepair (Awe, Ebert et al. 2020; Awe, Helmke, Aimers et al. 2020). When the royal palaces in the site's western acropolis began to fall apart, the few remaining members of the ruling family relocated their residences to Plaza H, a small courtyard in the northeastern corner of the site core (Awe, Ebert et al. 2020). Here, they constructed small platforms with perishable buildings that paled in comparison with their previous lofty palaces in the acropolis. In spite of these misfortunes, the remaining Cahal Pech elite made every effort to cling on to previous traditions. Small public offerings, to patron deities and ancestors, continued to be made in areas of the site that were no longer occupied (Aimers and Awe 2020; Awe, Ebert et al. 2020; Stemp and Awe 2020). When some members of the family passed away, they continued to bury them within "intrusive" graves in the site's Eastern Triadic Shrine (Awe, Ebert et al. 2020). At the death of what likely was the last ruler of the site, he was interred in a large tomb (Burial H1-1) constructed from cut stones scavenged from abandoned Late Classic buildings (Awe 2013; Awe, Ebert et al. 2020). In keeping with earlier Cahal Pech and Belize Valley cultural traditions, the deceased ruler was interred in a prone position with head to the south. A jadeite pendant of his necklace bore the image of the Maize God, and he wore this over a breastplate made of deer bones (Figure 10.12). By his feet were the skeletal remains of a small feline, possibly an ocelot, a clear reminder of the link between rulers and powerful felines. Other tangible manifestations of his royal status included large and exotic jadeite ear flares, five obsidian blades, and marine shells and shell beads. Around his upper torso and feet were several ceramic vessels, including his cacao drinking cup. Unlike his ancestors, however, his cup was no longer decorated with the primary standard sequences of the past. Instead, it had a band of repetitive pseudo-glyphs below the vessel rim, and a rather poorly drawn image of a standing male figure wearing a back rack and zoomorphic headdress. An AMS ^{14}C date obtained from one of the deer bones indicates that Cahal Pech's last ruler was interred in the tomb sometime between 710 and 875 cal CE (see Douglas et al. 2021). The Structure H1 tomb reflects the final attempt of the site's elite rulers to perpetuate their elevated statuses, and to rekindle the glories of the past.

Downriver from Cahal Pech, early facet Terminal Classic rulers at Baking Pot also continued their allegiance to Naranjo. These close ties, however, would gradually start to wane, likely falling victim to the various martial engagements that Naranjo was embroiled in. Naranjo's losing grip on its Belize Valley vassals is perhaps best reflected by

figure 10.12
Grave goods from Cahal Pech Burial H1-1. Photographs by Jaime Awe and Catharina Santasilia, courtesy of the BVAR Project.

Xunantunich, Stela 8   Xunantunich, Stela 9   Xunantunich, Stela 1

figure 10.13
Late to Terminal Classic monuments from Xunantunich: Stela 8, Stela 9, and Stela 1. Drawings by Ian Graham and Christophe Helmke, courtesy of the BVAR Project.

the Komkom Vase found in a peri-abandonment deposit at Baking Pot. This singular and unique vessel, which has one of the longest glyphic texts ever recorded in the Maya Lowlands, describes a series of military events that embroiled several of the major royal courts of the Terminal Classic central lowlands. Remarkably, the text that adorns this vase may render excerpts of a now-lost historical codex, partly explaining its style and calligraphy. Leading Naranjo's bellicose relationship with its competing neighbors was its penultimate liege, Itzamnaaj K'awiil (Helmke, Hoggarth, and Awe 2018; Martin and Grube 2008). In spite of his successes in battle, Itzamnaaj K'awiil's military engagements during a time of widespread challenges greatly affected Naranjo's supremacy over its earlier vassals, and together these forces contributed significantly to its waning regional dominance (Helmke, Beliaev, and Vepretskii 2020). But not all of Naranjo's external relations were similarly affected. Strong ties, for example, remained with some of its Belize Valley vassals, and this is reflected by Naranjo's continued gifting of special ceramics to the rulers of these allied polities. A polychrome vase that we discovered in a peri-abandonment deposit at Baking Pot's Group B palace complex provides an excellent example of this relationship. The hieroglyphic text on the barrel-shaped vase clearly identifies the original owner as Waxaklajun Ubah K'awil, the last known ruler of Naranjo.

Part of the story continues, some ten kilometers to the west, at Xunantunich, where its Stela 8 mentions the same contemporary ruler of Naranjo, as part of a period ending ritual in 820 CE. Together, the evidence from Baking Pot and Xunantunich suggests that even during this period of increasing decentralized power, Naranjo continued to court Belize Valley *ajawtaak* in its last "efforts to maintain the status quo and order of old" (Helmke 2019:41). Yet these adaptive processes were reflected differently at the different sites. During the initial decline of Naranjo's regional control, the royal house of Xunantunich appears to have reasserted its earlier autonomy, while at the same time maintaining some form of an alliance with its previous overlord. The weakened control of Naranjo, and Xunantunich's newfound freedom, are manifested by the erection of Stelae 1, 8, and 9 (Figure 10.13), and Altar 1 in Plaza A at Xunantunich (Helmke, Awe, and Grube 2010), and by renewed architectural activity within the site core (Awe, Helmke, Slocum et al. 2020; LeCount and Yaeger 2010).

Stela 8 (Figure 10.13), which celebrates the period ending date of 820 CE, depicts a local Xunantunich lord celebrating the period ending event with a ritual dance. The poorly preserved text on the monument also relates that the contemporary ruler of Naranjo, undoubtedly Waxaklajun Ubah K'awil, celebrated the event alongside the Xunantunich ruler (Helmke 2019:41; Helmke, Awe, and Grube 2010:110). Interestingly, the text is mute about the hierarchy of the two individuals, "making it very difficult to determine whether one is best seen as an overlord and the other as a vassal. As such, it may well be that both are here referred to on equal footing as royal homologues, jointly performing rituals and celebrations of the propitious period ending" (Awe, Helmke, Slocum et al. 2020:502). Stela 9 (Figure 10.13), which postdates Stela 8 by a decade, depicts the Xunantunich ruler standing tall and in full royal attire. Unlike Stela 8, however, the ruler on Stela 9 holds a *K'awiil* scepter in his hand rather than a lance. Helmke, Awe, and Grube (2010:113) note that it is "quite likely that both Stelae 8 and 9, separated by only ten years (and well within the biological range of one reign) . . . depict and name the same king, although he bears a longer titular string on Stela 9 (based on the total number of glyph blocks)."

Stela 1 (Figure 10.13), which dates to 849 CE, shares both parallels and differences with Stelae 8 and 9. Like the latter, Stela 1 portrays a standing male figure in full royal regalia, holding a small shield in one hand and a *K'awiil* scepter in the other. Similarities in the costumes of the male figures on both monuments suggest that they may represent the same ruler. Where Stela 1 diverges from earlier monuments is in "the disposition of its text and the replacement of the textual basal register with a bound and prostrate captive, upon which the ruler is shown standing" (Helmke, Awe, and Grube 2010:115). Another difference is that Stela 1 is paired with Altar 1, which bears a similar date of 849 CE. Altar 1 depicts a skeletal figure in front of a double column of glyphs. The glyphs "can be read as *pahsaj ub'aak ujo'l*, or literally "exhumed were the bones and the skull" (Helmke, Awe, and Grube 2010:119). Unfortunately, poor preservation of the following glyphs makes it impossible to determine the identity of whose remains were exhumed. In spite of this situation, the text on Stela 1 underscores the continued importance of human remains in the geopolitics of the ancient Maya, especially since comparable phrases are seen as part of exhumations that took place as part of bellicose interactions between polities or in anticipation of desecrations in the wake of war (see Grube and Schele 1994). As such, peering through these ritual expressions in the context of wars, we can tangentially see the continued import of ancestor veneration, and its continued use by Belize Valley monarchs for establishing and demonstrating their special ancestry and their right to rule. More importantly, these various pieces of evidence all suggest that the Belize Valley *ajawtaak* of the Terminal Classic period tried their best to perpetuate the long-established institution of divine rulership as well as the many traditions that accompanied this exalted social station.

Discussion and Conclusions

In this chapter, we examined more than three decades of accumulated archaeological data from central Belize in an effort to characterize the rise, apogee, and decline of rulership in this subregion of the Maya Lowlands. This rich and diverse body of data indicates that from the establishment of the first sedentary communities at the end of the Early Formative period, roughly between 1200 and 900 BCE, the heads of some lineages began to invest considerable resources in their personal aggrandizement to create social obligations that served to elevate their statuses within their communities. Besides sponsoring and celebrating public social and religious events, early aggrandizers may have also promoted cave rituals that helped to link them with sacred landscapes, deified spirits, and creation narratives.

By late Middle Formative times (750–300 BCE), early aggrandizers, now transformed into emerging rulers, began to commission the construction of monumental architecture, like E-Groups, and to celebrate and sponsor cyclical rituals that further reaffirmed and/or promoted their connection to the cosmos. The construction of E-Groups and elite residences at the center of expanding towns also served to establish these sites as the axis mundi of their communities. Other efforts toward this end included the conspicuous caching of exotic and symbolically laden objects along the centerline axes of E-Groups. The material record of these various activities demonstrates that the emerging rulers of the Late Middle Formative period continued to appropriate religious and cosmological concepts, and their associated rituals, to publicly express and manifest their elevated status and authority (Stuart 2005). Research at Cahal Pech indicates that these changes may have come at the expense of some household rituals, and that the latter were replaced by important communal petitions to deified spirits that were now publicly celebrated by emerging *ajawtaak*. These actions undoubtedly served to publicly demonstrate that fledgling kings had "special access to the divine realm and special responsibilities to intercede on behalf of their subjects" (Martin and Grube 2008:221). In many ways, these changes clearly align with Graeber's (2017) and Graeber and Sahlin's (2017:378) observation that the origins of political power are closely related to the appropriation and subsequent control of ritual and ceremonial events by incipient elites, and that the origins of royal politics and cosmology are inseparable.

By the onset of the Late Formative period, the now established *ajaw* of the Belize Valley continued to appropriate and use all forms of religious and cosmological knowledge for self-serving political purposes. This knowledge was incorporated into the construction of monumental architecture and public performances as instruments for demonstrating elevated elite rank and their hereditary right to rule. Besides Stela 9 from Cahal Pech, which depicts the site's ruler emerging from the maws of a supernatural being, nothing reflects this change better than Burial B4-3 and the sequential interment of elite individuals in Structure B1 at the site. The sequential burial of elites within the central structure of Eastern Triadic Shrines is a tradition typical of the Belize Valley, and it is a tradition that reflects the growing importance of publicly interring deceased rulers "in places where they could be linked with venerated ancestors" (McAnany 1995:132–133).

In the case of Burial B4-3 at Cahal Pech, the exhumation of an ancestor, his subsequent reburial along the central axis of a Late Formative pyramid, and the arrangement of his grave in a manner that associates him with the Maize God and the axis mundi is not just steeped with cosmological symbolism but also signals the establishment of the first *k'uhul ajawtaak* in central Belize. As McAnany (1995:132–133) previously noted, mortuary rituals that "stres[s] individuals and creat[e] ancestors, became more elaborate through the Formative period." The sequential elite burials in Structure B1 at Cahal Pech, and particularly Burial B4-3, provide clear evidence for McAnany's observation. At the same time, Burial B4-3 also demonstrates that the connection of ancestors with Maya creation narratives, and their association, if not identification, with the Maize God became an important heuristic device that was used by Maya rulers to manifest their "divine," "holy," or "sacred" statuses. We would like to think that the symbolic expression of these narratives at the end of the Formative period precedes their later Classic-period expression in the form of written theonyms and royal epithets, and of images on ceramic vessels that depict rulers in costumes that equate them with the Maize God.

In his study of dynastic politics at Tikal, Martin (2003:5) observed: "It would be premature to dub the Formative as truly 'predynastic,' but there is little question that the Classic placed an emphasis on dynastic rule that was either absent or weakly articulated in earlier times." Martin (2003:5) further noted, "The emergence of historical texts and personal portraits as well as changes in the style and use of monumental architecture—in particular its enhanced funerary function—reflect profound shifts in political rhetoric and ideology." Our data from the Belize Valley leads us to concur with both observations, but we would add that our data provides new evidence suggesting that these changes began to be manifested in Late Formative times. In spite of the precocity of these changes in the Belize Valley, what remains intriguing is that although some of the earliest carved Formative-period stelae in the lowlands have been discovered there and although there is evidence that local sites participated in "the tradition of inscribing stelae with calendrical notations as well as the application of dedicatory statements on ceramic vessels and other media" (Helmke 2019:36), the use of glyphic texts almost disappears during the transition from the Early Classic to the Late Classic period. What led to this change, when local rulers were using regnal names involving theonyms like their neighbors to the west and were still being interred in tombs with all the trappings of royalty? One explanation, previously offered by Helmke and Awe (2012), is that the waxing and waning of more powerful kingdoms and *k'uhul ajawtaak* to the west (Tikal, then Naranjo) and south (Caracol), as well as their efforts to extend their hegemonic control over the Belize Valley, may have impeded local rulers from making public written statements regarding their own exalted status. Another possible explanation for this situation, and one that aligns well with the comparison of the eastern Peten sites of Holmul and Naranjo by Tokovinine, Estrada Belli, and Fialko (this volume), is that Belize Valley rulers may have preferred to manifest their elevated status by constructing and interring their deceased ancestors in monumental funerary (Eastern Triadic) shrines rather than by displaying their position on carved and inscribed monuments. The relative epigraphic invisibility of rulership in some subregions of the Maya Lowlands is also highlighted in David Freidel's contribution to this volume. Freidel notes that a clear distinction can be made in the use of hieroglyphic inscriptions between the northern/eastern and the southern lowlands. Unlike southern kings, whose statuses and accomplishments were glorified on inscribed monuments, northern and eastern lieges apparently eschewed this tradition, a practice that echoes the concept of "adverse sacralization" described by Graeber and Sahlins (2017). The Late to Terminal Classic decline of regional seats of hegemonic power in the eastern Peten, and their waning control over previous vassals, eventually freed the *k'uhul ajawtaak* of the Belize Valley to manifest their status on an even footing with their previous overlords. This is made quite evident on stelae from Xunantunich, particularly Stela 8, which refers to rulers from Naranjo and Xunantunich as either "equals or independent allies" rather than as overlord and subjugated vassal (Awe, Helmke, Slocum et al. 2020:503). Another interesting dynamic evident on the Late to Terminal Classic monuments of the Belize Valley is that they eventually stop focusing specifically on rulers. Scrutiny of contemporaneous texts, instead, begins to revolve around three general themes or topics. In order of emphasis, these include the celebration of calendrical rituals (nearly 50 percent of the texts), followed by the deeds of kings, and the record of military engagements (a considerably smaller number, 14 percent, of monuments) (Helmke, Hoggarth, and Awe 2021; Martin 2020). Again, all three themes are evident on the monuments at Xunantunich (Awe, Helmke, Slocum et al. 2020; Helmke 2019; Helmke, Awe, and Grube 2010; Helmke, Hoggarth, and Awe 2021). Despite their renewed freedom, and the opportunity to once again participate fully in the various prerogatives of Classic-period kings, however, the celebration of Belize Valley rulers was short-lived, gradually brought to an end by the stressors that were beginning to affect the kingdoms in the central Maya Lowlands. Almost in denial of the dramatic changes that were consuming them at the end of the Classic period, local elites made every effort to preserve their past glory by clinging on to vestiges of their previous royal stations, perpetuating timeless rituals to celebrate the passing of important calendrical events. Some have suggested that Terminal Classic Maya of the Belize Valley adopted a decentralized council system of governance during this time, but data to support the latter are dubious at best, and not evident until historic times at sites such as Tipu (A. Chase and D. Chase 2021; Hoggarth et al. 2014). In the end, none of these efforts were successful, and two thousand years of history that witnessed descendants of aggrandizers slowly appropriate, amplify, then solidify their power over their communities gradually faded into the past.

Acknowledgments

The research conducted at Cahal Pech, Baking Pot, Lower Dover, and Xunantunich was made possible through the generous support of the Canadian commission to UNESCO, the Gordon Childe Fund of the University of London, the Tilden Family Foundation, the Social Sciences and Humanities Research Council of Canada, the National Science Foundation, and the Belize Ministry of Tourism and Culture. We are particularly grateful to Douglas Tilden for his continued support of our research and conservation efforts at Cahal Pech and Xunantunich, and to the many students and colleagues who have assisted us during the past thirty-three years of the BVAR Project. Last, but certainly not least, we extend our sincerest gratitude to our colleagues at the Belize Institute of Archaeology for their continued support of our ongoing investigations in central Belize.

REFERENCES CITED

Aimers, James J., Terry G. Powis, and Jaime J. Awe
- 2000 Preclassic Round Structures of the Upper Belize Valley. *Latin American Antiquity* 11(1):71–86.

Aimers, James J., and Prudence M. Rice
- 2006 Astronomy, Ritual, and the Interpretation of Maya "E-Group" Architectural Assemblages. *Ancient Mesoamerica* 17:79–96.

Audet, Carolyn M.
- 2006 Political Organization in the Belize Valley: Excavations at Baking Pot, Cahal Pech and Xunantunich. PhD dissertation, Vanderbilt University, Nashville.

Awe, Jaime J.
- 1992 Dawn in the Land Between the Rivers: Formative Occupation at Cahal Pech, Belize and Its Implications for Preclassic Development in the Maya Lowlands. PhD dissertation, Institute of Archaeology, University of London, London.
- 2008 Architectural Manifestations of Power and Prestige: Examples from Classic Period Monumental Architecture at Cahal Pech, Xunantunich and Caracol, Belize. *Research Reports in Belizean Archaeology* 5:159–174.
- 2013 Journey on the Cahal Pech Time Machine: An Archaeological Reconstruction of the Dynastic Sequence at a Belize Valley Polity. *Research Reports in Belizean Archaeology* 10:33–50.
- 2021 Archaeological Evidence for the Preclassic Origins of the Maya Creation Story and the Resurrection of the Maize God at Cahal Pech, Belize. In *The Myths of the Popol Vuh in Cosmology, Art, and Ritual*, edited by Holley Moyes, Allen Christenson, and Frauke Sachse, pp. 93–116. University Press of Colorado, Louisville.

n.d. The Evolution of Anthropomorphic Imagery at Cahal Pech, Belize and Its Implications for the Rise of Kingship in the Middle Preclassic Maya Lowlands. In *The Coming of Kings: A Reflection on the Forest of Kings*, edited by M. Kathryn Brown and Travis Stanton. University of Colorado Press, Louisville.

Awe, Jaime J., Claire E. Ebert, Julie A. Hoggarth, James J. Aimers, Christophe Helmke, John Douglas, and W. James Stemp

2020 The Last Hurrah: Examining the Nature of Peri-Abandonment Deposits and Activities at Cahal Pech, Belize. *Ancient Mesoamerica* 31(1):175–187.

Awe, Jaime J., Claire E. Ebert, W. James Stemp, M. Kathryn Brown, and James F. Garber

2021 Lowland Maya Genesis: The Late Archaic to Late Early Formative Transition in the Upper Belize River Valley. *Ancient Mesoamerica* 32(3):519–544.

Awe, Jaime J., Nikolai Grube, and David Cheetham

2009 Cahal Pech Stela 9: A Preclassic Monument from the Belize Valley. *Research Reports in Belizean Archaeology* 6:179–190.

Awe, Jaime J., Christophe Helmke, James J. Aimers, Claire E. Ebert, Julie A. Hoggarth, and W. James Stemp

2020 Applying Regional, Contextual, Ethnohistoric, and Ethnographic Approaches for Understanding the Significance of Peri-Abandonment Deposits in Western Belize. *Ancient Mesoamerica* 31(1):109–126.

Awe, Jaime J., Christophe Helmke, and Shawn G. Morton

2019 Beyond the Twilight Zone: Cave Exploration in the Macal River Valley, Belize. In *The Realm Below: Speleoarchaeological Investigations in the Macal River Valley, Belize*, edited by Christophe Helmke, pp. 20–73. Precolumbian Mesoweb Press, San Francisco.

Awe, Jaime J., Christophe Helmke, Diane Slocum, and Douglas Tilden

2019 Let's Talk of Graves, Eccentrics and Epitaphs: The Socio-Political Implications of Recent Discoveries at Xunantunich, Belize. *Research Reports in Belizean Archaeology* 16:57–74.

2020 Ally, Client or Outpost? Evaluating the Relationship between Xunantunich and Naranjo in the Late Classic Period. *Ancient Mesoamerica* 31(3):494–506.

Awe, Jaime J., Julie A. Hoggarth, and James J. Aimers

2017 Of Apples and Oranges: The Case of E-Groups and Eastern Triadic Architectural Assemblages in the Belize River Valley. In *Maya E Groups: Calendars, Astronomy, and Urbanism in the Early Lowlands*, edited by David A. Freidel, Arlen F. Chase, Anna Dowd, and Jerry F. Murdock, pp. 412–449. University Press of Florida, Gainesville.

Awe, Jaime J., and Marc Zender

2016 K'awiil Chan K'inich, Lord of K'an Hix: Royal Titles and Symbols of Rulership at Cahal Pech, Belize. *Mexicon* 38(6):157–165.

Becker, Marshall J.

1979 Priests, Peasants, and Ceremonial Centers: The Intellectual History of a Model. In *Maya Archaeology and Ethnology*, edited by Norman Hammond and Gordon R. Willey, pp. 3–20. University of Texas Press, Austin.

Blake, Michael, and John E. Clark

1999 The Emergence of Hereditary Inequality: The Case of Pacific Coastal Chiapas, Mexico. In *Pacific Latin America in Prehistory*, edited by Michael Blake, pp. 55–73. Washington State University Press, Pullman.

Boot, Erik

2017 The Chan Tuun Itzam: Epigraphic and Iconographic Observations on a Classic Maya Collective Theonym. *The PARI Journal* 17(3):9–20.

Brady, James E.

1995 A Reassessment of the Chronology and Function of Gordon's Cave #3, Copan, Honduras. *Ancient Mesoamerica* 6(1):29–38.

Brown, M. Kathryn

2003 Emerging Complexity in the Maya Lowlands: A View from Blackman Eddy, Belize. PhD dissertation, Southern Methodist University, Dallas.

2017 E-Groups and Ancestors: The Sunrise of Complexity at Xunantunich, Belize. In

Maya E Groups: Calendars, Astronomy, and Urbanism in the Early Lowlands, edited by David A. Freidel, Arlen F. Chase, Anna Dowd, and Jerry F. Murdock, pp. 386–411. University Press of Florida, Gainesville.

Brown, M. Kathryn, Jaime J. Awe, and James F. Garber

2018 The Role of Ideology, Religion, and Ritual in the Foundation of Social Complexity in the Belize River Valley. In *Pathways to Complexity: A View from the Maya Lowlands,* edited by M. Kathryn Brown and George Bey, pp. 87–116. University of Florida Press, Gainesville.

Brown, M. Kathryn, and George J. Bey III (editors)

2018 Conclusion: Charting the Pathways to Complexity in the Maya Lowlands. In *Pathways to Complexity: A View from the Maya Lowlands,* edited by M. Kathryn Brown and George J. Bey III, pp. 387–414. University of Florida Press, Gainesville.

Brown, M. Kathryn, and James F. Garber

2008 Establishing and Re-using Sacred Space: A Diachronic Perspective from Blackman Eddy, Belize. In *Ruins of the Past: The Use and Perception of Abandoned Structures in the Maya Lowlands,* edited by Travis W. Stanton and Aline Magnoni, pp. 147–170. University Press of Colorado, Boulder.

Chase, Arlen F., M. Charlotte Arnauld, Diane Z. Chase, Philippe Nondédéo, and Tsubasa Okoshi

2021 The Rupture of Classic Maya Divine Kingship from the Perspective of Postclassic Archaeology, Iconography, and Ethnohistory. In *Maya Kingship: Rupture and Transformation from Classic to Postclassic Times,* edited by Tsubaka Okoshi, Arlen F. Chase, Phillippe Nondédéo, and M. Charlotte Arnauld, pp. 291–310. University Press of Florida, Gainesville.

Chase, Arlen F., and Diane Z. Chase

2021 The Transformation of Maya Rulership at Caracol, Belize. In *Maya Kingship: Rupture and Transformation from Classic to Postclassic Times,* edited by Tsubaka Okoshi, Arlen F. Chase, Phillippe Nondédéo, and M. Charlotte Arnauld, pp. 224–245. University Press of Florida, Gainesville.

Chase, Diane Z., and Arlen F. Chase

1996 Maya Multiples: Individuals, Entries, and Tombs in Structure A34 of Caracol, Belize. *Latin American Antiquity* 7(1):61–79.

Clark, John E., and Michael Blake

1994 The Power of Prestige: Competitive Generosity and the Emergence of Rank Society in Lowland Mesoamerica. In *Factional Competition and Political Development in the New World,* edited by Elizabeth M. Brumfiel and John W. Fox, pp. 17–30. Cambridge University Press, Cambridge.

Coe, Michael D., Javier Urcid, and Rex Koontz

2015 *Mexico: From the Olmecs to the Aztecs.* 8th ed. Thames and Hudson, London.

Colas, Pierre Robert

2014 Personal Names: The Creation of Social Status among the Classic Maya. In *A Celebration of the Life and Work of Pierre Robert Colas,* edited by Christophe Helmke and Frauke Sachse, pp. 19–59. Anton Saurwein, Munich.

Colas, Pierre Robert, Christophe Helmke, Jaime J. Awe, and Terry G. Powis

2002 Epigraphic and Ceramic Analyses of Two Early Classic Maya Vessels from Baking Pot, Belize. *Mexicon* 24(2):33–39.

DeLance, Lisa L.

2016 Enchaining Kinship: Figurines and State Formation at Cahal Pech, Cayo, Belize. PhD dissertation, University of California, Riverside.

DeLance, Lisa L., and Jaime J. Awe

2021 The Complexity of Figurines: Ancestor Veneration at Cahal Pech, Cayo, Belize. In *Framing Complexity: Vantages from Formative Mesoamerica,* edited by Lisa L. DeLance and Garry M. Feinman, pp. 291–323. University of Colorado Press, Louisville; and Utah State University Press, Salt Lake City.

Digby, Adrian

1964 *Maya Jades.* British Museum, London.

Douglas, John, Brandi L. MacDonald, Claire E. Ebert, Jaime J. Awe, Laure Dussubieux, and Catherine E. Klesner
    2021   Fade to Black: The Implications of Mount Maloney Black Pottery from a Terminal Classic Deposit, Cahal Pech, Belize, Using a Comparative Multi-Method Compositional Approach. *Journal of Archaeological Science: Reports* 35, https://doi.org/10.1016/j.jasrep.2020.102666.

Ebert, Claire E.
    2017   Preclassic Maya Social Complexity and Origins of Inequality at Cahal Pech, Belize. PhD dissertation, Pennsylvania State University, University Park.

Ebert, Claire E., and Jaime J. Awe
    2020   Who Were the Early Preclassic Maya? Reassessing Key Questions about the Origins of Village Life in the Belize River Valley. *Research Reports in Belizean Archaeology* 17:273–286.

Ebert, Claire E, Julie A. Hoggarth, J. A., Jaime J. Awe, Brendan J. Culleton, and Douglas J. Kennett
    2019   The Role of Diet in Resilience and Vulnerability to Climate Change among Early Agricultural Communities in the Maya Lowlands. *Current Anthropology* 64(4):580–601.

Ebert, Claire E., James McGee, and Jaime J. Awe
    2021   Early Monumentality in the Belize River Valley: Excavations of a Preclassic E-Group at Cahal Pech, Belize. *Latin American Antiquity* 32(1):209–217.

Ebert, Claire E., Keith M. Prufer, Martha J. Macri, Bruce Winterhalder, and Douglas J. Kennett
    2014   Terminal Long Count Dates and the Disintegration of Classic Period Maya Polities. *Ancient Mesoamerica* 25:337–356.

Estrada Belli, Francisco
    2006   Lightning Sky, Rain, and the Maize God: The Ideology of Preclassic Maya Rulers at Cival, Peten, Guatemala. *Ancient Mesoamerica* 17(1):57–78.
    2011   *The First Maya Civilization: Ritual and Power before the Classic Period.* Routledge, London.

Fields, Virginia M., and Dorie Reents-Budet (editors)
    2005   *Lords of Creation: The Origins of Sacred Maya Kingship.* Los Angeles County Museum of Art, Los Angeles.

Flannery, Kent V., and Joyce Marcus (editors)
    1983   *The Cloud People: Divergent Evolution of the Zapotec and Mixtec Civilizations.* Academic Press, New York.

Freidel, David A., and Linda Schele
    1988   Kingship in the Late Preclassic Maya Lowlands: The Instruments and Places of Ritual Power. *American Anthropologist* 90(3):547–567.

Garber, James F.
    1992   A Baktun 8 Carved Stela from the Lowland Maya Site of Blackman Eddy, Belize. Paper presented at the 57th Annual Meeting of the Society for American Archaeology, Pittsburgh.

Garber, James F., and Jaime J. Awe
    2009   A Terminal Early Formative Symbol System in the Maya Lowlands: The Iconography of the Cunil Phase (110–900 BC) at Cahal Pech. *Research Reports in Belizean Archaeology* 6:151–159.

Garber, James F., M. Kathryn Brown, W. David Driver, David M. Glassman, Christopher J. Hartman, F. Kent Reilly III, and Lauren A. Sullivan
    2004   Archaeological Investigations at Blackman Eddy. In *The Ancient Maya of the Belize Valley: Half a Century of Archaeological Research*, edited by James F. Garber, pp. 48–69. University Press of Florida, Gainesville.

Giesey, Ralph E.
    1987   *Cérémonial et puissance souveraine: France, XVe–XVIIIe siècles.* Armand Colin, Paris.

Graeber, David
    2017   Notes on the Politics of Divine Kingship. In *On Kings*, edited by David Graeber and Marshall Sahlins, pp. 377–464. Hau Books, Chicago.

Graeber, David, and Marshall Sahlins
    2017   *On Kings.* Hau Books, Chicago.

Grube, Nikolai, and Linda Schele
    1994   Tikal Altar 5. *Texas Notes on Precolumbian Art, Writing, and Culture* 66:1–6.

Guernsey, Julia
    2010   Rulers, Gods, and Potbellies: A Consideration of Sculptural Forms and Themes from the Preclassic Pacific Coast and Piedmont of Mesoamerica. In *The

Place of Stone Monuments: Context, Use, and Meaning in Mesoamerica's Preclassic Transition, edited by Julia Guernsey, John E. Clark, and Barbara Arroyo, pp. 207–230. Dumbarton Oaks Research Library and Collection, Washington, D.C.

Guernsey, Julia, and Michael Love
- 2005   Late Preclassic Expressions of Authority on the Pacific Slope. In *Lords of Creation: The Origins of Sacred Maya Kingship*, edited by Virginia M. Fields and Dorie Reents-Budet, pp. 37–43. Los Angeles County Museum of Art, Los Angeles.

Halperin, Christina T.
- 2002   Caves, Ritual, and Power: Investigations at Actun Nak Beh, Cayo District, Belize. Master's thesis, Florida State University, Tallahassee.
- 2005   Social Power and Sacred Space at Actun Nak Beh. In *Stone Houses and Earth Lords: Maya Religion in the Cave Context*, edited by Keith M. Prufer and James E. Brady, pp. 71–90. University Press of Colorado, Boulder.

Hammond, Norman
- 1999   The Genesis of Hierarchy: Mortuary and Offertory Ritual in the Pre-Classic at Cuello, Belize. In *Social Patterns in Pre-Classic Mesoamerica*, edited by David C. Grove and Rosemary A. Joyce, pp. 49–66. Dumbarton Oaks Research Library and Collection, Washington, D.C.

Hansen, Richard
- 1991   *An Early Maya Text from El Mirador, Guatemala. Research Reports on Early Maya Writing* 37:19–32. Center for Maya Research, Washington, D.C.
- 2012   Kingship in the Cradle of Maya Civilization: The Mirador Basin. In *Fanning the Sacred Flame: Mesoamerican Studies in Honor of H. B. Nicholson*, edited by Matthew A. Boxt and Brian D. Dillon, pp. 139–172. University of Colorado Press, Boulder.

Healy, Paul F.
- 1974   The Cuyamel Caves: Preclassic Sites in Northeast Honduras. *American Antiquity* 39(3):435–447.
- 1990   Excavations at Pacbitun, Belize: Preliminary Report on the 1986 and 1987 Investigations. *Journal of Field Archaeology* 17(3):247–262.

Healy, Paul F., Jaime J. Awe, and Herman Helmuth
- 1998   Excavations at Caledonia (Cayo), Belize: An Ancient Maya Multiple Burial. *Journal of Field Archaeology* 25(3):261–274.

Helmke, Christophe
- 2012   Mythological Emblem Glyphs of Ancient Maya Kings. *Contributions in New World Archaeology* 3:91–126.
- 2019   Reading between the Lines: The Epigraphy of Central Belize. *Research Reports in Belizean Archaeology* 16:31–46.

Helmke, Christophe, and Jaime J. Awe
- 2008   Organización territorial de los antiguos mayas de Belice central: Confluencia de datos arqueológicos y epigráficos. *Mayab* 20:65–91.
- 2012   Ancient Maya Territorial Organization of Central Belize: Confluence of Archaeological and Epigraphic Data. *Contributions in New World Archaeology* 4:59–90.
- 2016a   Death Becomes Her: An Analysis of Panel 3, Xunantunich. *The PARI Journal* 16(4):1–14.
- 2016b   Sharper than a Serpent's Tooth: A Tale of the Snake-Head Dynasty as Recounted on Xunantunich Panel 4. *The PARI Journal* 17(2):1–22.

Helmke, Christophe, Jaime J. Awe, and Nikolai Grube
- 2010   The Carved Monuments and Inscriptions of Xunantunich. In *Classic Maya Provincial Politics: Xunantunich and Its Hinterlands*, edited by Lisa J. LeCount and Jason Yaeger, pp. 97–121. University of Arizona Press, Tucson.

Helmke, Christophe, Jaime J. Awe, Shawn G. Morton, and Gyles Iannone
- 2015   The Text and Context of the Cuychen Vase, Macal Valley, Belize. In *Maya Archaeology*, vol. 3, edited by Charles Golden, Stephen D. Houston, and Joel Skidmore, pp. 8–29. Precolumbian Mesoweb Press, San Francisco.

2019 Archaeological Investigations at Cuychen, Macal Valley, Belize. In *The Realm Below: Speleoarchaeological Investigations in the Macal River Valley, Belize*, edited by Christophe Helmke, pp. 74–121. Precolumbia Mesoweb Press, San Francisco.

Helmke, Christophe, Dmitri Beliaev, and Sergei Vepretskii

2020 The Litany of Runaway Kings: Another Look at Stela 12 of Naranjo, Guatemala. *The PARI Journal*, 21(2):1–28.

Helmke, Christophe, Julie A. Hoggarth, and Jaime J. Awe

2018 *A Reading of the Komkom Vase Discovered at Baking Pot, Belize*. Precolumbian Mesoweb Press, San Francisco.

2021 Deciphering the Collapse: An Account of Kingship in the Terminal Classic. In *Maya Kingship: Rupture and Transformation from Classic to Postclassic Times*, edited by Tsubaka Okoshi, Arlen F. Chase, Phillippe Nondédéo, and M. Charlotte Arnauld, pp. 106–130. University Press of Florida, Gainesville.

Hoggarth, Julie A., Brendan J. Culleton, Jaime J. Awe, and Douglas J. Kennett

2014 Questioning Postclassic Continuity at Baking Pot, Belize Using Direct AMC 14C Dating of Human Burials. *Radiocarbon* 56(3):1057–1075.

Houston, Stephen D., and Takeshi Inomata

2009 *The Classic Maya*. Cambridge University Press, Cambridge.

Houston, Stephen D., and David Stuart

1996 Of Gods, Glyphs and Kings: Divinity and Rulership among the Classic Maya. *Antiquity* 70:289–312.

Houston, Stephen D., and Karl A. Taube

2011 The Fiery Pool: Water and Sea among the Classic Maya. In *Ecology, Power and Religion in Maya Landscapes*, edited by Christian Isendahl and Bodil Liljefors Persson, pp. 17–38. A. Saurwein, Markt Schwaben.

Inomata, Takeshi

2016 Theories of Power and Legitimacy in Archaeological Contexts: The Emergent Regime of Power at the Formative Maya Community of Ceibal, Guatemala. In *Political Strategies in Pre-Columbian Mesoamerica*, edited by Sarah Kurnick and Joanne Baron, pp. 37–60. University Press of Colorado, Boulder.

Inomata, Takeshi, Daniela Triadan, Kazuo Aoyama, Victor Castillo, and Hitoshi Yonenobu

2013 Early Ceremonial Constructions at Ceibal, Guatemala and the Origins of Lowland Maya Civilization. *Science* 340:467–471.

Justeson, John S., and Peter Mathews

1990 Evolutionary Trends in Mesoamerican Hieroglyphic Writing. *Visible Language* 24(1):89–132.

Keller, Angela H.

2012 Creating Community with Shell. In *Chan: Ancient Maya Farming Community*, edited by Cynthia Robin, pp. 253–270. University Press of Florida, Gainesville.

LeCount, Lisa, David W. Mixter, and Borislava S. Simova

2017 Preliminary Thoughts on Radiocarbon Data from Actuncan's 2015 E-Group Excavations. In *The Actuncan Archaeological Project Report of the 2016 Field Season*, edited by Lisa LeCount and David W. Mixter, pp. 21–42. Report submitted to the Belize Institute of Archaeology, Belmopan.

LeCount, Lisa J., and Jason Yaeger (editors)

2010 *Classic Maya Provincial Politics: Xunantunich and Its Hinterlands*. University of Arizona Press, Tucson.

Lohse, Jon C., Jaime J. Awe, Cameron Griffith, Robert M. Rosenswig, and Fred Valdez Jr.

2006 Preceramic Occupations in Belize: Updating the Paleoindian and Archaic Record. *Latin American Antiquity* 17(2):209–226.

Marcus, Joyce

1998 *Women's Ritual in Formative Oaxaca: Figurine-Making, Divination, Death and the Ancestors*. Memoirs of the Museum of Anthropology 33. University of Michigan, Ann Arbor.

1999 Men's and Women's Ritual in Formative Oaxaca. In *Social Patterns in Pre-Classic Mesoamerica*, edited by David C. Grove and Rosemary A. Joyce, pp. 67–96.

Dumbarton Oaks Research Library and Collection, Washington, D.C.

2009 Rethinking Figurines. In *Mesoamerican Figurines: Small-Scale Indices of Large-Scale Social Phenomena*, edited by Christina T. Halperin, Katherine A. Faust, Rhonda Taube, and Aurore Giguet, pp. 25–50. University Press of Florida, Gainesville.

Martin, Simon

2003 In Line of the Founder: A View of Dynastic Politics at Tikal. In *Tikal: Dynasties, Foreigners, and Affairs of State*, edited by Jeremy A. Sabloff, pp. 3–46. School of American Research Press, Santa Fe.

2015 The Old Man of the Maya Universe: A Unitary Dimension to Ancient Maya Religion. In *Maya Archaeology*, vol. 3, edited by Charles Golden, Stephen D. Houston, and Joel Skidmore, pp. 186–227. Precolumbian Mesoweb Press, San Francisco.

2020 *Ancient Maya Politics: A Political Anthropology of the Classic Period, 150–900 CE*. Cambridge University Press, Cambridge.

Martin, Simon, and Nikolai Grube

2008 *Chronicle of the Maya Kings and Queens: Deciphering the Dynasties of the Ancient Maya*. 2nd ed. Thames and Hudson, London.

McAnany, Patricia A.

1995 *Living with the Ancestors: Kinship and Kingship in Ancient Maya Society*. University of Texas Press, Austin.

Miller, Mary Ellen, and Simon Martin

2004 *Courtly Art of the Ancient Maya*. Fine Arts Museum of San Francisco, San Francisco.

Mitchell, Patricia T.

2006 The Royal Burials of Buenavista del Cayo and Cahal Pech: Same Lineage, Different Palaces? Master's thesis, San Diego State University, San Diego.

Mixter, David

2016 Surviving Collapse: Collective Memory and Political Reorganization at Actuncan, Belize. PhD dissertation, Washington University, St. Louis.

Moyes, Holley

2006 The Sacred Landscape as a Political Resource: A Case Study of Ancient Maya Cave Use at Chechem Ha Cave, Belize, Central America. PhD dissertation, State University of New York, Buffalo.

Moyes, Holley, Laura Kosakowsky, Erin E. Ray, and Jaime J. Awe

2017 The Chronology of Ancient Maya Cave Use in Belize. *Research Reports in Belizean Archaeology* 14:327–338.

Novotny, Claire C.

2012 The Chan Community: A Bioarchaeological Perspective. In *Chan: Ancient Maya Farming Community*, edited by Cynthia Robin, pp. 231–252. University Press of Florida, Gainesville.

Novotny, Claire C., Jaime J. Awe, Catharina Santasilia, and Kelly J. Knudson

2018 Ritual Emulation of Ancient Maya Elite Mortuary Traditions during the Classic Period at Cahal Pech, Belize. *Latin American Antiquity* 29(4):641–659.

Okoshi, Tsubasa, Arlen F. Chase, Philippe Nondédéo, and M. Charlotte Arnauld (editors)

2021 *Maya Kingship: Rupture and Transformation from Classic to Postclassic Times*. University Press of Florida, Gainesville.

Peniche May, Nancy

2016 Building Power: Political Dynamics in Cahal Pech, Belize during the Middle Preclassic. PhD dissertation, University of California, San Diego.

Peniche May, Nancy, Lisa DeLance, and Jaime J. Awe

2018 The Middle Preclassic Figurines from Cahal Pech, Belize. *Ancient Mesoamerica* 30:221–234.

Pereira, Karen

2009 Plain but Not Simple: Middle Preclassic Stone Monuments of Naranjo, Guatemala. Master's thesis, University of Florida, Gainesville.

Porter, Mark L. B.

2020 Caching Aggrandizers: Ritual Caching Practices, Competitive Generosity, and the Rise of Inequality in the Preclassic Maya Lowlands. Master's thesis, Northern Arizona University, Flagstaff.

Powis, Terry G., Fred Valdez Jr., Thomas R. Hester, W. Jeffrey Hurst, and Stan M. Tarka Jr.
- 2002 Spouted Vessels and Cacao Use among the Preclassic Maya. *Latin American Antiquity* 13(1):85–106.

Prager, Christian M., and Geoffrey E. Braswell
- 2016 Maya Politics and Ritual: An Important New Hieroglyphic Text on a Carved Jade from Belize. *Ancient Mesoamerica* 27(2):267–278.

Rands, Robert L., and Barbara C. Rands
- 1965 Pottery Figurines of the Maya Lowlands. In *Archaeology of Southern Mesoamerica, Part 1*, edited by Gordon R. Willey, pp. 535–561. Vol. 2 of *Handbook of Middle American Indians*, edited by Robert Wauchope. University of Texas Press, Austin.

Rice, Prudence M.
- 2008 Time, Power, and the Maya. *Latin American Antiquity* 19(3):275–298.

Ringle, William, Tomás Gallareta Negrón, and George Bey III
- 2021 Stranger-Kings in Northern Yucatan. In *Maya Kingship: Rupture and Transformation from Classic to Postclassic Times*, edited by Tsubaka Okoshi, Arlen F. Chase, Phillippe Nondédéo, and M. Charlotte Arnauld, pp. 249–268. University Press of Florida, Gainesville.

Robin, Cynthia (editor)
- 2012 *Chan: Ancient Maya Farming Community*. University Press of Florida, Gainesville.

Robin, Cynthia, James Mierhoff, Caleb Kestle, Chelsea Blackmore, Laura J. Kosakowsky, and Anna C. Novotny
- 2012 Ritual in a Farming Community. In *Chan: Ancient Maya Farming Community*, edited by Cynthia Robin, pp. 113–132. University Press of Florida, Gainesville.

Saturno, William
- 2005 Centering the Kingdom, Centering the King: Maya Creation and Legitimization at San Bartolo. In *The Art of Urbanism: How Mesoamerican Kingdoms Represented Themselves in Architecture and Imagery*, edited by William L. Fash and Leonardo López Luján, pp. 110–134. Dumbarton Oaks Research Library and Collection, Washington, D.C.

Saturno, William A., Franco D. Rossi, and Boris Beltran
- 2018 Changing Stages: Royal Legitimacy and the Architectural Development of the Pinturas Complex at San Bartolo, Guatemala. In *Pathways to Complexity: A View from the Maya Lowlands*, edited by M. Kathryn Brown and George J. Bey III, pp. 315–335. University Press of Florida, Gainesville.

Saturno, William A., David Stuart, and Boris Beltran
- 2006 Early Maya Writing at San Bartolo, Guatemala. *Science* 311(5765):1281–1283.

Saturno, William A., Karl A. Taube, and David Stuart
- 2005 *The Murals of San Bartolo, El Peten, Guatemala, pt. 1, The North Wall*. Center for Ancient American Studies, Barnardsville, N.C.

Schele, Linda, and Mary Miller
- 1986 *The Blood of Kings: Dynasty and Ritual in Maya Art*. George Braziller, New York.

Sharer, Robert J., and Loa P. Traxler
- 2006 *The Ancient Maya*. 6th ed. Stanford University Press, Stanford.

Skaggs, Sheldon, Christophe Helmke, Jon Spenard, Paul F. Healy, and Terry G. Powis
- 2017 Some Observations and New Discoveries Related to Altar 3, Pacbitun, Belize. *Mexicon* 39(5):115–123.

Stemp, W. James, and Jaime J. Awe
- 2020 Point Counter Point: Interpreting Chipped Chert Bifaces in Terminal Classic "Problematic Deposits" from Structures A2 and A3 at Cahal Pech, Belize. *Ancient Mesoamerica* 31(1):161–174.

Stuart, David
- 1996 Kings of Stone: A Consideration of Ancient Stelae in Maya Ritual and Representation. *RES: Anthropology and Aesthetics* 29–30:148–171.
- 2005 Ideology and Classic Maya Kingship. In *A Catalyst for Ideas: Anthropological Archaeology and the Legacy of Douglas Schwartz*, edited by Vernon L. Scarborough, pp. 257–286. School of American Research Press, Santa Fe.

Stuart, David, and Stephen D. Houston
- 1994 *Classic Maya Place Names*. Dumbarton Oaks Research Library and Collection, Washington, D.C.

Taube, Karl A.
- 2000 Lightning Celts and Corn Fetishes: The Formative Olmec and the Development of Maize Symbolism in Mesoamerica and the American Southwest. In *Olmec Art and Archaeology in Mesoamerica*, edited by John E. Clark and Mary E. Pye, pp. 297–337. National Gallery of Art, Washington, D.C.
- 2005 The Symbolism of Jade in Classic Maya Religion. *Ancient Mesoamerica* 16(1):23–50.

Thompson, J. Eric S.
- 1927 *The Civilization of the Mayas*. Field Museum of Natural History, Chicago.

Urquizú, Mónica, and Heather Hurst
- 2011 The Murals of San Bartolo: A Window into the Art and Cosmovision of Precolumbian Man. *The PARI Journal* 12(2):8–13.

Wright, Mark A.
- 2011 A Study of Classic Maya Rulership. PhD dissertation, University of California, Riverside.

Yaeger, Jason, and M. Kathryn Brown
- 2019 Political Landscapes of the Upper Belize River Valley. *Research Reports in Belizean Archaeology* 16:21–30.

Yaeger, Jason, M. Kathryn Brown, Christophe Helmke, Marc Zender, Bernadette Cap, Christie Kokel Rodriguez, and Sylvia Batty
- 2015 Two Early Classic Elite Burials from Buenavista del Cayo, Belize. *Research Reports in Belizean Archaeology* 12:181–191.

Żrałka, Jarosław, Christophe Helmke, Simon Martin, Wiesław Koszkul, and Juan Luis Velásquez
- 2018 The Monolithic Monuments of Nakum, Guatemala. *The PARI Journal* 19(1):1–28.

11

Jaina Figurines

Contexts and Social Linkages on the Western Side of the Maya World

ANTONIO BENAVIDES C.

Archaeologically excavated figurines from Jaina total around 580 items. This figure doesn't consider those objects allegedly from the island, but only those with an archaeological provenience on the island. In addition to the large corpus of Jaina reproductions, archaeological figurines similar or practically identical to those from Jaina have been reported from settlements in central Veracruz and on the coasts of Tabasco, Campeche, and Yucatán. Jaina figurines encompass significant variation, not only in the manufacturing processes (molded and handmade) used for their construction but also in the dimensions, decoration, sex, and other kinds of representation of the figurines. These small objects reveal how the ancient inhabitants considered themselves and how they were seen by other ethnic groups. Their clothing and ornaments speak to their rank and activities. Most figurines represent adults who embody Maya ideals of beauty (with some significant deviations). Stratigraphic evidence indicates that the island of Jaina was humanly built, and several field seasons have yielded valuable data about the depositional contexts of Jaina figurines. Significantly, paste analyses of figurines through neutron activation reveal different sources for the raw materials used to craft the figurines.

Jaina is located forty kilometers north of Campeche city, on the western limit of the Hecelchakán municipality, in the Petenes Biosphere Reserve. The island is just seventy meters from the coast; it is not a big settlement, as it occupies less than one square kilometer (a little more than forty hectares), but the cultural heritage it contains tells us a lot about the Maya that lived there and in the vicinity of Jaina (Barba Meinecke 2003; Benavides 2007, 2010, 2012a; Fernández 1946; Moedano Koer 1946; Piña Chan 1948, 1968, 1996).

The central part of the Campeche state—the coast between Isla Aguada and the city of Campeche—is distinguished by the alternation of rocky shores, sandy beaches, and mangrove-covered sections. Archaeological surveys on the Campeche coast have reported many pre-Hispanic settlements, some of them dating back to the Preclassic

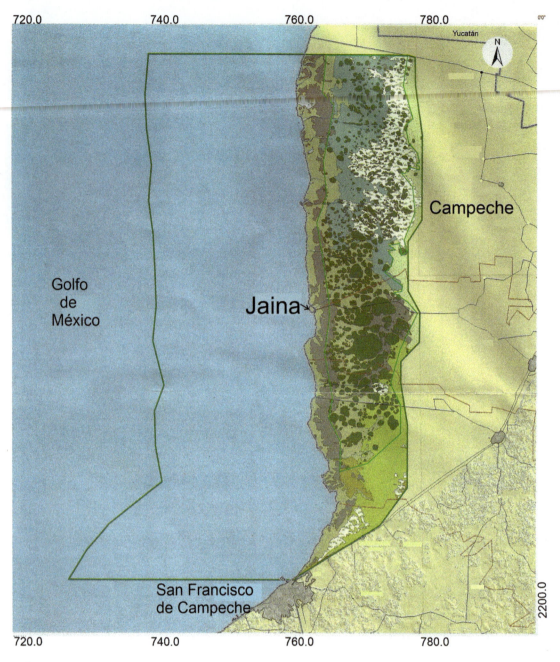

figure 11.1
Vegetation map, showing Jaina and its surrounding vegetation. Map by the Comisión Nacional de Áreas Naturales Protegidas (CONANP 2006).

period, such as Tixchel, Ulumal, Playa Esmeralda, Champoton, Niop, Chuncan, and Villa Madero (Benavides 2017; Eaton and Ball 1978). By contrast, from Campeche city to Celestún, there only existed a little more than one hundred kilometers of coast covered by mangrove during the Formative period.

Navigation along the southern Campeche shore was relatively easy. For instance, the journey around Carmen Island and north to Champoton was facilitated by the existence of several places to stop, replenish food and water, rest, and repair boats. But once in Campeche, journeys to the north

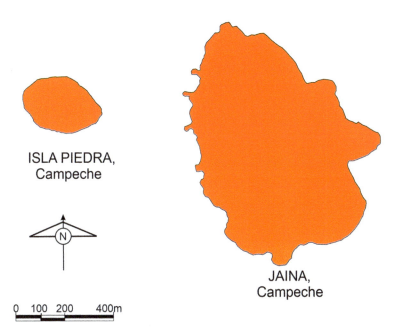

figure 11.2
Four examples of islands built by the ancient Maya. Drawing by Antonio Benavides C.

required intermediary points to rest and repair equipment. Crossing the mangrove forest that blankets the coast is an arduous task. Today, men need to open a trail several kilometers long (an average of twelve kilometers) before arriving on firm limestone soil (Figure 11.1). The Pre-Columbian solution was to build islands in the shallow offshore zone. In an environment of thick mangrove forests, Maya inventiveness utilized the narrow passages formed by the *petenes* (sweet water)[1] flowing to the sea. Farther on, they arrived at somewhat higher sectors where they could quarry *sascab*.[2] That material was hauled on thousands of canoe and cayuco trips, so that new shore spaces could be shaped (Benavides 2012a).

During the first centuries of the Common Era, the Maya created several artificial islands where they could alight on firm ground and perform daily activities. Today, those places are known as El Cuyo, Yukumbalan, Jaina, Nisyuc, Isla Piedras, Chisahscab, Yalton, Nunchukum, and Isla Uaymil (Andrews 1977, 1978a, 1978b) (Figure 11.2). But colonial times erased the memory of those efforts, and for this reason most of the current northern Campeche communities are far from the sea, located on limestone lands. Some of these locations are Kobén, Hampolol, Tenabo, Sodzil, Chunkanán, and Tankuché, among others (CONANP 2006). Commerce likely played a large role in stimulating the arduous task of creating near shore settlements, which provided useful and necessary places to stop after several hours of paddling. Northern Campeche coastal islands were like bridges helping to connect the northern and southern regions.

Jaina Figurines

An Island Built with *Sascab*

We have calculated the *sascab* contents of the less than half a square kilometer island. We considered its basic fill, as well as the fill of its monumental architectonic groups, several structures within the groups, and twenty platforms that once supported domestic units. We arrived at a figure of more than nine hundred thousand cubic meters. All the stratigraphic pits excavated at Jaina contain several levels of *sascab* fill. Different from the inland buildings, Jaina structures contain few rocks; they were basically built with *sascab* and finished with carved stones (Benavides 2014) (Figure 11.3).[3]

That quantity of *sascab* can be compared with other monumental constructions made of stone, such as the Governor's Platform at Uxmal, Coba's Great Platform, Edzna's Big Acropolis, and the Kinich Kak Moo structure at Izamal. Continuing this extrapolation, we can estimate that Jaina was built in about fifty years with the daily work of 570 persons, each working five effective hours per day. That likely happened between 400 and 600 CE. Moving *sascab* was a hard task, considering that laborers had to quarry the fill from high land about twelve kilometers from Jaina, then move it in canoes and place it where needed (to create more space or to build a platform or structure). Laborers covered the structure with cut stone, once again extracting, shaping, and transporting heavy rock before stuccoing and painting it.

The Settlement

The earliest human evidence registered at Jaina is from the Late Preclassic period (ca. 400 BCE–250 CE), in the form of ceramic fragments and Panel 3, which was found in 1999 reused as part of the east stairway of Structure 1. Panel 3 depicts a 5 Imix date in an early style only reported (until now) at Izapa and Kaminaljuyu (Benavides and

figure 11.3
Sascab fill of Jaina Structure 4. Photograph by Antonio Benavides C.

figure 11.4
Panel 3 with the 5 Imix date.
Photograph by Antonio Benavides C.

Grube 2002) (Figure 11.4). Similar items must have existed, but unfortunately destructive looting over many decades has destroyed the evidence. During the Early Classic period, there is continued evidence of occupation, as attested by ceramic fragments and evidence of building activity. Structure 4, for instance, exhibits rounded corners, rough building blocks, and a Peten molding on its first and second terraces. A radiocarbon estimate for this construction is 550 CE (Figure 11.5).[4] The apogee of construction and occupation at Jaina Island occurred during the Late Classic period (600–900 CE), when the island became one of the most relevant sites along the western coast of the peninsula, in parallel with the climax of the Puuc cities. The island had its own emblem glyph, containing the sign *caan* or sky (Figure 11.6). Stela 1 has been dated to 652 CE, and four radiocarbon dates correspond to the years 610, 645, 650, and 660 CE. (Two other stelae are known but have no calendrical dates.)

The eighth century at Jaina is attested by epigraphic references to several rulers discussed later in this chapter. The Terminal Classic period on the island has been dated between 800 and 1000 CE and for that time we have an 870 CE ^{14}C date. The Terminal Classic was a time of intense exchange with several Mesoamerican regions. During the Postclassic period, Jaina continued to be inhabited, as ceramic findings confirm. Some structures were modified; for example, the platforms defining the ballcourt were remodeled to create spaces for perishable structures. The island must have been abandoned before the European arrival, as there is no reference to it in the sixteenth-century chronicles.

figure 11.5
Structure 4, western view. Photograph by Antonio Benavides C.

figure 11.6
Jaina emblem glyph. Drawing by
Antonio Benavides C.

Over the next several centuries, Jaina was used only as a coastal reference point, notable for its jungle-covered big mounds. The British pirate William Dampier (1652–1715) visited Jaina in 1675, reporting on several mounds and writing that the place was eventually used by sea robbers (Dampier 1906).

The Calkini Codex (or Calkini Chronicle) is a copy of a sixteenth-century text written in Yucatec Mayan and relating to the western territories of the Yucatán Peninsula. It contains an indirect reference to Jaina. Historian José Tsubasa Okoshi Harada (2009) prepared an independent translation of the text that corroborates Miguel García Campillo's (1998) translation of several toponyms. Interestingly, both specialists refer to Pachcaan and Hinal in the Canul sea.

Pachcaan can be translated as "at the back of Caan/Sky," and today we know that Hinal corresponds to Jaina. The principal sign of the Jaina emblem glyph is that of sky. Hina/Hinal can be translated as "that was the house," a Postclassic name possibly alluding to the stone buildings of the island that were visible to those navigating near the shores of Jaina.

During the second part of the nineteenth century and in the first decades of the twentieth century, Jaina was heavily looted, especially by looters searching for figurines to satisfy the demand by the international black market. Many pieces found their way to collections, but also to different auction houses, galleries, and museums (Benavides 2012a; Miller 1975; O'Neal 2012; Sellen 2016). As a result, the island bears many scars in the form of irregular big and little holes. Due to the fine quality of many figurines, the island acquired fame—we can surmise that is the origin of the "Jaina style," an erroneous concept (more on this later), but one that rapidly spread.

The Society

How was it possible to organize a community to build a place where there was nothing but mangrove swamp? Undoubtedly, there was a form of rulership conjoining the efforts of several specialists in order to create a habitable place. Rulers may have appealed to the inventiveness of one or several leaders associated with special or supernatural forces. Dominion of a ruling family could have influenced a great number of individuals, enough to achieve impressive results. Association with divine entities must have played an important role, taking advantage of a shared cosmovision to project a common goal.

Rulers and their followers could not control natural forces (i.e., storms, vegetal growth, wind, and diurnal patterns), but they could modify their environment according to ideas of their leaders to shape an adequate order for the life of human beings. And that is what they achieved with the continuous work of several population groups. We do not know the identities of the first leaders to organize the society in order to build an island over an especially sacred space. Jaina was created out of the liminal space between the earth and the sea, between the places inhabited by divine beings dominating the wild habitat and those living in the underworld waters. But we recognize the presence, through the eighth century, of the Jol or Kimi family (skull/death), precisely Och Kimi, according to epigraphic information coming from Jaina, Cansacbe, and other contemporary settlements.

The epigraphy of a fluted and incised onyx bowl (PC.B.147) at Dumbarton Oaks provides information about Jaina's relationship with sites like Chichen Itza and Uaymil, but the island's emblem glyph also provides evidence of contacts with Santa Rosa Xtampak, Xcalumkin, Cansacbe, and maybe Belize. The Dumbarton Oaks vessel has been dated to 718 CE and depicts three characters: the ruler Lord Jol (Kimi), his wife (or mother?) Ix Mo', and Yiban, a scribe (Lacadena 2000). More than a decade later, Tokovinine (2012:121–129) suggested a more convincing interpretation—namely, that the vase was owned by Yiban and the other persons were his deceased mother and father (who emerge from centipede mouths, denoting that they belong to the underworld).

But there is also the Cansacbe column depicting the Sak Kimi nominal glyph. Cansacbe is located thirty kilometers southeast of Jaina, along a route that surely was covered with canoes. In 2022, we had the chance to supervise excavation of several mounds at Cansacbe, and despite the looting during the first half of the twentieth century, we found two interesting platforms containing numerous burials, some of them with ceramic materials and figurine fragments identical to those reported at Jaina.

Herbert Spinden (1975:196) published a drawing of a jade figurine with a glyphic inscription on its back that supposedly was held in Teobert Maler's collection. García Campillo (1998:48) read the glyphs as *yuhl, Waxaklahun Uba, Sak Kimi, Ch'ok, u nikil, Och Kimi, K'ul Kaan Ahau, Bakab* and proposed the following translation: "the pendant of Waxaklahun Uba Sak Kimi, young (prince), the son of Och Kimi, sacred lord of Kaan, Bakab."

Jaina's Sak Kimi sacred lord is also mentioned on a pair of jade quadrangular plaques retrieved from Chichen Itza's sacred cenote (Proskouriakoff 1974:pl. 49b) and on a shell pectoral probably found in a Belize settlement (Schele and Miller 1986:226). In this case, the inscription was read by García Campillo (1998:49, fig. 6g) as *yuhl, Sak Kimi, K'ul Kaan Ahau*, "the pendant of Sak Kimi, sacred lord of Kaan."

The shell pectoral displays a baroque design. Besides the lower section of glyphs, the larger upper text repeats the Sak glyph (T58, an adjective

figure 11.7
Figurine of a ruler with the war-serpent motif. Photograph by Antonio Benavides C.

that can indicate "white," "resplendent," or "pure") and the Kimi or Jol glyph (T1040, a noun meaning "skull"). As complements, they included several jaguar spots. Inside the skull's orbit is a cross (*k'an*; T281, an adjective indicating "yellow" or "precious") (Montgomery 2002). Sak Balam later ruled Jaina, as we read *Waxaklahun Uba, 12/13* [*sic*] . . . *Sak Balam K'ul Kaan Ahau* in the inscription of another jade pendant found at Uaymil, located twenty-five kilometers north of Jaina (Proskouriakoff 1974:fig. 13).

On the other hand, but complementary to Jaina's dynastic history, we return to the onyx vase and the mention of Yiban, possibly an *ah kuhuun* associated with the ruling family. The nominal clause of Muyal Chaak Kimi is painted on a vessel known as Grolier 53 in a private collection (Coe 1973:113; García Campillo 1998:51, fig. 9). It includes the *kaan* emblem glyph, which suggests that it refers to Jaina's dynasty.

The emergence and development of a dynasty at Jaina very probably occurred during the Early Classic period, when a leading family organized the necessary labor force to adequately transport thousands of *sascab* shipments to build the island. Stratified social organization and a centralized political system were supported by religion and directed by hereditary leaders (see Wengrow, this volume). Supernatural ideas related to nature, especially where the sea and the earth came together, shaped the ideological privileges of those ruling. The early history of the island is murky, but rulership is clear for Jaina and its surroundings during the eighth century.

The sacred quality of the rulers was legitimated by their association with different deities and with the ancestors, the founders of the society. This notion was basic for the privileged kinship relations (see Awe, Helmke, Ebert, and Hoggarth, this volume). By their sacred ancestry, the royal dynasties were superior, thus separating the aristocratic families from the common people on both political and economic levels.

It seems that several rulers were represented in the famous Jaina figurines. We identify them by the rich clothing they wear, as well as by the long-feather headdresses and accessories, especially the war-serpent motif so frequently associated with Terminal Classic lords (Figure 11.7). All of our examples show them seated, most of them on a throne, on a special bench, or partially inside a small but richly decorated enclosure. Two of them also depict human faces on their upper sections, which may be representations of ancestors.

The war-serpent motif (*Waxaklahun-Ubah-Kan*; 18-His Image-Serpent) is an old symbol known since the development of Teotihuacan (Schele and Freidel 1990; Taube 1992). It arrived at the Maya Lowlands at the end of the fourth century and was sometimes used by Maya elites to secure political dominion. This phenomenon is controversial and has been debated, but it is certain that the images represent war and the impulse to conquer lands and dominate people and resources.

Studying Sherds

An analysis of more than eighty thousand fragments retrieved during several seasons at Jaina has yielded a ceramic typology in which 21.7 percent of the sherds are gray, black, or orange fine wares. Most of the fragments (78.3 percent) are semi-fine and coarse wares; from this last cluster, 58.2 percent correspond to Celestún red ware, which we consider a local ceramic type,[5] while the other 20 percent is formed

figure 11.8
Jonuta woman with hands up. Photograph by Diana Arano R.

by several polychrome, bichrome, and monochrome wares (Ancona Aragón and Jiménez Alvarez 2005; Ancona Aragón, Sauri, and Reyes 2006; Brainerd 1958; Sauri, Jiménez Alvarez, and Benavides 2005). In this context, the complete figurines and their fragments constitute less than 1 percent of the sample. Analysis concentrated on fine pastes (non-carbonate temper), figurines, and polychrome ceramics.

Ronald L. Bishop, of the Smithsonian Institution, obtained 353 samples of ceramic pastes, thirty-nine of them taken from figurines. The samples underwent neutron activation analysis (NAA). The first identified provenance group is that of the Usumacinta Basin, including objects manufactured at Jonuta and carried to Jaina, where they were found in archaeological excavations (Alvarez Asomoza and Casasola 1985; Bishop 2003; Bishop

Jaina Figurines   293

a b

figure 11.9
Two female figurines from Comalcalco. Photographs by Antonio Benavides C.

et al. 2008; Bishop et al. 2006; Bishop, Blackman, and Sears 2006; Bishop, Sears, and Blackman 2005a, 2005b, 2012; Sears 2006) (Figure 11.8).

Molded figurines of women with their hands up were manufactured at Jonuta and exchanged at Jaina and Xcambó (Sierra Sosa 2004). The average distance between Jonuta and Xcambó is 650 kilometers. Among other forms, Jonuta's inventory of figurines includes molded women with their hands up, women praying, rectangular women, and funerary bundles placed on thrones (Gallegos 2009a).

The second ceramic group detected by NAA is called Comalcalco 1. Molded female figurines in a more hieratic pose but also with hands up are found in this group (Figure 11.9). Comalcalco was also an important figurine production center and some examples of its repertoire include musicians and dwarves (Miller 1985), standing or seated women, and figures with their hands up as if they were praying. Gallegos (2009b, 2011) distinguishes five groups of this last character, identifying a young fertility deity and indicating that some figurines were integrated into funerary offerings while others were discarded after being used in religious activities. Some of the figurines recovered at Comalcalco came from southern Veracruz.

The third ceramic group chemically detected by NAA is Comalcalco 3. Jaina figurines in that group include a male and female, both sitting on their legs, wearing necklaces, round earplugs, and complex headdresses (Figure 11.10).

A fourth ceramic group detected by NAA was manufactured many kilometers away from Jaina, somewhere in southern Veracruz. This finding reveals that many figurines looted from Jaina since the middle of the nineteenth century were originally manufactured in southern Veracruz, at least seven hundred kilometers away. Included among this

figure 11.10
Two seated figurines from Comalcalco. Photographs by Antonio Benavides C.

group is the 1886 item reported by Charnay (1978, 2019), some figurines excavated by Piña Chan in his 1947 and 1964 field seasons, and similar objects from the 1996–2005 explorations (Figure 11.11).

A fifth ceramic group identified by NAA is called Miscellaneous, as there is not sufficient chemical information to create a group cluster (Figure 11.12). The topic of Maya figurines becomes more complex when we remember that there existed other places in the Maya region where these objects were manufactured. For example, the northern foothills of the Chiapas Mountain range—the Palenque region— also developed a tradition of ceramic figurines (Benavides 2015; Flores Jiménez 2000, 2002; Rands and Rands 1965; Sharer 1983:381), with both molded and handmade representations.

On the other side of the Yucatán Peninsula, in southern Belize, there existed another Classic-period figurine tradition. Lubaantun researchers have reported representations of ballplayers, men on thrones, litter transportation, hunters, musicians, and women using grinding stones (Butler 1935; Hammond 1982; Joyce 1933).

At the site of Lagartero, around 150 kilometers south of Palenque, near Comitán, researchers Susanna Ekholm (1979) and Sonia Rivero Torres (2002) reported an abundant use of molds, animal figurines (especially dogs), and seated women with profusely decorated garments. Many women wore necklaces, chest ornaments, and bracelets.

The Peten sites also developed their own figurine traditions; in recent years, figurine numbers

figure 11.11
Five figurines from Veracruz retrieved at Jaina. Photographs by Antonio Benavides C.

figure 11.12
Miscellaneous figurines found at Jaina. Photographs by Antonio Benavides C.

have increased as research has continued at sites such as Aguateca (Triadan 2007; Valdés et al., 2001), Altar de Sacrificios (Willey 1972), Calakmul (Bishop, Ruiz Guzmán, and Folan 2000; Ruiz Guzmán 1998; Ruiz Guzmán, Bishop, and Folan 1999), Cancuén (Sears, Bishop, and Blackman 2005), Motul de San José (Halperin 2007, 2014), Nakum, Piedras Negras (Ivic de Monterroso 2002), Tikal (Becker 1973, 1983; Haviland 1965), Toniná (Becquelin and Baudez 1982; Halperin 2014), and Waká (Pérez Robles 2010; Pérez et al. 2015). Copan also had a figurine tradition (Hendon 2003). Since early times, figurine traditions provided an excellent mnemotechnic device that facilitated social memory of diverse actors (both human and supernatural), especially for illiterate members of society (Halperin, this volume).

Exchange Relations and Manufacture

Jaina was not only related to its hinterland but also to other distant regions, and thus we find cinnabar, basalt, obsidian, and jade from the Motagua Basin at the tiny island. Ceramic materials are abundant, and they arrived from nearby producers (Celestún ware) but also from the Grijalva–Usumacinta Basins as well as from central and southern Veracruz. We have also registered materials from the Chenes region (Cui orange polychrome, for example), Edzna, and the Puuc sites (slate wares) (Benavides 2016).

There is a continuity of images along the Veracruz–Campeche corridor, especially tripod dishes (often of fine-paste ceramics) with the representation of a feline or ballgame players. Turtles, owls, turkeys, and other birds are recurrent images but the models for these animals had their origin in central or southern Veracruz. Without a doubt, there was a substantial figurine market meeting the demands of both near and distant communities. Their ritual, ludic, or funerary use meant that figurines constantly had to be replaced, either because of breakage or placement within a burial assemblage. This demand augmented regional integration (see also Hutson, this volume).

A frequent problem with Jaina figurine analysis is the loss of archaeological context and thus the inability to associate the figurines with other artifacts forming the original assemblage. This research demonstrates not only the richness of contextual interpretation but also the enhanced precision of stratigraphic evidence in the consideration of production trajectories. For instance, specialists studying Maya figurines have generally supposed that the first items were handmade or modeled, with the addition of pastillage and incised details. Molded items were created as ceramic production advanced (Corson 1976:172; Piña Chan 1968:66). Finally, the production of molded separate sections gave way to articulated figurines. This seems to be a logical sequence—and as stratigraphic excavations did not demonstrate alternative trajectories at the island of Jaina, it was taken for granted (more on this soon).

For most of the terra-cotta figurines, there was a general post-firing painting, especially using white, blue, red, and yellow colors (in that frequency order). Many figurines are rattles, while others functioned as whistles (Benavides 2012b; Sambale 2000; Schele 1997). Now we will reconstruct part of Jaina's history by discussing complete figurines that were included in the neutron activation analysis and their burial contexts.

An Interesting Place

Playa Poniente is located west of the Zayosal Group and was severely affected by multiple destructive activities throughout the last two centuries. The architectonic group could have had masonry architecture enclosing a big plaza (Stelae Plaza) on its west side, where today we find the ruins of a nineteenth-century rustic villa. Excavations registered eight different *sascab* strata at Playa Poniente before reaching the phreatic level. The first two levels produced abundant coarse sherds as well as polychrome and incised sherds; there also were net weights, some chert artifacts, and a *Melongena* shell. We also found human bone fragments lacking any anatomical positioning. Their study revealed a male adult with no evidence of pathology. The third level began forty-six centimeters deep, with traces of a stucco floor. On that level, we collected bone fragments that, when analyzed, revealed two individuals: one not sexed and one male. At fifty-seven centimeters deep, we found four human burials with funerary offerings associated with each interment. They were placed at different depths, without disturbance and found in such a way that their consecutive deposit could not have been altered (Barba Meinecke 2003).

The first and uppermost burial was a female adult, between thirty-six and fifty-five years old and 1.43 meters tall. She was flexed on her left side; her skeleton and face were oriented to the south. Skull fragments and ulnas bore traces of cinnabar pigment. Her skull showed signs of pathology in the form of porotic hyperostosis and orbitalia sieve. Her teeth presented light wear, some tooth decay, and one abscess. Both femurs and tibias had periostitis. Her offering included a semi-fine-paste cooking pot, a whistle-figurine near her face, and two jade beads inside her mouth. Sampled for NAA, the figurine was classified as forming part of the lower Usumacinta Basin group and related to ceramics from Jonuta. The figurine represents a robust standing person with a rounded head and arms relaxed at both sides of the body. The form wears a simple loincloth, earplugs, and maybe a headdress. Erosion precludes more detail, but red (cinnabar) and blue pigments were visible.

A second burial is that of an infant, one or two years old, who was found at a depth of 98–120 centimeters with two figurines on its chest. Also associated with the infant burial are three vessels: two upside-down dishes protecting its skull, and a third vessel resting on its legs. The burial was flexed on the right side, oriented to the northwest–southeast. There was also a necklace formed by 299 *Spondylus* sp. beads and a pectoral of the same shell with two perforations. Further micro-excavation in the laboratory added two more adornments made of bone: a *bezote*, and two fragments of an earplug. The skull had tabular erect cranial deformation and was covered with traces of cinnabar.

Both modeled figurines from the second burial are seated figures. The female rests her arms on her knees. She wears a thick bracelet formed by round beads, a simple necklace, and circular earplugs. Her headdress seems to represent cloth with an "X" on the front. She wears a long skirt, and a short blouse shows her shoulders. There were no cinnabar traces, only whitewash. NAA indicates that the clay for the figurine came from the Comalcalco region (Figure 11.10). The second figurine of this burial is a seated male, wearing a simple loincloth with a bare chest. His arms are crossed over his torso. He wears an unassuming necklace, double earplugs, and a headdress simulating cloth decorated with a flower on the top. NAA indicates that the clay for this figurine also came from the Comalcalco region.

A fragmented vessel resting on the feet of the infant was restored; it was a fine-orange short-neck pot. The inverted dish covering the skull had no leg supports; its red body had a black bottom and base. This vessel was also analyzed, and results indicated a southern Veracruz clay provenience. The other dish had an annular support and a body with divergent walls. It was also manufactured with a fine-orange paste and NAA yielded a southern Veracruz origin.

Under the previous finding, we registered the fourth burial, also an infant but between three and four years old. The skull was covered with traces of cinnabar. Inside the mouth of the child was a shell phytomorphic spindle whorl. The skull was covered with a tripod dish; two other tripod dishes were placed near the feet, and three molded rattle-figurines were placed on the chest and among the arms. There were traces of cinnabar and whitewash throughout the burial interment. NAA analysis of the first rattle-figurine indicates that the paste came from southern Veracruz. A second molded figurine has a geometric form, lacks feet, and features arms raised to the sides. Covered with a thick whitewash, this figurine—also from southern Veracruz—lacked more observable details. A third figurine had been placed in the arms of the child and partially under an inverted vessel covering the head. Also geometric in form and without feet, the figurine featured upraised hands with palms showing. Probably female, her short skirt was decorated with diamond designs; a triangular blouse or *quechquemitl* features an anthropomorphic face with a mouth created by a perforation. Both wrists are covered with double bracelets of rounded beads. She wears earplugs and a semicircular headdress with rectangular designs in the center. Once again, the figurine had been whitewashed. NAA also indicated a southern Veracruz origin.

The vessel covering the head of the child was a tripod dish that had lost its supports; the exterior of the vessel is decorated with a jaguar head on one side, with the jaguar tail on the other. This kind of vessel is classified as Jaina ceramic type, Jaina variety, of the Dzitbalché ceramic group of the Fine Orange Isla ware.

Many researchers previously thought that this kind of ceramic was manufactured on the Campeche coast. A suitable region would be the southern boundary between Campeche and Tabasco. Petrographic fine-paste studies have proven that the clay banks around Jonuta contributed the raw material to make some of the figurines. However, recent studies of eleven sherds from the Dzitbalché group (of the Fine Orange Isla ware) were neutron activation analyzed and results indicated their Veracruz provenience.

Additionally, two tripod bowls with conic solid supports were found near the feet of the fourth burial. The bowls both feature a deep incised line under the rim and are decorated with several rounded segments. They are fine pastes and have been classified as Coast Chablekal-Tsicul style (Ancona Aragón 2008:160–167).[6] At Xcambó, this ceramic style has been dated to 500/550–700 CE and corresponds to the early Chablekal ceramic types (Peña and Sierra Sosa 2004). There are reports of Chablekal-Tsicul vessels with pastes coming from the Grijalva–Usumacinta Basin. But in the specific case of these two vessels, the NAA marks southern Veracruz as the origin for the paste.

The fifth burial was found in the deepest section (157 centimeters) of the northwest corner of the excavation unit—an infant two or three years old. Associated offerings included a fine-orange pot and a female figurine with molded and articulated arms. Near the feet, there were four beads carved from a big columella shell (possibly *Strombus* sp.). The arms of the infant embraced a figurine with a cylindrical body, which had perforations to hold arms and legs. The central section of the figurine features a rectangular design with six dots and lateral ribbons. The feet, including the soles and ankles, were covered with a thick whitewash. The arms are extended and both wrists wear bracelets. On the shirt, a triangular design is a schematic representation of a rain deity, with its goggles and mustache clearly visible. Whitewash covers the hands and wrists.

The figurine wears a necklace of thick rectangular beads. The hair has a central fringe with strands hanging down on both sides of the face. His circular earplugs bear traces of blue pigment. The simple headdress is rectangular. His mouth is slightly open, and the superior incisors are cut to form a triangle. The body was covered with whitewash. On sections where the whitewash is lost, there is blue pigment. It could have been originally painted blue and later covered with white (Figure 11.11d).

The fifth burial vessels can be dated to 500/550–700 CE on the basis of identified ceramic types; a charcoal sample recovered from an associated stucco floor yielded a date range of 570–645 CE. This basal date implies that the sequence of burials at Playa Poniente was deposited over two centuries.

As mentioned previously, stylistic studies of Jaina figurines often propose that molded figurines are later than handmade ones. Playa Poniente findings disagree with this proposal. According to the evidence obtained by recent stratigraphic excavations and radiocarbon dates, the oldest mold-made artifacts at Jaina came from Veracruz, with handmade figurines from the Chontalpa and the Usumacinta Basin arriving only later.

Figurines and Explanations

Contemplating the faces of rulership on Jaina figurines is complicated by the fact that many of the human figurines excavated from the island originally came from hundreds of kilometers away. These tiny pieces seem to reflect Maya features and were possibly fabricated according to ideas about how Maya people looked and what garments and attire they preferred. The principal interest lay in the detailing of the face and headdress, as hands and feet received less attention.

But not all the Jaina figurines depict Maya features, as many show another ethnic group, probably

figure 11.13
Four faces of male figurines from Jaina. Photographs by Antonio Benavides C.

the inhabitants of the central and southern regions of what is today called Veracruz, especially the Sotavento, Papaloapan, and Los Tuxtlas regions (Goldstein 1994).

An unsettled topic is the DNA analysis of the skeletons found at Jaina (Hernández Espinoza and Márquez Morfín 2007; López Alonso and Serrano Sánchez 1984; Tiesler and Cucina 2012). When completed, that information will help to determine if the island's population was only Maya or was hybrid, including people from different regions of the Gulf Coast.

Comparing facial traits (front and side views) can help to identify "typical" Maya phenotypes, but there are also other quite different phenotypes. Generally, it seems that Maya faces are vertically elongated. By contrast, other figurines show broad faces. Scarification is also common in Maya images

figure 11.14
Five representations of dwarves excavated at Jaina. Photographs by Antonio Benavides C.

(Figure 11.13). Something similar happens when dress is compared. It is difficult to find *quechquemitl* or triangular clothing associated with Maya faces. Headdresses also need more attention (Gallegos 2015; Halperin 2014).

When grave contents are analyzed, supposed portraits fail to reveal emblems of status or clear associations between burials and associated funerary items. For example, Carmen Cook de Leonard (1971, 2003) analyzed the association of dwarf figurines with burial age, sex, and other accoutrements. She found that dwarf figurines could accompany skeletons of normal infants, men, or women who had been interred with quite different elements (i.e., bowls, dishes, spindle whorls, jade beads, shell beads, earrings, other figurines, ceramic seals, obsidian artifacts, etc.) or only with a single dwarf figurine. Specific patterns elude analysis (Figure 11.14). The

Jaina Figurines 301

same pronounced variation exists within the burial assemblages we have excavated from the 1990s to the beginning of this century.

Final Comments

Jaina was not a place where figurines were manufactured. Some of the excavated objects could have been produced there, but the evidence suggests that many were imported. In fact, a large quantity of figurines arrived at Jaina, not only from relatively near regions, such as coastal Tabasco and the Usumacinta Basin, but also from farther regions, such as southern and central Veracruz.

While anthropomorphic figurines saw diverse uses in Mesoamerican societies (i.e., ludic, musical, construction offering, funerary deposit, etc.), the evidence indicates that their principal use at Jaina was to accompany the dead. Human burials associated with figurines have been documented at several coastal Campeche sites, including Los Guarixés, Villa Madero, Cansacbe, Jaina, Isla Piedras, and Uaymil,[7] but it seems to decrease in the Tabasco and Yucatán sites.[8]

With or without figurines, many Pre-Columbian people buried their dead under their homes. In the sixteenth-century, Diego de Landa wrote of the peninsular Maya: "They buried them inside their houses, or at the back of them, placing some idols in their graves" (Landa 1966:59). Surely, early colonial Yucatec Maya peoples considered it important to bury their ancestors nearby.

The idea of incorporating figurines into burial accoutrements could have emerged at inland sites in the Middle Grijalva Basin, around 150 kilometers south of the coast. Lowe (1998:98–101) reports burials with vessels and figurines from the Felisa phase (by the end of the Middle Preclassic period, 500–300 BCE) from sites at the confluence of the Grijalva and La Venta Rivers, and there are more examples from the Mechung phase (650–900 CE). During the later Late Classic period, figures in burials are commonly reported in an area known as La Mixtequilla, which is located forty to fifty kilometers from the Veracruz central coast at settlements such as El Zapotal, Dicha Tuerta, and Nopiloa (Ladrón de Guevara 2006; Medellín Zenil 1958, 1987).

Previous information indicates that the tradition of including figurines as part of grave goods could have extended to some coastal communities, arriving at the Campeche western littoral. In this context, it could also be significant that there are not many reports of burials with figurines in the Tabasco coastal sites (Gallegos and Armijo Torres 2004) or on the Yucatán northern coast. Of the more than five hundred burials excavated at Xcambó, only twenty-three anthropomorphic figurines were found (Jiménez Álvarez et al. 2006; Peña and Sierra Sosa 2004). Six figurines from Xcambó were found in construction fill, and only sixteen were associated with funerary items.

In other words, only 3.2 percent of Xcambó burials had figurines as part of the grave goods. By contrast, at Jaina, figurines are associated with burials more than 50 percent of the time, and frequently there is more than one figurine per burial. The differential figurine quantities at Jaina versus Xcambó could indicate less interest in figurines among communities located farther to the north. The existence of a burial tradition shared by the coastal settlements from the Veracruz, Tabasco, and Campeche coasts could help to explain why there are no burials with figurines in the inland settlements of the Yucatán Peninsula—in the central Puuc region, for example. Possibly inhabitants of the coastal communities shared beliefs and customs that were slightly different from their inland neighbors because they participated in a pluri-regional circuit of fast communication, giving them relatively easy access to luxury goods and, at the same time, a sense of cohesion or membership to the coastal ambit.

It is very probable that since the first centuries of the Common Era, some sites of the Campeche coast had strong links with Veracruz coastal settlements, apparently with scarce participation from coastal Tabasco sites (Ruz Lhuillier 1945). The Fine Orange Isla ceramic (from Veracruz) is common at Jaina and has also been reported at sites like Champoton (Ruz Lhuillier 1969:XXXVI 94), Isla Piedras (Eaton and Ball 1978), Villa Madero (Ceballos Gallareta 1998), Uaymil (Cobos 2012), Xlabarco, La Providencia,

Paso Holuntún, Xcambó (Jiménez Álvarez 2002), Dzibilchaltún, Becán (Ball 1977:42), Chicanná (Jiménez Álvarez 2002), Oxkintok (Jiménez Álvarez 2002), and Los Guarixés (Álvarez Aguilar 1985), but it seems that it is not found in Tabasco, though the forms and color palette are present in the Puxcagua style, which is dated to around 561 CE (Armijo, Gallegos, and Jiménez 2005).

It is also interesting that in the Usumacinta Basin (at Palenque, situated a little more than 110 kilometers from the sea), figurines are generally found in domestic units and are assumed to have ritual or festive uses. Sometimes exchanged, figurines from the Usumacinta Basin eventually were used as funerary goods (Flores Jiménez 2000; Goldstein 1980; López Bravo 2000; Nieto Calleja and Flores Jiménez 2013).

Contacts between Jaina and the Palenque region have been confirmed by the presence, on the island of Jaina, of the fine black Yalcox ceramic type. Ceramic vessels probably traveled by river to the sea via an Usumacinta tributary and were then incorporated into the coastal trading route that connected many sites between Veracruz and the peninsular coast. The journey from the Palenque region to Jaina covers a distance of around 410 kilometers. However, most of the sherds and vessels in the Jaina archaeological inventory came from the lower Usumacinta Basin and were manufactured between Tenosique and the sea. The river goes through communities like Balancan, Emiliano Zapata, and Jonuta, ending at Tres Brazos (in the Centla municipality) where it joins the Grijalva River and flows into the Gulf of Mexico.

At times, the figurines classifications derived from NAA and presented here coincide with figurine classifications or typologies proposed by earlier analysts (Corson 1976; Goldstein 1979; Piña Chan 1968). For future research, it is recommended that analysis include all artifacts from well-defined contexts. Such clarity will help us to obtain a better and more complete explanation. At the same time, it will be relevant to contrast formal groupings of the different provenience zones identified through NAA to verify their similarities and differences, independently from their provenience or archaeological context. This means that we need broader investigations so that we can link clay, place of manufacture, macroscopic typology, and context.

It is interesting to note that, as a rule, the figurines are barefoot; only some of them (for example, high-ranking officials) have adornments around their ankles or on their insteps. Moreover, the presence of female figurines is significant and serves to mute the patriarchal emphasis on male rulers, which is observable on the stelae of many royal courts. At the same time, the strong female presence in the figurines from Jaina reflects women's relevance in daily life not only as mothers but also as reproducers of Maya culture.

The many figurines documented at Jaina reveal their relevance for the ancient local people. The preference for figurines that also functioned as whistles or rattles helps to illuminate the role of figurines in diverse public and domestic ceremonies prior to their final use in accompanying the dead, as excavations have proven.

NOTES

1 *Peten* is a Maya word meaning "island"; it refers to a specific ecosystem near the sea that contains sweet water. It has different and taller trees and is surrounded by mangrove.
2 *Sascab* is a soft limestone material located under the Yucatán caprock. Like sand, *sascab* is compact when virgin, but is mixed with earth, sherds, sand, and other cultural waste when reused, as in the Jaina subsoil.
3 We decided to use our own calculations instead of Abrams and Bolland's (1999) labor-time estimates because we are proposing an alternative analysis.

4 The ^{14}C dates were processed by chemical engineer María Magdalena de los Ríos Paredes, of INAH's Dating Laboratory. In the cases presented here, we give the latest date of Oxcal calibration.

5 Classified as a local ceramic because of its high presence, but we have no evidence of kilns at the island.

6 The Chablekal-Tsicul ceramic style of the coast is integrated by fine black and gray composite silhouette bowls, composite silhouette bowls with "Z" angles, bowls, pots, and dishes with a marked divergent rim. Decoration is applied externally with geometric figures, parables, and pseudo glyphs bands. Gouged and incised deep designs made when the clay was fresh are common in this style (Ancona Aragón 2008:160).

7 Excepting Jaina, the quantity of burials with figurines reported at Los Guarixés and Villa Madero is low. Isla Piedras and Uaymil have suffered strong looting operations, but the presence of human bones and figurine and vessel fragments on the surface surely indicates that there were burials (Eaton and Ball 1978).

8 Xcambó, an excavated site on the northern Yucatán coast, is an exception (Sierra Sosa et al. 2014).

REFERENCES CITED

Abrams, Elliot M., and Thomas W. Bolland
  1999   Architectural Energetics, Ancient Monuments, and Operations Management. *Journal of Archaeological Method and Theory* 6(4):263–291.

Álvarez Aguilar, Luis Fernando
  1985   *El sitio arqueológico Los Guarixés*. Gobierno Municipal de Ciudad del Carmen, Campeche.

Alvarez Asomoza, Carlos, and Luis Casasola
  1985   *Las figurillas de Jonuta, Tabasco*. Instituto de Investigaciones Filológicas, Centro de Estudios Mayas, Universidad Nacional Autónoma de México, Mexico City.

Ancona Aragón, Iliana
  2008   La cerámica de pasta fina gris y negra de Jaina y Uaymil, Campeche como marcador de interacción social. BA thesis, Facultad de Ciencias Antropológicas de la Universidad Autónoma de Yucatán, Mérida.

Ancona Aragón, Iliana, and Socorro del Pilar Jiménez Alvarez
  2005   Las cerámicas gris y negra fina como marcadores de interacción en el litoral campechano. *Los investigadores de la cultura maya* 13(1):209–227.

Ancona Aragón, Iliana, Brenda Sauri, and Georgina Reyes G.
  2006   Las cerámicas de pasta fina noroccidental de la Península de Yucatán. *Los investigadores de la cultura maya* 14(2):481–490.

Andrews, Anthony P.
  1977   Reconocimiento arqueológico de la costa norte del estado de Campeche. *Boletín de la ECAUDY* 24:64–77.
  1978a Breve addenda al reconocimiento arqueológico de la costa norte del Estado de Campeche. *Boletín de la ECAUDY* 33: 40–43.
  1978b Puertos costeros del postclásico temprano en el norte de Yucatán. *Estudios de cultura maya* 11:75–93.

Armijo T., Ricardo, Miriam J. Gallegos, and Socorro Jiménez A.
  2005   La cerámica de pasta fina de Comalcalco, Tabasco, y su periferia: Temporalidad y relaciones culturales. *Los investigadores de la cultura maya* 13(1):189–208.

Ball, Joseph W.
  1977   *The Archaeological Ceramics of Becan, Campeche, Mexico*. Middle American Research Institute, Tulane University, New Orleans.

Barba Meinecke, Helena

    2003   Una visita al proyecto arqueológico Jaina en Campeche. *Investigadores de Mesoamérica* 3:52–72.

Becker, Marshall Joseph

    1973   Archaeological Evidence for Occupational Specialization among the Classic Period Maya at Tikal, Guatemala. *American Antiquity* 38:396–406.

    1983   Indications of Social Class Differences Based on the Archaeological Evidence for Occupational Specialization among the Classic Maya at Tikal, Guatemala. *Revista española de antropología americana* 13:29–46.

Becquelin, Pierre, and Claude-François Baudez

    1982   *Toniná: Une cité maya du Chiapas*, vol. 3. Editions Recherche sur les Civilisations, Paris.

Benavides C., Antonio

    2007   Jaina en el contexto de las poblaciones del Clásico en el occidente peninsular. In *La población prehispánica de Jaina: Estudio osteobiográfico de 106 esqueletos*, edited by Patricia Hernández and Lourdes Márquez, pp. 13–31. Instituto Nacional de Antropología e Historia, Mexico City.

    2010   Jaina, Campeche: Tiempos propuestos para su desarrollo prehispánico. In *La península de Yucatán: Investigaciones recientes y cronologías alternativas*, edited by Antonio Benavides and Ernesto Vargas, pp. 249–262. Universidad Autónoma de Campeche, Campeche.

    2012a   *Jaina: Ciudad, puerto y mercado*. Colección Justo Sierra 1. Gobierno del Estado de Campeche, Campeche.

    2012b   Jaina, Campeche, y la región de Los Tuxtlas, Veracruz. In *Arqueología de la costa de Campeche: La época prehispánica*, edited by Rafael Cobos, pp. 297–318. Universidad Autónoma de Yucatán, Mérida.

    2014   Jaina, una isla de sascab. In *Las grandes ciudades mayas de Campeche: Homenaje a Román Piña Chan*, edited by Enzia Verduchi, pp. 210–227. Turner Publicaciones, Madrid.

    2015   La Isla de Jaina y las figurillas de la costa campechana. In *Mayas: El lenguaje de la belleza*, edited by Karina Romero, pp. 16–29. Instituto Nacional de Antropología e Historia, Mexico City.

    2016   Investigaciones recientes en Jaina y Edzná, Campeche. In *Arqueología del norte de la península de Yucatán: Avances y exploraciones recientes*, edited by Lynneth Lowe and Tomás Pérez, pp. 129–150. Instituto de Investigaciones Filológicas, Universidad Nacional Autónoma de México, Mexico City.

    2017   Elementos prehispánicos del Municipio de Champotón. In *Champotón, 500 años de la mala pelea*, edited by Cornelio Sosa, pp. 25–108. Gobierno del Estado de Campeche, Ayuntamiento de Champotón, Campeche.

Benavides C., Antonio, and Nikolai Grube

    2002   Dos monolitos tempranos de Jaina, Campeche, México. *Mexicon* 24(5):95–97.

Bishop, Ronald L.

    2003   Five Decades of Maya Fine Orange Ceramic Investigation by INAA. In *Patterns and Processes: A Festschrift in Honor of Dr. Edward V. Sayre*, edited by Edward Sayre and Lambertus van Zelst, pp. 81–92. Smithsonian Center for Materials Research and Education, Washington, D.C.

Bishop, Ronald L., James Blackman, Antonio Benavides C., Socorro Jiménez, Robert Rands, and Erin Sears

    2008   Naturaleza material y evolución social en el norte y noroeste de las tierras bajas mayas. *Los investigadores de la cultura maya* 16(1):13–30.

Bishop, Ronald L., James Blackman, Donald Forsyth, William Folan, and Erin Sears

    2006   Observaciones iniciales sobre el consumo de la cerámica de Champotón. *Los investigadores de la cultura maya* 14(1):137–145.

Bishop, Ronald L., James Blackman, and Erin Sears

    2006   Report on the Neutron Activation Analysis of Pottery from Isla Jaina, Campeche, Mexico. National Museum of National History, Smithsonian Institution, Washington, D.C.

Bishop, Ronald L., Roberto Ruiz Guzmán, and William Folan
- 2000 Figurines and Musical Instruments of Calakmul, Campeche, Mexico: Their Chemical Classification. *Los investigadores de la cultura maya* 7(2):322–328.

Bishop, Ronald L., Erin Sears, and James Blackman
- 2005a Jonuta: Una ventana a la producción y distribución de pasta fina a finales del clásico maya. *Los investigadores de la cultura maya* 13(1):173–187.
- 2005b A través del río del cambio. *Estudios de cultura maya* 26:17–40.
- 2012 Cerámicas en el borde occidental de las tierras bajas mayas. In *Arqueología de la costa de Campeche: La época prehispánica*, edited by Rafael Cobos, pp. 187–213. Universidad Autónoma de Yucatán, Mérida.

Brainerd, George W.
- 1958 *The Archaeological Ceramics of Yucatan.* University of California Press, Berkeley.

Butler, Mary
- 1935 A Study of Maya Mould-Made Figurines. *American Anthropologist* 37:636–672.

Ceballos Gallareta, Teresa
- 1998 Informe preliminar del análisis cerámico de los materiales extraídos de la plataforma seis del sitio de Villa Madero, Campeche. Rescate arqueológico Autopista Campeche-Champotón, temporada 1991–1993. Centro INAH Campeche Technic Archive, Campeche.

Charnay, Desiré
- 1978 *Viaje a Yucatán a fines de 1886.* Fondo Editorial de Yucatán, Mérida.
- 2019 *Viajes a Yucatán: Expediciones ilustradas 1882, 1886.* Editorial Dante, Mérida.

Cobos, Rafael
- 2012 La arqueología de Uaymil, una comunidad costera del norte de Campeche. In *Arqueología de la costa de Campeche: La época prehispánica*, edited by Rafael Cobos, pp. 319–329. Universidad Autónoma de Yucatán. Mérida,

Coe, Michael D.
- 1973 *The Maya Scribe and His World.* The Grolier Club, New York.

CONANP
- 2006 *Programa de conservación y manejo: Reserva de la biosfera los petenes.* Comisión Nacional de Áreas Naturales Protegidas, Mexico City.

Cook de Leonard, Carmen
- 1971 Gordos y enanos de Jaina (Campeche, México). *Revista española de antropología americana* 6:57–84.
- 2003 Problemas arqueológico-geográficos de la Isla de Jaina, Campeche, México. *Investigadores de Mesoamérica* 3:82–97.

Corson, Christopher
- 1976 *Maya Anthropomorphic Figurines from Jaina Island, Campeche.* Ballena Press, Ramona, Calif.

Dampier, William
- 1906 *Dampier's Voyages.* 2 vols. E. P. Dutton, New York.

Eaton, Jack D., and Joseph W. Ball
- 1978 *Studies in the Archaeology of Coastal Yucatan and Campeche, Mexico.* Middle American Research Institute, Tulane University, New Orleans.

Ekholm, Susanna M.
- 1979 The Lagartero Figurines. In *Maya Archaeology and Ethnohistory*, edited by Norman Hammond and Gordon Willey, pp. 172–186. University of Texas Press, Austin.

Fernández, Miguel Angel
- 1946 Los adoratorios de la Isla de Jaina. *Revista mexicana de estudios antropológicos* 8: 243–260.

Flores Jiménez, María de los Ángeles
- 2000 Figurillas antropomorfas de Palenque. *Arqueología mexicana* 45:44–49.
- 2002 La organización social de los mayas palencanos a través de las figurillas. In *La organización social entre los mayas prehispánicos, coloniales y modernos: Memoria de la Tercera Mesa Redonda de Palenque*, edited by Vera Tiesler, Rafael Cobos, and Merle Greene, pp. 427–440. CONACULTA, Instituto Nacional de Antropología e Historia, Mexico City.

Gallegos G., Miriam
- 2009a Ataviando su identidad: La mujer prehispánica de Jonuta, Tabasco, México.

In *Identidades y cultura material en la región maya*, edited by Héctor Hernández and Marcos Pool, pp. 69–87. Universidad Autónoma de Yucatán, Mérida.

2009b   Manufactura, iconografía y distribución de figurillas en Comalcalco, Tabasco. In *XXII Simposio de Investigaciones Arqueológicas en Guatemala, 2008*, edited by Juan Pedro Laporte, Barbara Arroyo, and Héctor Mejía, pp. 1051–1061. Museo Nacional de Arqueología y Etnología, Guatemala City.

2011   Las jóvenes oradoras: Participación de la mujer prehispánica en la religión maya. In *Las mujeres mayas en la antigüedad*, edited by María Rodríguez-Shadow and Miriam López, pp. 41–70. Centro de Estudios de Antropología de la Mujer, Mexico City.

2015   Vestido, peinados e identidad de la mujer maya en el pasado. In *Mayas: El lenguaje de la Belleza*, edited by Karina Romero, pp. 38–45. Instituto Nacional de Antropología e Historia, Mexico City.

Gallegos G., Miriam, and Ricardo Armijo Torres

2004   La corte real de Joy Chan a través de las mujeres, hombres y dioses de barro: Estudio preliminar de género. *Los investigadores de la cultura maya* 12(2):304–318.

García Campillo, José Miguel

1998   Datos epigráficos para la historia de Jaina durante el periodo clásico. *Los investigadores de la cultura maya* 6(1):45–62.

Goldstein, Marilyn M.

1979   Maya Figurines from Campeche, México: Classification on the Basis of Clay Chemistry, Style, and Iconography. PhD dissertation, Columbia University, New York.

1980   Relationships between the Figurines of Jaina and Palenque. In *Third Palenque Round Table, 1978*, edited by Merle Greene Robertson, pp. 91–98. University of Texas Press, Austin.

1994   Late Classic Maya-Veracruz Figurines: A Consideration of the Significance of Some Traits Rejected in the Cultural Exchange. In *Seventh Palenque Round Table, 1989*, edited by Merle Greene Robertson and Virginia Fields, pp. 169–175. University of Texas Press, Austin.

Halperin, Christina T.

2007   Investigating Classic Maya Ritual Economies: Figurines from Motul de San José, Guatemala. Foundation for the Advancement of Mesoamerican Studies, http://famsi.org/reports/05045 Halperin01.pdf.

2014   *Maya Figurines: Intersections between State and Households*. University of Texas Press, Austin.

Hammond, Norman

1982   *Ancient Maya Civilization*. Rutgers University Press, Rutgers, N.J.

Haviland, William A.

1965   Prehistoric Settlement at Tikal, Guatemala. *Expedition* 7(3):14–23.

Hendon, Julia

2003   In the House: Maya Nobility and Their Figurine-Whistles. *Expedition* 45(3): 28–33.

Hernández Espinoza, Patricia O., and Lourdes Márquez Morfín (editors)

2007   *La población prehispánica de Jaina: Estudio osteobiográfico de 106 esqueletos*. Instituto Nacional de Antropología e Historia, Mexico City.

Ivic de Monterroso, Matilde

2002   Resultados de los análisis de las figurillas de Piedras Negras. In *XV Simposio de Investigaciones Arqueológicas en Guatemala, 2001*, edited by Juan Pedro Laporte, Héctor Escobedo, and Barbara Arroyo, pp. 480–494. Museo Nacional de Arqueología y Etnología, Guatemala City.

Jiménez Álvarez, Socorro

2002   La cronología cerámica del puerto maya de Xcambó, costa norte de Yucatán: Complejo cerámico Xcambó y Complejo cerámico Cayalac. BA thesis, Facultad de Ciencias Antropológicas de la Universidad Autónoma de Yucatán, Mérida.

Jiménez Álvarez, Socorro, Roberto Belmar Casso, Thelma Sierra Sosa, and Heajoo Chun Seu

2006   Estudio tecnológico de la cerámica de pasta fina Chablekal Temprano e Isla Fina del sitio costero de Xcambó, Yucatán. *Los investigadores de la cultura maya* 14(2): 501–515.

Joyce, T. A.
    1933   The Pottery Whistle Figurines of Lubantuun. *Journal of the Royal Anthropological Institute of Great Britain and Ireland* 63:xv–xxv.

Lacadena, Alfonso
    2000   Nominal Syntax and the Linguistic Affiliation of Classic Maya Texts. In *The Sacred and the Profane: Architecture and Identity in the Maya Lowlands*, edited by Pierre Colas, Kai Delvendahl, Marcus Kuhnert, and Annette Schubart, pp. 111–128. A. Saurwein, Markt Schwaben.

Ladrón de Guevara, Sara
    2006   *Museo de Antropología de Xalapa*. Editorial Raíces and Instituto Nacional de Antropología e Historia, Mexico City.

Landa, Diego de
    1966   *Relación de las cosas de Yucatán*. Editorial Porrúa, Mexico City.

López Alonso, Sergio, and Carlos Serrano Sánchez
    1984   Prácticas funerarias prehispánicas en la Isla de Jaina, Campeche. *Investigaciones recientes en el área maya* 2:441–452.

López Bravo, Roberto
    2000   La veneración de los ancestros en Palenque. *Arqueología mexicana* 45:38–43.

Lowe, Lynneth Susan
    1998   *El salvamento arqueológico de la presa de Mal Paso, Chiapas: Excavaciones menores*. Universidad Nacional Autónoma de México, Mexico City.

Medellín Zenil, Alfonso
    1958   *Cerámicas del Totonacapan*. Universidad Veracruzana, Xalapa.
    1987   *Nopiloa*. Exploraciones arqueológicas. Universidad Veracruzana, Xalapa.

Miller, Mary Ellen
    1975   *Jaina Figurines: Catalogue of an Exhibition Held by the Art Museum*. Princeton University, Princeton.

Miller, Virginia E.
    1985   The Dwarf Motif in Classic Maya Art. Mesoweb, https://www.mesoweb.com/pari/publications/RT06/Miller1985-OCR.pdf.

Moedano Koer, Hugo
    1946   Jaina: Un cementerio maya. *Revista mexicana de estudios antropológicos* 1–2:217–242.

Montgomery, John
    2002   *Dictionary of Maya Hieroglyphs*. Hippocrene Books, New York.

Nieto Calleja, Rosalba, and María Flores Jiménez
    2013   *Las figurillas de dos escondites de El Palacio de Palenque, Chiapas*. Dirección de Estudios Arqueológicos. Instituto Nacional de Antropología e Historia, Mexico City.

Okoshi Harada, Tsubasa
    2009   *Códice de Calkiní*. Universidad Nacional Autónoma de México, Mexico City.

O'Neil, Megan E.
    2012   Jaina-Style Figurines. In *Ancient Maya Art at Dumbarton Oaks*, edited by Joanne Pillsbury, Miriam Doutriaux, Reiko Ishihara-Brito, and Alexandre Tokovinine, pp. 399–425. Dumbarton Oaks, Washington, D.C.

Peña C., Agustín, and Thelma N. Sierra Sosa
    2004   Cronología y contexto en las figurillas de terracota de la costa del Golfo de México en Xcambó, Yucatán. *Los investigadores de la cultura maya* 12(1):210–225.

Pérez, Juan Carlos, Griselda Pérez, David Freidel, and Olivia Navarro-Farr
    2015   Waka', el reino del ciempiés: La reina K'abel y su historia recién descubierta. *Anales del Museo de América* 13:7–31.

Pérez Robles, Griselda
    2010   Una corte real: La restauración de 23 figurillas encontradas en el Entierro 39 de El Perú. *Proyecto Arqueológico El Perú-Waka': Informe no. 8, Temporada 2010*, edited by Mary Jane Acuña, pp. 5–29. Instituto de Antropología e Historia de Guatemala, Guatemala City.

Piña Chan, Román
    1948   *Breve estudio sobre la funeraria de Jaina, Campeche*. Gobierno del Estado, Campeche.
    1968   *Jaina: La casa en el agua*. Instituto Nacional de Antropología e Historia, Mexico City.

1996 Las figurillas de Jaina. *Arqueología mexicana* 18:52–59.

Proskouriakoff, Tatiana
- 1974 *Jades from the Cenote of Sacrifice, Chichen Itza, Yucatan*. Peabody Museum of Archaeology and Ethnology, Harvard University, Cambridge, Mass.

Rands, Robert, and Barbara Rands
- 1965 Pottery Figurines of the Maya Lowlands. In *Archaeology of Southern Mesoamerica*, edited by Gordon R. Willey, pp. 535–560. Vol. 2 of *Handbook of Middle American Indians*, edited by Robert Wauchope. University of Texas Press, Austin.

Rivero Torres, Sonia
- 2002 *Figurillas antropomorfas y zoomorfas del Juego de Pelota de Lagartero, Chiapas*. Universidad de Ciencias y Artes de Chiapas, Tuxtla Gutiérrez.

Ruiz Guzmán, Roberto
- 1998 Las figurillas e instrumentos musicales de Calakmul, Campeche: Descripción, análisis e interpretación: Una tentativa tipológica. BA thesis, Escuela Nacional de Antropología e Historia, Mexico City.

Ruiz Guzmán, Roberto, Ronald L. Bishop, and William J. Folan
- 1999 Las figurillas de Calakmul: Su uso funcional y clasificación sociocultural y química. *Los investigadores de la cultura maya* 7(1):37–49.

Ruz Lhuillier, Alberto
- 1945 *Campeche en la arqueología maya*. Acta anthropologica 1:2–3.
- 1969 *La costa de Campeche en los tiempos prehispánicos*. Instituto Nacional de Antropología e Historia, Mexico City.

Sambale, Thomas
- 2000 Die Jaina-Figurinen der Sammlung Jimeno des Ethnologischen Museums in Berlin. Master's thesis, University of Bonn, Bonn.

Sauri, Brenda, Socorro Jiménez Alvarez, and Antonio Benavides C.
- 2005 La naranja fina X de Jaina, Campeche, como parte de un sistema cerámico. *Los investigadores de la cultura maya* 13(1):229–243.

Schele, Linda
- 1997 *Rostros ocultos de los mayas*. Impetus Comunicación, Mexico City.

Schele, Linda, and David Freidel
- 1990 *A Forest of Kings: The Untold Story of the Ancient Maya*. William Morrow, New York.

Schele, Linda, and Mary Ellen Miller
- 1986 *The Blood of Kings: Dynasty and Ritual in Maya Art*. Kimbell Art Museum, Fort Worth.

Sears, Erin
- 2006 Las figurillas mayas del clásico tardío de sistemas de los ríos de Usumacinta/Pasión. *Los investigadores de la cultura maya* 14(2):389–402.

Sears, Erin, Ronald Bishop, and James Blackman
- 2005 Figurillas de Cancuén, Petén: El surgimiento de una perspectiva regional. In *XVIII Simposio de Investigaciones Arqueológicas en Guatemala, 2004*, edited by Juan Pedro Laporte, Barbara Arroyo, and Héctor Mejía, pp. 745–752. Museo Nacional de Arqueología y Etnología, Guatemala City.

Sellen, Adam T.
- 2016 Historia del coleccionismo arqueológico en la península de Yucatán durante el siglo XIX. In *Arqueología del norte de la península de Yucatán: Avances y exploraciones recientes*, edited by Lynneth Lowe and Tomás Pérez, pp. 13–36. Universidad Nacional Autónoma de México, Mexico City.

Sharer, Robert J.
- 1983 *The Ancient Maya*. Stanford University Press, Stanford.

Sierra Sosa, Thelma Noemí
- 2004 La arqueología de Xcambó, Yucatán, centro administrativo salinero y puerto comercial de importancia regional durante el Clásico. PhD dissertation, Facultad de Filosofía y Letras, Universidad Nacional Autónoma de México, Mexico City.

Sierra Sosa, Thelma, Andrea Cucina, Douglas Price, James Burton, and Vera Tiesler
- 2014 Vida y muerte en el puerto de Xcambó, Yucatán: Datos arqueológicos, mortuorios y poblacionales. In *The Archaeology of Yucatán*, edited by Travis W. Stanton, pp. 125–147. Archaeopress, Oxford.

Spinden, Herbert J.
- 1975 *A Study of Maya Art*. Introduction by Eric. S. Thompson. Dover Publications, New York.

Taube, Karl A.
- 1992 The Temple of Quetzalcoatl and the Cult of Sacred War at Teotihuacan. *RES: Anthropology and Aesthetics* 21:53–87.

Tiesler, Vera, and Andrea Cucina
- 2012 Etnicidad, relaciones interpoblacionales y patrones migratorios a lo largo de la costa de Campeche durante los periodos clásico y posclásico. In *Arqueología de la costa de Campeche: La época prehispánica*, edited by Rafael Cobos, pp. 67–95. Universidad Autónoma de Yucatán, Mérida.

Tokovinine, Alexandre
- 2012 Fluted and Incised Bowl. In *Ancient Maya Art at Dumbarton Oaks*, edited by Joanne Pillsbury, Miriam Doutriaux, Reiko Ishihara-Brito, and Alexandre Tokovinine, pp. 121–129. Dumbarton Oaks, Washington, D.C.

Triadan, Daniela
- 2007 Warriors, Nobles, Commoners and Beasts: Figurines from Elite Buildings at Aguateca, Guatemala. *Latin American Antiquity* 18(3):269–293.

Valdés, Juan Antonio, Mónica Urquizú, Héctor Martínez, and Carlos Díaz-Samayoa
- 2001 Lo que expresan las figurillas de Aguateca acerca del hombre y los animales. In *XIV Simposio de Investigaciones Arqueológicas en Guatemala, 2000*, edited by Juan Pedro Laporte, A. C. Suasnávar, and Barbara Arroyo, pp. 654–676. Museo Nacional de Arqueología y Etnología, Guatemala City.

Willey, Gordon R.
- 1972 *The Artifacts of Altar de Sacrificios*. Peabody Museum of Archaeology and Ethnology, Harvard University, Cambridge, Mass.

Postclassic and Contact-Period Maya Rulership

MARILYN A. MASSON

Postclassic rulership after 1000 CE, seldom considered in mainstream discussions of sacred and divine Maya kings and adjacent authorities, presents important parallels with the past, as highlighted in this chapter. This claim counters general assumptions, emphasizing disjunction, of the abandonment of divine rulers in the period in favor of secular emphases and council-style governance. Temporal differences have been well explored, and it is hard to ignore the lack of ruler-focused funerary temples and monumental center tombs in the Postclassic period. However, there is no denying that that rulers from Mayapan's domain (1150–1450 CE) forward legitimized their stations by claiming local authenticity, divine sanction, military prowess, and stranger origins through descent from legendary places or persons. Like their predecessors, they also claimed generous portions of their subjects' labor, products, possessions, and freedoms. While the growth of formal institutional means for participatory government, beginning with Chichen Itza, may distinguish the final, preconquest centuries from the past, this development may be best viewed as a shift in emphasis and scale. Such a shift did not involve the exclusion of kings and other authorities wielding political power.

As with many *ajawtaak* of the Classic period, Postclassic Maya rulers were pressed in their positions by the ranks of high-born noble allies, officials, and priests, who had both formal and informal (yet influential) roles in decision-making. In this period, some rulers negotiated with ruling council members, some presided over lesser vassal kings, some worked with authorities of quadripartite domains, some worked closely—with or against—powerful priests, and some rulers exerted supreme power as heirs of well-known dynasties. In this chapter, I review aspects of the authority and material representations of Postclassic and contact-period Maya *ajawob, halach winik, ajpop*, natural lords, real men, kings, and courts. Such rulers resided in fine palaces and their faces appear on royal art at major Maya centers. These are titles by which they were known, which were quickly suppressed by the Spanish

Crown in the sixteenth century in favor of the term "caciques" (Chuchiak, this volume). Most were men, but in the adjoining Gulf Coast region, at Xicalango, women could accede to lordship, accompanied by male regents (Scholes and Roys [1948] 1968:35). Noblewomen wielded political power and influence as the wives and mothers of rulers, as in the Classic period (Ardren, this volume). They co-presided opposite male designees at probable investiture rituals, flexed supernatural power, and are featured alongside males as founding ancestors.

Hieroglyphic texts referring to Postclassic rulers have scarcely survived, despite a prolific literary and artistic tradition of codices and plastered and painted murals vulnerable to erosion and destruction. For example, an entire glyphic panel, painted on stucco and witnessed by Thomas Gann on the Santa Rita murals, was vandalized and destroyed by locals before he had time to fully record it (Gann 1900:663). Franciscans burned hundreds of Maya hieroglyphic books, some of which may have held historical information (Chuchiak 2010:90; Love 1994:25–32). Debating the existence of written biographies for this period is thwarted, as most of the corpus of late Maya hieroglyphic writing was destroyed.

Biographical references to Postclassic Maya kings, governing elites, and ancestors exist in other formats, such as portraiture sculpture, architecture, and ethnohistorical sources. Although Postclassic-period ancestral temples were no longer built on the scale of earlier southern centers, ancestral claims perpetually asserted the right to rule into the colonial era, materialized in publicly visible oratories, shrines, portraits, and rituals. Noble descent remained critically important on literal and mythical grounds, declared on features within the monumental plazas of major capitals.

The recognition of "paramount" rulers within councils of noble authorities, alongside powerful military and priestly bureaucracies, in Late and Terminal Classic northern Yucatán paves the way for discussion of Postclassic and contact-period rulers (Restall 2001; Ringle, this volume; Ringle and Bey 2001). Nonetheless, Terminal Classic Maya northern kingship was different from southern Classic traditions (Cobos 2021; Ringle, Gallareta Negrón, and Bey 2021). Models for subsequent Postclassic political capitals had close historical relationships with their immediate northern predecessors (Proskouriakoff 1962:91). Changes from the Terminal Classic forward may be characterized as an amplification of bureaucratic institutions. However, Postclassic political organization after 1150 CE was not merely a copy of Puuc or Chichen Itza modes of governance. At this time, we see a shift that pulled older historical structures of rulership back into view. Mayapan's lords reestablished some earlier Maya traditions, such as stela erection. They claimed authenticity through a complex set of political and mythological structures rooted in recent (Itza) lore and emphasized their local legitimacy in contrast to previous regimes (Masson 2000:249–251; Peraza Lope and Masson 2014a:51–53). Given the diaspora of elites, nobles, and literati during the southern ninth-century collapse, followed by Chichen Itza's eleventh-century decline, it is not surprising that structures of authority were recombined in ways that drew on an array of older Maya area traditions.

Some problematic assumptions, briefly reviewed below, have impeded the study of Postclassic Maya rulership and models of societal complexity for this period. This chapter's discussion of the forms of power exerted by Postclassic lords and their representation underscores aspects of long-term structural reproduction—as well as changes—in Maya rulership. Topics explored here include the organization of political territories and capitals, ancestral commemoration, genealogical myths and histories, the entangled relationships of kings and priests, and the sacred burdens borne by rulers.

Pushing through Collapse Lenses

The Postclassic period (1150–1517 CE) is mostly left out of analyses of longer-term cycles of rulership, as is the contact period (1517–1542 CE), despite the opportunities presented by historical documents and eyewitness accounts prior to the conquest (e.g., Masson and Peraza Lope 2014a:11–13). Quezada's book (2014) on late Maya lords treads solid ground concerning Maya lords' loss of power during the second half of the 1500s (as does Hanks 2010), but Quezada's projections of late sixteenth-century structures to the final Pre-Columbian centuries and contact period are unfounded. A recent edited book on Maya kingship (Okoshi et al. 2021) considers the Postclassic period primarily from the perspective of Chichen Itza. Exceptions include a perspective from Santa Rita Corozal (D. Chase and A. Chase 2021) and a contribution by Okoshi (2021) that explores narratives of rulers' accountability to the governed in surviving mytho-historical texts.

Why is the Postclassic period too often excluded from long-term discussions of the power, authority, and complexity of Maya rulership? Jason Yaeger (2020:781) summarizes common characterizations of the Postclassic period, which has traditionally been defined primarily by what it lacks. To be fair, Yaeger was striving to summarize Mayanists' general views on the Classic-period collapse rather than discuss the Postclassic period. It is also true, however, that collapse narratives, by definition, negatively cast societies that follow in the aftermath. "Post" Classic society has long been regarded with low esteem, described as a "degenerate civilization" by Carnegie Institution archaeologists (Pollock 1962:17). Population decline is one of the factors that Yaeger cites. While true for the central, interior Maya Lowlands, areas within the states of Yucatán, Quintana Roo, Campeche, and northeastern Belize were densely occupied in the Terminal Classic, Postclassic, and at Spanish contact (Chamberlain 1948:12, 46, 48, 50, 51, 54, 60, 100–102; Masson 2000:253–264; Masson and Peraza Lope 2014b:frontispiece; Roys 1957). Do the abandonment of old centers and a reduction in monumental scale, as Yaeger observes, matter in terms of gauging collapse? Postclassic centers were built in new locations, and the architecture of this period often does not sit atop ancient platforms that provided extra volume and height. While buildings prior to the Postclassic period were larger, a better observation might be that monumental architecture continued to be built at centers across the lowlands. Rapidly founded sites like Mayapan contemporaneously constructed multiple buildings (and a great wall), distributing labor efforts horizontally rather than vertically. A reduction in public sculpture, also cited by Yaeger, does not hold true for political capitals like Mayapan, where works of art concentrate (Delgado Kú, Peraza Lope et al. 2021:166–168; Peraza Lope and Masson 2014a:77–87, 2014b:129–133, 2014c). One recently investigated temple at Mayapan yielded forty sculptures alone (Peraza Lope and Masson 2014b). While Yaeger correctly observes that the Postclassic period has fewer hieroglyphic stone monuments, the profusion of codices and murals attests to continued literacy.

It is difficult to quantify the reduction in sumptuary goods that Yaeger attributes to the Postclassic period, given the importance of metal artifacts such as effigy earrings, bells, and elaborate coiled rings (Paris 2021), as well as painted and modeled pottery and other ceramic and stone sculptural traditions (Masson 2009; Peraza Lope and Masson 2014b:112–113, 140–143, 2014c; Proskouriakoff 1962:figs. 5–12). Centers like Chetumal had substantial quantities of gold, seized by conquistadors (Roys [1943] 1972:52). An exquisite example of a ceramic effigy urn was among a rich assemblage of grave goods in an elite family tomb at Mayapan (Delgado Kú, Escamilla Ojeda et al. 2021:147–149; Paris 2021:fig. 13.8) (Figure 12.1). The face of this effigy attests to ideal noble conceptualizations of beauty and aesthetics. Comparisons of the Postclassic-period governing elites to those of earlier periods must be based on equivalent investigations of noble palaces. Lamentably, only one of Mayapan's seven most elaborate elite palaces has been excavated (Proskouriakoff and Temple 1955) (Figure 12.2). It had an impressive assemblage of sculptures and polychrome and effigy pottery (Peraza Lope and Masson 2014b:111–116, 2014c). A related variable listed by Yaeger is a decline in mortuary architecture and grave goods, yet Mayapan's monumental plaza is littered with ossuaries and oratories (funerary and/or ancestral monuments), and the city's elites built well-stocked tombs and shrines in their residential groups (Ruppert and Smith 1952, 1954; Smith 1962; Smith and Ruppert 1953, 1956).

Postclassic Maya society has also been unfairly characterized by Mayapan's collapse by around 1450 CE, a time of untold climatic hardship driving famine, pestilence, and, ultimately, warfare (Kennett

figure 12.1
Effigy urn from an elite child burial at Mayapan (Structure Q-39), with a face that demonstrates an example of ideal beauty for a youthful male entity (god, ancestor, or noble). Photograph courtesy of Marilyn A. Masson.

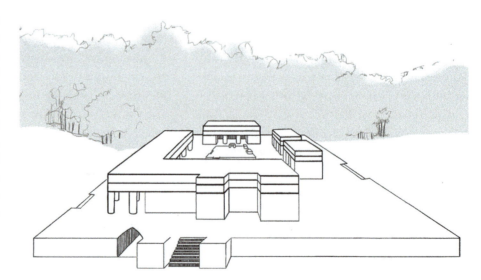

figure 12.2
One of Mayapan's three largest palatial residences, Structures R-86 to R-90, atop a platform through which a vaulted underground tunnel traverses; three structures have frontal gallery rooms, and the courtyard has a raised platform, shrines, and altars. Drawing by Sarah Moore, after Smith 1962:fig. 6.

et al. 2022; Masson 2021; Masson and Peraza Lope 2014c). For example, Quezada (2014:14–15) holds that the atmosphere of the Mayapan state was one of perpetual uncertainty and instability, and, after its fall, the land suffered a prolonged period of "instability and confusion." This view ignores the successes of the Mayapan regional state in unifying much of northwest Yucatán and profoundly influencing peninsula culture for three hundred years (1150–1450 CE), despite the challenges it faced toward the end of this period (Masson 2000, 2021; Masson and Peraza Lope 2014c).

Political Places

Quezada (2014:11, 21) sees little evidence for territoriality among the *batabil* of either the Postclassic or contact periods. He views the political organization of this time as based primarily on personal ties and allegiances to individual leaders. But this is a generic form of political affiliation, aspects of which can be found in many forms of governance. The personality, capabilities, longevity, and efficacy of individual Classic-period Maya rulers resulted in widely varying legacies (Martin and Grube 2008). Quezada, however, weights social relationships exclusively, to the point of denying the existence of territorial domains for late Maya polities. He ignores significant evidence for placemaking and landscape divisions that interwove politics with geography. Roads (with some *sacbes*), stone walls, monuments, shrines, and caves connected people, places, and history during the Postclassic and contact periods (Carosi 2020; Hare, Masson, and Peraza Lope 2014; Hutson and Welch 2016; Magnoni, Stanton, and Hutson 2014; Peraza Lope and Masson 2014a:42; Shaw 2001). Rotating calendrical celebrations, tied to places and political domains, served to regionally integrate rulers and nobles across the northern peninsula (Rice 2004; Roys [1933] 2008:86, 95–112). Boundaries can be perpetually contested (in ancient or modern states), underscoring their need for affirmation. The earliest conquistadors, such as Dávila and Montejo the Younger, were conscious of crossing the boundaries from one political territory to the next (e.g., Chamberlain 1948:100–101, 134), as was Cortés when he entered the Acalan polity (Scholes and Roys [1948] 1968:52–54). The Acalan polity spread geographically across seventy-six towns and villages, named in the Chontal text (Scholes and Roys [1948] 1968:52). K'iche' Maya land claims were recorded as early as the sixteenth century (Carmack 1977:2). A marked hierarchy distinguished principal patrilineages among royal and sub-royal K'iche', and the most important of these house societies were embodied by *nimja* (halls) that framed monumental plazas (Carmack 1977:11). These principal patrilineages also held estates (*chinamit*) and larger territorial expanses (*calpul*) under the jurisdictions of specific towns (Carmack 1977:13). I disagree with Quezada (2014:59–60) that the circumambulation of Xiu territorial boundaries in 1557 was a European introduction to Maya lords' conceptualization of spatial domains.

Jones (1998:93) makes a sound case for the territorial association of *kuch kab'al*, administered from a center. He equates Petén Itza Ajaw Kan Ek' with the *halach winik* lords of contact-period Yucatán. Subordinate to Peten rulers were petty kings, or vassal lords (referred to as *reyezuelos* in Peten ethnohistory), akin to the north's *batabil*, a title that some secondary Peten lords also held (Jones 1998:92). It has long been known that at least ten or eleven of the most powerful polities in Yucatán after the fall of Mayapan were ruled by *halach winikob* and that this office was hereditary (Roys [1943] 1972:59–60, 1957:162). *Batabil* were subordinate lords with bureaucratic duties, including funneling tribute and service to the *halach winik*; *batabil* were located within the capital (town of the *halach winik*) or at subject towns in his political domain.

At the very start of the colonial period in 1545 (twelve years prior to the Xiu treaty of 1557), Halach Winik Na Chi Kokom personally traversed the boundaries of Sotuta and resolved potential disputes with his peers from the Cochuah and Cupul domains (Roys 1957:60). Restall (2001:table 11.1) refers to an earlier such meeting in Calkini in 1530. Earlier in the contact period, in 1536, it was necessary for the Xiu to request permission to cross Sotuta lands during their ill-fated pilgrimage to Chichen

Itza (Tozzer 1941:54–55). These accounts reveal the importance of political boundaries prior to the conquest. The simultaneous existence of loosely organized, less hierarchical geographic areas lacking *halach winikob* (of the sort Quezada claims to have been the norm) has long been recognized (Restall 2001:table 11.2; Roys [1943] 1972:62–63). Power was unequally distributed among political families and actors, before and after Mayapan fell (Restall 2001).

Portraying and Remembering Individuals

Portraits of human faces littered the grounds of the monumental center at Mayapan prior to Carlos Peraza Lope's restoration of the center. Some sculptures likely represent the faces of Postclassic rulers, made during their lifetimes or as ancestral commemorations (Masson 2000:214–216, 221–225; Peraza Lope and Masson 2014a:81–85, 431–436). Many of these portrayals in stone, plaster, and ceramic sculpture assemblages lack identifying regalia of recognizable Maya gods (e.g., Schellhas 1904; Taube 1992). Instead, they present personalized faces and dress (Figure 12.3). Mayapan's monumental center evinces the theme of multiple actors (noble families, factions, deities) comprising the confederacy. The unity of the polity is exemplified within the Main Plaza, formed by the principal radial temple of K'uk'ulkan, the Round Temple, and the Temple of the Serpent Masks, and flanked by colonnaded hall groups, some with their own temples, shrines, and oratories (Proskouriakoff 1962). The floor assemblages, sculptures, and plans of these groups, including the halls, exhibit many unique attributes related to the design choices and activities of noble houses who built and used them (e.g., Milbrath and Peraza Lope 2003, 2009; Peraza Lope and Masson 2014a, 2014b). Some halls had ritual functions, with altars sanctified by caches; others had deity effigies installed in them by officials who assumed the burdens of celebrating calendrical intervals (Delgado Kú et al. 2021a:171; Peraza Lope and Masson 2014b:fig. 3.12; Winters 1955a). Calendrical celebrations also took place at the residences of high elites and at outlying ceremonial groups within Mayapan's walled urban landscape (Masson 2000:200–203; Masson et al. 2020; Peraza Lope and Masson 2014c). The colonnaded halls were surely the equivalents of long houses, *popol nah*, or *nimja*, as identified at earlier and contemporary Postclassic sites in the Maya area (Arnauld 2021; Carmack 1977:11; Ringle and Bey 2001; Ringle, Gallareta Negrón, and Bey 2021). The frontal gallery rooms of elite residences mimicked the form and, likely, the functions of colonnaded halls (Proskouriakoff and Temple 1955:294) (Figure 12.2).

Examples of portraits of historical actors or ancestors at Mayapan include six stone torsos from shrine Q-69 (part of the Hall Q-70 architectural group), idiosyncratically adorned with beads, cloth, pendants/mirrors, or pectoral collars (Figure 12.3). A set of three carved human stone heads from Hall Q-70 may have belonged to some of the torsos. Two of the heads sport feathered headdresses; the other wears a turban. Additional potential ancestral sculptures include a male and female pair from Hall Q-161. These are among examples from thirty-two public buildings and elite residences at the site (Peraza Lope and Masson 2014c:431–436, table 7.1). Stelae 7 and 14 (by Temples Q-152 and Q-126) portray full-bodied individuals that closely resemble the sculptures. Tenoned human head sculptures, present at four public buildings and one residence, have spikes that set them into architectural facades and depict faces similar to freestanding sculptures (Peraza Lope and Masson 2014c:table 7.2). Females as well as males are among the sculptures from colonnaded halls and other monumental buildings, suggesting the importance of women in politics and descent. Some shrines likely held the relics of revered ancestors, including skulls (Landa 1941:131). The headdresses of male stone sculptures and some effigy censers at Mayapan represent birds, reptilians, or jaguars, perhaps pertaining to military affiliations (Peraza Lope and Masson 2014c:435, 440, 457–458). Such examples, lacking distinctive deity markers, likely portray historical human faces of the ruling elite.

The upper room of the Itzmal Ch'en temple, in an outlying ceremonial group by the northeastern gate of Mayapan's wall, housed a pair of male and female ceramic urns (Figure 12.4), each seated on a box or mat throne like those exhibited in the Tulum

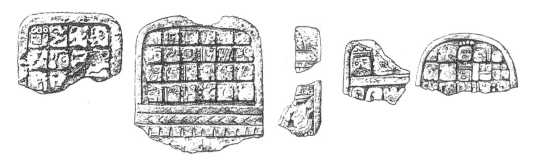

Stelae 2, 3, 4, 5, 6

Stelae 1, 2, 9

figure 12.3
Stelae from Mayapan with glyphic panels, seated lords, priestly attendants, and offerings, revealing the public portrayal of rulers in the context of calendrical rituals. Drawings by Tatiana Proskouriakoff (1962), including her published figures 12b, 12e–h (top row) and 12a, 12c, 12d (bottom row), reprinted with permission of the Carnegie Institution for Science.

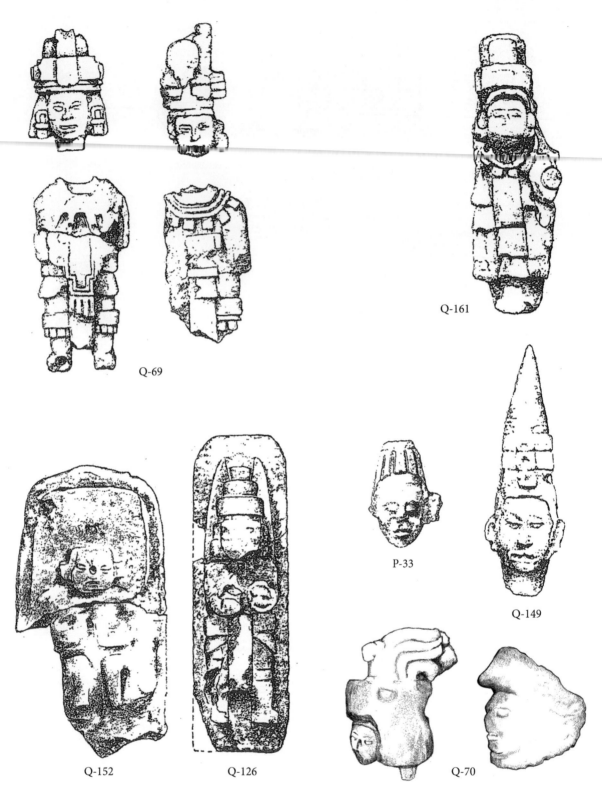

figure 12.4
Sculptures from Mayapán's monumental center, portraying the noble faces and dress of ruling elites, perhaps revered ancestors. Drawings by Tatiana Proskouriakoff (1962), including her published figures 9k, 9l, 9d, 9e (top left), 9b (top right), 11j, 11l (bottom left), and 8g, 8c (center right), reprinted with permission of the Carnegie Institution for Science; illustrations at the bottom right (from Structure Q-70) drawn by Sarah Moore, from photographs in possession of Marilyn A. Masson.

murals (Masson et al. 2020). This temple room also had a stone slab altar (or throne) supported by stucco figures with facial portraits of probable lineage ancestors important to the patrons of this group (Delgado Kú, Peraza Lope et al. 2021:fig. 6.7). Additional stucco portraiture graced the plaza shrine in front of the temple (Delgado Kú, Peraza Lope et al. 2021:fig. 6.11). Stucco ancestor portraits are found in temple and oratory rooms across the site's principal monumental center. Stalactites form the skeletal framework of these stucco portraits (e.g., Shook and Irving 1955:131; Winters 1955b:402). The symbolic association of cave stone "bones" with these sculptures was surely intentional, given that caves housed ancestors and gods, and served as entrances to their otherworldly domains.

Oratories sometimes have shaft ossuaries beneath the floors of their upper rooms (Shook 1953), as do small plaza-level shrines in front of temples (Shook 1954:259–262), further affirming the importance of ancestral commemoration at Mayapan. The genealogical histories of ruling families remained important, even if not recorded hieroglyphically in stone. Some historical text is implied by *tun* date sequences in the Paris Codex (Love 1994:28), and perhaps, the Santa Rita mural (Masson 2000:244–245); the same place glyph appears in the Paris and the Santa Rita mural (Love 1994:37). Aside from ancestor veneration, mythical dynastic histories reaching deeper into the past supported rulers' claims to power at Mayapan and into the contact period (Masson 2000:249–264; Restall 2001:370–375). The Feathered Serpent myth was particularly important (Landa 1941:23–24; Masson and Peraza Lope 2007; Peraza Lope and Masson 2014a:50, 54). Tracing descent from Mayapan remained important for lords and nobles of the colonial period (Quezada 2014:30; Tozzer 1941:24). For example, in Motul's history, Noh Cabal Pech declared himself a "close relative of the great lord at Mayapan" (Okoshi 2021:313). Note the singular reference to "the" great lord at Mayapan, implying a ruler. The ability to communicate with and conjure ancestral beings was not lost in the Postclassic period, including K'uk'ulkan, who was conjured during the Chic Kaban festival (Landa 1941:158; Tozzer 1941:143n685).

Kings and Priests

An examination of the role of priests belongs in any discussion of Postclassic Maya rulership. Priests were organized hierarchically and wielded considerable influence. Maya political lords were engaged in and sanctioned by public ritual, attended to by priests. Late Maya rulers were not exclusively secular and continued to be grounded in the divine. A gradation of divinity exists between the archetype of apotheosized god-kings on earth and rulers who claim descent from lineages "from heaven" (Scholes and Roys 1938:609; Tozzer 1941:9) whose political actions are proclaimed, and perhaps decided, by divination. The entanglement of lordly and priestly functions at contact signals the continued ritual importance and ritual practices of late Maya rulers (Jones 1998; Peraza Lope and Masson 2014a; Roys 1962). Priests, political officials, and their hereditary heirs were close kin within the families of Mayapan's governing nobility. These social ties crosscut bureaucratic roles and consolidated power. Grant Jones's (1998) well-known analysis of Peten Lakes politics identifies pairings of religious and political authorities. Such a set of nearly equivalent dual offices is not known for Mayapan, which had a cadre of resident priests, including some devoted especially to the Feathered Serpent entity (Peraza Lope and Masson 2014a:87).

Priests, while influential, were not as powerful as supreme political rulers (Jones 1998:101–102). As argued for Chichen Itza, they participated in king making, and they endowed titles on secondary lords in the realm through investiture (Peraza Lope and Masson 2014a). Accessions of Postclassic *k'atun* lords, appointed for twenty-year intervals, were attended by priests, who sometimes wore deity masks (Love 1994:18–25) (Figure 12.5). The Peten region's Ach Kat could have been *k'atun* priests (Jones 1998:101–102). Some Peten-area priests at contact viewed themselves as equal to the ruler, but in the sense that they represented dual aspects of the same persona, underscored by the close kin ties of priests and kings (Jones 1998:94). Priests represented a competing sector for power in the political realm—when in history has this not been the case?

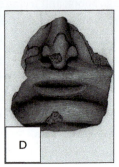
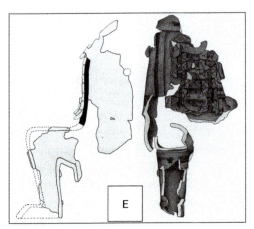
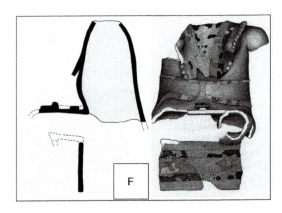

figure 12.5

Examples of ancestral sculptures from the Itzmal Ch'en temple group at Mayapan: a) upper temple sanctuary with the feet of three stucco portraits preserved; b) a stucco face (noble ancestor) found near the feet atop the temple; c) Itzmal Ch'en temple and its plaza shrine; d) stucco face found at a colonnaded hall facing the temple; and e–f) male and female effigy censers seated on thrones that were broken and discarded atop the temple. Photographs by Pedro Delgado Kú (a, c) and Bradley Russell (b); drawings by Wilberth Cruz Alvarado (d, e, f), courtesy of the Proyecto Económico de Mayapán.

A Xiu priest was the architect of Mayapan's final war and abandonment (Tozzer 1941:36).

Jones determined that a hierarchical model is more fitting for Peten Lakes rulership than a confederacy model, given evidence that kingdoms were ruled by a "small exclusive set of related kin who shared power with other groups only at their convenience or as a matter of political strategy" (Jones 1998:83). Robert Carmack characterized K'iche' rulership similarly. Although K'iche' political structure was in some ways oligarchical in that principle noble patrilineages officially participated in courtly administration, Carmack emphasizes that participants were ranked hierarchically. He states that the "Ajpop was a supreme ruler at Utatlan" and points out that only his close relatives could succeed him in office. His genealogy was closely reckoned, and he alone bore the nosepiece of rulership (Carmack 1977:14). Three other corulers, in practice, were his assistants, and their existence was essential to the narrative of four quadripartite divisions of the polity (Carmack 1977:15). Rulers of secondary sites, for example, two brothers of the king of Utatlan, recognized the Utatlan ruler as their superior (Carmack 1977:15). Beneath rulers, a host of principal men presided, often with specific responsibilities as tribute collectors, judges, or military captains (Carmack 1977:15). Priests were also accorded great respect in K'iche' society but ranked below the king; they served many specialized roles for the state (Carmack 1977:16).

Itzamkanac, the capital of Acalan, shared a similar quadripartite organization to that of Utatlan. Ruler Paxbolonacha called together advisory representatives from each town quarter to meet Cortés (Scholes and Roys [1948] 1968:52–54). Paxbolonacha was the sixth-generation ruler of Acalan. He held the title of *ajaw* (ruler/king) and was advised by lesser dignitaries beyond officials from the four divisions of the capital (Scholes and Roys [1948] 1968:55, 86). Quadripartite territorial and political divisions permeated the concepts of place and power for the political capitals of the Peten Itza, Utatlan, Itzamkanac, and northern Yucatán (Carmack 1977:18; Chuchiak 2001:145–146; Peraza Lope and Masson 2014a:52–53; Rice 2009:44; Scholes and Roys [1948] 1968:52–54).

Monumental architecture of Postclassic centers was intimately connected with mythical charters legitimizing the entitlements of lords to govern. At Mayapan, Utatlan, Tayasal, and Itzamkanac, principal pyramids dedicated to the Feathered Serpent dominated the built environments and perpetually reminded residents and visitors alike of the divine and stranger king mythic entitlements of rulership (Carmack 1977; Chase and Chase 2021; Jones 1998:73; Rice 2009:43; Scholes and Roys [1948] 1968:56). At these four capitals, other temples were devoted to deities associated with an array of different creation myths (Milbrath and Peraza Lope 2003; Peraza Lope and Masson 2014a).

More evidence of Postclassic Maya kings comes from K'iche' ethnohistory. The K'iche' ruling line, founded by Balam K'itze', began about 1225 CE and continued until the time of conquest in 1524. The most famous king (*ajpop*) was K'ikab, of the ninth generation, who ruled around 1475 CE (Carmack 1977:5–6). K'iche' rulers descended patrilineally from founding warlords. Lords held the title of *ajawab'*, and distinguished themselves with sacred royal emblems, feathers, gold ornaments, jade, feline claws, finely colored clothing, and ear plugs. They had restricted access to certain temples, were linked to founding and patron gods, and lived in palaces (Carmack 1977:6). Kings alone wore nosepieces, served as military leaders, were surrounded by guards and icons of the gods, and appointed members of the nobility to offices. K'iche' *ajpopib'* confirmed the accession of other kings, as for the polities of the Rabinal, Kaqchikel, and Tz'utujil, and they were the "first voice" in councils (Carmack 1977:13–14). The bundles of cremated kings were venerated. Kings married noblewomen from other centers and, in doing so, forged alliances (Carmack 1977:7). Other members of K'iche' society included vassals (*k'ajol*) who enjoyed few of the sumptuary privileges of the *ajawab'*. Merchants and artisans were esteemed and supported by patrons but were not nobles. The K'iche' had a complicated institution of slavery, a status for which there were multiple pathways and outcomes (Carmack 1977:7–8). Rural agrarian commoners represented an additional group that sometimes clashed with vassals over land claims. These rural farmers (*nimaq achi*) worked lands in the possession of the K'iche' lords long after the conquest (Carmack 1977:9).

Halach winikob in the contact and early colonial periods of Yucatán had similar rights and privileges, according to Roys ([1943] 1972:60–62). They ranked higher than priests, serving as inspectors of religious orders and authorizing major rituals. They owned slaves who worked their farms and cacao groves. They were supported by tribute from subject towns and received additional compensation for acting as judges. Some were transported on litters and accompanied by retinues. Subordinate *batabil* also were entitled to labor service in agriculture and construction. Some Mayapan kings had names or titles preserved in history. One may have been named K'uk'ulkan (Roys 1962:80). Another is referred to by a name or title, *Cotecpan*, a word that incorporates the Nahuatl term *tecpan* (government house, palace) and may have meant "man over everyone" (Roys 1962:55, 65; Smith 1962:182; Tozzer 1941:24).

Sacred Burdens, Sacred Sanctions

Postclassic lords commemorated passages of time. Grube argues that calendrical ritual became a major emphasis during the Terminal Classic period, compared to earlier (Classic-period) monuments that focused on life events of individual rulers (Grube 2021:48; Helmke, Hoggarth, and Awe 2021:115). However, Classic-period monuments regularly include those dedicated to calendrical period endings (e.g., Rice 2004:126–127). With the assistance of priests, Mayapan lords and subordinate officials continued the tradition of carrying the burdens of time and recording some of these acts in public art. Assuming this cargo obligated lords to sponsor celebrations (e.g., pageantry, performances, and feasts), fund shrine construction, and commission the production of ritual paraphernalia. Lords rotated the honor of hosting deities (and their material effigies) for periods such as the twenty-year *k'atun* as well as shorter intervals (D. Chase and A. Chase 2021:298; Landa 1941:138–166; Love 1994; Rice 2004:111–115; Rice and Rice 2018:30–31; Roys [1933] 2008:86, 95–112). Beyond Mayapan, *k'atun* celebrations were assumed by lords at smaller centers (Love 1994:25; Rice 2009:27, table 2.1). These occasions were marked by the setting of "stones," including stelae (Bolles 2003:205; Roys [1933] 2008:95–97). The contact-period Peten Itza also affirmed the partition of territory in terms of rotating localities for calendrical rituals. This practice integrated time, space, and politics (Jones 1998:102; Love 1994:25). The Santa Rita mural illustrates an assembly of lords from different places (place glyphs) perhaps bound together by similar calendrical duties. One scene of the mural features lords or ritualists, bearing an incense cone and a deity effigy, entering and leaving a shell-marked temple (Santa Rita) in which a jaguar supernatural presides (Masson 2000:247) (Figure 12.6). Mayapan's best-preserved stelae portray seated lords, aided by priests, commemorating *k'atun* periods (D. Chase and A. Chase 2021:298; Love 1994:10, 18, 25; Rice 2009:32) (Figure 12.3). High-ranking Maya elites, and presumably rulers, also let blood (D. Chase and A. Chase 2021:304).

Priests obviously shared the sacred burdens of the state with Postclassic Maya rulers, assisting in all the scenes just described. Priests were the literati of society and codices mostly reflect their concerns with time, astronomical cycles, and auguries (Vail 2006). Priests likely controlled the content of codices, and their choices are evident in the predominance of esoteric themes. Omission or minimalization of historical and political records could have been strategic. A similar scenario has been proposed for Classic-period Maya royals, who, along with their closest political allies, are the primary focus in courtly art, to the detriment of merchants (McAnany 2010:256–257) or priests (Zender 2004). Postclassic priests appeared in the guise of deities or wore god masks, as illustrated by some of the god-named assistants to the Paris Codex *k'atun* lords (Love 1994:21, 25) and the ritualists on the Tancah murals (Miller 1982:pl. 6). The seated ruler on Stela 1 at Mayapan wears a Chaahk mask (Figure 12.3), as do lords and other actors on the Tulum murals (Figure 12.5). Others at Tulum are without masks, sometimes wearing nose plugs of authority (Structures 5 and 16). The women in these murals are also unmasked and some of them bear nose plugs. The principal male in the Structure 16 mural (Figure 12.6a), receiving a bundle, is accompanied by masked, deity-attired male priests (Miller 1982:pls. 28, 37). Tulum Structure 16's scene suggests the bestowal of political office, framed by a serpent maw, a twisted serpent cord, and mat signs (Masson 2000:235; Miller 1982:pl. 37). The same bundle is passed from seated women to male lords in a pair of registers on Tulum Structure 5's mural (Figure 12.6b), framed by a k'awiil serpent, a starry celestial band, woven mat symbols of authority, and a watery underworld scene (Miller 1982:pl. 28). The Structure 5 program could reflect marriages, ancestors, founding myths, or sequential accessions involving the bestowal of the bundle. Most importantly, the Tulum murals show key events sanctioned by manifesting the sacred realm, using symbols that are reminiscent of earlier periods. Another example of the continued resonance of ancient symbols of authority includes the God K heads displayed in k'atun lord scenes of the Paris Codex (Figure 12.6c), as well as the caiman sky band throne upon which the lords sit (Love 1994:18, 36). Love (1994:87) also identifies the *Pauahtun* skybearers, a sky band, and celestial cords in the spiritual scene of the Paris Codex as elements of age-old Maya cosmological frameworks.

Political, Military, and Economic Authority

The political, military, and economic authority of Postclassic rulers has been explored in detail elsewhere (Masson and Peraza Lope 2014b; Peraza Lope and Masson 2014a; Piña Chan 1978; Restall 2001:365; Roys [1943] 1972, 1957, 1962). Taxation provided lords and officials beneath them with a baseline of regular goods such as cotton, other craft goods, and foodstuffs. Major marketplaces had judges and special buildings where agents of elites could make special exchanges (Chamberlain 1948:50). Subjects contributed architectural labor and cultivated lands of the lords (Okoshi 2021:313, citing De la Garza et al. 1983:269–270). Surpluses at the household level, for commoners (including crafting families) and elites (including tribute), were exchanged in the marketplace for items needed and desired (Masson et al. 2016). Sons of noble families engaged in long-distance mercantile trading expeditions (Landa 1941:39; Tozzer 1941:94–95), but merchants also operated within regions of the peninsula and at the community scale (Chamberlain 1948:91; Feldman 1978). Market exchange was an essential component of everyday life (Masson and Freidel 2012, 2013; Masson and Peraza Lope 2014d).

Warfare and raiding boosted the political power and economies of Postclassic peninsular polities (Peraza Lope and Masson 2014a:40; Roys [1943] 1972:66–70). Raiding brought captives who were often enslaved or traded to Gulf Coast slave markets (Roys [1943] 1972:34–35; Scholes and Roys 1938). Postclassic and contact-period lords made regional, multi-polity alliances and rallied subjects and allies for warfare (e.g., Roys [1943] 1972:68, 1962:47). During the contact period, allied polities joined together in campaigns against Montejo the Elder in the attack on Campeche and against Montejo the Younger at Chichen Itza (Chamberlain 1948:128, 135–141). These events refute Quezada's (2014:23) claim that Maya lords did not have the power to forge military alliances after Mayapan fell. The sacrifice of war captives was a conspicuous aspect of state theater at Mayapan (Peraza Lope and Masson 2014a:40, 91; Serafin and Peraza Lope 2007).

Tensions associated with feasts, discussed in other chapters of this book, are vividly illustrated by the Otzmal massacre event of the contact period. Lord Na Chi Kokom had his Xiu guests murdered in 1536, in retribution for the Xiu annihilation of Mayapan Kokom lords nearly one hundred years earlier (Tozzer 1941:54–55). The Xiu party had requested and received permission to pass through the Kokom polity territory of Sotuta during a ritual pilgrimage to Chichen Itza's cenote in the context of a period of severe droughts. The Kokom feasted the Xiu for three days, prior to killing them by setting their guesthouse aflame. Again, in 1545, the Kokom similarly feasted Xiu emissaries at a banquet at Otzmal before subsequently blinding them (Rice 2009:38). Otzmal was a rural estate of Na Chi Kokom. The existence of such properties attests to the affluence of contact-period lords who

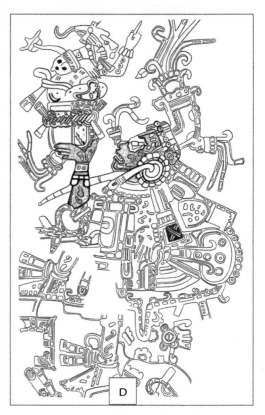

figure 12.6

The faces and dress of Maya lords assuming/conveying political offices or ritual burdens in segments of mural or codex scenes. Tulum Structure 16's mural (a) shows an initiate (center), accompanied by a Chaahk-masked priest (right) and receiving offerings and a bundle from another (probable) priest (left). Tulum Structure 5's mural (b) illustrates a conferral of the bundle between a seated female (right) and a standing male (left). A *k'atun* lord (c, figure on right) in the Paris Codex sits on a caiman sky band throne, aided by a standing priest. A lord (d), carrying an effigy bundle, ascends the stair of a temple on the Santa Rita murals, while his predecessor (not shown) exits the temple from the other side. Illustrated renderings by Sarah Moore, after Miller 1982:pls. 28, 37; Gann 1900:pl. XXX; and Paris Codex (Bibliothèque Nationale de France, http://www.famsi.org/mayawriting/codices/paris.html, pl. 3.

had residences at political capitals as well as countryside retreats. Occasions for assembling regional lords involved the gifting of cloth and currency (e.g., cacao beans and strands of shell and greenstone), as for the Xiu treaty of 1557 (Okoshi 2021:316, 319; Quezada and Okoshi Harada 2001:57–58).

Sumptuary goods also distinguished rulers at the time of contact. Gold, turquoise, and fine metal items were restricted to the highest elites (Chamberlain 1948:47, 104; D. Chase and A. Chase 2021:302; Smith and Ruppert 1956:figs. 8, 10, 11), as were sculptures with hieroglyphic inscriptions (Proskouriakoff and Temple 1955:298). Postclassic and contact-period lords were elaborately adorned in cloth, shell, metals, complex headdresses (and masks), and face/body paint or tattoos, and they traveled with entourages (D. Chase and A. Chase 2021:295). Art of the period attests to their rich and colorful presentations (Figure 12.5). The two largest palaces at Mayapan were built atop platforms that had vaulted tunnels running beneath them (Proskouriakoff and Temple 1955; Smith 1962:198, fig. 6), setting them above and apart from the city's populace (Figure 12.2).

With the abandonment of centers in the context of warfare, conquest, or other strife, elites carried their treasure with them (Chamberlain 1948:104; Love 1998:13; Tozzer 1941:39). Ultimately, such valuables likely found their way into the early colonial economy. A cist burial at one of Mayapan's palatial residences was opened just prior to abandonment. A cache of deity effigy censers, too large and fragile for hasty transport, was placed into this mortuary chamber (Proskouriakoff and Temple 1955). The occasion may also have been cause for the removal of ancestral bundles or relics and valued grave goods. A number of altar caches at Mayapan's monumental central public buildings were systematically removed not long after the city's abandonment, given that roof collapse materials cover them (Shook 1954:268; Winters 1955a:384). These deposits may have been mined during the early colonial period as part of a search for metals. Mayapan's metal axes were also likely carried off, as they are extremely scarce at the site. The hoarding of such objects is known from at least two early colonial Maya sites in Belize (Oland 2014; Simmons, Pendergast, and Graham 2009).

Discussion

"We have kings, oh noble lords, King Cocom, Naum Pech, King Pech, Namax Chel, King Chel . . . of Dzinzantun. Foreign warriors, . . . we here are the Itza." So stated Nacon Cupul, lord of the Cupul polity, addressing Montejo the Younger in 1532, in response to a request that they subordinate themselves to the king of Castile and Christianity (Chamberlain 1948:136). This insider statement claims the status of kings for contact-period rulers. López de Cogolludo ([1688] 1867–1868) wrote: "What is certain is that . . . [Yucatan had previously] . . . been subject to one supreme lord and king, and thus ruled by a monarchical government, until the disloyalty of some vassals caused the division . . . all this land was called Mayapan from the name of the principal city, where the king had his court . . ." (Roys 1962:32).

D. Chase and A. Chase (2021:309) suggest that the Classic-period form of divine kingship was an anomaly in the context of long-term Maya political history. In their view, the extensive and prosperous periods bracketing the Classic period functioned well without the political convention of divine kingship, written, literally, in stone. Nonetheless, some aspects of divine sanction were maintained for Postclassic and contact-period rulers. They were ritualists with special relationships to temples and other monumental buildings. They were lords of time presiding over the wheel of the *k'atun* cycle. They commissioned deity effigies for calendrical and other ritual displays from artisans in their employ (Delgado Kú, Escamilla Ojeda et al. 2021:148). They commemorated and enshrined their ancestors in monumental public settings; ancestral sculptural faces perpetually asserted the genealogical credentials of ruling elites. They proclaimed affiliation with the K'uk'ulkan founder stranger king narrative along with locally specific heroic histories. Closely heeled by priests, late Maya lords assumed the bundles and burdens of office on thrones framed by symbolism such as serpent maw portals, crocodilian thrones, and layered earthly, underworld, and celestial realms. Some sons of lords became priests, representing an investment in complementary, centralized sources of social power within privileged kin groups. Other sons voyaged distantly in merchant canoes, buttressing the economic resources of their families. Rulers and aspiring nobles proclaimed their social distance and political entitlement by covering themselves with symbols of wealth, power, and divinity. Like their Classic-period predecessors, they were war leaders and the architects of military campaigns, with their triumphs heralded in ceremonious captive sacrifice in monumental political capitals. Divine and priestly sanctions of rulership were clearly reinforced by such explicit expressions of the state's capacity for violence. Carmack (1977:18) long ago recognized parallels between the K'iche' and Mayapan states, in that their rulers controlled the "warfare, tribute collection, legal process, and economic affairs of the provinces from the political center." Most notably, rulers of both capitals called for principal leaders from subordinate territories to reside for lengthy periods of time within the capital, an effective policy to subdue dissent and foster unity (Carmack 1977:18).

Kingship was "constantly changing" at Caracol (A. Chase and D. Chase 2021:244), and this was likely true for many kingdoms in Maya history, including the Postclassic and colonial Yucatán. State unity and allegiance is negotiated perpetually among rulers, influential nobility, and members of the general populace. The droughts, famines, and other climatic hardships of the late 1300s pushed Mayapan to its limits, establishing the conditions that set the stage for a revolt from within the council (the Xiu) in the 1450s. The Xiu's usurpation ultimately destroyed the capital and regional polity. It is interesting that colonial documents, drawing on Xiu sources, frame such acts as representing the moral high ground, appealing to social contractual obligations of rulers to subject peoples (Okoshi 2021:316). Clearly, this language was part of a rallying cry for mustering support for the great battle that broke down the city walls of Mayapan (Roys 1962:47–48). Afterward, this narrative justified the wanton massacre of Kokom lords and the destruction of a city so well remembered and legendary that contact-period lords reckoned their heritage back to its governors.

Mayapan, along with Postclassic and contact-period Maya rulership in general, should not be assessed solely on the saga of its dramatic collapse. The Mayapan polity arose from the ashes within a century after Chichen Itza's fall and reigned much of the peninsula for around three hundred years. The first two centuries of this regime were significantly prosperous and stable. Maya rulers of the Postclassic and contact eras are best evaluated by their practices, the material signifiers of their power and personhood, and who they said they were. The hieroglyphic record of Classic-period kings represents a rich, if seductive, set of source material, however incomplete in terms of the structures and players of governance. For later Maya kings, few carved stone records herald their histories, but fortunately, illuminating glimpses are provided in colonial-era documents regarding Yucatán's last independent rulers at the time of European contact.

REFERENCES CITED

Arnauld, M. Charlotte
    2021   Classic to Postclassic Maya Rulership: Changes in Military-Courtly Institutions. In *Maya Kingship: Rupture and Transformation from Classic to Postclassic Times*, edited by Tsubaka Okoshi, Arlen F. Chase, Phillippe Nondédéo, and M. Charlotte Arnauld, pp. 133–151. University Press of Florida, Gainesville.

Bolles, David (editor)
    2003   *Post Conquest Mayan Literature: Based on Pre-Columbian Sources.* Labyrinthos, Lancaster, Calif.

Carmack, Robert M.
    1977   Ethnohistory of the Central Quiche: The Community of Utatlan. In *Archaeology and Ethnohistory of the Central Quiche,*

edited by Dwight T. Wallace and Robert M. Carmack, pp. 1–19. Institute for Mesoamerican Studies, State University of New York, Albany.

Carosi, Gaia

2020 La red de los caminos en Yucatán, siglo XVI: Una propuesta de análisis a partir de las fuentes coloniales. *Journal of Latin American Geography* 19(4):91–111.

Chamberlain, Robert S.

1948 *The Conquest and Colonization of Yucatan, 1517–1550*. Carnegie Institution of Washington, Washington, D.C.

Chase, Arlen F., and Diane Z. Chase

2021 The Transformation of Maya Rulership at Caracol, Belize. In *Maya Kingship: Rupture and Transformation from Classic to Postclassic Times*, edited by Tsubaka Okoshi, Arlen F. Chase, Phillippe Nondédéo, and M. Charlotte Arnauld, pp. 224–248. University Press of Florida, Gainesville.

Chase, Diane Z., and Arlen F. Chase

2021 The Rupture of Classic Maya Divine Kingship from the Perspective of Postclassic Archaeology, Iconography, and Ethnohistory. In *Maya Kingship: Rupture and Transformation from Classic to Postclassic Times*, edited by Tsubaka Okoshi, Arlen F. Chase, Phillippe Nondédéo, and M. Charlotte Arnauld, pp. 291–310. University Press of Florida, Gainesville.

Chuchiack, John F.

2001 Pre-Conquest Ah Kinob in a Colonial World: The Extirpation of Ideology and the Survival of the Maya Priesthood in Colonial Yucatan, 1563–1697. *Acta mesoamericana* 12:135–160.

2010 Writing as Resistance: Maya Graphic Pluralism and Indigenous Elite Strategies for Survival in Colonial Yucatan, 1550–1750. *Ethnohistory* 57(1):86–116.

Cobos, Rafael

2021 Rulers at Chichen Itza at the End of the Classic Period: Their Continuity as Seen in Iconography and Architecture. In *Maya Kingship: Rupture and Transformation from Classic to Postclassic Times*, edited by Tsubaka Okoshi, Arlen F. Chase, Phillippe Nondédéo, and M. Charlotte Arnauld, pp. 269–290. University Press of Florida, Gainesville.

De la Garza, Mercedes, Ana Luisa Izquierdo, María del Carmen León, and Tolita Figueroa (editors)

1983 *Relaciones histórico-geográfica de la gobernación de Yucatán*, vol. 1. Universidad Autónoma de México, Mexico City.

Delgado Kú, Pedro C., Bárbara del C. Escamilla Ojeda, Marilyn A. Masson, Carlos Peraza Lope, Bradley W. Russell, and Douglas J. Kennett

2021 Household Archaeology Within and Outside of Mayapán's Monumental Center. In *Settlement, Economy, and Society, at Mayapan, Yucatan, Mexico*, edited by Marilyn A. Masson, Timothy S. Hare, Carlos Peraza Lope, and Bradley W. Russell, pp. 119–155. University of Pittsburgh, Center for Comparative Archaeology, Pittsburgh.

Delgado Kú, Pedro C., Carlos Peraza Lope, Marilyn A. Masson, Bárbara del C. Escamilla Ojeda, Wilberth A. Cruz Alvarado, and Bradley W. Russell

2021 Architecture and Sculptures of a Colonnaded Hall and Temple at the Itzmal Ch'en Group, Mayapán. In *Settlement, Economy, and Society, at Mayapan, Yucatan, Mexico*, edited by Marilyn A. Masson, Timothy S. Hare, Carlos Peraza Lope, and Bradley W. Russell, pp. 155–183. University of Pittsburgh, Center for Comparative Archaeology, Pittsburgh.

Feldman, Lawrence H.

1978 Moving Merchandise in Protohistoric Central Quauhtemallan. In *Mesoamerican Communication Routes and Cultural Contacts*, edited by Thomas A. Lee and Carlos Navarette, pp. 7–17. New World Archaeological Foundation, Provo, Utah.

Gann, Thomas

1900 Mounds in Northern Honduras. *Nineteenth Annual Report of the Bureau of American Ethnology 1897–1898*, pt. 2: 655–692.

Grube, Nikolai
- 2021 Nostalgic Kings: The Rhetoric of Terminal Classic Maya Inscriptions. In *Maya Kingship: Rupture and Transformation from Classic to Postclassic Times*, edited by Tsubaka Okoshi, Arlen F. Chase, Phillippe Nondédéo, and M. Charlotte Arnauld, pp. 35–50. University Press of Florida, Gainesville.

Hanks, William F.
- 2010 *Converting Words: Maya in the Age of the Cross*. University of California Press, Berkeley.

Hare, Timothy S., Marilyn A. Masson, and Carlos Peraza Lope
- 2014 The Urban Cityscape. In *Kukulcan's Realm: Urban Life at Postclassic Mayapán*, by Marilyn A. Masson and Carlos Peraza Lope, pp. 149–185. University Press of Colorado, Boulder.

Helmke, Christophe, Julie A. Hoggarth, and Jaime J. Awe
- 2021 Deciphering the Collapse: An Account of Kingship in the Terminal Classic. In *Maya Kingship: Rupture and Transformation from Classic to Postclassic Times*, edited by Tsubaka Okoshi, Arlen F. Chase, Phillippe Nondédéo, and M. Charlotte Arnauld, pp. 106–132. University Press of Florida, Gainesville.

Hutson, Scott R., and Jacob Welch
- 2016 Neighborhoods at Chunchucmil. In *The Ancient Urban Maya: Neighborhoods, Inequality, and Built Form*, by Scott R. Hutson, pp. 97–138. University Press of Florida, Gainesville.

Jones, Grant D.
- 1998 *The Conquest of the Last Maya Kingdom*. Stanford University Press, Stanford.

Kennett, Douglas J., Marilyn A. Masson, Carlos Peraza Lope et al.
- 2022 Drought-Induced Civil Conflict among the Ancient Maya. *Nature Communications* 13:3911, doi.org/10.1038/s41467-022-31522-x.

Landa, Diego de
- 1941 *Relaciones de las cosas de Yucatan*. Translated by Alfred Tozzer. Peabody Museum of Archaeology and Ethnology, Harvard University Press, Cambridge, Mass.

López de Cogolludo, Diego
- (1688) *Historia de Yucatan*. 2 vols. 3rd ed. 1867–1868 M. Aldana Rivas, Mérida.

Love, Bruce
- 1994 *The Paris Codex: Handbook for a Maya Priest*. University of Texas Press, Austin.

Magnoni, Aline, Travis W. Stanton, and Scott R. Hutson
- 2014 The Importance of Place and Memory in the Maya Past: The Variable Appropriation of Ancient Settlement at Chunchucmil and Yaxuná, Yucatán, during the Terminal Classic. In *The Archaeology of Yucatán*, edited by Travis W. Stanton, pp. 457–466. Archaeopress, Oxford.

Martin, Simon, and Nikolai Grube
- 2008 *Chronicle of the Maya Kings and Queens: Deciphering the Dynasties of the Ancient Maya*. 2nd ed. Thames and Hudson, New York.

Masson, Marilyn A.
- 2000 *In the Realm of Nachan Kan: Postclassic Maya Archaeology at Laguna de On, Belize*. University Press of Colorado, Boulder.
- 2009 Appendix: Inventory and Lot Descriptions from Carnegie Institution Current Reports on Mayapan. In *The Carnegie Maya II: Carnegie Institution of Washington Current Reports, 1952–1957*, edited by John Weeks, pp. 553–609. University of Colorado Press, Boulder.
- 2021 Resiliency and Cultural Reconstitution of the Postclassic Mayapan Confederacy and Its Aftermath. In *Mesoamerican Archaeology: Theory and Practice*, edited by Julia Hendon, Rosemary Joyce, and Lisa Overholtzer, pp. 278–314. Wiley/Blackwell, Hoboken, N.J.

Masson, Marilyn A., and David A. Freidel
- 2012 An Argument for Classic Era Maya Market Exchange. *Journal of Anthropological Archaeology* 31:455–484.
- 2013 Wide Open Spaces: A Long View of the Importance of Maya Market Exchange. In *Merchants, Trade and Exchange in the Pre-Columbian World*, edited by Kenneth G. Hirth and Joanne Pillsbury, pp. 201–208. Dumbarton Oaks Research Library and Collection, Washington, D.C.

Masson, Marilyn A., Timothy S. Hare, Carlos Peraza Lope, Bárbara C. Escamilla Ojeda, Elizabeth H. Paris, Betsy Kohut, Bradley W. Russell, and Wilberth Cruz Alvarado

    2016   Household Craft Production in the Prehispanic Urban Setting of Mayapan, Yucatan, Mexico. *Journal of Archaeological Research* 24(3):229–274.

Masson, Marilyn A., and Carlos Peraza Lope

    2007   Kukulkan/Quetzalcoatl, Death God, and Creation Mythology of Burial Shaft Temples at Mayapán. *Mexicon* 29(3):77–85.

    2014a   Archaeological Investigations of an Ancient Urban Place. In *Kukulcan's Realm: Urban Life at Ancient Mayapán*, by Marilyn A. Masson and Carlos Peraza Lope, pp. 1–38. University Press of Colorado, Boulder.

    2014b   *Kukulcan's Realm: Urban Life at Ancient Mayapán.* University Press of Colorado, Boulder.

    2014c   Militarism, Misery, and Collapse. In *Kukulcan's Realm: Urban Life at Ancient Mayapán*, by Marilyn A. Masson and Carlos Peraza Lope, pp. 521–540. University Press of Colorado, Boulder.

    2014d   The Economic Foundations. In *Kukulcan's Realm: Urban Life at Ancient Mayapán*, by Marilyn A. Masson and Carlos Peraza Lope, pp. 269–424. University Press of Colorado, Boulder.

Masson, Marilyn A., Carlos Peraza Lope, Wilberth Cruz Alvarado, and Susan Milbrath

    2020   Effigy Censer Smashing and Termination Rituals at a Mayapan Ceremonial Group. In *A Forest of History: The Maya after the Emergence of Divine Kingship*, edited by T. Stanton and M. K. Brown, pp. 204–235. University of Colorado Press, Boulder.

McAnany, Patricia A.

    2010   *Ancestral Maya Economies in Archaeological Perspective.* Cambridge University Press, Cambridge.

Milbrath, Susan, and Carlos Peraza Lope

    2003   Revisiting Mayapan: Mexico's Last Maya Capital. *Ancient Mesoamerica* 14:1–46.

    2009   Clash of Worldviews in Late Mayapan. In *Maya Worldviews at Conquest*, edited by Leslie Cecil and Timothy W. Pugh, pp. 183–204. University of Colorado Press, Boulder.

Miller, Arthur G.

    1982   *On the Edge of the Sea: Mural Painting at Tancah-Tulum, Quintana Roo, Mexico.* Dumbarton Oaks, Washington, D.C.

Okoshi, Tsubasa

    2021   Colonial Maya Discourse on the Rupture and Transformation or Continuity of Pre-Columbian Kingship: An Ethnohistorical Analysis. In *Maya Kingship: Rupture and Transformation from Classic to Postclassic Times*, edited by Tsubaka Okoshi, Arlen F. Chase, Phillippe Nondédeo, and M. Charlotte Arnauld, pp. 311–326. University Press of Florida, Gainesville.

Okoshi, Tsubasa, Arlen F. Chase, Philippe Nondédéo, M. Charlotte Arnauld (editors)

    2021   *Maya Kingship: Rupture and Transformation from Classic to Postclassic Times.* University Press of Florida, Gainesville.

Oland, Maxine H.

    2014   With the Gifts and Good Treatment that He Gave Them: Elite Maya Adoption of Spanish Material Culture at Progresso Lagoon, Belize. *International Journal of Historical Anthropology* 18(4):643–667.

Paris, Elizabeth H.

    2021   Molding Identity at Mayapan: The Multifaceted Uses of Metal at an Urban Center. In *Settlement, Economy, and Society at Mayapan, Yucatan, Mexico*, edited by Marilyn A. Masson, Timothy S. Hare, Carlos Peraza Lope, and Bradley W. Russell, pp. 315–335. University of Pittsburgh, Center for Comparative Archaeology, Pittsburgh.

Peraza Lope, Carlos, and Marilyn A. Masson

    2014a   Politics and Monumental Legacies. In *Kukulcan's Realm: Urban Life at Ancient Mayapán*, by Marilyn A. Masson and Carlos Peraza Lope, pp. 39–104. University Press of Colorado, Boulder.

    2014b   An Outlying Temple, Hall, and Elite Residence. In *Kukulcan's Realm: Urban Life at Ancient Mayapán*, by Marilyn A. Masson and Carlos Peraza Lope, pp. 105–148. University Press of Colorado, Boulder.

2014c   Religious Practice. In *Kukulcan's Realm: Urban Life at Ancient Mayapán*, by Marilyn A. Masson and Carlos Peraza Lope, pp. 425–520. University Press of Colorado, Boulder.

Piña Chan, Román

1978   Commerce in the Yucatec Peninsula: The Conquest and Colonial Period. In *Mesoamerican Communication Routes and Culture Contacts*, edited by T. A. Lee and C. Navarrete, pp. 37–48. Brigham Young University, Provo, Utah.

Pollock, H. E. D.

1962   Introduction. In *Mayapán, Yucatan, Mexico*, edited by Harry E. D. Pollock, Ralph Roys, Tatiana Proskouriakoff, and A. Ledyard Smith, pp. 1–24. Carnegie Institution of Washington, Washington, D.C.

Proskouriakoff, Tatiana

1962   Civic and Religious Structures of Mayapán. In *Mayapán, Yucatan, Mexico*, edited by Harry E. D. Pollock, Ralph Roys, Tatiana Proskouriakoff, and A. Ledyard Smith, pp. 87–164. Carnegie Institution of Washington, Washington, D.C.

Proskouriakoff, Tatiana, and Charles R. Temple

1955   A Residential Quadrangle—Structures R-85 to R-90. *Current Reports* 29:289–362. Carnegie Institute of Washington, Washington, D.C.

Quezada, Sergio

2014   *Maya Lords and Lordship: The Formation of Colonial Society in Yucatan 1350–1600*. University of Oklahoma Press, Norman.

Quezada, Sergio, and Tsubasa Okoshi Harada

2001   *Papeles de los Xiu de Yaxá, Yucatán*. Centro de Estudios Mayas, Instituto de Investigaciones Filológicas, Universidad Autónoma de México, Mexico City.

Restall, Matthew

2001   The People of the Patio: Ethnohistoric Evidence of Yucatec Maya Royal Courts. In *Royal Courts of the Maya*, vol. 2, *Data and Case Studies*, edited by Takeshi Inomata and Stephen D. Houston, pp. 335–90. Westview Press, Boulder, Colo.

Rice, Prudence M.

2004   *Maya Political Science: Time, Astronomy and the Cosmos*. University of Texas Press, Austin.

2009   The Kowoj in Geopolitico-Ritual Perspective. In *The Kowoj: Identity, Migration, and Geopolitics in the Late Postclassic Petén, Guatemala*, edited by Prudence M. Rice and Don S. Rice, pp. 21–54. University Press of Colorado, Boulder.

Rice, Prudence M., and Don S. Rice

2018   Classic-to-Contact-Period Continuities in Maya Governance in Central Petén, Guatemala. *Ethnohistory* 65(1):25–50.

Ringle, William M., and George J. Bey III

2001   Post-Classic and Terminal Classic Courts of the Northern Maya Lowlands. In *Royal Courts of the Maya*, vol. 2, *Data and Case Studies*, edited by Takeshi Inomata and Stephen D. Houston, pp. 266–307. Westview Press, Boulder, Colo.

Ringle, William M., Tomás Gallareta Negrón, and George J. Bey III

2021   Stranger-Kings in Northern Yucatan. In *Maya Kingship: Rupture and Transformation from Classic to Postclassic Times*, edited by Tsubaka Okoshi, Arlen F. Chase, Phillippe Nondédéo, and M. Charlotte Arnauld, pp. 249–268. University Press of Florida, Gainesville.

Roys, Ralph L.

(1933) 2008   *The Book of Chilam Balam of Chumayel*. Forgotten Books, London.

(1943) 1972   *The Indian Background of Colonial Yucatan*. University of Oklahoma Press, Norman.

1957   *The Political Geography of the Yucatan Maya*. Carnegie Institution of Washington, Washington, D.C.

1962   Literary Sources for the History of Mayapan. In *Mayapán, Yucatan, Mexico*, edited by Harry E. D. Pollock, Ralph Roys, Tatiana Proskouriakoff, and A. Ledyard Smith, pp. 1–24. Carnegie Institution of Washington, Washington, D.C.

Ruppert, Karl, and A. L. Smith

1952   Excavation in House Mounds at Mayapan. *Current Reports* 4:45–66.

Carnegie Institution of Washington, Washington, D.C.

1954 Excavations in House Mounds at Mayapan: III. *Current Reports* 17:27–52. Carnegie Institution of Washington, Washington, D.C.

Schellhas, Paul

1904 *Representation of Deities in the Maya Manuscripts*. Peabody Museum of Archaeology and Ethnology, Harvard University, Cambridge, Mass.

Scholes, France V., and Ralph L. Roys

1938 Fray Diego de Landa and the Problem of Idolatry in Yucatan. In *Cooperation in Research*, pp. 585–620. Carnegie Institution of Washington, Washington, D.C.

(1948) 1968 *The Maya Chontal Indians of Acalan-Tixchel*. University of Oklahoma Press, Norman.

Serafin, Stanley, and Carlos Peraza Lope

2007 Human Sacrificial Rites among the Maya of Mayapán: A Bioarchaeological Perspective. In *New Perspectives on Human Sacrifice and Ritual Body Treatments in Ancient Maya Society*, edited by Vera Tiesler and Andrea Cucina, pp. 232–250. Springer, New York.

Shaw, Justine M.

2001 Maya Sacbeob: Form and Function. *Ancient Mesoamerica* 12:261–272.

Shook, Edwin M.

1953 The X-Coton Temples at Mayapan. *Current Reports* 11:207–221. Carnegie Institute of Washington, Washington, D.C.

1954 Three Temples and Their Associated Structures at Mayapan. *Current Reports* 14:254–291. Carnegie Institute of Washington, Washington, D.C.

Shook, Edwin M., and William N. Irving

1955 Colonnaded Buildings at Mayapan. *Current Reports* 22:127–224. Carnegie Institute of Washington, Washington, D.C.

Simmons, Scott, David M. Pendergast, and Elizabeth Graham

2009 The Context and Significance of Copper Artifacts in Postclassic and Early Historic Lamanai, Belize. *Journal of Field Archaeology* 34(1):57–75.

Smith, A. Ledyard

1962 Residential and Associated Structures at Mayapan. In *Mayapan, Yucatan, Mexico*, by Harry E. D. Pollock, Ralph L. Roys, Tatiana Proskouriakoff, and A. Ledyard Smith, pp. 165–320. Carnegie Institution of Washington, Washington, D.C.

Smith, A. Ledyard, and Karl Ruppert

1953 Excavations in House Mounds at Mayapan: II. *Current Reports* 10:180–206. Carnegie Institution of Washington, Washington, D.C.

1956 Excavations in House Mounds at Mayapan: IV. *Current Reports* 36:471–528. Carnegie Institution of Washington, Washington, D.C.

Taube, Karl A.

1992 *The Major Gods of Ancient Yucatan*. Dumbarton Oaks Research Library and Collection, Washington, D.C.

Tozzer, Alfred M.

1941 Notes on Landa's *Relaciones de las cosas de Yucatan*. Peabody Museum of Archaeology and Ethnology, Harvard University, Cambridge, Mass.

Vail, Gabrielle

2006 The Maya Codices. *Annual Review of Anthropology* 35:497–519.

Winters, Howard

1955a Excavation of a Colonnaded Hall at Mayapan. *Current Reports* 31:381–396. Carnegie Institute of Washington, Washington, D.C.

1955b Three Serpent Column Temples and Associated Platforms at Mayapan. *Current Reports* 32:397–424. Carnegie Institute of Washington, Washington, D.C.

Yaeger, Jason

2020 Collapse, Transformation, Reorganization: The Terminal Classic Transition in the Maya World. In *The Maya World*, edited by Scott Hutson and Traci Ardren, pp. 777–793. Routledge, London.

Zender, Marc

2004 A Study of Classic Maya Priesthood. PhD dissertation, University of Calgary, Alberta.

Denying the Rights of "Natural Lords"
Maya Elite Struggles for Rewards and Recognition in Colonial Yucatán, 1550–1750

JOHN F. CHUCHIAK IV

Captain don Juan Chan, cacique and natural lord and governor of the town of Chancenote and lord over his subjects in the province of Yucatán, says that his father and grandparents were natural lords of the said peoples, and as such they were attended to with all their tributes in time of their gentility until they came to the knowledge of the holy gospel; and then they gave obedience to your majesty and to the governors who by order of your majesty have gone to that land . . .

Probanza de don Juan Chan, 1622,
Archivo General de Indias (AGI), México, 140, r. 2

In June 1618, don Juan Chan, the *batab* and natural lord of the Maya *cah* of Chancenote, appeared before Spanish officials in Mérida and presented a *probanza* of his merits and services to the Spanish Crown. This *probanza* gave "proof" of his noble lineage and the military and religious service that he and his son, don Francisco Chan, rendered in favor of the Crown and the Christian religion (Quezada 1989:41–44) (Figure 13.1).

Juan Chan's grandfather, Nahau Chan, served as the legitimate *halach uinic,* or supreme native lord, of the region before the conquest. In the *probanza*, certified witness testimony corroborated more than thirty years of active service in conducting military expeditions to bring back Maya idolaters who had fled Spanish colonialism.[1] Based on the formula necessary to receive the grant of a coat of arms, don Juan Chan had every reason to believe that he would receive this privilege, as he descended from natural lords of the Chancenote region, maintained a loyal and active military service on the part of the Spanish Crown, and aided in the Christianization, conversion, and *reducción* of pagan Maya. Many earlier caciques had received royally sanctioned coats of arms for much less. However, two years later, the royal response came in the form of a *cédula*, signed in Madrid and dated February 14, 1622, in which King Philip IV recognized Chan's merits, writing to the governor of Yucatán that he should favor him as an inspiration to other Maya leaders:

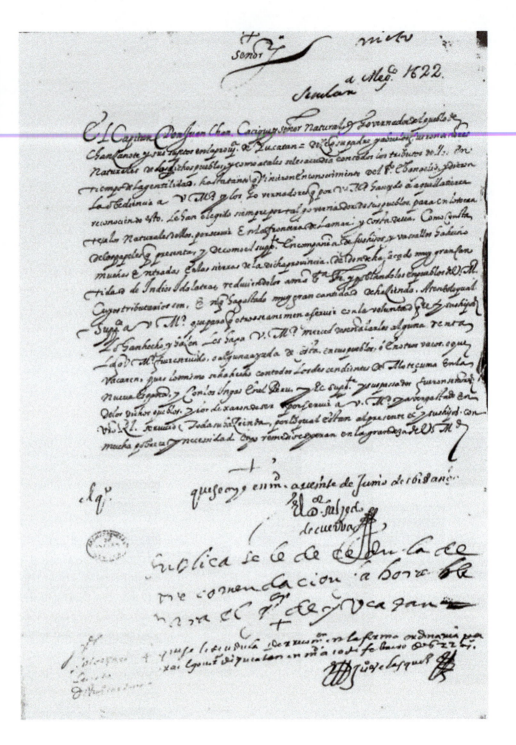

figure 13.1
Probanza de méritos de cacique Don Juan Chan, 1618–1622. AGI, México, 140.

Based on his merits, and so that other Indians will also be inspired to serve with the will and similar desire that he and his sons have served us . . . I have decided to bestow favor on him and award him some revenue and an annuity to be paid from the revenues of royal towns . . . and this is fitting because the same has been done for all of the descendants of Montezuma in New Spain and with those of the Incas in Peru and seeing that he and his ancestors were also natural lords of the said towns . . . it is my will that don Juan Chan should receive the royal favor and that you, our governor, should occupy him in offices related to my service and honor . . . [2]

Nevertheless, this royal *cédula* of recommendation fell short of granting don Juan Chan the privilege of receiving a coat of arms, a symbol of Spanish prestige given to those Indigenous collaborators who during the conquest, or subsequent military and religious campaigns, had served the Crown loyally.

What is most surprising in this case is not that don Juan Chan did not receive a grant of a coat of arms, but rather, that not a single Maya conquistador or Indigenous collaborator with the Spanish colonial regime in Yucatán ever successfully petitioned for a coat of arms (see Chuchiak 2007:175–225, 2013:277–302). Surrounded by regions such as Guatemala and Oaxaca, in which Indigenous conquistadors received formal grants of coats of arms in recognition of their valuable services (Castañeda de la Paz 2008, 2009, 2010; Luque Talaván and Castañeda de la Paz 2006:68–73; Oudijk and Restall 2008), the absence of a single royally sanctioned Indigenous coat of arms for the region of Yucatán is a strange anomaly.

Pre-Hispanic Maya Concepts of Shields and Heraldic Emblems

> For defense they had shields which they made out of reeds, which they split and wove with much care... and which were fitted with deer skin.
>
> Fray Diego de Landa,
> *Relación de las cosas de Yucatán*, 1566

Although a specifically European importation, Spanish coats of arms and their symbolism would not be completely foreign to the Maya. Emblematic shields and banners existed in Mesoamerica before the arrival of the Spaniards. Robert Haskett and others have commented that the shields of warriors showed "emblems indicating geographic origin, or ethnic affiliation" (Haskett 2005:222). The Spanish conquistadors identified the insignias and other symbols on the Native warriors' shields as true heraldic symbols (Domínguez Torres 2013:21–22). Moreover, in the Maya region, early colonial observers mistook many of the Classic Maya emblem glyphs and other carvings of shields and banners in the inscriptions as true coats of arms (Houston, Chinchilla Mazariegos, and Stuart 2001:43–44). An anonymous Dominican friar wrote about several inscriptions in the Maya ruins of Toniná, Chiapas, that he viewed as "coats of arms" as late as 1711, stating that "many of these shields have been taken to the Town of Ocozingo where I have seen them: and noticing in the characters that the shields have as their *Orla*, more than just letters, they seemed to me to be figures or hieroglyphs that mean actions or events" (Anonymous 1892:109).

The shield, in all its variations, seems to have been an integral part of pre-Hispanic Maya war iconography. Maya shields were used in other instances to emphasize the martial skills or glory of a Maya ruler (Bassie-Sweet 2021). The symbol of the shield is so intricately related to warfare in Maya iconography that Berthold Riese (1982:279–281) first believed that the "Flint-Shield" (*took' pakal*) glyph indicated a raid or act of warfare. More recent scholars have examined the use and iconography of Maya shields in warfare in greater depth (Martin 2020:157–159; Stone and Zender 2011:86–87). The most common form of Maya shield (*pakal* in Classic Maya or *max* in colonial Yucatec Maya) was a flexible type, either round, square, or rectangular in design (Figure 13.2).

Based on their depictions on stelae and polychrome vases, Maya shields were most probably made from wooden or wicker bases and covered with wood or animal hide that was painted and adorned with feathers and emblematic images related to war and capture. Diego de Landa described Postclassic Maya shields, saying that "for defense they had shields which they made out of reeds, which they split and wove with much care" (Tozzer 1941:121). For the Maya, the imagery on shields held special symbolic significance, like the emblems emblazoned on Spanish coats of arms. Moreover, the shape and styles of Classic Maya shields seem to be emblematic of a specific site, city, polity, or noble dynasty (Webster 1989). The iconography on these shields further illustrates their connection to warfare, as the Maya painted or decorated their shields with mythical images of animals, beasts, or abstract war motifs (Figure 13.3). Images related to death are

figure 13.2
Typical types of Classic Maya emblematic shields: K5772, K5827, and K8566. Justin Kerr Maya archive, Dumbarton Oaks, Trustees for Harvard University, Washington, D.C.

Square and Rectangular Shields

| Crossed Bones Symbols K 2036 | Skull with Missing Mandible K 2036 | Geometric Patterns K 3984 | Geometric Patterns K 2036 | Geometric Pattern K 4549 | Geometric Pattern K 6416 |

Death Imagery   *Geometric Designs*

Round Shields

| Shield & Knotted Mat Symbols K 4549 | Jaguar Spot Symbols K 4549 | Iconographic Symbols K 4549 | Iconographic Symbols K 1116 | Skull/Death Symbols K 5772 | Geometric Patterns K 1365 | Geometric Patterns K 638 | Geometric Patterns K 6416 |

Iconographic Symbols   *Geometric Designs*

figure 13.3
Heraldic-style images emblazoned on Classic Maya shields. Justin Kerr Maya archive, Dumbarton Oaks, Trustees for Harvard University, Washington, D.C.

frequently emblazoned on Classic Maya shields, including crossed bones and skulls (both universal symbols of death), the *cimi* death symbol, and other geometric designs whose significance is not yet understood (Chuchiak n.d.). All of these images may have also served to frighten the enemy, thereby aiding the owner in battle.

Furthermore, Maya city-states had their own emblem glyphs that served, like coats of arms, to symbolize a polity with place-linked titles, and sometimes with symbols of a ruling lineage (Martin 2020; Mathews 1991:19–29). As William Ringle notes (this volume), decorative mosaic masks, or similar emblematic symbols, may have served at Puuc Maya sites as emblematic markers of the administrative or military status of structures, giving hints to elite use of these buildings. Similarly, Maxime Lamoureux-St-Hilaire and Patricia A. McAnany note (this volume) that it was not unusual for Maya nobles to adopt "the titles, practices, and regalia of hegemonic courts," including their emblems and other symbols. Based on these precontact understandings of the emblematic nature of certain shields, masks, or other imagery, the post-conquest Maya of Yucatán came to recognize and appreciate the symbolism and prestige gained by the display and use of a Spanish coat of arms (Haskett 2005:222).

The Nature of *Cacicazgos* and the Status of "Natural Lords" in the Maya Region

> The chieftains were absolute in ruling, and they executed their commands with great rigor.
> Relación de algunas costumbres, 1582,
> AGI, México, 110

In order to explain why no legitimate grants of coats of arms exist for the "natural lords" of the Maya region of Yucatán, it is necessary to first examine the differences between the precontact nature of *cacicazgos* in the Maya region and Central Mexico. The Indigenous rulers of New Spain, regardless of whether they were called *tlatoani*, *batab*, or *cazonci*, all governed complex hierarchically stratified societies (Luque Talaván 2004; Menegus Bornemann 1999). The differences between the Central Mexican Nahua lords and the Maya lords of Yucatán focused many times on each Native nobility's access to or lack of patrimonial property and their claims to traditional rights over the tribute and services of their vassals (Menegus Bornemann 1999:601–602). The Maya nobility of Yucatán apparently had little access to patrimonial land holdings (Quezada 1993, 2005). Although some scholars have recently begun to examine this issue of patrimonial landholdings among the preconquest Maya (Masson, this volume), the fact remains that none of the contact-era Maya made any attempt to claim recognition from the earliest Spanish colonial authorities of these patrimonial land rights for their noble lineages. There is no denying the evidence for the existence of territorial domains for late Maya polities (Masson, this volume), but what is absent is the contact-era Maya nobles' claims of independent landed patrimonial property belonging to their lineages apart from the communal holdings of the communities they ruled.[3] Evidence exists for noble Maya claims for their control over tribute and the labor services of their precontact vassals, but no documentation survives for noble claims to precontact extensive patrimonial landholdings for themselves, except for claims of control over the usufruct of certain natural resources, such as the salt beds of the northern peninsula (MacKinnon and Kepecs 1989) and some cacao groves in other areas (Terry et al. 2022).[4]

The conservation of the Native lords in their positions of rulership at first served a very clear and pragmatic purpose, since these lords served as a natural linkage between the Spanish and the Indigenous world (Menegus Bornemann 1999:614). Nevertheless, the Spanish Crown, demanding complete sovereignty over the political life of the colony, could not officially recognize that these Indigenous nobles were "kings" or "natural lords." As early as 1538, the Crown prohibited these surviving rulers from calling themselves "natural lords" or "kings," instead mandating that they should be called caciques.[5]

From this early period onward, the Crown limited the functions and inherent privileges attached to caciques. In Yucatán in 1552, the royal *oidor* and *visitador* Tomás López Medel drastically changed the role of the Maya nobility in the *cacicazgos*. During his visitation of the province, he reduced the number of Native lords and *principales*, and ordered the release of all their Native slaves, thus taking from the Maya caciques much of their wealth, which had been traditionally held in slaves and tribute-paying retainers (Chuchiak 2018). The judge directly attacked the existence of the Maya nobles, stating that "because a great number of leaders causes confusion and discord, and so it is among the natives of this province due to the many *principales*, and nobles, who rise up in each town ... therefore, I command by this order there may be no more than six in any town" (Ancona 1889:539).

The next blow to the powers and privileges of the Maya nobility came in the 1560s, when the *alcalde mayor*, don Diego de Quijada, further attacked the powers and privileges of the Maya caciques by regulating and lowering the amount of tribute and labor services for Maya commoners.[6] Since the Maya caciques did not hold any patrimonial lands, and since their wealth resided mainly in their access to slaves, Native labor, and tribute, these reforms destroyed the basis of the caciques' prosperity (Quezada 1993; Quezada and Rugeley 2014).

Although the *cabildo* system of government was introduced in the 1560s, it did not take root formally in Yucatán until the 1580s, mostly due to the local *batabob*, who resisted the Spanish attempts to limit their functions and privileges.[7] Nevertheless, by the 1590s, the Spanish government in Yucatán had shifted away from their initial policy of maintaining the traditional Maya elite in the position of Indigenous *gobernador* of the towns. The powers of the natural lords were limited again with the forced disappearance of the figure of the pre-Hispanic regional Native lord, or *halach uinic* (provincial lords, or the "Great Lords").[8] By the late 1580s, the few Maya *halach uinicob* who had survived the conquest lost their effective control over their regional provinces. This act effectively ended the reigns of these pre-Hispanic "kings" as provincial lords, as they were ultimately reduced to holding the powers and prestige of a simple local town cacique or *batab*.

The nature of the pre-Hispanic Maya caciques' powers and their traditional style of government greatly impacted the colonial caciques' abilities or failures to claim certain privileges and tributes after the conquest. Those regions and caciques in New Spain who did not have access to formal claims of patrimonial territories or landholdings, or clear natural rights to receive the labor and tribute of their vassals, would find it difficult to claim these rights in the newly forming governments of the colonial period. Moreover, without the ability to claim these "natural rights" as "Native patrimonial lords," the colonial Indigenous nobility's ability to successfully petition the Crown for and receive privileges and other rewards was severely curtailed.

Grants of Coats of Arms to Indigenous Conquistadors and Collaborators

> Abiding by all the above and considering that you are a faithful vassal and a good Christian, so that you and your descendants shall be more honored, and so that other chieftains shall be encouraged to serve us, it is our mercy and will to give you a coat of arms in recognition of your services.
>
> Cédula real para don Miguel,
> Indio cacique de Cicaztenango,
> en la Provincia de Guatemala, June 30, 1543

From the first forays into overseas territories, Spanish explorers and conquerors began to ask the king of Spain for several privileges in recognition of their services. To this end, the applicants submitted to the king and the Council of the Indies thick bundles of documents called *probanzas de méritos y servicios*, or "proofs of merits and services," which contained notarized testimonies and affidavits testifying to the petitioners' exploits and services in the New World (Chuchiak 2001, 2002; Macleod 1998).[9] In contrast to the Spanish conquistadors, who started making requests for coats of arms shortly after the initial conquests of the 1520s, the Indigenous conquistadors petitioned for this privilege only beginning in the mid-sixteenth century (Castañeda de la Paz 2009:128). In the case of Indigenous petitioners, the grants were awarded most often because the Indigenous lords personally asked for them (Gibson 1967:165–167). These Indigenous petitions were made possible by a solid knowledge of Spanish forms of law on the part of the petitioners (Castañeda de la Paz 2009:128; Gibson 1967:165). Both the Spaniards and the Indigenous peoples held a very high regard for coats of arms and the high prestige and value of possessing one was evident in the Americas from the beginning (Haskett 2005:222–231; see also Domínguez Torres 2013).

Generally, these *probanzas* served as the prerequisite for formally petitioning grants of coats of arms, and in them the *principales* specified their noble ascendancy; their role in the conquest, pacification, and settlement of the recently conquered lands; and their contributions of people, arms, and monetary expenses related to the military campaigns (Castañeda de la Paz 2013:71–72; Domínguez Torres 2013:31; Oudjik 2013). The procedure to request a municipal coat of arms normally began with the Indigenous *cabildo*, or town council, writing a petition to be presented before the king (Castañeda de la Paz 2009:129). Then, a specially formed committee of *principales* personally took the request to Spain and afterward brought the concessions of privileges back to New Spain to be presented to the viceroy. Upon the return of a successful delegation, a special ceremony of obedience would be performed, followed by the presentation of the concessions to the Indigenous *cabildo* (Castañeda de la Paz 2009:128–129; Gibson 1991:156–158). If individuals made a request for a coat of arms, the procedure was the same: the interested party would submit a petition to the colonial authorities, who sent it to Spain. As has been illustrated by other scholars, the prestige, power, and symbolic significance of grants of coats of arms to Indigenous rulers remained a coveted reward for loyal service to the Crown throughout Mesoamerica (see Castañeda de la Paz 2013; Chuchiak 2013; Haskett 2005; Roskamp 1998, 2003, 2010; Roskamp and Monzón 2020; Roskamp, Monzón, and Warren 2009; Wood 1998a, 1998b, 1998c, 2003; Wood and Noguez Ramírez 1998).

Early Grants of Coats of Arms to Indigenous Collaborators in Guatemala, 1520s–1540s

> For we are informed that you, don Gaspar, chief of the towns of Teculitlan, which are in the province of Guatemala, have served us in what has been offered, especially in seeking together with fray Pedro de Angulo, and other religious of the Order of Santo Domingo, in bringing peace and in our service and in knowledge of our Holy Catholic Faith to the natural Indians of the said provinces of Teculitlan and Lacandón . . . [and] our mercy and will is to give you by arms a shield.
>
> Cédula real para don Gaspar,
> Indio cacique de Teculitlan,
> en la Provincia de Guatemala, June 30, 1543

Although most coats of arms awarded to Indigenous rulers in New Spain went to the rulers of Central Mexican city-states such as Tlaxcala and Texcoco, a few examples of the early awarding to caciques in the Maya region did occur (Castañeda de la Paz 2009:137–138, 145–146; Luque Talaván and Castañeda de la Paz 2006:68–73; Wood 2003). The initial grants of coats of arms to Maya nobles from Guatemala were made based on a combination of their military aid during the conquest, their acceptance of the Christian faith, and their aid in the conversion of other pagan Maya groups. This was not out of line with traditional Castilian customs, which equated the concept of nobility and the granting of a coat of arms with merits or actions in war, or in the defense or spread of the faith against the infidel, such as in the Spanish reconquest (Menéndez Pidal 2008). All of these coats of arms were granted by *cédulas* signed on June 30, 1543.[10] As the royal *cédulas* explain, the grants for the Guatemalan Maya caciques were specifically for their aid to the Dominican friar Pedro de Angulo in his religious *reducciones* of the Maya of the Teculitlan and Lacandon regions.[11] The Dominican friar praised these Maya caciques for their efforts on his behalf even in his own *probanza*.[12] Fray Pedro de Angulo's missionary efforts would later gain him appointment to the post of Bishop of the Verapaz region.[13] For their part in the expedition, five Maya caciques received a grant of a series of related coats of arms, all of which shared

Coat of arms of cacique don Jorge of Tecpanatitlan (Sololá, Guatemala) Granted June 30, 1543	Coat of arms of caciques don Pedro and Don Diego Zacatepeque, Guatemala Granted June 30, 1543	Coat of arms of cacique don Gaspar of Teculitlan Guatemala Granted June 30, 1543	Coat of arms of cacique don Miguel of Cicaztenango Guatemala Granted June 30, 1543
(A) Shield A (Lamina xxxiv, 2)	(B) Shield B (Lamina xxxv, 6)	(C) Shield C (Lamina xxxv, 5)	(D) Shield D (Lamina xxxv, 2)

figure 13.4
Coats of arms granted to Guatemalan caciques in 1543. Reproduced from Paz y Meliá 1892.

similar characteristics emphasizing their true conversion to Christianity and their aid in the missionary's efforts (Figure 13.4).

Similar grants of coats of arms with the words "Ave Maria" and other religious inscriptions in Latin clearly emphasized the new faith of these loyal Maya caciques (Luque Talaván and Castañeda de la Paz 2006:68–73). Moreover, as Domínguez Torres (2013) argued, and the Spanish heraldic scholar Riquer (1996) noted earlier, similar types of Latin religious inscriptions were granted on the coats of arms of converted Jews in later medieval Spain to allude to the new faith of the recipient. This obvious transplantation of Spanish heraldic symbolism to the New World by grants of coats of arms to Indigenous people became a conscious effort on the part of the Crown to make sense of the place of their new vassals within the greater Spanish world.

Nevertheless, what is most remarkable about the case of the Indigenous coats of arms from the Maya region is the general absence of any subsequent grants after the middle of the 1540s, a decade of widespread Maya rebellions that led colonial officials to doubt the loyalty and commitment to the conversion of local lords (Chuchiak 2004; Gosner 1992; Lovell 2005; Patch 1998, 2002). Those Maya caciques and other noblemen who would seek privileges and the coats of arms in recognition of their merits and services on behalf of the Crown after the 1550s would find their efforts futile. Those unlucky loyal Maya caciques would be caught up in the changes in royal policy toward Indigenous nobles that occurred with the abdication of the Emperor Charles V and the ascension to the throne of his son, King Philip II (Cruz Pazos 2005; Mira Caballos 2003; Rojas 2007).

Attempts at Attaining Privileges by the "Natural Lords" of Yucatán, 1550–1700

> The witness knows the said don Juan Kauil . . . and has long known about him because don Juan Caamal, cacique and governor who was of the town of Sisal, was the one who first governed it . . . and that he and his ancestors had come from Mexico to populate this land of Yucatán, and that they were the ones who populated Chichen Itza

and made the buildings that are in that place, very sumptuous ... and they populated it with people, and they were lords of these provinces, and they ruled and lorded over them for many years.

Testimonio en la probanza
de don Juan Kauil, 1618

Petitions and *probanzas de méritos* from Maya caciques in colonial Yucatán began shortly after the conquest. By the 1550s, Maya *batabob* throughout the peninsula petitioned for privileges on the basis of their role in the Spanish conquest and the conversion. It is notable that most of the surviving petitions and *probanzas* of Maya caciques come from those in the western portion of Yucatán, which had earlier submitted to the Spaniards and then aided in the conquest of the eastern peninsula (Figure 13.5). Notably absent in the colonial records are *probanzas* of the Maya caciques of the eastern lineages such as the Cocom, Couoh, and Chan families, which had led the bitter resistance and spearheaded several major colonial revolts (for a larger discussion, see Chuchiak 2004:48–50; Gorissen 2007). As Figure 13.5 illustrates, only the petition of don Juan Chan exists for the eastern region in the colonial records.

Even for those Maya caciques who could offer proof of their loyalty and faithful service to the Crown, the cost of the entire process remained prohibitive. It is not surprising that no single Yucatec Maya community sought to pay the expense of seeking a grant of a coat of arms for their own towns. Even Maya caciques as individuals would have had a difficult time pulling together the financial resources to formally make an official *probanza* and have it sent to Spain (Hillerkuss 1993). By the 1570s, Maya caciques did not officially receive any income, other than from the small amount that they were given as tribute from their townspeople in recognition of their title or lordship (Okoshi Harada 2003). In the case of the Xiu, this amounted in Mani to no more than an annual payment of thirty

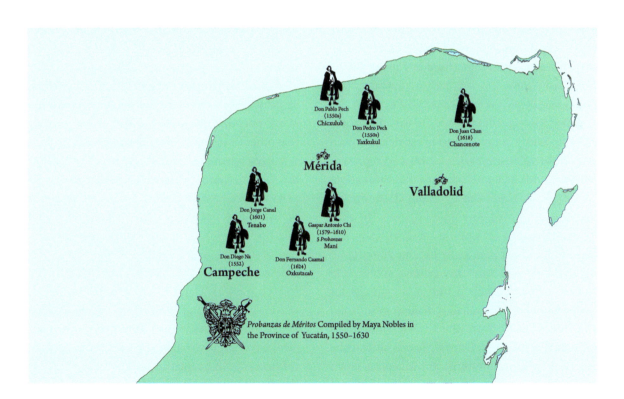

figure 13.5
Probanzas de méritos compiled by Maya nobles from the province of Yucatán, 1550–1630. Map and images drawn and illustrated by John F. Chuchiak IV.

Denying the Rights of "Natural Lords" 341

pesos in agreement between the community and the caciques (Quezada and Okoshi Harada 2001). Without patrimonial landholdings, the Maya caciques' earnings came mainly from their control of labor, and they would be hard-pressed to pay the expenses necessary to make a *probanza*. Moreover, since a cacique wishing to make a *probanza* had to appear in person (or through a properly authorized and paid deputy with a formal power of attorney) before the local provincial governor or other regional Spanish magistrate, distance became an important means of reducing the frequency of the petitions (cf. Borah 1983:237). For Maya caciques living anywhere from thirty or more leagues away from Mérida, the trip to the city alone would take almost a week. Individuals or communities at greater distances had the costs of preparing and presenting their *probanzas* complicated by the addition of the costs of travel and stay in the capital or local Spanish town. For a Maya community, the cost of sending a delegation could be shared among all members of the town. For an individual Maya cacique, on the other hand, the costs of the travel, provisions, and necessary services such as the notarization of documents would be prohibitive. The cost of the paper and notarized documents alone could easily consume a cacique's annual salary (see Borah 1983:53–63; Owensby 2008:50–58).

Also, the legal climate of the times had changed, and Charles V's ready interest in receiving embassies of Native Mesoamerican lords and representatives from Indigenous communities throughout New Spain was replaced by Philip II's desire for tighter control over his empire. By 1563, the ability of Indigenous caciques to travel to Spain and petition the court personally became restricted.[14] All caciques and other Indigenous nobles who wished to present their petitions or requests for coats of arms in person had to request permission and direct license from the Crown. Indigenous towns and nobles from Central Mexico, close to the seat of the political power in the kingdom, could more easily visit the audiencia in Mexico City and request these permissions to travel directly from the viceregal authorities. The distance and travel costs involved were minimal. Native nobles and caciques from the Maya region, on the other hand, had the added filter of having to first petition their local provincial governor and, if given the permission, then pay the expenses for the difficult trip to the viceregal capital and request permission from the audiencia to present their petition personally in Spain. The costs of this process, the administrative distances involved, and the local colonial authorities' lack of interest in pursuing or aiding in the processing of Maya noblemen's cases often forced the Native petitioners to lose hope and abandon their efforts.[15]

Few Maya nobles pursued the granting of royal privileges and pensions with more vigor than don Gaspar Antonio Chi, a descendant on his mother's side of the ancient Maya lineage of the Xiu of Mani (Okoshi Harada 2001). Chi spent many long years, and a fortune, compiling more than five *probanzas* of his merits and services to the Crown from 1579 to 1610 (Quezada and Torres Trujillo 2010:15–32). As his case exemplifies, even hard-won concessions of partial privileges from the Crown were often ignored or removed from the petitioner by the local governors. Chi complained bitterly about the burdens of the costs of his many *probanzas* (Jakeman 1952:1–29). If Gaspar Antonio Chi, one of the best-paid local Maya nobles due to his official position as general interpreter for the province, could not afford pursuing his privileges, then it was unlikely that other less wealthy Maya nobles would.

Even when able to make a formal petition to the Crown, many petitioners revealed more of a preoccupation with gaining a pension or *ayuda de costa* than in acquiring the prestige of a coat of arms.[16] For instance, don Jorge Canul, the cacique of Tenabo, and a relative of the ruling pre-Hispanic noble lord of the town, *Ah Naum Canul*, in 1589 used his claim to direct noble lineage of pre-Hispanic natural lords of his region and his merits and services to the Church and Crown not for the request of a coat of arms, but for the practical necessity of having his nobility recognized so that he and his children could be freed from their tribute burden.[17] The singular merits of don Jorge's discovery and denunciation of the plot and rebellion organized by the Maya nobleman don Andres

Cocom alone should surely have led the cacique to expect that his petition would be granted and his merits rewarded. Although the local Spanish governor, don Antonio de Voz Mediano, granted his petition and issued an order exempting him and his sons from paying tribute, don Jorge still had to personally write to the Crown and request confirmation of this order (Quezada and Torres Trujillo 2010:34). On October 25, 1601, the cacique wrote to the Crown requesting the confirmation of the tribute exemptions. Unluckily for don Jorge Canul, he owed his tribute burden to a private Spanish *encomendero*, Baltasar Pacheco Dorantes, and not the Crown. The rather terse response of the Crown to his *probanza* was a subsequent order for the local governor to explain his granting of a tribute exemption to don Jorge Canul and his concern that the tribute exemption could "result in the prejudice and damage to a third party."[18] In his favor, the Crown did request that if the exemption was not confirmed, then the local governor should inform the Crown "in case it is not appropriate to grant him this mercy, then you should inform us of something else that could be done for them."[19] Apparently the economic interests of the *encomendero* trumped the necessity of Philip III to reward the Canul lineage for their loyal services. No further documentation exists in the case, but don Jorge Canul did not receive any other privileges though his case apparently merited them.

In another instance, the Maya cacique don Pablo Pech of the town or *cah* of Chicxulub (baptized post-1553, after the López Medel *visita*) claimed that he and his children had been granted the privileges of *indios hidalgos*. Pech claimed: "we were the chief and lords in this land when there was not yet the Holy Church in these regions; when these lands were not yet ruled by the Spaniards; in the times when they did not gather for worship" (Pech 1936:24). In order to prove his case, he wrote, in Maya, a famous historical chronicle called the *Crónica de Chac Xulub Chen*, with its claims of his nobility and his loyal services to the Crown. In his chronicle of the conquest, he commented: "I was the prince and ruler in this village, in this land of Chac Xulub Chen, when our lord the Adelantado arrived in the region, in the year 1529 [sic] . . . We received them with words of peace and gave tributes, veneration, and food to the captains of the Spaniards" (Pech 1936:20). Don Pablo Pech alludes to the submission of proof of his merits, though no surviving *probanzas* exist in the archives: "I was called don Pablo Pech and then they stopped naming me Nakuk Pech. The main chiefs and lords were made *hidalgos* by the captains, when they settled here in the region, and we were the first to pay tribute to the foreign lords. Afterward, we were given power by God and by the king who ruled. We beget nobles and all my children will be nobles until the sun should burn out and destroy itself" (Pech 1936:22–23).

A similar petition and historical chronicle of the merits and services of another member of the Pech lineage, don Pedro Pech from the town of Yaxkukul, also exists with claims to nobility and proof of similar merits and services (Martínez Hernández 1926; Restall 1998:104–128). Even more remarkable was the fact that don Pedro Pech traveled back to Spain in early 1543 as the leader of a delegation of fifty Maya caciques who the Spanish *procurador* and brother-in-law of the conquistador Montejo, don Alonso López, took with him to Spain (Molina Solís 1896:695–696). Although don Pedro Pech resided at the Spanish court while the Guatemalan caciques received their own coats of arms, there is no surviving record of any similar grant in recognition of don Pedro Pech's services to the Crown.

Apparently, the Maya dignitaries did not receive much help from their Spanish companions. In fact, the Spanish *procurador* and his companions who accompanied the delegation showed little respect for the Maya nobles, and even less interest in helping to advance their case for rewards of their services. Alonso López showed so much disrespect toward the Maya caciques while at the Spanish court that he vulgarly referred to one of the leading members of the embassy upon his return to Yucatán simply as "Valladolid" because the cacique had resided for some time at court in the Spanish city of Valladolid pursuing his own petitions or *probanzas* (Molina Solís 1896:696). According to some sources, even though this cacique rose in the estimation of the

table 13.1

Probanzas de méritos y servicios submitted by caciques and Maya nobles in Yucatán, 1550–1630. Source: AGI, Justicia, 245 and 253; AGI, Indiferent General, 746; and AGI, México, 104, r. 3, 105-a, 105-b, 118, 130, and 131.

INDIGENOUS MAYA PETITIONER	TOWN / CAH OF PETITIONER	DESCENDANT OF PRE-HISPANIC RULING ELITE	YEARS OF PROBANZA / PETITION	PRIVILEGES SOUGHT OR GRANTED	COAT OF ARMS GRANTED
Don Diego Nah	Campeche	Yes	1550s	Recognition of noble status	No
Don Pedro Pech	Yaxkukul	Yes (*Ah Tunal Pech*)	1550s	Recognition of noble status, freedom from tribute	No
Don Pablo Pech	Chac Xulub Chen	Yes (*Ah Kom Pech*)	1550s	Recognition of noble status, freedom from tribute	No
Gaspar Antonio Chi	Mani	Yes (*Ah Mochan Xiu*)	1579–1610	Pension for life, freedom from tribute, license to carry arms and ride a horse	No
Don Jorge Canul	Tenabo	Yes (*Ah Naum Canul*)	1589–1601	Freedom from tribute from *encomendero* (denied)	No
Don Juan Kauil	Sisal	Yes	1618	Recognition of noble status, freedom from tribute	No
Don Juan Chan	Chancenote	Yes (*Ah Nahau Chan*)	1618–1622	Recognition of noble status, freedom from tribute, license to carry arms and ride a horse	No
Don Fernando Caamal	Oxkutzcab	No	1624	Freedom from tribute, license to carry arms	No

conquistador's son, Francisco de Montejo *el mozo*, who took him as one of his servants, López continued to harbor little respect for him, and he reportedly had another Maya murder this same nobleman a few years later.

Several other Maya caciques and noblemen submitted their own *probanzas* between 1550 and 1630, requesting privileges and other exemptions, but none of them were successful in gaining the coveted grant of a coat of arms (Table 13.1). Nevertheless, throughout the rest of the colonial period, the Maya began to appropriate, adapt, and modify for their own uses many of the heraldic symbols of Spanish power and prestige legitimately denied to them.

Apocryphal Elite Maya Appropriations of Spanish Heraldic Symbols, 1550–1750

What I can certify is that this patent and coat of arms exists today in the Royal Houses of Mani, and they painted the event on that blazon and those from that town cherish this painting very much.

Fray Diego López de Cogolludo,
Historia de Yucatán, 1688

Seeing that the Maya recognized the prestige conveyed by the display of coats of arms imagery, it is not surprising that the Maya elite appropriated and illicitly created apocryphal coats of arms and other

figure 13.6
The apocryphal coat of arms of the Xiu lineage of Mani, ca. 1580s. Reproduced from López de Cogullodo 1688: bk. 3, ch. VI, fol. 133.

heraldic images for their own use and for the use of their Indigenous communities. Just like the Maya adaptations of Spanish documentary and petitionary forms, this apocryphal use of aspects of Spanish heraldry was done out of a desire to Mayanize these symbols of colonial prestige and claim them for the local Maya elite and their Indigenous towns (Chuchiak 2010, 2013:277–281). It was apparently not uncommon for Indigenous communities or noblemen to invent, fabricate, or otherwise copy coats of arms granted to other individuals as a means of usurping the prestige and privileges attached to these items (Castañeda de la Paz 2013; Haskett 1996:100; Oudjik 2013). One striking case of an apparent Maya nobleman's appropriation of Spanish heraldry and the apocryphal creation of a coat of arms occurred in the last quarter of the sixteenth century in the region of the Maya town of Mani (Figure 13.6).

It is possible and even probable that this apocryphal Xiu coat of arms may have been designed by Gaspar Antonio Chi for submission with a later *probanza de méritos* as an example of the shield he may have wished to have granted to him by the Crown. Obsessed with proving his own connection to the ancient lineage of the pre-Hispanic Xiu rulers of Mani, it is known that Chi drew and elaborated a similarly hybridized Franciscan-styled "Tree of Jesse" for the Xiu lineage (Figure 13.7).[20]

The Xiu family was one of the sixteen prominent noble Maya families that dominated the Yucatán Peninsula by the sixteenth century (Cortez 1995:2;

Denying the Rights of "Natural Lords"   345

figure 13.7
Xiu family tree, ca. 1560s–1570s, reproduced from William Gates and Charles Bowditch, Xiu Chronicles (1919):8–9.

Okoshi Harada 2001, 2003; Quezada and Okoshi Harada 2001). The primary function of the Xiu family tree was to promote the interests of the family members by emphasizing the history of the family as lords in perpetuity, citing frequent reference to their earlier lordly status (Cortez 1995:4). The iconography of the drawing indicates that the Indigenous author had a level of understanding of both Christian and Mesoamerican ideology (Cortez 1995:5–6). This genealogical drawing, together with the pages within the Xiu family chronicle in which it is presently contained, falls into the category of colonial documents known as *probanzas de hidalguía* or "proofs of nobility." As Cortez (1995:6) has noted, these were a "recital of services to the Crown by a claimant for a pension or land grant, supported by sworn statements of witnesses as to the truth of the claimant's contentions." When effective, these colonial documents enabled the holder, and his/her extended family, to claim the status of *hidalgo* (nobility) with all its privileges. The hereditary status of Indigenous nobility was "recognized by the Spanish throughout the entire colonial period" and it became equated with the Spanish notion of the noble *hidalgo* (Luque Talaván 2004:11–12).

The handwriting of the annotations on this so-called Xiu family tree, executed sometime in the 1560s or 1570s, closely resembles the handwriting on one historical relation that we know for sure was penned by Gaspar Antonio Chi (Strecker and Artieda 1978:89–111). From a comparative analysis, it appears that the similar style of handwriting used in the names of the Maya caciques on this shield also belonged to Gaspar Antonio (Cortez 1995:74). Moreover, if Chi was the author of this apocryphal shield, then he would no doubt have chosen to highlight the two most important figures—*Ah Napot Xiu* and *Ah Kin Chi*, his uncle and his father—by placing them at the top of the bordure. It is also illustrative that in his *probanzas*, the initial *interrogatorio* focuses on tying himself and his lineage through his mother's side to these two important Maya leaders. On the Xiu family tree, the author (probably Gaspar Antonio) was again careful to note his relationship to his mother, *Ix Kukum Xiu*, with the annotation "mother of Gaspar Antonio." In his *probanza*, Chi specifically asked that all witnesses testify to the following:

> If they know Gaspar Antonio Chi, interpreter of the natives of this land, and if they had met Ah Kulel Chi, father of the said Gaspar Antonio, and Ah Mochan Xiu, grandfather of the said Gaspar Antonio, and if they know that he was the legitimate son of the said Ah Kulel Chi, and grandson of the said Ah Mochan Xiu, who were the lords of Mani and its province, and that they were the first who gave obedience to the king, our Lord and his captains in his name. And if the witnesses know as it turned out that the said Ah Kulel Chi, father of the said Gaspar Antonio, was caught and killed by the natives of the town of Sotuta, and they should state what they know, saw, or heard.[21]

The Apocryphal Xiu Coat of Arms of Mani (ca. 1550s–1570s)

> This province of Yucatán, which the natives call *Maya*, was ruled in ancient times by a Supreme Lord, and the last of these was Tutul Xiu, who was Lord of Mani, and he ruled over a very populous head town.
>
> Gaspar Antonio Chi Xiu,
> Relación de algunas costumbres, 1582

Familiar enough with the basics of Spanish heraldry, Gaspar Antonio Chi may have created both the Xiu family tree and an apocryphal Xiu coat of arms in tribute to the deeds of his ancestors that he alluded to as testimony of his nobility in his *probanzas*. It is most probable that Chi drew the initial image of this coat of arms during his residency in Mani as its Indigenous governor from 1571 to 1573. The author emphasized his father's figure (*Ah Kin Chi*) as one of the central two trophy heads (see Figure 13.6). He is placed at the top of the bordure (blinded by arrows as he recounts in his *probanza*) flanked by the most important leader in the Mani region of the time, his uncle *Ah Napot Xiu*. The coat of arms offered visual proof of their merits and their connection to Gaspar Antonio, even though testimony to this fact remained somewhat in doubt in his own *probanza* (Quezada and Torres Trujillo 2010:9–28).

The Native artist who designed this shield imagery obviously hoped to emphasize the Xiu dynasty's loyalty to the Spaniards, who at the cost of their own lives attempted to force other Maya groups to accept allegiance to Spain and convert to Christianity. It was not uncommon for Indigenous caciques to fabricate official Spanish coats of arms for their family to bolster their own personal status (Wood 1998c:225). As Wood (2003:57) observed, "coats of arms represent one of the most interesting and instructive symbols of power that indigenous people adopted and modified." Maya modifications of Spanish symbolism included the infusion of the armorial structure with encoded Indigenous images as illustrated here in the apocryphal coat of arms designed to represent the nobility of the Xiu lineage.

On the coats of arms granted to Spanish conquistadors in colonial New Spain, the Crown usually replaced the traditional ordinaries (bars, crosses, saltires, etc.) with figurative arms that included "severed heads of Moors or Indians, mountains, and rivers" as examples representative of the historical events or unfamiliar landscapes of the region conquered (Weckmann and López-Morillas 1992:146–147). However, in the Xiu shield, the Indigenous artist's use of heraldic symbols violated the typical rules of Spanish heraldry, which dictated that trophy heads serve as a symbol of vanquished enemies. Soldiers who participated in the conquest commonly used heraldic heads of Indians as decorations, in a number proportional to the number of Indigenous leaders whom they defeated (Figure 13.8). In a conscious and explicit inversion of this Spanish heraldic rule, the Xiu artist in Mani instead used the symbols of "trophy" heads as a tribute to those noble Xiu lords who sacrificed their lives in the service of the Crown of Spain.[22]

Along with this inversion, the Indigenous author of the shield (most probably Chi himself) included an ornately drawn image of a tree, which occupies the entire central charge of the escutcheon. Although plants are extremely common in European heraldry and figure among the earliest charges designed for coats of arms, this Indigenous rendering is obviously of a local tree from the region (Riquer 1942). The central significance of this tree is the focal point of the presentation. The image may even refer to the mythical sacred Maya world tree, or *yax cheel cab* (Knowlton and Vail 2010). The first securely dated textual reference to the existence of the *yax cheel cab* "is Gaspar Antonio Chi Xiu's mention of pre-Hispanic cross symbols as the *arbol verde del mundo* (green tree of the world) in the *Relación histórico-geográfica* for the town of Maní" (Knowlton and Vail 2010:722). Chi's account asserts that stones worked to represent this "green tree of the world were in fact representations of the cross of Christ and that their construction was a new phenomenon introduced by the prophet Chilam Balam in Maní as a prophecy of the coming of Christianity" (Knowlton and Vail 2010:722).

The Franciscan historian fray Diego López de Cogolludo, who spent time in the convent of Mani, made a copy of the Xiu coat of arms and included it as the only printed image in his famous *Historia de Yucatán* published in 1688. He wrote: "what I can certify is that today in the royal cabildo hall in the town of Mani, the natives there have as their own coat of arms a painted image of this whole event, painted in the form of a coat of arms" (López de Cogolludo 1688:132). So important was this coat of arms for the prestige of the Xiu elite that they guarded a large cotton *lienzo* with this image in their own town *cabildo* hall well into the nineteenth century. In 1842, the American diplomat and adventurer John Lloyd Stephens saw an image of the painted coat of arms during a visit to Mani:

> The Indians brought a copy of Cogolludo, wrapped up and treasured with great care in the *casa real*. This did not astonish us much, and they opened the book and pointed out a picture, the only one in it, being a representation of the murder of the ambassadors of Tutul Xiu; and while we were looking at it, they brought out and unrolled on the floor an old painting on cotton cloth, being the original from which Cogolludo had the engraving made. The design was a coat of arms bordered with the heads of the murdered ambassadors, one of which has an arrow fixed in the temple, intended to represent the ambassador who had his eyes put out with this weapon. In the

figure 13.8
Coat of arms of Hernán Cortés, with a string displaying seven heads representing the caciques of towns that he conquered; compare with Figure 13.6. Drawing from fifth sheet of grant, Library of Congress, Washington, D.C.

center is a tree growing out of a box, representing the sapote tree at Sotuta, under which the murder was committed, and which, the Indians say, is still standing (Stephens 1843:2:260).

Stephens continued: "the painting had evidently been executed by an Indian, and probably very near the time of the occurrence which it was intended to commemorate. Cogolludo refers to it as an ancient and interesting relic in his time, and, of course, it is much more so now. It is an object of great reverence among the Indians of Mani" (Stephens 1843:2:261). What is more interesting to note is that

fray López de Cogolludo himself earlier connected Gaspar Antonio Chi to the *lienzo*, stating in his same *Historia de Yucatán*:

I have seen in a royal cédula dated the 6th of September 1599 which refers to another cédula from 1593 which specifically mentions this event which is painted on this shield, and this order gives a pension of 200 pesos to Gaspar Antonio, by reason of his serving as General Interpreter, as well as for being the grandson of Tutul Xiu and the son of Ah Kin Chi, who had his eyes taken out with an arrow . . . and this event described there is painted

Denying the Rights of "Natural Lords" 349

according to the image that I have made into an engraving here (López de Cogolludo 1688:132).

If indeed Gaspar Antonio was the author of this apocryphal coat of arms, then he curiously adapted his use of the Spanish heraldic system to his own Native understandings of the pictorial representation of elite Maya imagery, like that found in other clandestine Maya books of Chilam Balam. Stephens's description of the tree image as referring to the sacred sapote tree at Sotuta is interesting, but it does not preclude that the central tree may have served two purposes or may have had a dual Maya/Spanish conflated meaning (Barteet 2018). Stephens's description suggests that Gaspar Antonio's assertion that the "green tree of the world" served to presage the arrival of Christianity might have been his own attempt to sanitize, or christianize, a Maya message for a Spanish or Christian audience. This tantalizing possibility suggests that Maya images like this world tree could be polyvalent and serve to imbue the apocryphal Maya coat of arms with multiple meanings for both the Maya and Spanish world.

In many ways, this shield is a transfiguration, or an inversion of the proper style and use of addendum and other Spanish heraldic imagery. Gaspar Antonio Chi used trophy heads not as symbols of his family's vanquishing of its enemies, but instead to represent his dynastic lineage's sacrifices in service of the Spaniards. Gaspar Antonio aided in the compilation of the *Relaciones histórico-geográficas* questionnaires during the period from 1579 to 1582, at the same time that he was also compiling his first *probanza* to send to the Crown to request privileges for himself.[23] We should not be surprised then to see even in the *Relaciones,* including in the relation of the city of Mérida, Chi suggested that the Spanish authors should focus on the early Xiu prophecies of the imminent arrival of Christianity. Under Gaspar Antonio's influence, the authors of the *Relación de la ciudad de Mérida* wrote:

> There were some provinces that never gave war, but rather received the Spaniards in peace, especially the province of Tutulxiu [Tutul Xiu], whose head town was the town of Mani... which was where a few years before the Spaniards came to conquer this land a principal Indian, who was a priest, called Chilam Balam and a great prophet and diviner, foretold them that in a short time white bearded people would come from where the Sun rises, and that they would bring up a sign like this [+], to which their gods could not resist... and that these people were to come to lord over the earth, and that those who received them with peace would not be wronged by any and those who waged war with them would be killed, and that the natives of the land would leave their idols behind... and that they made this sign of the cross of carved stone and put them in the patios of their temples where all could see them, and he [Chilam Balam] told them that this was the green tree of the world, and many people came to see it as a novel thing, and it seemed that they have venerated this sign from then on (Garza 1983:1:69).

Manipulating the historical message behind these passages, no doubt for his own benefit, Chi might have thought that these compilations would have reached the Crown before his own *probanza,* allowing them, as they were written by Spaniards, to serve as valuable testimony of his own merits and services. No better example exists of the successful manipulation on the part of a Maya Indigenous nobleman of the written history of the Spaniards.

Observers may argue that the early apocryphal uses of Spanish heraldic imagery by the Maya during the sixteenth and early seventeenth centuries reveal an apparent lack of understanding of the nature of Spanish heraldry and the rules and common types of Spanish coats of arms. Still, as the shield of the Xiu illustrates, the symbols and other addenda were conflated with Maya concepts and symbolism, not in disregard of the proper style of Spanish heraldic symbolism, but rather as an apparent conscious decision by Maya authors.

Nevertheless, a coat of arms that possibly began as an individually designed family crest eventually came to serve as a communal image painted on a *lienzo* that the town of Mani claimed

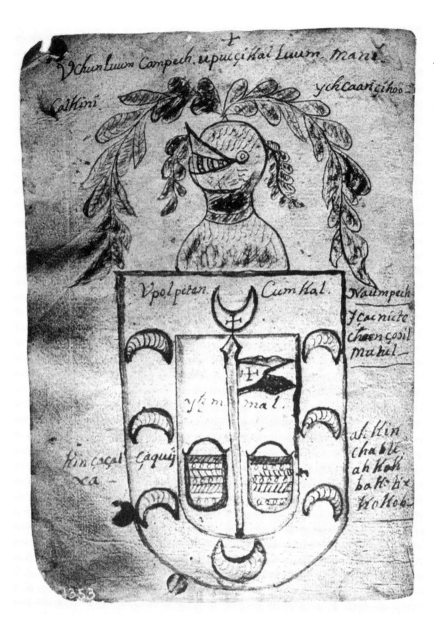

figure 13.9
The armorial bearings of Yucatán, in the Book of Chilam Balam of Chumayel, eighteenth century. Reproduced from George Byron Gordon, *The Book of Chilam Balam of Chumayel* (Philadelphia, 1913), 5:25.

as its municipal coat of arms in 1688. The case of the apocryphal Xiu shield is unique among the Yucatec Maya, in terms of an attempted usurpation or creation of a Spanish-style coat of arms to represent a noble lineage.

The Apocryphal Coat of Arms of Yucatán in the Chilam Balam of Chumayel

Other examples of apocryphal coat of arms imagery also exist in the clandestine Maya books of Chilam Balam. Indigenous communities often made dubious claims that they had been awarded a coat of arms by the king for their valuable services, which served the purpose of transforming Spanish heraldic symbols into "symbols of indigenous corporate legitimacy" (Haskett 1996:100). One of the few clear examples of this type of later eighteenth-century appropriation and apocryphal use of Spanish heraldry in colonial Yucatán occurred in an illustration in the Maya Book of Chilam Balam of Chumayel (Figure 13.9).

The Maya not only used this symbol of nobility and prestige in their book, claiming the legitimacy brought by similar shields to their holders, but they also interpreted the shield as conveying a symbolic map of political space. The image serves a conflated

Denying the Rights of "Natural Lords" 351

figure 13.10
Coat of arms granted to conquistador Francisco de Arceo, conqueror of Yucatán and *encomendero* of the Maya town of Pustunich in the province of Mani; compare with Figure 13.9. AGN, Indiferente Virreinal, Mercedes caja-exp:3196-013.

Maya purpose of mapping the political divisions of colonial Yucatán and emphasizing the centrality of Mani, and thus the Xiu Maya elites' claims to hegemony, based not only on their ancient lineage but also on their alliance and early aid to the Spanish regime (Solari 2013). The style and format of this Maya shield closely resembles the most common type of Spanish coat of arms designed for the local conquistadors of Yucatán.

The centrality of Maya appropriation of possible Christian symbolism (i.e., the Christian flag in the center of the shield from the Chilam Balam of Chumayel) and the possible reference to the "green tree of the world," as interpreted by Gaspar Antonio as symbolizing the Chilam Balam prophecy of the arrival of Christianity in the Mani region, tend to show a colonial Maya obsession with portraying their elite lineages as good and true faithful Christians. Since a denial or lack of a coat of arms meant that a petitioner did not successfully convince the Spanish world of one's services, or true conversion, these Christian images on the apocryphal shields from the province of Mani no doubt served to emphasize the noble Xiu lineage's dedication to the new Christian faith. It is also interesting to note that all the surviving examples of apocryphal coat of arms imagery mimicking the Spanish style of heraldry come from the province and region of Mani. No other Maya region, or noble lineage, had better claims to merit the eventual granting of a coat of arms in recognition for their loyal service during the conquest and conversion of the Maya. Still, even more interesting is the fact that as early as 1549, the Maya of the Mani region would have come into direct contact with Spanish heraldic imagery in the form of the local Spanish *encomendero* Francisco de Arceo's display of his own blazon, awarded to him for his service in the early conquest of Yucatán in 1534 (Figure 13.10).

The centrality of the Xiu Maya town of Mani, at the "heart" of the land in this shield image in the Chilam Balam of Chumayel, illustrates what Hans Roskamp (2003:328) has argued for his own analysis of the *escudo de armas* of Tzintzuntzan, that the elite Maya scribe's inclusion of this apocryphal coat of arms not only served a simple emblematic function but also composed "a pictographic document with a message that was clear." In the Maya Book of Chilam Balam of Chumayel, that message served to emphasize the supremacy of the Xiu of the Mani region and their dedication and true conversion to the Christian religion.

These appropriations of Spanish heraldically inspired symbolism and their combination with local Maya concepts of elite dynastic rulership show how the colonial Maya subordinated the new Spanish ruling culture's values and prestige imagery and refashioned them into appropriated Maya forms of expression of the new colonial faces of rulership.

Illicit Maya Appropriations of the Habsburg Royal Arms and Double-Headed Eagle

> The Maya by name, the Maya people, they were named Christians, and all the bearings and burdens of their lands were ordered by Saint Peter and the King and Emperor.
>
> The Book of Chilam Balam of Chumayel

One of the most important symbols of Spanish heraldry adapted and appropriated by the Maya was the symbol of the double-headed eagle of the Spanish Habsburg dynasty (De Ridder 1994). The officially sanctioned use of this symbol only occurred from the 1520s to the end of the 1560s. The conquest of Yucatán was not officially completed until 1546, with the final suppression of the last great Maya rebellion. Only ten years later, the Emperor Charles V abdicated, and his son Philip II began to phase out the use of the imagery of the double-headed eagle after the 1560s.[24]

But where did the Maya acquire their understanding of Spanish heraldic imagery? Joaquín Galarza believes that many of the coats of arms in the *Techialoyan* manuscripts of Central Mexico added crests adapted from official Spanish documents and books they had seen (Galarza 1987:91–94). Native Maya elites, like Gaspar Antonio Chi (who had a Spanish education and early access to the libraries of the Franciscan convents), would also have observed Spanish crests in books bearing images of heraldry. Still, as early as 1480, the Spanish Crown prohibited individuals who did not belong to the royal family from using these symbols either in part or in whole, except by specific royal grant (Domínguez Torres 2013:26–28). In order to legally display the imperial arms, specific *cédulas* had to be issued authorizing the use of the royal arms.[25] Spaniards believed that the placement, presentation, and use of the royal coat of arms symbolized possession, but it also served as a symbol of promises of protection and vassalage (Green and Dickason 1989:3–17). Nevertheless, unique public Maya adaptations of the royal arms, most of which were not sanctioned by official royal grant, occurred frequently in the peninsula.

Although Maya artisans continued to have easy access to images of the Spanish royal coat of arms from the reign of Philip II onward, the remaining Habsburg monarchs of Spain refrained from using the double-headed eagle on their shields. Instead, the right to bear this imagery reverted to the Austrian branch of the Habsburg family, who continued to use the double-headed eagle (Wheatcroft 1997). Nowhere in any of the official documentation extant in colonial Yucatán did the heraldic imagery of the Habsburg double eagle appear. When Spanish sealed paper arrived in the colony by royal mandate after 1638, it did not display the Habsburg arms and even then, sealed paper was not used routinely in colonial papers in Yucatán until the middle of the seventeenth century.[26]

The Habsburg monarchs—Philip II, Philip III, Philip IV, and Charles II, whose reigns spanned from 1556 to 1700—all used the aforementioned coat of arms that was devoid of the imperial crown and the double-headed eagle of the empire. Still, the double-headed eagle of the early Habsburgs continued to appear in error in imagery throughout New Spain. As several scholars earlier noted, the Spanish viceroys of New Spain took special care that the double-headed eagle of the empire appeared on every major public work undertaken, not only out of respect for the Habsburg monarchs but also as the assertion of Spain's claims to supremacy over the Natives (Stevenson 1909:3). So prevalent was the misuse of the imperial double-headed eagle in New Spain throughout the later sixteenth and early seventeenth century, even Chinese ceramics from the Manila galleon trade, influenced by Mexican designs from the western coasts near Acapulco, continued to use the double-headed eagle image (Castro 1988:29; Kuwayama 1997). However, after 1700 and the end of the Habsburg dynasty, even these illicit uses apparently ceased. As a matter of fact, most modern art historians have argued that objects bearing the double-headed eagle predate 1700.[27] As we will see, colonial Maya usages of the symbol continued long after the end of the Habsburg period.

The public displays of civic coats of arms in Spain, some of the most elaborate in Europe, typically conveyed the symbolism of protection, and the display of the royal crest "invoked temporal political support" (Haskett 2005:222). It appears that the use of apocryphal coats of arms, as well as the use and illicit display of the Habsburg royal arms, served as a type of protective amulet for the Maya. The double-headed eagle symbol appears frequently in the woven material of the Maya region of Mexico and Guatemala. It appears that the symbol of the reigning Habsburg dynasty in Spain during the conquest "entered forcefully into the indigenous imagination" (Artes de México 1996:84). In the Guatemalan Highlands, the Maya continue to weave the Habsburg double-headed eagle into their clothing and draw it on their buildings. The K'iche' Maya even today, with the royal Spanish connotations long gone from their collective memories, still believe that these double-headed eagle symbols protect their community (Lowie 1985).

In many churches and surviving colonial structures, colonial Maya artisans used and prominently displayed the double-headed eagle without direct royal permission, which would never have occurred in a public monument created by and for Spaniards. What is interesting to note is that all these assimilations of the Habsburg double eagle occurred in distant Maya parishes, far from the oversight of the Spanish towns of Mérida, Campeche, or Valladolid. Many of these public displays of ornately carved double-headed eagles in the Maya region postdate the end of the Habsburg dynasty (Figure 13.11).[28] It appears that for the Maya craftsmen and artisans, the Habsburg eagle continued to play a major role as a symbol of prestige long after the end of Habsburg rule.

If this is the case, it is also not surprising that colonial texts, written in Maya languages from throughout the Maya region, often also contain fictitious or apocryphal uses of the royal coat of arms, the double-headed Habsburg eagle, or both. The embellishment of Indigenous-language histories such as primordial titles with Habsburg symbols was not confined to Central Mexico. An imperial Habsburg crest emblazoned on the chest of a double-headed eagle embellishes the K'iche' *Título de Totonicapán* (Carmack and Mondloch 1983). Another K'iche' Maya title, the *Título de K'oyoi*, appropriates a similar imperial coat of arms (Carmack 1973:266; Haskett 1996:104). This *Título de K'oyoi*, probably written at Utatlan by the K'oyoi rulers from the second most important K'iche' Maya town of Quetzaltenango, may also be an apocryphal use of this symbol, since no petitions or *probanzas* are known to exist for this region (Carmack 1973:266). A third Guatemalan colonial document, written sometime between the 1550s and 1560s, also reveals the use of a two-headed eagle emblem that represents the royal title granted by the Crown to the lords of Momostenango (Carmack 1973:63). Art historian Donald Robertson (1975:255) had earlier argued that such coats of arms represented the authority of the Spanish government for the Guatemalan Maya (Figure 13.12).

Even more interesting is the fact that Habsburg double-eagle imagery also appears in the clandestine cave art of the Maya region. The images appear in caves and cenotes, where archaeological evidence has shown that the colonial Maya continued to perform idolatrous ceremonies related to the rites of rulership and noble lineages (Stone 1995, 1997a:33–42, 1997b). Three Yucatecan caves to date have been found to contain colonial drawings of

figure 13.11
Examples of Maya appropriations of the Habsburg double-headed eagle on local architecture, 1636–1750. Map drawn and illustrated with photographs by John F. Chuchiak IV.

Habsburg eagles, along with other presumably elite Maya drawings of lords put there by Native Maya. It has been postulated that there was an elite ritual significance in the clandestine usage of the symbol of the double-headed eagle for the colonial Maya (Stone 1987, 1997b).[29] In the symbols and powers of the "stranger king" (see Baron, this volume; Lamoureux-St-Hilaire and McAnany, this volume; Masson, this volume), the Maya found for political purposes that "foreign identification could be an asset, and its pedigree could be assumed in a formulaic way." For instance, the association of the K'iche' and Kaqchikel Maya ruling elite with "foreign" sources of power occurs repeatedly in early colonial Native language documents. The same is the case with Mexican intruders in Yucatán, or the foreigners who are often said to come from the mythical land Zuyua, usually described as Tollan Zuyua (Stone 1989:167).

In the case of the Xiu of Yucatán, Maya claims of foreign pedigree were cultivated by a ruling elite in a way that reveals a more fundamental attitude toward warfare, rank, and political power, which some scholars have suggested stretches back to the Classic period, when warlords of "foreign" pedigree formed exclusive dynastic lines. Rank differentiation and political legitimacy, the faces of Maya rulership, were achieved through claimed affiliation with prestigious foreign polities or even the memory of such polities (Stone 1989:167). According to Segovia Liga, the cryptic Maya passages in the Chilam Balam books known as the language of Zuyua may be a case in point that reveals the conflated nature of the Maya historical representation of foreign historic origins.[30]

Numerous instances of the clandestine use of the imported double-headed Habsburg eagle also appear throughout the Maya region on public architecture, private texts, and primordial titles, and in caves, where the Maya elite continued to celebrate idolatrous religious ceremonies long into the colonial period (Figure 13.13). There is also evidence that the Habsburg double-headed eagle may have been used on more perishable items, as a common motif in Maya weaving and wood carving. The royal arms and other apocryphal images were frequently carved into the lintels and walls of the homes of the Maya caciques and used by individual *batabs* as visible claims of their lineage. The Maya in Yucatán

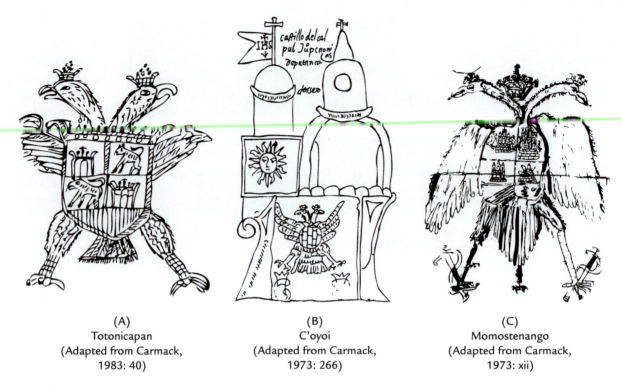

(A)
Totonicapan
(Adapted from Carmack, 1983: 40)

(B)
C'oyoi
(Adapted from Carmack, 1973: 266)

(C)
Momostenango
(Adapted from Carmack, 1973: xii)

figure 13.12
Use of double-headed Habsburg eagles in Guatemalan Maya *títulos*, 1550–1590. Drawings by John F. Chuchiak IV, adapted from Carmack 1973:XII, 266; Carmack and Mondloch 1983:40.

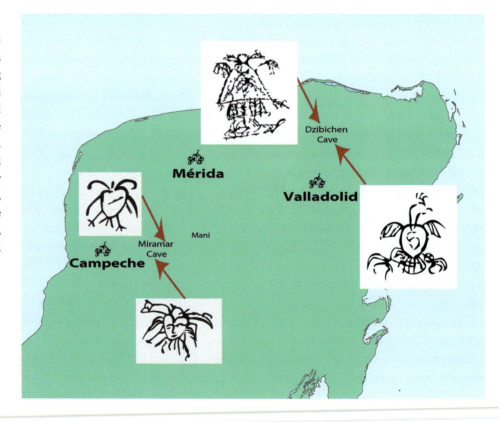

figure 13.13
Clandestine Maya uses of the Habsburg double-headed eagle and royal arms in ritual cave art, ca. 1550–1750. Map illustrated with drawings by John F. Chuchiak IV, adapted from Stone 1995:figs. 4-81, 4-82, 4-86, 4-87.

continued to reproduce the Habsburg double-headed eagle on objects such as the leather carving placed on chairs used by the elite as late as 1808 (Gontar 2003:183–187).

The continued use of these symbols served, as Robert Haskett observed among the primordial titles from Central Mexico, as a type of protective talisman for the community (Haskett 1996:113). Just as the Central Mexican coats of arms were seen to grant Nahua communities their "nobility" and "rulership," the apocryphal Maya uses of the royal arms were an attempt to claim the same security and title to nobility. Even after the arrival of the Bourbon monarchy, Yucatec Maya craftsmen, artists, and anonymous cave graffiti testify to the power and endurance of the double eagle as a Maya symbol of protection and prestige.

Conclusion

> Then you will see them, they are coming, and they will be the governors... Those of the two-day thrones, those of the two-day mats, in these painful years, in the crooked times, in truth it will be the end of the true Lords, the True Maya men.
>
> The Book of Chilam Balam of Chumayel

There are several reasons why the Maya nobility from Yucatán never received grants of formal coats of arms. The absence of patrimonial property is perhaps the most significant aspect that differentiates this region from the rest of Mesoamerica (Menegus Bornemann 2009:359–378). After the Crown restricted their control over labor in 1552, most Maya caciques did not receive any income, other than a small amount given as tribute from their townspeople in recognition of their lordship, and thus they were unable to cover the costs of petitioning. The interminable struggles between the Spanish-imposed town councils in Yucatán and the old pre-Hispanic Maya ruling elite hampered any early attempts at unity in Maya communities, which remained necessary to petition successfully for a grant of a civic coat of arms. The nobles found it difficult to receive community support for the creation of their own *probanzas*.

Moreover, the complex nature of pre-Hispanic leadership in the region of Yucatán confused the situation, as the Spanish understood it, of the rights and privileges of the Maya "natural lords." Unlike in Mexico and Peru, where the supreme Indigenous ruler or dynasty controlled a vast centralized state, in pre-Hispanic Yucatán a very complex patchwork of warring provinces and petty city-states existed (Okoshi Harada 2000:28–37). Maya power was decentralized and divided among rival factions. The peninsula was under the control of sixteen different hereditary lords. The situation was similar in Coatzacoalcos, Chiapas, Tabasco, and Honduras, which also saw no grants of coats of arms for Indigenous conquistadors and collaborators of the Spanish. The conquests of these regions were of a long and difficult nature, as previously "conquered" regions had to be reentered and reconquered many times. One-time peaceful caciques and communities that had accepted Spanish sovereignty later threw off their allegiance to the Spaniards and rebelled.

Indigenous petitioners had to give incontrovertible proof of their steadfast loyalty and sincere and early Christian conversion to merit the granting of a coat of arms. The proof required relied mostly on Spanish testimonies and certified eyewitness reports of surviving Spanish conquistadors, who recounted the voluntary and active role of the Indigenous petitioners in supporting and advancing both the Spanish military conquest and conversion of a region. In the case of the Indigenous caciques from the Verapaz, they received the active support of the Dominican missionaries for their own appeals for coats of arms. The Franciscan friars in Yucatán were not as supportive as the Dominicans in Guatemala. Few Maya caciques could count on Franciscan support, mostly due to the continued idolatry among the Yucatec Maya nobility from the 1550s to the 1590s. The discovery of the Maya nobility's betrayal of their Christianity precluded active Franciscan support for even the most important Maya elite like the Xiu. Don Francisco de Montejo Xiu himself was one of those caciques whom the Franciscan ecclesiastical judges condemned for idolatry in 1562.

But nobility could also be acquired by lineage, merits, or knowledge (Menegus Bornemann and Aguirre Salvador 2005:23). Many Maya caciques from Yucatán, like Gaspar Antonio Chi, made attempts to claim all three merits and services, yet still they were ultimately unsuccessful in their claims for nobility and the privileges of a coat of arms. The Crown chose to recognize ancient traditional lineages, but it also chose to only award new privileges to those Native lords who voluntarily and incontrovertibly collaborated. By means of the granting of coats of arms, the Crown sought to ensure that it had loyal servants in the Americas. The *cédulas* and coats of arms granted to Indigenous nobility in New Spain often alluded to the motivational aspect of the grant of arms, which the Crown intended to serve as "a symbol for others to animate them to serve us" (358n11). Indigenous nobles who successfully petitioned also expected to receive other privileges, such as the recognition of their ancient lineage, which ensured that their grants and coats of arms would be hereditary, as well as other rewards such as lands, goods, or pensions (Menegus Bornemann and Aguirre Salvador 2005:25).

Moreover, if coats of arms were only given to those who could incontrovertibly prove their loyal services as well as their good Christian conversion, then the Xiu family would have been disqualified. This is probably part of the reasoning behind the Crown's lack of desire to award even the persistent Gaspar Antonio Chi a formal recognized coat of arms. His close family ties to the Xiu might have made him suspect in the eyes of the Spanish authorities.

As the Spaniards continued to restrict the Maya caciques' access to power, more of the traditional nobles sought refuge by continuing to manipulate access to the sacred by the exercise of traditional Maya religion and ceremonies that the Spaniards called idolatrous (Chuchiak 2003). In 1561, the aforementioned Don Francisco de Montejo Xiu, the hereditary ruler of the Xiu town of Mani, was brought up on charges of drunkenness and rape. Further evidence of sacrificed deer legs and other offerings found in a cave near Mani touched off the infamous Franciscan inquisition led by the provincial fray Diego de Landa. Quickly, after the summer of 1561, the Xiu leadership of the region fell out of favor.[31]

They were replaced with non-noble Maya town governors, the so-called two-day holders of the mat. The Yucatec scribes of the colonial period, in their clandestine books of Chilam Balam, complained bitterly about the "two-day holders of the mat" or usurpers, the non-noble, imposed town *gobernadores* and other *cabildo* officials, who had no claims to noble lineage nor any connection to the pre-Hispanic legitimacy of past rulers. Thus, the number of Maya elites and their towns that could lay legitimate claim to true meritorious service on behalf of the Crown and Catholic religion was further reduced.

In the end, even don Juan Chan, whom the Crown recognized as a *señor natural*, was not rewarded with the grant of an individual coat of arms for his loyal service. Although many earlier caciques from Guatemala earned individual coats of arms for much less, don Juan Chan, who conducted more than four decades of similar loyal service, received nothing more than a simple royal *cédula*, recognizing him as "equal in all measure with the heirs of Montezuma and the Incas," equal in all things save for the respect and nobility that a grant of a coat of arms would have brought. Don Juan Chan, don Pablo Pech, the exasperated Gaspar Antonio Chi, and many other Maya caciques and collaborators were left without any legitimate royal recognition of their ancient lineage and their valuable services to the Crown. In response, Maya *batabob* and *al mehenob* sought to appropriate, albeit illicitly and sometimes secretly, the heraldic symbols of Spanish power. If the Spanish Crown would not grant them legitimate coats of arms to recognize their lineage, then they, as enterprising colonial Indigenous elites, would invent their own shields. The surviving examples of Maya apocryphal shields and the illicit use of heraldic imagery in cave ceremonies and the Chilam Balam books serve as a living testimony to the resilience and tenacity of the local Maya elite to adapt and adopt Spanish symbols of power for their own local uses.

NOTES

1 For the *probanza*, see the Relación de los méritos y servicios de don Juan Chan, cacique del pueblo de Chancenote, Archivo General de Indias (AGI), México, 140.

2 Real Cédula de recomendación al cacique don Juan Chan, AGI, Indiferente General, 450, libro A6, fols. 270r–270v.

3 The Mani Land Treaty of 1557, the earliest known Yucatec Maya document in alphabetic script, is a case in point. In August 1557, don Francisco de Montejo Xiu and other Maya nobles from the Mani region marked out the boundaries of their communities' landholdings, stating clearly that the lands marked out were communally held, not the patrimonial holdings of the lords themselves.

4 The *batab* of Caucel, don Francisco Euan, attested that the government of the city of Mayapan had put his ancestors on the coast in charge of the salt beds there and of the distribution of salt (Restall et al. 2023:189). Fray Diego de Landa reported that based on Euan's testimony the Audiencia of Guatemala ordered that all those who went to those regions to collect salt should pay a fee to the lords of Caucel (Restall et al. 2023:189). It appears that Euan submitted a *probanza* to the *audiencia* in Guatemala. Euan had been an assistant to the friars, knowing and likely working with Landa. If the *probanza* was sent and approved by the *audiencia* of Guatemala, it was sent very early (between 1550 and 1559) and may still exist in the archives of Guatemala.

5 *Recopilación de leyes de los reinos de las Indias* (Madrid, 1681), libro VII, título 7, ley 5.

6 For numerous Maya cacique complaints against the *alcalde mayor*, see Auto del alcalde mayor don Diego Quijada sobre el asunto de indios de servicio, Mérida, 1561, AGI, Justicia, 244.

7 The system of *cabildo* government and the fixing of a standard tribute quota occurred during the visitation of the province by Judge don Diego García de Palacio (Ortíz Yam and Quezada 2009). For a discussion of the significance of these reforms in terms of tribute, see Bracamonte Sosa and Solís Robleda 1996:189.

8 For an excellent analysis of the desperate nature of colonial Maya caciques' attempts to hold on to power through their creation of the *Lenguage de Zuyua*, see Segovia Liga 2008.

9 For the royal legislation on the *probanzas de méritos*, see *Recopilación de leyes de los reinos de las Indias* (Madrid, 1681), libro II, título 33, leys 1–20, fols. 291–294.

10 For the early grants to Maya caciques from Guatemala for their aid in the religious *reducciones* of the Lacandon in the Verapaz region, see Paz y Meliá 1892. Especially relevant here are the grants of arms to don Jorge of Tecpanatitan, 1543 (Paz y Meliá 1892:249–250); don Gaspar of Teculatlan, 1543 (Paz y Meliá 1892:265); don Pedro and don Diego, caciques of Zacatepeque, Guatemala, 1543 (Paz y Meliá 1892:266); and don Miguel of Cicaztenango [Quetzaltenango], 1543 (Paz y Meliá 1892:267). For the grant to Juan de Apobazt, cacique of Atitlán, Guatemala, see Escudo de Juan de Apobazt, cacique de Atitlán, provincia de Guatemala, AGI, Mapas y Planos, Escudos, 24.

11 For a description of this religious reduction conducted by de Angulo and local Maya perceptions of the activities of the Dominicans, see Bricker 1981:35–36.

12 Información de oficio y parte de fray Pedro de Angulo, Dominico, 1560, AGI, Guatemala, 111, n. 12.

13 See Real Cédula a fray Pedro de Angulo, de la Orden de Santo Domingo, de la Orden de Santo Domingo, ordenándole que envíe al Consejo de Indias, información de la vida, costumbres y linaje a fin de presentarla en Roma pues se le ha propuesto para el Obispado de la provincia de Verapaz, por sus muchos méritos y conocimiento de los naturales, 9 de junio, 1558, AGI, Indiferente General, 425, l. 23, fol. 399r.

14 *Recopilación de leyes de los reinos de las Indias* (Madrid, 1681), libro VI, título 7 ("de los caciques"), ley xvii, fol. 291.

15 The difficulties of presenting a petition are illustrated in the Carta y petición de los indios mexicanos, 1576, AGI, México, 100.

16 In four of his five official *probanzas*, Gaspar Antonio Chi Xiu focused his petition on the specific granting of a royal pension in reward for his merits and services to the Spanish Crown and Christian faith. See AGI, México, 104, r. 3 (November 22, 1580); AGI, México, 105-B, r. 4 (October 11, 1581); AGI, México, 105-B, r. 4 (October 12, 1581); AGI, México, 118, r. 2 (1598); and AGI, México, 118, r. 3 (April 23, 1599).

17 See Probanza de don Jorge Canul, cacique del pueblo de Tenabo, 1589, AGI, México, 131.
18 See marginal note written in 1601 on the document Real cédula sobre la petición del cacique don Jorge Canul sobre los tributos, AGI, México, 131.
19 AGI, México, 131.
20 For information on similar "Tree of Jesse" images in New Spain and their significance and prevalence, see Russo 1998.
21 See Petición y probanza de Gaspar Antonio al gobernador Alonso Ordóñez sobre el aumento de su ayuda de costa a 200 pesos, Mérida, October 25, 1594, AGI, México, 118, r. 3.
22 Weckmann and López-Morillas (1992:148) did not realize that the Xiu were inverting the proper Spanish heraldic symbolism of conquered trophy heads for their own purposes and erroneously interprets this Maya coat of arms as "an allusive coat of arms . . . granted to the city of Mani, in Yucatán, with a bordure showing the severed heads of thirteen caciques . . . of Zotuta, whom they the inhabitants of Mani had defeated in aid of the Spaniards . . ."
23 See Probanza de Gaspar Antonio Chi, November 22, 1580, AGI, México, 104, r. 3.
24 Although Charles V chose Philip II's arms before 1548, his selection of his royal arms was done in connection with his son's future role as king of Spain and sovereign of the Netherlands. On January 16, 1556, Charles V abdicated the crowns of Castile, Leon, Aragon, Sicily, and parts of the New World to Philip. If Philip II would have become emperor of the Holy Roman Empire, he too would have continued to use the double-headed eagle of the empire in his arms. As fate had it, upon Charles V's abdication, the use of the double-headed eagle passed on to the Austrian branch of the family, removing Philip II's legitimacy in his continued use of the double-headed eagle (see Gasten 2005:223). Nevertheless, artists and other craftsmen in Europe and the Americas continued to erroneously use the double-headed eagle in the armorial bearings of Philip II (Gasten 2005:223). The official coinage of Philip II immediately removed the double-headed eagle from its symbolism even in Europe.
25 In 1544, for example, Charles V granted don Alonso Tito Uchi Inca, the son of Huascar and the grandson of Huayna Capac, the right to display his coat of arms over the door of his house with "una aguila real con dos cabezas coronadas." This type of royal permission to use the Habsburg coat of arms was rare and reserved most often only for the hereditary descendants of Montezuma or the Inca rulers (see Cummins 2002:264n126).
26 On December 28, 1638, a decree established as obligatory the employment of the sealed paper. For the regulations of sealed paper and its introduction in 1638, see *Leyes de Indias*, libro VIII, Estancos, ley 18. To avoid falsification, the seals on the sealed paper had to be changed every two years. Nevertheless, even with the changes in the design of the "seal," the Habsburg double eagle never appeared on any of the seals.
27 In reference to a church facade in Chiapas, Sidney Markman (1984:172n20) wrote "basing their conclusions on the use of the Habsburg double-headed eagle motif which appears in the central bay of the third story of the façade (fig. 95–97) some art historians have placed the west façade in the 17th century with the year 1700 as the last possible date BEFORE which it could have been built." Markman also noted (1984:20) that in the Maya region "this motif continued to enjoy popularity long after the Habsburg dynasty had ceased to rule the Spanish Empire."
28 Thomas DaCosta Kaufmann (2004:293–294) noted in reference to the use of the double-headed imperial eagle that "although the motif may have become widely diffused, decontextualized, and thus ultimately used simply as a form of decoration, the examples from Ecuador adduced here already indicate that not all double eagles on facades can be interpreted as being merely decorative, some have meaning."
29 According to Andrea Stone (1989:167), claims of foreign affiliation "were a favored form of propping up elite hierarchies in Yucatán from at least the terminal classic." Even after the conquest, the Yucatec Maya, like other groups in Mesoamerica, were quick to adopt emblems of imperial Spanish rule, such as royal crowns and the Habsburg eagle, to represent Indigenous notions of supreme authority.
30 As Segovia Liga argues (2008), this cryptic language of Zuyua, supposedly connected to the distant Central Mexican origins of the Mexicanized Maya elite of postclassic Yucatán, was refashioned during the later sixteenth and early seventeenth century during a time of major attacks on the privileges of the Maya caciques. The Maya elite looked to this arcane

language of their foreign past to reinvent and teach it to the Spanish governor of Yucatán, don Carlos de Luna y Arellano (1602–1611), who would then see that they were the "true Maya men" (*Hahil Maya Uinic*).

31 Proceso que hizo el doctor Diego Quijada contra los caciques de la provincia de Mani sobre decir se emborracharon, October 26, 561, AGI, Justicia, 248.

REFERENCES CITED

Ancona, Eligio
- 1889 *Historia de Yucatán, desde la época más remota hasta nuestros días*, vol. 2, *La dominación española [1542–1811]*. J. J. Roviralta, Mérida.

Anonymous
- 1892 *Isagoge histórico apologético general de todas las Indias y especial de la provincia Sn. Vicente Ferrer de Chiapa y Goathemala de el orden de Predicadores: Libro inédito hasta ahora, que, con motivo de la celebración del cuarto centenario del descubrimiento de América, ha mandado publicar el gobierno de la república de Guatemala*. Tip. de T. Minuesa de los Ríos, Madrid.

Artes de México
- 1996 *Artes de México* 34–35. Universidad Nacional Autónoma de México, Mexico City.

Barteet, C. Cody
- 2018 Maya Heraldic Arms: The Merging of Spanish and Maya Visual Cultures in the Memorial Shield to the Massacre at Otzmal. *Konsthistorisk Tidskrift* 87(1):23–44.

Bassie-Sweet, Karen
- 2021 *Maya Gods of War*. University Press of Colorado, Louisville.

Borah, Woodrow
- 1983 *Justice by Insurance: The General Indian Court of Colonial México and the Legal Aides of the Half-Real*. University of California Press, Berkeley.

Bracamonte Sosa, Pedro, and Gabriela Solís Robleda
- 1996 *Espacios mayas de autonomía: El pacto colonial en Yucatán*. Universidad Autónoma de Yucatán, Mérida.

Bricker, Victoria R.
- 1981 *The Indian Christ, the Indian King: The Historical Substrate of Maya Myth and Ritual*. University of Texas Press, Austin.

Carmack, Robert M.
- 1973 *Quichean Civilization: The Ethnohistoric, Ethnographic, and Archaeological Sources*. University of California Press, Berkeley.

Carmack, Robert M., and James L. Mondloch
- 1983 *Título de Totonicapán: Texto, traducción y comentario*. Universidad Nacional Autónoma de México, Instituto de Investigaciones Filológicas, Centro de Estudios Mayas, Mexico City.

Castañeda de la Paz, María
- 2008 Privileges of the "Others": The Coats of Arms Granted to Indigenous Conquistadors. In *The International Emblem: From Incunabula to the Internet; Selected Proceedings from the Eighth International Conference of the Society for Emblem Studies*, edited by Simon McKeown, pp. 283–316. Cambridge Scholars, Newcastle.
- 2009 Central Mexican Indigenous Coats of Arms and the Conquest of Mesoamerica. *Ethnohistory* 56(1):125–161.
- 2010 Heráldica indígena: Iconografía tipo códice en los escudos de armas tepanecas. *Arqueología mexicana* 105:70–75.
- 2013 Los escudos de armas de Tlaxcala: Un recorrido por su rico repertorio heráldico. In *Los escudos de armas indígenas: De la colonia al México independiente*, edited by María Castañeda de la Paz and Hans Roskamp, pp. 71–107. El Colegio de Michoacán, Zamora.

Castro, Nuno de
 1988 *Chinese Porcelain and the Heraldry of the Empire*. Civilização, Barcelos.

Chuchiak IV, John F.
 2001 Self-Promotion or Valid Historical Narratives? Reexamining the "Relaciónes de Méritos" as Sources of Juridical Proof in Idolatry Trials in Yucatán, 1570–1780. Paper presented at the American Historical Association Annual Meeting, Boston.
 2002 Toward a Regional Definition of Idolatry: Reexamining Idolatry Trials in the *Relaciónes de Méritos* and Their Role in Defining the Concept of *Idolatria* in Colonial Yucatan, 1570–1780. *Journal of Early Modern History* (6):140–167.
 2003 "It Is Their Drinking That Hinders Them": *Balché* and the Use of Ritual Intoxicants among the Colonial Yucatec Maya, 1550–1780. *Estudios de cultura maya* 24:137–172.
 2004 Cuius Regio Eius Religio: Yucatec Maya Nativistic Movements and the Religious Roots of Rebellion in Colonial Yucatán, 1547–1697. *Ketzalcalli* 1(1):44–59.
 2007 Forgotten Allies: The Origins and Role of Native Mesoamerican Auxiliaries and Indios Conquistadores in the Conquest of Yucatán, 1526–1550. In *Indian Conquistadors: Native Militaries in the Conquest of Mesoamerica*, edited by Michel Oudijk and Laura Matthew, pp. 175–225. University of Oklahoma Press, Norman.
 2010 Writing as Resistance: Maya Graphic Pluralism and Indigenous Elite Strategies for Survival in Colonial Yucatán, 1550–1750. *Ethnohistory* 57(1):87–116.
 2013 Anhelo de un escudo de armas: La falta de concesiones de escudos de armas indígenas mayas y la iconografía apócrifa de la heráldica colonial en Yucatán. In *Los escudos de armas indígenas: De la Colonia al México independiente*, edited by María Castañeda de la Paz and Hans Roskamp, pp. 273–308. El Colegio de Michoacán, Zamora.
 2018 Human Plunder: The Role of Maya Slavery in Postclassic and Early Conquest Era Yucatán, 1450–1550. Paper presented at the 82nd Annual Meeting of the Society for American Archaeology, Washington, D.C.
 n.d. Spears, Shields and Stars: A Study in the Nature of the Weapons and Tactics of Classic Maya Warfare. Under review.

Cortez, Constance
 1995 Gaspar Antonio Chi and the Xiu Family Tree. PhD dissertation, University of California, Los Angeles.

Cruz Pazos, Patricia
 2005 Nobles indígenas y mestizos: El acceso al poder en los pueblos de indios de la Nueva España. In *Estudios sobre América: Siglos XVI–XX*, edited by Antonio Gutiérrez Escudero and María Luisa Laviana Cuetos, pp. 1499–1506. Universidad de Sevilla, Seville.

Cummins, Tom
 2002 *Toasts with the Inca: Andean Abstraction and Colonial Images on Quero Vessels*. University of Michigan Press, Ann Arbor.

De Ridder, Rob
 1994 Karl V, Keizer van de Maya's: Het wapenschild van Karel V in de Mayaliteratuur. *Spiegel Historiael* 29(9):371–376.

Domínguez Torres, Mónica
 2013 Los escudos de armas indígenas y el lenguaje heráldico castellano a comienzos del siglo XVI. In *Los escudos de armas indígenas: De la Colonia al México independiente*, edited by María Castañeda de la Paz and Hans Roskamp, pp. 21–47. El Colegio de Michoacán, Zamora.

Galarza, Joaquín
 1987 *In amoxtli, in tlacatl / El libro, el hombre: Codices y vivencias*. Seminario de Escritura Indígena Tradicional, Mexico City.

Garza, Mercedes de la
 1983 *Relaciones histórico-geográficas de la gobernación de Yucatán: Mérida, Valladolid y Tabasco*. 2 vols. Instituto de Investigaciones Filológicas, Centro de Estudios Mayas, Universidad Nacional Autónoma de México, Mexico City.

Gasten, Andrea
    2005   The Kingship of Philip and Mary: Some Remarks on the Presentation and Heraldry and the Special Circumstances Surrounding the King's Window of Gouda. In *The Seventh Window: The King's Window Donated by Philip II and Mary Tudor to Sint Janskerk in Gouda*, edited by Wim de Groot, pp. 215–226. Verloren, Hilversum.

Gibson, Charles
    1967   *Tlaxcala in the Sixteenth Century*. Stanford University Press, Stanford.
    1991   *Tlaxcala en el siglo XVI*. Gobierno del Estado de Tlaxcala, Tlaxcala.

Gontar, Cybèle Trione
    2003   The Campeche Chair in the Metropolitan Museum of Art. *Metropolitan Museum Journal* 38:183–212.

Gorissen, Matthias
    2007   Fear, Conspiracy, and Rebellion in Early Colonial Yucatán: The Enemy Without, the Enemy Within. *Jahrbuch für Geschichte Lateinamerikas* 44:67–91.

Gosner, Kevin
    1992   *Soldiers of the Virgin: The Moral Economy of a Colonial Maya Rebellion*. University of Arizona Press, Tucson.

Green, L. C., and Olive Patricia Dickason
    1989   *The Law of Nations and the New World*. University of Alberta Press, Edmonton.

Haskett, Robert
    1996   Paper Shields: The Ideology of Coats of Arms in Colonial Mexican Primordial Titles. *Ethnohistory* 43(1):99–126.
    2005   *Visions of Paradise: Primordial Titles and Mesoamerican History in Cuernavaca*. University of Oklahoma Press, Norman.

Hillerkuss, Thomas
    1993   Los méritos y servicios de un maya yucateco principal del siglo XVI y la historia de sus probanzas y mercedes. *Estudios de la historia novohispana* 13:9–39.

Houston, Stephen D., Oswaldo Fernando Chinchilla Mazariegos, and David Stuart
    2001   *The Decipherment of Ancient Maya Writing*. University of Oklahoma Press, Norman.

Jakeman, M. Wells
    1952   *The "Historical Recollections" of Gaspar Antonio Chi: An Early Source-Account of Ancient Yucatan*. Brigham Young University, Provo, Utah.

Kaufmann, Thomas DaCosta
    2004   *Toward a Geography of Art*. University of Chicago Press, Chicago.

Knowlton, Timothy W., and Gabrielle Vail
    2010   Hybrid Cosmologies in Mesoamerica: A Reevaluation of the Yax Cheel Cab, a Maya World Tree. *Ethnohistory* 57(4):709–739.

Kuwayama, George
    1997   *Chinese Ceramics in Colonial Mexico*. University of Hawai'i Press, Honolulu.

López de Cogolludo, Fray Diego
    1688   *Historia de Yucatán*. J. García Infanzon, Madrid.

Lovell, George
    2005   *Conquest and Survival in Colonial Guatemala: A Historical Geography of the Cuchumatán Highlands, 1500–1821*. McGill-Queen's University Press, Montreal.

Lowie, Robert H.
    1985   *Evolution in Textile Design from the Highlands of Guatemala*. University of California Press, Berkeley.

Luque Talaván, Miguel
    2004   Tan príncipes e infantes como los de Castilla: Análisis histórico-jurídico de la nobleza indiana de origen prehispánico. *Anales del Museo de América* 12:9–34.

Luque Talaván, Miguel, and María Castañeda de la Paz
    2006   Escudos tlaxcaltecas: Iconografía prehispánica y europea. *Arqueología mexicana* 14(82):68–73.

MacKinnon, J. Jefferson, and Susan M. Kepecs
    1989   Prehispanic Saltmaking in Belize: New Evidence. *American Antiquity* 54(3):522–533.

Macleod, Murdo
    1998   Self-Promotion: The *Relaciones de méritos y servicios* and Their Historical and Political Interpretation. *Colonial Latin American Historical Review* 7(1):25–42.

Markman, Sidney David
  1984 *Architecture and Urbanization in Colonial Chiapas, Mexico*. American Philosophical Society, Philadelphia.

Martin, Simon
  2020 *Ancient Maya Politics: A Political Anthropology of the Classic Period, 150–900 CE*. Cambridge University Press, Cambridge.

Martínez Hernández, Juan
  1926 *Crónicas mayas: Crónica de Yaxkukul*. Nuevos Talleres de la Compañía Tipográfica Yucateca, Mérida.

Mathews, Peter
  1991 Classic Maya Emblem Glyphs. In *Classic Maya Political History: Hieroglyphic and Archaeological Evidence*, edited by T. Patrick Culbert, pp. 19–29. Cambridge University Press, Cambridge.

Menegus Bornemann, Margarita
  1999 El gobierno de los indios en la Nueva España, siglo XVI: Señores o Cabildo. *Revista de Indias* 59:599–617.
  2009 La territorialidad de los cacicazgos y los conflictos con terrazqueros y los pueblos vecinos en el siglo XVIII. In *Prácticas populares, cultura política y poder en México, siglo XIX*, edited by Brian F. Connaughton, pp. 359–378. Universidad Autonoma Metropolitana, Unidad Iztapalapa, Mexico City.

Menegus Bornemann, Margarita, and Rodolfo Aguirre Salvador
  2005 *El cacicazgo en Nueva España y Filipinas*. Plaza y Valdés, Mexico City.

Menéndez Pidal, Faustino
  2008 *La nobleza en España: Ideas, estructuras, historia*. Fundación Cultural de la Nobleza Española, Madrid.

Mira Caballos, Esteban
  2003 Indios nobles y caciques en la Corte real española, siglo XVI. *Temas americanistas* 16:1–15.

Molina Solís, Juan Francisco
  1896 *Historia del descubrimiento y conquista de Yucatán: Con una reseña de la historia antigua de esta península*. Impr. Y lit. R. Caballero, Mérida.

Okoshi Harada, Tsubasa
  2000 Análisis de la organización político territorial de los mayas peninsulares del Posclásico tardío: Una nueva perspectiva. *Los investigadores de la cultura maya* 1–6(8):28–37.
  2001 Gaspar Antonio Chi Xiu: El que "perpetuó" la imagen de los Xiu. *Acta mesoamericana* 12:59–72.
  2003 Vivir en dos mundos: Los gobernantes mayas yucatecos del siglo XVI. In *Cuarto Congreso Internacional de Mayistas*, pp. 85–95. Centro de Estudios Mayas, Instituto de Investigaciones Filológicas, Universidad Nacional Autónoma de México, Mexico City.

Ortíz Yam, Inés, and Sergio Quezada (editors)
  2009 *Visita de Diego García del Palacio a Yucatán, 1583*. Instituto de Investigaciones Filológicas, Centro de Estudios Mayas, Universidad Nacional Autónoma de México, Mexico City.

Oudjik, Michel R.
  2013 Falsificaciones de escudos de armas indígenas en el Estado de México (siglo XVIII). In *Los escudos de armas indígenas: De la Colonia al México independiente*, edited by María Castañeda de la Paz and Hans Roskamp, pp. 169–194. El Colegio de Michoacán, Zamora.

Oudjik, Michel R., and Matthew Restall
  2008 *La conquista indígena de Mesoamérica: El caso de don Gonzalo Mazatzin Moctezuma*. Secretaría de Cultura del Estado de Puebla, Universidad de las Américas, Puebla.

Owensby, Brian
  2008 *Empire of Law and Indian Justice in Colonial Mexico*. Stanford University Press, Stanford.

Patch, Robert
  1998 Culture, Community, and Rebellion in the Yucatec Maya Uprising of 1761. In *Native Resistance and the Pax Colonial in New Spain*, edited by Susan Schroeder, pp. 63–83. University of Nebraska Press, Lincoln.

2002 *Maya Revolt and Revolution in the Eighteenth Century*. M. E. Sharpe, Armonk, N.Y.

Paz y Meliá, Antonio
1892 *Nobiliario de conquistadores de Indias*. Impr. de M. Tello, Madrid.

Pech, Nakuk
1936 *Historia y crónica de Chac-Xulub-Chen*. Edited by Héctor Pérez Martínez. Departamento de Bibliotecas de la Secretaría de Educación Pública, Mexico City.

Quezada, Sergio
1989 Don Juan Chan: Un cacique yucateco anti-idólatra. *Mayab* 5:41–44.
1993 *Pueblos y caciques Yucatecos, 1550–1580*. El Colegio de México, Mexico City.
2005 El cacique yucateco: Un señorío sin territorio (siglo XVI). In *El cacicazgo en Nueva España y Filipinas*, by Margarita Menegus Bornemann and Rodolfo Aguirre Salvador, pp. 70–86. Plaza y Valdés, Mexico City.

Quezada Sergio, and Tsubasa Okoshi Harada
2001 *Papeles de los Xiu de Yaxá, Yucatán*. Universidad Nacional Autónoma de México, Mexico City.

Quezada, Sergio, and Terry Rugeley
2014 *Maya Lords and Lordship: The Formation of Colonial Society in Yucatán, 1350–1600*. University of Oklahoma Press, Norman.

Quezada, Sergio, and Anabel Torres Trujillo
2010 *Tres nobles mayas yucatecos*. Instituto de Cultura de Yucatán, Mérida.

Restall, Matthew
1998 *Maya Conquistador*. Beacon Press, Boston.

Restall, Matthew, Amara Solari, John F. Chuchiak IV, and Traci Ardren
2023 *The Friar and the Maya: Diego de Landa and the Account of the Things of Yucatan*. University Press of Colorado, Boulder.

Riese, Berthold
1982 Kriegsberichte der Klassischen Maya. *Baessler-Archiv*, n.F., 30:255–321.

Riquer, Martín de
1942 *Manual de heráldica española*. Apolo, Barcelona.

1996 *Heráldica castellana en tiempos de los reyes católicos*. Biblioteca Filológica Quaderns Crema, Barcelona.

Robertson, Donald
1975 Techialoyan Manuscripts and Painting, with a Catalog. In *Handbook of Middle American Indians*, vol. 14, pt. 3, *Guide to Ethnohistorical Sources*, edited by Howard F. Cline, pp. 253–280. University of Texas Press, Austin.

Rojas, José Luis de
2007 La nobleza indígena de México ante la conquista española. *Trocadero* (19):55–68.

Roskamp, Hans
1998 *La historiografía indígena de Michoacán: El lienzo de Jucutácato y los títulos de Carapan*. Research School CNWS, School of Asian, African, and Amerindian Studies, Leiden.
2003 Los títulos primordiales de Carapan: Legitimación e historiografía en una comunidad indígena de Michoacán. In *Autoridad y gobierno indígena en Michoacán*, edited by Carlos Paredes Martínez y Marta Terán, vol. 1, pp. 305–359. El Colegio de Michoacán, Zamora.
2010 Memoria, identidad y legitimación en los títulos primordiales de la región tarasca. In *Caras y máscaras de México étnico: Las formaciones del estado mexicano*, edited by Andrew Roth Seneff, pp. 39–53. El Colegio de Michoacán, Zamora.

Roskamp, Hans, and Christina Monzón
2020 El título primordial tarasco de Tócuaro, Michoacán. *Tlalocan* 25:287–342.

Roskamp, Hans, Christina Monzón, and J. Benedict Warren
2009 La memoria de don Melchor Caltzin (1543): Historia y legitimación en Tzintzuntzan, Michoacán. *Estudios de historia novohispana* 40:21–55.

Russo, Alessandra
1998 El renacimiento vegetal: Árboles de Jesé entre el viejo y nuevo mundo. *Anales del Instituto de Investigaciones Estéticas* 20:5–39.

Segovia Liga, Argelia
    2008   Los indios del Mariscal: Revisión de un manuscrito yucateco del siglo XVII. Thesis, Universidad Nacional Autónoma de México, Mexico City.

Solari, Amara
    2013   *Maya Ideologies of the Sacred: The Transfiguration of Space in Colonial Yucatan.* University of Texas Press, Austin.

Stephens, John L.
    1843   *Incidents of Travel in Yucatan.* 2 vols. Harper and Brothers, New York.

Stevenson, Cornelius
    1909   An Old Mexican Bandeja. *Bulletin of the Pennsylvania Museum* 7(25):1–6.

Stone, Andrea
    1987   Cave Painting in the Maya Area. *Latin American Indian Literatures Journal* 3(1):95–108.
    1989   Disconnection, Foreign Insignia, and Political Expansion: Teotihuacan and the Warrior Stelae of Piedras Negras. In *Mesoamerica after the Decline of Teotihuacan, AD 700–900*, edited by Richard A. Diehl and Janet Catherine Berlo, pp. 153–172. Dumbarton Oaks Research Library and Collection, Washington, D.C.
    1995   *Images from the Underworld: Naj Tunich and the Tradition of Maya Cave Paintings.* University of Texas Press, Austin.
    1997a   Regional Variation in Maya Cave Art. *Journal of Cave and Karst Studies* 59(1):33–42.
    1997b   Prehispanic Cave Utilization among the Maya. In *The Human Use of Caves*, edited by C. Bonsall and C. Tolan-Smith, pp. 201–206. British Archaeological Reports, Oxford.

Stone Andrea, and Marc Zender
    2011   *Reading Maya Art: A Hieroglyphic Guide to Ancient Maya Painting and Sculpture.* Thames and Hudson, New York.

Strecker, Matthias, and Jorge Artieda
    1978   La relación de algunas costumbres (1582) de Gaspar Antonio Chi. *Estudios de historia novohispana* 6:89–111.

Terry, Richard E., Bryce M. Brown, Travis W. Stanton, Traci Ardren, Tanya Cariño Anaya, Justin Lowry, and José Francisco Osorio León et al.
    2022   Soil Biomarkers of Cacao Tree Cultivation in the Sacred Cacao Groves of the Northern Maya Lowlands. *Journal of Archaeological Science: Reports* 11(4):103331.

Tozzer, Alfred
    1941   *Landa's Relación de las cosas de Yucatán: A Translation.* Peabody Museum of American Archaeology and Ethnology, Harvard University, Cambridge, Mass.

Webster, David
    1989   The Study of Maya Warfare: What It Tells Us About the Maya and What It Tells Us About Maya Archaeology. In *Lowland Maya Civilization in the Eighth Century AD*, edited by Jeremy A. Sabloff and John S. Henderson, pp. 415–444. Dumbarton Oaks Research Library and Collection, Washington, D.C.

Weckmann, Luis, and Frances M. López-Morillas
    1992   *The Medieval Heritage of Mexico.* Fordham University Press, New York.

Wheatcroft, Andrew
    1997   *The Habsburgs: Embodying Empire.* Penguin, New York.

Wood, Stephanie
    1998a   El problema de la historicidad de títulos y los códices del grupo Techialoyan. In *De tlacuilos y escribanos: Estudios sobre documentos indígenas coloniales del centro de México*, edited by Xavier Noguez Ramírez and Stephanie Wood, pp. 167–221. El Colegio Mexiquense and El Colegio de Michoacán, Mexico City.
    1998b   Testaments and Títulos: Conflict and Coincidence of Cacique and Community Interests in Colonial Mexico. In *Dead Giveaways: Indigenous Testaments of Colonial Spanish America*, edited by Matthew Restall and Susan Kellogg, pp. 85–111. University of Utah Press, Salt Lake City.

1998c The Social versus Legal Context of Nahuatl Títulos. In *Native Traditions in the Postconquest World*, edited by Elizabeth Hill Boone, pp. 201–231. Dumbarton Oaks Research Library and Collection, Washington, D.C.

2003 *Transcending Conquest: Nahua Views of Spanish Colonial Mexico*. University of Oklahoma Press, Norman.

Wood, Stephanie, and Xavier Noguez Ramírez (editors)

1998 *De tlacuilos y escribanos: Estudios sobre documentos indígenas coloniales del centro de México*. El Colegio de Michoacán, Zamora.

14

Toward a New Framework for Comparing Ancient and Modern Forms of Social Domination (or, "Whatever Happened to the Archaic State?")

DAVID WENGROW[1]

Introduction: The Elementary Forms of Domination

Not so long ago, a comparative study of Classic Maya (or ancient Egyptian, Shang, etc.) kingship would most likely have been framed as part of a broader investigation into the "origins of the state." It seems worth reflecting on why that is no longer assumed to be the case. Part of the answer may reside in the inability of archaeologists and anthropologists—after more than half a century of debate—to arrive at a coherent definition of the "archaic state," which encompasses such diverse cases as ancient Egypt, Mesopotamia, China, and Mesoamerica; alternately, it may reside in their willingness to settle for definitions that are sufficiently vague to encompass all these cases but, as a result, tell us very little of significance about the similarities and differences between them (compare, for example, Feinman and Marcus 1998:4–6; Jennings and Earle 2016; Trigger 2003; Yoffee 2005; note the critical observations by Ur 2016:486–487, and Scheidel's (2013:16) concession

that any attempt to define the common characteristics of early states "inevitably paints with a frightfully broad brush"). Perhaps part of the answer also lies in the growing fragility of states on the contemporary world stage, or what Susan Strange (1996) has called "the retreat of the state," making it increasingly difficult to view "states" (however defined) as a logical culmination of human social evolution. For those seeking instructive comparisons between ancient and modern forms of domination, "the state," in short, is becoming something of a shopworn concept (Graeber and Sahlins 2017:456).

With hindsight, perhaps the greatest appeal of those earlier debates was precisely their insistence on comparing modern and historical (sometimes even ancient) political arrangements. After all, there is a lineage of sorts here because modern nation-states since the Age of Revolution have been based on the principle of popular sovereignty—that is, the idea that the same power once held by absolute monarchs is now held by an entity called "the people." Of course, modern states are also more than that.

They may, perhaps, be best viewed as an amalgam of institutional elements that came together at a recent point in history—broadly the mid-seventeenth through the nineteenth century—and are now in the process of drifting apart again (cf. Bayart 2007). Those elements, which we will shortly define in more detail, comprise not just sovereignty but also a central administrative apparatus (or bureaucracy) and formal arenas of political competition (most often in the form of national elections). What has interested scholars for more than a century is precisely how and why those heterogeneous elements coalesced to produce a form of governance that is now ubiquitous.

Searching for the "origins of the state" in ancient Mexico, Egypt, China, or Peru is usually a matter of trying to find a point in time when sovereign power became harnessed to an administrative apparatus, forming internally specialized and mutually reinforcing organs of government (a competitive political field is considered somewhat optional). In what follows, I will be questioning the underlying teleology of this approach and suggesting an alternative one, based on a new framework for analyzing and comparing forms of social domination, which encompasses both ancient and modern cases (further discussed in chapter ten of Graeber and Wengrow 2021). We might begin with the—no doubt, obvious—point that there is no particular reason to see the global distribution of modern nation-states as the culmination of a millennial process of political evolution, since their "spread" has been anything but evolutionary in character (assuming we reject a Spencerian definition of evolution as "survival of the fittest"). More often it has been the result of imposition by armed conquest, colonialism, and empire, abetted by the enslavement, mass murder, and dispossession of entire populations.

Turning directly to the three basic institutional components of the modern state—sovereignty, bureaucracy, and political competition—it seems noteworthy that all three are elaborations of elementary forms of social domination, which can be found operating just as well on the scale of domestic households, families, or local groups. Sovereignty is, in the last resort, control over the legitimate use of violence in a given territory. Absolute sovereigns, just like domestic patriarchs, stand outside and beyond the moral order that applies to others in their domain; throughout history, most kingdoms and empires have modeled themselves on the patriarchal organization of households ("patrimonial systems" in the sense of Weber [1922] 1978; for the rhetorical nature of such modeling and its lack of fit with the realities of gender relations in such systems, see Ardren, this volume; Joyce 2008; McAnany and Masson, this volume). Administrative power rests on control over the circulation of knowledge or information, which may be esoteric as well as bureaucratic (and, of course, bureaucracy can and often does itself take on an esoteric cast), while competitive politics comes down to the exercise of individual charisma (i.e., one's ability to attract followers and put down rivals).

On reflection, it seems clear that access to violence, knowledge, and charisma defines the very possibilities of social domination (Graeber and Wengrow 2021:362–367). Imagine a hypothetical world where everyone is immune to physical force—structural inequalities would be harder to maintain, but they could still be based on privileged access to information or on qualities of personal attractiveness. Or try the same thought experiment again, starting in a world where nobody can keep secrets, and so on. Since the modern state is defined by a combination of sovereignty, bureaucracy, and a competitive political field, it seems natural to examine history in this light. But as soon as we attempt to do this, it becomes apparent that there is no particular reason why these three principles should go together, let alone reinforce each other in the particular fashion we have come to expect from governments today. In fact, as we will begin to show in what follows, the elementary forms of domination have entirely separate origins and histories, often appearing in opposition to one another.

As an initial illustration, it is becoming clear—in light of archaeological evidence from Iraq, Turkey, and neighboring countries—that in Uruk-period Mesopotamia, bureaucratically ordered societies of the river valleys (including some of the world's earliest cities and their colonial offshoots) are to be contrasted with much smaller, aristocratic polities that emerged in the surrounding hill country (e.g., at Arslantepe, Başur Höyük), both during and directly after an initial phase of urban expansion in the late fourth millennium BCE (Frangipane 2016). As currently reconstructed by archaeologists, these aristocratic societies of the highlands comprised warrior-leaders who vied for the loyalty of retainers through spectacular contests—reflected in the presence of royal burials containing great quantities of wealth and personal weaponry, as well as human victims killed for the occasion—but who also appear to have rejected the very principles of urban administration (Frangipane 2006, 2012; Hassett and Sağlamtimur 2018). It could be argued that "states" first emerged in this region when the two forms of authority (the bureaucratic-administrative order of the floodplains, and the political-charismatic order of the highlands) merged together in the Early Dynastic period; but even in later centuries, there is little to suggest that the rulers of Mesopotamian city-states achieved a significant measure of sovereignty, or even made any such claims (see Richardson 2012). We are, therefore, still a long way from anything like an embryonic version of the modern state.

Conversely, it is possible to point to historical examples of polities where sovereignty existed in highly concentrated and localized forms, but in the absence of an administrative apparatus or any formal arena of political competition. The "divine kingship" of the Shilluk of South Sudan and of the Natchez (Théoloël) of Louisiana are two cases in point. In each, royal power was centered on capitals—respectively, the *reth*'s compound at Fashoda (now called Kodok, in West Nile province) and the "Great Village" of the Natchez (now known as the Fatherland Site, in Adams County)—containing shrines where rulers followed an elaborate schedule of daily rituals and where complex installation ceremonies were performed. The royal households of the Shilluk and Natchez were also located in their respective capitals, each comprising an eclectic mixture of royal wives (who often wielded considerable influence) and other kin, servants, dependents, and retainers. Within these rather small domains, the Shilluk *reth* and the Natchez "Great Sun" wielded absolute power of command: they could order summary executions and appropriate goods pretty much as they had a mind to. Yet in both cases, a variety of sources, both ethnographic and archaeological, confirm that these sovereigns lacked any effective way of extending or stabilizing power beyond the immediate perimeter of the royal court—or even beyond their physical person. Such arrangements led to situations where, for much of the year, the area around the Shilluk and Natchez capitals became depopulated, as subjects got as far away as they could from their ostensible rulers, leading very different—and generally much freer—lives elsewhere (Graeber and Sahlins 2017:65–138, 390–398, with further references).

In what follows, we will consider the possibility that—when looking at those times and places in human history usually taken to mark "the origins of the state"—we may, in fact, be seeing how very different kinds of power crystallized, each with its own peculiar juxtaposition of violence, knowledge, and charisma. One way to test the value of a new approach is to see if it helps explain what had previously seemed to be anomalous cases. In this instance, that means ancient polities that mobilized and organized great numbers of people at the behest of elites, but do not seem to fit any of the usual definitions of a state; or that are clearly organized around certain principles we associate with states, but just as clearly lacking in others. The inability of researchers to account for such entities is striking, and history so full of examples, that one begins to wonder if their "anomalous" status is largely an artifact of our own conceptual limitations. To begin exploring an alternative framework of analysis, and given the regional focus of the present volume, let us start with the Olmec.

Politics as Charismatic Sport: The Olmec Case

Precisely defining the Olmec has proved to be a difficult problem for archaeologists. Early twentieth century scholars referred to it as an artistic or cultural "horizon," largely because it wasn't clear how else to describe a style—identified by certain common types of pottery, anthropomorphic figurines, and stone sculpture—that appeared between 1500 and 1000 BCE across an enormous area, straddling the Isthmus of Tehuantepec, and including Guatemala, Honduras, and much of southern Mexico. Whatever the Olmec were, they seemed to represent the "mother culture," as it came to be known, of all later Mesoamerican civilizations, having invented the region's characteristic calendar systems, glyphic writing, and ceremonial ballgames (Pool 2007).

At the same time, there was no reason to assume that the Olmec were a unified ethnic or even political group. Archaeologists later came to understand that there was, in fact, an Olmec heartland in the marshlands of Veracruz, where the swamp cities of San Lorenzo and La Venta arose along the fringes of Mexico's Gulf Coast. But the internal structure of these Olmec cities is still poorly understood. Most seem to have been centered on ceremonial precincts, including massive earthen platforms and, later, pyramid mounds (ballcourts having so far proved elusive) surrounded by extensive suburbs. Monumental centers such as these stood in relative isolation, amid an otherwise fragmented and relatively unstructured landscape of small maize-farming settlements and seasonal forager camps (Rosenswig 2017; a picture liable to change, perhaps, with the application of LiDAR survey in Tabasco and Veracruz).

In no sense was Olmec society egalitarian, as there were clearly marked elites (Clark 1997; Drucker 1981). Pyramids, plazas, and monuments designed to be viewed from afar suggest that, at least in certain times of year, those elites could draw upon extensive resources of skill and labor. As Warren Hill and John Clark (2001) argue, it seems reasonable to envisage a fairly direct relationship between competitive games—drawing participants and spectators from a wide hinterland—and the rise of an Olmec aristocracy, owing not least to the production of colossal heads, laboriously sculpted in basalt, that appear to be portraits of Olmec leaders wearing the leather helmets of ballplayers emblazoned with "individualizing insignia" (Clark 2004:213; see also Blomster 2012 for the connection between competitive ballgames and Olmec rulership and its codification in images). All of the known examples are sufficiently similar that each seems to reflect some ideal standard of male beauty; but each is also different enough to be seen as a unique portrait of a particular champion (in this respect, Wilk's [2004] comparison between Olmec politics and modern beauty pageants seems very apposite).

In other respects, ties between center and periphery appear superficial. As Robert Rosenswig (2010) observes, the decline of the first great Olmec city at San Lorenzo seems to have had very little impact on the wider regional economy. With their intense fusion of political competition and organized spectacle, it is easy to appreciate why the Olmec are often seen as cultural progenitors of later Mesoamerican kingdoms and empires; but there is little evidence that Olmec polities themselves ever created an infrastructure for dominating a large population. So far as anyone knows, their rulers did not command a stable military or administrative apparatus, which might have allowed them to extend their power throughout a wider hinterland; instead, they presided over a remarkable spread of cultural influence radiating from ceremonial centers, which may only have been densely occupied on specific occasions (such as ballgames) scheduled in concert with the demands of the agricultural calendar (and largely empty at other times).

In other words, if these were "states" in any sense at all, then they are probably best defined as seasonal versions of what Clifford Geertz (1980) once called "theatre states," where organized power was realized only periodically, in grand but fleeting spectacles, and anything we might consider "statecraft"—from diplomacy to the stockpiling of resources—existed in order to facilitate the rituals and ceremonies, rather than the other way around.

Chavín de Huántar: An "Empire" Built on Images?

In South America, we find a somewhat analogous situation. Before the Inka, a whole series of polities in the Peruvian Andes and adjacent coastal drainages are identified tentatively as "states" in the scholarly literature. None used writing, at least in any form that modern researchers can recognize, but from 600 CE onward many employed knotted strings for record-keeping and probably other forms of notation too. Monumental centers of some kind already existed in the Río Supe region in the third millennium BCE. Later, between 1000 and 200 BCE, a single center at Chavín de Huántar, in the northern highlands of Peru, extended its influence over a much larger area (Conklin and Quilter 2008). This "Chavín Horizon" gave way to three distinct regional cultures—Wari, Tiwanaku, and Moche—associated with urban polities of differing types and organization.

Jeffrey Quilter and Michele Koons (2012) have discussed how the first Europeans to study the remains of these early Peruvian polities, in the late nineteenth and early twentieth centuries, tended to assume that any city or set of cities with monumental art and architecture that exerted "influence" over a surrounding region must be the capitals of states or empires. As with the Olmec, however, a surprisingly large proportion of that "influence" seems to have come in the form of images—distributed, in the Andean case, on small ceramic vessels, objects of personal adornment, and textiles—rather than in the spread of administrative, military, and commercial institutions, or their associated technologies.

Consider Chavín de Huántar itself, located high in the Mosna Valley of the Peruvian Andes. Archaeologists once believed Chavín to have been the core of a pre-Inka empire in the first millennium BCE; a "state" controlling a hinterland that reached to the Amazonian rainforest to the east and the Pacific coast to the west, encompassing all the intervening highlands and coastal drainages in between. Such power seemed commensurate with the scale and sophistication of Chavín's cut-stone architecture, its unrivaled abundance of monumental sculpture, and the appearance of its motifs on pottery, jewelry, and fabric across the wider region, but, as Quilter and Koons note, little evidence has since emerged to suggest that Chavín really was some kind of "Rome of the Andes."

To better define the kind of polity that Chavín was requires a closer look at its imagery (see also Burger 2003; Weismantel 2013). Unlike that of the Olmec (see Tate 2012), the art of Chavín does not readily lend itself to the reconstruction of pictorial narratives, nor does it appear to be a pictographic writing system. Chavín images are complex in other ways, and clearly they were not for the uninitiated. Crested eagles curl in on themselves, vanishing into a maze of ornament; human faces grow snake-like fangs, or contort into feline grimaces. Only after some study do even the most elementary forms reveal themselves to the untrained eye. With due attention, the modern viewer can begin to tease out recurrent images of tropical forest animals—jaguars, snakes, caimans—but just as the eye attunes to them, they slip back from the field of vision, winding in and out of each other's bodies, or merging into complex patterns.

Some of these images are described in the literature as "monsters," but they have nothing in common with the simple composite figures—centaurs, griffins, and the like—that feature in visual narratives on ancient Greek vases or Mesopotamian sculpture, or their Moche equivalents. We are in another kind of visual world altogether. It is the realm of the shape-shifter (cf. Severi 2015), where no body is ever stable or complete and where diligent mental training is required to tease out structure from what seems at first to be visual mayhem. A wealth of circumstantial evidence relates the experience of Chavín art to altered states of consciousness. At Chavín itself, snuff spoons, small ornate mortars, and bone pipes have been found, and among its carved images are sculpted male figures with fangs and snake headdresses, holding aloft the stalk of the San Pedro cactus. This plant is the basis of *Huachuma*, a mescaline-based infusion still made in the region today, that induces psychoactive visions. Other carved figures, all of them apparently male, are surrounded by images of vilca leaves (*Anadenanthera* sp.), which contain a powerful hallucinogen. Released when the leaves are ground up and snorted, it induces a gush of mucus from the nose, as faithfully depicted on sculpted heads that line the walls of Chavín's major temples (Burger 2011; Torres 2008).

Little in Chavín's monumental landscape really seems concerned with secular government at all. There are no obvious military fortifications or administrative quarters. Almost everything that survives seems connected with ritual performance and the revelation or concealment of esoteric knowledge (Rick 2017). Consider the Old Temple, with its stone labyrinths and hanging staircases, which seem designed for individual trials, initiations, and vision quests—tortuous journeys ending at narrow corridors, large enough for only a single person, beyond which lies a tiny sanctum containing a monolith, El Lanzón, carved with dense tangles of images. It resides at the heart of a darkened maze, illuminated by slats, where no single viewer could ever grasp the totality of its form or meaning (Weismantel 2013).

Defining "First Order Regimes"

If Chavín was in any sense an "empire," it was an empire built on control over images linked to esoteric knowledge. While this was also true of Olmec rulership, the latter presents a distinct emphasis on spectacle, competition, and the personal attributes of political leaders, which has no obvious equivalent in the Chavín case. Clearly, our use of the term "empire" is about as loose as it could possibly be. Neither, so far as we can tell, was remotely similar to the Roman or Han, or indeed the Inka and Aztec empires. Nor do they fulfill any of the important criteria for "statehood"—at least not on most standard sociological definitions (monopoly of violence, levels of administrative hierarchy, and so forth). The usual recourse is to describe such regimes instead as "complex chiefdoms," but this seems hopelessly inadequate as well. Instead, we propose to look at these otherwise puzzling cases through the lens of our three elementary principles of domination—control of violence (or sovereignty), control of knowledge, and charismatic politics—to examine how each stresses a particular form of domination to an exceptional degree and develops it on an unusually large scale.

In the case of Chavín, power over a large and dispersed population seems to have been about retaining control over certain kinds of knowledge, something perhaps not that far removed from the idea of "state secrets" found in later bureaucratic regimes, although the content was obviously very different, and there was apparently very little in the way of military force to back it up. In the Olmec tradition, power was about certain formalized ways of competing for personal recognition in an atmosphere of play laced with risk—a prime example of a large-scale competitive political field, but again in the absence of territorial sovereignty or evidence for an administrative apparatus. No doubt there was a certain degree of personal charisma, spectacle, and jockeying too at Chavín; no doubt among the Olmec, too, some did obtain influence by their command of arcane knowledge (as strongly indicated, for example, by the contents of buried offerings at La Venta [Tate 1998]); neither case gives us reason to think anyone was asserting a strong principle of sovereignty.

We might refer to these as "first order regimes" because they seem to be organized around one of the three elementary forms of domination (knowledge control, for Chavín; charismatic politics for the Olmec) to the relative neglect, but not exclusion, of the other two. To fully illustrate the model, an obvious next question, then, is whether there are also examples of the third possible variant—that is, societies that develop a principle of sovereignty (i.e., grant an individual or small group a monopoly on the right to use violence with impunity) and take it to rather extreme lengths, without either an apparatus for controlling knowledge or any sort of competitive political field. In fact, there are, and we have already mentioned two: the Shilluk of South Sudan, and the Natchez of southern Louisiana (the latter representing the only undisputed historical case of divine kingship north of the Rio Grande). The rulers of these polities enjoyed an absolute power of command that would have satisfied a Sapa Inka or Egyptian pharaoh, but they had little capacity to extend that power beyond their immediate physical ambit. It has never occurred to anyone to refer to such an arrangement as a "state."

So far, then, we have seen how each of the three principles we began with—violence, knowledge, and charisma—could, in "first order regimes" of domination, become the basis for political structures that in some ways resemble what we think of as a state, but in others clearly do not. Now let's turn instead to the sort of cases that are usually considered to be more straightforward examples of archaic states or empires: Old Kingdom Egypt, Early Dynastic Mesopotamia, Shang China, Inka Peru, and the Classic Maya. These cases are often compared in order to define a stage or threshold in human social evolution—"the archaic state," "early civilization," or "social complexity." Here instead we will attempt to view them, in a preliminary way, through the lens of our three principles of domination, to see how much they really have in common. We might begin by noting significant parallels between Egypt and Peru, which are all the more remarkable considering their strikingly different topographies—the flat and easily navigable Nile, as compared with the "vertical archipelagos" of the Andes.

Some Salient Differences in the Forms of "Early States" from China to Mesoamerica

Old Kingdom Egypt and the Inka Empire demonstrate what can happen when the principle of sovereignty is armed with a bureaucracy and manages to extend itself across a territory in a more or less uniform manner. Accordingly, they are often invoked as primordial examples of state formation. There are other similarities as well, which go down to uncanny details, like the mummification of dead rulers, the way mummified rulers continued to maintain their own rural estates, and how living kings were treated as gods who had to make periodic tours of their domains. Both societies shared a certain antipathy to urban life. Their capitals were really ceremonial centers, stages for royal display, with relatively few permanent residents, and their ruling elites preferred to imagine their subjects as living in a realm of bucolic estates and hunting grounds (Kolata 1997; cf. Baines 1997, 2003).

All of this, however, only serves to underline the degree to which other "early states" followed entirely different paths. Early Dynastic Mesopotamia was made up of dozens of city-states of varying sizes, each governed by its own charismatic warrior-king, all vying constantly for dominance. Only occasionally would one ruler gain enough of an upper hand to create something that might be described as the beginnings of a unified kingdom or empire. The cities they ostensibly ruled over had been around for centuries: commercial hubs with strong traditions of self-governance, each with its own city-gods, who presided over local systems of temple administration. Kings, in this case, almost never claimed to be gods, but rather the god's vicegerent and sometimes heroic defender on earth: in short, they were delegates of sovereign power that resided properly in heaven (Wengrow 2010; Winter 2008). The result was a dynamic tension between two principles, which, as we noted earlier, originally arose in opposition to one another: the administrative order of the river valleys, and the heroic/charismatic politics of the surrounding highlands. Sovereignty, in the last resort, belonged to the gods alone.

The Classic Maya Lowlands were different again. To be a ruler (*ajaw*) was to be a hunter and god impersonator of the first rank, a warrior whose body, on entering battle or during dance rituals, became host to the spirit of an ancestral hero, deity, or dreamlike monsters (Freidel, Schele, and Parker 1993:293–336; Houston and Inomata 2009:193–217; Schele and Freidel 1990). The degree to which Maya rulership was supported by a stable administration is contested and may have varied considerably (Masson [2002] notes this as an issue "for which the least data and the strongest opinions exist"). While royal households were internally structured according to quite elaborate ranks and offices, there is little to suggest that Classic Maya sovereigns possessed an extensive bureaucratic apparatus for the wider management of their subjects' affairs (Inomata 2001; cf. Foias 2013:112–164). *Ajawtaak* seem to have been tiny squabbling gods, and if anything was projected into the cosmos, in the Classic Maya case, it was precisely the principle of bureaucracy.

With the emergence of hereditary rulership, the Maya cosmos itself came to be imagined as a kind of administrative hierarchy governed by predictable laws: an intricate set of celestial or subterranean wheels within wheels, such that it was possible to establish the exact birth and death dates of major divinities thousands of years in the past—the deity

Muwaan Mat, for instance, was born on December 7, 3121 BCE, seven years before the creation of the current universe—even if it would never occur to rulers to register the numbers, wealth, or birth dates of their own subjects (cf. Rice 2004:56–74; Stuart 2011). As McAnany (2019:57) suggests, with reference to the southern Maya Lowlands, the enfolding of royal action within cosmic time—as well as eliciting great outlays of aesthetic and intellectual labor—may mask a "tacit recognition of the fragility of rulership." Here we can draw a further contrast with Mesopotamia, where administration was a pervasive feature of earthly government, while the cosmos, far from being predictably organized, was inhabited by gods whose actions came in the form of unexpected interventions, and frequently chaotic ruptures, in human affairs (Jacobsen 1976).

Do these various polities, in spite of their differences, have any common features? Some basic generalizations can be made. All deployed spectacular violence at the pinnacle of the system, and, as we noted earlier, all to some degree mimicked the patriarchal organization of households. In every case, the apparatus of government stood on top of some kind of division of society into classes. But these common elements could just as well have existed without or prior to the creation of central government—as demonstrated by ethnohistorical cases, such as the Indigenous societies of the Pacific Northwest coast—and even when such government was established, the various common features could take on very different forms. In Mesopotamian cities, for instance, social class was often based on land tenure and mercantile wealth. Temples doubled as city banks and factories, and there were powerful societies of merchants. We know much less about such matters in the Maya Lowlands, but what we do know suggests that power was based less on the control of land or commerce than on the ability to control flows of people directly, through intermarriage and the personal bonds of loyalty between lords and lesser nobles (Martin 2020). Hence the focus, in Classic Maya politics, on capturing high-status rivals in warfare as a form of "human capital" (or what McAnany [2010:278–283] calls "tribute ransom," which is something that hardly features in Mesopotamian sources).

Looking at China only seems to complicate things further. In the time of the late Shang, from 1200 to 1000 BCE, Chinese society did share certain features with the other canonical "early states," but considered as an integrated whole, it is entirely unique. Like Inka Cuzco, the Shang capital at Anyang was designed as a "pivot of the four quarters"—a cosmological anchor for the entire kingdom, laid out as a grand stage for royal ritual. Like both Cuzco and the Egyptian capital of Memphis, the city served as home to the royal cemeteries and their attached mortuary temples, as well as a living administration. Anyang's industrial quarters produced enormous quantities of bronze vessels and jades, used in communing with ancestors (Bagley 1999). But in most important ways, we find little similarity between the Shang and either Old Kingdom Egypt or Inka Peru.

Shang rulers did not claim sovereignty over an extended area. They could not travel safely, let alone issue commands, outside a narrow band of territories clustered on the middle and lower reaches of the Yellow River, not far from the royal court (Shaughnessy 1989). Even there, one is left with a sense that Shang rulers did not claim sovereignty in the same sense as Egyptian, Peruvian, or even Maya ones. The clearest evidence is the exceptional importance of divination in the early Chinese state (Flad 2008). Any royal decision—whether related to war, alliances, the founding of new cities, or even such apparently trivial matters as extending royal hunting grounds—could only proceed if approved by the ultimate authorities, the gods and ancestral spirits, and there was no absolute assurance that such approval would be forthcoming in any given case (Keightley 1999; Yuan and Flad 2005). Shell and bone oracles were stored for consultation, and while it is possible that writing was used for everyday purposes on perishable media that don't survive, there is as yet no clear evidence at this time for other forms of administrative archives that became so typical of later Chinese dynasties, nor much in the way of an elaborate administrative apparatus at all (for a slightly different view, see Haicheng [2014:183], who talks of the Shang state "bureaucratizing the form taken by communication with the spirits").

Like the Classic Maya, Shang rulers routinely waged war to acquire stocks of living human victims for sacrifices. Rival courts to the Shang had their own ancestors, sacrifices, and diviners, and while they appear to have recognized the Shang as paramount, especially in ritual contexts, there seemed to be no contradiction between this and actually going to war with them, if they felt there was sufficient cause. This rivalry helps explain the lavishness of Shang funerals and the mutilation of captive bodies; their rulers were still, in a sense, playing the agonistic games typical of a heroic society, competing to outshine and humiliate their rivals (Campbell 2014). Such a situation is inherently unstable, and eventually, one rival dynasty, the Western Zhou, managed to definitively defeat the Shang and to claim for itself the Mandate of Heaven.

Defining "Second Order Regimes"

At this point, it should be clear that what we are really talking about is not the "origins of the state," in the sense of the emergence, in embryonic form, of a single, novel institution that would become a constant feature of human history across multiple continents, growing and evolving into modern forms of government. We are speaking instead of broad regional systems. It just happens, in the case of Egypt and the Andes, that an entire system became united (at least some of the time) under a single authority, but this was actually a fairly unusual arrangement. More common were situations such as those in Shang China, where unification was largely theoretical; or Mesopotamia, where regional hegemony rarely lasted for longer than a generation or two; or the Classic Maya, where there was a protracted struggle between two main power blocs, neither of which could ever quite overcome the other.

In terms of the specific theory we have been developing here, where the three elementary forms of domination—control of violence, control of knowledge, and charismatic authority—can each crystallize into its own institutional form (sovereignty, administration, and agonistic politics), almost all of these "early states" could be more accurately described as "second order regimes" of domination. If "first order regimes" like the Olmec, Chavín, or Natchez each developed only one part of the triad, in the typically far more violent arrangements of "second order regimes," two of the three principles of domination were brought together in some spectacular and unprecedented way. Which two it was seems to have varied from case to case. Egypt's first rulers combined literate administration and sovereignty (the latter amply illustrated by the spectacular violence, including the ritual killing of human victims, that went on around early royal tombs) (Wengrow 2006:218–258, 266–269); Mesopotamian kings navigated between administrative order and heroic politics; their individual qualities and achievements were said to be recognized by the gods and physically marked in the virility and allure of the ruler's body (Winter 1996). Classic Maya *ajawtaak* fused heroic politics with sovereignty; Halperin (this volume) discusses some permutations of this in Maya royal costume, where featherwork expresses the cumulative memory of specific heroic deeds, while jade ornaments signify transcendent aspects of royal sovereignty.

We should emphasize that it is not as if any of these principles were entirely absent in any one case: in fact, what often seems to have happened is that two of them crystallized into institutional forms—reinforcing one another as the basis of government—while the third form of domination was largely pushed out of the realm of human affairs altogether, and displaced onto the nonhuman cosmos (as with divine sovereignty in China and Mesopotamia, or the cosmic bureaucracy of the Classic Maya). Equally, when we speak of an absence of charismatic politics in Old Kingdom Egypt or Inka Peru, we are talking about the lack of a "star system" or "hall of fame"—with institutionalized rivalries between warlords, local magnates, and so on. We are most certainly not speaking of an absence of individual personalities.

Conclusions: Rethinking Some Basic Premises of Political Evolution

Social scientists and political philosophers have been debating the "origins of the state" for over a century. The fact that the world, at the present time, is almost entirely covered by states makes it easy to write as if this outcome was inevitable and to project current institutional arrangements backward, assuming these came into existence once societies attained a certain degree of "complexity." It is sometimes asserted, for example, that states begin when certain key functions of government—military, administrative, and judicial—pass into the hands of full-time specialists (e.g., Turchin et al. 2018). This makes sense if we assume that an agricultural surplus "freed up" a significant portion of the population from the onerous responsibility of securing adequate amounts of food, and it suggests the beginning of a process that would lead to our current global division of labor. Yet almost none of the regimes we've been considering were actually staffed by full-time specialists. Most obviously, none seem to have had a standing army, and warfare was largely a business for the agricultural offseason (see, for example, Richardson 2012 and Schrakamp 2010 on Mesopotamia; Van Tuerenhout 2002 for the Classic Maya; and more generally, Meller and Schefik 2015).

Priests and judges rarely worked full time; in fact, most government institutions in Old Kingdom Egypt, Shang China, and Early Dynastic Mesopotamia were staffed by a rotating workforce, whose members had other lives as managers of rural estates, traders, or any number of different occupations. We might even ask to what degree many of these "early states" were themselves largely seasonal phenomena (cf. Scott 2017:15, as well as some useful qualifications to this point by Hutson, this volume). Like warfare, the business of government tended to concentrate strongly upon certain times of year: some months were full of building projects, pageants, festivals, census taking, oaths of allegiance, trials, and spectacular executions, but in others a king's subjects scattered to attend to the more urgent needs of planting, harvesting, and pasturage. This doesn't mean these kingdoms weren't real: they were capable of mobilizing, or for that matter killing and maiming, thousands of human beings. It just means their reality was, in effect, sporadic.

As the sociologist Philip Abrams pointed out long ago, to understand the realities of power, whether in modern or ancient societies, is to acknowledge the gap between what elites claim they can do and what they are actually able to do. Not making this distinction has led social scientists and archaeologists up countless blind alleys, because the state is "not the reality which stands behind the mask of political practice. It is itself the mask which prevents our seeing political practice as it is." To understand the latter, he argued, we must attend to "the senses in which the state does not exist rather than to those in which it does" (Abrams 1977:58). As we can now see, these points apply just as forcefully to ancient political regimes as they do to modern ones—if not more so. What we call the "modern state" is simply one particular amalgam of sovereignty, administration, and competitive politics, one way that our three elementary principles of domination happened to come together, but this time with a notion that sovereignty (the power of kings) is held by an entity called "the people" (or "the nation"), that bureaucracies exist for the benefit of said "people," and where a variation on aristocratic contests and prizes has come to be relabeled as "democracy." Nothing, we suggest, was inevitable about any of this, nor was it the only possible result of societies increasing in demographic scale, density, or organizational complexity.

We might briefly return to our initial point about orders of magnitude: that the basic components of modern states are institutional versions of elementary forms of social domination that can be found operating just as well at the level of domestic households or small family groups. This matters because scale itself—in the simple, demographic sense of raw numbers of people living together in dense concentrations or large organized systems—is often invoked as a causal factor in the entrenchment of social hierarchies and structural inequality. Here we might make two final observations, based on evidence that has emerged from the archaeological record in recent decades. Contemporary archaeology shows that rather than emerging as a "package" of institutional features, sovereignty, competitive politics, and specialized administration first appear, in various parts of the world, in isolation from each other, among demographically small groups, long before their incorporation into centralized forms of governance. Consider, for example, the small-scale kingdoms of predynastic Egypt (Baines 1995; Friedman 2008), the warrior aristocracies in Bronze Age Europe (Treherne 1995), or the village bureaucracies of Late Neolithic (Halaf-'Ubaid period) Mesopotamia (Akkermans and Verhoeven 1995; Ferioli et al. 1994). Second, these same institutional features appear to be either lacking or highly attenuated in at least some of the world's earliest known cities. Here consider, for instance, the "mega-sites" of Trypillia, Ukraine (Müller, Rassmann, and Videiko 2016), the first cities of the Indus Valley (Green 2020), or the later phases of urban life at Teotihuacan in the Valley of Mexico (Froese, Gershenson, and Manzanilla 2014; and see, more generally, Graeber and Wengrow 2021).

A new picture seems to be emerging of what was once called "state formation." If we might venture one final generalization, it seems likely that the most productive studies of the roots of systemic domination in human societies will begin not at the level of cities, ceremonial centers, or regional confederacies but at the small scale, at the level of gender relations, age groups, and domestic servitude—the kind of relationships that contain at once the greatest intimacy, and also the deepest forms of structural violence (cf. Hutson, this volume; McAnany and Masson, this volume). In pursuing such studies, it will be important to distinguish the elementary forms of social domination, tracing how they historically came together and drifted apart, examining the affinities and the tensions between them in different cases, and considering how "social domination operates at the household level in order to facilitate its operations at the societal level" (Ardren, this volume). This, we suggest, can provide a more compelling way to look at the history of social power on a global scale than chasing that eternal phantasm, the "origins of the state."

NOTE

1 The present chapter develops ideas and arguments that are the outcome of my collaborative research with David Graeber (1961–2020), culminating in our coauthored book, *The Dawn of Everything: A New History of Humanity* (Graeber and Wengrow 2021; notably chapter 10, "Why the State Has No Origin: The Humble Beginnings of Sovereignty, Bureaucracy and Politics"). David had originally intended to join me at the symposium Faces of Rulership in the Maya Region; the responsibility for any departure from or elaborations to our jointly published work rests with me alone.

REFERENCES CITED

Abrams, Philip
  1977 Notes on the Difficulty of Studying the State. *Journal of Historical Sociology* 1(1):58–89.

Akkermans, Peter M. M. G., and Mark Verhoeven
  1995 An Image of Complexity: The Burnt Village at Late Neolithic Sabi Abyad, Syria. *American Journal of Archaeology* 99(1):5–32.

Bagley, Robert
    1999   Shang Archaeology. In *Cambridge History of Ancient China*, edited by Michael Loewe and Edward L. Shaughnessy, pp. 124–231. Cambridge University Press, Cambridge.

Baines, John
    1995   Origins of Egyptian Kingship. In *Ancient Egyptian Kingship*, edited by D. O'Connor and D. Silverman, pp. 95–156. Brill, Leiden.
    1997   Kingship before Literature: The World of the King in the Old Kingdom. In *Selbstverständnis und Realität*, edited by R. Gundlach and C. Raedler, pp. 125–186. Harrassowitz, Wiesbaden.
    2003   Early Definitions of the Egyptian World and Its Surroundings. In *Culture Through Objects: Ancient Near Eastern Studies in Honour of P. R. S. Moorey*, edited by T. F. Potts, M. Roaf, and D. Stein, pp. 27–57. Griffith Institute, Oxford.

Bayart, Jean-François
    2007   *Global Subjects: A Political Critique of Globalization*. Polity Press, Cambridge.

Blomster, Jeffrey P.
    2012   Early Evidence of the Ballgame in Oaxaca, Mexico. *Proceedings of the National Academy of Sciences* 109(21):8020–8025.

Burger, Richard L.
    2003   The Chavin Horizon: Chimera or Socioeconomic Metamorphosis. In *Latin American Horizons*, edited by Don S. Rice, pp. 41–82. Dumbarton Oaks Research Library and Collection, Washington, D.C.
    2011   What Kind of Hallucenogenic Snuff Was Used at Chavín de Huántar? An Iconographic Identication. *Journal of Andean Archaeology* 31(2):123–140.

Campbell, Roderick
    2014   Transformations of Violence: On Humanity and Inhumanity in Early China. In *Violence and Civilization: Studies of Social Violence in History and Prehistory*, edited by Roderick Campbell, pp. 94–118. Oxbow, Oxford.

Clark, John E.
    1997   The Arts of Government in Early Mesoamerica. *Annual Review of Anthropology* 26:211–234.
    2004   The Birth of Mesoamerican Metaphysics: Sedentism, Engagement, and Moral Superiority. In *Rethinking Materiality: The Engagement of Mind with the Material World*, edited by Elizabeth DeMarrais, Chris Gosden, and Colin Renfrew, pp. 205–224. McDonald Institute for Archaeological Research, Cambridge.

Conklin, William J., and Jeffrey Quilter (editors)
    2008   *Chavín: Art, Architecture, and Culture*. Cotsen Institute of Archaeology, Los Angeles.

Drucker, Philip
    1981   On the Nature of Olmec Polity. In *The Olmec and Their Neighbors: Essays in Memory of Matthew W. Stirling*, edited by Elizabeth P. Benson, pp. 29–47. Dumbarton Oaks Research Library and Collection, Washington, D.C.

Feinman, Gary, and Joyce Marcus (editors)
    1998   *Archaic States*. School of American Research Press, Santa Fe.

Ferioli, Piera, Enrica Fiandra, Gian Giacomo Fissore, and Marcella Frangipane
    1994   *Archives Before Writing*. Scriptorium, Rome.

Flad, Rowan
    2008   Divination and Power: A Multiregional View of the Development of Oracle Bone Divination in Early China. *Current Anthropology* 49(3):403–437.

Foias, Antonia E.
    2013   *Ancient Maya Political Dynamics*. University Press of Florida, Gainesville.

Frangipane, Marcella
    2006   The Arslentepe "Royal Tomb": New Funerary Customs and Political Changes in the Upper Euphrates Valley at the Beginning of the Third Millennium BC. *Scienze Dell'Antichità* 14(1):169–194.
    2012   Fourth Millennium Arslantepe: The Development of a Centralised Society without Urbanisation. *Origini* 34:19–40.
    2016   The Development of Centralised Societies in Greater Mesopotamia and

Freidel, David, Linda Schele, and Joy Parker
- 1993 *Maya Cosmos: Three Thousand Years on the Shaman's Path*. William Morrow, New York.

Friedman, Renée F.
- 2008 Excavating Egypt's Early Kings: Recent Discoveries in the Elite Cemetery at Hierakonpolis. In *Egypt at Its Origins 2*, edited by B. Midant-Reynes and Y. Tristant, pp. 1157–1194. Peeters, Leuven.

Froese, Tom, Carlos Gershenson, and Linda R. Manzanilla
- 2014 Can Government Be Self-Organized? A Mathematical Model of the Collective Social Organization of Ancient Teotihuacan, Central Mexico. *PLoS ONE* 9(10):e109966.

Geertz, Clifford
- 1980 *Negara: The Theatre State in Nineteenth-Century Bali*. Princeton University Press, Princeton.

Graeber, David, and Marshall Sahlins
- 2017 *On Kings*. Hau, Chicago.

Graeber, David, and David Wengrow
- 2021 *The Dawn of Everything: A New History of Humanity*. Farrar, Straus and Giroux, New York.

Green, Adam S.
- 2020 Killing the Priest-King: Addressing Egalitarianism in the Indus Civilization. *Journal of Archaeological Research* 29(2):153–202.

Haicheng, Wang
- 2014 *Writing and the Ancient State: Early China in Comparative Perspective*. Cambridge University Press, Cambridge.

Hassett, Brenna R., and Haluk Sağlamtimur
- 2018 Radical "Royals"? New Evidence from Başur Höyük for Radical Burial Practices in the Transition to Early States in Mesopotamia. *Antiquity* 92:640–654.

Hill, Warren, and John E. Clark
- 2001 Sports, Gambling, and Government: America's First Social Compact? *American Anthropologist* 103(2):331–245.

the Foundation of Economic Inequality. *Tagungen des Landesmuseums für Vorgeschichte Halle* 13.

Houston, Stephen D., and Takeshi Inomata
- 2009 *The Classic Maya*. Cambridge University Press, Cambridge.

Inomata, Takeshi
- 2001 King's People: Classic Maya Courtiers in Comparative Perspective. In *Royal Courts of the Ancient Maya*, vol. 1, *Theory, Comparison, and Synthesis*, edited by Takeshi Inomata and Stephen D. Houston, pp. 27–53. Westview Press, Boulder, Colo.

Jacobsen, Thorkild
- 1976 *The Treasures of Darkness: A History of Mesopotamian Religion*. Yale University Press, New Haven.

Jennings, Justin, and Timothy Earle
- 2016 Urbanization, State Formation, and Cooperation: A Reappraisal. *Current Anthropology* 57(4):474–493.

Joyce, Rosemary A.
- 2008 *Ancient Bodies, Ancient Lives: Sex, Gender, and Archaeology*. Thames and Hudson, New York.

Keightley, David N.
- 1999 The Shang: China's First Historical Dynasty. In *Cambridge History of Ancient China*, edited by Michael Loewe and Edward L. Shaughnessy, pp. 232–291. Cambridge University Press, Cambridge.

Kolata, Alan
- 1997 Of Kings and Capitals: Principles of Authority and the Nature of Cities in the Native Andean State. In *The Archaeology of City States: Cross-Cultural Approaches*, edited by D. L. Nichols and T. H. Charlton, pp. 245–254. Smithsonian Institution Press, Washington, D.C.

Martin, Simon
- 2020 *Ancient Maya Politics: A Political Anthropology of the Classic Period, 150–900 CE*. Cambridge University Press, Cambridge.

Masson, Marilyn
- 2002 Review of *Royal Courts of the Ancient Maya*, vol. 1, *Theory, Comparison, and Synthesis*, edited by Takeshi Inomata and Stephen D. Houston. *Ethnohistory* 49(2):454–456.

McAnany, Patricia A.
- 2010 *Ancestral Maya Economies in Archaeological Perspective*. Cambridge University Press, New York.
- 2019 Fragile Authority in Monumental Time: Political Experimentation in the Classic Maya Lowlands. In *The Evolution of Fragility: Setting the Terms of the Debate*, edited by Norman Yoffee, pp. 47–60. McDonald Institute for Archaeological Research, Cambridge.

Meller, Harald, and Michael Schefik
- 2015 *Krieg: Eine Archäologische Spurensuche*. Landesmuseum für Vorgeschichte, Halle (Saale).

Müller, Johannes, Knut Rassmann, and Mykhailo Videiko (editors)
- 2016 *Trypillia Mega-Sites and European Prehistory, 4100–3400 BCE*. Routledge, London.

Pool, Christopher A.
- 2007 *Olmec Archaeology and Early Mesoamerica*. Cambridge University Press, Cambridge.

Quilter, Jeffrey, and Michele Koons
- 2012 The Fall of the Moche: A Critique of Claims for South America's First State. *Latin American Antiquity* 23(2):127–143.

Rice, Prudence M.
- 2004 *Maya Political Science: Time, Astronomy, and the Cosmos*. University of Texas Press, Austin.

Richardson, Seth
- 2012 Early Mesopotamia: The Presumptive State. *Past and Present* 215:3–49.

Rick, John W.
- 2017 The Nature of Ritual Space at Chavín de Huántar. In *Rituals of the Past: Prehispanic and Colonial Case Studies in Andean Archaeology*, edited by Silvana Rosenfeld and Stefanie L. Bautista, pp. 21–50. University Press of Colorado, Boulder.

Rosenswig, Robert M.
- 2010 *The Beginnings of Mesoamerican Civilization: Inter-regional Interaction and the Olmec*. Cambridge University Press, Cambridge.
- 2017 Olmec Globalization: A Mesoamerican Archipelago of Complexity. In *The Routledge Handbook of Archaeology and Globalization*, edited by Tamar Hodos, pp. 177–193. Routledge, London.

Scheidel, Walter
- 2013 Studying the State. In *The Oxford Handbook of the State in the Ancient Near East and Mediterranean*, edited by Peter Fibiger Bang and Walter Scheidel, pp. 5–58. Oxford University Press, Oxford.

Schele, Linda, and David A. Freidel
- 1990 *A Forest of Kings: The Untold Story of the Ancient Maya*. William Morrow, New York.

Schrakamp, Ingo
- 2010 *Krieger und Waffen im frühen Mesopotamien. Organisation und Bewaffnung des Militärs in frühdynastischer und sargonischer Zeit*. Philipps-Universität, Marburg.

Scott, James C.
- 2017 *Against the Grain: A Deep History of the Earliest States*. Yale University Press, New Haven.

Severi, Carlo
- 2015 *The Chimera Principle: An Anthropology of Memory and Imagination*. Translated by Janet Lloyd. Hau Books, Chicago.

Shaughnessy, Edward L.
- 1989 Historical Geography and the Extent of the Earliest Chinese Kingdom. *Asia Minor* 2(2):1–22.

Strange, Susan
- 1996 *The Retreat of the State*. Cambridge University Press, Cambridge.

Stuart, David
- 2011 *The Order of Days: Unlocking the Secrets of the Ancient Maya*. Three Rivers Press, New York.

Tate, Carolyn E.
- 1998 La Venta's Stone Figurines and the Olmec Body Politic. In *Memorias del Tercer Simposio Internacional de Mayistas*, pp. 335–358. Instituto de Investigaciones Filologicas, Universidad Nacional Autónoma de México, Mexico City.
- 2012 *Reconsidering Olmec Visual Culture: The Uborn, Women, and Creation*. University of Texas Press, Austin.

Torres, Constantino Manuel
　2008　Chavín's Psychoactive Pharmacopoeia: The Iconographic Evidence. In *Chavín: Art, Architecture, and Culture*, edited by William J. Conklin and Jeffrey Quilter, pp. 237–257. Cotsen Institute of Archaeology, Los Angeles.

Treherne, Paul
　1995　The Warrior's Beauty: The Masculine Body and Self-Identity in Bronze Age Europe. *Journal of European Archaeology* 3(1):105–144.

Trigger, Bruce
　2003　*Understanding Early Civilizations*. Cambridge University Press, Cambridge.

Turchin, Peter, Harvey Whitehouse, Andrey Korotayev, Pieter François, Daniel Hoyer, Peter Peregrine, Gary Feinman, Charles Spencer, Nikolay Kradin, and Thomas E. Currie
　2018　Evolutionary Pathways to Statehood: Old Theories and New Data [pre-print], https://doi.org/10.31235/osf.io/h7tr6.

Ur, Jason
　2016　Commentary on *Urbanization, State Formation, and Cooperation: A Reappraisal*, by Justin Jennings and Timothy Earle. *Current Anthropology* 57(4):487–488.

Van Tuerenhout, Dirk
　2002　Maya Warfare: Sources and Interpretations. *Civilisations* 50:129–152.

Weber, Max
　(1922) 1978　*Economy and Society*. Edited by Guenther Roth and Claus Wittich. University of California Press, Berkeley.

Weismantel, Mary
　2013　Inhuman Eyes: Looking at Chavín de Huantar. In *Relational Archaeologies: Humans, Animals, Things*, edited by Christopher Watts, pp. 21–41. Routledge, London.

Wengrow, David
　2006　*The Archaeology of Early Egypt: Social Transformations in North-East Africa, c. 10000 to 2650 BC*. Cambridge University Press, Cambridge.
　2010　*What Makes Civilization? The Ancient Near East and the Future of the West*. Oxford University Press, Oxford.

Wilk, Richard
　2004　Miss Universe, the Olmec and the Valley of Oaxaca. *Journal of Social Archaeology* 4(1):81–98.

Winter, Irene J.
　1996　Sex, Rhetoric, and the Public Monument: The Alluring Body of Naram-Sin of Agade. In *Sexuality in Ancient Art: Near East, Egypt, Greece, and Italy*, edited by Natalie Boymel Kampen and Bettina Bergmann, pp. 11–26. Cambridge University Press, Cambridge.
　2008　Touched by the Gods: Visual Evidence for the Divine Status of Rulers in the Ancient Near East. In *Religion and Power: Divine Kingship in the Ancient World and Beyond*, edited by Nicole Brisch, pp. 75–102. Oriental Institute of the University of Chicago, Chicago.

Yoffee, Norman
　2005　*Myths of the Archaic State: Evolution of the Earliest Cities, States, and Civilizations*. Cambridge University Press, Cambridge.

Yuan, Jing, and Rowan Flad
　2005　New Zooarchaeological Evidence for Changes in Shang Dynasty Animal Sacrifice. *Journal of Anthropological Archaeology* 24(3):252–270.

15

Relationships of Command

From Sovereignty to Anarchy

SCOTT R. HUTSON

Shortly after the symposium schedule was publicized, I came across a droll reaction on social media. The comment read: "Finally, Mesoamericanists paying attention to Maya rulers!" True, Maya rulers have hogged the spotlight for almost as long as people have studied the ancient Maya. But this quip misses all the research that has successfully put rulers into what I and others have called a relational framework (Brück 2001; Hendon 2010; Hutson 2010; Thomas 2000). As many of the papers in this symposium show, a clear-eyed glance at the face of rulership reveals not a single ruler but a multitude of faces. As David Freidel puts it in his paper, "rulership, relations, and royal courts were entangled for the ancient Maya . . . as they were everywhere"(28). And the faces of this community include not just human faces but faces of stone and ceramic, wood and wind, smoke and spirits.

Rulership involves a motley crew of participants who are active and consequential in a variety of ways. This stance, which shines in many of the papers, has, of course, gained favor among political anthropologists and theorists working far beyond Mesoamerica. The key concept here is sovereignty, and it is now very clear that sovereignty is, in a word, compromised. At face value, sovereignty suggests ultimate power. The commonplace understanding of sovereignty holds that sovereign nations possess untrammeled dominion, "subordinated to no earthly authority" within the bounds of their territory. Yet in the last decades, anthropologists and others have exposed the porosity of national sovereignty (Bonilla 2017; Hansen and Stepputat 2005, 2006; Kauanui 2017). Institutions and actors at the global level (nongovernmental organizations, terrorist networks, multinational corporations), the local level (vigilantes, mafiosi, guerillas), and in between (hackers, pirates) have left the authority of nation-states quite trammeled, even if aspects of this authority remain effective. If we take a different definition of sovereignty, we come to a similar conclusion. For example, David Graeber explores the sovereignty of rulers as the ability to carry out arbitrary violence with impunity (Graeber and

Sahlins 2017). This is not terribly dissimilar to the Foucaultian take on sovereignty, more recently continued in the work of Giorgio Agamben (1998). Yet as Graeber reveals in his chapter on the Shilluk of South Sudan, subjects wage a constant, if hidden, war on the sovereign. This war does not just circumscribe the sovereign's abilities and powers—it constitutes the nation itself. Thus, the faces of regular people always refract themselves in the faces of rulership. As a memorial to Graeber (2004), let's not forget that he was the most committed anarchist anthropologist at least since Al Brown (Radcliffe-Brown [1922] 1944) and Marcel Mauss ([1925] 1966). If we also remember that anarchism involves challenging domination, inequality, and structures of violence, then recognizing anarchist tendencies in the contested faces of rulership does not produce a distorted view of the ancient Maya. Relationships of command find themselves on a spectrum between anarchy and sovereignty.

Probably one of the most obvious ways in which the faces of rulership include more than the portrait of a single sovereign is the possibility of rule by council. Freidel, Lamoureux-St-Hilaire and McAnany, and Ringle all mention the possibility of ruling councils in northern Yucatán, with Freidel proposing an Early Classic council at Yaxuna that selected the ruler and Ringle mentioning council houses at Puuc sites. Rule by council is also likely at Chunchucmil in the fifth and sixth centuries (Dahlin 2009). A point of interest here is chronology. In the case of Labna, the council house predates the throne room in the palace. This is also the case at Ek' Balam, where a proposed council house predates the reign of Ukit Kan Le'k Tok' (Bey and May Ciau 2014; Vargas de la Peña et al. 2020). It could be added that Yaxuna's less visible monarchs from the Early Classic were followed by traditional dynastic monarchs at Coba in the Late Classic. Thus, we have a narrative of council rule giving way to dynastic rulership by the end of the Classic period. This is the reverse of what has occasionally been proposed at southern lowlands sites such as Copan, where Fash and others (Fash, Andrews, and Manahan 2004; Fash et al. 1992) proposed the emergence of a council toward the end of the city's history. In the western Peten, the growing presence of *cahals* in the Late Classic could also be read as an inflationary increase of personnel whose role in governance was now deemed important enough for them to be named and depicted on carved monuments. In her chapter, Joanne Baron carries this narrative of the broader distribution of authority into the Postclassic period, making the case for a democratization and decentralization of patron gods. Masson identifies Mayapan's colonnaded halls as council houses (*popol nah*) while also highlighting ethnographic evidence for single rulers. Archaeologists have made the case for democratization in other parts of Mesoamerica, such as the Postclassic Tlaxcallan state (see also Knab and Pohl 2019 on Cholula). Fargher, Blanton, and Heredia Espinoza (2010) describe this state as led by a council of between 50 and 150 members, selected largely on the basis of merit, who made decisions by consensus after speeches and debate. The archaeological signature of council rule and collective action in Tlaxcala (Fargher et al. 2020) differs substantially from what we normally see in the Maya area, where wealth gradients are higher and patrimonial rhetoric is greater.

Despite these scattered possibilities, regimes headed by dynastic rulers outnumbered ruling councils in the Classic-period lowlands. Therefore, any robust argument that the face of rulership was relational and multiple must traffic directly in those cases of a ruling king or queen. The chapters by Ardren and Lamoureux-St-Hilaire and McAnany give us a start here. Ideologies of gender complementarity rightly highlight that women were indispensable to the reproduction of patriarchal societies, even if states that promoted such ideologies exploited women's labor and rewarded women less than men (Hutson, Hanks, and Pyburn 2013; Joyce 1993). Indeed, even today, this so-called ideology still performs as an ideology. In other words, it fools us. As Ardren (this volume) writes, "the obvious biological ramifications of male and female artistic pairings has fooled scholars into both overemphasizing the function of Maya queens as generators of heirs and underemphasizing the ideological role of queens in the fundamental reproduction of elite political and cosmological order" (148). Beyond the mere reproductive dutifulness of queens, Ardren underscores the way that female sexuality endangered the cosmic order, threatening to "destabilize official and sanctioned reproduction, and thus patrilineal succession and dynastic claims to authority" (153). Thus, princesses shape the patrilines they marry into, moving them (trapping them?) to spend significant symbolic, architectural, and artistic energy to maintain a status quo. Though this effort circumscribes the power of sexuality, it is also clear that sexuality circumscribes, even burdens, the patriline by necessitating this expenditure.

If Ardren's chapter shifts the face of rulership to pairings and webs of gendered relations within the polity, then Lamoureux-St-Hilaire and McAnany expand that face to include actors beyond the polity. Their point is not just that kings and queens are sometimes strangers, in some cases literally coming from beyond the polity. They argue in a fully relational mode that rulership in one polity must always be understood in terms of neighboring polities: "Maya regimes did not emerge in isolation, but rather through interactions with neighbors, leading to both foundational alliances and antagonisms" (120). La Corona's kings spent time at Calakmul and received Calakmul princesses as brides.

Lamoureux-St-Hilaire and McAnany's treatment of stranger kings opens a productive dialogue with Graeber and Sahlins's repackaging of the concept. In the Maya world, rulers like K'inich Yax K'uk' Mo' at Copan or Yax Nuun Ahiin I at Tikal clearly qualify as strangers of various types and their dynastic successors often highlight this. Masson notes that Mayapan's kings also claimed stranger origins. Yet as Lamoureux-St-Hilaire and McAnany note, if we understand strangerhood in terms of geography, queens are more often strangers than kings. This alerts us to a blind spot in Graeber and Sahlins's text. While Graeber dwells on queens in Madagascar (Graeber and Sahlins 2017:257–258), Graeber and Sahlins (2017:4) clearly frame stranger kingship as archetypally male. Ardren (this volume) fleshes out the allure of queens as strangers, proposing that they bring to the local polity not just a diffuse taste of what Mary Helms (1993:7) refers to as the "cosmologically-charged outside" but connections with rather specific deities and rituals from beyond the realm and the "magical aptitude" (Ardren, this volume) for performing them. Ardren also locates the allure of a stranger queen in the context of patriarchal control of sexuality, noting that a stranger queen's sexual past might be largely unknown to her host polity, posing less of a threat.

There are other ways in which the Maya data necessitate a makeover of the stranger king model. To be sure, many aspects of the model fit what we know about Maya rulership, and it is useful to sketch these concordances. Stranger kings are hunters, much like the Maya culture heroes Hunahpu and Xbalanque. Stranger kings commit an exploit that violates the norms of kinship, just as Hunahpu and Xbalanque battle their older brothers and grandmother (see also the examples of fratricide in Maya creation myths discussed in Chinchilla Mazariegos 2017:160). Maya kingdoms from Classic-period Tikal to the Postclassic K'iche' royal courts drew power from a variety of non-local Tollans. Stranger kingship, like most Maya rulership, "does not work on proprietary control of the subject people's means of existence so much as on the beneficial or awe-inspiring effects of royal largesse, display, and prosperity" (Graeber and Sahlins 2017:15). In other words, a ruler's power is based not so much in land as in people, a point that John Chuchiak makes in his chapter. This perspective clashes with the view of sovereignty as grounded in control over territory. Indeed, Graeber and Sahlins (2017:7) explicitly adopt a different view of sovereignty, stating that its essence is not untrammeled dominion within polity boundaries but rather divine rulership. They define divine as the ability to act like a god, which implies absolute power in theory, but triggers several forms of circumscription in practice.

Control over territory marks another moment in which Maya rulers might part company with the stranger king model. The earthworks on the northern hinterland of Yaxchilan imply a concern with control over territory in the face of Piedras Negras (Golden and Scherer 2006). The Tikal earthworks, initially thought of as defensive (Puleston and Callendar 1967) then ruled as follies (Webster et al.

2007), have come back into focus as territorial markers in the context of the "watchful" settlement patterns and defensive features recently documented among Tikal's neighbors at the western end of the Buenavista Valley (Doyle, Garrison, and Houston 2012; Garrison, Houston, and Alcover Firpi 2019). Locally grounded patron deities, deftly covered by Baron (this volume), also suggest that Maya rulers were deeply rooted in place. This groundedness complements the notion that the body of the Maya ruler is the axis mundi, centering the cosmos that orbits it (Houston and Cummins 2004:367). Masson (this volume) marshals diverse evidence for the existence of territorial boundaries in the Postclassic.

Thus, we hit a crossroads: royal courts can get a boost from stranger kings and queens, yet indigeneity, being rooted in the local, matters. Several emblem glyphs that refer to dynasties derive from toponyms, ostensibly anchoring Maya rulers in place, though other emblems float unmoored from spatial referents, such as the Kaanul shift from Dzibanche to Calakmul or the Mutul peregrination from Tikal to Dos Pilas to Aguateca to Ixlu. The chapter by Tokovinine, Estrada Belli, and Fialko exemplifies this paradox, showing how the neighboring polities of Holmul and Naranjo chose opposite strategies with regard to place. They show that Holmul rulers attempted to legitimate themselves by claiming ties with foreign powers such as Teotihuacan and the Kaanuls. Rulers at Naranjo, on the other hand, highlight the temporal depth of the local Sa'al dynasty, hoard local landscapes, and keep themselves anchored in place even when literally on the move. Tokovinine, Estrada Belli, and Fialko have done a brilliant job of extracting meaning from admittedly murky text and art. In the end, the best path at this crossroads is to view strangerhood and indigeneity not as conflicting principles, but as complementary strategies sometimes used separately, sometimes in tandem. The trick to building this into a model is to figure out which local and historical circumstances affect how these two forces are deployed and in what ratio.

The stranger king model may also need a Maya makeover when it comes to farming. Sahlins insists that, in the stranger king formation, stranger kings are not of the land and do not work the land (Graeber and Sahlins 2017:188–195). Yet even if Hunahpu and Xbalanque were hunters, many Maya rulers portray themselves as farmers. Maya rulers describe their oversight of the passage of *k'atuns* as if they were harvesting time (Houston and Stuart 2001). They perform scattering rituals as if they were scattering agricultural seed (Stuart 2020:645). They lay out their royal compounds as farmers delimit their milpas (Davenport and Golden 2016:193). Agricultural rhetoric is, in fact, not foreign to stranger kings, many of whom participate in food production as the guarantors of rain. Graeber (Graeber and Sahlins 2017:106) notes that the Shilluk kings of South Sudan worked a few symbolic fields and followed the same agricultural cycles as their subjects.

The takeaway point with regard to agricultural rhetoric is not how closely the Maya fit the mold of the stranger king, but rather how rulers create connections with their subjects. Agricultural symbolism is only one of the ways that rulers attempted to align themselves with practices intelligible to their subjects. Rulers often appropriated the tropes of authority—ancestor worship, caching behavior, cosmology—from folk traditions that have been documented among humble households (McAnany 1995; Robin 2013). Lisa Lucero (2003:523) states this position clearly: "[e]merging Maya rulers expanded family-scale rites, especially dedication, termination, and ancestor veneration rituals, into larger communal ceremonies." Such appropriations legitimate rulership as a continuation of long-established traditions that everyone understands. Feasting should be added to the list of activities that underscore commonalities among (and intelligibility between) ruler and ruled. As Morell-Hart (this volume) remarks, feasting occurs at all rungs of the social ladder.

Such strategies of highlighting inclusivity and commonality compare well with the notion that the body politic includes all subjects. Two chapters in this volume refer to the concept of the body politic. Ernst Kantorowicz clarified the notion of the body politic in *The King's Two Bodies* (1957). Whereas the ruler's mortal, physical "body natural" can die and decay, the body politic outlasts the individual life of a particular ruler. Awe, Helmke, Ebert, and Hoggarth place the concept of the ruler's two bodies—one mortal, one institutional—in their very title: "The king is dead, long live the king." Halperin explicitly cites Kantorowicz and persuasively shows that a ruler's feathered cape, subject to decay, pertains to the body natural and signifies the individual deeds of the ruler. On the other hand, jade adornments persist, are inherited, and therefore signify the enduring, undying office of divine kingship, the body politic.

Tension exists in the concept of the body politic. The divine aspects of the Maya body politic fit with the notion that the ruler is a *persona mixta*, endowed with both spiritual and secular powers. Yet some of Kantorowicz's sources (1957:13), dating to the early seventeenth century and before, suggest that the body politic consists not only of the mystical, undying office but also the subjects of the polity, a formulation that would reappear in Thomas Hobbes's notion of the Leviathan (see also Hansen and Stepputat 2005:5–6). Certain late medieval European rulers were given a ring during investiture, signifying a marriage with the polity and further highlighting the linkage between ruler and ruled (Kantorowicz 1957:215; see also Scott 1976:77). For the Maya area, Houston and Stuart (2001:61) note that the ruler is part of a collectivity with the people.

Much like the paradox within the concept of the body politic, attempts to highlight the commonalities between ruler and ruled—to demonstrate that all operate within the same moral community (Houston et al. 2003)—stand in tension with the ruler's need to display uniqueness as a credential for sovereignty (Kurnick 2016:20). Previous work frames Maya rulers as unique because they have hotter souls, sensory distinctiveness, and closer connections with gods (Houston and Stuart 1996; Houston, Stuart, and Taube 2006). Several chapters in the volume expand upon this concept of exceptionalism. Morell-Hart writes: "Through food practices, rulers presented themselves as rulers in ways that were understood by other rulers . . . as well as by the ruled and the divine" (233). Likewise, Halperin convincingly argues that rulers' costumes distinguished them, sensu Bourdieu, in two ways: capes memorialized a ruler's military triumphs, creating a unique biography, and jade adornments "anchored the king's body in a longstanding legacy of divine dynastic history" (208). Halperin's point builds on the work of David Freidel, who for many years has construed jade and *Spondylus* adornments from Late Preclassic caches as the insignia of royalty.

Yet the more that a ruler's blood or bodily adornments set them apart from the rest, the more risk they ran of their power being blunted or curtailed. As Freud wrote in *Totem and Taboo* (1918), the ruler's tremendous power leads his subjects to distrust him and to justify the use of surveillance over him. Graeber and Sahlins call this adverse sacralization. Divine rulers have total power, but only when they are physically present. Thus, it is in the interest of a ruler's subjects to restrict the ruler's movements. They do so, and get away with it, by extolling the ruler as sacred, which is to say, set apart. The imposition of taboos (dicta that rulers must remain cloistered, not to be looked upon, etc.) literally sets the ruler apart, to the point of isolation. Taboos work like a pair of golden handcuffs. They flatter the wearer, treating the ruler as a truly special, transcendent being while at the same time drastically restricting agency. Thus, as Graeber argued, ruler and ruled are in a constant tug-of-war between divinity and sacredness. Rulers prefer to be divine (which is to say powerful), while subjects prefer their ruler to be sacred (which is to say impotent). Freidel follows this logic when he discusses invisibility of rulers as a form of adverse sacralization. Yet Friedel makes the creative move of suggesting that when Tikal rulers like Yax Ehb Xook first broke out of the mold and made themselves visible at the dawn of the Classic period, they swerved not from the strictures imposed by their own subjects, but by other rulers. Specifically, Freidel argues that Kaanul regime kings sought to destroy or control this new form of royal visibility by desecrating Tikal's North Acropolis.

To avoid adverse sacralization, rulers will want to circulate, to perform, to be seen (Scott 2012:22). This involves building relationships that link them directly with people beyond the court. Whereas portrayals of the ruler as a farmer might build a sort of imagined community with subjects, the physical copresence of rulers and subjects at events like ballgames, feasts, war ceremonies, and processions establishes face-to-face communities (Inomata 2006:807). These kinds of associations are the stuff of politics, in the sense of the creation of a legitimate political order. Yet encounters between rulers and ruled can be seen through divergent lenses. One lens, fashioned by writers like Foucault ([1975] 1977) and Agamben (1998), holds that encounters such as feasts and the presentation of war captives are a form of violence, either symbolic or physical, that sets the terms of subjection (Smith 2011:421). Another lens, fashioned by authors like Allport (1954) and Putnam (2000), views face-to-face contacts as opportunities to build trust and to create values held in common (Golden and Scherer 2013; Hutson and Welch 2019; Inomata 2006:808).

The chapters in this volume make room for both approaches; sovereignty can be built on both trust and violence. As Baron has argued, both rulers and ruled participate in the veneration of patron gods, thus building a community identity (see also Baron 2016:124). The Jaina figurines discussed by Benavides can, in many ways, be seen as a performance of sovereignty. These figurines very often depict royalty and they are widespread, appearing in 50 percent of the burials. As Benavides argues, the figurines are like a window that allows us to imagine private and public ceremonies where different social classes participated. To me, this comes close to the penetration of the practices of sovereignty into the everyday (Smith 2011:421), but since Benavides and his colleagues find these in burials, we are left to speculate about the social contexts in which they performed before being taken out of circulation. The best performances—the ones that engender trust or cause spectators to buy into the legitimacy of the sovereign—develop from two-way communication between rulers and ruled. When Mayanists talk about a charismatic ruler, we often think of charisma as a trait that a performer possesses. Alternatively, we should see charisma not as a possession but as a relationship. Charisma is listening carefully to the audience, noticing what works and what doesn't, and improvising or modifying the next iteration of the performance (Scott 2012:25). Thus, in a healthy sovereignty, the audience reciprocally shapes the performance. Only the most powerful ruler can afford to have tin ears.

Freidel's paper shifts us from trust-based sovereignty to violence-based sovereignty. He marshals evidence of the exercise of sovereignty through embodied violence. A stranger king arrived at Yaxuna in the fifth century, decapitated the local king, and killed his wife and nine others, all of whom were placed in a tableau macabre that we now refer to as Burial 24. The conqueror gathered the local family's royal jewels, smashed them with an axe, and, on top of it all, placed a raptor diadem representing, according to Freidel, the "living agency" of Spearthrower Owl. This use of the vanquished rulers' corpses as a canvas on which to rewrite who is in charge shows the brutal face of rulership, stripped down to its most elemental forms of power and violence. Of course such performances of sovereignty are sporadic at best. Maya states, as David Wengrow (this volume) intimates, may well have been seasonal phenomena. In other words, much like early government institutions in Old Kingdom Egypt, Shang China, and Early Dynastic Mesopotamia, Maya administrators and priests may not have been full time. Simon Martin (2020) certainly confirms the seasonal employ of war captains. As Morell-Hart notes, however, successful politics requires constant iteration, not seasonal iteration. This is the central message of Bruno Latour's *Reassembling the Social* (2005): the practices of sovereignty are not enacted constantly enough to be able to stand on their own. They are propped up by a network of agents, many of them material. I would definitely include the figurines discussed by Benavides, the capes and adornments discussed by Halperin, and the coats of arms discussed by Chuchiak as actants of this sort. Coats of arms such as the Habsburg double eagle are an intriguing case. Spanish viceroys placed these on nearly all major public works as a way of asserting Spanish sovereignty in New Spain, yet Maya people illicitly created their own royal coats of arms (usually in places far removed from Spanish settlements) to boost their own claim to nobility. Portrait stelae play even greater roles in literally concretizing the evanescent faces of rulership. As Stuart (1996:159) argued many years ago, rulers attempted to advance the perception that their likeness, carved in stone, in some way embodied or acted as an extension of their royal person, such that their presence in a plaza endured beyond the sporadic moments in which the ruler showed a face in the flesh.

Built environments also "operate as technologies of governmental ordering and control" (Smith 2011:424). Key examples here are fortifications (Golden and Scherer 2006) and causeways (Hutson and Welch 2021), not to mention the buildings explored in the chapter by Ringle. Triangulating among the Codz Pop at Kabah and the Nunnery Quadrangle and Adivino Sub at Uxmal, Ringle makes a compelling argument for royal versus military associations of different buildings and parts of buildings. Carvers adorned military quarters, such as the east rooms of the Codz Pop and the east building of the Nunnery, with a simple lattice pattern of stonework. They adorned royal quarters, like the north building of the Nunnery, with the more elaborate brocaded lattice pattern. This distinction highlights the aesthetics of subjection in the sense that the beautiful stonework of the royal buildings can evoke the kinds of sentiments that inspire dedication to the ruler (Smith 2011:424).

Feasting is, of course, an exemplary practice of sovereignty from a number of angles. At its most basic level, Lamoureux-St-Hilaire and McAnany note that when rulers host feasts and invite a broad range of guests, they create relationships that link the royal court with non-noble people. Morell-Hart alludes to the extensive amount of work that goes into a feast. Expanding on this, overcoming the challenges of putting on a feast linked all manner of people (farmers, gardeners, hunters, fishers, cooks, servers, and potters) into a working team. If participation in building a monumental temple creates solidarity and trust (Golden and Scherer 2013), so would the work of preparing feast after feast after feast. Yet in the same moment that feasts create inclusive linkages, they highlight unequal power relations. How people are seated, who is served first, who is excluded from the feast entirely—all of these define relations of hierarchy. As Morell-Hart notes, the choice of what foods to serve at a feast helps establish an aesthetics of distinction. Thus, feasts do the political work of creating, reiterating, and indoctrinating people into relations of subjection. Furthermore, simply to be invited and to be served establish relations of indebtedness. To take a word from Lamoureux-St-Hilaire and McAnany, the ruler's goal is to entangle their subjects.

It is worth dwelling on the concept of entanglement, as it illuminates an issue that is at the very core of a relational approach to the faces of rulership. Rulers undoubtedly attempt to entangle subjects, but we often overlook the myriad ways in which subjects entangle their rulers and rulers entangle themselves, sometimes intentionally, sometimes unintentionally. As I alluded to before, the economic, social, and ritual practices of nonnobles actually structure, and even entrap, the ruler. In order to comply with a moral order and to position themselves as leaders worth following, rulers may have little choice but to seize on and emulate cultural standards not of their own making (Houston and Inomata 2009:158–159; Sheets 2009:159). Legitimacy depends upon rulers subjecting themselves to traditions and understandings coming from the bottom up, such as quadripartite worldviews, the centrality of farming, and covenants with other-than-human beings. The evidence reported by Jaime Awe and coauthors stands as clear testimony that the emerging *ajawtaak* of the Late Middle Formative at Cahal Pech were operating under a ritual program clearly organized around folk understandings such as a layered cosmos and the narrative of the Maize God's decapitation, resurrection, and ascent to the heavens. These standards provided a script that to some degree constrained how rulers could act (Inomata 2006). As Morell-Hart argues in her chapter, the expectation that a ruler should follow performative routines at all costs can be seen as a form of entrapment. As an example, rulers continued to host feasts in Terminal Classic times, when such lavish expenditures would have exacerbated shortages of resources and tightened the economic noose around their necks. This particular form of entrapment is, of course, a central pillar of the scapegoat model of rulership (Iannone 2016). As soon as the ruler fails to "discharge the duties of his position by ordering the course of nature for the people's benefit," wrote Frazer (1911:7), the devotion and homage that his subjects "had hitherto lavished on him cease and are changed into hatred and contempt; he is ignominiously dismissed and may be thankful if he escapes with his life. Worshipped as a god one day, he is killed as a criminal the next."

The original and perhaps most potent way in which rulers were entrapped has to do with their relations with other-than-human beings. Maya rulers clearly operated within what Sahlins (Graeber and Sahlins 2017:24) called a cosmic polity, where "the life-giving means of people's existence were supplied by 'supernatural' beings of extraordinary powers: a polity thus governed by so-called 'spirits'—though they had human dispositions, often took human bodily forms, and were present within human experience." In his work with Linda Schele, Freidel was one of the first to clarify this for students of the ancient Maya (Schele and Freidel 1990). Maya cosmic polities involved covenants that bound humans to other-than-human beings. Human leaders fulfilled covenants through continuing payments that took the form of caches of valuable foods and objects. At Cahal Pech, as reported by Awe and colleagues (this volume), these offerings included marine shell, obsidian flakes, jadeite objects, cave pearls, faunal remains, and ceramic vessels incised with *k'an* crosses, lightning, and Principal Bird Deity motifs. Moving into the Classic period, Baron's work highlights the covenantal relations that rulers maintained with patron deities. Such deities oversaw the passage of time and took credit for military victories (Baron 2016:127). At the same time, such deities, like most Maya supernaturals, should not be seen as massively exalted or hallowed. In a sense, they are down to earth, fallible, and flawed (Baron, this volume; Houston and Inomata 2009). Rulers used them just as they used rulers. As Baron has argued for La Corona, rulers created new patron deities when it was expedient. Rulers were obliged to care for patron deities but could also leverage their privileged relations as caretakers to claim resources from the populace. Yet rulers did not monopolize these deities. Baron shows that many different actors venerated them. Household archaeology shows not a monopoly of contact with supernaturals but actors from across the social spectrum practicing covenantal relations at home (Hutson, Lamb, and Medina 2017; Robin 2013; Zaro and Lohse 2005), potentially undercutting the authority of rulers.

Conclusion

Political relations within ancient Maya city-states were sometimes divisive, sometimes cohesive, and usually both. Rulers played one courtier off another, courtiers shared or withheld information from rulers for personal gain, nobles jockeyed for the betterment of their factions and kin, nonnobles calculated whom to support with their labor and resources, and actors across the social spectrum pressed advantage and resisted exploitation (Houston and Inomata 2009; Hutson 2013; Lucero 2007; Scott 1990). At the same time, leaders and their subjects worked together to build networks of trust. Rulers upheld covenants with other-than-human forces; sponsored feasts; performed feats of violence; and mobilized sacred knowledge, bodily *hexis*, jade, feathers, shells, carved stones, polychrome murals, and painted pots to substantiate and materialize their divine exceptionalism. Subjects demanded leaders, held them accountable, provided the backing to make rulership possible, graded and certified their performances, and constituted the body politic, which, like James Scott's idea of the moral community, may have only ever gained partial legitimacy, and only part of the time. But rulership survived, careening unsteadily between the poles of anarchy and sovereignty, as long as it met minimal, commonly held standards of fairness, correctness, and belief (Inomata 2016a, 2016b; Scott 1976). The body politic, the face of rulership, the ship of state—whatever we call it—involved the participation, willing and unwilling, of a vast array of actors, each with a small hand on the keel, and these chapters highlight the creativity the ancient Maya used in painting a very inclusive face of rulership.

REFERENCES CITED

Agamben, Giorgio
- 1998 *Homo Sacer: Sovereign Power and Bare Life*. Stanford University Press, Stanford.

Allport, Gordon W.
- 1954 *The Nature of Prejudice*. Addison Wesley, Reading, Mass.

Baron, Joanne P.
- 2016 Patron Deities and Politics among the Classic Maya. In *Political Strategies in Pre-Columbian Mesoamerica*, edited by Sarah Kurnick and Joanne P. Baron, pp. 121–152. University Press of Colorado, Boulder.

Bey III, George J., and Rossana May Ciau
- 2014 The Role and Realities of Popol Nahs in Northern Maya Archaeology. In *The Maya and Their Central American Neighbors: Settlement Patterns, Architecture, Hieroglyphic Texts, and Ceramics*, edited by Geoffrey E. Braswell, pp. 335–355. Routledge, New York.

Bonilla, Yarimar
- 2017 Unsettling Sovereignty. *Cultural Anthropology* 32(3):330–339.

Brück, Joanna
- 2001 Monuments, Power, and Personhood in the British Neolithic. *Journal of the Royal Anthropological Institute* 7:649–667.

Chinchilla Mazariegos, Oswaldo
- 2017 *Art and Myth of the Ancient Maya*. Yale University Press, New Haven.

Dahlin, Bruce H.
- 2009 Ahead of Its Time? The Remarkable Early Classic Maya Economy of Chunchucmil. *Journal of Social Archaeology* 9(3):341–367.

Davenport, Bryce, and Charles Golden
- 2016 Landscapes, Lordships, and Sovereignty in Mesoamerica. In *Political Strategies in Pre-Columbian Mesoamerica*, edited by Sarah Kurnick and Joanne P. Baron, pp. 37–60. University Press of Colorado, Boulder.

Doyle, James, Thomas Garrison, and Stephen Houston
- 2012 Watchful Realms: Integrating GIS Analysis and Political History in the Southern Maya Lowlands. *Antiquity* 86(333):792–807.

Fargher, Lane F., Ricardo R. Antorcha-Pedemonte, Verenice Y. Heredia Espinoza, Richard E. Blanton, Aurelio López Corral, Robert A. Cooke, John K. Millhauser, Marc D. Marino, Iziar Martínez Rojo, Ivonne Pérez Alcántara, and Angelica Costa
- 2020 Wealth Inequality, Social Stratification, and the Built Environment in Late Prehispanic Highland Mexico: A Comparative Analysis, https://doi-org.libproxy.albany.edu/10.1016/j.jaa.2020.101176

Fargher, Lane F., Richard E. Blanton, and Verenice Y. Heredia Espinoza
- 2010 Egalitarian Ideology and Political Power in Prehispanic Central Mexico: The Case of Tlaxcallan. *Latin American Antiquity* 21:227–251.

Fash, Barbara, William Fash, Sheree Lane, Rudy Larios, Linda Schele, and David Stuart
- 1992 Investigations of a Classic Maya Council House at Copan, Honduras. *Journal of Field Archaeology* 19:419–442.

Fash, William L., E. Wyllis Andrews IV, and Kam Manahan
- 2004 Political Decentralization, Dynastic Collapse, and the Early Postclassic in the Urban Center of Copan, Honduras. In *The Terminal Classic in the Maya Lowlands: Collapse, Transition and Transformation*, edited by Arthur A. Demarest, Prudence M. Rice, and Don S. Rice, pp. 260–287. University Press of Colorado, Boulder.

Foucault, Michel
- (1975) 1977 *Discipline and Punish: The Birth of the Prison*. Vintage Books, New York.

Frazer, James
- 1911 *The Golden Bough: A Study in Magic and Religion*, pt. 2, *Taboo and the Perils of the Soul*. 3rd ed. MacMillan, London.

Freud, Sigmund
- 1918 *Totem and Taboo: Resemblances between the Psychic Life of Savages and Neurotics*. Moffat Yard, New York.

Garrison, Thomas, Stephen D. Houston, and Omar Alcover Firpi
- 2019 Recentering the Rural: Lidar and Articulated Landscapes among the Maya. *Journal of Anthropological Archaeology* 53:133–146.

Golden, Charles W., and Andrew Scherer
- 2006 Border Problems: Recent Archaeological Research along the Usumacinta River. *PARI Journal* 7(2):1–16.
- 2013 Territory, Trust, Growth, and Collapse in Classic Period Maya Kingdoms. *Current Anthropology* 54(4):397–435.

Graeber, David
- 2004 *Fragments of an Anarchist Anthropology.* Prickly Paradigm Press, Chicago.

Graeber, David, and Marshall Sahlins
- 2017 *On Kings.* Hau Books, Chicago.

Hansen, Thomas Blom, and Finn Stepputat
- 2005 *Sovereign Bodies: Citizens, Migrants and States in the Postcolonial World.* Princeton University Press, Princeton.
- 2006 Sovereignty Revisited. *Annual Review of Anthropology* 35:295–315.

Helms, Mary W.
- 1993 *Craft and the Kingly Ideal: Art, Trade and Power.* University of Texas Press, Austin.

Hendon, Julia A.
- 2010 *Houses in a Landscape: Memory and Everyday Life in Mesoamerica.* Duke University Press, Durham.

Houston, Stephen D., and Tom Cummins
- 2004 Body, Presence, and Space in Andean and Mesoamerican Rulership. In *Ancient Palaces of the New World: Form, Function and Meaning*, edited by Susan Toby Evans and Joanne Pillsbury, pp. 359–398. Dumbarton Oaks Research Library and Collection, Washington, D.C.

Houston, Stephen D., Hector L. Escobedo, Mark Child, Charles Golden, and Rene Muñoz
- 2003 The Moral Community: Settlement Transformation at Piedras Negras, Guatemala. In *Social Construction of Ancient Cities*, edited by Monica L. Smith, pp. 212–253. Smithsonian Books, Washington, D.C.

Houston, Stephen D., and Takeshi Inomata
- 2009 *The Classic Maya.* Cambridge University Press, Cambridge.

Houston, Stephen D., and David Stuart
- 1996 Of Gods, Glyphs, and Kings: Divinity and Rulership among the Classic Maya. *Antiquity* 70:289–312.
- 2001 Peopling the Classic Maya Court. In *Royal Courts of the Ancient Maya*, vol. 1, *Theory, Comparison, and Synthesis*, edited by Takeshi Inomata and Stephen D. Houston, pp. 54–83. Westview Press, Boulder, Colo.

Houston, Stephen D., David Stuart, and Karl Taube
- 2006 *The Memory of Bones: Body, Being and Experience among the Classic Maya.* University of Texas Press, Austin.

Hutson, Scott R.
- 2010 *Dwelling, Identity and the Maya: Relational Archaeology at Chunchucmil.* Altamira, Lanham, Md.
- 2013 Recap: Four Reasons for Relationality. In *Classic Maya Political Ecology: Resource Management, Class Histories, and Political Change in Northwestern Belize*, edited by Jon C. Lohse, pp. 211–225. Cotsen Institute, University of California, Los Angeles.

Hutson, Scott R., Bryan K. Hanks, and K. Anne Pyburn
- 2013 Gender, Power, and Politics in Early States. In *Companion to Gender Prehistory*, edited by Diane Bolger, pp. 45–67. Blackwell, Oxford.

Hutson, Scott R., Celine Lamb, and David Medina
- 2017 Political Engagement in Household Ritual among the Maya of Yucatan. In *Beyond Integration: Religion and Politics in the Ancient Americas*, edited by Sarah Barber and Arthur A. Joyce, pp. 165–188. Routledge, London.

Hutson, Scott R., and Jacob A. Welch
- 2019 Old Urbanites as New Urbanists? Mixing at an Ancient Maya City. *Journal of Urban History* 47(4):812–831.
- 2021 Roadwork: Long Distance Causeways at Uci, Yucatan, Mexico. *Latin American Antiquity* 32(2):310–330.

Iannone, Gyles
    2016   Cross-Cultural Perspectives on the Scapegoat King: The Anatomy of a Model. In *Ritual, Violence, and the Fall of the Classic Maya Kings*, edited by Gyles Iannone, Brett A. Houk, and Sonja A. Schwake, pp. 23–60. University Press of Florida, Gainesville.

Inomata, Takeshi
    2006   Plazas, Performers and Spectators: Political Theaters of the Classic Maya. *Current Anthropology* 47:805–842.
    2016a   Concepts of Legitimacy and Social Dynamics: Termination Rituals and the Last King of Aguateca, Guatemala. In *Ritual, Violence and the Fall of the Classic Maya Kings*, edited by Gyles Iannone, Brett A. Houk, and Sonja A. Schwake, pp. 89–107. University Press of Florida, Gainesville.
    2016b   Theories of Power and Legitimacy in Archaeological Contexts: The Emergent Regime of Power at the Formative Maya Community of Ceibal, Guatemala. In *Political Strategies in Pre-Columbian Mesoamerica*, edited by Sarah Kurnick and Joanne P. Baron, pp. 37–60. University Press of Colorado, Boulder.

Joyce, Rosemary A.
    1993   Women's Work: Images of Production and Reproduction in Prehispanic Southern Central America. *Current Anthropology* 34(3):255–274.

Kantorowicz, Ernst Hartwig
    1957   *The King's Two Bodies: A Study in Medieval Political Theology*. Princeton University Press, Princeton.

Kauanui, J. Kēhaulani
    2017   Sovereignty: An Introduction. *Cultural Anthropology* 32(3):323–329.

Knab, Timothy J., and John M. D. Pohl
    2019   Round and Round We Go: Cholula, Rotating Power Structures, Social Stability, and Trade in Mesoamerica. In *Interregional Interaction in Ancient Mesoamerica*, edited by Joshua D. Englehardt and Michael D. Carrasco, pp. 292–312. University Press of Colorado, Louisville.

Kurnick, Sarah
    2016   Paradoxical Politics: Negotiating the Contradictions of Political Authority. In *Political Strategies in Pre-Columbian Mesoamerica*, edited by Sarah Kurnick and Joanne P. Baron, pp. 3–36. University Press of Colorado, Boulder.

Latour, Bruno
    2005   *Reassembling the Social*. Oxford University Press, Oxford.

Lucero, Lisa J.
    2003   The Politics of Ritual: The Emergence of Classic Maya Kings. *Current Anthropology* 44(4):523–558.
    2007   Classic Maya Temples, Politics, and the Voice of the People. *Latin American Antiquity* 18(4):407–428.

Martin, Simon
    2020   *Ancient Maya Politics: A Political Anthropology of the Classic Period, 150–900 CE*. Cambridge University Press, Cambridge.

Mauss, Marcel
    (1925) 1966   *The Gift: Forms and Functions of Exchange in Archaic Societies*. Routledge, London.

McAnany, Patricia A.
    1995   *Living with the Ancestors: Kinship and Kingship in Ancient Maya Society*. University of Texas Press, Austin.

Puleston, Dennis E., and Donald W. Callendar
    1967   Defensive Earthworks at Tikal. *Expedition* 9(3):40–48.

Putnam, R. D.
    2000   *Bowling Alone: The Collapse and Revival of American Community*. Simon and Schuster, New York.

Radcliffe-Brown, Alfred Reginald
    (1922) 1944   *The Andaman Islanders*. FreePress, Glencoe, Ill.

Robin, Cynthia
    2013   *Everyday Life Matters: Maya Farmers at Chan*. University Press of Florida, Gainesville.

Schele, Linda, and David A. Freidel
    1990   *A Forest of Kings: The Untold Story of the Ancient Maya*. William Morrow, New York.

Scott, James C.

1976 *The Moral Economy of the Peasant: Rebellion and Subsistence in Southeast Asia.* Yale University Press, New Haven.

1990 *Domination and the Arts of Resistance.* Yale University Press, New Haven.

2012 *Two Cheers for Anarchism.* Princeton University Press, Princeton.

Sheets, Payson

2009 When the Construction of Meaning Preceded the Meaning of Construction: From Footpaths to Monumental Entrances in Ancient Costa Rica. In *Landscapes of Movement: Trails, Paths, and Roads in Anthropological Perspective*, edited by James E. Snead, Clark L. Erikson, and J. Andrew Darling, pp. 158–179. University of Pennsylvania Museum of Archaeology and Anthropology, Philadelphia.

Smith, Adam T.

2011 Archaeologies of Sovereignty. *Annual Review of Anthropology* 40:415–432.

Stuart, David

1996 Kings of Stone: A Consideration of Stela in Ancient Maya Ritual and Representations. *RES: Anthropology and Aesthetics* 29/30:148–171.

2020 Maya Time. In *The Maya World*, edited by Scott R. Hutson and Traci Ardren, pp. 624–647. Routledge, London.

Thomas, Julian

2000 Reconfiguring the Social, Reconfiguring the Material. In *Social Theory in Archaeology*, edited by Michael Brian Schiffer, pp. 143–155. University of Utah Press, Salt Lake City.

Vargas de la Peña, Alejandra Alonso Olvera, Victor R. Borges Castillo, and Alfonso Lacadena Garcia-Gallo

2020 Ek' Balam: A Maya City in the Urban Landscape of Yucatan. In *The Ancient Maya World*, edited by Scott R. Hutson and Traci Ardren, pp. 364–384. Routledge, New York.

Webster, David L., Tim Murtha, Kirk D. Straight, Jay Silverstein, Horacio Martinez, Richard Terry, and Richard Burnett

2007 The Great Tikal Earthwork Revisited. *Journal of Field Archaeology* 32(1):41–64.

Zaro, Gregory, and Jon C. Lohse

2005 Agricultural Rhythms and Rituals: Ancient Maya Solar Observation in Hinterland Blue Creek, Northwestern Belize. *Latin American Antiquity* 16(1):81–98.

CONTRIBUTORS

Traci Ardren is professor of Anthropology at the University of Miami. Her research focuses on issues of identity and other forms of symbolic representation in the archaeological record, especially the ways in which differences are explained through gender. She is codirector of the Proyecto de Interacción Política del Centro de Yucatán, at the Classic Maya site of Yaxuna, in Yucatán, where she investigates the ways ancient road systems allowed for the flow of information and ideas as well as how culinary tourism and modern foodways intersect. She also codirects the Matecumbe Chiefdom Project in the Florida Keys, which explores the unique historical ecology of Pre-Columbian south Florida. Her most recent book is *Everyday Life in the Classic Maya World* (2023). She grew up in and around the Ringling Museum of Art, and the many ways in which objects are allowed to convey our wants and needs is a lifelong fascination.

Jaime Awe is professor of Anthropology at Northern Arizona University, director emeritus of the Belize Institute of Archaeology, and recipient of the Society for American Archaeology Award for Excellence in Latin American and Caribbean Archaeology. He received his PhD from the Institute of Archaeology, University College London. He is codirector of the Belize Valley Archaeological Reconnaissance (BVAR) project, which investigates human-environment interaction, preceramic Mesoamerica, Formative-period cultural complexity, Maya ritual cave use, and the factors that impacted the rise, apogee, and decline of Maya civilization. He also invests considerable professional efforts in the conservation and management of Belize's tangible cultural heritage, public archaeology, and heritage education.

Joanne Baron is a postdoctoral fellow in Pre-Columbian art and archaeology at Dumbarton Oaks. Her research investigates political and economic strategies among ancient Maya kingdoms. In addition to the analysis of Maya art and hieroglyphic writing, she has carried out archaeological fieldwork on several projects in Belize, Honduras, and Guatemala, including directing the La Florida Archaeology Project in Peten from 2013 to 2019. She has published extensively on Classic Maya patron deity cults and on the monetization of the Maya economy in the seventh and eighth centuries. Her most recent investigations have examined religious and economic themes represented on Classic Maya pottery as part of the Kerr Photographic Archive Project at Dumbarton Oaks.

Antonio Benavides C. is a research professor at the Instituto Nacional de Antropología e Historia, Campeche, which he led as director in 1987 and from 2016 to 2018. He received his doctoral degree in Mesoamerican Studies from the Universidad

Nacional Autónoma de México. He began his career as an archaeologist at the sites of Coba, Ecab, Tulum, and Xelha in Quintana Roo, then worked at Chacmultun, Oxkintok, and Kom in Yucatán. Since 1985, he has directed research, excavation, and consolidation projects in Campeche at the sites of Edzna, Jaina, Xcalumkin, Uxul, Dzehkabtun, and Santa Rosa Xtampak. He also directed a maintenance program at scarcely known sites like Sabana Piletas, Chunchimay, Ichmac, Ramonal, Puerto Rico, Hwasil, Xcochkax, Xuelen, and Chelemi.

John F. Chuchiak IV is Distinguished Professor of Colonial Latin American History; director of the Honors College; director of the Latin American, Caribbean, and Hispanic Studies program; and the Rich and Doris Young Honored College Endowed Professor at Missouri State University. He is a corresponding member of both the Mexican Academy of History and the Guatemalan Academy of Geography and History. Among his publications are numerous books and articles on colonial Maya ethnohistory and the history of the Mexican Inquisition, including *El castigo y la reprensión: El juzgado del Provisorato de Indios y la extirpación de la idolatría maya en el obispado de Yucatán, 1563–1763* (2022); *Text and Context: Analyzing Colonial Yucatec Maya Texts and Literature in Diachronic Perspective* (2009, with Antje Gunsenheimer and Tsubasa Okoshi Harada); *The Inquisition in New Spain, 1536–1820* (2012); *Los edictos de fe del Santo Oficio de la Inquisición de la Nueva España* (2018, with Luis René Guerrero Galván); and *The Spanish Inquisition: Fact and Fiction* (forthcoming). Currently, he is completing a book entitled *Unlikely Allies: Mayas, Spaniards and Pirates in Colonial Yucatán, 1550–1750*, on the role of Maya militias in colonial defenses against piracy in colonial Yucatán.

Claire Ebert is assistant professor of Anthropology at the University of Pittsburgh. Her research integrates methods and approaches in environmental archaeology, biogeochemistry, and spatial analysis to explore the complex dynamics between people and their environments throughout the Holocene in Mesoamerica. She is particularly interested in the emergence of complexity among the earliest lowland Maya agricultural communities during the Formative period, as well as in subsequent forms of urban and economic growth. Her current research projects in the upper Belize River Valley explore the stable isotope ecology of agriculture and the role of diet in resilience to climate change, and also feature lidar remote sensing analyses and pottery and obsidian geochemical sourcing analyses.

Francisco Estrada Belli is research professor at the Middle American Research Institute at Tulane University. He holds a PhD in archaeology from Boston University. His research focuses on the archaeology of the Preclassic- and Classic-period Maya and on the application of remote sensing methods in archaeology. Since 2000, he has directed multidisciplinary research at Holmul and other sites in the northeastern Peten; he currently collaborates with INAH's project at Dzibanche and Ichkabal, Mexico. His publications include *The First Maya Civilization: Ritual and Power before the Classic Period* (2011), "Ancient Lowland Maya Complexity as Revealed by Airborne Laser Scanning of Northern Guatemala" in *Science* (2018, with Marcello A. Canuto et al.), "Palaeoenvironmental, Epigraphic and Archaeological Evidence of Total Warfare among the Classic Maya" in *Nature Human Behaviour* (2019, with David Wahl et al.), "Chochkitam: A New Classic Maya Dynasty and the Rise of the Kaanu'l (Snake) Kingdom" in *Latin American Antiquity* (2022, with Alexandre Tokovinine), and "Architecture, Wealth, and Status in Classic Maya Urbanism Revealed by Airborne Lidar Mapping" in *Journal of Archaeological Science* (2023).

Vilma Fialko is an archaeologist with the Instituto de Antropología e Historia in Guatemala. Since 2002, she has directed fieldwork at Naranjo and documented the damage caused by looting and the challenges looting creates for understanding this dynastic center. Additionally, she has conducted excavations at "wetland communities" in the central Peten to clarify the use of wetlands for intensive agricultural purposes during pre-colonial times. Her research interests include the technology of food production as well as the distribution and significance of E-Group architecture. She has over fifty published scientific articles and chapters.

David Freidel received his PhD in anthropology from the Graduate School of Arts and Sciences at Harvard University in 1976. He taught at Southern Methodist University between 1975 and 2007, and at Washington University in St. Louis between 2008 and 2022. He directed research at Cerros (Cerro Maya) in Belize, Yaxuna in Yucatán, and El Peru-Waka', Peten. He has been studying Maya kingship since 1975. He focuses on Maya rulership as discerned through contextual analysis of complex ritual deposits. He is an iconographer of Maya material symbol systems and interested in Maya ancient history.

Christina Halperin is associate professor in the Department of Anthropology at the Université de Montréal. Her research examines ancient Maya politics from the perspectives of household political economies, gender, materiality, and everyday life. She has published extensively on topics such as ceramic figurines, textile production, chemical analysis of ceramics, architecture, and landscape archaeology. Her most recent book, *Foreigners among Us: Alterity and the Making of Ancient Maya Societies* (2023), draws renewed attention to intercultural connections and critically assesses who and how "Others" were constituted in ancient Maya societies. She is the author of *Maya Figurines: Intersections between State and Household* (2014), one of the first books to comprehensively investigate figurines across the southern Maya Lowlands, and the primary editor of *Vernacular Architecture of the Pre-Columbian Americas* (2017) and *Mesoamerican Figurines: Small-Scale Indices of Large-Scale Social Phenomena* (2009).

Christophe Helmke is associate professor of American Indian Languages and Cultures at the Institute of Cross-Cultural and Regional Studies at the University of Copenhagen. He holds a PhD in Archaeology from University College London. He teaches undergraduate and graduate courses on the archaeology, epigraphy, iconography, and languages of Mesoamerica. Besides Maya archaeology and epigraphy, his primary research interests include the Pre-Columbian use of caves, Mesoamerican writing systems and rock art, and comparative Amerindian mythology.

Julie Hoggarth is associate professor of Anthropology at Baylor University. She conducts research on identifying the timing and processes of the breakdown in political systems and demographic decline at the end of the Classic period in the Belize River Valley. Her research fuses archaeological investigations with demography, history, geography, and other fields and is strongly focused on chronology building. She is also working on comparative archaeology projects on human-environment interactions in North and South America.

Scott Hutson is professor of Anthropology at the University of Kentucky. He began his scholarly career as an archaeologist in Oaxaca, Mexico, but, thanks to Tim Beach and Bruce Dahlin, he got permanently sidetracked into field research in the northern Maya Lowlands. He focuses on household archaeology, settlement patterns, demography, urbanism, economic anthropology, ritual practice, governance, and the contemporary socio-politics of academic archaeology. His recent books include *The Ancient Urban Maya* (2016), *Ancient Maya Commerce: Multidisciplinary Research at Chunchucmil* (2017), and *The Maya World* (2020, edited with Traci Ardren). His most-cited papers came out in the late 1990s and focus on techno-shamanism.

Maxime Lamoureux-St-Hilaire is assistant professor of archaeology in the Department of Sociology and Anthropology at Mount Royal University, Calgary, Alberta, Canada. He is also editor-in-chief of *The Mayanist* journal. He obtained his PhD from Tulane University (2018) and his MA from Trent University (2011). He has done fieldwork in Belize, Guatemala, Mexico, Honduras, Canada, and the United States. His research has focused on political institutions, regal palaces, GIS, and geoarchaeology. In particular, he is interested in the structure of Classic Maya regimes and the architectural institutions that articulated these ancient political communities. He is currently developing a slow archaeological project in Dolores, Guatemala, in collaboration with the local heritage community. He has published the coedited volume *Detachment from Place: Beyond an Archaeology of Settlement Abandonment* (2020). He has published in the *Journal of Anthropological Archaeology, Latin American Antiquity, Ancient Mesoamerica,* and *Geoarchaeology.* He wrote most of his dissertation, "Palatial Politics: The Classic Maya Royal Court of La Corona, Guatemala," at Dumbarton Oaks as a junior fellow from 2017 to 2018.

Marilyn Masson is a historical anthropologist and archaeologist whose current research projects focus on resiliency and social transformations in the face of environmental and political disjunction from the Terminal Classic through colonial periods in northern Yucatán. This research engages the archaeology of the majority from the study of daily life, social diversity, hybridity, and household economies of ordinary people in town and countryside settings. In Mexico, she collaborates with an international team of researchers and local assistants. Most recently, this team launched new investigations at two remote, rural Maya mission towns of sixteenth-century date. She has authored or coedited three recent books, *Kukulcan's Realm: Urban Life at Ancient Mayapan* (2014, with Carlos Peraza Lope), *The Real Business of Ancient Maya Exchange* (2020, with David Freidel and Arthur Demarest), and *Settlement, Economy, and Society at Mayapan, Yucatan, Mexico* (2021, with Timothy Hare, Carlos Peraza Lope, and Bradley Russell).

Patricia McAnany (PhD 1986, University of New Mexico) is Kenan Eminent Professor of Anthropology at the University of North Carolina, Chapel Hill. She is the recipient of the 2022 A. V. Kidder Award from the American Anthropological Association. She has received both research and community-impact grants from the National Science Foundation, National Geographic Society, Archaeological Institute of America, and the Z. Smith Reynolds Foundation. A Maya archaeologist, she is co-investigator of Proyecto Arqueológico Colaborativo del Oriente de Yucatán, a community-archaeology project focused on the Preclassic through contemporary community of Tahcabo, Yucatán. As the executive director of a UNC-CH program called InHerit: Indigenous Heritage Passed to Present (www.in-herit.org), she works with local communities throughout the Maya region and beyond to provide opportunities to dialogue about cultural heritage and to magnify Native voices in education and heritage conservation. She is the author/coauthor of many journal articles, books, and book chapters, including *Maya Cultural Heritage: How Archaeologists and Indigenous Communities Engage the Past* (2016).

Shanti Morell-Hart is associate professor of Anthropology at Brown University. Her published research has focused on ancient foodways; the origins and impacts of agriculture in the development of societies; the contributions of plants to ritualized activity and healthcare; the range and diversity of quotidian ethnobotanical practices; and transformations in human-environment relationships, especially as related to narratives of "collapse" and resilience. She has engaged in funded research in Mexico (Chiapas, Oaxaca, and Quintana Roo), as well as projects in Honduras and Guatemala. She is founding coeditor of *Archaeology of Food and Foodways,* coeditor of *Mesquite Pods to Mezcal: 10,000 Years of Oaxacan Cuisines* (2024), and recently completed the book *Gastronomic Heritage: Stakes in Antiquity,* which investigates the role of archaeogastronomy in narratives of food security, revitalization, and resilience.

William Ringle received his PhD from Tulane University, then became a member of the Anthropology department at Davidson College until 2019. His research has focused on the archaeology of northern Yucatán. Between 1984 and 1999, he codirected the Ek' Balam (Yucatán) project with George J. Bey, and since 2000 has been a codirector of the

Bolonchen Regional Archaeological Project with Bey and Tomás Gallareta Negrón. His interests include settlement and landscape archaeology, mapping (particularly digital applications), early urbanism and political organization, and Mesoamerican iconography. He also has a strong interest in the development of Mesoamerican internationalism during the Terminal Classic/Epiclassic period, particularly as manifested at Chichen Itza and in the Puuc region of Yucatán.

Alexandre Tokovinine is an anthropological archaeologist and specializes in Maya archaeology and epigraphy. His doctoral dissertation (2008) at Harvard University centered on Classic Maya place-names. Other research projects include 3D documentation of Classic Maya monuments and contributions to *Ancient Maya Art at Dumbarton Oaks*. He is a research associate of the Corpus of Maya Hieroglyphic Inscriptions. He currently holds an appointment of associate professor at the University of Alabama. His primary research interest concerns the transformations of the ancient complex societies in the context of the Maya civilization. He has been relying on a combination of archaeological, textual, and visual data to explore the Indigenous concepts of place, memory, and identity, as well as specific historical trajectories of individual polities and broader regional networks. The field component of the project has been centered on the region of the ancient cities of Holmul and Naranjo in Guatemala and Dzibanche in Mexico.

David Wengrow is professor of Comparative Archaeology at the Institute of Archaeology, University College London, and has been a visiting professor at New York University, the University of Auckland, and the University of Freiburg. In 2023, he was awarded the Albertus Magnus Professorship by the University of Cologne. David has conducted archaeological fieldwork in Africa and the Middle East. He is the author of numerous academic articles and three books, including *The Archaeology of Early Egypt* (2006) and *What Makes Civilization?* (2010); he is coauthor of *The Dawn of Everything: A New History of Humanity* (2021), a finalist for the Orwell Prize for Political Writing.

INDEX

Figures are indicated by italicized page numbers; tables are indicated by "t" following the page numbers.

A

Abrams, Philip, 378
Acalan polity, 180–181, 185, 315, 321
accession ceremonies, 204
Actuncan, 258, 263, *263*
Actun Halal Rockshelter, 254
Acuña, Mary Jane, 30
Adams, Richard E. W., 67
Adivino pyramid (Uxmal), *124*; Advino-sub and, 89–90, *89*, *91*, 101, 391; built over range structure, 124; "Chenes" Temple, 79, *81*, 82, 105; mask as speaking podium, 83; mask nose from, *80*; mask similarity to House of the Governor and Codz Pop masks, 107
adornment. *See* costuming and adornment, royal
adverse sacralization, 4t, 15, 27–28, 274, 389
Agamben, Giorgio, 386, 390
aggrandizers in Belize Valley in late Early Formative to early Middle Formative period (1200–750 BCE), 251t, 252–255
agriculture: ancestors, agricultural land claims, and, 231; fertility rituals, 254; rulers portrayed as farmers, 388; rural farmers under K'iche' rulers, 322. *See also* food and culinary practice
Ah Bolon Tz'acab. *See* K'awiil (God K)
Ahktuun, 129
Aimers, James J., 258
Ajaw Jatz'oom (Spearthrower Owl), 39–40, 390
Ajaw Kan Ek', 315
ajawtaak, 28, 32, 272–274, 375, 377; emerging in late Middle Formative period (750–300 BCE), 251t, 255–258, 273, 391; "first order regimes" in Classic Maya Lowlands, 375; fully established by start of Christian era, 264; *k'uhul ajawtaak* in early and late Classic periods (300–800 CE), 251t, 264–268, 273; in Late Formative period (300 BCE–300 CE), 251t, 258–264,

273; perpetuators in Terminal Classic period (800–900 CE), 251t, 269–272, 275; Postclassic period, 311; "second order regimes" in Classic period, 377
Aj K'ahk' O' Chahk (god), 53, 178
aj k'uhuun (title), 127, 131, 174
Ajnumsaaj Chan K'inich, 59, 62–64; as child ruler, 64; compound of, 66–69, *66*; Naranjo Stela 48 and, 50, *50*, 64, 69; palace, *65*; titles of, 70, *70*; vessel from reign of, *67*, *68*
Aj Pakal Tahn (priest), 179
Aj Sak Teles (Bonampak king), 199, *199*
alliance and conflict, 15, 27–46, 387; afterlife of invisible rulers (bundling and bundle shrines), 28–34; Early Classic rulers in the north, 34–36; invisible and anonymous rulers of the north, 27–28, 30–31; Kaanul regime, origins of, 36–38; Kaanul rulers' move to visibility, 38–40; marriage alliances for royal daughters, 145, 146; Preclassic lowland rulers and queens, 30–34
Allport, Gordon W., 390
anarchism, 386
ancestors, 4t; agricultural land claims and, 231; bundling and, 4t, 28–34, 321, 323, *324*; burial establishing hierarchy of, 262; cessation of household rituals to petition, 251, 257, 262; communication with deceased ancestors, 262; concurrence of ancestors and gods, 51, 51–52; deflation over time, 8; feeding of, 4t, 239; female fertility rites and, 254; jade ornaments and, 191; Mayapan, 319; orchards and, 231; Postclassic period, 312, 319, 325; problems created by, 8; royal ancestors distinguished from patron gods, 15; shift to local deities, 237; of stranger queens, 146; veneration, 7, 15, 54. *See also* conjuring
Andrews, Anthony, 232
Andrews, E. Wyllys, 33
Andrieu, Chloé, 12
Angulo, Pedro de (bishop), 339
anonymity of rulers, 27–28, 31–32
Appadurai, Arjun, 226

403

Arceo, Francisco de, 352, *352*
archaic state, 375; difficulty in defining, 369
architectural expansion, stranger ruler precipitating, 11, 123, 126
Ardren, Traci, 14, 141, 234, 238, 379, 386–387; *Ancient Maya Women*, 7
Atlantean gods, 261
authenticity and authentication, 2, 3, 8, 10, 11, 312
Auxaual, 180–181
Awe, Jaime J., 10, 249; on aggrandizement, 233, 254; on attempts to control Belize Valley, 274; on Cahal Pech *ajawtaak*, 391; on Cahal Pech offerings, 392; on Cahal Pech Stela 9, 262; on chocolate pot spouts, 262; on cycles of rulership at Belize Valley sites, 16; on Middle Preclassic period at Cahal Pech, 257; on royal residences, 264–265; on ruler's two bodies (mortal and institutional), 388–389; on Xunantunich receiving reward for being Naranjo war ally, 267; on Xunantunich Stelae 8 and 9, 272
Aztecs, 148, 149, 160, 374; feathered capes, 194, 199, 202, 204

B

Bahlam Jol-Witzna, 68, 71
Bajlaj Chan K'awiil, 122–123
Baking Pot, 264, 265, 267, 269–272; Komkom vase of, 67, 68, 74, 271
Balam K'itze', 321
ballplayers and ballcourts, 60, 69, 267–268, 297, 371–372
Baluun K'awiil (god), 177
Baron, Joanne, 10, 15, 173, 237, 386, 388, 390, 392
Barrientos, Tomás, 126–127
batabil lords, 315, 322, 337, 355
Beach, Timothy, 236
Béjar, Diego de (fray), 181
Beliaev, Dmitri, 38
Belize: under foreign control in ninth century, 179; invisible rulers of, 27, 28; Mayapan's relationship with, 185; ; population levels in Terminal Classic through Spanish contact, 313; relationship with other major hegemonies, 16; Tulix Mul, 64; Yukatek and, 174
Belize Valley, 249–283; aggrandizers in late Early Formative to early Middle Formative period (1200–750 BCE), 251*t*, 252–255, 273; *ajawtaak* emerging in late Middle Formative period (750–300 BCE), 251*t*, 255–258, 273, 391; *ajawtaak* in Late Formative period (300 BCE–300 CE), 251*t*, 258–264, 273; compared to Naranjo, 274; diachronic changes and rulership in, 250–252, 251*t*; Eastern Triadic Shrines, 255, 258–259, 264–266, 273; Jaina and, 291, 295; *k'uhul ajawtaak* in early and late Classic period (300–800 CE), 251*t*, 264–268, 273; map, *250*; monuments shifting focus from rulers to calendrical rituals, 274; perpetuators in Terminal Classic period (800–900 CE), 251*t*, 269–272, 275. *See also* Baking Pot; Blackman Eddy; Cahal Pech; Xunantunich
belt heads, 50–51, 72, 205
Benavides Castillo, Antonio, 16, 17, 285, 390
Berlin, Heinrich, 6, 120

Bey, George J., III, 11, 28, 105, 125, 126, 134, 183
bird entities and imagery, 55, 57, 68, 297, 316; bird-human hybrid, 55, 57, 153, 204
bird feathers. *See* feathered capes
Bird Jaguar IV, 147
Bishop, Ronald L., 293–294
black clothing, popularity in Europe, 192–193, *193*
Blackman Eddy, 16, 250; aggrandizers in late Early Formative to early Middle Formative period (1200–750 BCE), 252–255; *ajawtaak* emerging in late Middle Formative period (750–300 BCE), 255–258; *ajawtaak* in Late Formative period (300 BCE–300 CE), 258, 264; *k'uhul ajawtaak* in early and late Classic period (300–800 CE), 265; Middle Preclassic E-Group, 255; Stela 1, 265; Structure B1-5th, 257
Blake, Michael, 254
Blanton, Richard E., 9, 11, 13, 386
Blomster, Jeffrey P., 372
bloodletting, 13, 110n5, 149–150, 159, 175, 179, 202, 203, 218, 229, *229*, 239, 322
Bolles, John S., 101, 103, 104
Bonampak: cacao tributes depiction, 231; feathered cape depiction (Lintel 3), 195, 199, *199*; Panel 1, 204; Stela 1, 199; Stela 2, *229*
Books of Chilam Balam. *See* Chilam Balam books
Boot, Erik, 79, 182
Bourdieu, Pierre, 191–192, 193, 389
Braswell, Geoffrey E., 183
Braudel, Ferdinand, 192
Brown, Al, 386
Brown, M. Kathryn, 254, 257, 264
Budsilhá, 227
Buenavista, 264
Buenavista Valley, 388
Buenavista vase, 267
built environment. *See* royal body in built environment
bundles pertaining to ancestors, 4*t*, 28–34, 321, 323, 324
bureaucracies, 4*t*, 10–12, 312, 370; little evidence to support existence in Classic period, 375; of modern state, 370; power residing in knowledge and information, 370; of river valleys, 375; state secrets and, 374

C

Caamal, Fernando, 344*t*
cacao, 179, 231, 232–233, 238
caciques, 312, 333, 338; coats of arms granted to Guatemalan caciques, 335, 339–340, *340*; origin of term, 337
Cahal Pech, 16, 250; aggrandizers in late Early Formative to early Middle Formative period (1200–750 BCE), 252–255; *ajawtaak* emerging in late Middle Formative period (750–300 BCE), 255–258, 273, 391; *ajawtaak* in Late Formative period (300 BCE–300 CE), 258–264; bone ring inscriptions, 266–267, *266*; Caracol's influence on, 266; E-Group, 255, *256*, 258; *k'uhul ajawtaak* in early and late Classic period (300–800 CE), 264–268; last ruler's burial, 269, *270*; offerings to gods and ancestors, 252, 253, 259–262, *260*, 265, 266–267, 268,

269, *270*, 273, 392; perpetuators in Terminal Classic period (800–900 CE), 269–272; Plaza B, 255, *256*, *257*; Stela 9, 262–263, *263*, 273; Structure A1, 258, 267–268; Structure B1, *259*, 273; Structure B4, *252*, *255*

Calakmul, 37, 52; complementarity of male and female elites, 148; expansion of dominance, 184, 186; figurines and, 297; Kaanul royal dynasty transfer from Dzibanche to, 53, 71, 126–127, 176, 388; location of, 12; Naranjo conquered by, 160; palace size, 127; patron god appearing at El Peru, 176; patron god effigies from, 175; patron god version of the vision/waterlily serpent, 182; princesses of, marriage into La Corona, 11, 157, 158–160, 167, 387; reliance on archaeological evidence at, 12; Stela 33, 39; Stela 51, *202*, 204; wars of expansion, 158, 159–160, 162

calendrical notations and rituals, 6, 159, 162, 178–179, 181, 183, 185–186, 274, 275; Olmec invention of, 372; Postclassic period, 315–317, 322, 325

Calkini Codex, 290

Campeche: figurines and, 285, 297, 299, 302; population levels in Terminal Classic through Spanish contact, 313; relationship with Peten, 16; settlements, 285–287; Spanish attack on, 323; as terra incognita, 119

Cancuén, 176, 297

Cansacbe, 291, 302

Canul, Jorge, 342–343, 344t

Canuto, Marcello A., 126–127

captives, 13, 14, 50, 105, 160, 165, 195, 323, 376. *See also* sacrifices

Caracol: Altar 21, 38; *audiencias* of, 264–265; blood ties with Tikal royalty, 121; Caana temple complex, 264; constantly changing kingship of, 11, 326; hieroglyphic stairway section, 53; influence on Belize Valley sites, 264, 265–266; Kaanul coopting patron deity cults of, 176; Naranjo and, 160, 267; patron gods, 184; seeking to expand control in Belize Valley, 274. *See also* Chichen Itza mosaic masks

Carmack, Robert, 321, 326

Carter, Nicholas, 179, 195

Casa Colorada, 111n10. *See also* Chichen Itza mosaic masks

cave pearls, 252, 254, 392

cave rituals, 254, 273, 319, 354–355, *356*, *357*, 358

Ceibal, 120, 238; A-3 stela program, 180, 186; Cache 108, 255; directional gods, 180; E-Group, 255–258

cenotaphs, 15, 32

centipedes, 93, 154; serpent-centipede, 159

Central Mexico, 83, 337, 342, 353, 354, 357

ceramics: Andean culture and, 373; Celestún red ware, 286, 293, 297; Chablekal-Tsicul style, 299, 304n6; with dedicatory inscriptions, 265; feathered capes in Late Classic polychrome ceramic scenes, 195; Fine Orange Isla ware, Dzitbalché ceramic group, 299, 302; fine-paste ceramic vessels of Formative period, 252–254, 259; grave goods in Late Formative period, 259; lack of polychrome ceramics at northern sites, 134; Late Classic ceramic vases, 195, *203*, 204; lip-to-lip vessels, 259, 261, 262; Puuc Slate, 132; Puxcagua style, 303; redwares, 120; spouted ceramic vessels, 262; Tepeu 1 Saxche Orange polychrome, 66; Yalcox type, 303

Cerros: Cache 1 (Structure 6), 30, 32, *33*; Cache 6B, 204; expanding population and cosmological foundations of rulership, 16; Ichkabal and, 37; jade diadems in headdresses, 204; Structure 5C-2nd, 29, 30, 32, 37

Certeau, Michel de, 238

Chaak (God B), 79, 110n5, 180, *324*

Chaan Muan (Bonampak king), 199, *199*

Chahk rain deity (La Sufricaya Stela 1), *56*, 57

Chak Ak' Paat Kuy, 126–129

Chakanbakan, 37

Chakaw Nahb Chan, 127, *128*

Chaksinkin royal jades, 33–34

Chak Tok Wayaab, 55, 57, 59, 71

Chak Took Ich'aak I (Tikal), 40

Champoton, 286, 302

Chan (Belize Valley), 257–259, 341

Chan, Francisco, 333

Chan, Juan, 333–335, 341, 344t, 358; *Probanza de méritos de cacique*, 333–334, *334*

Chan, Nahau, 333

Chan family, 341

Chan te' Ajaw ("four lords"), 177

Chan te' Ch'oktaak ("four princes"), 177

charisma, 4t, 8, 390; nonhuman faces of the sacred and, 14; Olmec and Chavín as examples of power based on, 374; political competition and, 370; politics of highlands and, 375; royal charisma, experience of, 130, 133

Charles II (king of Spain), *193*, 353

Charles V (Holy Roman emperor, king of Spain), *193*, 340, 342, 353, 360nn24–25

Charles VIII, death of, 249

Charnay, Desiré, 295

Chase, Diane Z. and Arlen F., 325

Chavín de Huántar (Peru), 372–374, 377

Chechem Ha Cave, 254

Cheetham, David, 262

Chenes-style monster-maw masks, 79–82, *81*, 88, 105, *107*

Chenes-style Adivino temple. *See* Adivino pyramid

Chetumal, 313

Chi, Ah Kin, 347, 349

Chiapa de Corzo, 30, 204

Chiapas, 121, 227, 295, 335, 357

Chicanna mask with mat sign, 83, *84*

Chichen Itza: apogee and decline of, 174, 312, 326; campaign against Montejo the Younger, 323; comparing Postclassic period to, 313; corbelled vaults with feathered serpents, 126; formal institutional form of governance, 311; fusion of building styles in Late Terminal Classic periods, 126; Initial Series Lintel, 104, 183; Itza foodways in Postclassic period, 238; Jaina and, 291; map, *182*; military leaders depicted with feathered capes, 195, 204; Osario, 99, *101*; patron gods, 181–183, *182*, 185; priests, role of, 319; Sacred Cenote, 205, *207*, 323; Spanish attack on, 323; Structure 3D7, 99, 101, 105; Temple of the Jaguar (Atlantean Columns), 105, 195, *201*, 204; Temple of the Jaguar (lower), 195; Temple of the Jaguar (upper), 195, *200*; Temple of the Little Tables, 80; Thousand Columns Group, 105; Uxmal predating, 123; Venus Temple, 107, 110n7

INDEX 405

Chichen Itza mosaic masks, 12, 77, 79, *80*, 83, 97–110, *98–100*; Caracol, 100, *100*, 104, 105, 108; Casa Colorada, 97, *98*, 100, 101, 104; Castillo, 97, *99*, 101, 108; Chenes-style monster-maw masks, 105, *107*; compared to Puuc masks, 97–101, *107*; emergence theme, 100–101, 105–110, *106*; House/Temple of the One Lintel, 97, 104; House/Temple of the Three Lintels, 97, *98*, 101, 104; House/Temple of the Four Lintels, 104; La Iglesia, 101, 105, *106*, 110n9; Las Monjas, 97, *100*, 101–103, *102*, 104–105, *107*; Modified Florescent style, 97, *99*, 101, 105; nose rolls, 100, 110n9, 111n11; Pure Florescent style, 97, *98*, 101, 103, 104–105
Chih Ka' K'awiil, 53, 71
Chijchan (Snake Deer), 36
Chilam Balam books, 157, 183, 184, 185, 357; apocryphal coat of arms of Yucatán in, 351–353, *351*; complaints against two-day holders of the mat, 358; language of Zuyua in, 355, 360n30
Chilam Balam (prophet), 348, 350, 352, 357
Chinchilla Mazariegos, Oswaldo, 151, 152–154, 387
Chi Stone Throne Palace, 37
Chi Xiu, Gaspar Antonio, 342, 344t, 345, 347–350, 352, 353, 358, 359n16
chocolate pots, 259, 262
Chok Watab (god), 104
Ch'olti'an. *See* Classic Ch'olti'an
Chontal, 48; Acalan Chontal, 180–181, 185; as ninth-century powerbrokers, 179–180; patron gods, 178–181, 185, 186; Paxbolon-Maldonado Papers recording language of, 180; speakers of language, 174, 178
Chontal text, 315
Christianity, conversion and missionaries, 181, 333, 339–340, 348, 350, 352–353, 358
Chuchiak, John F., IV, 5, 17, 235, 333, 387, 390
Chuwaaj Fire God, 68
Cival, 37, 38; decline of, 55; Holmul's link to, 54; Middle Preclassic emerging elite's construction of E-Group, 258; Stela 2, 263, *263*
Clark, John E., 121, 204, 254, 372
class, social, 14, 17, 34, 264; class differences common to all early polities, 376
Classic Ch'olti'an, 174–182; group using language of, 174; patron gods, 175–178, 184, 185–186
Classic period: divine rulers, 325; dynastic form of rulership, 386; Early Classic rulers in the north, 34–36; emblematic shields, 335–337, *336*; fusing heroic politics with sovereignty, 377; helmet crown of Early Classic period, 30; Jaina settlement, 289, 302; *k'uhul ajawtaak* in early and late Classic period (300–800 CE), 251t, 264–268, 273; political networks, 129–130, *129*, 27–46, 47, 48; power struggle of two main blocs, 377
coats of arms, 17, 333, 337, 390; appropriation of Spanish heraldic symbols (1550–1750), 344–353, 360n22; Chilam Balam books' apocryphal coat of arms of Yucatán, 351–353, *351*; to Francisco de Arceo, 352, *352*; to Guatemalan Indigenous collaborators, 335, 339–340, *340*; held in high regard by Spaniards and Indigenous peoples, 339; to Indigenous conquistadors and collaborators, 338–340; motivational aspect of grant of, 358; to Oaxacan caciques, 335; to Spanish conquistadors, 338, 348, 352, *352*; trophy heads in, 348. *See also probanzas de méritos y servicios*
Coatzacoalcos, 357
Coba, 125, 148; stranger queens, 155; traditional dynastic monarchs, 386
Cocom, Andres, 342–343
Cocom dynasty, 18, 108, 184, 325, 341
Codz Pop, 82, 85–87, 391; compared to Las Monjas, 101, 103; developed throne complex, 89–90, *89*; as living structure, 103; location of masks, 87, *87*; mask similarity to Nunnery and House of the Governor masks, 90, 107, 108, *109*, 391; mask variety, 83; Mayapan masks echoing, 108–110, *109*; military offices, 93–97, *94–95*, 104; "profile masks," 90, *92*; as sorcery houses, 79
Coe, William R., 39
Colman, Arlene, 204
colonialism: *cabildo* system of government, 338, 339, 359n7; negative effects on knowledge of Maya culture, 5, 325; Yucatán, 333–367. *See also* coats of arms
Colonnette architecture, 77–79, *78*
Comalcalco, 17; cultural mixing, 181; emblem glyph, 179; figurines, 294, *294–295*, 298; Yukatekan version of god at, 182
Comayagua, Honduras, 205
complementarity, 148–149, *149*, 155, 165, 386
conjuring, 13, 14, 79, 151, 153
contact period. *See* Postclassic and contact period
Contreras, Diego de, 5
Cook, James, 203
Cook de Leonard, Carmen, 301
Copan: Altar Q, *52*, 53; blood ties with Tikal royalty, 121; council rule at end of city's history, 386; on division of Maya world, 180, 181; dynastic founders, 126, 387; fifth-century genealogy, 39; figurines, 297; Itzamkanac at, 181; jade ornament brought from Palenque to, 205; map of region and stelae, 177, *177*; Papagayo step, *50*, 51; patron gods, 176–177; patron god version of the vision/waterlily serpent, 182; royal court, 7; Stela 2, *50*, 51; Stela 7, 177–178; Stela 10, 177; Stela 13, 177; Stela B, 177; Stela J, *50*, 51; Temple 10L-22, 79; Teotihuacan imagery at, 234
Corozal. *See* Santa Rita
corporate regimes, 9–10, 11, 72
Cortés, Hernán, 180–181, 315, 321; coat of arms, 349
Cortez, Constance, 347
cosmic bureaucracy, 18, 377
Cosmic Vase (Rio Azul), 67
cosmology, 9; in Formative-period Belize Valley, 252, 254; in late Middle Formative-period Belize Valley, 255, 257, 258, 273; old cosmology continuing into Postclassic period, 323; parallels of Inka Cuzco with Shang dynasty China, 376; royal politics involving, 14, 273, 392; ruler as axis mundi, 388
costuming and adornment, royal, 16–17, 152, 191–223, 390; Andean culture and, 373; bodily dress, 191–194; duck-billed Mexican wind deity, 180; leafy capes, 202, *203*; Mexica emperors, cape and jewels of, 199–202; nosepieces, 321; Postclassic elite dress, 325, 326;

Postclassic metal artifacts, 313, 325; rulers identifiable by, 28, 389; trophy head pendants, 195, *196*. *See also* feathered capes; headbands/headdresses; jade ornaments; Maize God

Cotecpan, 322

councils and secondary political officials, 4*t*, 10, 254, 275, 386; Acalan, 321; Postclassic period, 311, 312

Couoh family, 341

Courtly Art of the Ancient Maya (exhibition), 7

creation narrative/myth, 252, 254, 255, 265, 321, 387

crocodile motif, 227, 252, 259, 261, *261*, 262

Cuello, 264

culinary practice. *See* feasting; food and culinary practice

Cupul polity, 315, 325

D

Dampier, William, 290

Dávila, Gil González, 315

Davletshin, Albert, 51

death symbolism, *336*, 337

deep-time ancestry, 4*t*, 8, 206

Deer Cowrie, *35*, 36

Delgado, Hilda, 153

Dickson, D. Bruce, 2

Digby, Adrian, 262

divine exceptionalism of rulers, 18, 389

divine rulers, 8, 249, 389; in Belize Valley, 267–268; Classic period, 325; as foundation of social and cosmic order, 60; as "imitations of gods," 29, 31, 174; of Natchez, 371, 374; parallels of Inka and ancient Egypt, 375; role of, 119, 173; theonyms and, 267, 274; transformation into, 31

divine vs. sacred rulership, 8, 14, 319, 375, 389

Domínguez Torres, Mónica, 340

Dos Caobas, 178

Dos Pilas: Ix Wak Jalam Chan from, 13, 123; leaf cape depiction, 202, *203*; Mutul peregrination from Tikal to, 388; stranger queen from, at Naranjo, 160, 162, 167

double-headed eagle. *See* Habsburg dynasty

Dresden Codex, 48, *49*

dress, royal. *See* costuming and adornment, royal

droughts, 7, 235, 236, 239, 323, 326

dual sovereignty, 3*t*, 8, 11–12, 119, 123, *129*, 129–130, 133, 135, 173

Dunning, Nicholas, 236

dynastic rulership: accession ceremonies, 204; council rule yielding to, 385; institutionalization of, 28; most common form of rulership in Classic period, 386; polygyny's effect on, 147. *See also* hereditary rulership; *specific names of dynasties*

Dzibanche, 36–39, *52*, 53, 59, 71–72, 126, 158, 176, 388

Dzidz Yam, Edber, 156–157

E

ear flares, 30, 34, *35*, 55, 79, 82, 97, 104, 163, 259, 269

Eastern Triadic Shrines, 255, 258–259, 264–266, 273

Ebert, Claire E., 10, 16, 233, 249, 388–389

E-Group constructions, 16, 62, 65, 121, 255–259, 273

Ek' Balam, 5; acropolis, 88; council house predating throne room, 386; pyramidal shrines to patron deities, 124–125; seated figure and Chenes-style masks, 105, *107*; stranger king, 11

Ekholm, Susanna, 295

El Achiotal (Peten), 30, 37

elites and nobles: female elites, 141, 146, 148; food practices and serving pieces, 233–235; gender parallelism in Aztec society, 148; masked heads, 100–101, 103; Olmec society, 372; Postclassic period, 313, 321; rituals sponsored by emerging rulers, 257–258; role of, 1; titles of nobles in Peten, 315; upward nobility, 117, 119, 123, 135. *See also* hierarchy

El Lanzón of Old Temple (Chavín de Huantar, Peru), 374

El Mirador, 36–38, 263

El Palmar, 176, 177

El Peru-Waka', 38–40; Deer Cowrie amulet in tomb, 36; patron god effigies from, 175; patron god from Calakmul appearing at, 176; Stela 15, 39; Stela 44, 38

El Porton Structure J7-4B-2, 175

emblem glyphs, 6–7, 63, 120, 122–123, 179, 388; for *ajaw*, 264; Flint-Shield glyph, 335; mistaken for coats of arms, 335; polities symbolized by, 337

emergence theme (masked heads), 90, *100*, 100–101, 105–110, *106*, 110n9

"Endless Drunkenness Fire O' (bird) Chahk," 50

Ensor, Bradley, 145

Entrada of Sihyaj K'ahk', 34, 36

entradas, 5, 14, 125, 126

environmental factors: in crises of Late Classic rulers, 7; in regional interdependencies and commercial exchange, 12. *See also* droughts

Estrada Belli, Francisco, 10, 47, 388; on ancestral monuments, 15; on legitimation, 233; on Naranjo expansion of realm, 176, 274; on royal legitimacy, 12; on shrines to patron gods, 175, 178; on vesting of royal identity, 15

Euan, Francisco, 359n4

exogamy, 119, 120, 122–123, 135, 145, 155, 165

eye surrounds, 82, 97, 101, 103, 111n11

F

Fargher, Lane F., 386

Fash, William L., 386; *Scribes, Warriors, and Kings*, 7

feasting, 2, 3*t*, 11, 16, 130–134, 226–228, 235, 388, 391; creation of social indebtedness, 235, 391; patron-client mode, 237; as pretext for massacre, 235, 323, 390. *See also* food and culinary practice

feathered capes, 16, 191, 194–204, 210–217*t*, 218n1; Bonampak depiction, 199, *199*; Calakmul depiction, 202, 204; change in styles and generational differences, 197–199; Chichen Itza depictions, 195, 200–201, 204; decomposition of, 197–199; disappearance of feather workers in Spanish colonial period, 208; as indication of heroic deeds, 199, 377, 389; as indication of wealth and prestige, 202; Late Classic depictions, 195, *196*, 204; Piedras Negras depiction, 195, *198*; trophy head pendants and, 195, *196*; types of feathers used, 203–204 feathered serpents, 12, 79, *80*, 90, *100*, 105–107, 183, 195. *See also* K'uk'ulkan (Feathered Serpent)

Feinman, Gary M., 9

feminism, 142, 143

fertility, 9, 154, 159, 294; female fertility rites, 254. *See also* sexuality, female

Fialko, Vilma, 10, 47, 388; on ancestral monuments, 15; on legitimation, 233; on Naranjo expansion of realm, 170, 274; on royal legitimacy, 12; on shrines to patron gods, 175, 178; on vesting of royal identity, 15

figurines, 16–17; disappearance in Late Preclassic period, 262; Lagartero, 295; Middle Formative, 259–262, *260*; as mnemotechnic device, 297; in private rituals and used by women, 254, 257; ritual or funerary use, 297, 303. *See also* Jaina figurines

"first order regimes," 374–375

flame eyebrow motif, 252, *253*

Flower Mountain, 68, 79

Foias, Antonia, 237–238

Foliated Ajaw Jaguar, 39–40

food and culinary practice, 225–247; *atoles*, 233; cacao, 179, 231, 232–233, 238; crop resilience, 236; culinary specialists, 228; fair market prices, 238; fish and seafood, 231–232; food ingredients, 227; food offerings to gods and the deceased, 4*t*, 231; food preparation and culinary equipment, 16, 130–133, *134*, 226, 227, 391; funerary practices and, 231, 239; imagery of lavish foodstuffs, 237; impermanence of food, 239; inside the gilded cage, 238–239; marriage negotiation and food offerings, 232; meats (including deer), 231, 233; rulership and culinary lies, 237–238, 388, 391; scarcity, 16, 225, 235–236, 237, 239, 326; spice mixtures, 231; stranger rulers and, 234, 239; supernatural nourishment, 228–231; supply chain breakdown, 236; tamales, 233. *See also* feasting; gastropolitics

Formative period, 9, 12; aggrandizers in late Early Formative to early Middle Formative period (1200–750 BCE), 250, 251*t*, 252–255, 273; *ajawtaak* emerging in late Middle Formative period (750–300 BCE), 251*t*, 255–258, 273, 391; *ajawtaak* in Late Formative period (300 BCE–300 CE), 251*t*, 258–264, 273; architectural changes of, 258; female effigies of, 254; lowland rulers and queens, 30–34; relational politics in southern and northern lowlands, 120–121; ritual and feasting activities, 18

Foucault, Michel, 386, 390

Frazer, James, 392

Freidel, David, 10, 27, 153–154; on cenotaphs, 15; on class strife, 34; comparing southern and northern use of hieroglyphic inscriptions, 274; on Dzibanche transformations, 71–72; on jade and spondylus adornments as royal insignia, 389; *Maya Cosmos* (with Schele and Parker), 29; on relationship of Maya people and the divine, 228–229; on royal alliance and conflict, 15, 27; on rulership, relations, and royal courts, 385; selection of rulers, 11; on serpent with jaguar claws, 158; on shaman-kings, 249, 392; on sovereignty based on violence, 390; on state councils in northern Yucatán, 386

funerary practices. *See* mortuary practices

G

galactic mimesis, 3*t*, 117, 119, 135; Habsburgs paralleling Maya, 195; in north, 123–126; in south, 126–129; upward nobility and, 123

Galarza, Joaquin, 353

Gallareta Cervera, Tomás, 123, 134

Gallareta Negrón, Tomás, 11, 28, 88, 125, 126, 183

Gallegos, Miriam J., 294

Gann, Thomas, 312

Garber, James F., 252, 254, 257, 264

García Barrios, Ana, 237

García Campillo, Miguel, 290, 291

Gaspar (cacique of Teculitlan, Guatemala), 339, *340*

gastropolitics, 225–247; defined, 226; in elite performance, 233–235; "gastropolitik," 237; in haute cuisine, 231–233; multiple embodiments of, 239; pomp and, 235. *See also* feasting; food and culinary practice

Geertz, Clifford, 235, 372

gender roles, 7, 13–14, 17, 141, 159; complementarity and, 148–149, *149*, 155, 165, 386; de-stabilization of women's relationships and, 146; female breast and, 153; inverted vase signifying mother and wife, 156, *157*; mother–son bond as touchstone of Classic Maya culture, 156; in portraiture of Maya queens, 149–151, *150*; reproductive power of women, 156–157, 166. *See also* queens; sexuality, female; stranger queens

God C, 174

God D, 55, 79, 174

God G (K'inich Ajaw), 174

God G1, 83, *84*, 88, 90, 100, *100*, 110n5, 180

God K. *See* K'awiil

God L, 197

God N, 174, 261

God S, 152–153

gods and goddesses: blood offerings to, 236, 239; dual nature of Classic-period gods, 174; food offerings to, 4*t*, 231, 392; goddesses as lunar and earth deities, 149; valuable objects as offerings to, 392. *See also* patron gods; *specific god by name or letter designation*

Graeber, David, 2, 4; on adverse sacralization, 274, 389; *The Dawn of Everything* (with Wengrow), 9, 18; on dichotomy between stranger kings and queens, 135, 387; on divine rulers imitating gods, 31, 174, 387; on divine rulers' power, 173, 273; on divine stranger kingship, 117, 123, 387; on divine vs. sacred kings, 8; on endurance of kingship, 12; on galactic mimesis, 195; on gender dynamics of rulership, 13; on invisible rulers of the north, 27; on meta-human powers in deep antiquity, 29; on nonhuman faces of sacred authority, 14–15; *On Kings* (with Sahlins), 2; on political economy of kingship, 130; on sovereignty of rulers as ability to commit violence with impunity, 385–386; on upward nobility, 11

Grijalva-Usumacinta Basins, 297, 299, 302, 303

Grube, Nikolai, 37, 39, 262, 272, 322; *Chronicle of the Maya Kings and Queens* (with Martin), 7

Grupo Magana (Huntichmul), 105

Guatemala: coats of arms to Indigenous collaborators, 335, 339–340, *340*, 357; double-headed Habsburg eagles in,

354, *356*, 357; early stone monuments in, 32; queenship as cultural phenomenon in, 142; Tiquisate region, masks from, 83

Guenter, Stanley, 38, 158, 179

Guernsey, Julia, 30, 264

Gulf Coast: Chontal language and, 174; Jaina's ties to, 17, 300; slave markets, 323. *See also* Tabasco

Gutierrez, Maria Eugénia, 156–157

H

Ha' K'in Xook, *198*, 205

Habsburg dynasty: double-headed eagle imagery passed to Austrian branch after Charles V's abdication, 360n24; Maya appropriations of royal arms and double-headed eagle, 353–357, *355–356*, 360nn27–29, 390; royal family clothing, 192–193, *193*, 195

Halach Winik lords, 315, 322, 333

Halakal, 182–183

hallucinogenics in Chavín's culture, 373

Halperin, Christina T., 16, 17, 152, 191, 233, 237–238, 377, 389, 390

Hansen, Richard D., 121

Hare, Timothy S., 184

Harrison-Buck, Eleanor, 145

Haskett, Robert, 335, 357

Hauberg Stela, 175

headbands/headdresses, 30, 34, 55, 63, 64, 68, 90, 111n11, 325; disk, 103, 104; feathered, 104; flowered, indicating Itsamna (God D), 79; with jade diadems, 204, *206*; in male graves at Chan, 259; serpent, 17; snake, 373

"Hearth" Chan Ahk of Naranjo, 50–51, *50–51*

Helmke, Christophe, 10, 249; on aggrandizement, 233; on attempts to control Belize Valley, 274; on Cahal Pech Stela 9, 263; on cycles of rulership at Belize Valley sites, 16; on Kaanul, 38; on ruler's two bodies (mortal and institutional), 388–389; on Xunantunich receiving reward for being Naranjo war ally, 267; on Xunantunich Stelae 8 and 9, 272

Helms, Mary, 387

Heredia Espinoza, Verenice Y., 386

hereditary rulership, 249–283, 375; absence of, 125; perpetuators in Terminal Classic period (800–900 CE), 251t, 269–272, 275

Herzfeld, Michael, 193

hierarchy, 3t, 5, 9, 18, 72, 120–123, 141–142, 226, 315, 321, 337, 374–375, 378. *See also* gender roles

hieroglyphic literacy, 5, 31

Hill, Warren, 372

Hina/Hinal, 290

Hobbes, Thomas, 389

Hocart, A. M., 14

Hoggarth, Julie A., 10, 16, 233, 236, 249, 388–389

Holmul (royal court), 70–72, 274; ancestral monuments, 15; Kaanul incorporating of, 57; royal legitimacy of, 12; Teotihuacan connection, 59, 388

Holmul site, 53–62; Building A, Group II, 57–60, *58*, 60–61, 62, 68; Building B, Group II, 54, *54*, 55; Building B, phase I, 30; Building C, Group II, *54*, 55, 57; Building D, Group I, *54*, 59, *67*, 72; compared to Naranjo, 59, 70–71, 388; construction phases, burials, and caches, 57–59, *58–59*, 62, *67*; dynastic shrine (Group II), 62; funeral shrines (Group I), 62; La Sufricaya palace, 55–56, 57, 71; map of archaeological sites, *55*; map of political centers, *48*; Ruin X (main pyramid of local E-Group), 62. *See also* La Sufricaya palace

Honduras, 180, 205, 357

household rituals to petition ancestors, cessation of, 251, 257, 262

House of the Governor (Uxmal), 79, 87, *109*; Chenes-style monster-maw mask, 105; developed throne complex, 89, 90; mask similarity to Nunnery and Codz Pop masks, 90, 107, 108, *109*, 391; mosaic mask, 85; "profile masks," 90, 92, 93; Venus Temple and, 110n7

House/Temple of the Four Lintels (Chichen Itza), 97, 104, 183. *See also* Chichen Itza mosaic masks

House/Temple of the One Lintel, 97. *See also* Chichen Itza mosaic masks

House/Temple of the Three Lintels. *See* Chichen Itza mosaic masks

Houston, Stephen D., 14, 154–155, 225, 227, 229, 234, 238, 267, 389

Huachuma (mescaline-based infusion), 373

Hummingbird God of Naranjo, *67*, 69

hummingbirds, 15, 55, 64, 67–70, 153

Hunac Ceel, 185

Hunahpu, 387, 388

Hun Yeh Winik Chaak (Sun God as One Tooth Person), 34

Hutson, Scott R., 18, 385

Hux Bolon Chahk, 53

Hux Yop Huun, *54*, 55, 57

hypogamy, 11, 123, 126, 135, 165

I

Ichkabal, 37

Ihk' Miin SNB (Square-Nosed Beast), 64, 65

incensarios, 83, 85

Indigenous past, celebration of, 5–6

Indus Valley, 379

inequality, 255; institutionalized, 17, 18, 34; symbols of, 10. *See also* gender roles; hierarchy

inheritance and successors, 7, 8; absence of inherited sacred rulership, 125; female sexuality as threat to, 153; heavy investments in hereditary rulership, 126; jade ornaments, 16, 204–205, *205*; K'iche' patrilineages, 315, 321–322; male entitlement, 13; polygyny and, 147; Postclassic period, 312; titles, privileges, and capacities of rulers, 16. *See also* dynastic rulership; hereditary rulership

initiation ceremonies, 28, 30, 31, 33, 105, 202, 374

Inka Peru, 29, 375; lack of charismatic politics, 377; parallels with Shang dynasty China, 376; parallels with Old Kingdom Egypt, 375

Inomata, Takeshi, 121, 227, 238, 255, 258, 267

insect, supernatural, 153

International style. *See* Toltec/International style

investiture rites, 8, 12, 103, 105, 108, 312

islands built by ancient Maya, 285, *287*, 287. *See also* Jaina

Isla Piedras, 287, *287*, 302, 304n7
Isla Uaymil, 287, *287*, 291, 292, 302, 304, 304n7
Itsamna (God D), 79
Itzamkanac (capital of Acalan), 180–181, 321
Itzam Kokaaj (God D), 55, 57, 71
Itzamnaaj (the creator), 32, 153
Itzamnaaj K'awiil, 66, 271
Ix Ahku'ul Patah, 229
Ix K'abal Xook, 13
Ix Kukum Xiu, 347
Ixlu, 179, 180, 388
Ix Naah Ek', 126
Ix Ti' Kaan, 126
Ix Tz'ihb Winik, 126
Ix Wak Jalam Chan, 13, 62, 64, 123, 160–163, *161*, 167
Ix Yax Chiit Ju'n Witz' Noh Kan, 229
Izapa, 30, 262

J

jadeite: beads representing kernels of maize, 257; male remains in tombs with, 259
jade ornaments, 16, 191, 204–208; Chaksinkin royal jades, 33–34; connecting king to dynasty, 389; diminished importance in Postclassic period, 208; elite status of, 204; head belt, 51; Holmul Building B in Group II, 54; Jaina and, 297; pectoral (Dumbarton Oaks), 204, *205*; pectoral (Nakum Burial 1), 206–208, *207*; Piedras Negras heirloom jade pendant, 205, *207*; in Red Queen's tomb, 163; *sak hu'n* diadems, 204, *206*; transcendence of ruler indicated by, 377; Uaymil pendant, 292; Yaxuna tableau, queen wearing crown with, 34, *35*, 36
Jaguar God of the Underworld (Chuwaaj Fire God), 64, 68, 180, 195
jaguar mountain, 54
Jaina, 285–310; as built island, 285, *287*, 288, *288*; Dumbarton Oaks onyx bowl from, 291, 292; emblem glyph, 289, *290*, 291, 292; exchange relations and manufacture, 297–299, 302; Kimi dynasty, 291, 292; La Mixtequilla and, 302; maps and location, *286–287*; relationship with Palenque, 17; rulers and society, 291–293; settlement, 288–291; Stela 1, *289*; Structure 1, 288, *289*; Structure 4, 288–289, *288*, *290*
Jaina figurines, 16–17, 390; burial levels and, 297–299, 302; dwarf representations, 301, *301*; examples, 294–295, *294–296*, 298; explanations, 299–302; fragments, 293–297; future research needs, 303; Jonuta woman with hands up, *293*, 294; looting, 291; males faces and scarification, 300, *300*; as rattles and whistles, 297; of rulers, 291; similar figurines from Veracruz, 17, 285, 294–295, *296*, 300; types of, 285; war-serpent motif, 292, 293
James, Liz, 142
Jarosław, Źrałka, 263
jewel ornaments, 32. *See also* costuming and adornment, royal; jade ornaments
Jo' Chan Naah, 63, 66
Jones, Grant D., 185, 315, 319, 321

Jonuta, 17, 293–294, 298; woman figurine with hands up, *293*, 294
Joyce, Rosemary A., 148, 205
Juun Ixim. *See* Maize God
Juxtlahuaca Cave, 254

K

Kaanul dynasty: ancestral spirits, unleashing of, 154; as corporate regime, 72; Dos Pilas and, 123; foreign places as sources of divine authority, 121; incorporating Holmul region, 57; La Corona and, 126–129, 131, 133; legitimating practices of, 71–72; Naranjo and, 64, 123; origins of, 36–38; Palenque and, 164; princesses of, marriage into subordinate court of allied cities, 11, 147, 157–159, 167; rebuilding and consolidating influence after epic wars, 159; transfer from Dzibanche to Calakmul state, 53, 71, 126–127, 388; visibility of early rulers, 38–40; war with Tikal, 39, 159. *See also specific rulers*
Kabah: coalition with Uxmal, 107; dating construction from hieroglyphics, 107–108, 108t, 110n8; East Group masks, 85–87, *87*; food preparation area, 134; mask placement, 97; "profile masks," 92; roof combs, 87; warrior sculptures, 11, 93. *See also* Codz Pop
K'ab'al Xook (Yaxchilan queen), 147, 166
K'ahk' Ti' Chi'ch', 38
K'ahk' Tiliw Chan Chahk, 50, 63, 64, 162–163, 195
K'ahk' Way Na', 127
K'ak'upakal (Chichen Itza ruler), 183
kaloomte' status, 39–40, 49, 53; adoption of apical title of, 121; Chontal-style names and, 179; female ruler with, 13, 142, 143t, 165; *ix kaloomte'* of stranger queen, 158–159, 163
Kaminaljuyu, 263
K'an II, 265
k'an cross, 252, *253*, 392
Kantorowicz, Ernst: *The King's Two Bodies*, 191, 192, 388–389
k'atun lords, 319–323, 324, 388
Kaufmann, Thomas DaCosta, 360n28
Kauil, Juan, 340–341, 344t
k'awiil/k'awiilil, 50, 52, 52–53
K'awiil (God K), 52–53, *52*, 174; arrival at Tikal (La Sufricaya Structure 1 Mural 7), 56, 57; "conjuring K'awiil" as metaphor, 155; long-nosed deity, 79; mask nose at Xkipche, 83, *84*; queens drawing spiritual authority from association with, 155; as theonym used by rulers, 267; in Tulum murals, 321
K'awiil Chan K'inich, 267
Keegan, William, 144, 145
Keller, Angela H., 259
Kellogg, Susan, 148, 149
Kelly, Mary Kate, 38
Kennedy, John F. and Jacqueline, 193–194, *194*, 209
K'iche' rulership, 315, 321–322, 326, 354–355, 387
K'ikab (Postclassic king), 321
Kimi family, 291, 292
kinam, 156

K'inchil Kab, 68
kings. *See* rulers; stranger rulers
K'inich Ahkal Mo' Nahb (young royal male), 202
K'inich Ajaw (God G/sun god), 174
K'inich as theonym used by rulers, 267
K'inich Janaab Pakal I. *See* Pakal I
K'inich Tajal Tuun/Chahk, 59
K'inich Yax K'uk' Mo'. *See* Yax K'uk' Mo (ruler of Copan)
k'in mask markings, 79, *80*
kinship, 11, 144–145
Kiuic: dual sovereignty, 11; Dzunun Plaza, 134; feasting, 227; finished veneer stones and, 134; hypogamy, 123; Kuche palace, 134; mosaic mask noses, 83; pyramid built over earlier structure, 124, *125*; Yaxche sector, 134
K'iyel Janab (Sacul king), 195
Klein, Cecelia, 160
Knowlton, Timothy, 156–157
Kokom polity, 323, 326
Komkom vase, 67, 68, 74, 271
Koons, Michele, 373
Kowalewski, Stephen A., 9
Kowalski, Jeff Karl, 110n1
Kowoj, 185
kuch kab'al, 315
k'uh, 50–53, *50*, 60, 64, 69, 174
k'uhul ajaw (sacred ruler), 6, 14, 202, 208
k'uhul ajawtaak: in early and late Classic periods (300–800 CE), 251t, 264–268, 273. *See also ajawtaak*
K'uk'ulkan (Feathered Serpent): importance of, 183, 185–186; Mayapan and, 184, 316, 319, 321, 322; Postclassic pyramids dedicated to, 321; as shared founding deity, 15, 325
Kupprat, Felix A., 38
Kurnick, Sarah, 173

L
Labna Palace, 11; council house predating throne room, 386; "Las Pulgas," 134; mask locations, 83, 85, *86*, 96; mask motifs, 79, *80–81*, 96; military offices, 93, *94*, 96, 97, 104; serpents with feathered bodies, 90; tripartite throne room, 88, *88*, 90; warrior depictions, 97
Lacanjá Tzeltal, 227
La Corona: dual sovereignty, 11, 16; Element 56 (hieroglyphic monument), 126, *128*, 129; Elements 55 and 59, 127, *128*; galactic mimesis in, 126–129; Kaanul and, 11, 126–129, 133; map, *127, 131*; meal and feast preparation, 16, 130–133, 227; Panel 6, 153–154, *154*, 158–159; patron-client mode of feasting, 237; patron gods, 15, 176, 178, 392; regal palace, *127*, 130–133, *131–132*; shift from ancestors to patron deities, 71; stranger queens, 155, 158–160, 167, 387; temples of patron gods, 175–176
Lady of Itzan, 122
Lady Six Sky. *See* Ix Wak Jalam Chan
Lady Ti' (Third Snake Lady) (stranger queen at La Corona), 158–159, 160
Lagartero figurines, 295
La Iglesia, 101, 103–105, *106*. *See also* Chichen Itza mosaic masks

Lamat markings, 79, 90
Lamoureux-St-Hilaire, Maxime, 10, 11, 16, 117, 157, 337, 386, 387, 391
Landa, Diego de (bishop), 134, 183, 184, 302, 335, 358, 359n4
Las Monjas: Chenes-style monster-maw mask, 105, *107*; floor plan, 101–103, *102*; military activities, 104–105; patron gods, 104, 183. *See also* Chichen Itza mosaic masks
Latour, Bruno: *Reassembling the Social*, 390
La Venta, 32, 204, 372, 374
legitimation, 391; among Puuc cities, 108; of Belize Valley rulers, 265; defined, 47; K'awiil connected to dynastic legitimacy, 155; of kingship, 249; of queens and of stranger queens, 155, 162. *See also* authenticity and authentication; royal body in built environment
Lem Aat/Lem Neh cult, 68
Lem? Tz'unun Tok Suutz', 265
Lem Witz Nal, 68
Liendo Stuardo, Rodrigo, 125
lightning motif, 53, 252, *253*
local place/community, 9; patron gods and, 176, 186
López, Alonso, 343–344
López de Cogolludo, Diego, 325; *História de Yucatán*, 344, 348–350
López Domingo, Leidy Marily, 144
López Medel, Tomás, 338
López-Morillas, Frances M., 360n22
Los Guarixés, 302, 303, 304n7
Love, Michael, 264, 323
Lowe, Lynneth Susan, 302
Lucero, Lisa, 388
Luzzadder-Beach, Sheryl, 236

M
Maize God: at Cerros, 32; decapitation and resurrection of, 255, 257; Dressing of, 149–151, *150*, 155; El Achiotal masks and, 30; as father of Hero Twins, 262; as gender ambiguous or intersexed, 151–152; greenstone pendants in Late Formative burials and, 259, 273; importance to Maya rulers, 273–274, 391; jadeite pendant with image of, 269; jade ornaments and, 204, 208; Middle Classic period, 257; in Pinturas shrine wall mural, 31; queens choosing to embody, 155, 159; in San Bartolo murals, 264
Maler, Teobert, 291
Mam deity, 54
mangrove forest, 285–287
Mani. *See* Xiu dynasty
Manos Rojas: Structure 1A1, 79, *81*, 82; Structure 2A1, 105; Uxmal and, 107
maps: Belize Valley, *250*; Chichen Itza, *182*; Copan, *177, 177*; Holmul, *48, 55*; Jaina, *286–287*; La Corona, *127, 131*; Maya area, *118*; Mesoamerica, *122*; Naranjo, *48, 63*
Marcus, Joyce, 6, 254, 262
market exchange, 12; Jaina, 297–299, 302; Postclassic period, 323
Markman, Sidney, 360n27
marriages. *See* queens; stranger queen
Martin, Simon, 2; on *ajawtaak* with its king, 34; *Ancient Maya Politics*, 7; on Calakmul palace size, 127; on

INDEX 411

Chontal Maya, 179–180; *Chronicle of the Maya Kings and Queens* (with Grube), 7; on divine vs. sacred rulership, 14; on dynastic politics at Tikal, 274; on Dzibanche, 38; on early ninth-century crisis, 126; on gender dynamics of rulership, 13; on gods, 174, 228; on hegemonic balance of power, 239; on Kaanul rulers, 38, 39; on political networks of courts, 16; on polygyny, 147; on rejection of primogeniture, 146; on stranger queens, 158; on warfare's timing with food shortages and dry periods, 236, 390

masculinity, 194–204

masks, 77–115; to "animate" space of noble or military personage, 104; on belt heads, 50; on buildings, 29–30; on bundles, 30; El Mirador and other Peten sites' god masks, 37–38; *k'in* mask markings, 79, *80*; Lamat markings, 79, 90; as political symbols, 83, 104; priests wearing deity masks, 319, 322, *324*; stucco, 12, 110n2, 255, 258; *tun* markings, 79, *80*. See also Chichen Itza mosaic masks; emergence theme; Puuc mosaic masks

Masson, Marilyn A., 1, 7–8, 10, 17, 108, 184, 311, 375, 386–388

Mathews, Peter, 39

Mauss, Marcel, 238, 386

Maya exceptionalism, 119, 389

Mayapan: ceramic effigy urn, 313, *314*; collapse, 313–315, 321, 326; construction, 313, 316; deity veneration, shifts in, 173, 183, 184; feasting, 227, 236; grave goods, 313; Itzmal Ch'en temple, 316–319, *320*; K'iche' rulership's parallels with, 326; literacy, 313; mask resembling earlier Puuc masks, 108–110, *109*; monumental center sculptures, 313, 316; palatial and elite residences, 313, *314*, 316, 325; patron gods, 184–186; political structure, 226; portraits, 316–319, *317–318*, 390; removal of burial goods and altar caches around time of city's abandonment, 325; Round Temple, 316; sacrifice of war captives at, 323; salt distribution rights, 359n4; stable multigenerational ruling structure, 184, 311, 315, 326; stela erection, 312, 316, *317*, 322; stranger kings, 387; Structure Q-151, 108–110, *109*; Structure Q-152, 184; Temple of the Serpent Masks, 316; Temple Q-162, 184; Xiu rulers, 108, 326

McAnany, Patricia A., 1, 10, 11, 16, 117; on feasting and interaction with non-nobles, 391; on interment of deceased related to agricultural claims of ancestors, 231; on mortuary rituals, 273; on regalia and emblems, 337; on royal action within cosmic time, 376; on state councils in northern Yucatán, 386; on stranger queens, 157, 387; on tribute ransom, 376; on women's indispensability in patriarchal societies, 387

McGinn, John J., 39

men: jade worn by royal males, 205, 208; masculinity, 194–204; as sole wearers of feathered capes, 195–196. See also military; warriors

Mérida, 5, 333, 342, 350

Mesoamerica: map, *122*; Olmecs as mother culture of all Mesoamerican civilizations, 372; symbol system, 252

Mesopotamian Early Dynastic period, 18, 370–371, 375; compared to Maya governance, 376; part-time nature of government workforce, 390; "second order regime" of administrative order and heroic politics, 377; village bureaucracies of Late Neolithic period, 379; wealth and land control, importance of, 376

Mexica emperors, cape and jewels of, 199–202

Mihesuah, Devon, 142–143, 144

Milbrath, Susan, 108

military, 11, 93–97, *94–96*, 104–105, 111n13; feathered capes and, 194–204; kings as leaders of, 321, 326, 335, 375; Mayapan, 316; Postclassic and contact period, 323. See also warriors

Miller, Mary Ellen: *Blood of Kings: Dynasty and Ritual in Maya Art* (with Schele), 6, 249

Moche culture, 373

Modified Florescent style (Chichen Itza masks), 97–101, *99*, 105

monkeys, 68, 174

Montejo, Francisco de (the Elder), 323

Montejo, Francisco de ("the Younger"/ el Mozo), 315, 323, 325, 343–344

Montejo Xiu, Franciso de, 357, 358, 359n3

monuments, 3*t*, 7; bundling and, 30; cosmological authentication of specific places and, 10; earliest Mayan constructions, 120; in Late Preclassic period, 32, 258. See also specific sites

Moon Goddess, 34–36, 149, 152, 204

Morell-Hart, Shanti, 16, 225, 388, 389–391

Morley, Sylvanus G., 117

mortuary practices, 17, 28, 179, 231, 239; burials in late Middle Preclassic Belize Valley, 257; cremation or exhumation/reburial in Formative period, 252, 273; parallels of Shang dynasty China, Inka Cuzco, and Egyptian Memphis, 376; shared by Veracruz, Tabasco, and Campeche coasts, 302

mosaic masks: Formative period (Belize Valley), 252. See also Chichen Itza mosaic masks; Puuc mosaic masks

mother-son bond as touchstone of Classic Maya culture, 156, 160

Motul de San José, 121, 180, 297, 319

mountains, 53–72; as zoomorphs, 79

mouth mirrors, 30

mutuality. See complementarity; stranger rulers

Mutul dynasty, 13, 121, 122–123, 125, 388

Muwaan Jol (Tikal), 40

Muwaan Mat (deity), 375–376

Muwaan Mat (ruling name for Lady Sak K'uk'), 164

mythology: female reproductive power and, 157; female sexuality and, 147, 151–154; Hero Twins, 152, 261, 262; of intersexed or nonbinary deity, 152; of Mayapan rulers, 312, 319; queenship and, 145, 148–155; Quetzalcoatl, 183; sacred Maya world tree, 348, 350; serpents and centipedes in, 154. See also creation narrative/myth

N

Naatz Chan Ahk, 63

Na Chi Kokom, 315, 323–325

Nacon Cupul, 325

Nah, Diego, 344*t*

Nahua, 48, 184, 337, 357

Nahuatl peoples and language, 178, 179, 183, 194, 322

Nakbe, 32, 37, 263–264
Nakum, 180; figurines, 297; heirloom jade pectoral, 206–208, *207*; Stela 4, 263
Naranjo (royal court): Calakmul and, 160, 176; Caracol and, 160, 267; compared to Belize Valley, 274; compared to Holmul, 59; decline in Terminal Classic period, 269; Dos Pilas stranger queen at, 160; duration of dynasty for thirty-four rulers, 62; emblem glyphs, 63; expansion and aggression of, 62, 71, 176, 271, 274, 388; influence on Belize Valley sites, 264, 267, 269; Ix Wak Jalam Chan as stranger queen at, 123; last known ruler (Waxaklajun Ubah K'awil), 271–272; patron god effigies from, 175; royal ancestors merged with local divine founder, 52; royal ancestors vs. patron gods, 15; royal legitimacy of, 12; stranger queens, 13, 155, 160–163, *161*, 167; Tikal and, 71, 162; waning influence, 271; Xunantunich's Stela 8 equating Naranjo and Xunantunich rulers, 272, 274
Naranjo site, 62–70; Altar 1, 64, *65*; ancestral monuments, 15; Aurora structure, 66, 67–69, *69*, 175; B-15 pyramid, 65–66; C-9 structure, 178; Central Acropolis, 65–66, *69*, 71, *72*; compared to Holmul, 59, 70–71, 388; deep-time places, 62, 64; feathered cape depictions, 195; Guacamaya structure, 66, 68–69, *69*; map of political centers, *48*; map of sacred landscape, *63*; Maxam, *63*, 64–65; North Acropolis, 64; reference to sovereignty of, 123; Stela 2, 64, *65*; Stela 8, *65*; Stela 11, 195; Stela 21, 195; Stela 22, *63*; Stela 23, *50*, 50–51; Stela 24, 62, *65*, *161*; Stela 29, 62; Stela 38, 64, *65*; Stela 40, 64; Stela 43, 51, *51*, 64; Stela 45, *51*, 62–63; Stela 46, *63*, 64; Stela 48, 50–51, *50*, 64, 69; Structure B-4, *65*; Structure C-9, 62, 64, 175, 178; Structures A14–A16, 62, *63*, 64–65; triadic acropolis, 62
Naranjo-Yaxha wars, 68
Natchez of Louisiana, 371, 374, 377
Nim li Punit, 68, 267
nobles. *See* elites and nobles
Noh Cabal Pech, 319
Noj Peten (capital of Peten Itza), 185
nonhuman faces of sacred authority, 14–15
north-south divide, 12, 15, 117–119; construction scale and elaboration, 134
nosepieces, 321
Novelo Rincón, Gustavo, 89, 90, 93, 134
Nunnery Quadrangle (Uxmal): developed throne complex, 89, 90; Feathered Serpent masked head, 100, *100*; masks and "profile masks," 83, 90, 92; mask similarity to Codz Pop and House of the Governor masks, 90, 107, 108, 391; masks reflecting function of architectural space, 104; Mayapan masks echoing, 108–110, *109*; military offices, 93, *94*, 104–105, 111n13; Pure Florescent mask, 98, 101; as sorcery houses, 79

O

Oaxaca, Mexico, 254, 262, 335
Och Kimi, 291
Okoshi, Tsubaka, 290; *Maya Kingship: Rupture and Transformation from Classic to Postclassic Times*, 2–4, 313
Old Creator shaman's solar bird avatar, 31
Old Kingdom Egypt. *See* Egypt

Olmecs, 30, 32, 34, 120, 206; compared to Chavín culture, 373, 374; as "first order regime," 377; as mother culture of all Mesoamerican civilizations, 372; politics as charismatic sport, 371–372
origin deities with features of both genders, 149
origins of the state, 369–370, 371, 377, 378
"otherness," 3t, 9, 47–53, *49*, 71, 157, 162. *See also* stranger queens; stranger rulers
Otzmal massacre, 323–325
owls, 93, 297
Oxkintok, 36, 303
Oxtotitlan Cave, 254

P

Pacbitun, 264, 265
Pachcaan, 290
Pacheco Dorantes, Baltasar, 343
Pacific Northwest Coast Indigenous societies, 376
Paddler Gods, 66, 177
Painted Ruler List, 38, 39
Pakal I (king of Palenque): ancestors as fruit-bearing trees, *230*, 231; ancestor shrines and, 7; death mask of, 6; headdress with jade diadems, 206; marriage to Red Queen (stranger queen), 156, 163–165, 167; tomb/sarcophagus of, 6, 52, 53, 60, 92, 93
Palenque dynasty, 5, 38–39; capes of young royal males, 202, *203*; expansion of dominance, 179; female rulers of, 13; jade ornament brought from Palenque to Copan, 205; local names in, 9; Oval Palace Tablet, 163; patron deities of, 15, 110n5, 175; patron god veneration ceremonies, 175; Red Queen from, 156; stranger queens, 163–165, *164*, 167; Tablet of the Foliated Cross, *80*; Tablet of the Slaves, 165; ties with Jaina, 17; tourism and, 6; war with Kaanul dynasty, 164. *See also specific rulers*
Palenque site: Cross Group temples, 175; Panel of the Cross, 38; Temple of the Inscriptions, 6, 52, 92, 175, 178; Temple XXI throne panel, 202, *203*; Yukatekan version of god at, 182
Paris Codex, 319, 322, 323, *324*
Parker, Joy: *Maya Cosmos* (with Freidel and Schele), 29
Pasión, 122, 257
Paso del Macho, 120
patrilineality of queens, 144–148, *146*, 155–156, 162
patrilocality, 145–146
patrimonial systems: failure to institutionalize in Proto-Classic period, 28; modeled on patriarchal organization of households, 370, 379; ruler and rhetoric of Classic Maya texts, 7, 9, 13; Yucatán's lack of patrimonial property, 337–338, 342, 357
patron gods, 4t, 15, 173–190, 392; benefits of, 176; Chichen Itza, 181–183, *182*; Chontal Maya, 178–181, 185; Classical-period gods becoming, 174; Classic Ch'olti'an veneration of, 175–178; definition of, 174–175; effigies of, 175, 184, 186; effigy censer fragments at Postclassic sites, 175, 184, 325; expansion of pantheon, 178, 392; feeding of, 175; local community and rulers, importance for, 176, 186; Mayapan, 184–185; Peten Itza, 185; rulers as caretakers of, 173, 186, 392; shrines to, 104, 124, 175;

spatial distribution (local community vs. whole polity), 176–178; of stranger queens, 146; temples, recognition of, 175; temporal distribution, 178; veneration prevalent across Mesoamerica, 173, 175; Yukatek Maya, 181–185

Paxbolon, Pablo, 180
Paxbolonacha (Acalan ruler), 321
Paxbolon-Maldonado Papers, 179, 180–181
Pech, Pablo, 343, 344*t*, 358; *Crónica de Chac Xulub Chen*, 343
Pech, Pedro, 343, 344*t*
Peraza Lope, Carlos, 108, 184, 316
Peregrine, Peter N., 9
Perez, Griselda, 38
Perez, Juan Carlos, 38
period ending rituals, 39, 40, 62, 146, 159, 176, 179, 180, 204, 272
perpetuators in Terminal Classic period (800–900 CE), 251*t*, 269–272, 275
Peru, 372–374. *See also* Inka
Petén Itza, 185, 315, 319–321, 322
Peten region, Guatemala, 36–38; Altar de Sacrificios, 297; Belize Valley compared to, 257, 274; costly plants in, 231; expanding population and cosmological foundations of rulership, 16; figurines, 17, 295–297; under foreign control in ninth century, 179; Mayapan's relationship with, 185; priests, role of, 319; titles of nobles, 315; Triadic Groups, 259; Yucatán's relationship with, 16. *See also specific urban sites*
Philip II (king of Spain), 340, 342, 343, 353, 360n24
Philip III (king of Spain), 353
Philip IV (king of Spain), 333–334, 353
Piedras Negras, 6; apical title, adoption of, 121; feathered cape depicted on king, 195, *198*; figurines, 297; food consumption across various classes of society, 232; heirloom jade ornament, 205, *207*; Itzamkanac at, 181; in military actions for control over eastern Tabasco, 179; scaffold accession thrones of stelae, 34; Stela 2 (Ruler 3), *198*, 205; Stela 4 (Ruler 3), 205; Stela 7 (Ruler 3), 195, *198*; Stela 10 (Ruler 4), 205; Stela 12 (Ruler 7), 195, *198*; Stela 13 (Ha' K'in Xook), *198*, 205; Stela 40 (Ruler 4), 205; Yaxchilan and, 387
Piña Chán, Román, 295
Pinturas shrine murals (San Bartolo), 30–32, *31–32*, 264
Plank, Shannon E., 104
Playa Poniente, 297–299
political affairs. *See* relational politics in southern and northern lowlands; *specific sites, dynasties, and time periods*
political economy of kingship, 130
polygyny, 123, 146–148, 156, 166
Porter, Mark L. B., 257
Postclassic and contact period, 17, 311–331; ancestor commemoration, 312, 325; collapse narratives, 313; compared to Chichen Itza, 313; Jaina settlement, 289; lack of ruler-focused funerary temples and monumental center tombs, 311; little study of rulership during, 250, 312–313; market exchange, 323; placemaking, 315; political, military, and economic authority, 323–325, *324*; political organization, 315–316, 386; population levels, 313; portraits, 316–319, *317–318*, 390; priests, role of, 319–322, *324*; rulership, 319–322; sacred burdens of the state, 322–323, 325; shared founding deities, 15, 325

pottery. *See* ceramics
Preclassic Maya. *See* Formative period
pre-Inka empire, 373–374
presentations of kingship, 10–17. *See also* costuming and adornment; feasting
priesthood: in Postclassic period, 319–322, *324*; role of, 10–11, 179; ruler priests, 249
primogeniture, 146
Principal Bird Deity, 55, 57, 68, 392; Cunil-phase, 252, *253*; merged with God N, 174; stucco masks with, 258
probanzas de hidalguía (proofs of nobility), 347
probanzas de méritos y servicios, 333, 334, 338–345, *341*, 344*t*, 347, 350; prohibitive costs of, 341, 342, 357
Proskouriakoff, Tatiana A., 6, 108
Pure Florescent style of masks, 97–101, *98*, 103, 104–105
Putnam, R. D., 390
Puuc cities, 11, 107–108; architectural style used throughout, 123–125, 183; commensal politics, 133–134; continuous construction, 134; council houses, 386; Fluorescence, 174; Huntichmul Structure, *78*; Jaina and, 297; shared burial traditions, 302
Puuc mosaic masks, 12–13, 77–97; as animate creatures, 79–82, *81*; architectural placement of, 82–83, 85–97; butterflies, 83, *85*; Chenes-style monster-maw masks, 105; compared to Chichen Itza mosaic masks, 97–101, 107; considerations, 82–83; as emblematic markers, 337; glyphs, 79, *80*; grape bunches and, 79; long-nosed, 79, 83; marking rooms and doorways, 82–83, 90; with mat signs, 83, *84*; nose rolls, 83, *85*; noses with mat signs, 83; as political symbols, 83, 104; "profile masks," 90, *92*; single tooth, 83; as steps, 77, 83, 89; as zoomorphic mountains, 79. *See also* Codz Pop; House of the Governor; Labna Palace; Nunnery Quadrangle
pyramids: built over earlier structures, 124, *125*; burial of deceased rulers in, 265; burial of Palenque queen in, 163; Great Pyramid (Uxmal), 83, *84*, 90, 110n9; Ichkabal, 37; Naranjo, 62, 64, 65, 66; Olmec, 372; in Postclassic centers, 321; Principal Bird Deity and, 55; as shrines, 15. *See also* Adivino pyramid

Q

quadripartite worldview, 180, 185, 258, 261, *261*, 311, 321, 391
quatrefoil motif, 252, *253*, 254
queens, 141–172; as co-rulers, 142; depicted in service roles, 149; exchange of royal brides, 9, 14; inverted vase imagery, 156, *157*; with *kaloomte'* title, 13, 142, 143*t*, 165; motherhood as avenue to power, 156; mythology and, 148–155; no Maya word for, 142; parentage statements revealing names of, 156, 159, 163, 267; patrilineality, 144–148, *146*, 155, 162; regents, queen mothers chosen as, 156, 162, 165; reproductive expectations for male heir, 155, 165; role of, 1, 3*t*, 142, 156; sexuality and dynastic success, 147, 155–157; textile arts and, 208; titles of,

141, 142, 143t; in warrior dress, 155, 160. *See also* royal women; stranger queens
Quetzalcoatl, 183, 184. *See also* K'uk'ulkan (Feathered Serpent)
Quetzaltenango, 354
Quezada, Sergio, 5, 17, 312–313, 315, 316, 323
Quijada, Diego de, 338
Quilter, Jeffrey, 373
Quintana Roo, 36, 37, 119, 313

R
rain deities, 57, 70, 208, 278, 299
range structures, 78, 87–89, 101, 124–125, 127
realpolitik, 237
rebirth, 93, 149, 151, 152, 158, 265
Red Queen at Palenque, 156, 163, *164*, 165
Reese-Taylor, Kathryn, 13, 160
Reilly, Kent, 30
Relación de la ciudad de Mérida, 350
Relaciones histórico-geográficas, 350
relational framework, 385–396; council rule yielding to dynastic rulership, 386; entanglement and, 391; entrapment of ruler and, 4t, 391–392; legitimacy and, 391; sovereignty and, 385–386. *See also* rulers; stranger queens; stranger rulers; *specific locations and time periods*
relational politics in southern and northern lowlands, 117–140; background, 117–120; Classic period, 120–123; commensal politics and political communication, 130, 239; conquest and colonization, 119; exogamous marriages, 119; hierarchy, 120; local politics, 129–130; north's commensal politics, 133–134; north's galactic mimesis, 123–126; Preclassic period, 120–121; royal commensal politics at La Corona, 130–133; south's galactic mimesis, 126–129; stranger rulership and schismogenesis, 120–123; upward nobility and galactic mimesis, 123
Restall, Matthew, 9, 10, 315
Rice, Prudence M., 258
Riese, Berthold, 335
Ringle, William M., 6, 10, 11, 77; on architecture and construction, 28, 391; on Chichen Itza's participation in galactic mimesis, 123–124; on Ek' Balam entombment of Ukit Kan Lek Tok', 125; on Feathered Serpent tradition, 183; on mask symbolism, 12–13, 105, 183, 337; on state councils in northern Yucatán, 386; on stranger kings, 126
Río, Antonio del, 5
Rio Azul tomb paintings, 67, 68
Rio Bec region, masks from, 83
Río Supe region, monumental centers in, 373
Riquer, Martín de, 340
ritual death and resurrection, 28, 30, 33. *See also* rebirth
rituals, 2; accompanying or preceding rulership, 9; cave rituals, 254, 273, 319, *356*, *357*, *358*; Chavín culture and, 374; equinox, 179; at monumental places, 10; public performances, 255; stabilizing royal power, 15. *See also* bloodletting; investiture rites; mortuary practices; sacrifices

Rivero Torres, Sonia, 295
Robertson, Donald, 354
Robin, Cynthia, 257
roofing, 67–68, 87, 100, 110–111, 134
Rosenswig, Robert, 372
Roskamp, Hans, 353
royal body in built environment, 47–76; Holmul's landscape, 53–62; landscape-authority connection, 47; legitimating strategies among Classic Maya, 47–53; Naranjo landscape, 62–70
royal courts, 7, 28, 120, 130. *See also specific sites*
royal women, 142; distortion of role by use of borrowed language, 147; high-status burials, 14; jade worn by, 205, 208; Jaina figurines and, 303; malnutrition of, 148; patronage and, 142; Postclassic period, 312; as religious specialists, 159; Sun God interactions with, 152; textiles and, 208; as war booty, 162; as warriors, 13, 159, 160; in Xicalango, 312. *See also* queens; stranger queens
Roys, Ralph, 181, 322
Rubenstein, Meghan, 83, 90, 97, 103
rulers: ability to access spirit world, 249; *ajawtaak* emerging in late Middle Formative period (750–300 BCE), 251t, 255–258, 273, 391; *ajawtaak* in Late Formative period (300 BCE–300 CE), 251t, 258–264, 273; alignment with their subjects, 388; as axis mundi, 388; as caretakers of supernaturals, 4t, 229; definition of, 2; deity impersonation by, 29, 31, 174; Formative period, aggrandizers in (1200–750 BCE), 250, 251t, 252–255, 273; gender not indicated in titles of, 13; as gods' viceregents, 375; invisible and anonymous, 27–28, 30–32, 389; Jaina, 291–293; *k'uhul ajawtaak* in early and late Classic periods (300–800 CE), 251t, 264–268, 273; mummification, 375; mythic rationale for transformation of rulers, 34; perpetuators in Terminal Classic period (800–900 CE), 251t, 269–272, 275; recognition by their subjects, 28, 391; relationship to patron gods, 4t, 175, 176, 186, 389; relationship to subject peoples and lands, 4t, 18, 388–389; shaman-kings, 249, 392; symbolic extravagance, 237; theonyms, use of, 181, 251, 267, 274; uniqueness of, 389; use of term, 1; violence and power, 390. *See also ajawtaak*; sovereignty; *specific periods, dynasties, and locations*
Ruler Sky Lifter, 39
Ruppert, Karl, 105
Ruz Lhuillier, Alberto, 6

S
Sa'aal, 63–64, *63*, 70, 388
Saak/Xaak Witz, 67, 68
sacred rulers, 8, 50; divine vs. sacred rulership, 8, 14, 319, 375, 389
sacrifices, 2; blood sacrifices, 159; Egypt's first rulers engaging in, 377; leafy capes associated with, 202, *203*; Shang dynasty China waging war to acquire captives for, 377; tomb of Red Queen containing sacrificial victims, 163; single projecting tooth on masks and, 83, 110n5; of war captives, 323, 326, 377
Sacul Stela 6, 195

Sáenz Vargas, Cesar, 90
Sahagún, Bernardino de, 202
Sahlins, Marshall, 2, 4; on adverse sacralization, 274, 389; on cosmic polity, 273, 392; on dichotomy between stranger kings and queens, 135, 387; on divine rulers imitating gods, 31, 174, 387; on divine stranger kingship, 117, 123, 173, 387; on dual sovereignty, 173; on endurance of kingships, 12; on galactic mimesis, 195; on invisible rulers of the north, 27; on kingship and kinship, 144; on meta-human powers in deep antiquity, 29; on nonhuman faces of sacred authority, 14–15; *On Kings* (with Graeber), 2; on political economy of kingship, 130; on stranger kingship, 8, 121–122, 388; on stranger queen, 157; on upward nobility, 11
Sak Balam, 292
Sak Chuween, 63
Sak Kimi, 291
Sak K'uk' (Palenque queen), 163–165, *206*
San Bartolo, 11, 34, 37, 38; *ajawtaak*'s establishment, 264; Dressing of Maize Deity (mural), 149–151, *150*, 155; jade diadems in headdresses, 204; Pinturas shrine murals, 30–32, *31–32*, 264; Structure Sub-1A, AJAW grapheme with *tz'ul* markings, 48, *49*
San José Mogote, figurines from, 262
San Lorenzo, 372
San Pedro cactus and *Huachuma*, 373
Santa Rita (Corozal), 313; murals, 312, 319, 322, 324
Saturno, William A., 31
Sayil, 134
Schele, Linda, 39, 79, 228–229, 249, 392; *Blood of Kings: Dynasty and Ritual in Maya Art* (with Miller), 6, 249; *Maya Cosmos* (with Freidel and Parker), 29
Schellhas, Paul, 52, 174
Scherer, Andrew, 229
schismogenesis, 3*t*, 117, 119, 120–123, 135
Schmidt, Peter J., 105
Scholes, France V., 181
Scott, James, 392
"second order regimes," 377
Second Snake Lady (stranger queen at La Corona), 158
Segovia Liga, Argelia, 355, 360n30
Seler, Eduard, 79, 110n1
Selz Foundation Yaxuna Project, 33, 34
serpents: headdresses, 17; with jaguar claws, 158; masks, 79, 82; serpent-centipede, 159; in Tulum murals, 321; vision serpent, 154; warriors and, 105; war-serpent motif, *292*, *293*. *See also* feathered serpents
settler colonialism, 144
sexuality, female: dynastic success and, 155–157, 158, 386; need for control, 13, 133, 142, 147, 151, 153, 158, 167, 386, 387; potency of, 147, 151–155, 166
shamans, 7, 31, 249; shaman-kings, 249, 392
Shang dynasty (China), 375–377; part-time nature of government workforce, 378, 390; Zhou's overthrow of, 377
Sharer, Robert J., 175, 254
shell symbolism, 30, 32–36, *35*, 152, 202, 254–256, 259, 291
shields and heraldic emblems, pre-Hispanic, 335–337, *336*

Shilluk of South Sudan, 13, 371, 374, 386, 388
Sihó, 227
Sihyaj Chan K'awiil II, 39
Sihyaj K'ahk', 34, 39–40; on Tikal Stela 31, 52, 53
sky bands, 82, 102, 105, 323, *324*
Sky Witness (Kaanul ruler), 36, 38
slavery, 321, 322; slave trade, 323; Spaniards releasing slaves held by Maya nobles, 338
Slocum, Diane, 267
Smith, Adam T., 12, 47
snake imagery, 36, 373
social domination, comparison of ancient and modern forms of, 369–383; Shang period in China, 376–377; Classic Maya politics, importance of social bonds, 376; comparison of Inka Peru and Old Kingdom Egypt, 375; democracy, 378; divine rulers, 371; elementary forms of domination, 369–371; empire built on images, 372–374; esoteric knowledge as basis of empire, 374; "first order regimes," 374–375; Mesopotamian statecraft, 370–371; modern nation-states assumed to be culmination of evolutionary process, 369–370; modern state defined as combination of sovereignty, bureaucracy, and competitive politics, 370; new picture of state formation, 379; Olmecs and politics as charismatic sport, 371–372; origins of the state, 369–370, 371, 377; regional hegemony as anomaly, 377; rethinking basic premises of political evolution, 378–379; salient differences in early state forms, 371, 375–376; seasonal nature of government work, 378; "second order regimes," 377; social class structure as common feature, 376; violence as common denominator, 376; writing ancient history backwards from current state arrangement, 378
Sotuta, 315–316, 323, 347, 350
south-north divide. *See* north-south divide
sovereignty: absolute sovereigns, 370, 374; blended in concept of stranger queen or king, 157, 165, 167; depiction linking to legitimacy, 50; as divine domain, 375, 377; enactment of, 130; of modern state, 370; political machinery of, 12, 18; popular, 369, 378; porosity of, 385; relational framework and, 385; Shang rulers and, 376; trust and violence as dual basis for, 390
Spaniards: complete sovereignty over colonies, 337; dismantling of extant architecture and destruction of texts and monuments, 5; Inquisition into lapsed conversions, 358; loss of authority of natural lords under, 17, 337–338, 357; Mayan societies compared to Spanish kingdoms, 5; royal dress during Golden Age of the Spanish Empire, 192. *See also* colonialism; Postclassic and contact period
Spearthrower Owl (Ajaw Jatz'oom), 39–40, 390
Speed, Shannon, 144
Spinden, Herbert, 291
statecraft. *See* social domination
Stephens, John Lloyd, 348–349, 350
stingray spines, 55, 229, *229*, 259
Stone, Andrea, 153, 360n29
Strange, Susan: *The Retreat of the State*, 369

stranger queens, 3t, 13–14, 36, 122, 125, 135, 157–165, 387; ability to improve bloodline of new home, 155; ancestors and patron gods of, 146, 157; benefits of marriage with, 158, 167; dichotomy with stranger kings, 135; expectations placed upon, 156, 165; as forced marriages, 163, 166; at La Corona, 158–160, 167; at Naranjo, 160–163, 167; at Palenque, 163–165, 167; power of the Other, 157, 162; as queen mother in most powerful position in Maya court, 156; relocation into new polity, 146, 157, 165–166, *166*

stranger rulers, 3t, 8, 28, 47, 134, 387; Auxaual as, 181; Classic period, 120–123; complementarity and mutual benefit, 123, 387, 388; divine powers, 117, 129, 173; early colonial period and, 355; exogamous marriages and, 119; foodstuffs and, 234, 239; La Corona and, 126–129; land ownership and, 129; Mayapan's kings, 387; patron gods transferring with, 183–184; Preclassic period, 120–121; schismogenesis and, 122–123; in Tikal, 39–40. *See also* stranger queens

Stuart, David, 34, 79, 104, 110n5, 155, 180, 389–391; *The Order of Days*, 7

stucco masks, 12, 110n2, 255, 258

Suhler, Charles, 33, 34

Sun God: depiction of, 152–153, *152–153*, 153, 258; El Achiotal masks and, 30; God G, 174; "Hearth" Chan Ahk transformed into, 51; ruler equated with, 263–264; Tajal Wayaab, 56, 57; in Ya, 34

supernatural entities: feasts and, 229; power of, 10, 157; royal women's ability to contact, 163, 166; rulers in role of mediators with, 14–15. *See also* ancestors; *specific gods*

T

Tabasco, 174, 179, 285, 299, 302–303, 357

Tajal Wayaab Sun God (La Sufricaya Stela 6), 56, 57

Takalik Abaj, 262, 263

Tancah murals, 322

Taube, Karl A., 31, 79, 174, 262

taxes or tributes, 130, 341–343, 357; tribute exemptions, 342–343

Techialoyan manuscripts, 353

Temple of the Warriors (Chichen Itza): feathered capes and military, 195; masks, 99, 101, 107

Teotihuacan: corporate structure of, 9–10; Dos Pilas and, 123; foodstuffs from Tepantitla compound murals, 234, *234*; historical impact of interventions, 8–9; Holmul rulers' connection to, 59, 388; La Sufricaya adopting architectural style of, 57; as mega city but lacking a full institutional package, 379; Moon Goddess, 34–36, *35*; Naranjo and, 123; nose rolls on *incensarios*, 83; Street of the Dead, 125; Tikal and, 121; war-serpent motif, 293; Yaxuna and, 36

Terminal Classic period: commemoration of passage of time, 322; decline/collapse during, 269, 274; definition of, 174; feasting, 391; feathered capes, 194; Jaina settlement, 289; little study of rulership during, 250; mosaic masks of, 12, 77, 108; northern kingship compared to southern Classic traditions, 312; perpetuators in Belize Valley (800–900 CE), 251t, 269–272, 275; population dispersion, 135; rulership changes in, 236, 251t, 254; shared founding deities, 15; Tollans, 108; Uxmal hegemonic influence in, 123; war-serpent motif, 293

theonyms, use of, 181, 251, 267, 274

Third Snake Lady (Lady Ti') (stranger queen at La Corona), 158–159, 160

T'ho (royal court), 5

Thompson, J. Eric, 7; *The Rise and Fall of Maya Civilization*, 6, 249

"Three Gods" rural center, 163, 165

Ti' (Sa'aal), 63, 64

Tikal, 37–39; affiliations with, 121; *ajawtaak*'s establishment, 264; Altar 2, 202; Burial 10, 238; Burial 85, 39, 204; cacao vessel, 238; conquest of Naranjo, 71; deluge of evidence from, 6; dynastic founders, 126; earthworks as territorial markers, 387–388; expansion of dominance, 184, 186, 274; feasting, 227, 234; female rulers of, 13; figurines, 297; foreign foods served at, 234, 238; Holmul rulers and, 57; influence on Belize Valley sites, 264; jade diadems in headdresses, 204; Lintel 2, Temple IV, 64, *65*; Mutul peregrination to Dos Pilas from, 388; North Acropolis, 30, 39, 40, 64, 389; patron god effigies, 175; patron god version of the vision/waterlily serpent, 182; royal ancestors merged with local divine founder, 52; Stela 10, 195; Stela 22, 52, 53, 68; Stela 29, 39; Stela 31, 39–40, *51–52*, 53; Stela 34, 195; surnames in ninth century, 179; Temple VI (Temple of the Inscriptions), 175; Uxmal compared to, 123; visibility of rulers, 389; war with Kaanul, 39, 159; war with Naranjo, 162

Ti' K'awiil (Kaanul king), 127, *128*

Tilden, Douglas, 267

Tipan Chen Uitz, 267–268

Tipu, 275

Título de K'oyoi (K'iche' title), 354

Título de Totonicapan (K'iche' title), 354

Tixchel, 181, 286

Tlaloc masks, 90, *91*, 180

Tlaxcala, 9, 10, 339, 386

Tokovinine, Alexandre, 10, 47, 388; on ancestral monuments, 15; on Dumbarton Oaks onyx bowl from Jaina, 291; on feasting changes over time, 237; on legitimation, 233; on Naranjo expansion of realm, 176, 274; on royal legitimacy, 12; on shrines to patron gods, 175, 178; on vesting of royal identity, 15

Tollan Zuyua, 355, 360n30

Toltec: butterfly symbolism, 83; as feather workers, 194; influence on political centers, 97; mask use, 107

Toltec/International style, 97, 183

Toniná, 297, 335

toponyms, use of, 388

Tortuguero, 179, 181

Toscano Hernández, Lourdes, 89, 134

Tovilla, Martin, 218n4

Traxler, Loa P., 254

tributes. *See* taxes or tributes

Trypillia Ukraine, 379

Tulum: masks, 111n14; murals, 316–319, 322–323, *324*

INDEX 417

Turner, Terrence, 191
turtle shells and imagery, 30–31, 33, 34, 227, 262, 266–267, 297
Tutul Xiu. *See* Xiu dynasty of Mani
Tuub'al, 162–163
Tuun K'ab Hix (Kaanul king), 158
Tzahb Chan Yopaat Macha', 59, 60
Tz'akab Ajaw. *See* Red Queen at Palenque
Tzik'in Bahlam, 51, 63
tz'ul, 48–50, *49*

U

Uaxactun, 30, 121, 234
Uaymil. *See* Isla Uaymil
ubaahil aan, 51–52, *51*
Ucanal, 179–180
Ukit Kan Le'k, 88
Ukit Kan Le'k Tok', 125, 386
Unen Bahlam (of Tuub'al), 162
Unen Bahlam (queen of Tikal), 39–40
Unen K'awiil, 179
Upakal K'inich (young royal male), 202, *203*
Ursua, General, 185
Usumacinta Basin, 293, 297–299, 302, 303
Utatlan, 321, 354
Uxmal: compared to Tikal, 123; corbelled vaults with feathered serpents, 126; Dovecote, Structure S mask, 83, *84*, 110n9; Great Pyramid, 83, *84*, 90, 110n9; hegemonic influence of, 123–124; Pajaros complex, 87, 90, 107; Puuc cities and, 107–108; Queen of Uxmal, 90, *91*; structures similar to Codz Pop, 89. *See also* House of the Governor; Nunnery Quadrangle

V

Valladolid, 5, 343
Vargas Pacheco, Ernesto, 181
Velásquez, Erik, 38
Vepretski, Sergei, 38
Veracruz: exchange relations with Jaina, 297–299; figurines and, 17, 285, 294–295, *296*, 300, 302
vilca leaves, hallucinogen from, 373
Villa Madero, 286, 302, 304n7
Volta, Beniamino, 183
Voz Mediano, Antonio de, 343

W

Waká, 38, 40, 297
Wak Chanal Muyal Witz, 57
Wak Chan K'awiil, 38
Wak Ihk' . . . Huun Nal Pek Sa'aal, 62–64
Wak Jalam Chan Ajaw, 155, 162, 163, 167
Walker, Debra, 37
warfare. *See* military; *specific sites, dynasties, etc.*
war gods, 158
warrior queens, 13, 159, 160
warriors, 11, 93, *96*, 97, 105; capes awarded for achievements, 199; fighting in agricultural off-season, 378; rulers as, 375; shields and emblems, 335–336. *See also* military

war-serpent motif, 292, 293
Waterlily Serpent deity, 180, 182
Wat'ul K'atel ("GI-K'awiil"), 180, 238
Waxaklahun Uba Sak Kimi, 291–292
Waxaklajun Ubah K'awil, 271–272
Waxaklajuun Ubaah Kaan (war god), 158
wayib (patron deity temples), 175
Weber, Max, 370
Webster, David, 238
Weckmann, Luis, 360n22
Wengrow, David, 17–18, 145, 166, 208, 369, 390; *The Dawn of Everything* (with Graeber), 9
Wiinte' Naah, 53, 59, 62, 71
Wind God, 177–178, 180, 184, 208
Winzenz, Karon, 218n2
wits mask markings, 79, *80*
Witzna, 68, 71
women. *See* gender roles; queens; royal women; stranger queens
Wood, Stephanie, 348
Wright, Mark A., 258

Xaak/Saak Witz, 68
Xbalanque, 387, 388
Xcalumkin, 123, 125, 181, 291
Xcambó, 294, 299, 302, 303, 304n8
Xculoc, 125
Xicalango, 312
Ximenez, Francisco, 152
Xiu, Ah Mochan, 347
Xiu, Ah Napot, 347
Xiu, Gaspar Antonio Chi. *See* Chi Xiu, Gaspar Antonio
Xiu dynasty of Mani: coat of arms, 17, 345, *345*, 347–351; fall from favor under Spaniards, 358; family tree, 345–347, *346*; foreign pedigree claims of, 355; Mayapan and, 108, 321, 326; Mexican ancestry of, 126; Otzmal massacre of, 323; territorial boundaries, 315–316; tribute in colonial period, 341–342; uprising against Cocom rule, 184
Xiu treaty (1557), 315, 325
Xiu uprising, 184, 326
Xkipche, mask nose from, 83, *84*
Xochiquetzal (goddess), 152
Xocnaceh, 124
"X-O markings," 97
Xquic (goddess), 152–153
Xuenkal, 234
Xunantunich, 16, 52, 53, 250; aggrandizers in Belize Valley in Formative period (1200–750 BCE), 252, 255; *ajawtaak* emerging in late Middle Formative period (750–300 BCE), 255, 257; *ajawtaak* in Late Formative period (300 BCE–300 CE), 259, 264; Altar 1, 272; E-Group constructions, 255, 257, 259; feasting, 227; female remains in royal court shrine, 13; *k'uhul ajawtaak* in early and late Classic periods (300–800 CE), 267–268; monuments, 264, 274; mortuary practices, 257; perpetuators in Terminal Classic period (800–900 CE), 271–272; Stela 1, *271*, 272; Stela 8 referring to rulers from Naranjo as equals, 271–272, *271*, 274; Stela 9, *271*, 272; Structure A9 tomb, 267

Y

Yaeger, Jason, 313
Yajaw Chan Muwaahn II, *229*
Yajawte' K'inich II, 265
Yax Bolon Chahk, 50–51
Yax Chich Kan (vision/waterlily serpent), 182–183
Yaxchilan, 6; complementarity of male and female elites, 148; feathered cape depiction, *197*; female royal at, 13; Lintel 25, *52*; patron gods, 178; polygamy at, 146–147; royal women on panels, 153–155; sixth-century genealogy, 39; Stela 11, *49*, 50, *52*, 60, 70; stranger queens, 155; Structure 23, 166; Temple 3, 175; territorial concerns, 387
Yax Ehb Xook (ruler of Tikal), 28, 39, 40, 389
Yaxha, 50, 162–163, 206
Yax K'uk' Mo (ruler of Copan), *52*, 387
Yax Mayuy Chan Chahk, 64
Yax Nuun Ahiin I (ruler of Tikal), *51*, 387
Yax Uk'uk'um K'awiil ("Green-feathered K'awiil"), 182–183
Yaxuna, 33–36, 386, 390; Burial 23, Structure 6F-3, *34*, *35*, 36; Burial 24, Structure 6F-4, 34–36, *35*, 390; New Order conqueror's treatment of prior ruler and queen, 36; tableau in Burial 24 (Structure 6F-4), queen wearing crown with, 34, *35*; underrepresented due to fewer or poorly preserved records, 36
Yaxuun Bahlam, *49*, 50, 52–53
Yiban (scribe), 291, 292
Yohl Ik'nal (queen of Palenque), 155, 156, 163–164
Yucatán, 5; appropriation of Habsburg royal arms and double-headed eagle, 353–357, *355–356*, 360nn27–29; appropriation of Spanish heraldic symbols (1550–1750), 344–353, 360n22; betrayal of Christianity in, 357; coat of arms of, 351–353, *351*; *See also specific sites*; council system of governance in Late Postclassic, 254; decentralized power in pre-Hispanic period, 357; figurines and, 285, 290, 302; Franciscan inquisition under Diego de Landa, 358; idolatrous cave ceremonies after conversion and use of double-headed eagle, 354–355, *356*, 357, 358; lack of patrimonial property, 337, 342, 357; Mani Land Treaty (1557), 359n3; natural lords' attempts to attain privileges (1550–1700), 340–344; population levels in Terminal Classic through Spanish contact, 313; postcontact nature of *cacicazgos*, 338; precontact nature of *cacicazgos*, 337; *probanzas de méritos y servicios* compiled from, 340–344, *341*, 344t; quadripartite worldview, 321; rulers in contact and early colonial periods, 322, 326; Spanish conquest competed (1546), 353, 357; spouted ceramic vessels, 262
Yuhknoom Ch'een II, 38, 39
Yuhknoom Yich'aak K'ahk, 126
Yukatek, 178–179, 180–181; patron gods, 181–185, 186; Yukatekan languages, 174
Yuknoom Took' K'awiil, 202, *202*

Z

Zací (royal court), 5
Zacpeten, 185, 229
Zactam–Xicalango, 48, 49
Zapote Bobal vessel, *67*, 68
Zender, Marc, 179

DUMBARTON OAKS PRE-COLUMBIAN SYMPOSIA AND COLLOQUIA

PUBLISHED BY DUMBARTON OAKS, WASHINGTON, D.C.

The Dumbarton Oaks Pre-Columbian Symposia and Colloquia Series volumes are based on papers presented at scholarly meetings sponsored by the Pre-Columbian Studies program at Dumbarton Oaks. Inaugurated in 1967, these meetings provide a forum for the presentation of advanced research and the exchange of ideas on the art and archaeology of the ancient Americas.

Further information on the Dumbarton Oaks Pre-Columbian series and publications can be found at www.doaks.org/publications.

Dumbarton Oaks Conference on the Olmec, edited by Elizabeth P. Benson, 1968

Dumbarton Oaks Conference on Chavín, edited by Elizabeth P. Benson, 1971

The Cult of the Feline, edited by Elizabeth P. Benson, 1972

Mesoamerican Writing Systems, edited by Elizabeth P. Benson, 1973

Death and the Afterlife in Pre-Columbian America, edited by Elizabeth P. Benson, 1975

The Sea in the Pre-Columbian World, edited by Elizabeth P. Benson, 1977

The Junius B. Bird Pre-Columbian Textile Conference, edited by Ann Pollard Rowe, Elizabeth P. Benson, and Anne-Louise Schaffer, 1979

Pre-Columbian Metallurgy of South America, edited by Elizabeth P. Benson, 1979

Mesoamerican Sites and World-Views, edited by Elizabeth P. Benson, 1981

The Art and Iconography of Late Post-Classic Central Mexico, edited by Elizabeth Hill Boone, 1982

Falsifications and Misreconstructions of Pre-Columbian Art, edited by Elizabeth Hill Boone, 1982

Highland-Lowland Interaction in Mesoamerica: Interdisciplinary Approaches, edited by Arthur G. Miller, 1983

Ritual Human Sacrifice in Mesoamerica, edited by Elizabeth Hill Boone, 1984

Painted Architecture and Polychrome Monumental Sculpture in Mesoamerica, edited by Elizabeth Hill Boone, 1985

Early Ceremonial Architecture in the Andes, edited by Christopher B. Donnan, 1985

The Aztec Templo Mayor, edited by Elizabeth Hill Boone, 1986

The Southeast Classic Maya Zone, edited by Elizabeth Hill Boone and Gordon R. Willey, 1988

The Northern Dynasties: Kingship and Statecraft in Chimor, edited by Michael E. Moseley and Alana Cordy-Collins, 1990

Wealth and Hierarchy in the Intermediate Area, edited by Frederick W. Lange, 1992

Art, Ideology, and the City of Teotihuacan, edited by Janet Catherine Berlo, 1992

Latin American Horizons, edited by Don Stephen Rice, 1993

Lowland Maya Civilization in the Eighth Century AD, edited by Jeremy A. Sabloff and John S. Henderson, 1993

Collecting the Pre-Columbian Past, edited by Elizabeth Hill Boone, 1993

Tombs for the Living: Andean Mortuary Practices, edited by Tom D. Dillehay, 1995

Native Traditions in the Postconquest World, edited by Elizabeth Hill Boone and Tom Cummins, 1998

Function and Meaning in Classic Maya Architecture, edited by Stephen D. Houston, 1998

Social Patterns in Pre-Classic Mesoamerica, edited by David C. Grove and Rosemary A. Joyce, 1999

Gender in Pre-Hispanic America, edited by Cecelia F. Klein, 2001

Archaeology of Formative Ecuador, edited by J. Scott Raymond and Richard L. Burger, 2003

Gold and Power in Ancient Costa Rica, Panama, and Colombia, edited by Jeffrey Quilter and John W. Hoopes, 2003

Palaces of the Ancient New World, edited by Susan Toby Evans and Joanne Pillsbury, 2004

A Pre-Columbian World, edited by Jeffrey Quilter and Mary Ellen Miller, 2006

Twin Tollans: Chichén Itzá, Tula, and the Epiclassic to Early Postclassic Mesoamerican World, edited by Jeff Karl Kowalski and Cynthia Kristan-Graham, 2007

Variations in the Expression of Inka Power, edited by Richard L. Burger, Craig Morris, and Ramiro Matos Mendieta, 2007

El Niño, Catastrophism, and Culture Change in Ancient America, edited by Daniel H. Sandweiss and Jeffrey Quilter, 2008

Classic Period Cultural Currents in Southern and Central Veracruz, edited by Philip J. Arnold III and Christopher A. Pool, 2008

The Art of Urbanism: How Mesoamerican Kingdoms Represented Themselves in Architecture and Imagery, edited by William L. Fash and Leonardo López Luján, 2009

New Perspectives on Moche Political Organization, edited by Jeffrey Quilter and Luis Jaime Castillo B., 2010

Astronomers, Scribes, and Priests: Intellectual Interchange between the Northern Maya Lowlands and Highland Mexico in the Late Postclassic

Period, edited by Gabrielle Vail and Christine Hernández, 2010

The Place of Stone Monuments: Context, Use, and Meaning in Mesoamerica's Preclassic Transition, edited by Julia Guernsey, John E. Clark, and Barbara Arroyo, 2010

Their Way of Writing: Scripts, Signs, and Pictographies in Pre-Columbian America, edited by Elizabeth Hill Boone and Gary Urton, 2011

Past Presented: Archaeological Illustration and the Ancient Americas, edited by Joanne Pillsbury, 2012

Merchants, Markets, and Exchange in the Pre-Columbian World, edited by Kenneth G. Hirth and Joanne Pillsbury, 2013

Embattled Bodies, Embattled Places: War in Pre-Columbian Mesoamerica and the Andes, edited by Andrew K. Scherer and John W. Verano, 2014

The Measure and Meaning of Time in Mesoamerica and the Andes, edited by Anthony F. Aveni, 2015

Making Value, Making Meaning: Techné in the Pre-Columbian World, edited by Cathy Lynne Costin, 2016

Smoke, Flames, and the Human Body in Mesoamerican Ritual Practice, edited by Vera Tiesler and Andrew K. Scherer, 2018

Sacred Matter: Animacy and Authority in the Americas, edited by Steve Kosiba, John Wayne Janusek, and Thomas B. F. Cummins, 2020

Teotihuacan: The World Beyond the City, edited by Kenneth G. Hirth, David M. Carballo, and Barbara Arroyo, 2020

Waves of Influence: Pacific Maritime Networks Connecting Mexico, Central America, and Northwestern South America, edited by Christopher S. Beekman and Colin McEwan, 2022

Reconsidering the Chavín Phenomenon in the Twenty-First Century, edited by Richard L. Burger and Jason Nesbitt, 2023

Faces of Rulership in the Maya Region, edited by Patricia A. McAnany and Marilyn A. Masson, 2024